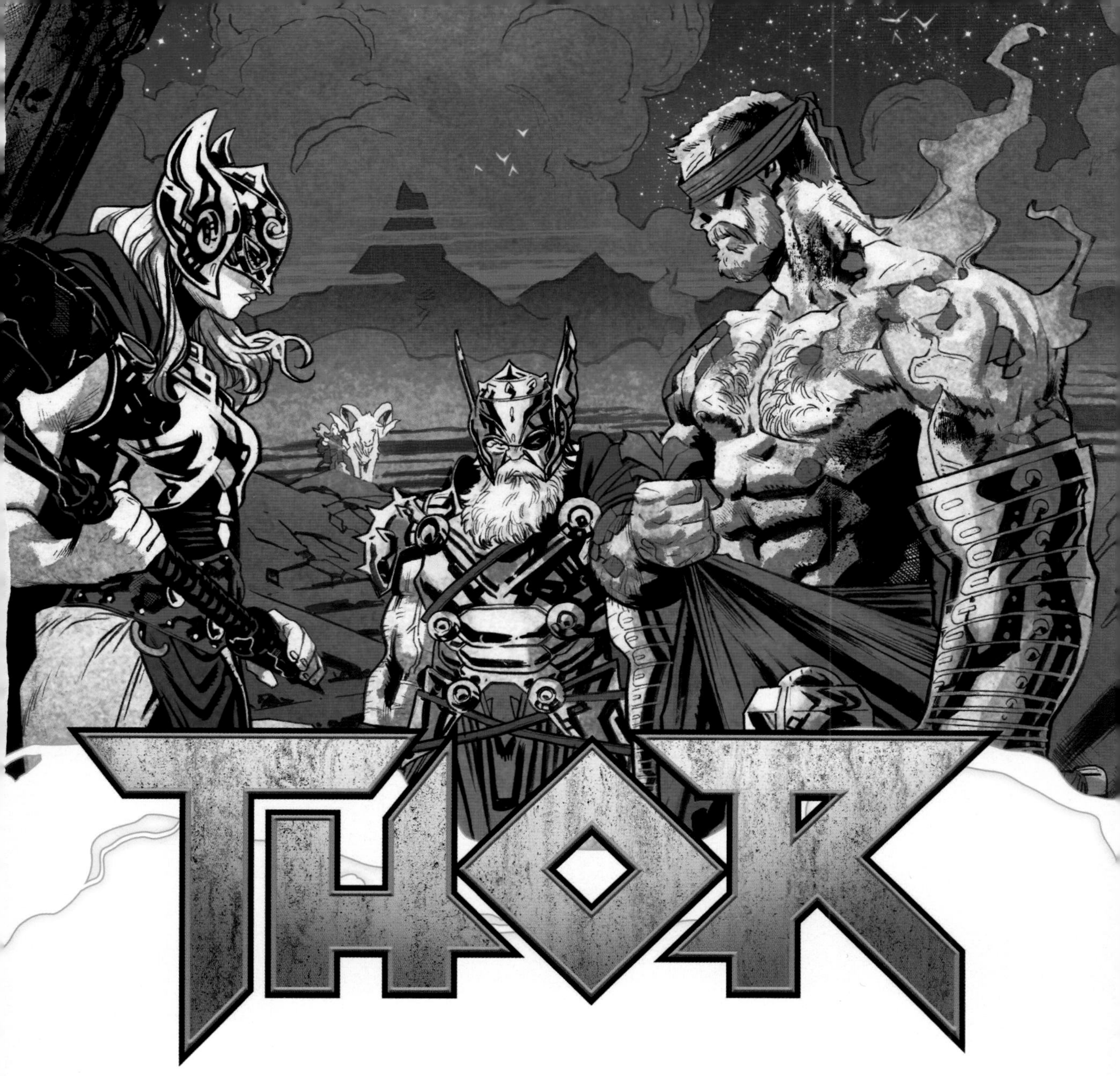

THOR

THOR IS BACK. WHILE STILL UNWORTHY OF LIFTING HIS HAMMER, MJOLNIR,
HE IS ONCE MORE THE GOD OF THUNDER.

BUT MUCH ELSE HAS CHANGED. AFTER LAYING WASTE TO NINE OF THE TEN REALMS,
MALEKITH AND HIS ALLIES — INCLUDING LOKI'S OWN BIRTH FATHER, KING LAUFEY OF THE
FROST GIANTS — HAVE FINALLY INVADED THE LAST REALM: MIDGARD.

THE GODS OF ASGARD HAVE BANDED TOGETHER WITH THE HEROES OF EARTH TO FIGHT
MALEKITH'S INVASION. FINALLY REPENTANT FOR HIS ROLE IN BUILDING MALEKITH'S ARMY,
LOKI INTERVENED TO SAVE HIS ADOPTED MOTHER FREYJA FROM THE ASSAULT. AND THUS
FOR LOKI, GOD OF MISCHIEF, THE WAR SEEMINGLY CAME TO A SWIFT END…

…WHEN LAUFEY PICKED HIM UP AND ATE HIM.

THOR CREATED BY **STAN LEE**, **LARRY LIEBER** & **JACK KIRBY**

COLLECTION EDITOR: **JENNIFER GRÜNWALD**
ASSISTANT EDITOR: **DANIEL KIRCHHOFFER**
ASSISTANT MANAGING EDITOR: **MAIA LOY**
ASSISTANT MANAGING EDITOR: **LISA MONTALBANO**
VP PRODUCTION & SPECIAL PROJECTS: **JEFF YOUNGQUIST**
SVP PRINT, SALES & MARKETING: **DAVID GABRIEL**
EDITOR IN CHIEF: **C.B. CEBULSKI**

THOR BY JASON AARON VOL. 5. Contains material originally published in magazine form as THOR (2018) #12-16 and KING THOR (2019) #1-4. First printing 2021. ISBN 978-1-302-93158-2. Published by MARVEL WORLDWIDE, INC., a subsidiary of MARVEL ENTERTAINMENT, LLC. OFFICE OF PUBLICATION: 1290 Avenue of the Americas, New York, NY 10104. © 2021 MARVEL No similarity between any of the names, characters, persons, and/or institutions in this magazine with those of any living or dead person or institution is intended, and any such similarity which may exist is purely coincidental. **Printed in China.** KEVIN FEIGE, Chief Creative Officer; DAN BUCKLEY, President, Marvel Entertainment; JOE QUESADA, EVP & Creative Director; DAVID BOGART, Associate Publisher & SVP of Talent Affairs; TOM BREVOORT, VP, Executive Editor; NICK LOWE, Executive Editor, VP of Content, Digital Publishing; DAVID GABRIEL, VP of Print & Digital Publishing; JEFF YOUNGQUIST, VP of Production & Special Projects; ALEX MORALES, Director of Publishing Operations; DAN EDINGTON, Managing Editor; RICKEY PURDIN, Director of Talent Relations; JENNIFER GRÜNWALD, Senior Editor, Special Projects; SUSAN CRESPI, Production Manager; STAN LEE, Chairman Emeritus. For information regarding advertising in Marvel Comics or on Marvel.com, please contact Vit DeBellis, Custom Solutions & Integrated Advertising Manager, at vdebellis@marvel.com. For Marvel subscription inquiries, please call 888-511-5480. **Manufactured between 8/27/2021 and 11/8/2021 by R.R. DONNELLEY ASIA PRINTING SOLUTIONS, CHINA.**

10 9 8 7 6 5 4 3 2 1

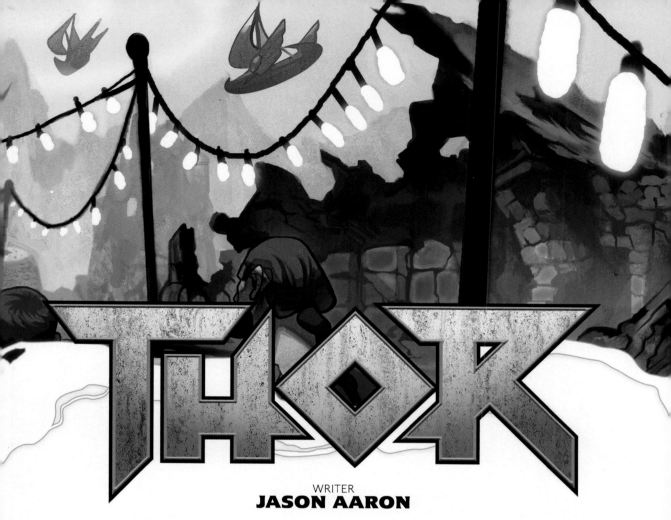

THOR

WRITER
JASON AARON

— THOR #12-13 & #15-16 —

ARTIST
MIKE DEL MUNDO

COLOR ARTISTS
MIKE DEL MUNDO WITH
MARCO D'ALFONSO (#13, #15-16)

COVER ART
MIKE DEL MUNDO

— KING THOR #1-4 —

ARTIST
ESAD RIBIĆ

COLOR ARTIST
IVE SVORCINA

ADDITIONAL ART, #3
DAS PASTORAS

ADDITIONAL ART, #4
GABRIEL HERNANDEZ WALTA
& CHRIS O'HALLORAN;
ANDREA SORRENTINO & DAVE STEWART;
CHRIS BURNHAM & NATHAN FAIRBAIRN;
NICK PITARRA & MICHAEL GARLAND;
AARON KUDER & LAURA MARTIN;
OLIVIER COIPEL & LAURA MARTIN;
RUSSELL DAUTERMAN & MATTHEW WILSON;
AND MIKE DEL MUNDO

COVER ART
ESAD RIBIĆ

— THOR #14 —

ARTIST
SCOTT HEPBURN

COLOR ARTIST
MATTHEW WILSON

COVER ART
MIKE DEL MUNDO

LETTERER
VC's JOE SABINO

ASSOCIATE EDITOR
SARAH BRUNSTAD

EDITOR
WIL MOSS

EXECUTIVE EDITOR
TOM BREVOORT

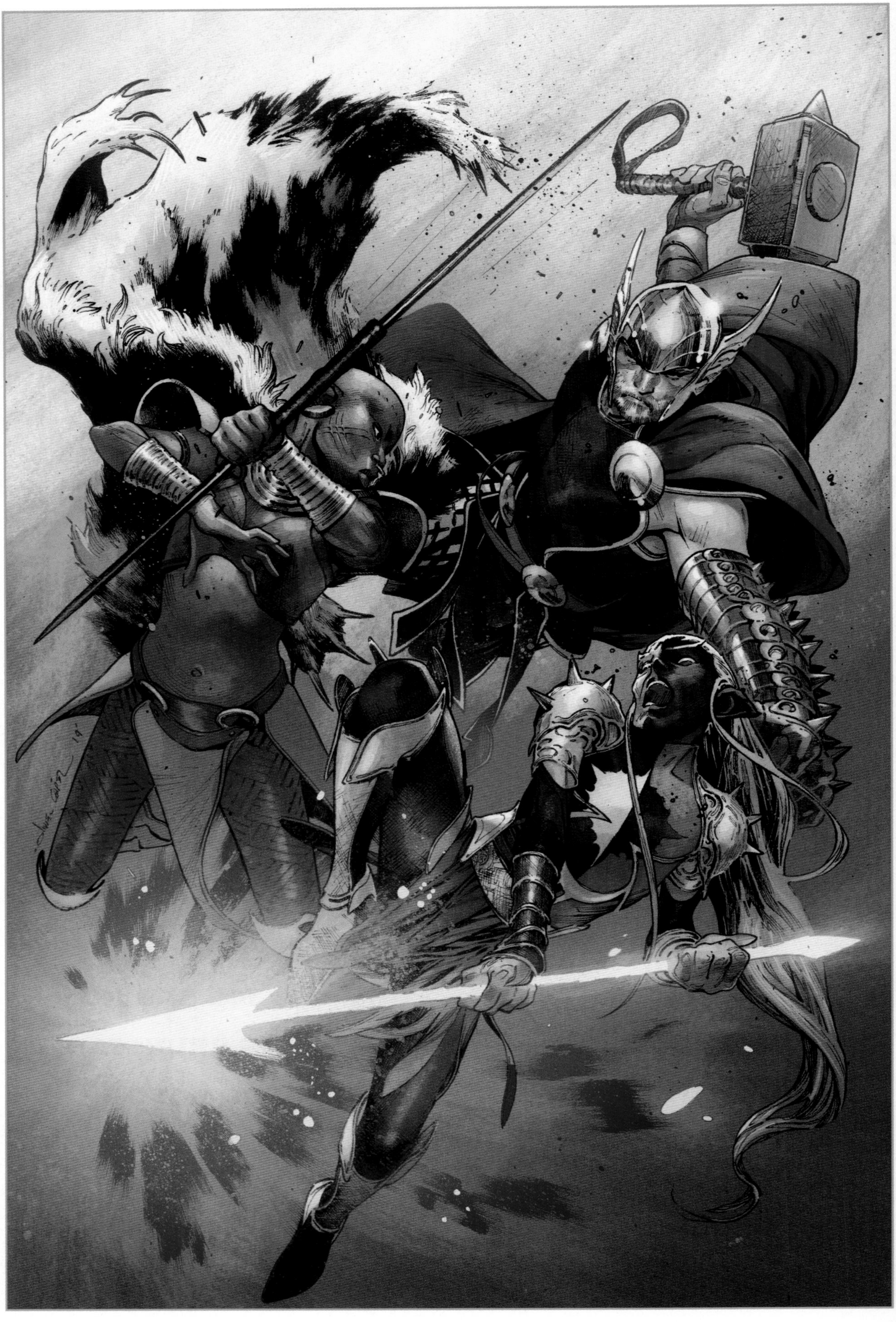

THOR #12 VARIANT
BY **OLIVIER COIPEL** & **MATTHEW WILSON**

— 12 —

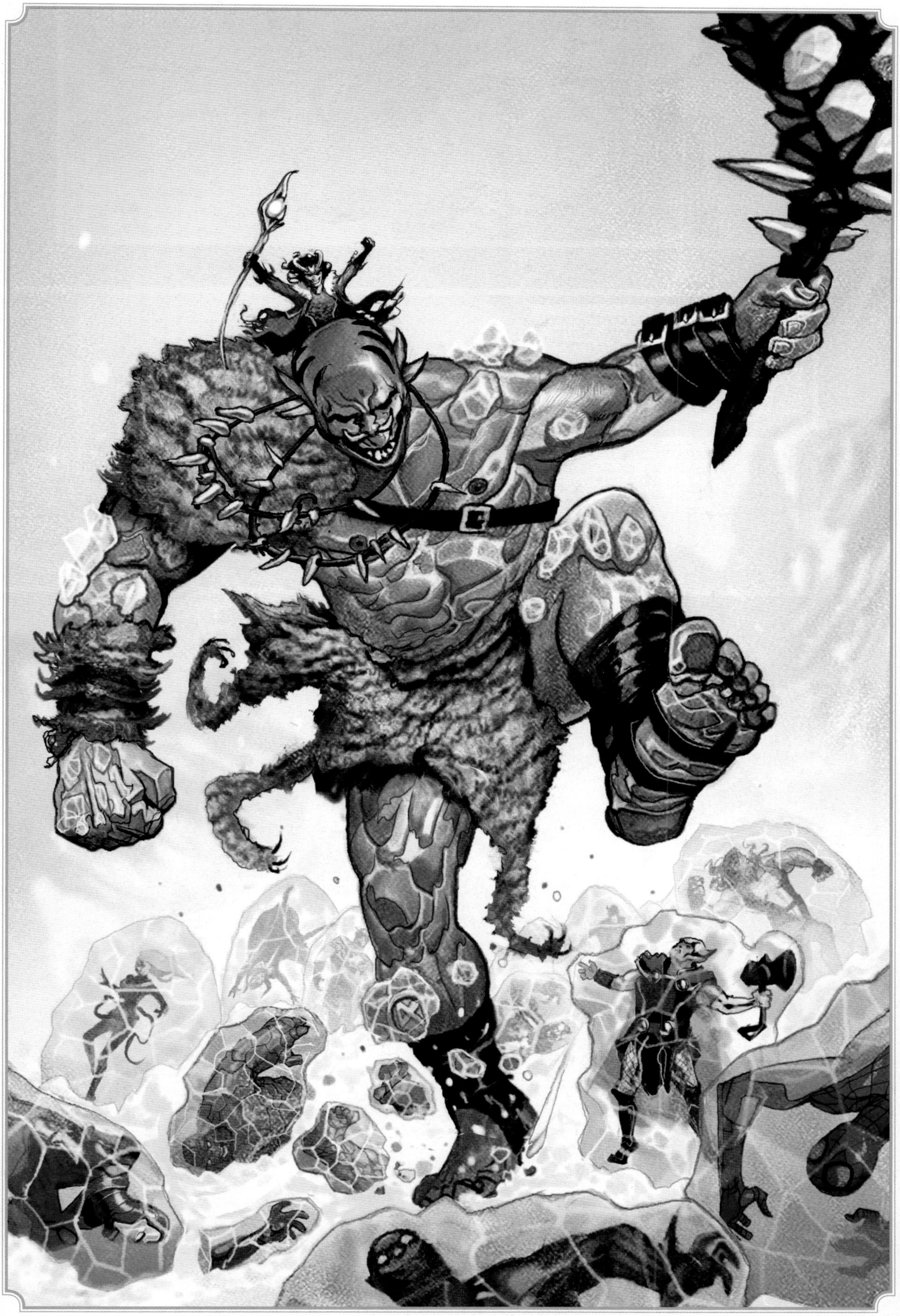

THE WAR OF THE LOKIS

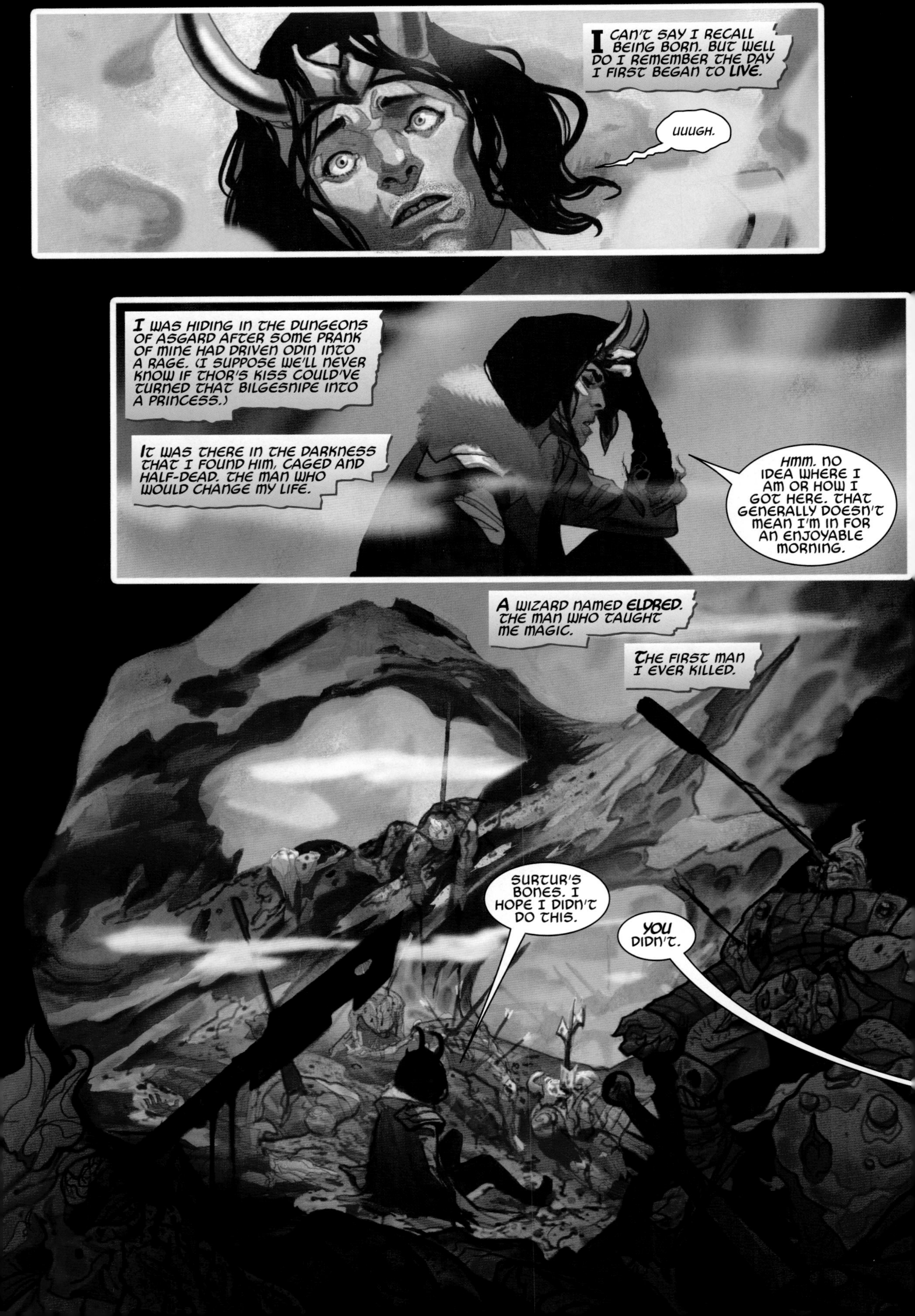
I CAN'T SAY I RECALL BEING BORN. BUT WELL DO I REMEMBER THE DAY I FIRST BEGAN TO LIVE.
UUUGH.
I WAS HIDING IN THE DUNGEONS OF ASGARD AFTER SOME PRANK OF MINE HAD DRIVEN ODIN INTO A RAGE. (I SUPPOSE WE'LL NEVER KNOW IF THOR'S KISS COULD'VE TURNED THAT BILGESNIPE INTO A PRINCESS.)
IT WAS THERE IN THE DARKNESS THAT I FOUND HIM, CAGED AND HALF-DEAD. THE MAN WHO WOULD CHANGE MY LIFE.
HMM. NO IDEA WHERE I AM OR HOW I GOT HERE. THAT GENERALLY DOESN'T MEAN I'M IN FOR AN ENJOYABLE MORNING.
A WIZARD NAMED ELDRED. THE MAN WHO TAUGHT ME MAGIC.
THE FIRST MAN I EVER KILLED.
SURTUR'S BONES. I HOPE I DIDN'T DO THIS.
YOU DIDN'T.

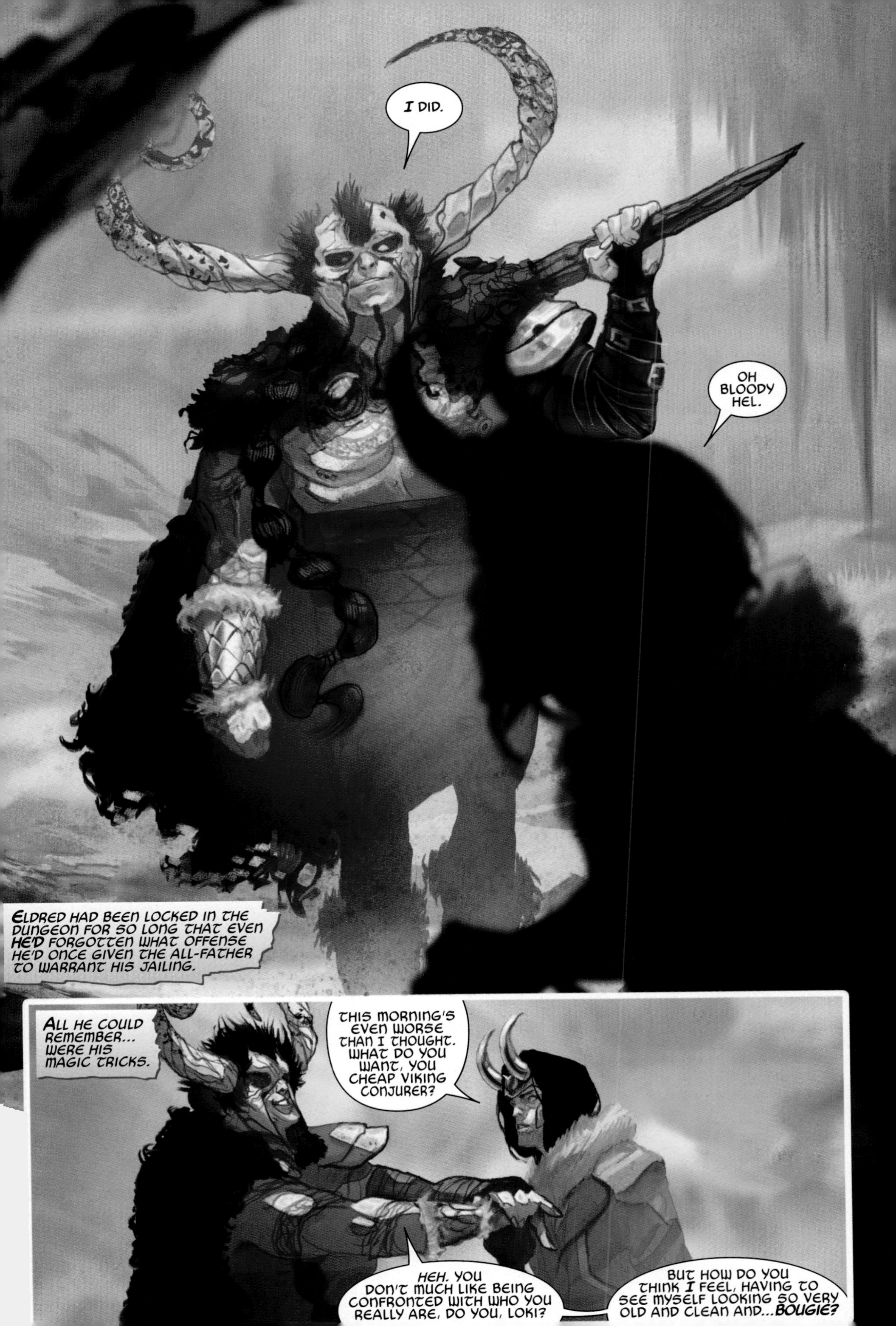
I DID.
OH BLOODY HEL.
ELDRED HAD BEEN LOCKED IN THE DUNGEON FOR SO LONG THAT EVEN HE'D FORGOTTEN WHAT OFFENSE HE'D ONCE GIVEN THE ALL-FATHER TO WARRANT HIS JAILING.
ALL HE COULD REMEMBER... WERE HIS MAGIC TRICKS.
THIS MORNING'S EVEN WORSE THAN I THOUGHT. WHAT DO YOU WANT, YOU CHEAP VIKING CONJURER?
HEH. YOU DON'T MUCH LIKE BEING CONFRONTED WITH WHO YOU REALLY ARE, DO YOU, LOKI?
BUT HOW DO YOU THINK I FEEL, HAVING TO SEE MYSELF LOOKING SO VERY OLD AND CLEAN AND...BOUGIE?

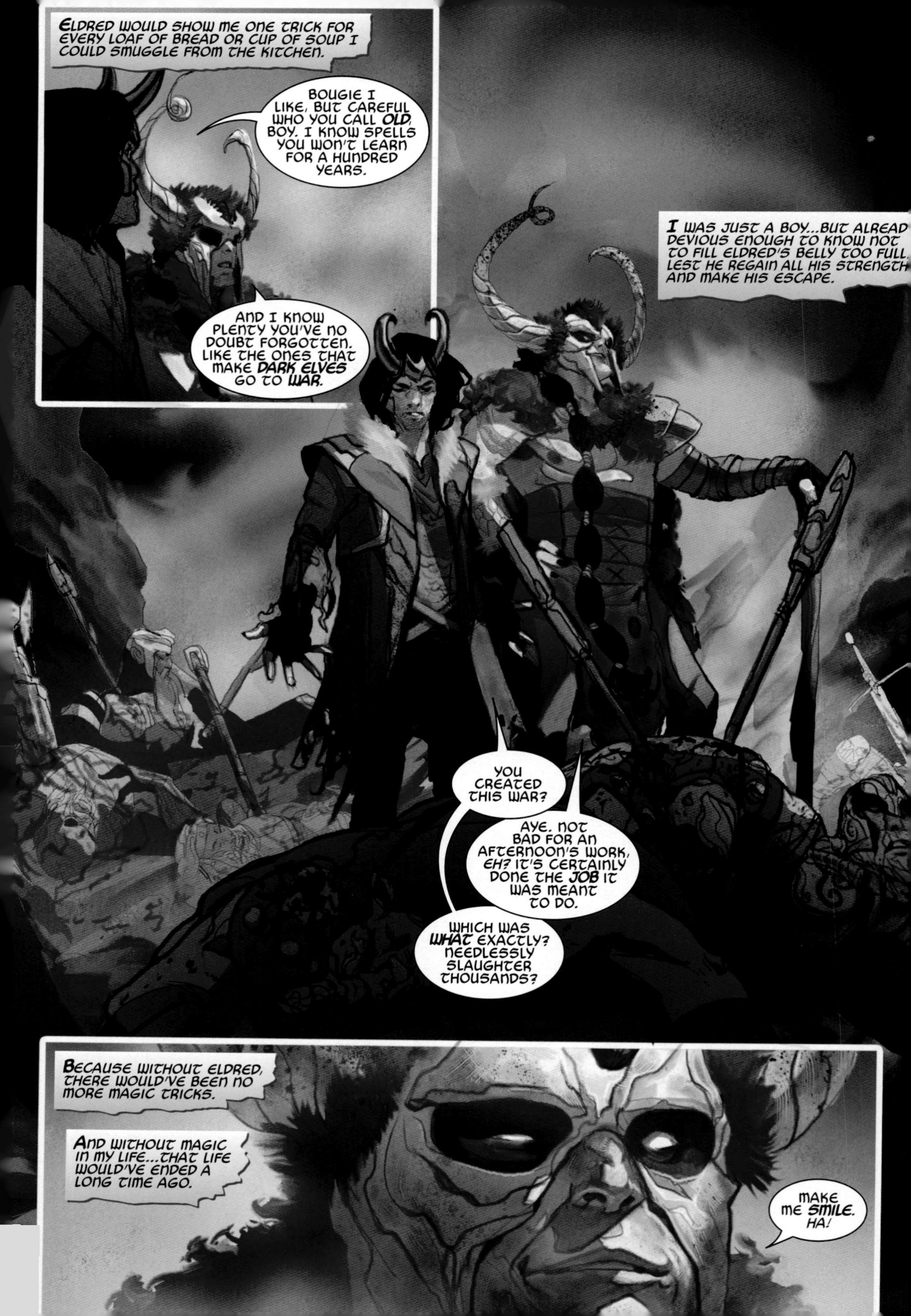
ELDRED WOULD SHOW ME ONE TRICK FOR EVERY LOAF OF BREAD OR CUP OF SOUP I COULD SMUGGLE FROM THE KITCHEN.
BOUGIE I LIKE, BUT CAREFUL WHO YOU CALL OLD, BOY. I KNOW SPELLS YOU WON'T LEARN FOR A HUNDRED YEARS.
AND I KNOW PLENTY YOU'VE NO DOUBT FORGOTTEN. LIKE THE ONES THAT MAKE DARK ELVES GO TO WAR.
I WAS JUST A BOY...BUT ALREAD DEVIOUS ENOUGH TO KNOW NOT TO FILL ELDRED'S BELLY TOO FULL, LEST HE REGAIN ALL HIS STRENGTH AND MAKE HIS ESCAPE.
YOU CREATED THIS WAR?
AYE. NOT BAD FOR AN AFTERNOON'S WORK, EH? IT'S CERTAINLY DONE THE JOB IT WAS MEANT TO DO.
WHICH WAS WHAT EXACTLY? NEEDLESSLY SLAUGHTER THOUSANDS?
BECAUSE WITHOUT ELDRED, THERE WOULD'VE BEEN NO MORE MAGIC TRICKS.
AND WITHOUT MAGIC IN MY LIFE...THAT LIFE WOULD'VE ENDED A LONG TIME AGO.
MAKE ME SMILE. HA!

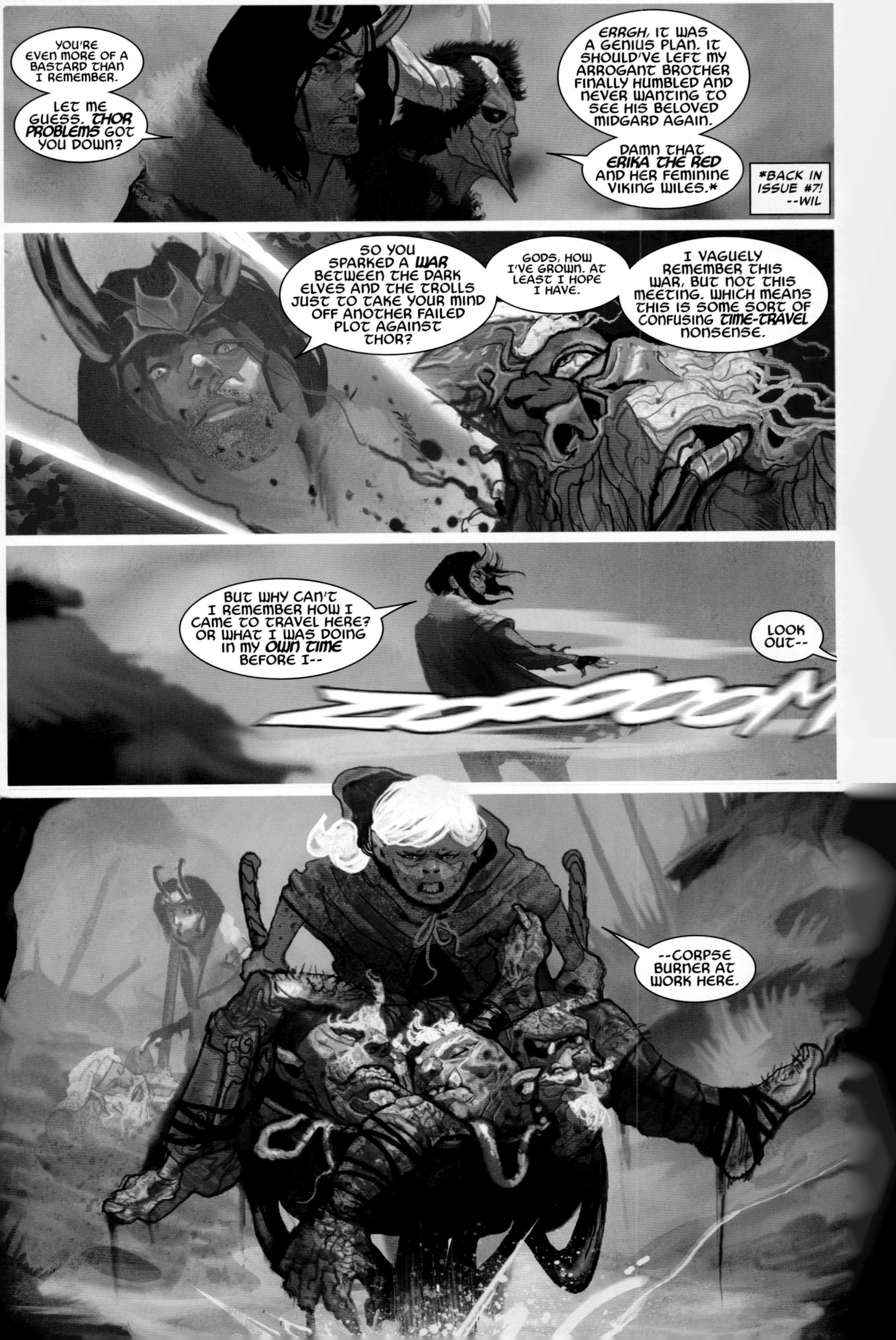
YOU'RE EVEN MORE OF A BASTARD THAN I REMEMBER.
LET ME GUESS. THOR PROBLEMS GOT YOU DOWN?
ERRGH, IT WAS A GENIUS PLAN. IT SHOULD'VE LEFT MY ARROGANT BROTHER FINALLY HUMBLED AND NEVER WANTING TO SEE HIS BELOVED MIDGARD AGAIN.
DAMN THAT ERIKA THE RED AND HER FEMININE VIKING WILES.*
*BACK IN ISSUE #7! --WIL
SO YOU SPARKED A WAR BETWEEN THE DARK ELVES AND THE TROLLS JUST TO TAKE YOUR MIND OFF ANOTHER FAILED PLOT AGAINST THOR?
GODS, HOW I'VE GROWN. AT LEAST I HOPE I HAVE.
I VAGUELY REMEMBER THIS WAR, BUT NOT THIS MEETING. WHICH MEANS THIS IS SOME SORT OF CONFUSING TIME-TRAVEL NONSENSE.
BUT WHY CAN'T I REMEMBER HOW I CAME TO TRAVEL HERE? OR WHAT I WAS DOING IN MY OWN TIME BEFORE I--
LOOK OUT--
ZOOOOOOM
--CORPSE BURNER AT WORK HERE.

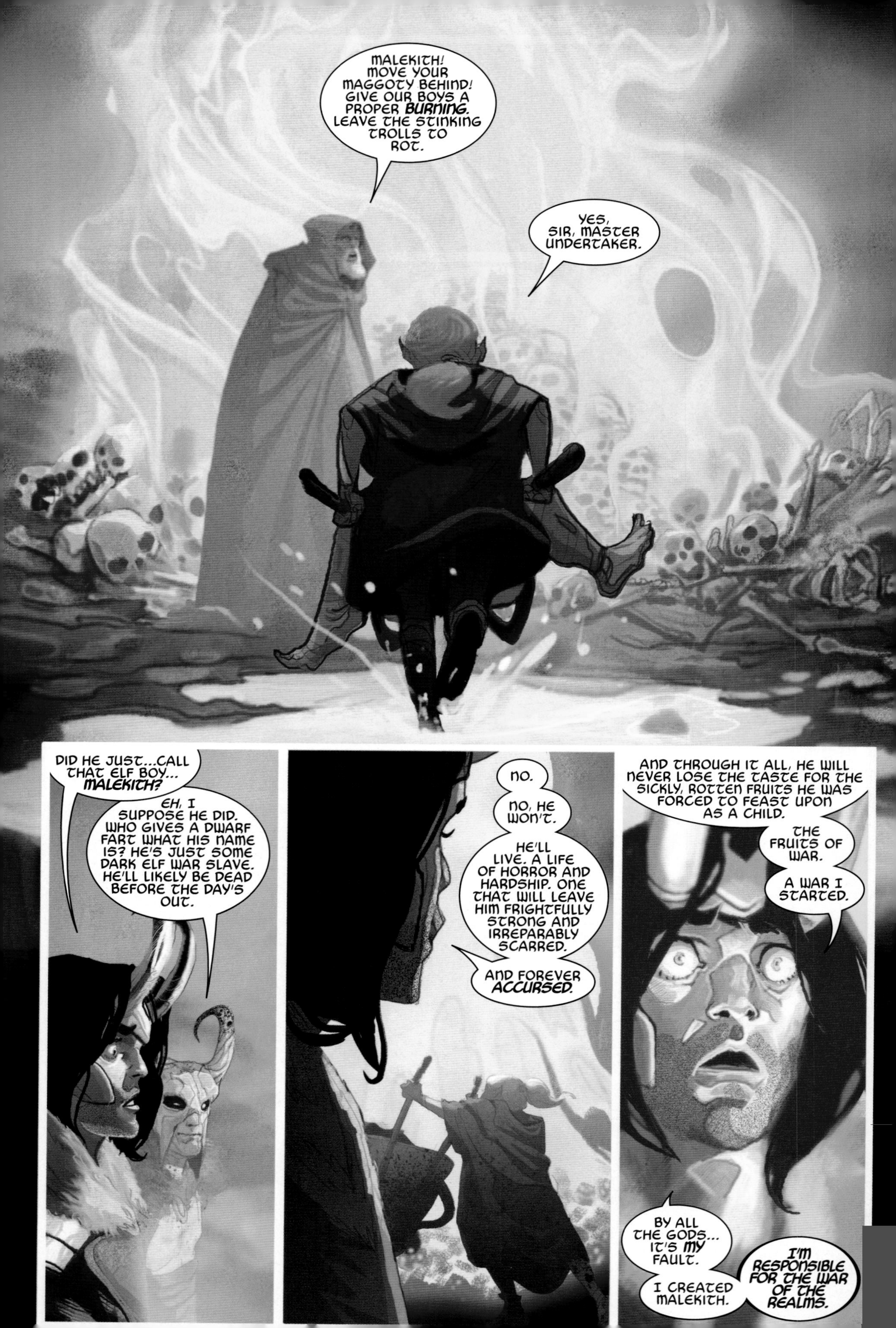
MALEKITH! MOVE YOUR MAGGOTY BEHIND! GIVE OUR BOYS A PROPER BURNING. LEAVE THE STINKING TROLLS TO ROT.
YES, SIR, MASTER UNDERTAKER.
DID HE JUST...CALL THAT ELF BOY... MALEKITH?
EH, I SUPPOSE HE DID. WHO GIVES A DWARF FART WHAT HIS NAME IS? HE'S JUST SOME DARK ELF WAR SLAVE. HE'LL LIKELY BE DEAD BEFORE THE DAY'S OUT.
NO.
NO, HE WON'T.
HE'LL LIVE. A LIFE OF HORROR AND HARDSHIP. ONE THAT WILL LEAVE HIM FRIGHTFULLY STRONG AND IRREPARABLY SCARRED.
AND FOREVER ACCURSED.
AND THROUGH IT ALL, HE WILL NEVER LOSE THE TASTE FOR THE SICKLY, ROTTEN FRUITS HE WAS FORCED TO FEAST UPON AS A CHILD.
THE FRUITS OF WAR.
A WAR I STARTED.
BY ALL THE GODS... IT'S MY FAULT.
I CREATED MALEKITH.
I'M RESPONSIBLE FOR THE WAR OF THE REALMS.

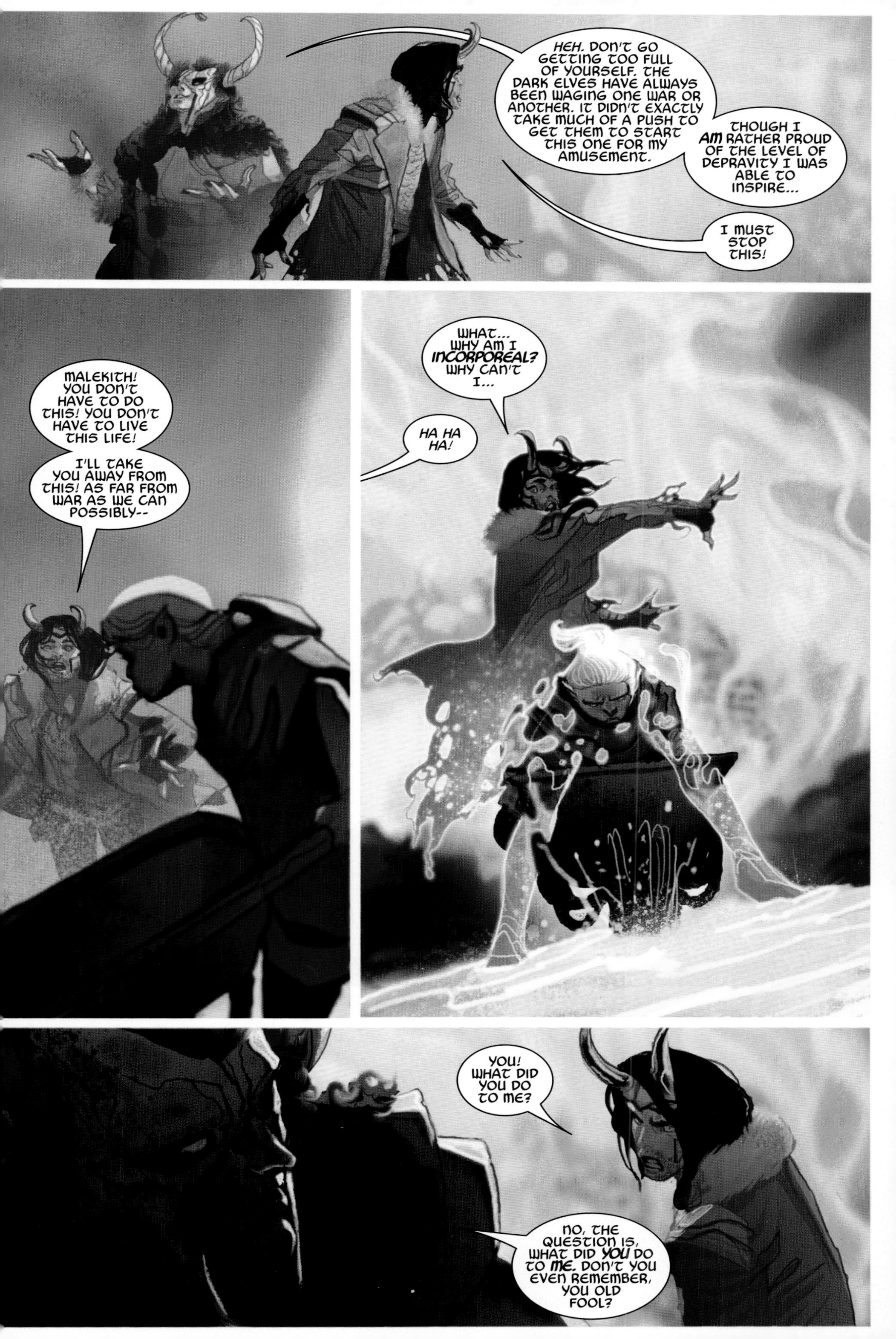
HEH. DON'T GO GETTING TOO FULL OF YOURSELF. THE DARK ELVES HAVE ALWAYS BEEN WAGING ONE WAR OR ANOTHER. IT DIDN'T EXACTLY TAKE MUCH OF A PUSH TO GET THEM TO START THIS ONE FOR MY AMUSEMENT.
THOUGH I AM RATHER PROUD OF THE LEVEL OF DEPRAVITY I WAS ABLE TO INSPIRE...
I MUST STOP THIS!
MALEKITH! YOU DON'T HAVE TO DO THIS! YOU DON'T HAVE TO LIVE THIS LIFE!
I'LL TAKE YOU AWAY FROM THIS! AS FAR FROM WAR AS WE CAN POSSIBLY--
WHAT... WHY AM I INCORPOREAL? WHY CAN'T I...
HA HA HA!
YOU! WHAT DID YOU DO TO ME?
NO, THE QUESTION IS, WHAT DID YOU DO TO ME. DON'T YOU EVEN REMEMBER, YOU OLD FOOL?

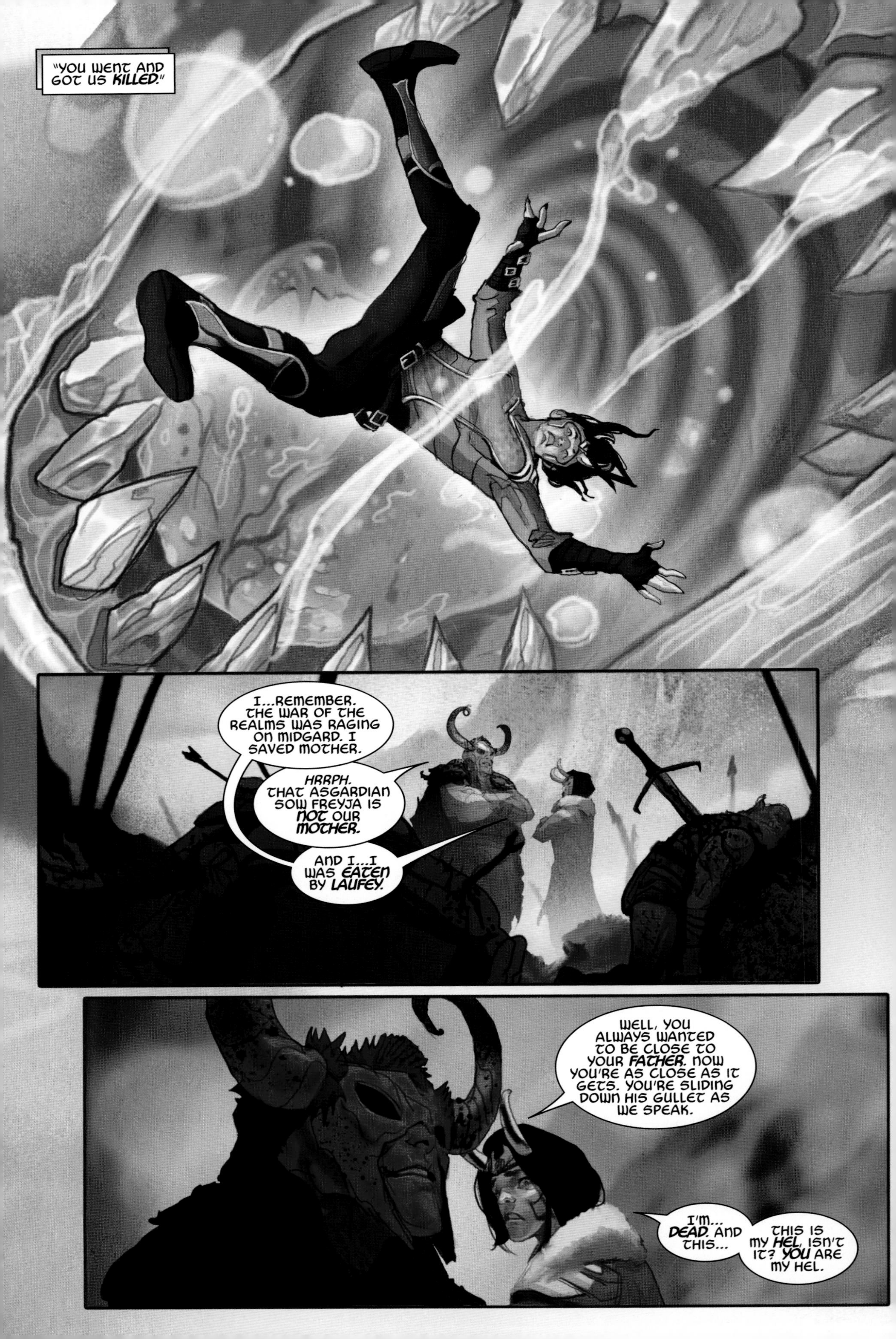
"YOU WENT AND GOT US KILLED."
I...REMEMBER. THE WAR OF THE REALMS WAS RAGING ON MIDGARD. I SAVED MOTHER.
HRRPH. THAT ASGARDIAN SOW FREYJA IS NOT OUR MOTHER.
AND I...I WAS EATEN BY LAUFEY.
WELL, YOU ALWAYS WANTED TO BE CLOSE TO YOUR FATHER. NOW YOU'RE AS CLOSE AS IT GETS. YOU'RE SLIDING DOWN HIS GULLET AS WE SPEAK.
I'M... DEAD. AND THIS...
THIS IS MY HEL, ISN'T IT? YOU ARE MY HEL.

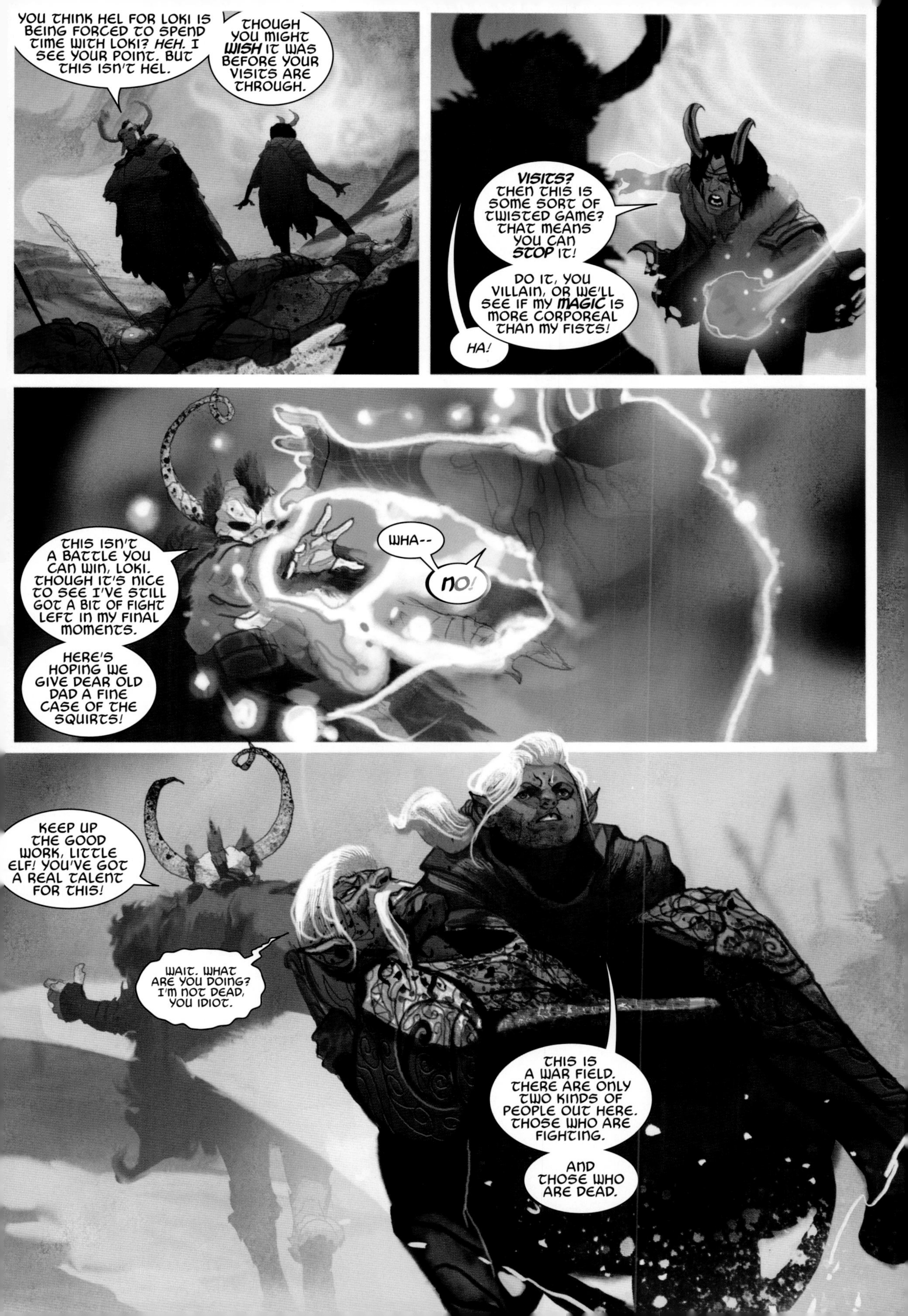

YOU THINK HEL FOR LOKI IS BEING FORCED TO SPEND TIME WITH LOKI? *HEH.* I SEE YOUR POINT. BUT THIS ISN'T HEL.
THOUGH YOU MIGHT *WISH* IT WAS BEFORE YOUR VISITS ARE THROUGH.
VISITS? THEN THIS IS SOME SORT OF TWISTED GAME? THAT MEANS YOU CAN *STOP* IT!
DO IT, YOU VILLAIN, OR WE'LL SEE IF MY *MAGIC* IS MORE CORPOREAL THAN MY FISTS!
HA!
THIS ISN'T A BATTLE YOU CAN WIN, LOKI. THOUGH IT'S NICE TO SEE I'VE STILL GOT A BIT OF FIGHT LEFT IN MY FINAL MOMENTS.
HERE'S HOPING WE GIVE DEAR OLD DAD A FINE CASE OF THE SQUIRTS!
WHA--
NO!
KEEP UP THE GOOD WORK, LITTLE ELF! YOU'VE GOT A REAL TALENT FOR THIS!
WAIT. WHAT ARE YOU DOING? I'M NOT DEAD, YOU IDIOT.
THIS IS A WAR FIELD. THERE ARE ONLY TWO KINDS OF PEOPLE OUT HERE. THOSE WHO ARE FIGHTING.
AND THOSE WHO ARE DEAD.

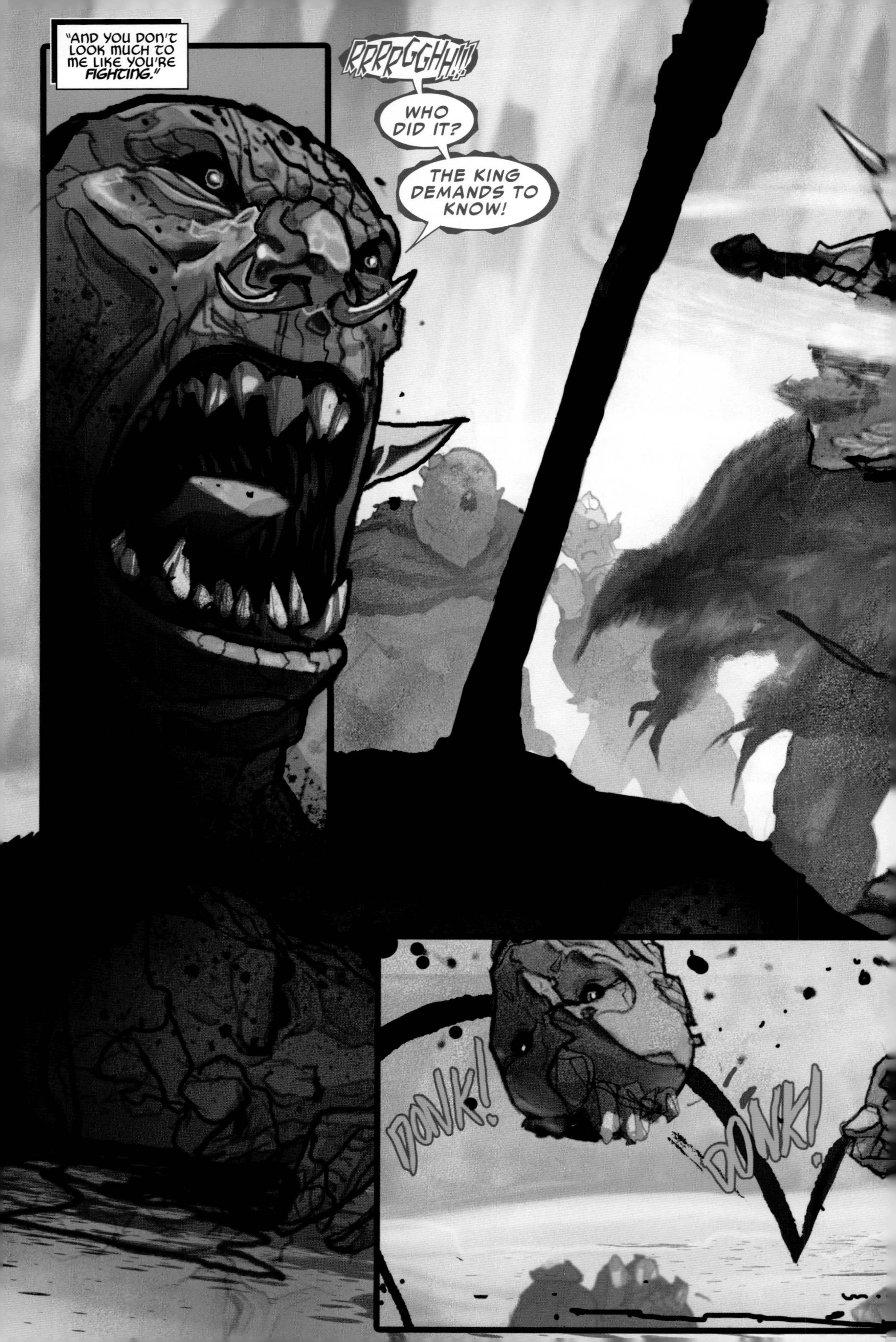
"AND YOU DON'T LOOK MUCH TO ME LIKE YOU'RE FIGHTING."
RRRRGGHH!!!
WHO DID IT?
THE KING DEMANDS TO KNOW!
DONK!
DONK!

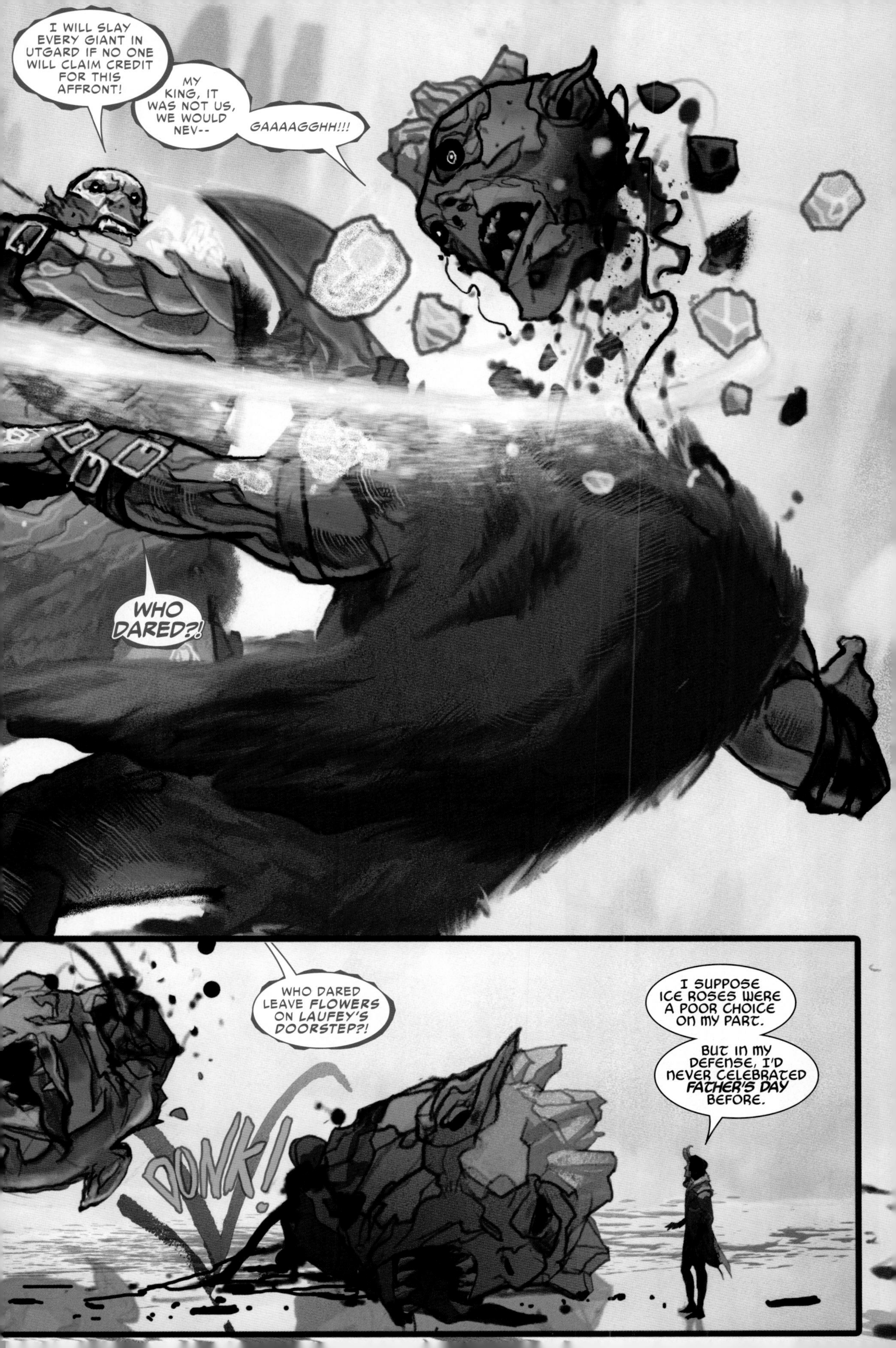
I WILL SLAY EVERY GIANT IN UTGARD IF NO ONE WILL CLAIM CREDIT FOR THIS AFFRONT!
MY KING, IT WAS NOT US, WE WOULD NEV--
GAAAAGGHH!!!
WHO DARED?!
WHO DARED LEAVE *FLOWERS* ON *LAUFEY'S* DOORSTEP?!
DONK!
I SUPPOSE ICE ROSES WERE A POOR CHOICE ON MY PART.
BUT IN MY DEFENSE, I'D NEVER CELEBRATED ***FATHER'S DAY*** BEFORE.

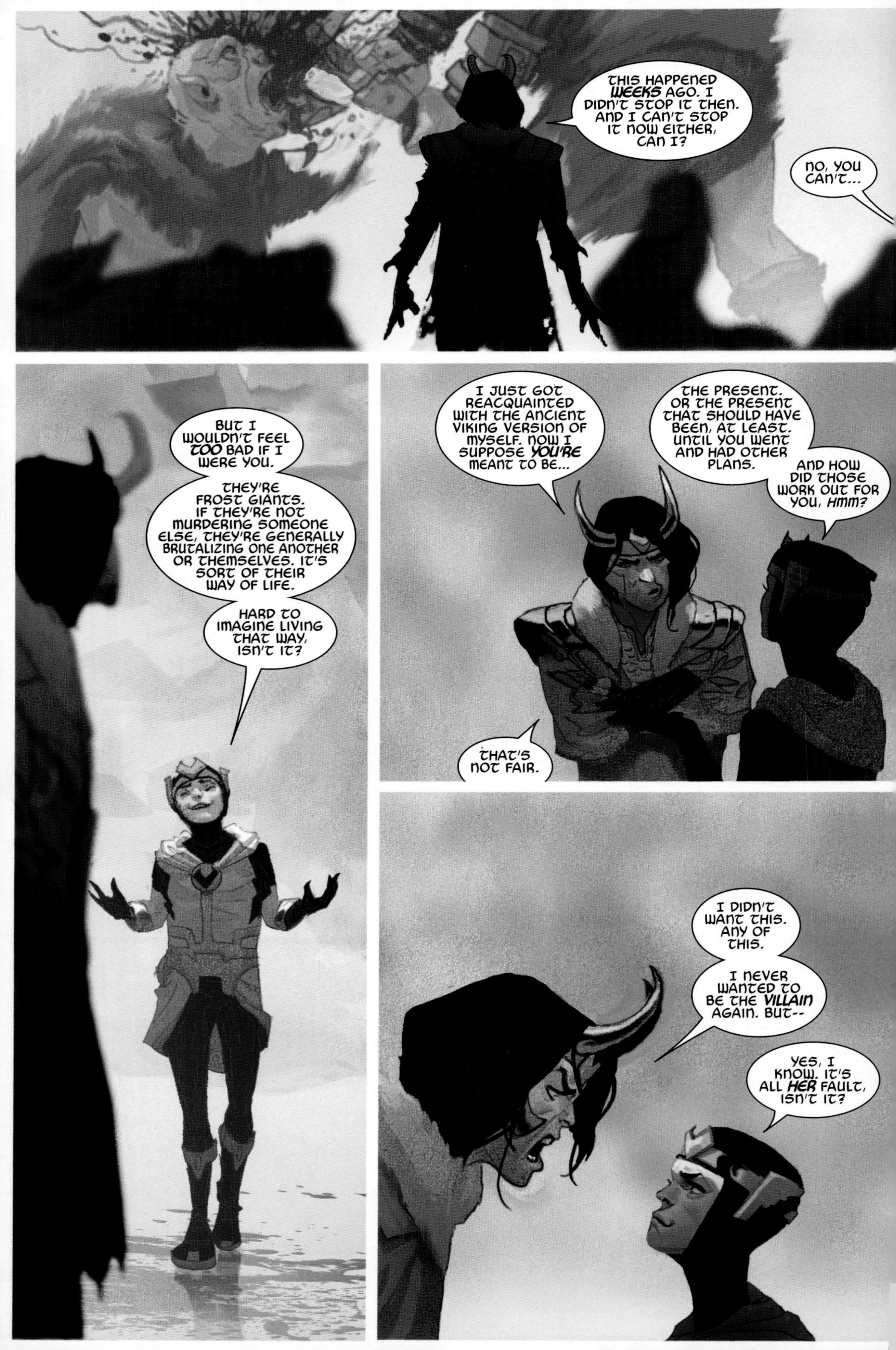
THIS HAPPENED WEEKS AGO. I DIDN'T STOP IT THEN. AND I CAN'T STOP IT NOW EITHER, CAN I?
NO, YOU CAN'T...
BUT I WOULDN'T FEEL TOO BAD IF I WERE YOU.
THEY'RE FROST GIANTS. IF THEY'RE NOT MURDERING SOMEONE ELSE, THEY'RE GENERALLY BRUTALIZING ONE ANOTHER OR THEMSELVES. IT'S SORT OF THEIR WAY OF LIFE.
HARD TO IMAGINE LIVING THAT WAY, ISN'T IT?
I JUST GOT REACQUAINTED WITH THE ANCIENT VIKING VERSION OF MYSELF. NOW I SUPPOSE YOU'RE MEANT TO BE...
THE PRESENT. OR THE PRESENT THAT SHOULD HAVE BEEN, AT LEAST. UNTIL YOU WENT AND HAD OTHER PLANS.
AND HOW DID THOSE WORK OUT FOR YOU, HMM?
THAT'S NOT FAIR.
I DIDN'T WANT THIS. ANY OF THIS.
I NEVER WANTED TO BE THE VILLAIN AGAIN. BUT--
YES, I KNOW. IT'S ALL HER FAULT, ISN'T IT?

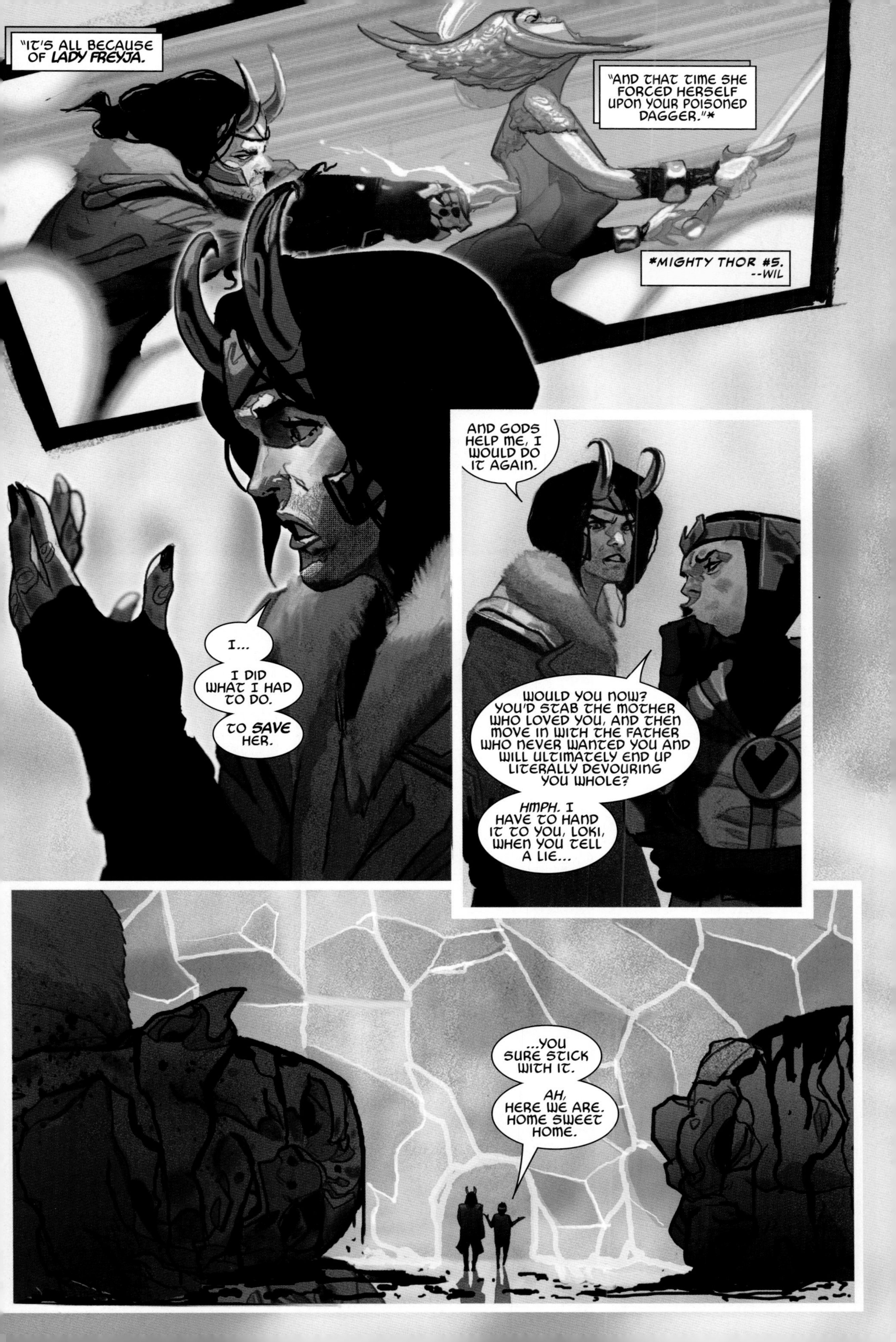
"IT'S ALL BECAUSE OF LADY FREYJA.
"AND THAT TIME SHE FORCED HERSELF UPON YOUR POISONED DAGGER."*
*MIGHTY THOR #5. --WIL
I...
I DID WHAT I HAD TO DO.
TO SAVE HER.
AND GODS HELP ME, I WOULD DO IT AGAIN.
WOULD YOU NOW? YOU'D STAB THE MOTHER WHO LOVED YOU, AND THEN MOVE IN WITH THE FATHER WHO NEVER WANTED YOU AND WILL ULTIMATELY END UP LITERALLY DEVOURING YOU WHOLE?
HMPH. I HAVE TO HAND IT TO YOU, LOKI, WHEN YOU TELL A LIE...
...YOU SURE STICK WITH IT.
AH, HERE WE ARE. HOME SWEET HOME.

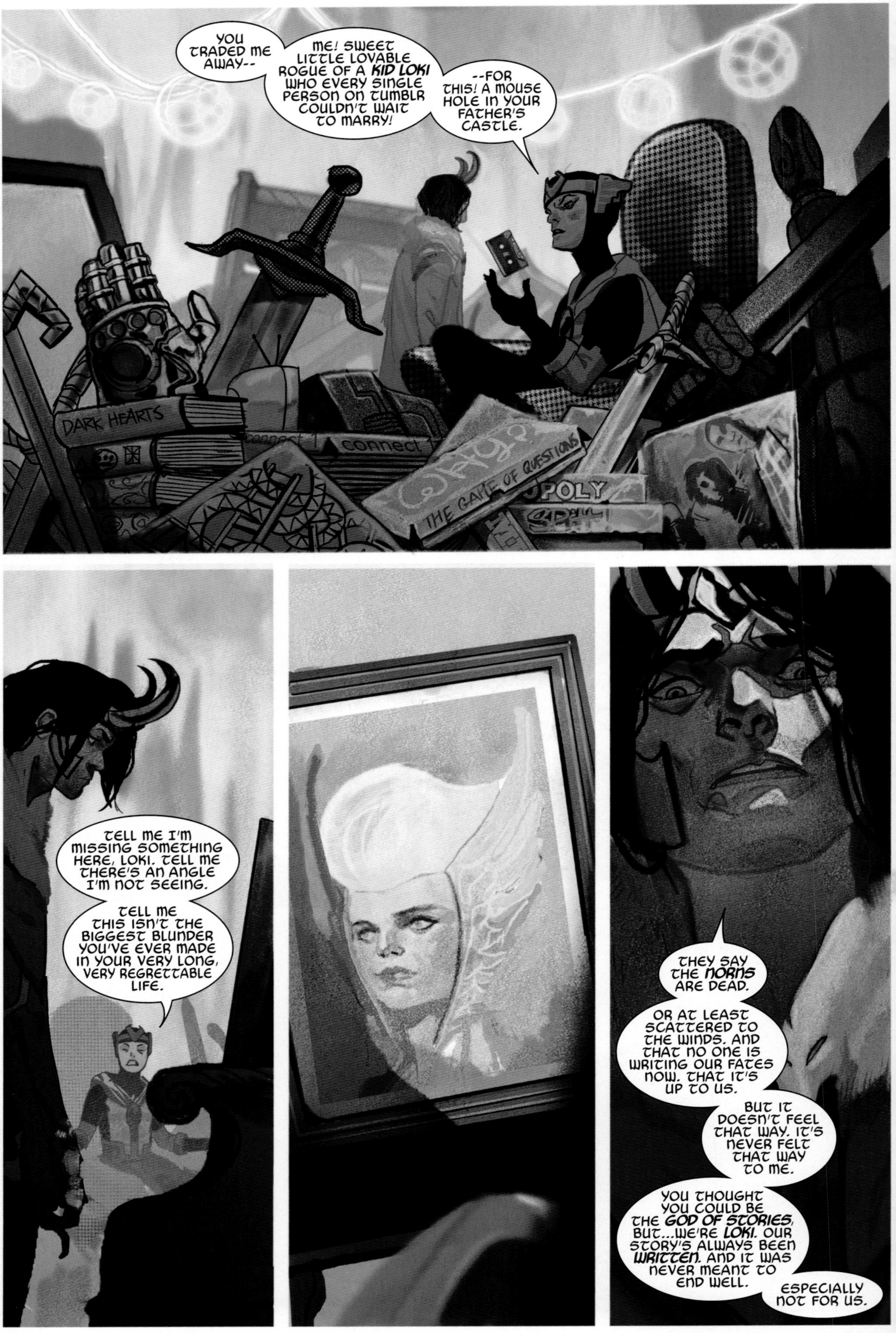
YOU TRADED ME AWAY--
ME! SWEET LITTLE LOVABLE ROGUE OF A KID LOKI WHO EVERY SINGLE PERSON ON TUMBLR COULDN'T WAIT TO MARRY!
--FOR THIS! A MOUSE HOLE IN YOUR FATHER'S CASTLE.
DARK HEARTS
connect 4
connect 4
WHY?
THE GAME OF QUESTIONS
POLY
TELL ME I'M MISSING SOMETHING HERE, LOKI. TELL ME THERE'S AN ANGLE I'M NOT SEEING.
TELL ME THIS ISN'T THE BIGGEST BLUNDER YOU'VE EVER MADE IN YOUR VERY LONG, VERY REGRETTABLE LIFE.
THEY SAY THE NORNS ARE DEAD.
OR AT LEAST SCATTERED TO THE WINDS. AND THAT NO ONE IS WRITING OUR FATES NOW. THAT IT'S UP TO US.
BUT IT DOESN'T FEEL THAT WAY. IT'S NEVER FELT THAT WAY TO ME.
YOU THOUGHT YOU COULD BE THE GOD OF STORIES, BUT...WE'RE LOKI. OUR STORY'S ALWAYS BEEN WRITTEN. AND IT WAS NEVER MEANT TO END WELL.
ESPECIALLY NOT FOR US.

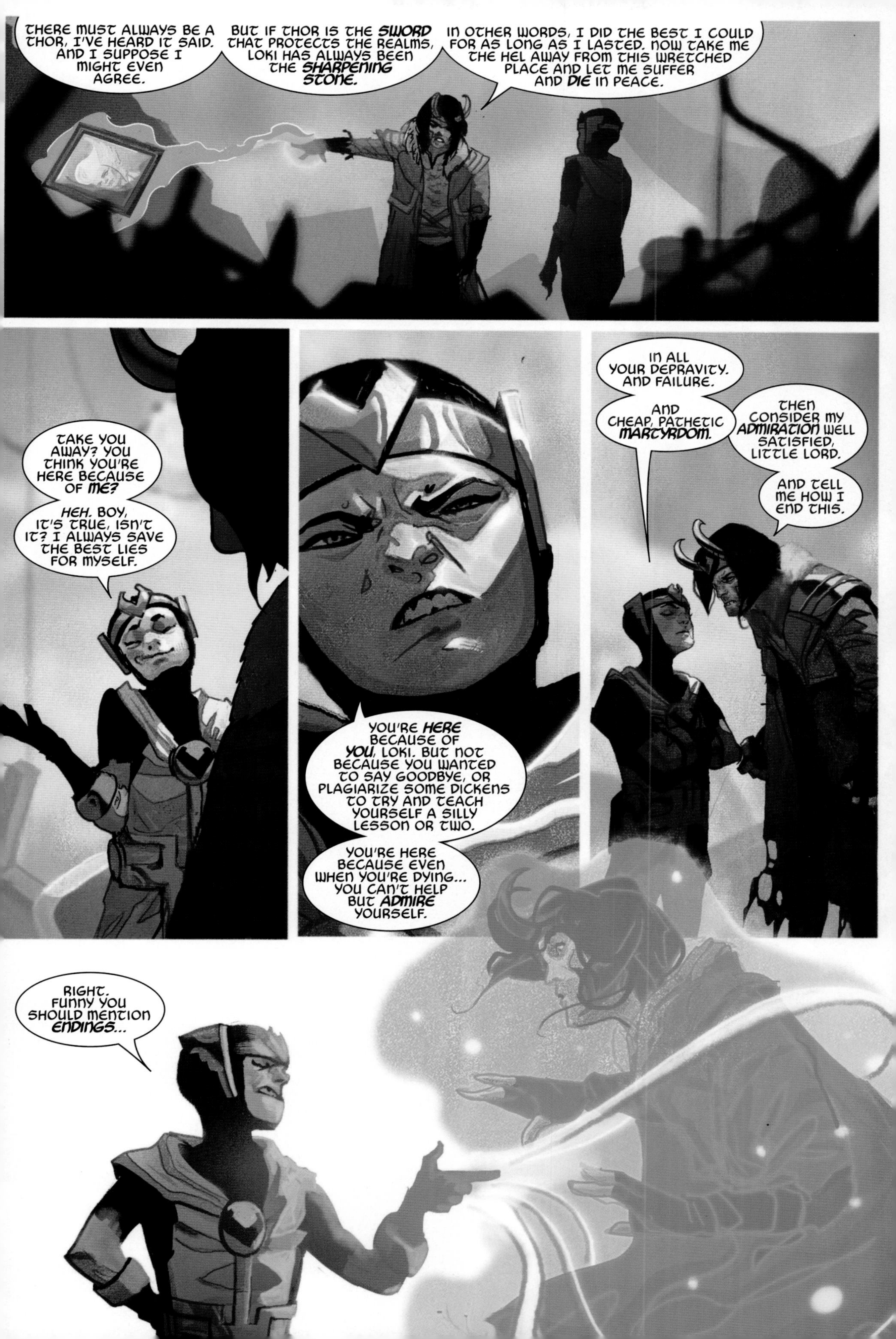
THERE MUST ALWAYS BE A THOR, I'VE HEARD IT SAID. AND I SUPPOSE I MIGHT EVEN AGREE.
BUT IF THOR IS THE SWORD THAT PROTECTS THE REALMS, LOKI HAS ALWAYS BEEN THE SHARPENING STONE.
IN OTHER WORDS, I DID THE BEST I COULD FOR AS LONG AS I LASTED. NOW TAKE ME THE HEL AWAY FROM THIS WRETCHED PLACE AND LET ME SUFFER AND DIE IN PEACE.
TAKE YOU AWAY? YOU THINK YOU'RE HERE BECAUSE OF ME?
HEH. BOY, IT'S TRUE, ISN'T IT? I ALWAYS SAVE THE BEST LIES FOR MYSELF.
YOU'RE HERE BECAUSE OF YOU, LOKI. BUT NOT BECAUSE YOU WANTED TO SAY GOODBYE, OR PLAGIARIZE SOME DICKENS TO TRY AND TEACH YOURSELF A SILLY LESSON OR TWO.
YOU'RE HERE BECAUSE EVEN WHEN YOU'RE DYING... YOU CAN'T HELP BUT ADMIRE YOURSELF.
IN ALL YOUR DEPRAVITY. AND FAILURE.
AND CHEAP, PATHETIC MARTYRDOM.
THEN CONSIDER MY ADMIRATION WELL SATISFIED, LITTLE LORD.
AND TELL ME HOW I END THIS.
RIGHT. FUNNY YOU SHOULD MENTION ENDINGS...

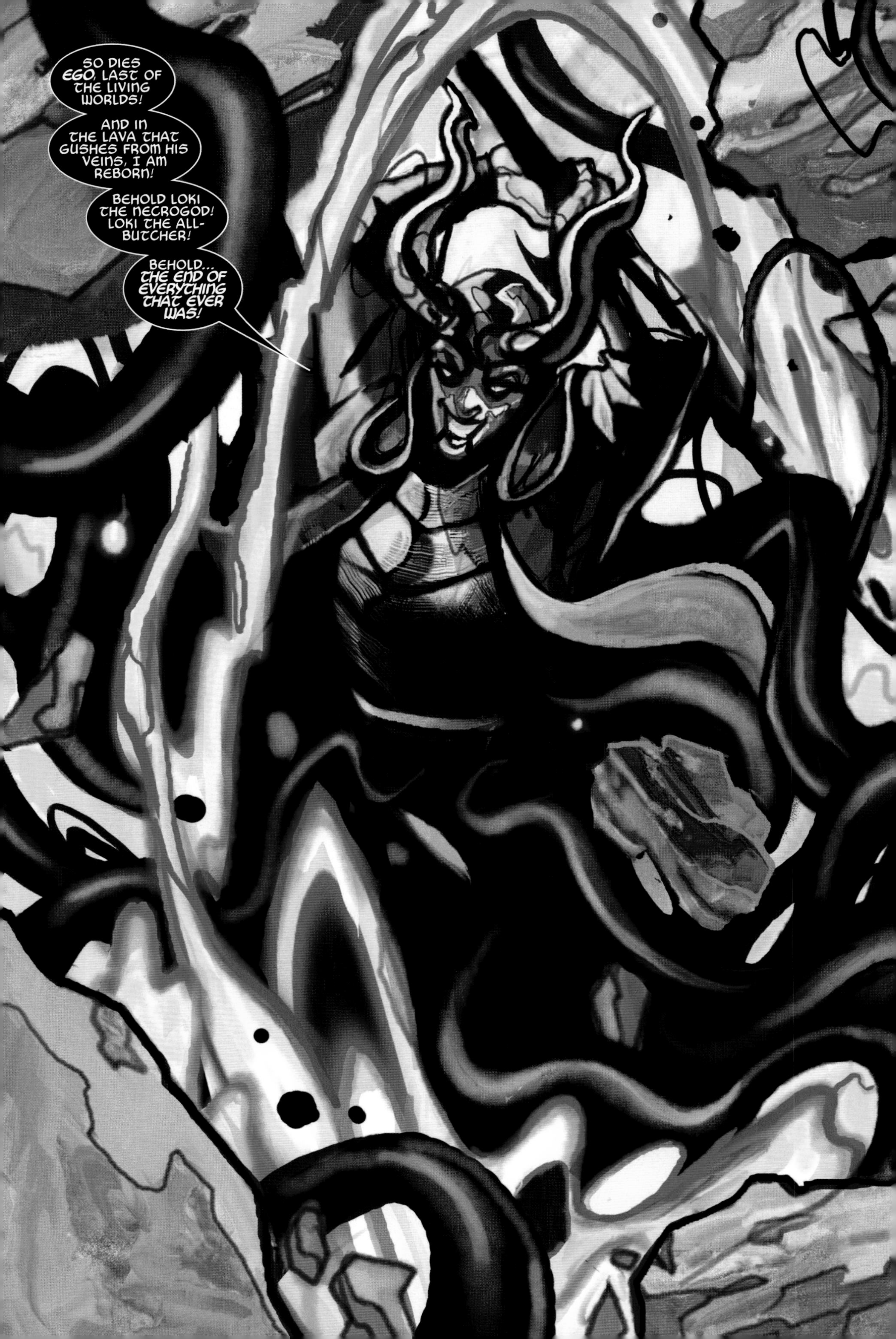
SO DIES EGO, LAST OF THE LIVING WORLDS!
AND IN THE LAVA THAT GUSHES FROM HIS VEINS, I AM REBORN!
BEHOLD LOKI THE NECROGOD! LOKI THE ALL-BUTCHER!
BEHOLD... THE END OF EVERYTHING THAT EVER WAS!

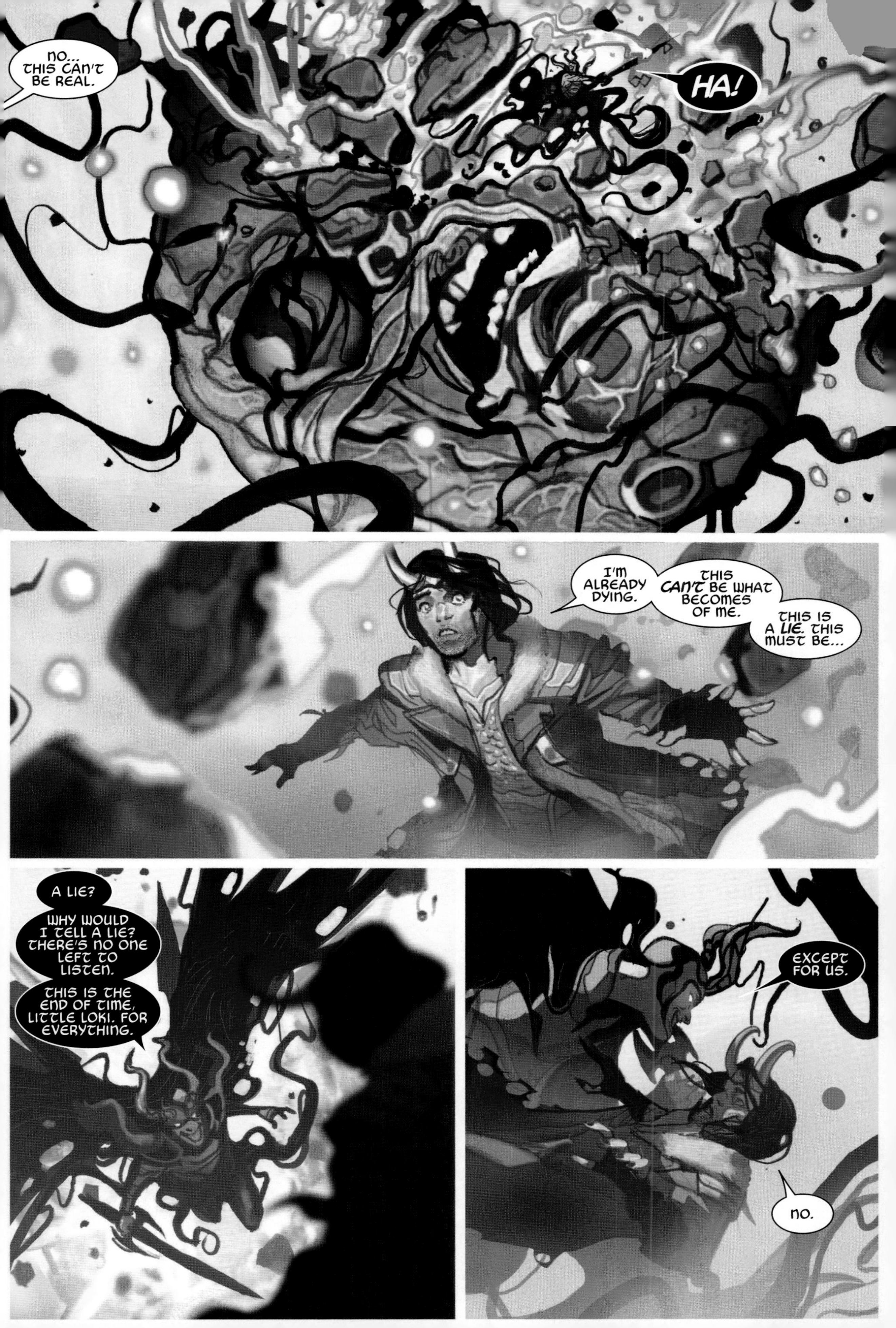
NO... THIS CAN'T BE REAL.
HA!
I'M ALREADY DYING.
THIS CAN'T BE WHAT BECOMES OF ME.
THIS IS A LIE. THIS MUST BE...
A LIE?
WHY WOULD I TELL A LIE? THERE'S NO ONE LEFT TO LISTEN.
THIS IS THE END OF TIME, LITTLE LOKI. FOR EVERYTHING.
EXCEPT FOR US.
NO.

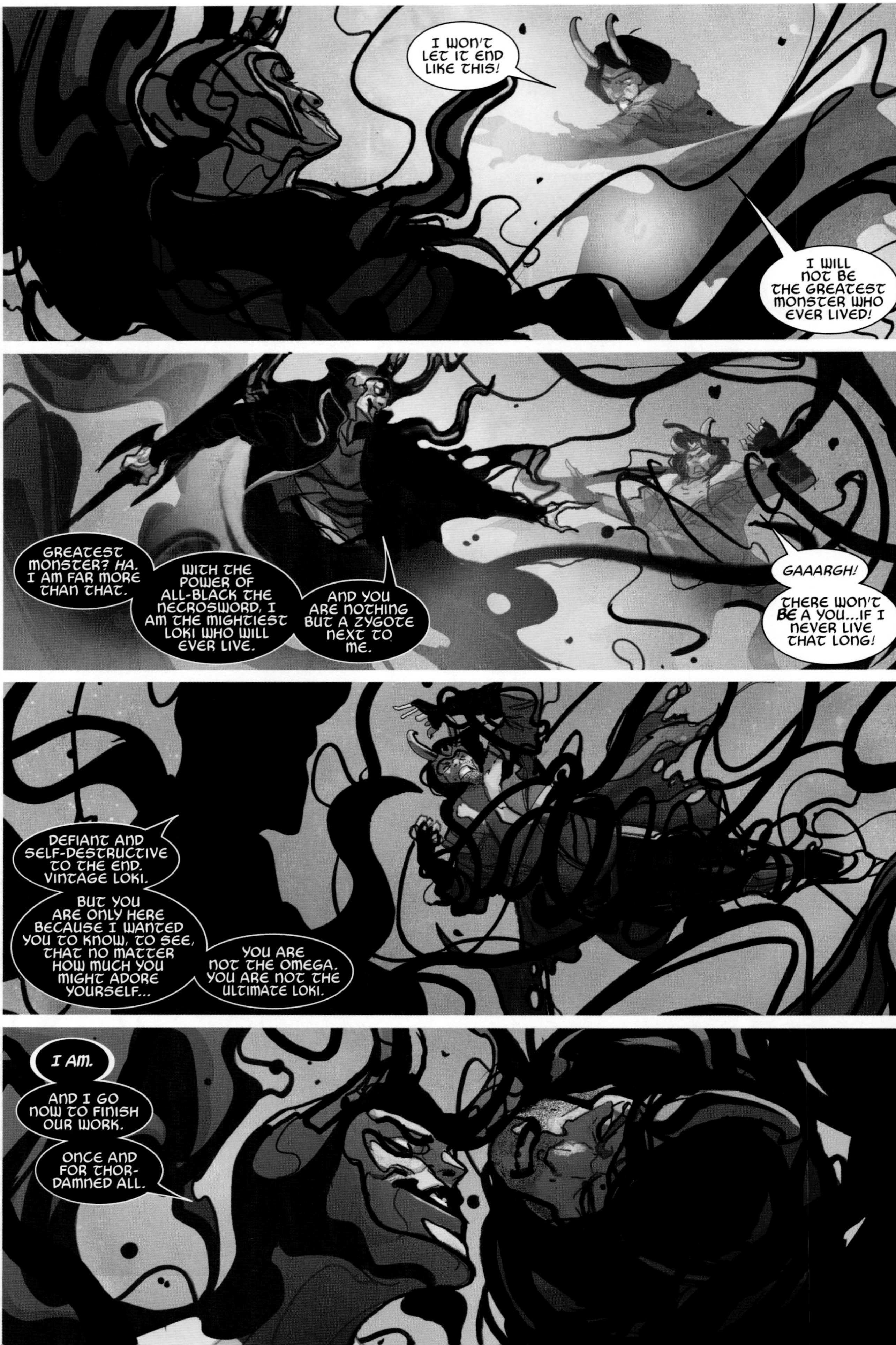
I WON'T LET IT END LIKE THIS!
I WILL NOT BE THE GREATEST MONSTER WHO EVER LIVED!
GREATEST MONSTER? HA. I AM FAR MORE THAN THAT.
WITH THE POWER OF ALL-BLACK THE NECROSWORD, I AM THE MIGHTIEST LOKI WHO WILL EVER LIVE.
AND YOU ARE NOTHING BUT A ZYGOTE NEXT TO ME.
GAAARGH!
THERE WON'T BE A YOU...IF I NEVER LIVE THAT LONG!
DEFIANT AND SELF-DESTRUCTIVE TO THE END. VINTAGE LOKI.
BUT YOU ARE ONLY HERE BECAUSE I WANTED YOU TO KNOW, TO SEE, THAT NO MATTER HOW MUCH YOU MIGHT ADORE YOURSELF...
YOU ARE NOT THE OMEGA. YOU ARE NOT THE ULTIMATE LOKI.
I AM.
AND I GO NOW TO FINISH OUR WORK.
ONCE AND FOR THOR-DAMNED ALL.

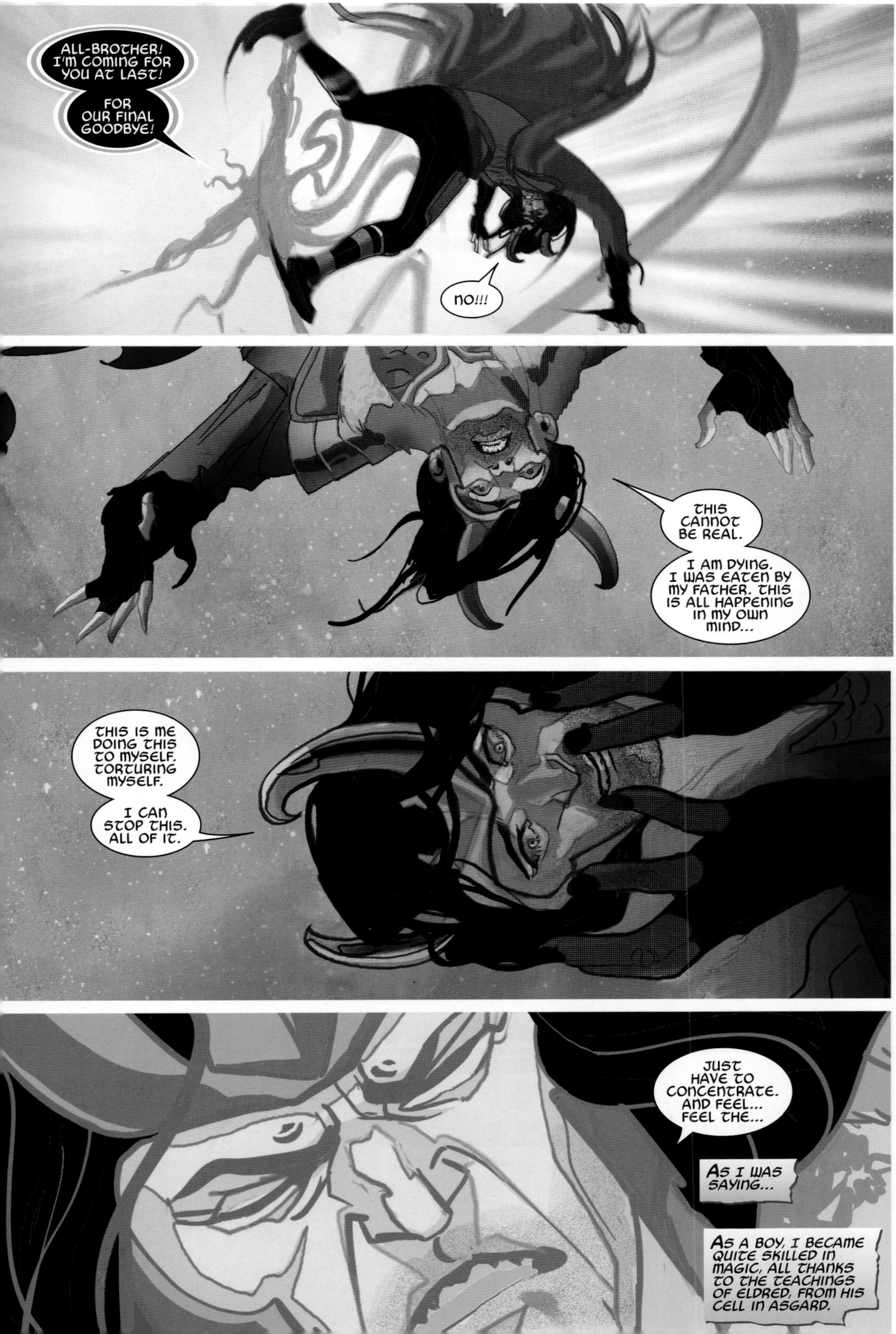

ALL-BROTHER! I'M COMING FOR YOU AT LAST!
FOR OUR FINAL GOODBYE!
NO!!!
THIS CANNOT BE REAL.
I AM DYING. I WAS EATEN BY MY FATHER. THIS IS ALL HAPPENING IN MY OWN MIND...
THIS IS ME DOING THIS TO MYSELF. TORTURING MYSELF.
I CAN STOP THIS. ALL OF IT.
JUST HAVE TO CONCENTRATE. AND FEEL... FEEL THE...
AS I WAS SAYING...
AS A BOY, I BECAME QUITE SKILLED IN MAGIC, ALL THANKS TO THE TEACHINGS OF ELDRED, FROM HIS CELL IN ASGARD.

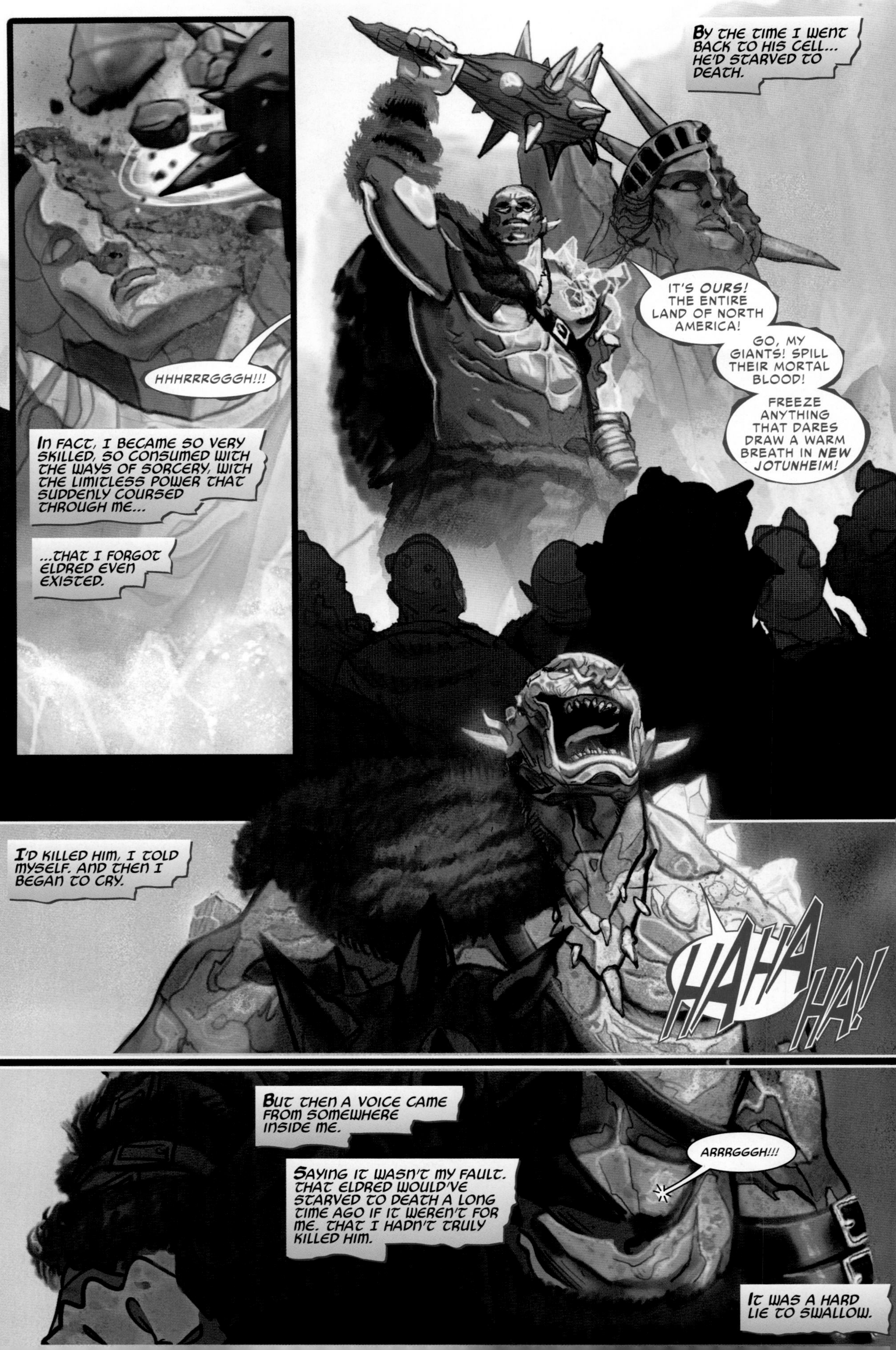
HHHRRRGGGH!!!
IN FACT, I BECAME SO VERY SKILLED, SO CONSUMED WITH THE WAYS OF SORCERY, WITH THE LIMITLESS POWER THAT SUDDENLY COURSED THROUGH ME...
...THAT I FORGOT ELDRED EVEN EXISTED.
BY THE TIME I WENT BACK TO HIS CELL... HE'D STARVED TO DEATH.
IT'S OURS! THE ENTIRE LAND OF NORTH AMERICA!
GO, MY GIANTS! SPILL THEIR MORTAL BLOOD!
FREEZE ANYTHING THAT DARES DRAW A WARM BREATH IN NEW JOTUNHEIM!
I'D KILLED HIM, I TOLD MYSELF. AND THEN I BEGAN TO CRY.
HAHAHA!
BUT THEN A VOICE CAME FROM SOMEWHERE INSIDE ME.
SAYING IT WASN'T MY FAULT. THAT ELDRED WOULD'VE STARVED TO DEATH A LONG TIME AGO IF IT WEREN'T FOR ME. THAT I HADN'T TRULY KILLED HIM.
ARRRGGGH!!!
IT WAS A HARD LIE TO SWALLOW.

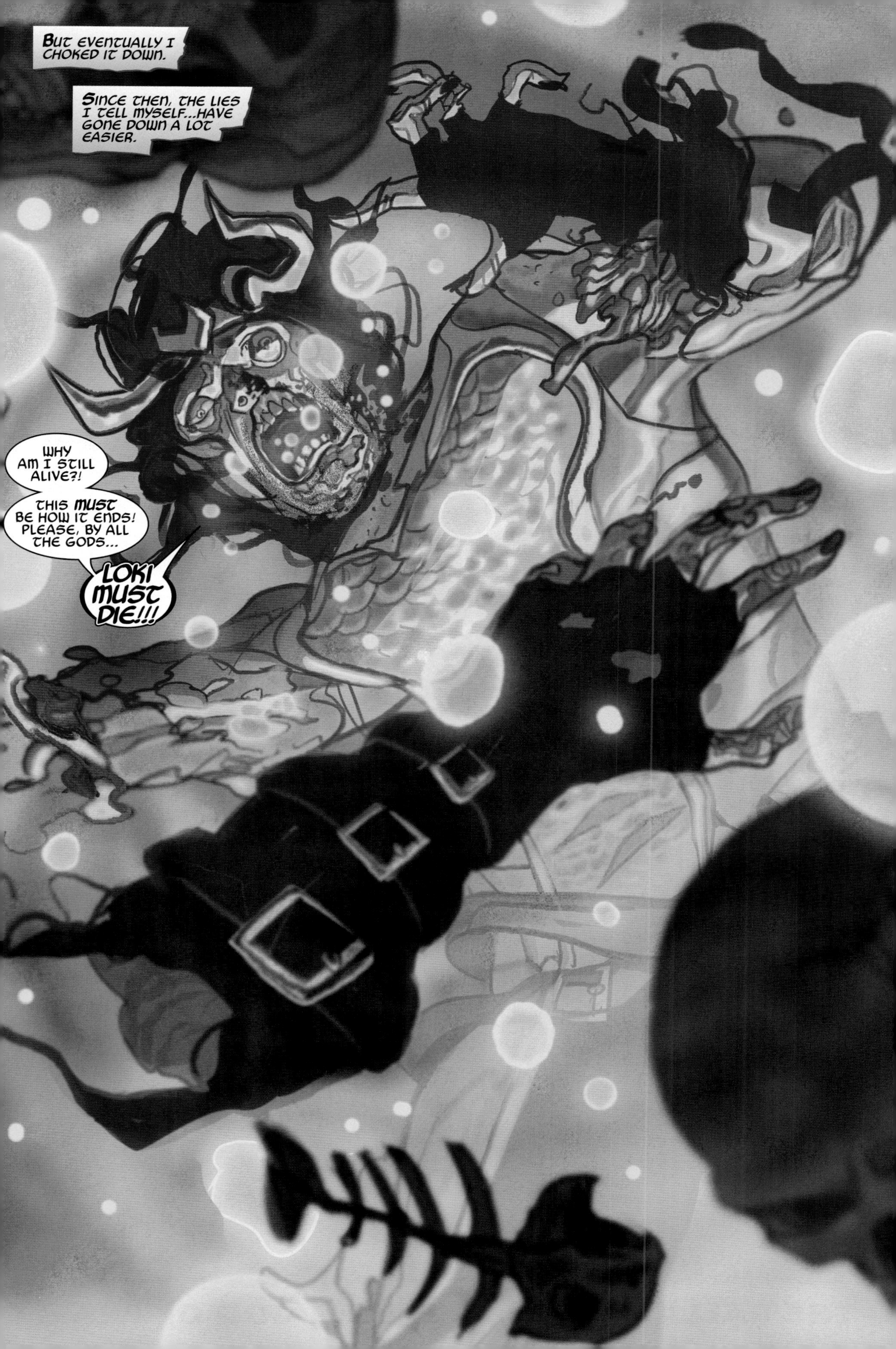
But eventually I choked it down.
Since then, the lies I tell myself...have gone down a lot easier.
Why am I still alive?!
This must be how it ends! Please, by all the gods...
Loki must die!!!

13

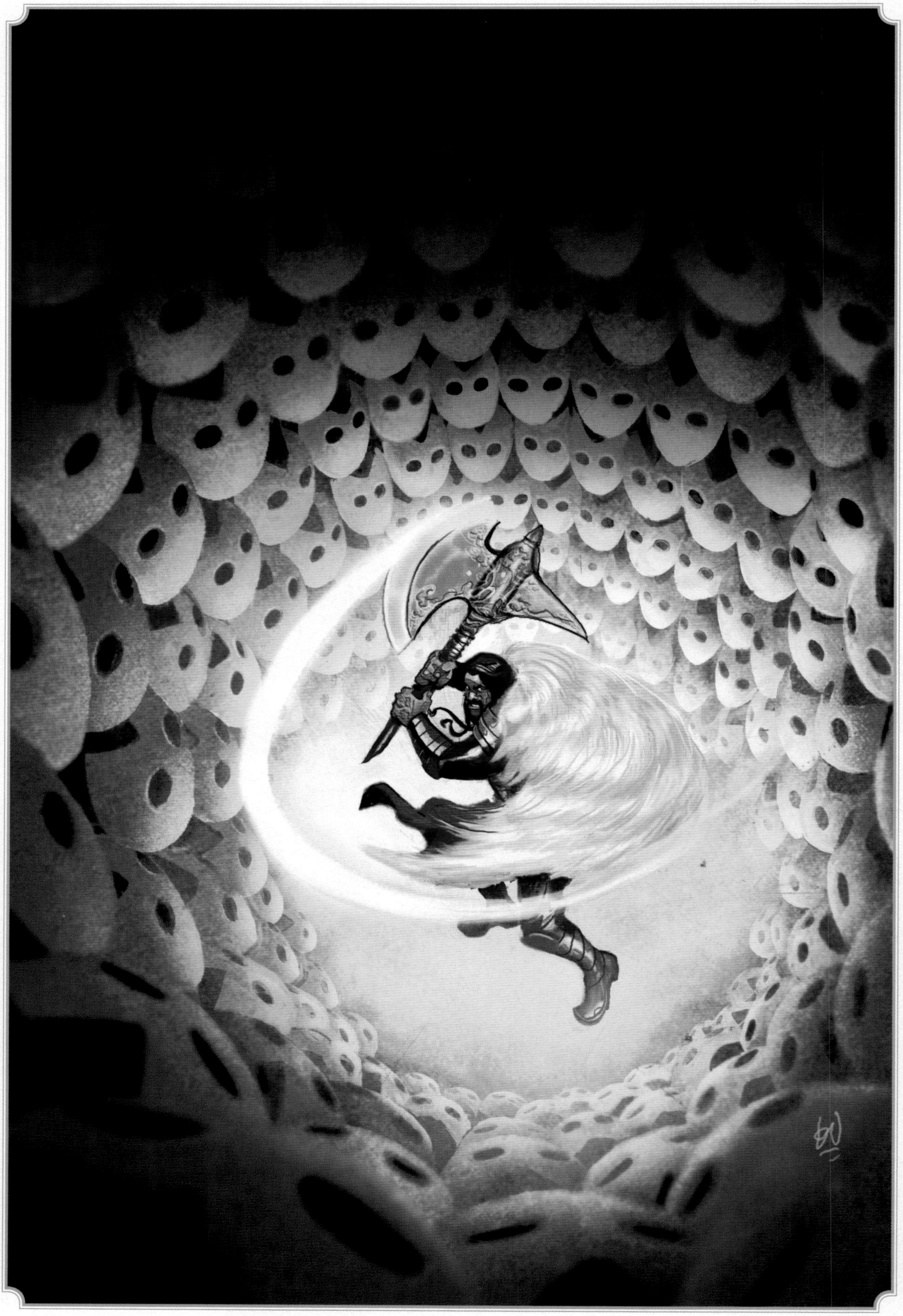

THE BALLAD OF CUL BORSON, GOD OF FEAR

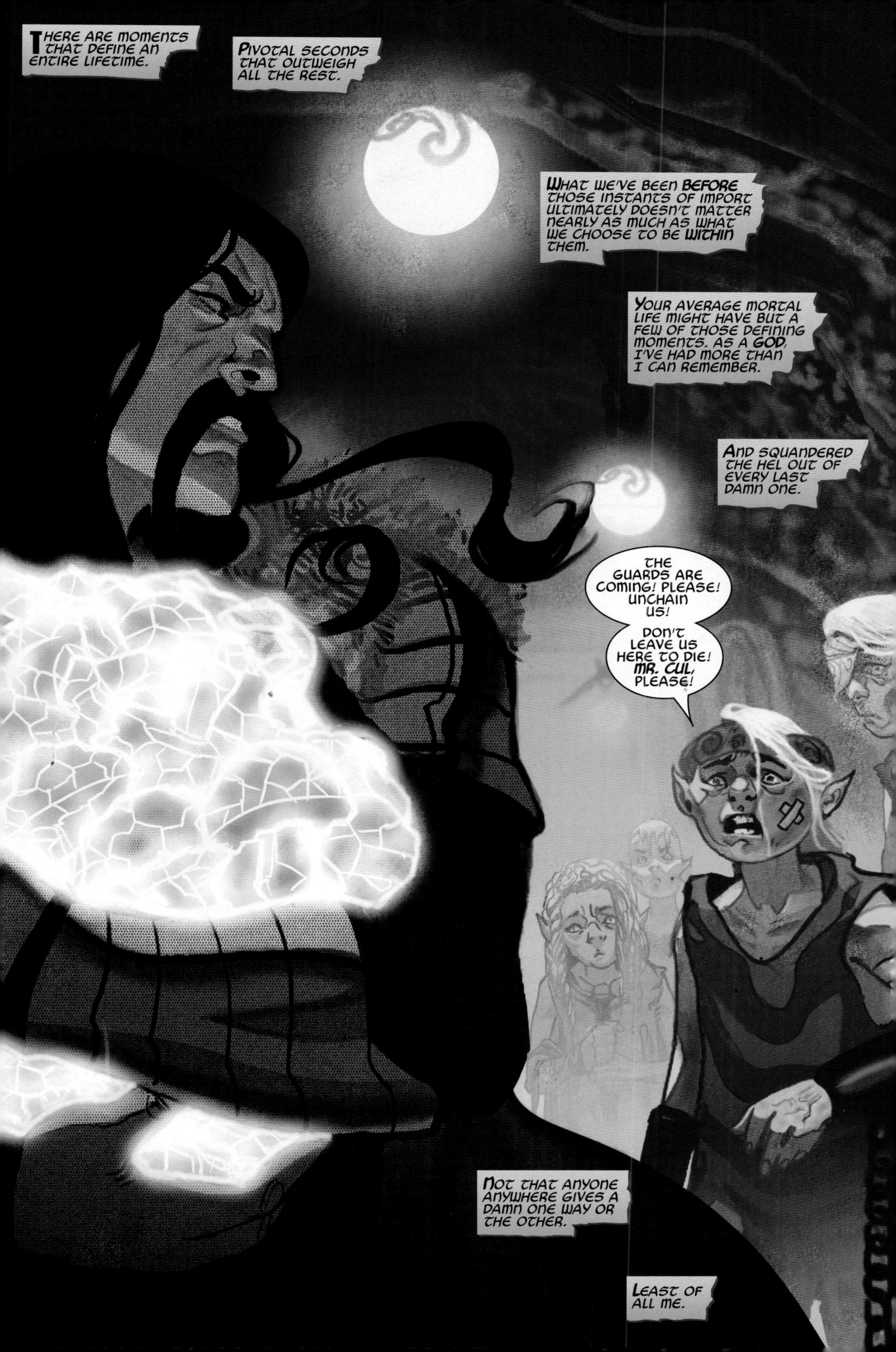
There are moments that define an entire lifetime.
Pivotal seconds that outweigh all the rest.
What we've been BEFORE those instants of import ultimately doesn't matter nearly as much as what we choose to be WITHIN them.
Your average mortal life might have but a few of those defining moments. As a GOD, I've had more than I can remember.
And squandered the Hel out of every last damn one.
The guards are coming! Please! Unchain us!
Don't leave us here to die! MR. CUL, please!
Not that anyone anywhere gives a damn one way or the other.
Least of all me.

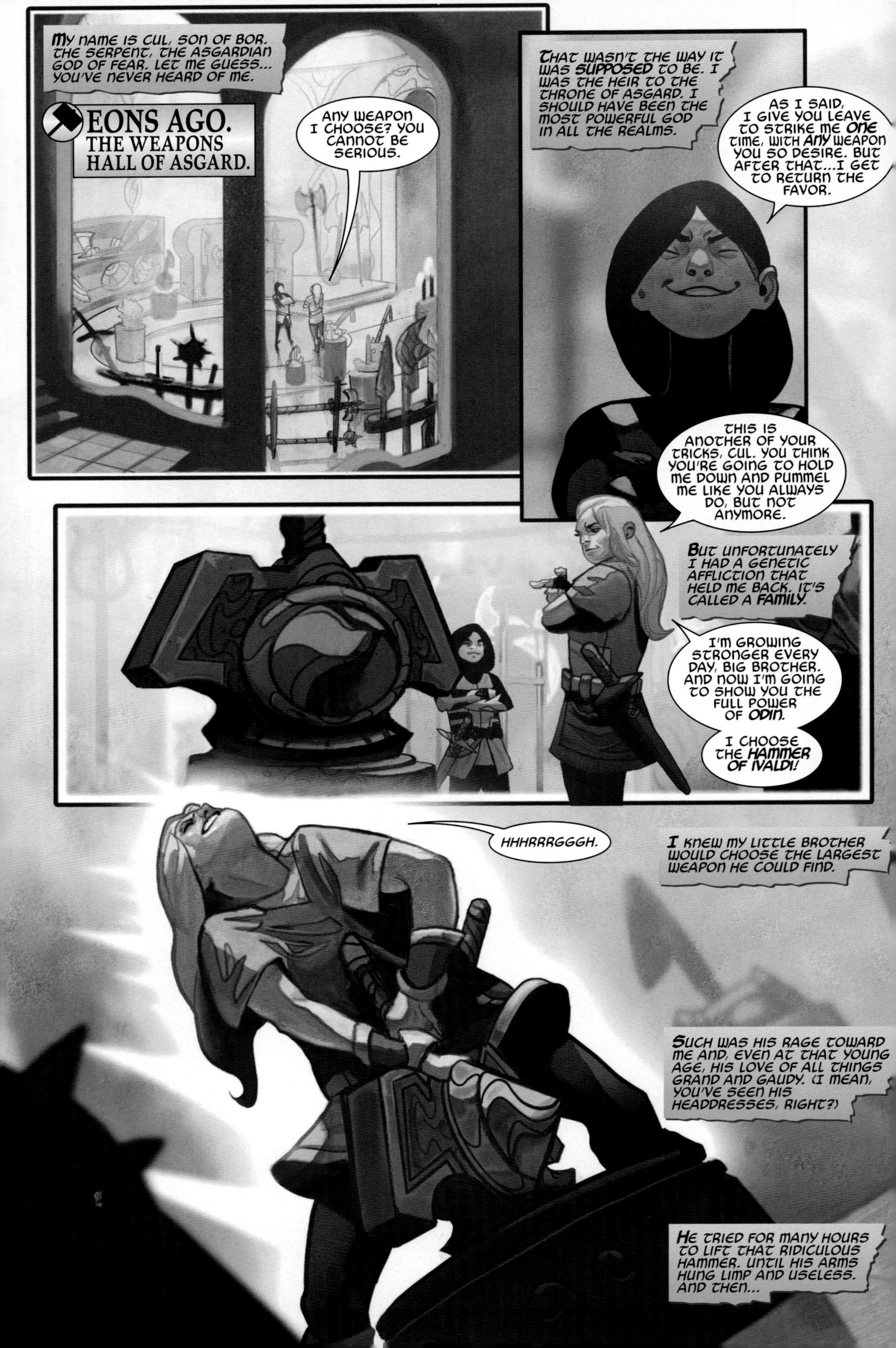
My name is Cul, son of Bor. The Serpent, the Asgardian god of fear. Let me guess... you've never heard of me.
EONS AGO. THE WEAPONS HALL OF ASGARD.
Any weapon I choose? You cannot be serious.
That wasn't the way it was supposed to be. I was the heir to the throne of Asgard. I should have been the most powerful god in all the realms.
As I said, I give you leave to strike me one time, with any weapon you so desire. But after that...I get to return the favor.
This is another of your tricks, Cul. You think you're going to hold me down and pummel me like you always do, but not anymore.
But unfortunately I had a genetic affliction that held me back. It's called a family.
I'm growing stronger every day, big brother. And now I'm going to show you the full power of Odin.
I choose the Hammer of Ivaldi!
HHHRRRGGGH.
I knew my little brother would choose the largest weapon he could find.
Such was his rage toward me and, even at that young age, his love of all things grand and gaudy. (I mean, you've seen his headdresses, right?)
He tried for many hours to lift that ridiculous hammer. Until his arms hung limp and useless. And then...

I CANNOT. CANNOT LIFT IT. CANNOT LIFT... ANYTHING.

SO... YOU FORFEIT YOUR STRIKE. WHICH MAKES IT...

...MY TURN.

DO YOUR WORST, BROTHER. HIT ME WITH WHATEVER CUDGEL OR MACE YOU LIKE. YOU'LL NEVER MAKE ME SHED ANOTHER TEAR. I'D RATHER DIE FIRST.

OH, YOU WON'T DIE.

YOU'LL MERELY WISH YOU HAD.

AND THEN I WHISPERED IN HIS EAR.

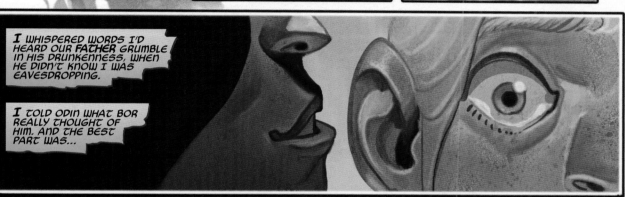

I WHISPERED WORDS I'D HEARD OUR FATHER GRUMBLE IN HIS DRUNKENNESS, WHEN HE DIDN'T KNOW I WAS EAVESDROPPING.

I TOLD ODIN WHAT BOR REALLY THOUGHT OF HIM. AND THE BEST PART WAS...

...MOST OF IT WAS TRUE.

DAMN YOU, BROTHER. DAMN YOU TO THE FROZEN DEPTHS OF HEL.

WHY ARE YOU LIKE THIS, CUL?

BY "THIS," YOU MEAN VICTORIOUS?

BUT...YOU DIDN'T EVEN HIT ME WITH A WEAPON.

OH, I DID INDEED.

THE STRONGEST WEAPON IN THIS ENTIRE ARMORY. THE WEAPON I WIELD BETTER THAN ANY GOD IN ASGARD.

I HIT YOU WITH YOUR OWN FEARS, LITTLE ODIN.

UNTIL NEXT TIME, BROTHER.

I LIKED TO REMIND MY BROTHER OF HIS PLACE IN THE ORDER OF SUCCESSION. TO REMIND HIM THAT I WOULD BE HIS ALL-FATHER SOMEDAY. I SUPPOSE MY ONLY MISTAKE...

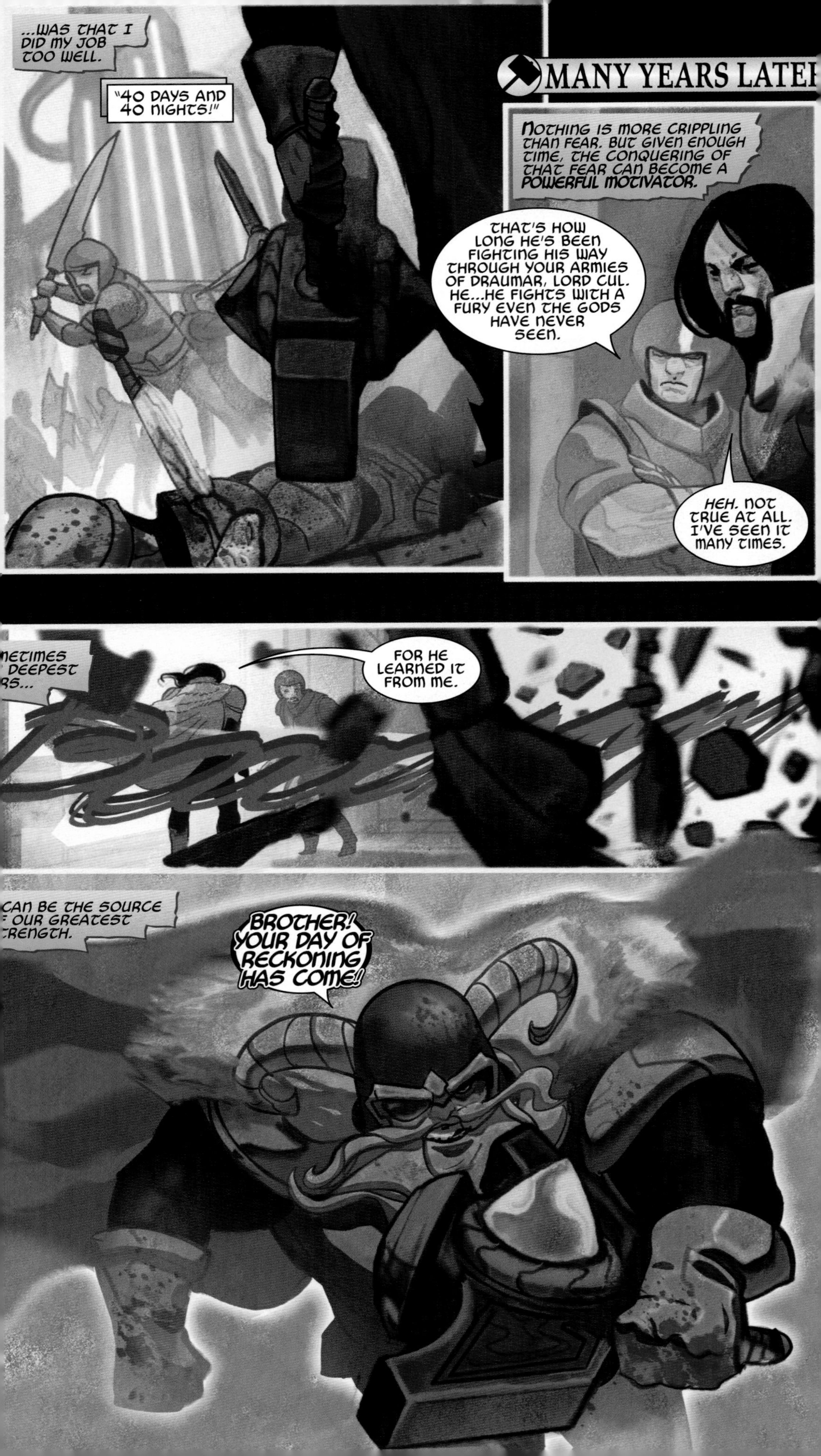
...WAS THAT I DID MY JOB TOO WELL.
"40 DAYS AND 40 NIGHTS!"
MANY YEARS LATE
NOTHING IS MORE CRIPPLING THAN FEAR. BUT GIVEN ENOUGH TIME, THE CONQUERING OF THAT FEAR CAN BECOME A POWERFUL MOTIVATOR.
THAT'S HOW LONG HE'S BEEN FIGHTING HIS WAY THROUGH YOUR ARMIES OF DRAUMAR, LORD CUL. HE...HE FIGHTS WITH A FURY EVEN THE GODS HAVE NEVER SEEN.
HEH. NOT TRUE AT ALL. I'VE SEEN IT MANY TIMES.
NETIMES DEEPEST RS...
FOR HE LEARNED IT FROM ME.
CAN BE THE SOURCE F OUR GREATEST TRENGTH.
BROTHER! YOUR DAY OF RECKONING HAS COME!

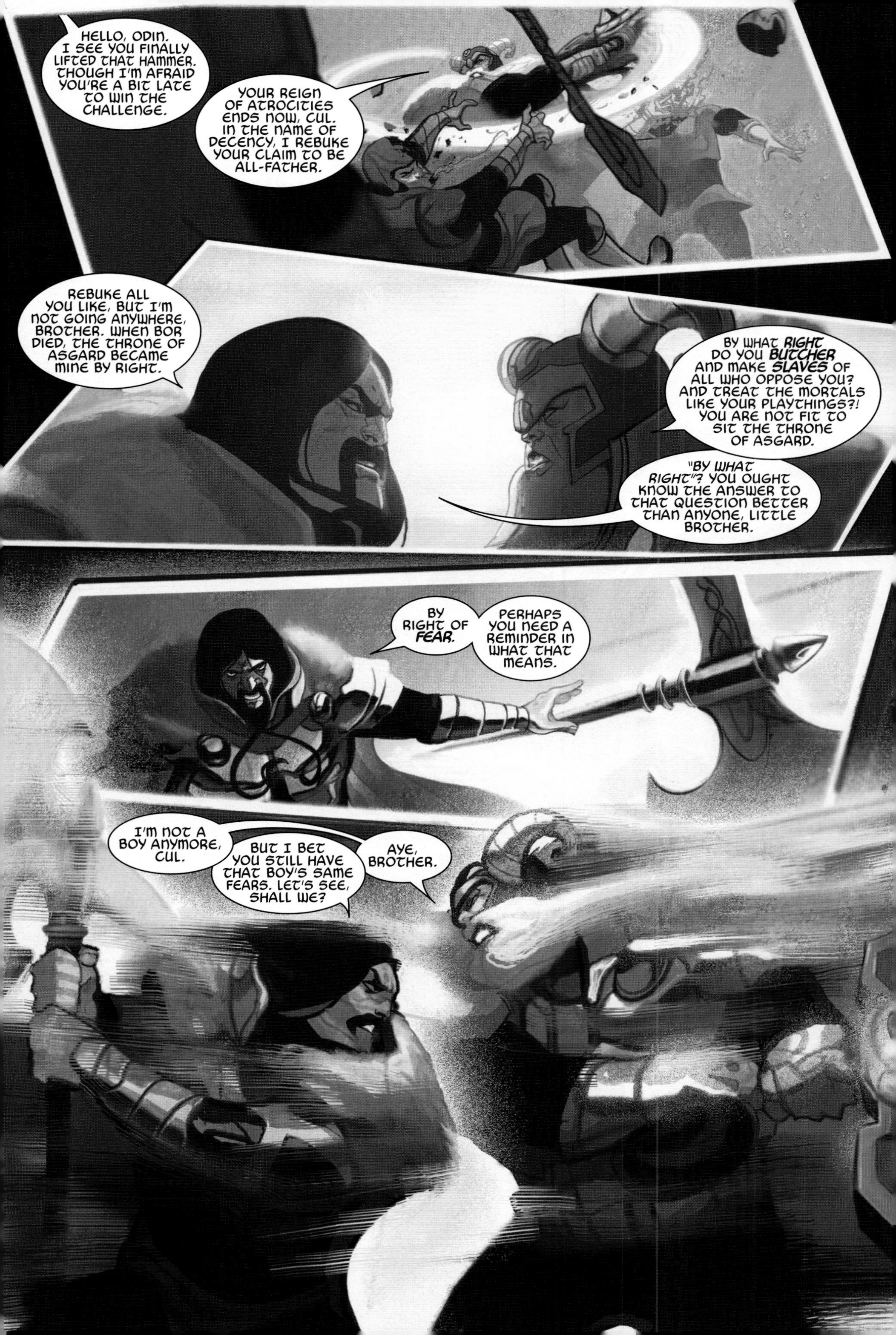
HELLO, ODIN. I SEE YOU FINALLY LIFTED THAT HAMMER. THOUGH I'M AFRAID YOU'RE A BIT LATE TO WIN THE CHALLENGE.
YOUR REIGN OF ATROCITIES ENDS NOW, CUL. IN THE NAME OF DECENCY, I REBUKE YOUR CLAIM TO BE ALL-FATHER.
REBUKE ALL YOU LIKE, BUT I'M NOT GOING ANYWHERE, BROTHER. WHEN BOR DIED, THE THRONE OF ASGARD BECAME MINE BY RIGHT.
BY WHAT RIGHT DO YOU BUTCHER AND MAKE SLAVES OF ALL WHO OPPOSE YOU? AND TREAT THE MORTALS LIKE YOUR PLAYTHINGS?! YOU ARE NOT FIT TO SIT THE THRONE OF ASGARD.
"BY WHAT RIGHT"? YOU OUGHT KNOW THE ANSWER TO THAT QUESTION BETTER THAN ANYONE, LITTLE BROTHER.
BY RIGHT OF FEAR.
PERHAPS YOU NEED A REMINDER IN WHAT THAT MEANS.
I'M NOT A BOY ANYMORE, CUL.
AYE, BROTHER.
BUT I BET YOU STILL HAVE THAT BOY'S SAME FEARS. LET'S SEE, SHALL WE?

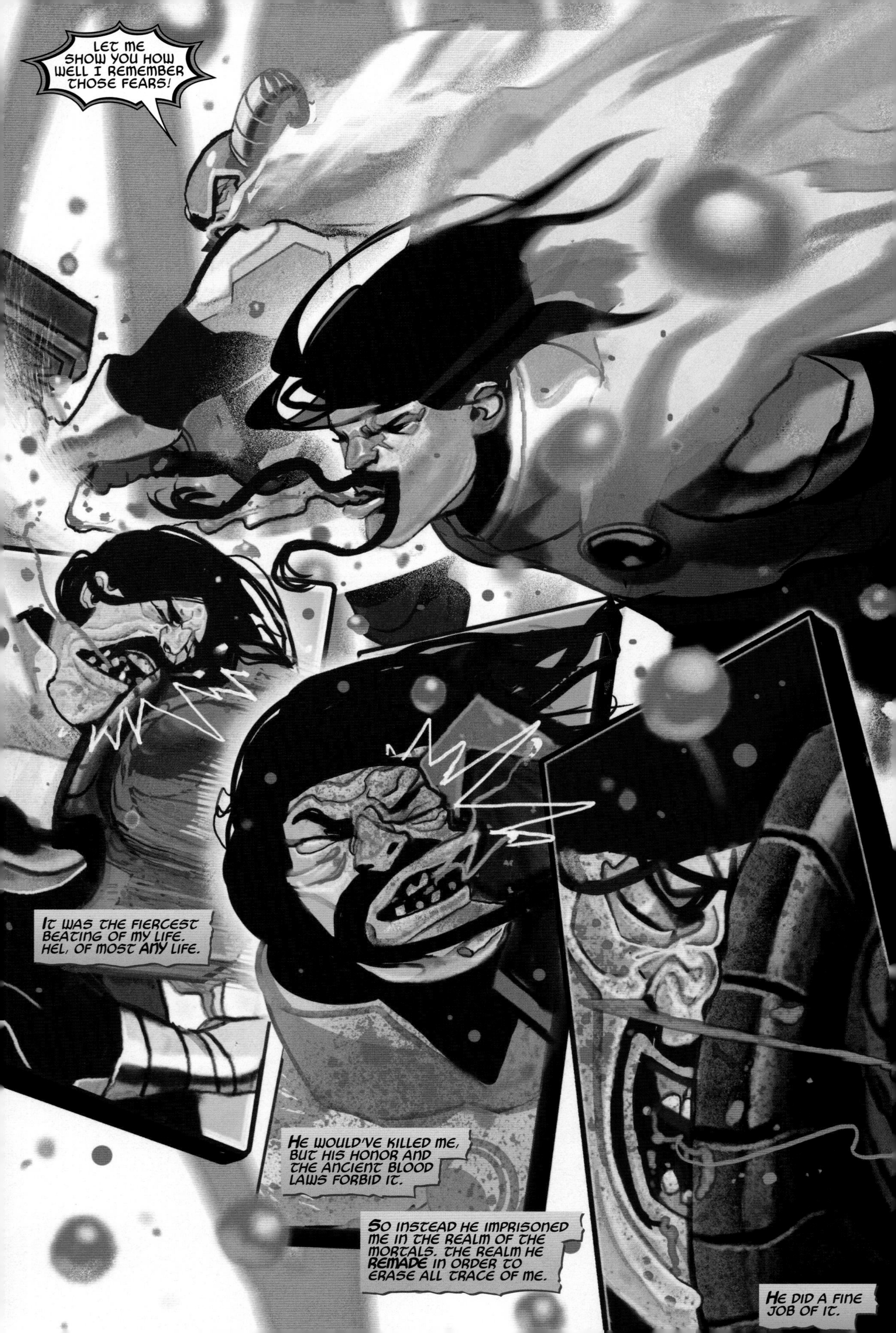
LET ME SHOW YOU HOW WELL I REMEMBER THOSE FEARS!
IT WAS THE FIERCEST BEATING OF MY LIFE. HEL, OF MOST ANY LIFE.
HE WOULD'VE KILLED ME, BUT HIS HONOR AND THE ANCIENT BLOOD LAWS FORBID IT.
SO INSTEAD HE IMPRISONED ME IN THE REALM OF THE MORTALS. THE REALM HE REMADE IN ORDER TO ERASE ALL TRACE OF ME.
HE DID A FINE JOB OF IT.

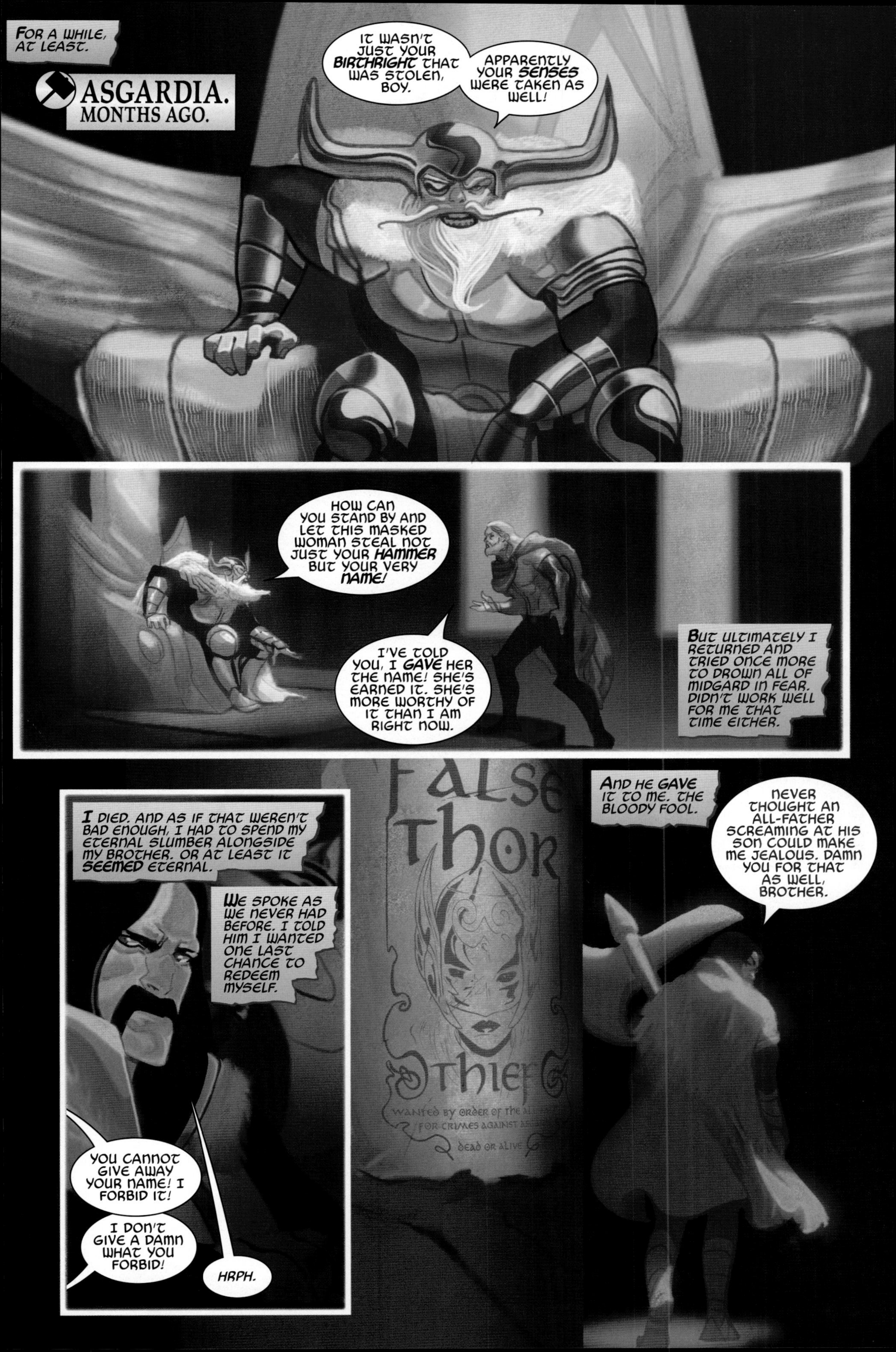

FOR A WHILE, AT LEAST.
ASGARDIA. MONTHS AGO.
IT WASN'T JUST YOUR BIRTHRIGHT THAT WAS STOLEN, BOY.
APPARENTLY YOUR SENSES WERE TAKEN AS WELL!
HOW CAN YOU STAND BY AND LET THIS MASKED WOMAN STEAL NOT JUST YOUR HAMMER BUT YOUR VERY NAME!
I'VE TOLD YOU, I GAVE HER THE NAME! SHE'S EARNED IT. SHE'S MORE WORTHY OF IT THAN I AM RIGHT NOW.
BUT ULTIMATELY I RETURNED AND TRIED ONCE MORE TO DROWN ALL OF MIDGARD IN FEAR. DIDN'T WORK WELL FOR ME THAT TIME EITHER.
I DIED. AND AS IF THAT WEREN'T BAD ENOUGH, I HAD TO SPEND MY ETERNAL SLUMBER ALONGSIDE MY BROTHER. OR AT LEAST IT SEEMED ETERNAL.
WE SPOKE AS WE NEVER HAD BEFORE. I TOLD HIM I WANTED ONE LAST CHANCE TO REDEEM MYSELF.
YOU CANNOT GIVE AWAY YOUR NAME! I FORBID IT!
I DON'T GIVE A DAMN WHAT YOU FORBID!
HRPH.
False Thor
Thief
WANTED BY ORDER OF THE ALL
FOR CRIMES AGAINST AS
DEAD OR ALIVE
AND HE GAVE IT TO ME. THE BLOODY FOOL.
NEVER THOUGHT AN ALL-FATHER SCREAMING AT HIS SON COULD MAKE ME JEALOUS. DAMN YOU FOR THAT AS WELL, BROTHER.

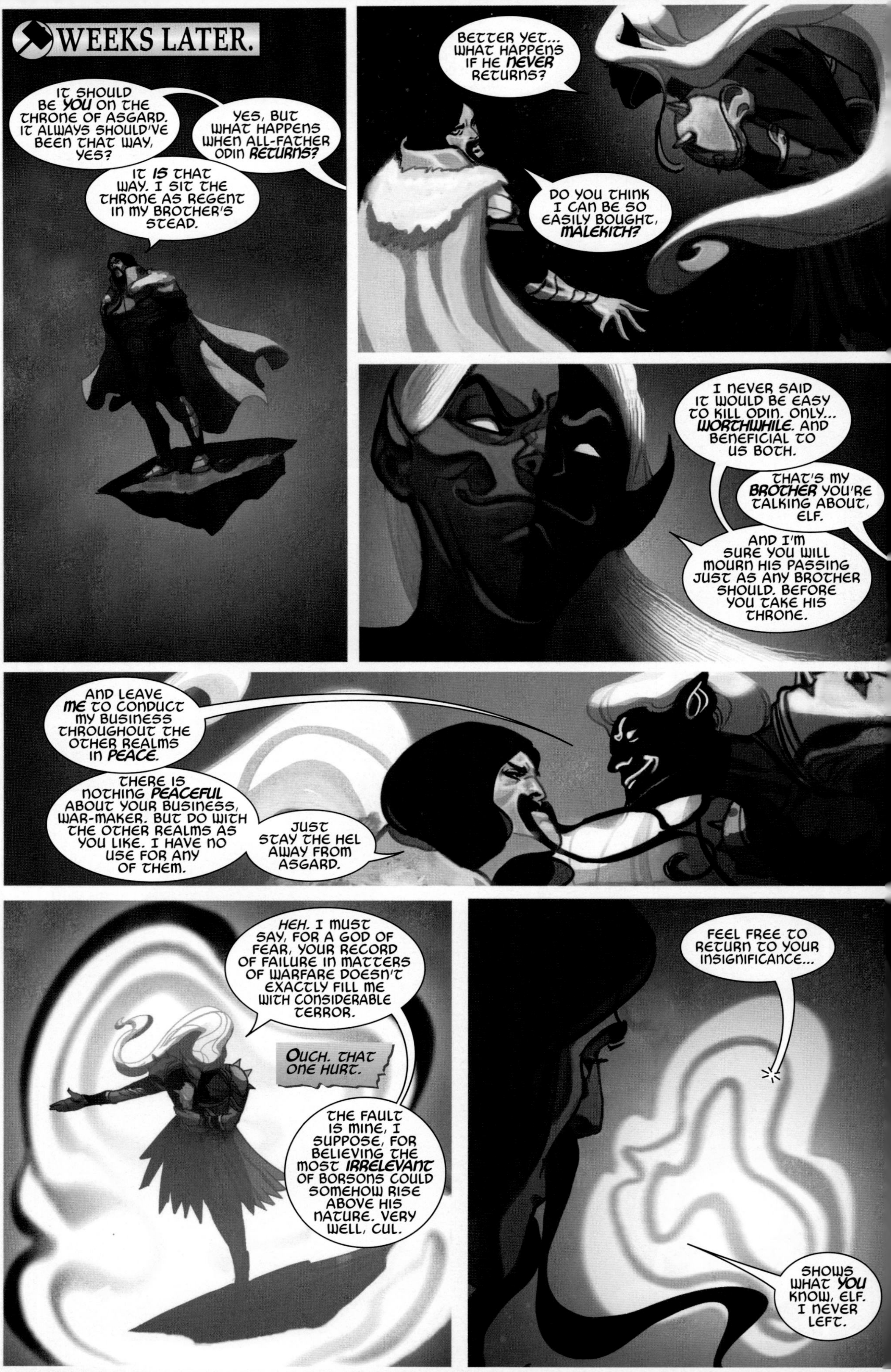
WEEKS LATER.
IT SHOULD BE YOU ON THE THRONE OF ASGARD. IT ALWAYS SHOULD'VE BEEN THAT WAY, YES?
YES, BUT WHAT HAPPENS WHEN ALL-FATHER ODIN RETURNS?
IT IS THAT WAY. I SIT THE THRONE AS REGENT IN MY BROTHER'S STEAD.
BETTER YET... WHAT HAPPENS IF HE NEVER RETURNS?
DO YOU THINK I CAN BE SO EASILY BOUGHT, MALEKITH?
I NEVER SAID IT WOULD BE EASY TO KILL ODIN. ONLY... WORTHWHILE. AND BENEFICIAL TO US BOTH.
THAT'S MY BROTHER YOU'RE TALKING ABOUT, ELF.
AND I'M SURE YOU WILL MOURN HIS PASSING JUST AS ANY BROTHER SHOULD. BEFORE YOU TAKE HIS THRONE.
AND LEAVE ME TO CONDUCT MY BUSINESS THROUGHOUT THE OTHER REALMS IN PEACE.
THERE IS NOTHING PEACEFUL ABOUT YOUR BUSINESS, WAR-MAKER. BUT DO WITH THE OTHER REALMS AS YOU LIKE. I HAVE NO USE FOR ANY OF THEM.
JUST STAY THE HEL AWAY FROM ASGARD.
HEH. I MUST SAY, FOR A GOD OF FEAR, YOUR RECORD OF FAILURE IN MATTERS OF WARFARE DOESN'T EXACTLY FILL ME WITH CONSIDERABLE TERROR.
OUCH. THAT ONE HURT.
THE FAULT IS MINE, I SUPPOSE, FOR BELIEVING THE MOST IRRELEVANT OF BORSONS COULD SOMEHOW RISE ABOVE HIS NATURE. VERY WELL, CUL.
FEEL FREE TO RETURN TO YOUR INSIGNIFICANCE...
SHOWS WHAT YOU KNOW, ELF. I NEVER LEFT.

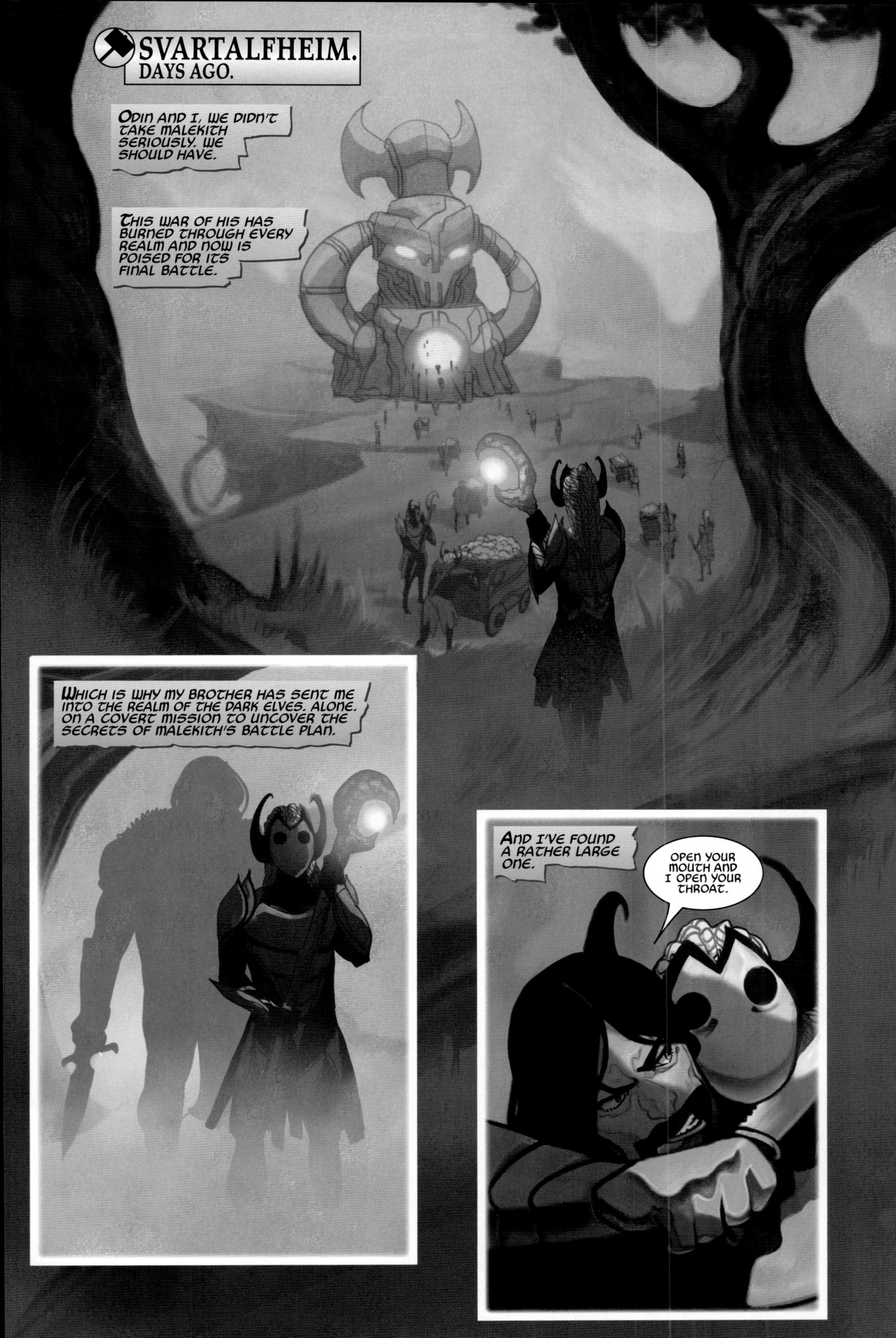
SVARTALFHEIM.
DAYS AGO.
ODIN AND I, WE DIDN'T TAKE MALEKITH SERIOUSLY. WE SHOULD HAVE.
THIS WAR OF HIS HAS BURNED THROUGH EVERY REALM AND NOW IS POISED FOR ITS FINAL BATTLE.
WHICH IS WHY MY BROTHER HAS SENT ME INTO THE REALM OF THE DARK ELVES. ALONE. ON A COVERT MISSION TO UNCOVER THE SECRETS OF MALEKITH'S BATTLE PLAN.
AND I'VE FOUND A RATHER LARGE ONE.
OPEN YOUR MOUTH AND I OPEN YOUR THROAT.

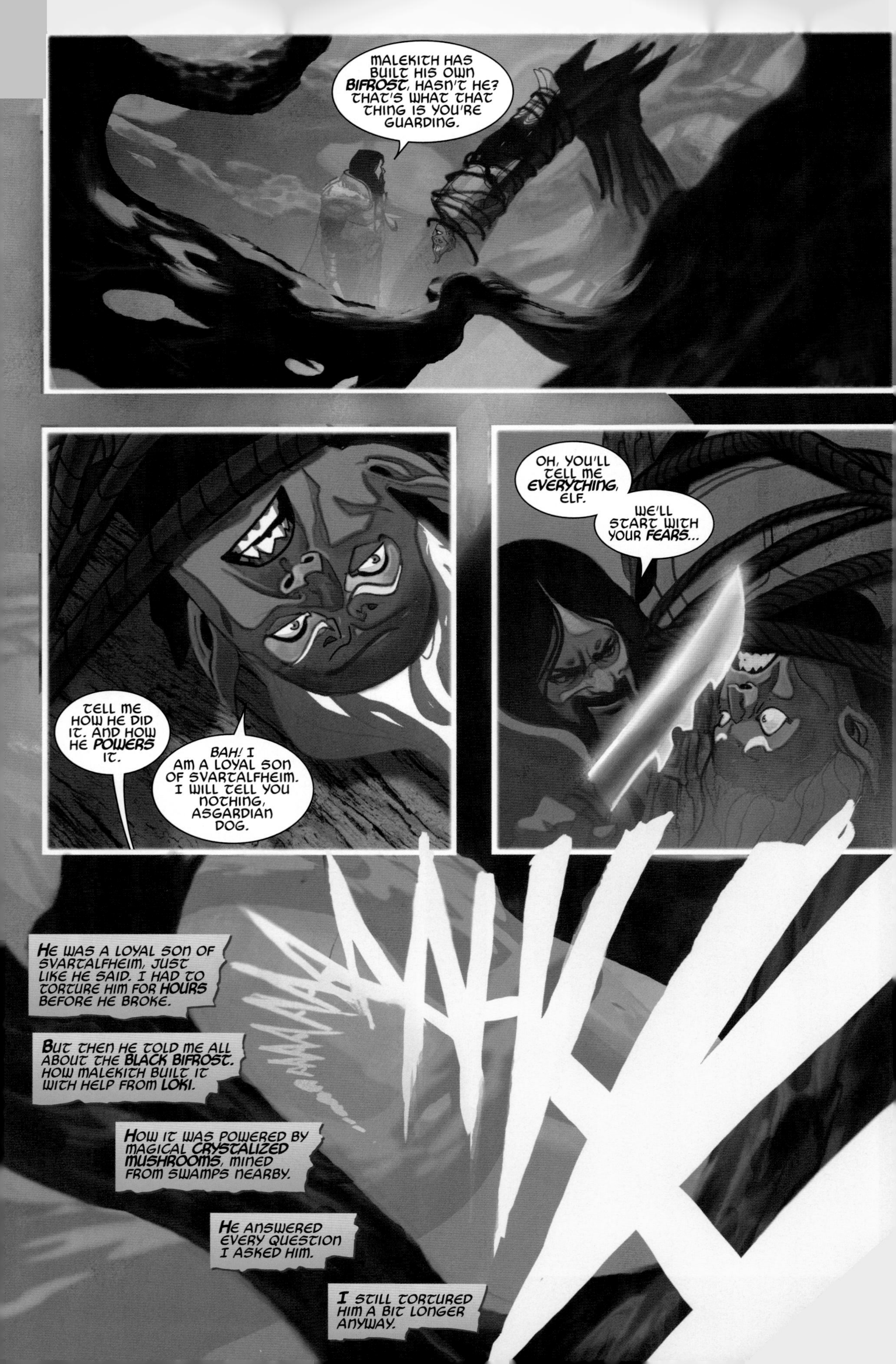
MALEKITH HAS BUILT HIS OWN BIFROST, HASN'T HE? THAT'S WHAT THAT THING IS YOU'RE GUARDING.
TELL ME HOW HE DID IT. AND HOW HE POWERS IT.
BAH! I AM A LOYAL SON OF SVARTALFHEIM. I WILL TELL YOU NOTHING, ASGARDIAN DOG.
OH, YOU'LL TELL ME EVERYTHING, ELF.
WE'LL START WITH YOUR FEARS...
HE WAS A LOYAL SON OF SVARTALFHEIM, JUST LIKE HE SAID. I HAD TO TORTURE HIM FOR HOURS BEFORE HE BROKE.
BUT THEN HE TOLD ME ALL ABOUT THE BLACK BIFROST. HOW MALEKITH BUILT IT WITH HELP FROM LOKI.
HOW IT WAS POWERED BY MAGICAL CRYSTALIZED MUSHROOMS, MINED FROM SWAMPS NEARBY.
HE ANSWERED EVERY QUESTION I ASKED HIM.
I STILL TORTURED HIM A BIT LONGER ANYWAY.

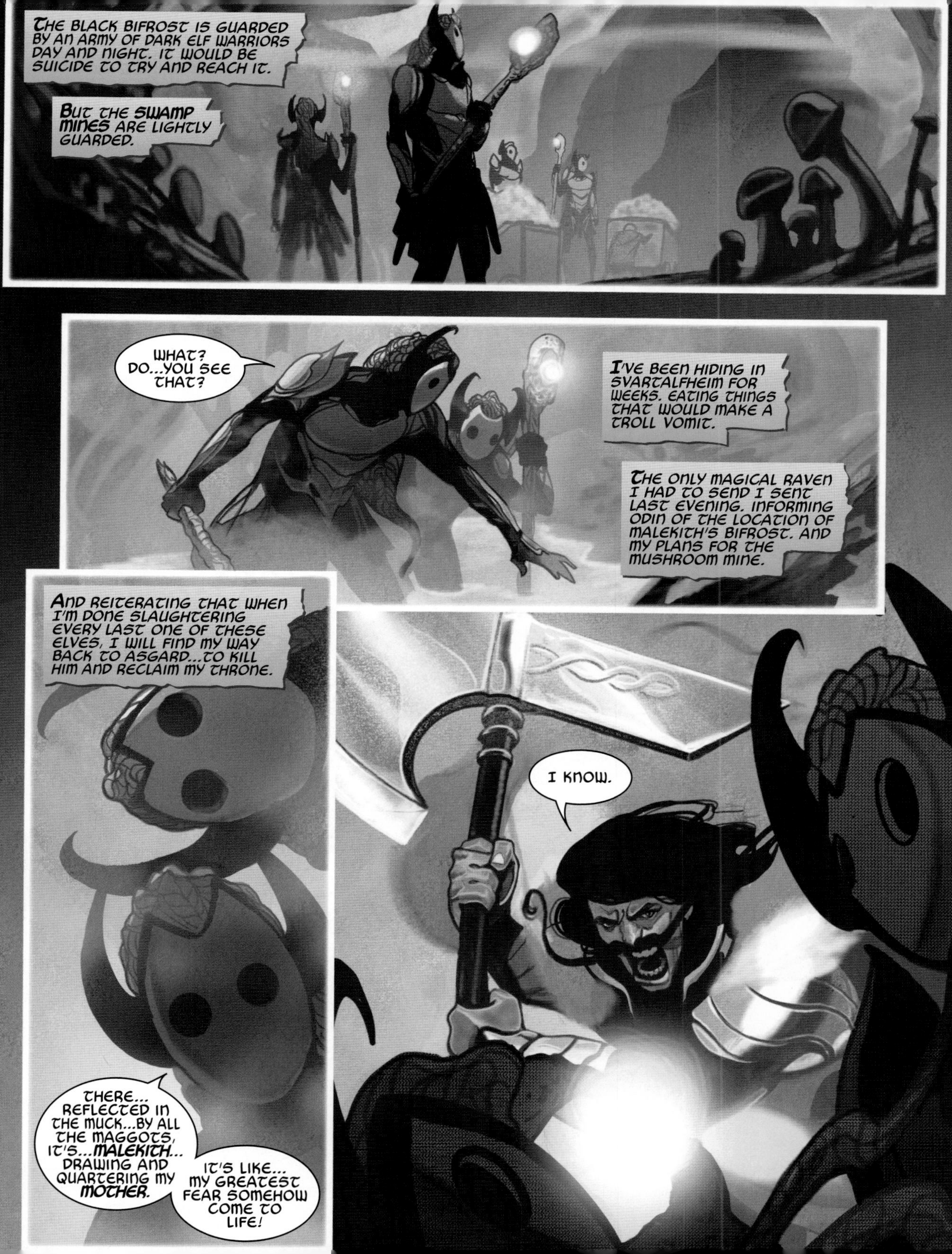
THE BLACK BIFROST IS GUARDED BY AN ARMY OF DARK ELF WARRIORS DAY AND NIGHT. IT WOULD BE SUICIDE TO TRY AND REACH IT.
BUT THE SWAMP MINES ARE LIGHTLY GUARDED.
WHAT? DO...YOU SEE THAT?
I'VE BEEN HIDING IN SVARTALFHEIM FOR WEEKS. EATING THINGS THAT WOULD MAKE A TROLL VOMIT.
THE ONLY MAGICAL RAVEN I HAD TO SEND I SENT LAST EVENING. INFORMING ODIN OF THE LOCATION OF MALEKITH'S BIFROST. AND MY PLANS FOR THE MUSHROOM MINE.
AND REITERATING THAT WHEN I'M DONE SLAUGHTERING EVERY LAST ONE OF THESE ELVES, I WILL FIND MY WAY BACK TO ASGARD...TO KILL HIM AND RECLAIM MY THRONE.
THERE... REFLECTED IN THE MUCK...BY ALL THE MAGGOTS, IT'S...MALEKITH... DRAWING AND QUARTERING MY MOTHER.
IT'S LIKE... MY GREATEST FEAR SOMEHOW COME TO LIFE!
I KNOW.

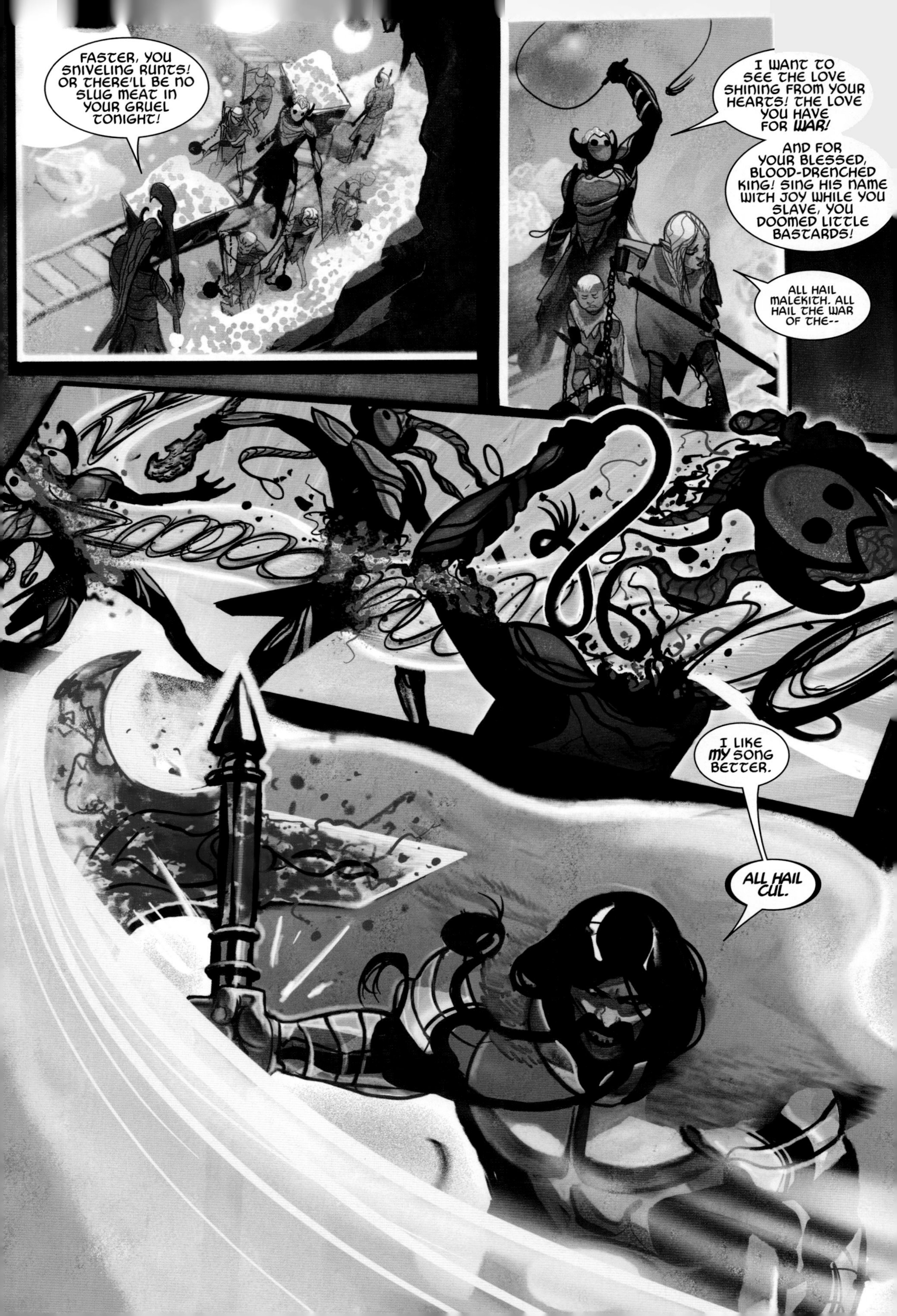
FASTER, YOU SNIVELING RUNTS! OR THERE'LL BE NO SLUG MEAT IN YOUR GRUEL TONIGHT!
I WANT TO SEE THE LOVE SHINING FROM YOUR HEARTS! THE LOVE YOU HAVE FOR WAR!
AND FOR YOUR BLESSED, BLOOD-DRENCHED KING! SING HIS NAME WITH JOY WHILE YOU SLAVE, YOU DOOMED LITTLE BASTARDS!
ALL HAIL MALEKITH. ALL HAIL THE WAR OF THE--
I LIKE MY SONG BETTER.
ALL HAIL CUL.

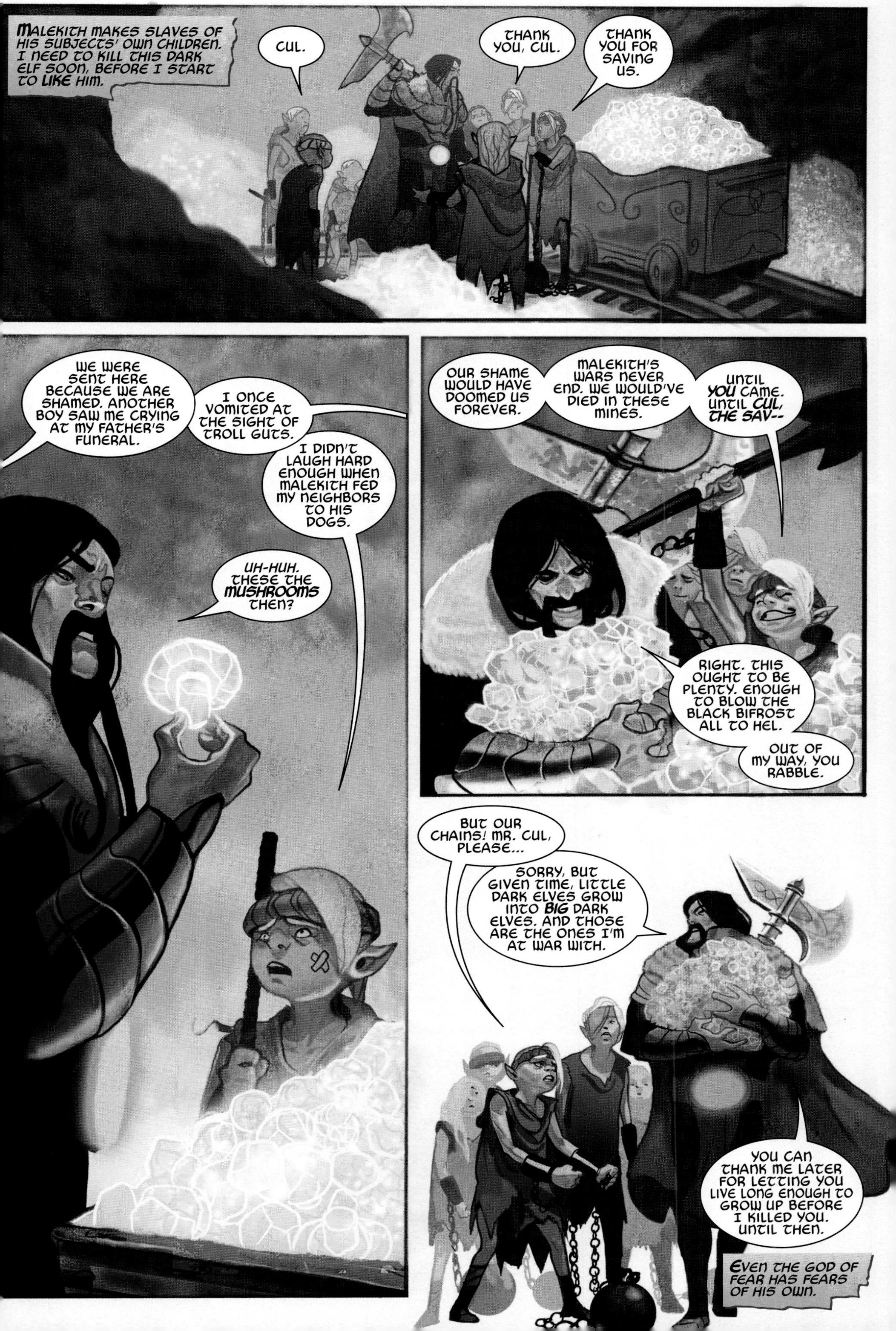
Malekith makes slaves of his subjects' own children. I need to kill this dark elf soon, before I start to LIKE him.
Cul.
Thank you, Cul.
Thank you for saving us.
We were sent here because we are shamed. Another boy saw me crying at my father's funeral.
I once vomited at the sight of troll guts.
I didn't laugh hard enough when Malekith fed my neighbors to his dogs.
Uh-huh. These the MUSHROOMS then?
Our shame would have doomed us forever.
Malekith's wars never end. We would've died in these mines.
Until YOU came. Until CUL, THE SAV--
Right. This ought to be plenty. Enough to blow the Black Bifrost all to Hel.
Out of my way, you rabble.
But our chains! Mr. Cul, please...
Sorry, but given time, little dark elves grow into BIG dark elves. And those are the ones I'm at war with.
You can thank me later for letting you live long enough to grow up before I killed you. Until then.
Even the God of Fear has fears of his own.

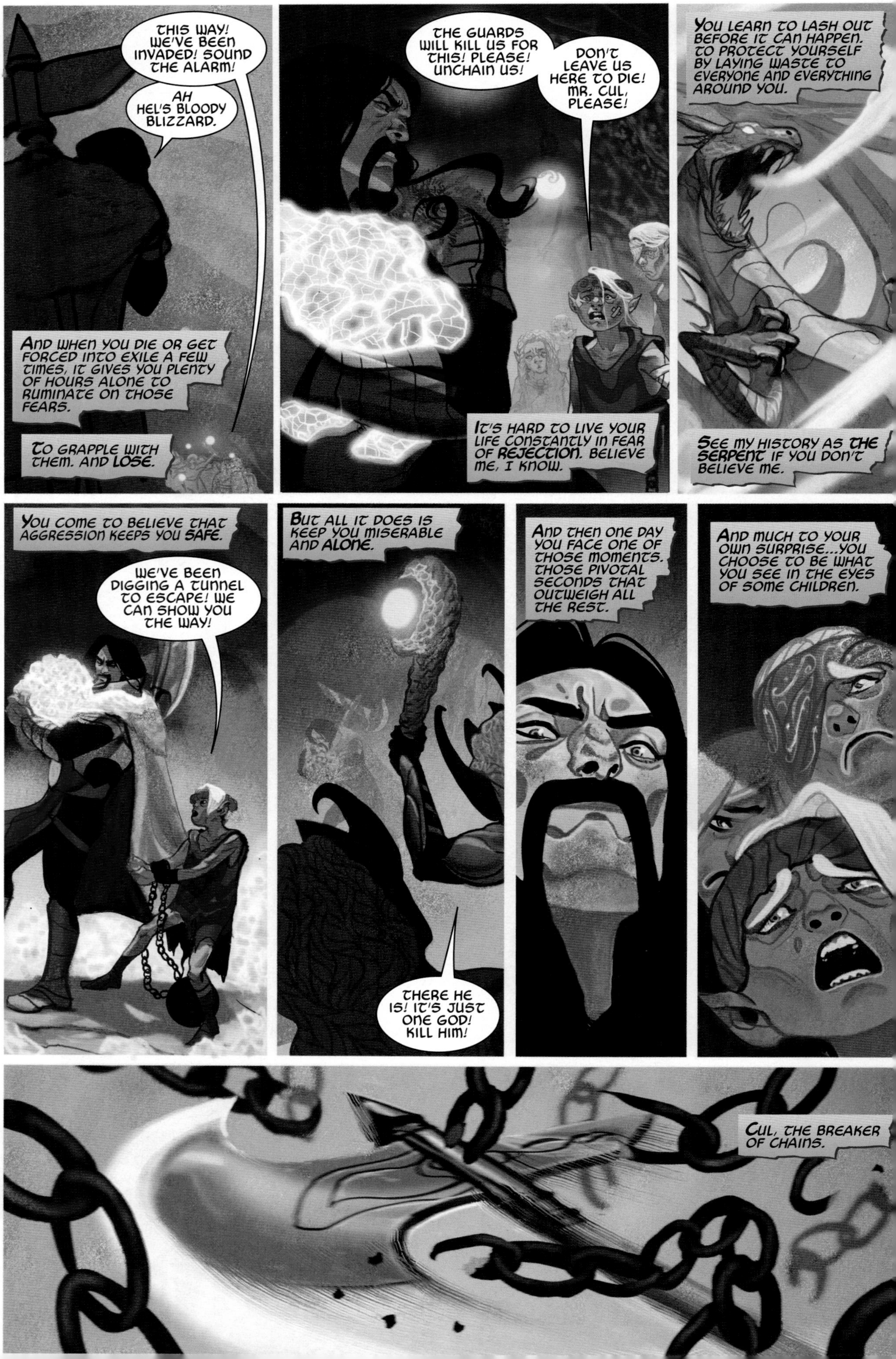
THIS WAY! WE'VE BEEN INVADED! SOUND THE ALARM!
AH HEL'S BLOODY BLIZZARD.
AND WHEN YOU DIE OR GET FORCED INTO EXILE A FEW TIMES, IT GIVES YOU PLENTY OF HOURS ALONE TO RUMINATE ON THOSE FEARS.
TO GRAPPLE WITH THEM. AND LOSE.
THE GUARDS WILL KILL US FOR THIS! PLEASE! UNCHAIN US!
DON'T LEAVE US HERE TO DIE! MR. CUL, PLEASE!
IT'S HARD TO LIVE YOUR LIFE CONSTANTLY IN FEAR OF REJECTION. BELIEVE ME, I KNOW.
YOU LEARN TO LASH OUT BEFORE IT CAN HAPPEN. TO PROTECT YOURSELF BY LAYING WASTE TO EVERYONE AND EVERYTHING AROUND YOU.
SEE MY HISTORY AS THE SERPENT IF YOU DON'T BELIEVE ME.
YOU COME TO BELIEVE THAT AGGRESSION KEEPS YOU SAFE.
WE'VE BEEN DIGGING A TUNNEL TO ESCAPE! WE CAN SHOW YOU THE WAY!
BUT ALL IT DOES IS KEEP YOU MISERABLE AND ALONE.
THERE HE IS! IT'S JUST ONE GOD! KILL HIM!
AND THEN ONE DAY YOU FACE ONE OF THOSE MOMENTS. THOSE PIVOTAL SECONDS THAT OUTWEIGH ALL THE REST.
AND MUCH TO YOUR OWN SURPRISE...YOU CHOOSE TO BE WHAT YOU SEE IN THE EYES OF SOME CHILDREN.
CUL, THE BREAKER OF CHAINS.

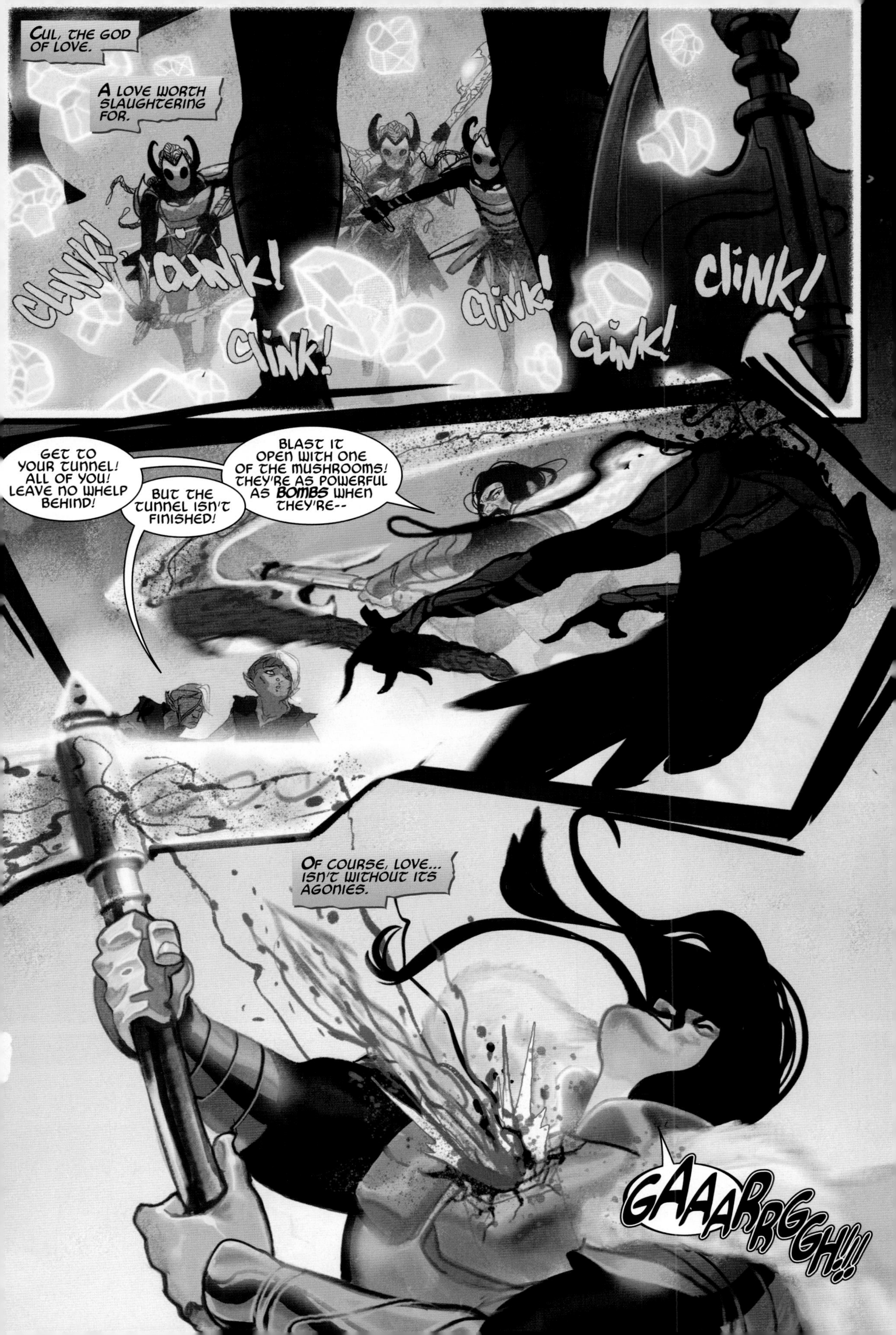
CUL, THE GOD OF LOVE.
A LOVE WORTH SLAUGHTERING FOR.
CLINK!
CLINK!
CLINK!
CLINK!
CLINK!
CLINK!
GET TO YOUR TUNNEL! ALL OF YOU! LEAVE NO WHELP BEHIND!
BUT THE TUNNEL ISN'T FINISHED!
BLAST IT OPEN WITH ONE OF THE MUSHROOMS! THEY'RE AS POWERFUL AS BOMBS WHEN THEY'RE--
OF COURSE, LOVE... ISN'T WITHOUT ITS AGONIES.
GAAARRGGH!!!

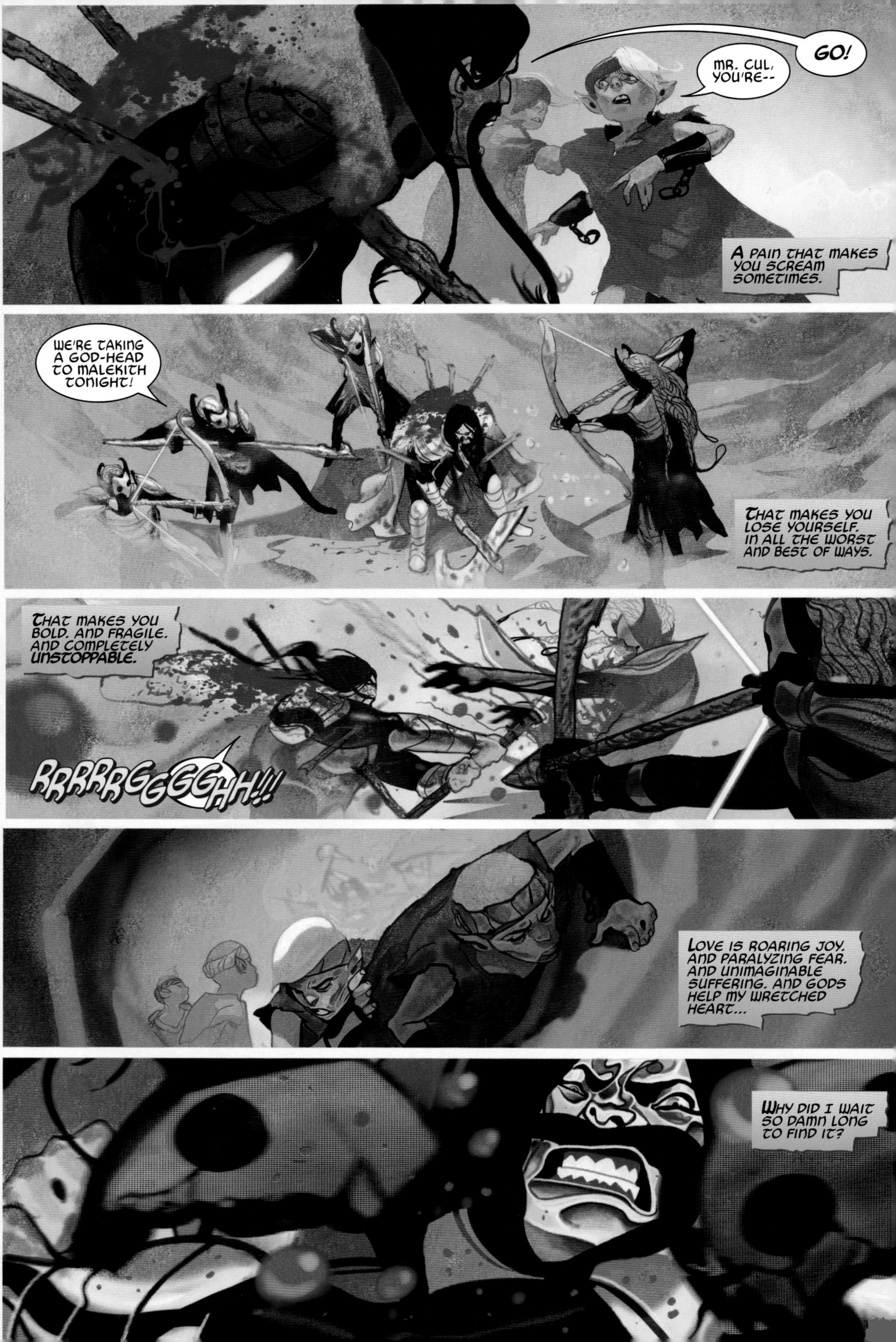
MR. CUL, YOU'RE--
GO!
A PAIN THAT MAKES YOU SCREAM SOMETIMES.
WE'RE TAKING A GOD-HEAD TO MALEKITH TONIGHT!
THAT MAKES YOU LOSE YOURSELF. IN ALL THE WORST AND BEST OF WAYS.
THAT MAKES YOU BOLD. AND FRAGILE. AND COMPLETELY UNSTOPPABLE.
RRRRRGGGGHH!!!
LOVE IS ROARING JOY. AND PARALYZING FEAR. AND UNIMAGINABLE SUFFERING. AND GODS HELP MY WRETCHED HEART...
WHY DID I WAIT SO DAMN LONG TO FIND IT?

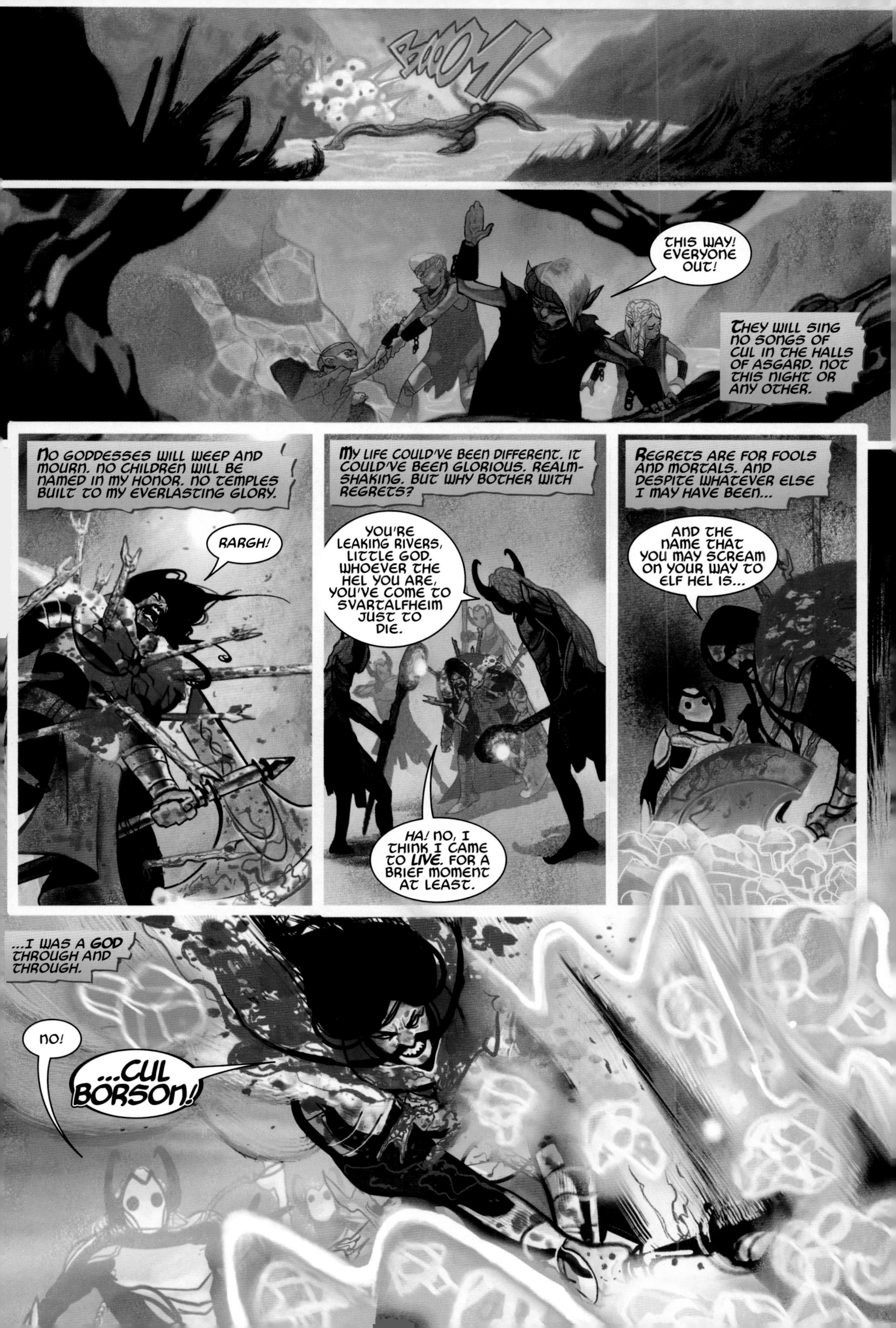
BOOM!
THIS WAY! EVERYONE OUT!
THEY WILL SING NO SONGS OF CUL IN THE HALLS OF ASGARD. NOT THIS NIGHT OR ANY OTHER.
NO GODDESSES WILL WEEP AND MOURN. NO CHILDREN WILL BE NAMED IN MY HONOR. NO TEMPLES BUILT TO MY EVERLASTING GLORY.
RARGH!
MY LIFE COULD'VE BEEN DIFFERENT. IT COULD'VE BEEN GLORIOUS. REALM-SHAKING. BUT WHY BOTHER WITH REGRETS?
YOU'RE LEAKING RIVERS, LITTLE GOD. WHOEVER THE HEL YOU ARE, YOU'VE COME TO SVARTALFHEIM JUST TO DIE.
HA! NO, I THINK I CAME TO LIVE. FOR A BRIEF MOMENT AT LEAST.
REGRETS ARE FOR FOOLS AND MORTALS. AND DESPITE WHATEVER ELSE I MAY HAVE BEEN...
AND THE NAME THAT YOU MAY SCREAM ON YOUR WAY TO ELF HEL IS...
...I WAS A GOD THROUGH AND THROUGH.
NO!
...CUL BÖRSON!

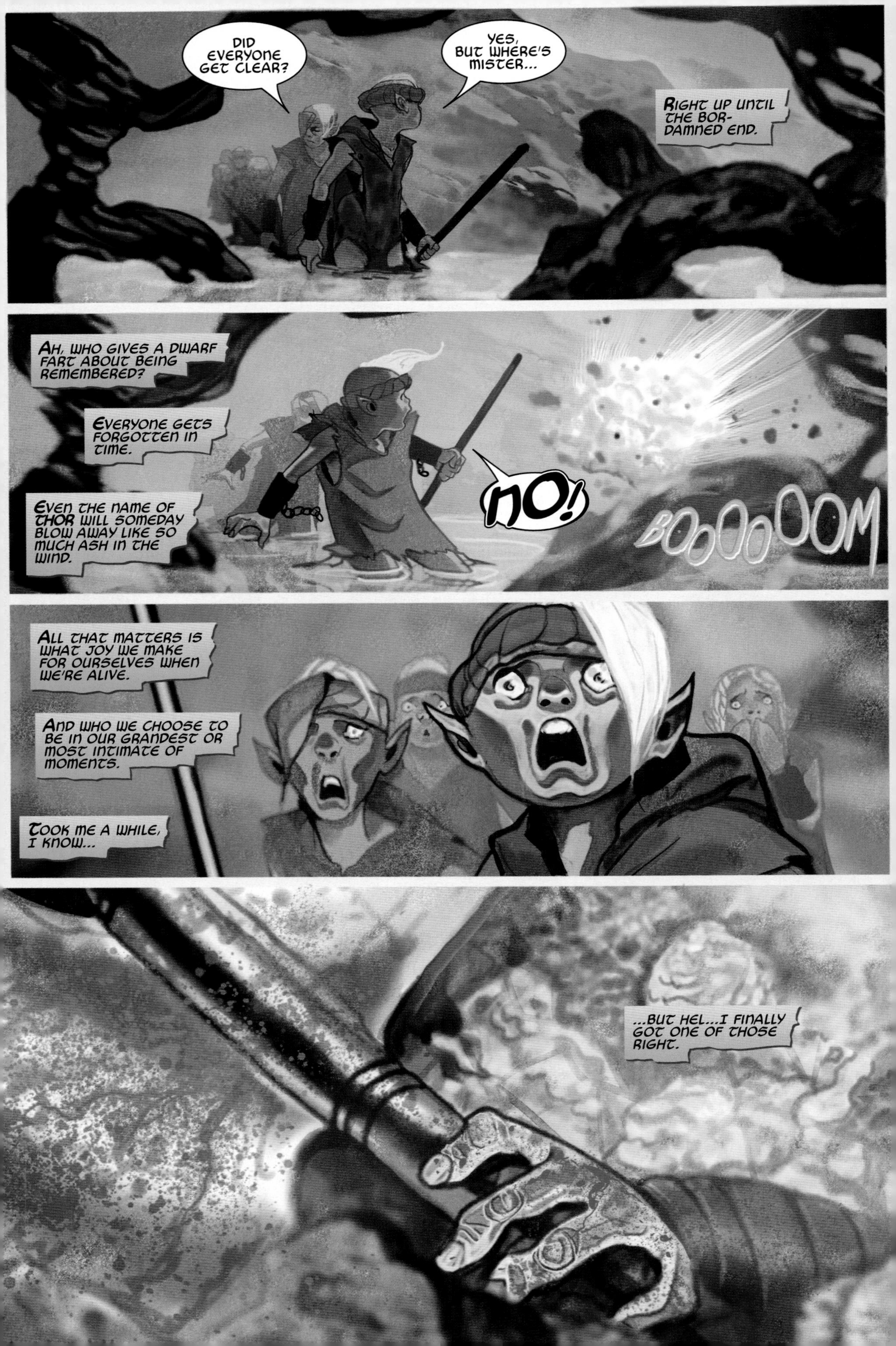
DID EVERYONE GET CLEAR?
YES, BUT WHERE'S MISTER...
RIGHT UP UNTIL THE BOR-DAMNED END.
AH, WHO GIVES A DWARF FART ABOUT BEING REMEMBERED?
EVERYONE GETS FORGOTTEN IN TIME.
EVEN THE NAME OF THOR WILL SOMEDAY BLOW AWAY LIKE SO MUCH ASH IN THE WIND.
NO!
BOOOOOOOM
ALL THAT MATTERS IS WHAT JOY WE MAKE FOR OURSELVES WHEN WE'RE ALIVE.
AND WHO WE CHOOSE TO BE IN OUR GRANDEST OR MOST INTIMATE OF MOMENTS.
TOOK ME A WHILE, I KNOW...
...BUT HEL...I FINALLY GOT ONE OF THOSE RIGHT.

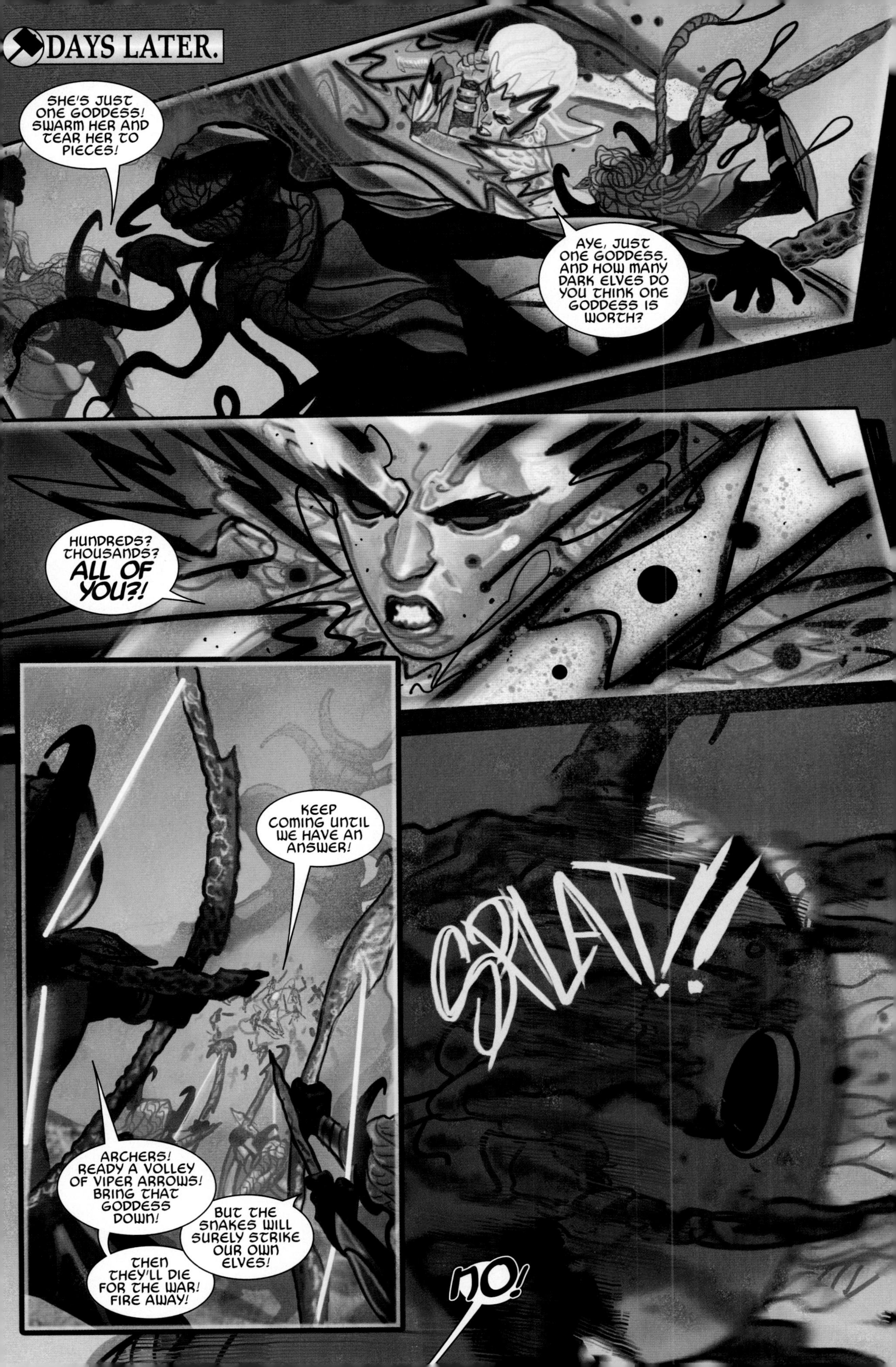
DAYS LATER.
SHE'S JUST ONE GODDESS! SWARM HER AND TEAR HER TO PIECES!
AYE, JUST ONE GODDESS. AND HOW MANY DARK ELVES DO YOU THINK ONE GODDESS IS WORTH?
HUNDREDS? THOUSANDS? ALL OF YOU?!
KEEP COMING UNTIL WE HAVE AN ANSWER!
ARCHERS! READY A VOLLEY OF VIPER ARROWS! BRING THAT GODDESS DOWN!
BUT THE SNAKES WILL SURELY STRIKE OUR OWN ELVES!
THEN THEY'LL DIE FOR THE WAR! FIRE AWAY!
SPLAT!!
NO!

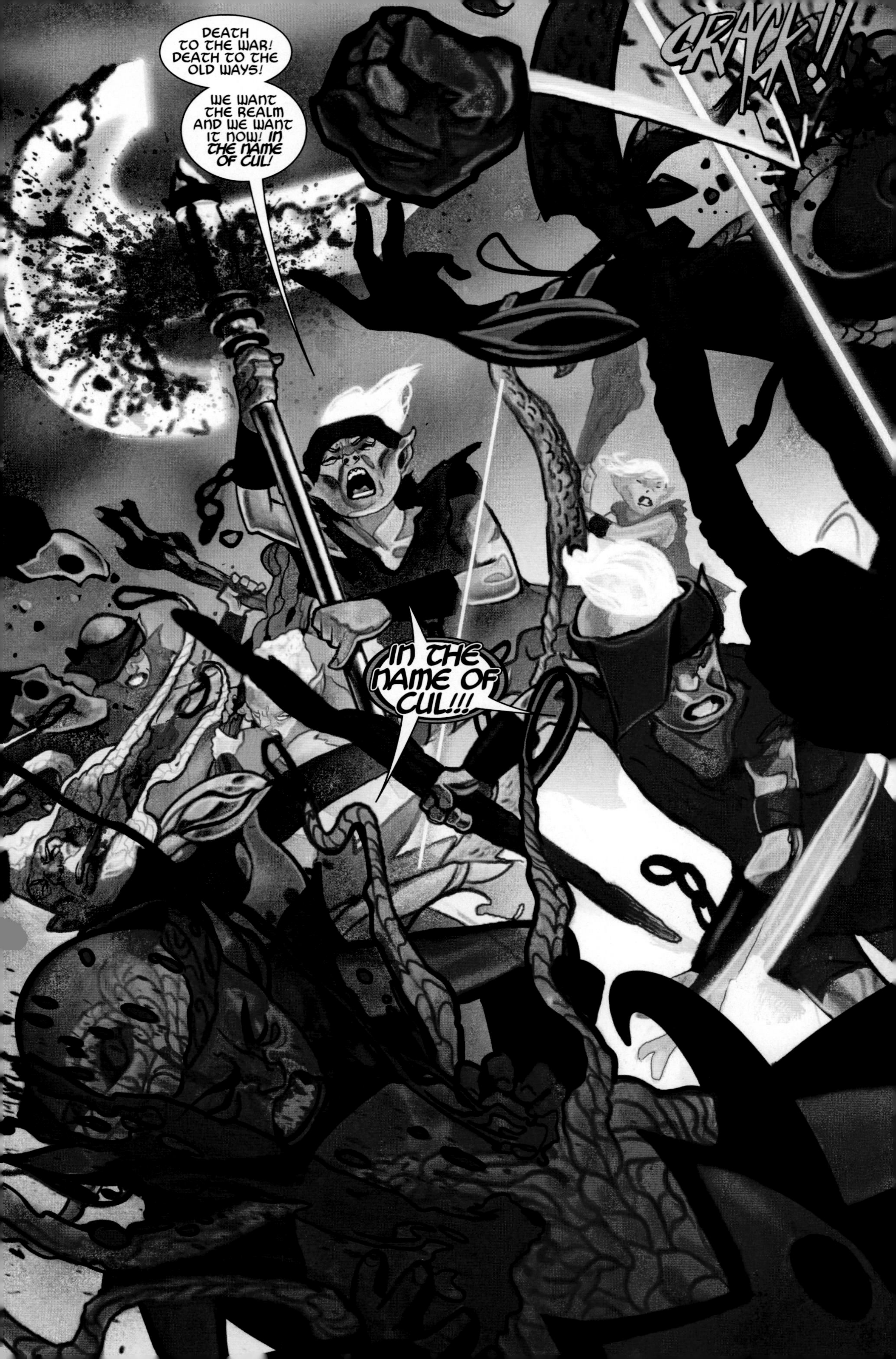
CRACK!!
DEATH TO THE WAR! DEATH TO THE OLD WAYS!
WE WANT THE REALM AND WE WANT IT NOW! *IN THE NAME OF CUL!*
IN THE NAME OF CUL!!!

— 14 —

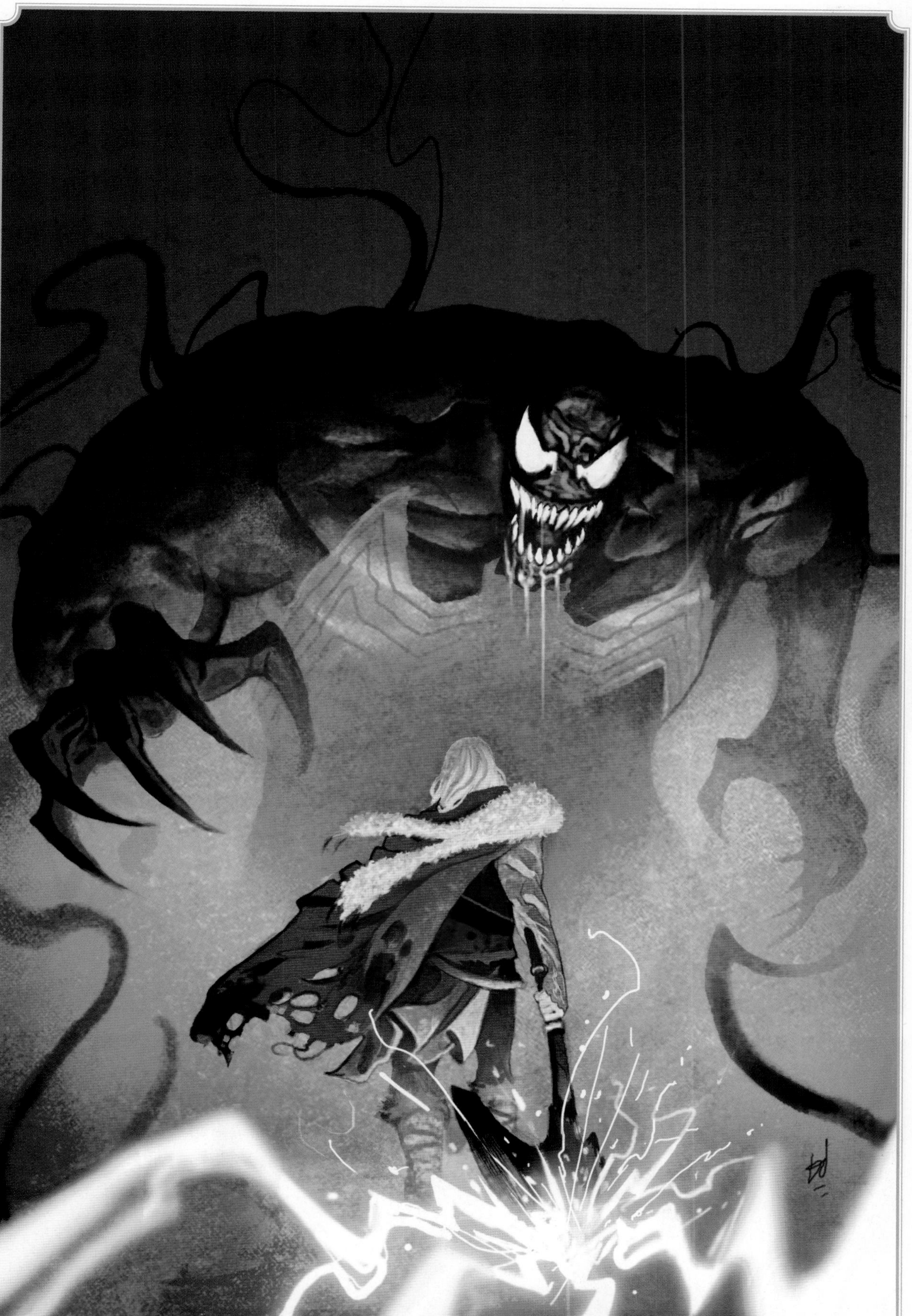

TO HEL WITH HAMMERS

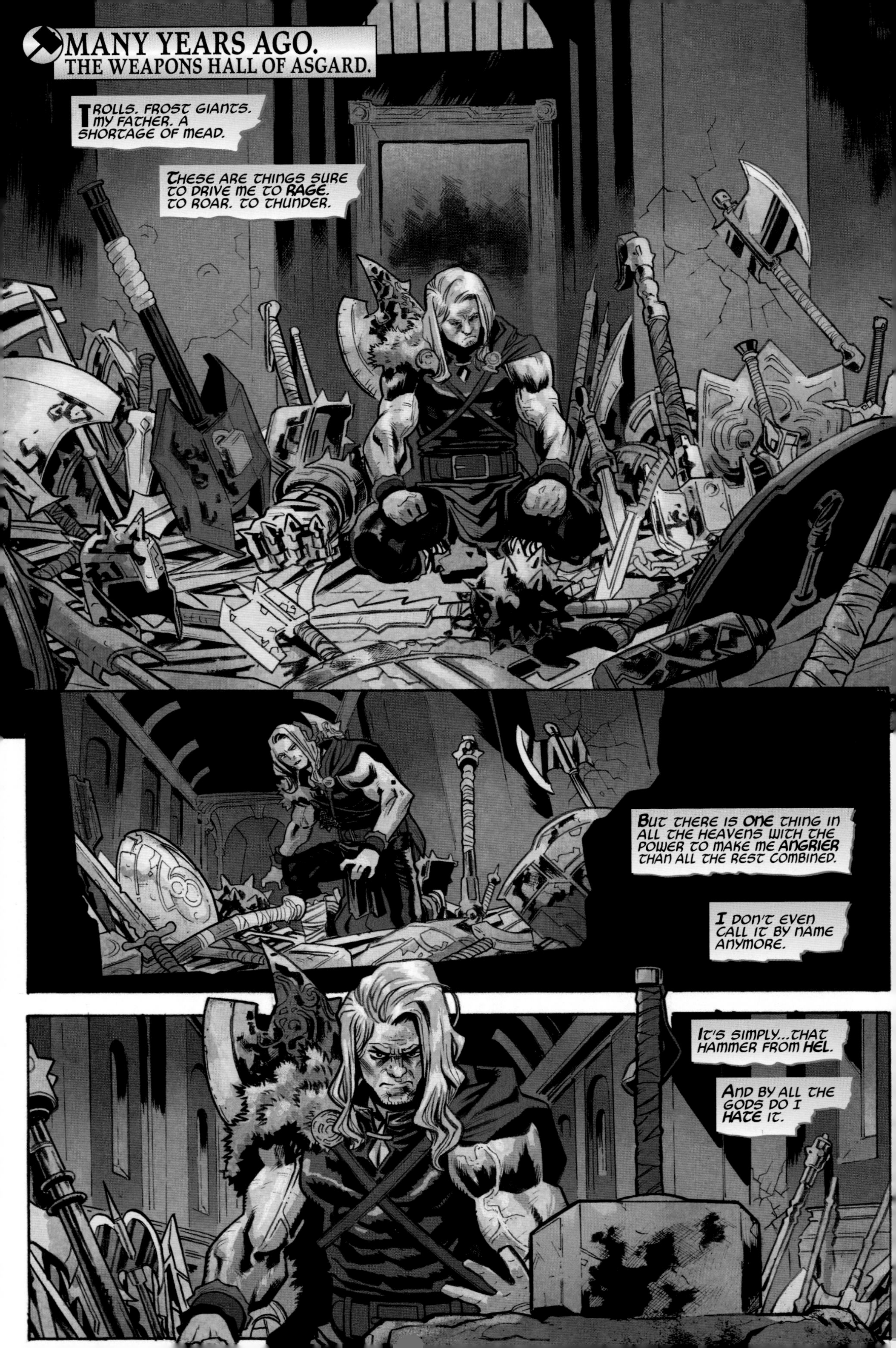
MANY YEARS AGO.
THE WEAPONS HALL OF ASGARD.
TROLLS. FROST GIANTS. MY FATHER. A SHORTAGE OF MEAD.
THESE ARE THINGS SURE TO DRIVE ME TO RAGE. TO ROAR. TO THUNDER.
BUT THERE IS ONE THING IN ALL THE HEAVENS WITH THE POWER TO MAKE ME ANGRIER THAN ALL THE REST COMBINED.
I DON'T EVEN CALL IT BY NAME ANYMORE.
IT'S SIMPLY...THAT HAMMER FROM HEL.
AND BY ALL THE GODS DO I HATE IT.

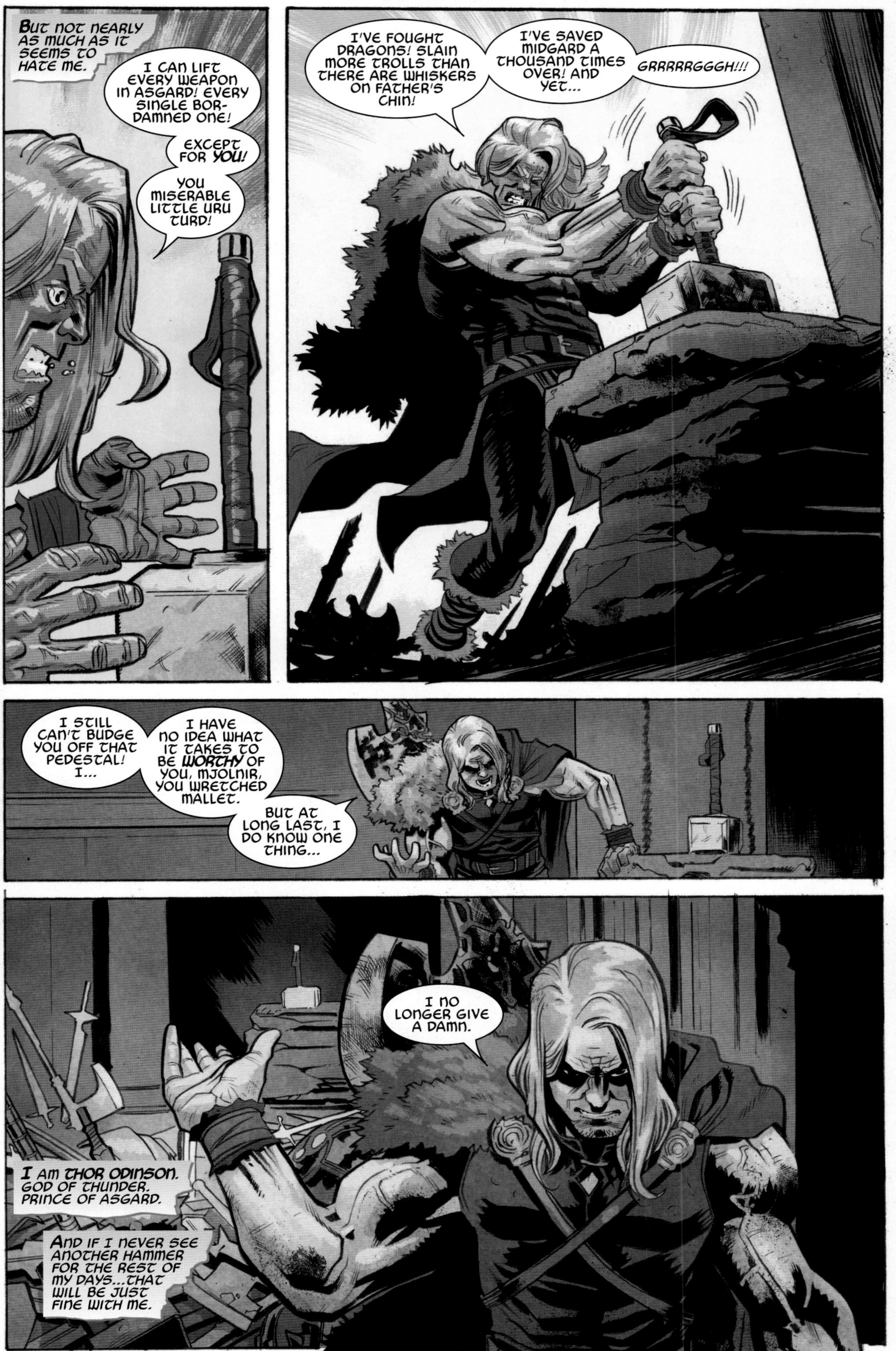

But not nearly as much as it seems to hate me.
I can lift every weapon in Asgard! Every single Bor-damned one!
Except for YOU!
You miserable little Uru turd!
I've fought dragons! Slain more trolls than there are whiskers on father's chin!
I've saved Midgard a thousand times over! And yet...
GRRRRRGGGH!!!
I still can't budge you off that pedestal! I...
I have no idea what it takes to be WORTHY of you, Mjolnir, you wretched mallet.
But at long last, I do know one thing...
I no longer give a damn.
I am THOR ODINSON. God of thunder. Prince of Asgard.
And if I never see another hammer for the rest of my days...that will be just fine with me.

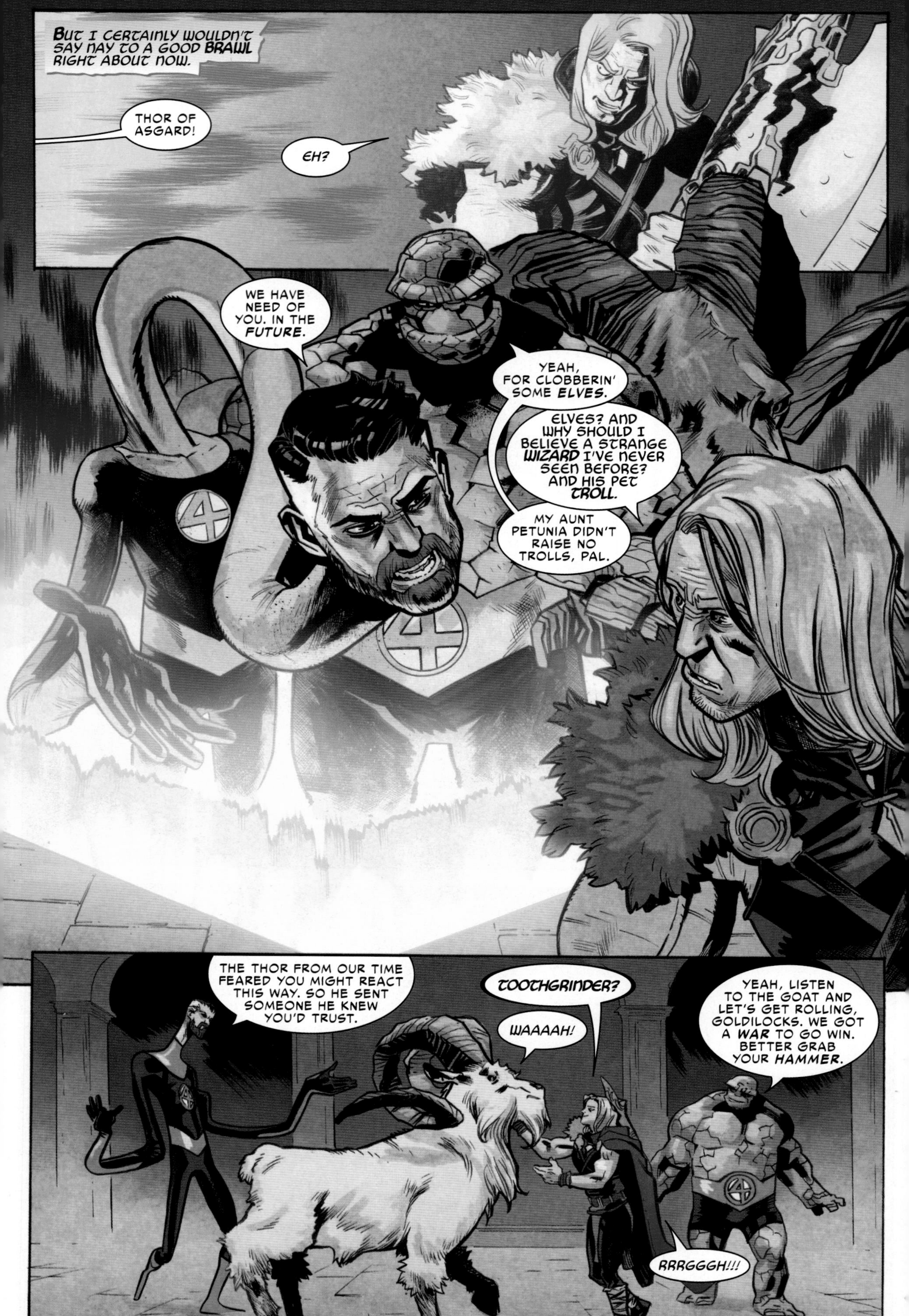
BUT I CERTAINLY WOULDN'T SAY NAY TO A GOOD BRAWL RIGHT ABOUT NOW.
THOR OF ASGARD!
EH?
WE HAVE NEED OF YOU. IN THE FUTURE.
YEAH, FOR CLOBBERIN' SOME ELVES.
ELVES? AND WHY SHOULD I BELIEVE A STRANGE WIZARD I'VE NEVER SEEN BEFORE? AND HIS PET TROLL.
MY AUNT PETUNIA DIDN'T RAISE NO TROLLS, PAL.
THE THOR FROM OUR TIME FEARED YOU MIGHT REACT THIS WAY. SO HE SENT SOMEONE HE KNEW YOU'D TRUST.
TOOTHGRINDER?
WAAAAH!
YEAH, LISTEN TO THE GOAT AND LET'S GET ROLLING, GOLDILOCKS. WE GOT A WAR TO GO WIN. BETTER GRAB YOUR HAMMER.
RRRGGGH!!!

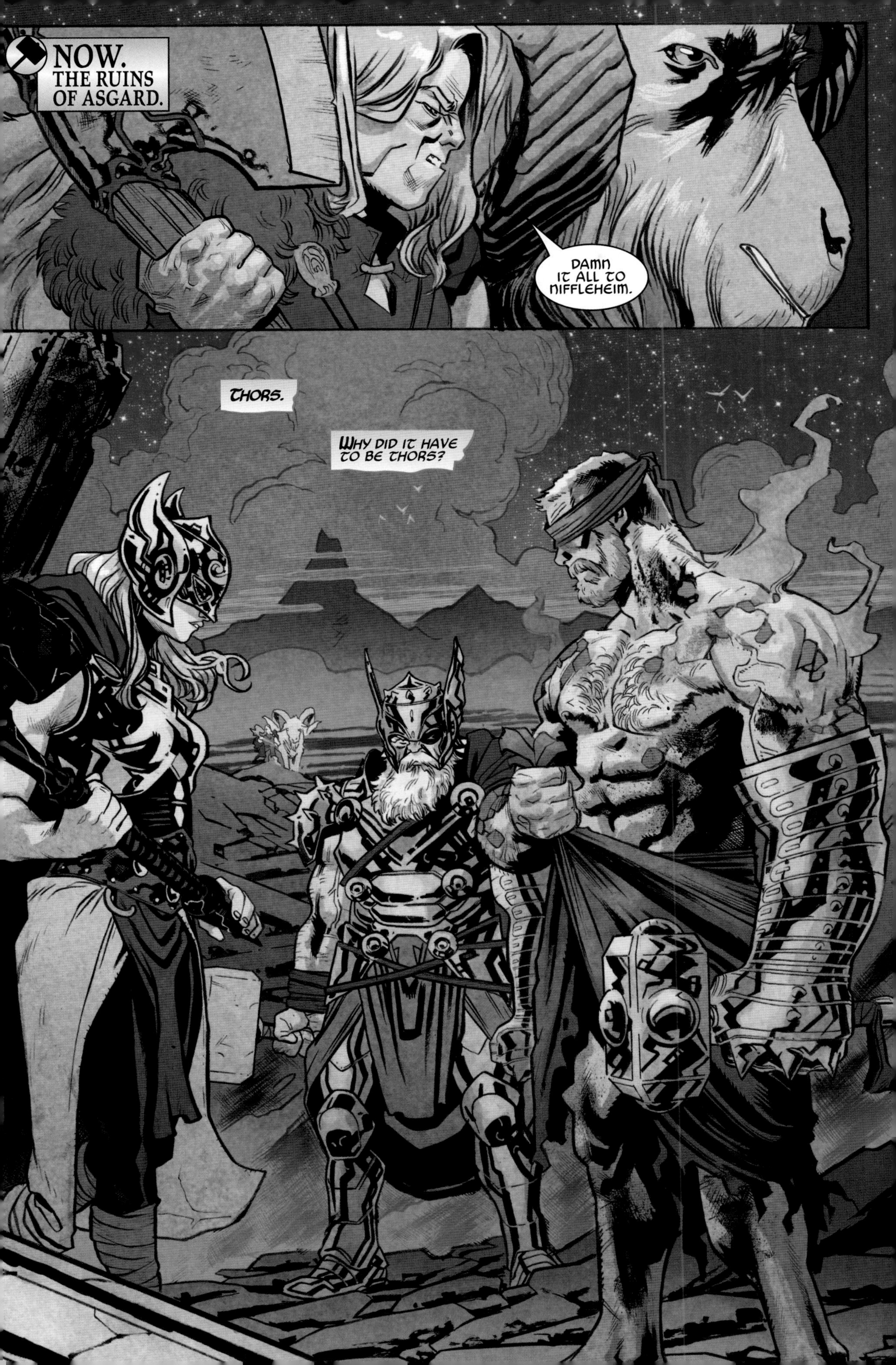
NOW. THE RUINS OF ASGARD.
DAMN IT ALL TO NIFFLEHEIM.
THORS.
WHY DID IT HAVE TO BE THORS?

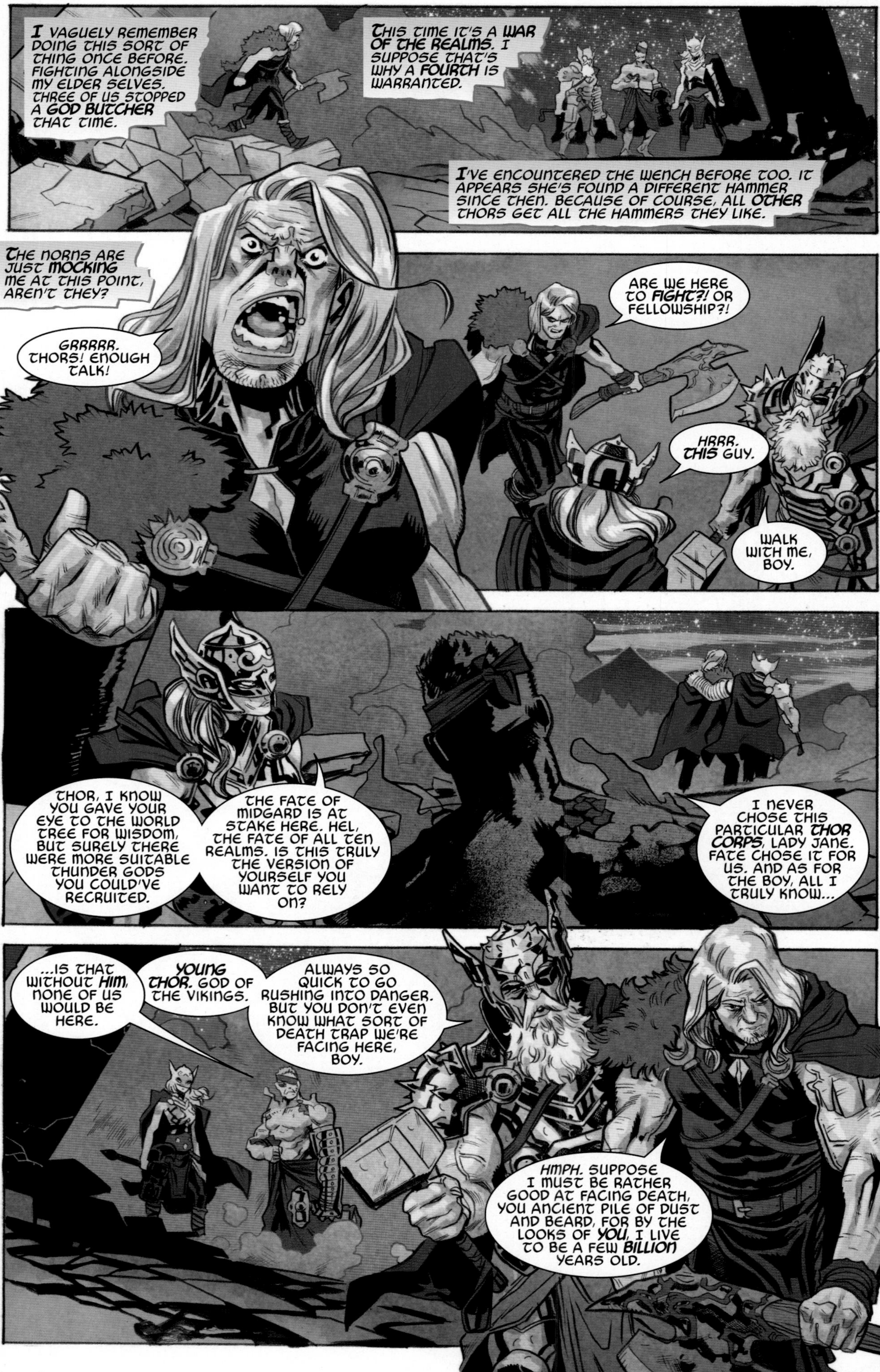

I VAGUELY REMEMBER DOING THIS SORT OF THING ONCE BEFORE. FIGHTING ALONGSIDE MY ELDER SELVES. THREE OF US STOPPED A GOD BUTCHER THAT TIME.
THIS TIME IT'S A WAR OF THE REALMS. I SUPPOSE THAT'S WHY A FOURTH IS WARRANTED.
I'VE ENCOUNTERED THE WENCH BEFORE TOO. IT APPEARS SHE'S FOUND A DIFFERENT HAMMER SINCE THEN. BECAUSE OF COURSE, ALL OTHER THORS GET ALL THE HAMMERS THEY LIKE.
THE NORNS ARE JUST MOCKING ME AT THIS POINT, AREN'T THEY?
GRRRRR. THORS! ENOUGH TALK!
ARE WE HERE TO FIGHT?! OR FELLOWSHIP?!
HRRR. THIS GUY.
WALK WITH ME, BOY.
THOR, I KNOW YOU GAVE YOUR EYE TO THE WORLD TREE FOR WISDOM, BUT SURELY THERE WERE MORE SUITABLE THUNDER GODS YOU COULD'VE RECRUITED.
THE FATE OF MIDGARD IS AT STAKE HERE. HEL, THE FATE OF ALL TEN REALMS. IS THIS TRULY THE VERSION OF YOURSELF YOU WANT TO RELY ON?
I NEVER CHOSE THIS PARTICULAR THOR CORPS, LADY JANE. FATE CHOSE IT FOR US. AND AS FOR THE BOY, ALL I TRULY KNOW...
...IS THAT WITHOUT HIM, NONE OF US WOULD BE HERE.
YOUNG THOR. GOD OF THE VIKINGS.
ALWAYS SO QUICK TO GO RUSHING INTO DANGER. BUT YOU DON'T EVEN KNOW WHAT SORT OF DEATH TRAP WE'RE FACING HERE, BOY.
HMPH. SUPPOSE I MUST BE RATHER GOOD AT FACING DEATH, YOU ANCIENT PILE OF DUST AND BEARD, FOR BY THE LOOKS OF YOU, I LIVE TO BE A FEW BILLION YEARS OLD.

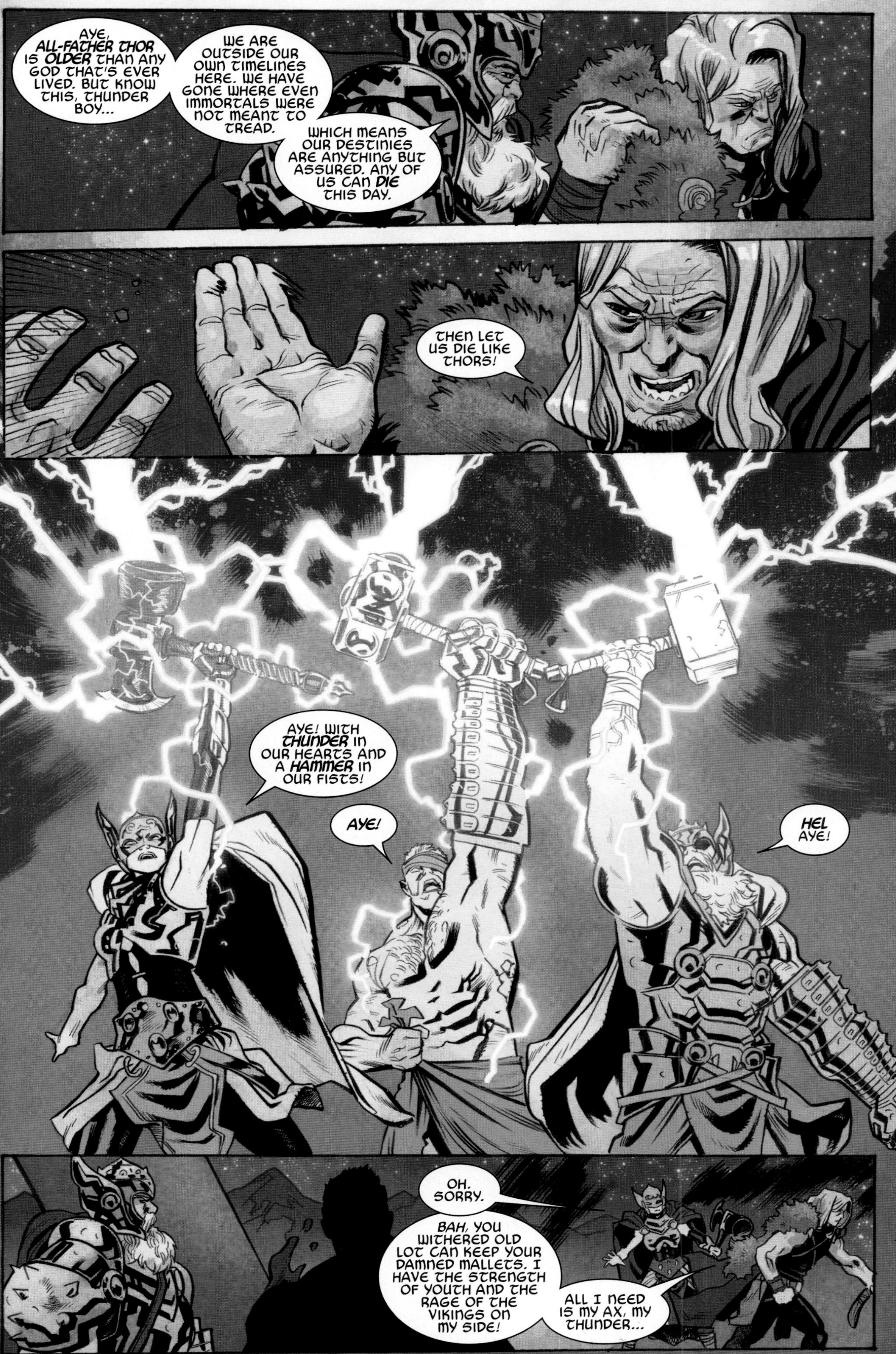
AYE, ALL-FATHER THOR IS OLDER THAN ANY GOD THAT'S EVER LIVED. BUT KNOW THIS, THUNDER BOY...
WE ARE OUTSIDE OUR OWN TIMELINES HERE. WE HAVE GONE WHERE EVEN IMMORTALS WERE NOT MEANT TO TREAD.
WHICH MEANS OUR DESTINIES ARE ANYTHING BUT ASSURED. ANY OF US CAN DIE THIS DAY.
THEN LET US DIE LIKE THORS!
AYE! WITH THUNDER IN OUR HEARTS AND A HAMMER IN OUR FISTS!
AYE!
HEL AYE!
OH. SORRY.
BAH, YOU WITHERED OLD LOT CAN KEEP YOUR DAMNED MALLETS. I HAVE THE STRENGTH OF YOUTH AND THE RAGE OF THE VIKINGS ON MY SIDE!
ALL I NEED IS MY AX, MY THUNDER...

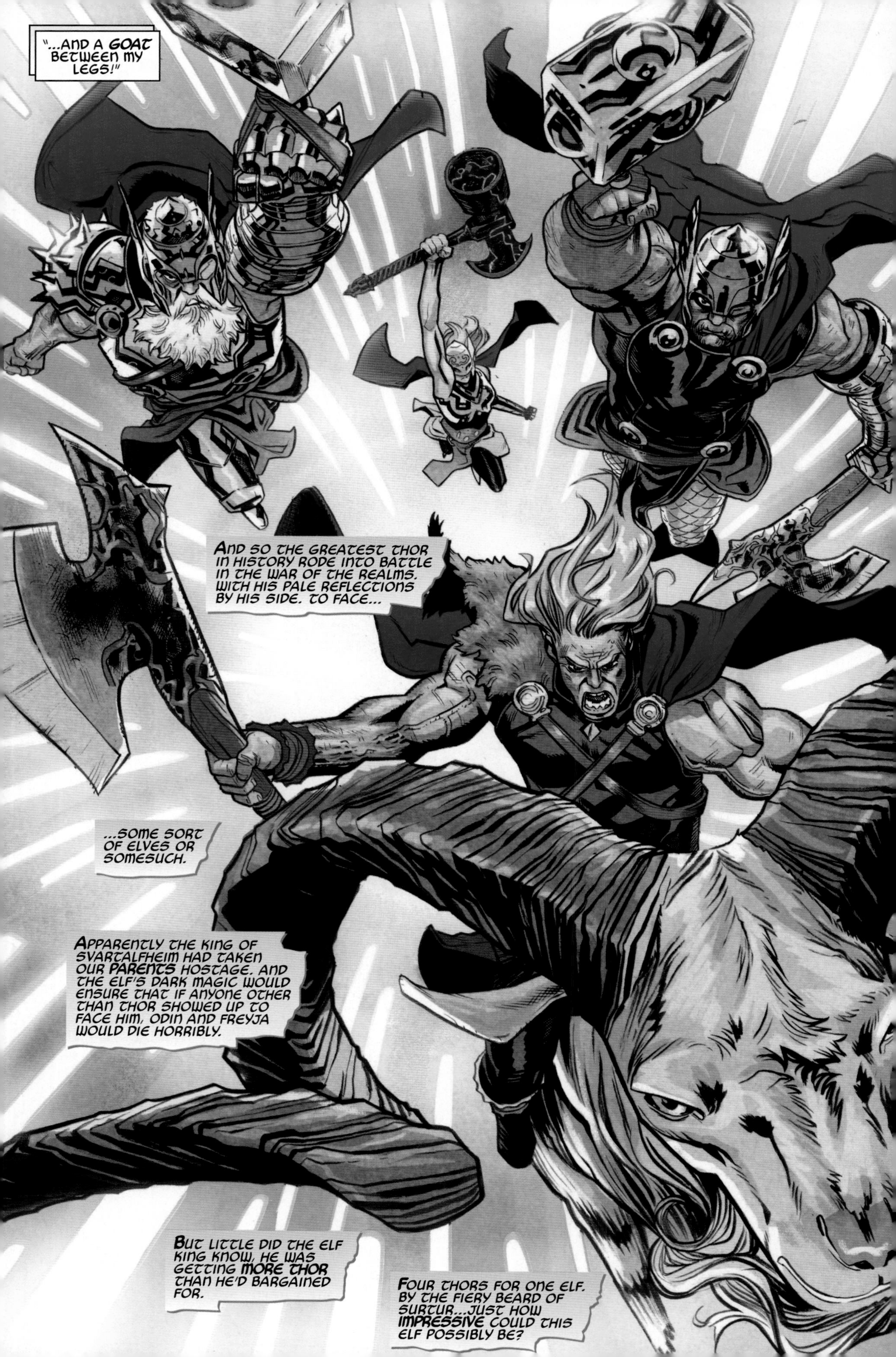
"...AND A GOAT BETWEEN MY LEGS!"
AND SO THE GREATEST THOR IN HISTORY RODE INTO BATTLE IN THE WAR OF THE REALMS. WITH HIS PALE REFLECTIONS BY HIS SIDE. TO FACE...
...SOME SORT OF ELVES OR SOMESUCH.
APPARENTLY THE KING OF SVARTALFHEIM HAD TAKEN OUR PARENTS HOSTAGE. AND THE ELF'S DARK MAGIC WOULD ENSURE THAT IF ANYONE OTHER THAN THOR SHOWED UP TO FACE HIM, ODIN AND FREYJA WOULD DIE HORRIBLY.
BUT LITTLE DID THE ELF KING KNOW, HE WAS GETTING MORE THOR THAN HE'D BARGAINED FOR.
FOUR THORS FOR ONE ELF. BY THE FIERY BEARD OF SURTUR...JUST HOW IMPRESSIVE COULD THIS ELF POSSIBLY BE?

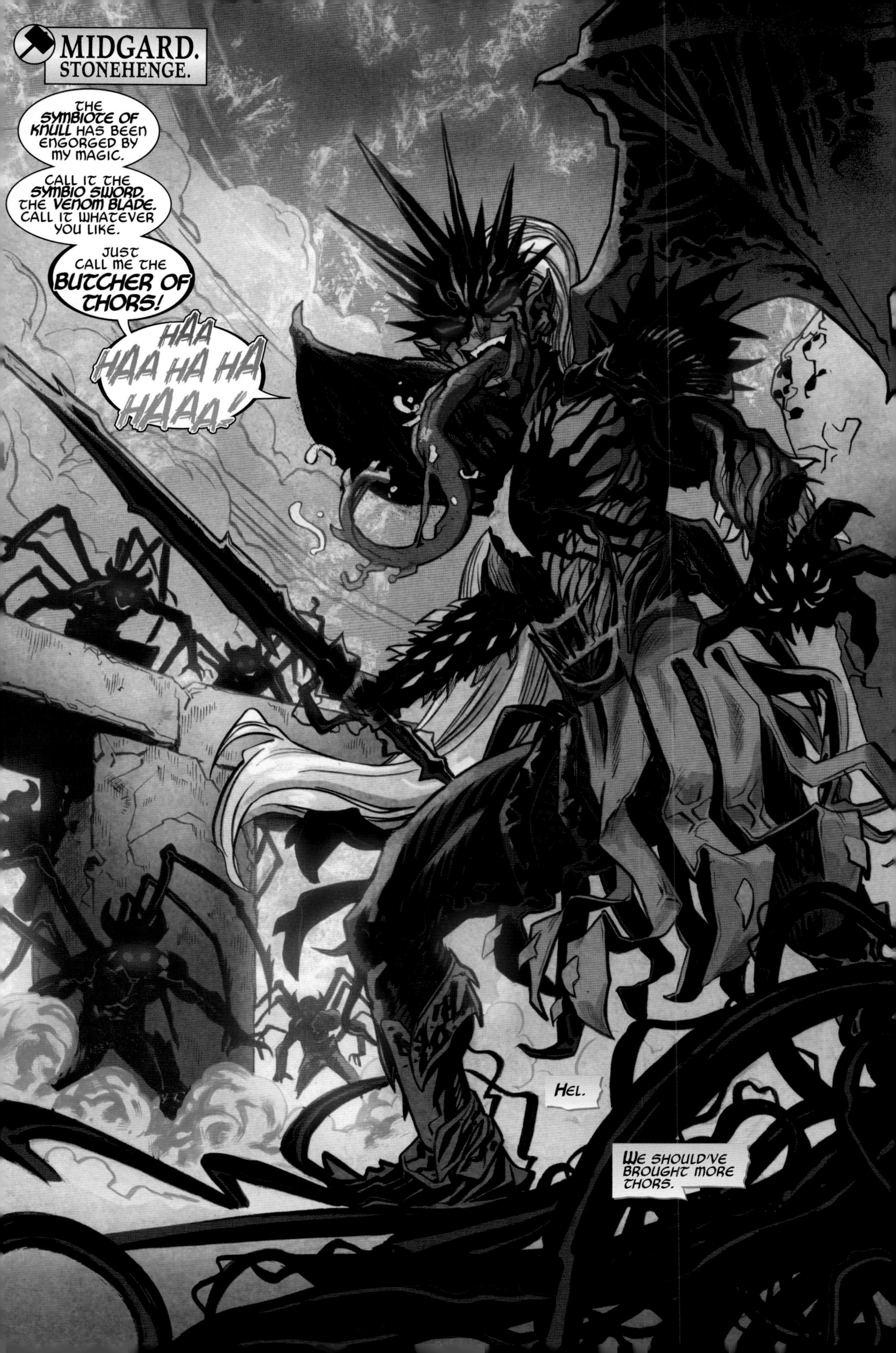
MIDGARD.
STONEHENGE.
THE SYMBIOTE OF KNULL HAS BEEN ENGORGED BY MY MAGIC.
CALL IT THE SYMBIO SWORD. THE VENOM BLADE. CALL IT WHATEVER YOU LIKE.
JUST CALL ME THE BUTCHER OF THORS!
HAA HAA HA HA HAAA!
HEL.
WE SHOULD'VE BROUGHT MORE THORS.

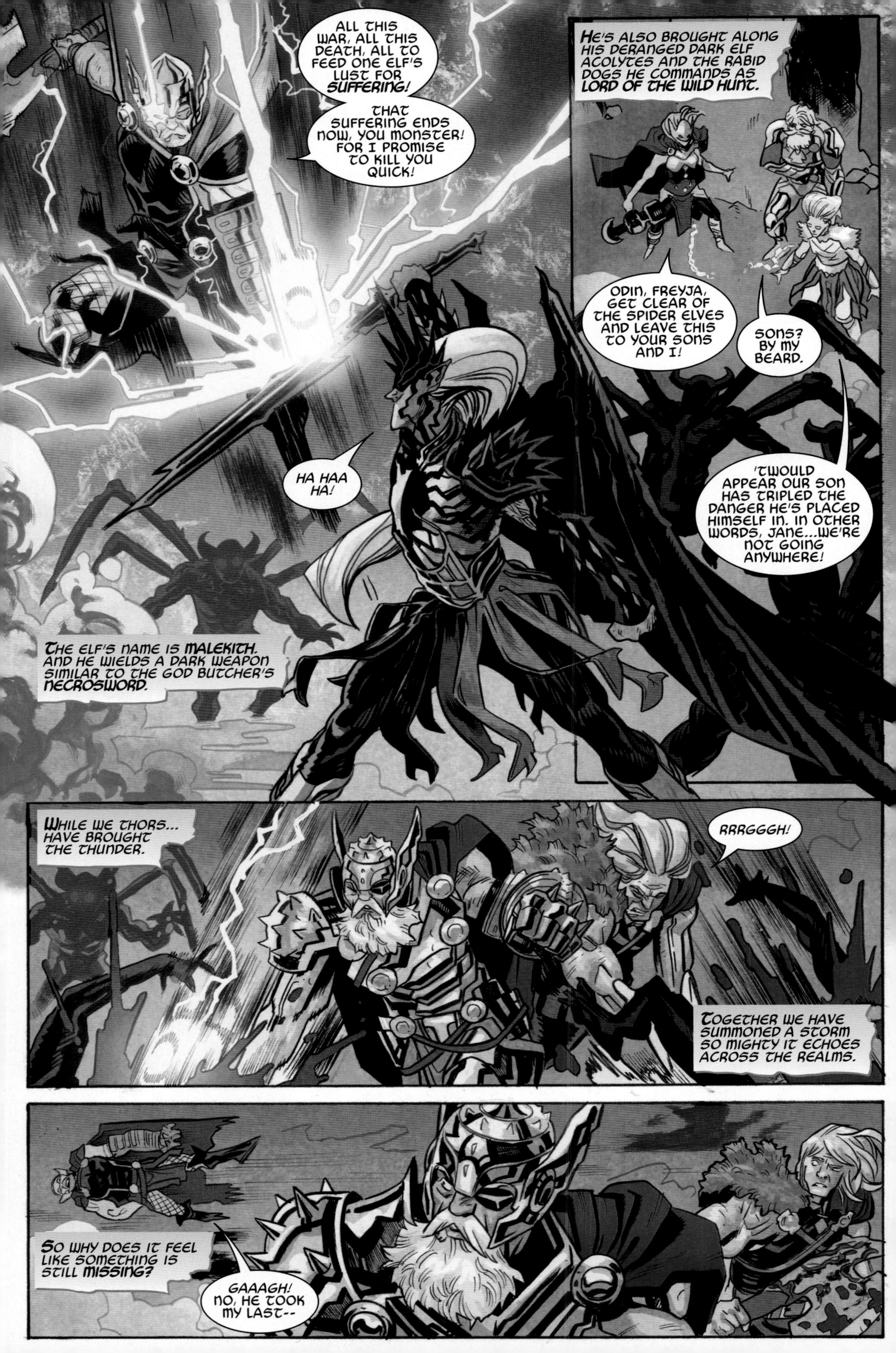
ALL THIS WAR, ALL THIS DEATH, ALL TO FEED ONE ELF'S LUST FOR SUFFERING!
THAT SUFFERING ENDS NOW, YOU MONSTER! FOR I PROMISE TO KILL YOU QUICK!
HE'S ALSO BROUGHT ALONG HIS DERANGED DARK ELF ACOLYTES AND THE RABID DOGS HE COMMANDS AS LORD OF THE WILD HUNT.
ODIN, FREYJA, GET CLEAR OF THE SPIDER ELVES AND LEAVE THIS TO YOUR SONS AND I!
SONS? BY MY BEARD.
'TWOULD APPEAR OUR SON HAS TRIPLED THE DANGER HE'S PLACED HIMSELF IN. IN OTHER WORDS, JANE...WE'RE NOT GOING ANYWHERE!
HA HAA HA!
THE ELF'S NAME IS MALEKITH. AND HE WIELDS A DARK WEAPON SIMILAR TO THE GOD BUTCHER'S NECROSWORD.
WHILE WE THORS... HAVE BROUGHT THE THUNDER.
RRRGGGH!
TOGETHER WE HAVE SUMMONED A STORM SO MIGHTY IT ECHOES ACROSS THE REALMS.
SO WHY DOES IT FEEL LIKE SOMETHING IS STILL MISSING?
GAAAGH! NO, HE TOOK MY LAST--

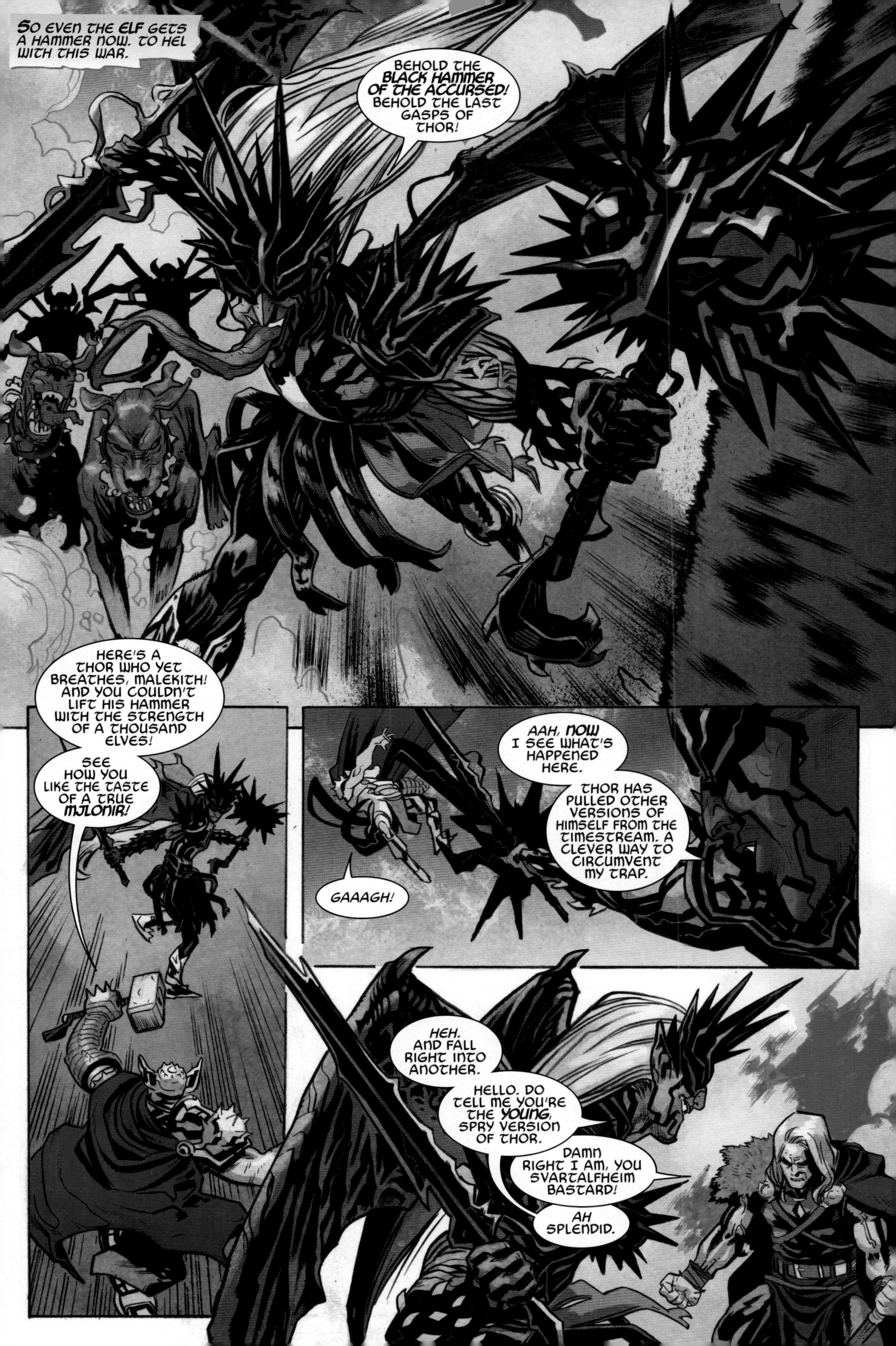
SO EVEN THE ELF GETS A HAMMER NOW. TO HEL WITH THIS WAR.
BEHOLD THE BLACK HAMMER OF THE ACCURSED! BEHOLD THE LAST GASPS OF THOR!
HERE'S A THOR WHO YET BREATHES, MALEKITH! AND YOU COULDN'T LIFT HIS HAMMER WITH THE STRENGTH OF A THOUSAND ELVES!
SEE HOW YOU LIKE THE TASTE OF A TRUE MJOLNIR!
AAH, NOW I SEE WHAT'S HAPPENED HERE.
THOR HAS PULLED OTHER VERSIONS OF HIMSELF FROM THE TIMESTREAM. A CLEVER WAY TO CIRCUMVENT MY TRAP.
GAAAGH!
HEH. AND FALL RIGHT INTO ANOTHER.
HELLO. DO TELL ME YOU'RE THE YOUNG, SPRY VERSION OF THOR.
DAMN RIGHT I AM, YOU SVARTALFHEIM BASTARD!
AH SPLENDID.

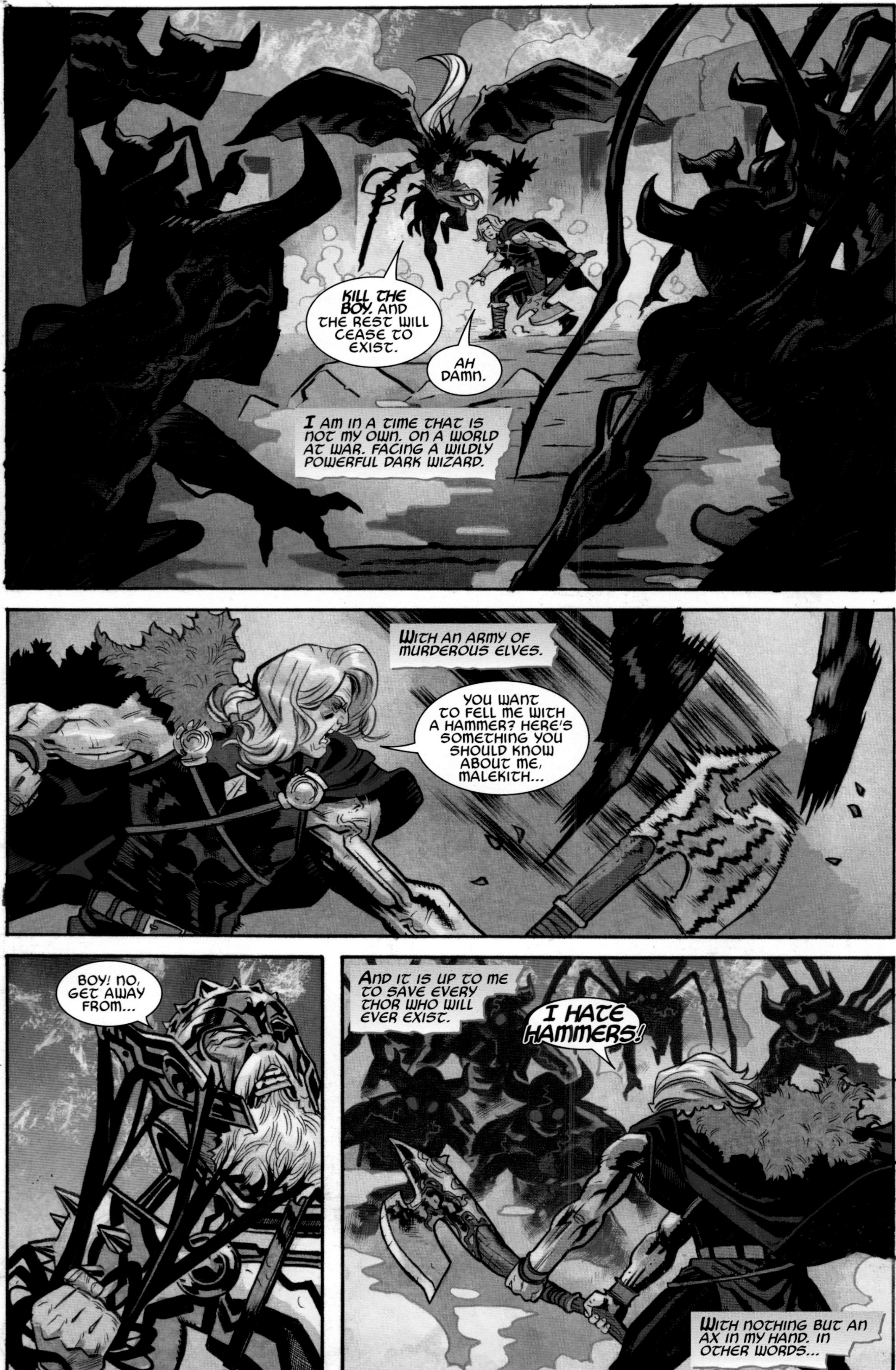

KILL THE BOY. AND THE REST WILL CEASE TO EXIST.
AH DAMN.
I AM IN A TIME THAT IS NOT MY OWN. ON A WORLD AT WAR. FACING A WILDLY POWERFUL DARK WIZARD.
WITH AN ARMY OF MURDEROUS ELVES.
YOU WANT TO FELL ME WITH A HAMMER? HERE'S SOMETHING YOU SHOULD KNOW ABOUT ME, MALEKITH...
BOY! NO, GET AWAY FROM...
AND IT IS UP TO ME TO SAVE EVERY THOR WHO WILL EVER EXIST.
I HATE HAMMERS!
WITH NOTHING BUT AN AX IN MY HAND. IN OTHER WORDS...

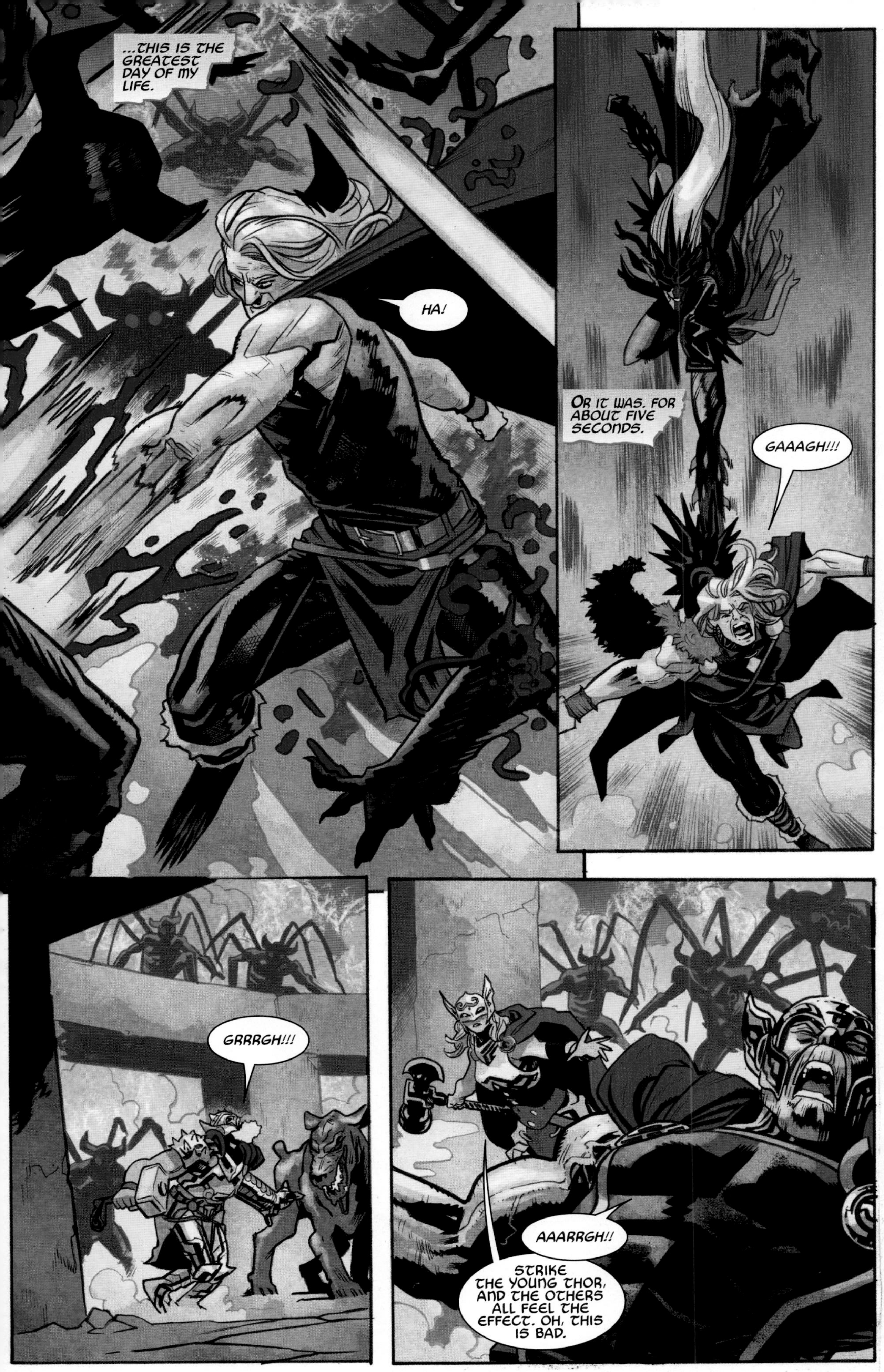
...THIS IS THE GREATEST DAY OF MY LIFE.
HA!
OR IT WAS. FOR ABOUT FIVE SECONDS.
GAAAGH!!!
GRRRGH!!!
AAARRGH!!
STRIKE THE YOUNG THOR, AND THE OTHERS ALL FEEL THE EFFECT. OH, THIS IS BAD.

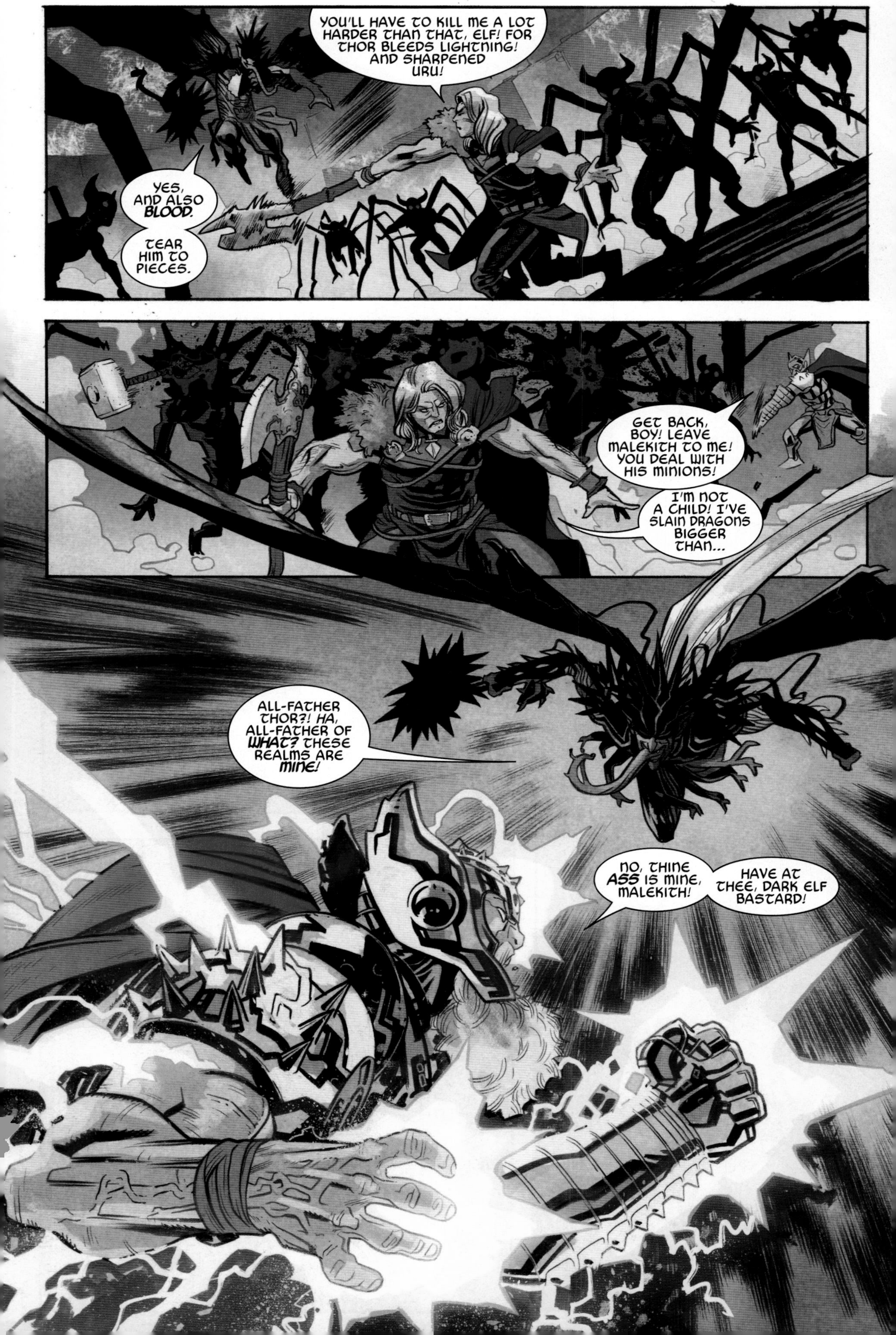

YOU'LL HAVE TO KILL ME A LOT HARDER THAN THAT, ELF! FOR THOR BLEEDS LIGHTNING! AND SHARPENED URU!
YES, AND ALSO BLOOD.
TEAR HIM TO PIECES.
GET BACK, BOY! LEAVE MALEKITH TO ME! YOU DEAL WITH HIS MINIONS!
I'M NOT A CHILD! I'VE SLAIN DRAGONS BIGGER THAN...
ALL-FATHER THOR?! HA, ALL-FATHER OF WHAT? THESE REALMS ARE MINE!
NO, THINE ASS IS MINE, MALEKITH!
HAVE AT THEE, DARK ELF BASTARD!

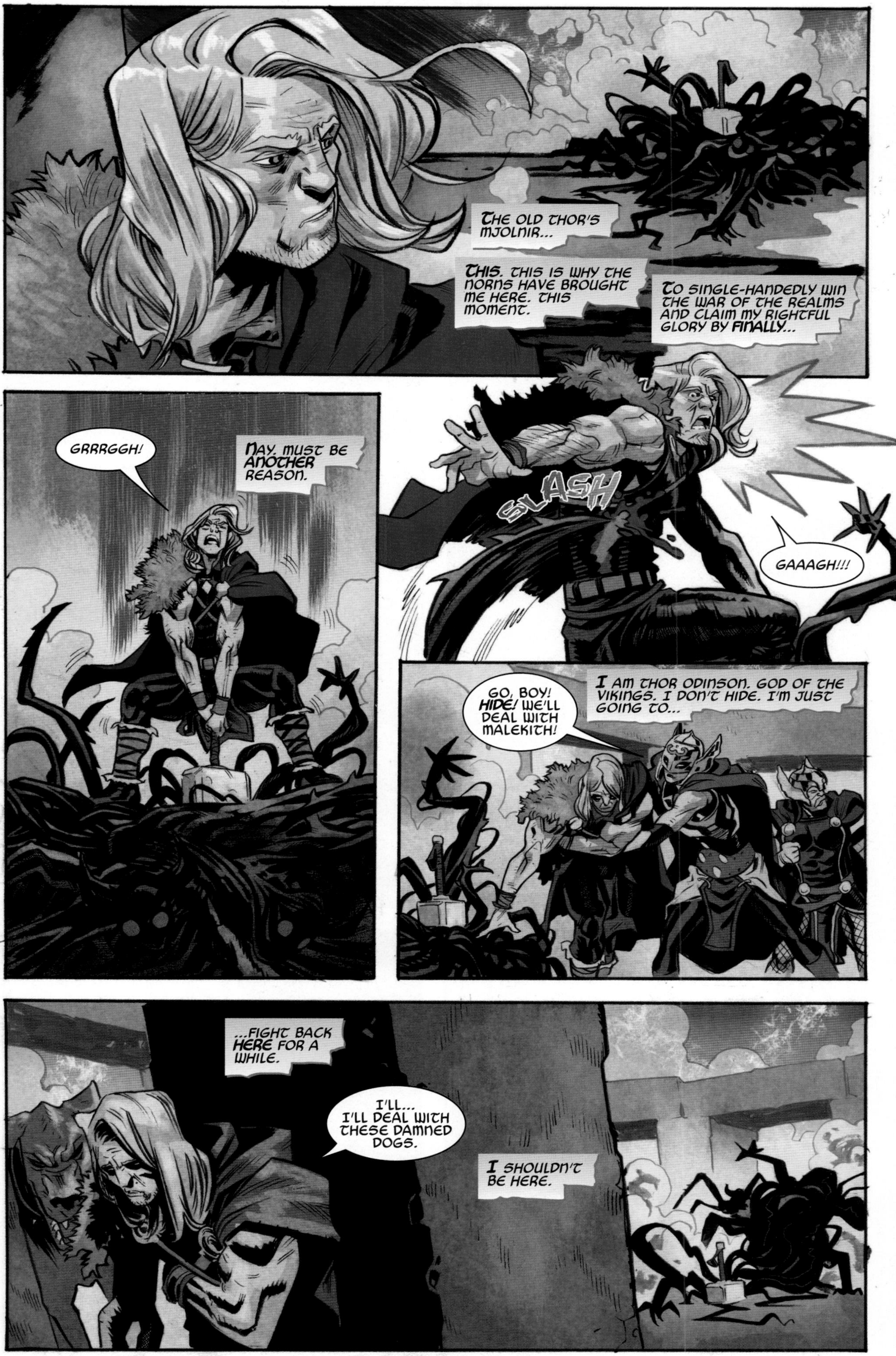
THE OLD THOR'S MJOLNIR...
THIS. THIS IS WHY THE NORNS HAVE BROUGHT ME HERE. THIS MOMENT.
TO SINGLE-HANDEDLY WIN THE WAR OF THE REALMS AND CLAIM MY RIGHTFUL GLORY BY FINALLY...
GRRRGGH!
NAY. MUST BE ANOTHER REASON.
SLASH
GAAAGH!!!
GO, BOY! HIDE! WE'LL DEAL WITH MALEKITH!
I AM THOR ODINSON. GOD OF THE VIKINGS. I DON'T HIDE. I'M JUST GOING TO...
...FIGHT BACK HERE FOR A WHILE.
I'LL... I'LL DEAL WITH THESE DAMNED DOGS.
I SHOULDN'T BE HERE.

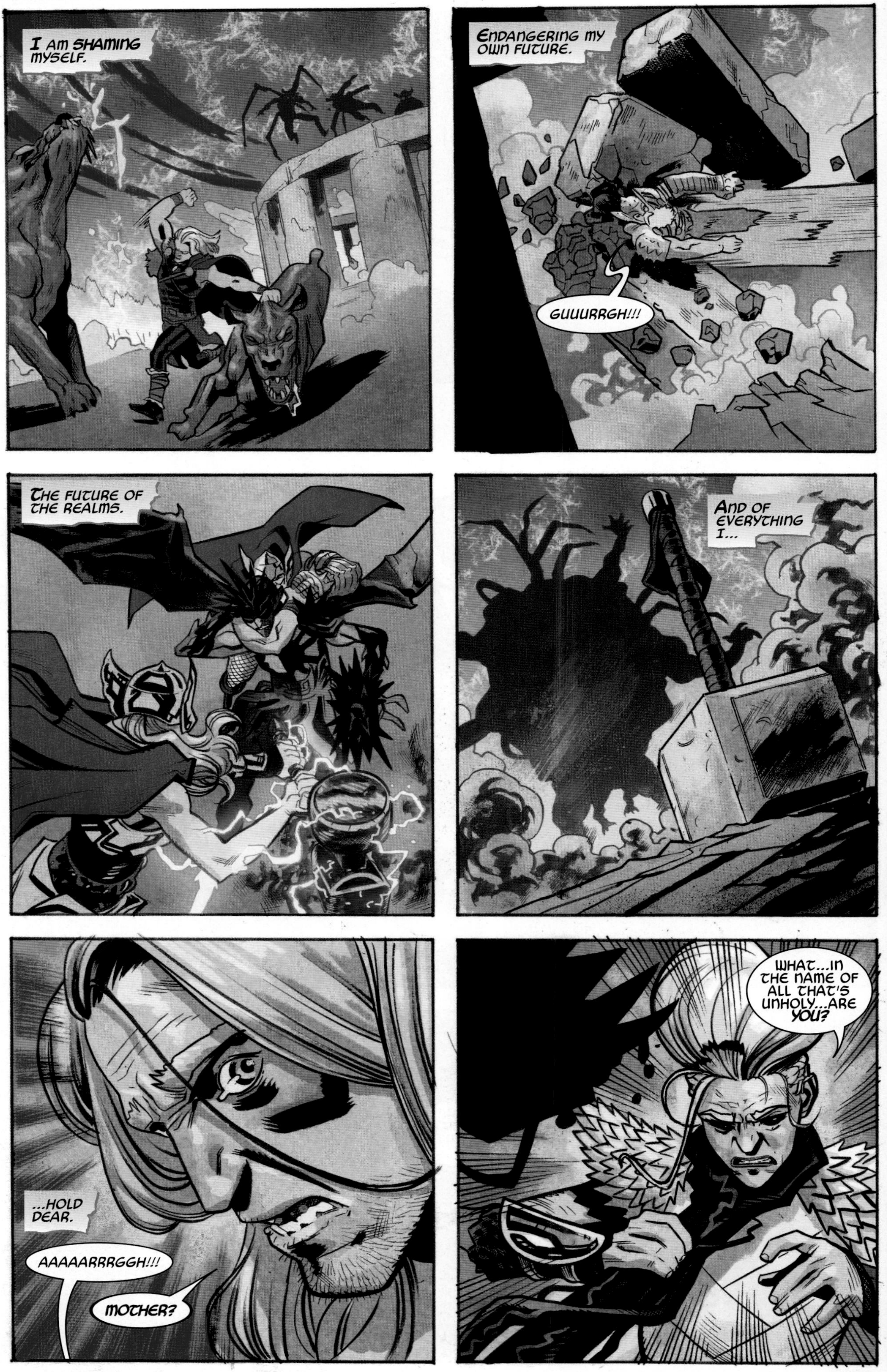
I AM SHAMING MYSELF.
ENDANGERING MY OWN FUTURE.
GUUURRGH!!!
THE FUTURE OF THE REALMS.
AND OF EVERYTHING I...
...HOLD DEAR.
AAAAARRRGGH!!!
MOTHER?
WHAT...IN THE NAME OF ALL THAT'S UNHOLY...ARE YOU?

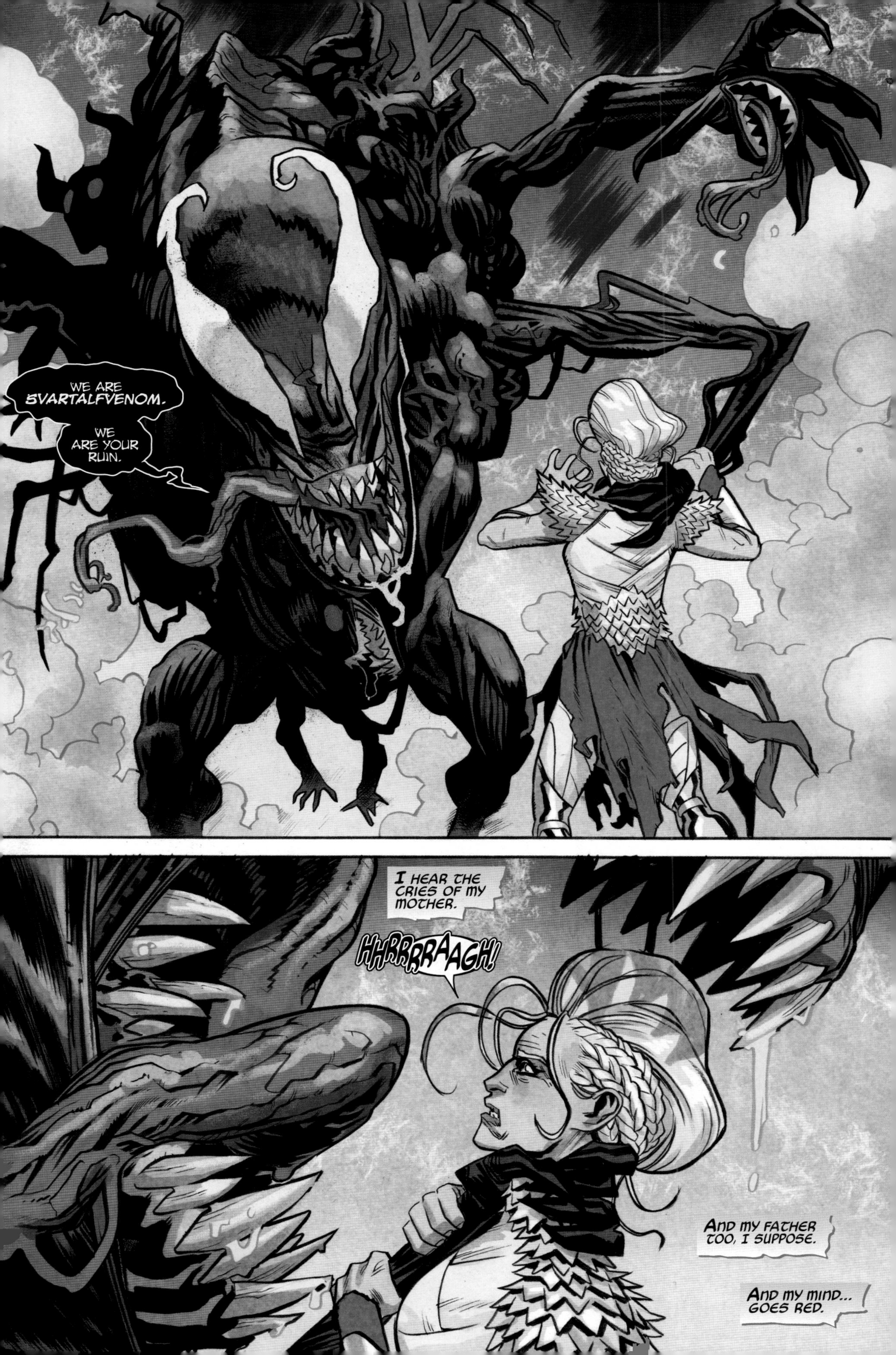
WE ARE SVARTALFVENOM.
WE ARE YOUR RUIN.
I HEAR THE CRIES OF MY MOTHER.
HHRRRRAAGH!
AND MY FATHER TOO, I SUPPOSE.
AND MY MIND... GOES RED.

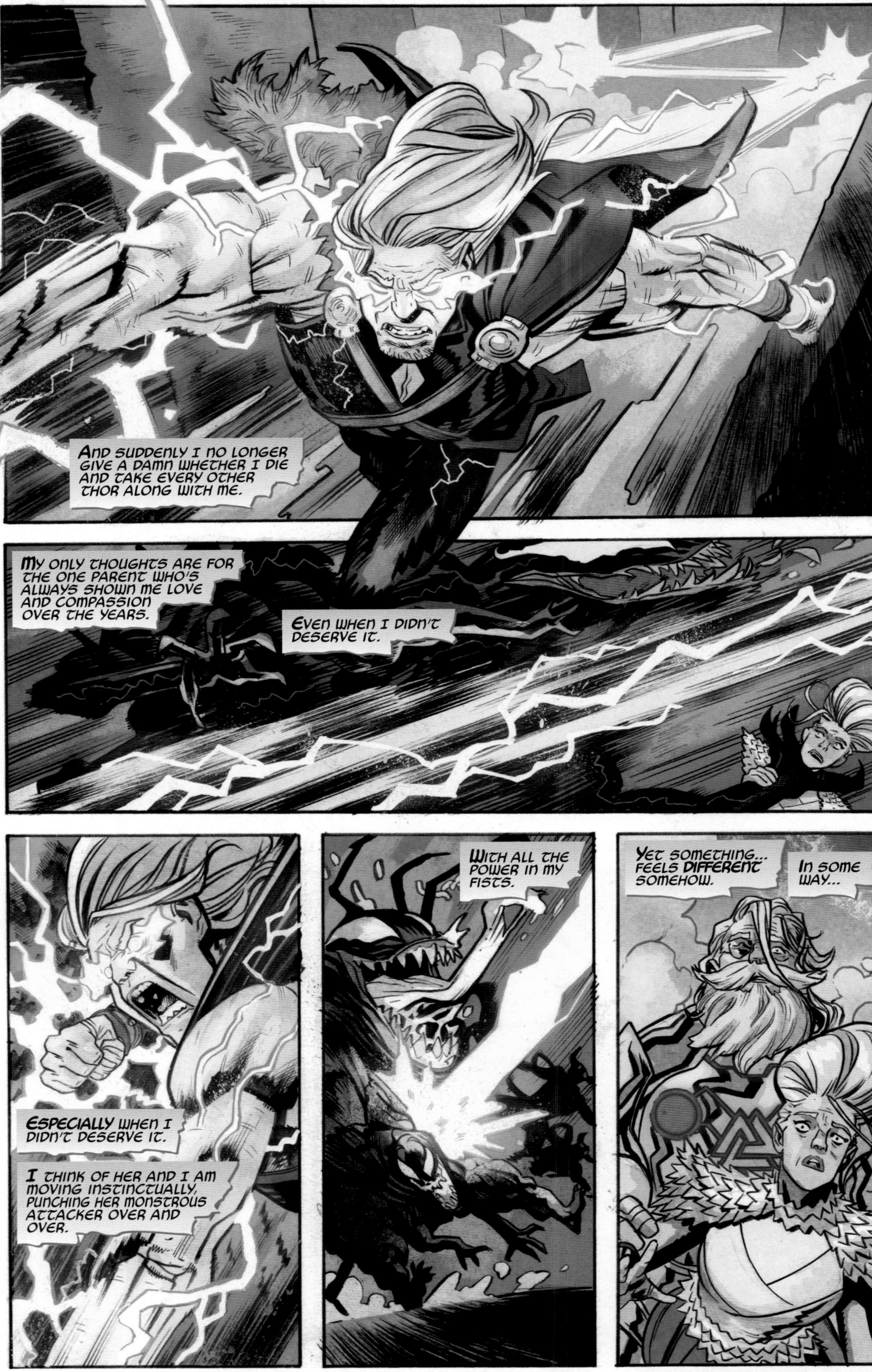

AND SUDDENLY I NO LONGER GIVE A DAMN WHETHER I DIE AND TAKE EVERY OTHER THOR ALONG WITH ME.
MY ONLY THOUGHTS ARE FOR THE ONE PARENT WHO'S ALWAYS SHOWN ME LOVE AND COMPASSION OVER THE YEARS.
EVEN WHEN I DIDN'T DESERVE IT.
ESPECIALLY WHEN I DIDN'T DESERVE IT.
I THINK OF HER AND I AM MOVING INSTINCTUALLY, PUNCHING HER MONSTROUS ATTACKER OVER AND OVER.
WITH ALL THE POWER IN MY FISTS.
YET SOMETHING... FEELS DIFFERENT SOMEHOW.
IN SOME WAY...

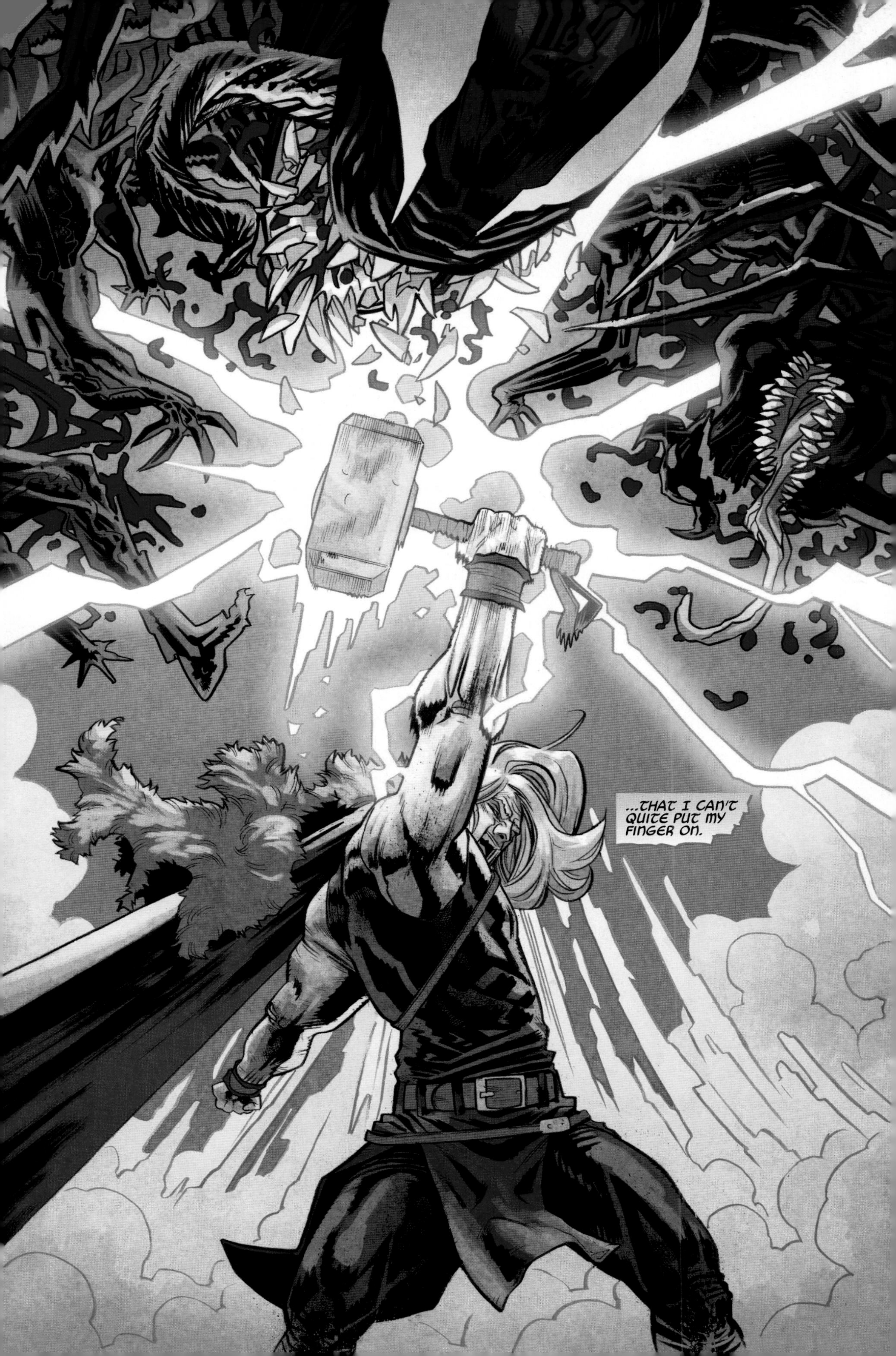
...THAT I CAN'T QUITE PUT MY FINGER ON.

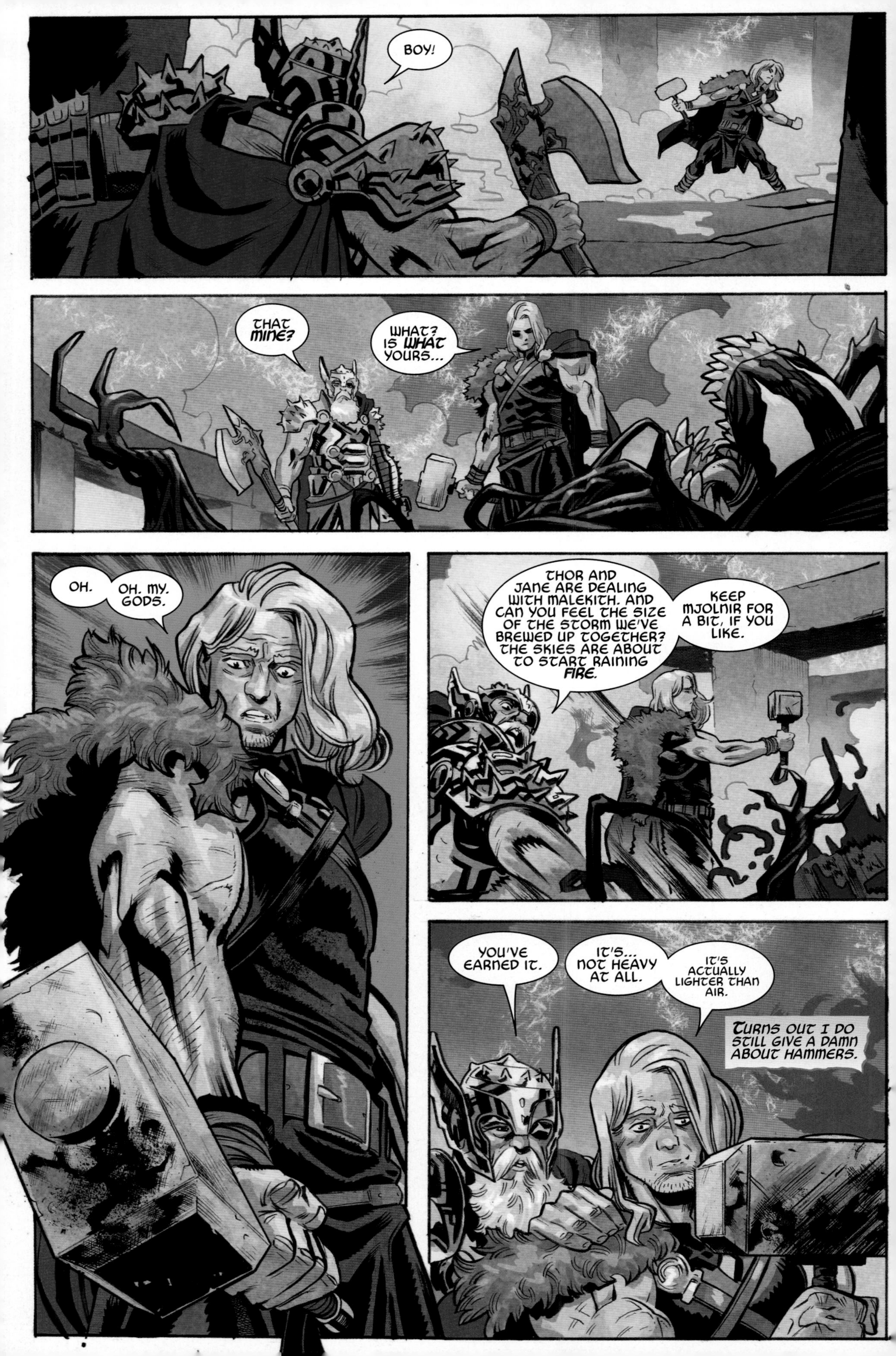
BOY!
THAT MINE?
WHAT? IS WHAT YOURS...
OH.
OH. MY. GODS.
THOR AND JANE ARE DEALING WITH MALEKITH. AND CAN YOU FEEL THE SIZE OF THE STORM WE'VE BREWED UP TOGETHER? THE SKIES ARE ABOUT TO START RAINING FIRE.
KEEP MJOLNIR FOR A BIT, IF YOU LIKE.
YOU'VE EARNED IT.
IT'S... NOT HEAVY AT ALL.
IT'S ACTUALLY LIGHTER THAN AIR.
TURNS OUT I DO STILL GIVE A DAMN ABOUT HAMMERS.

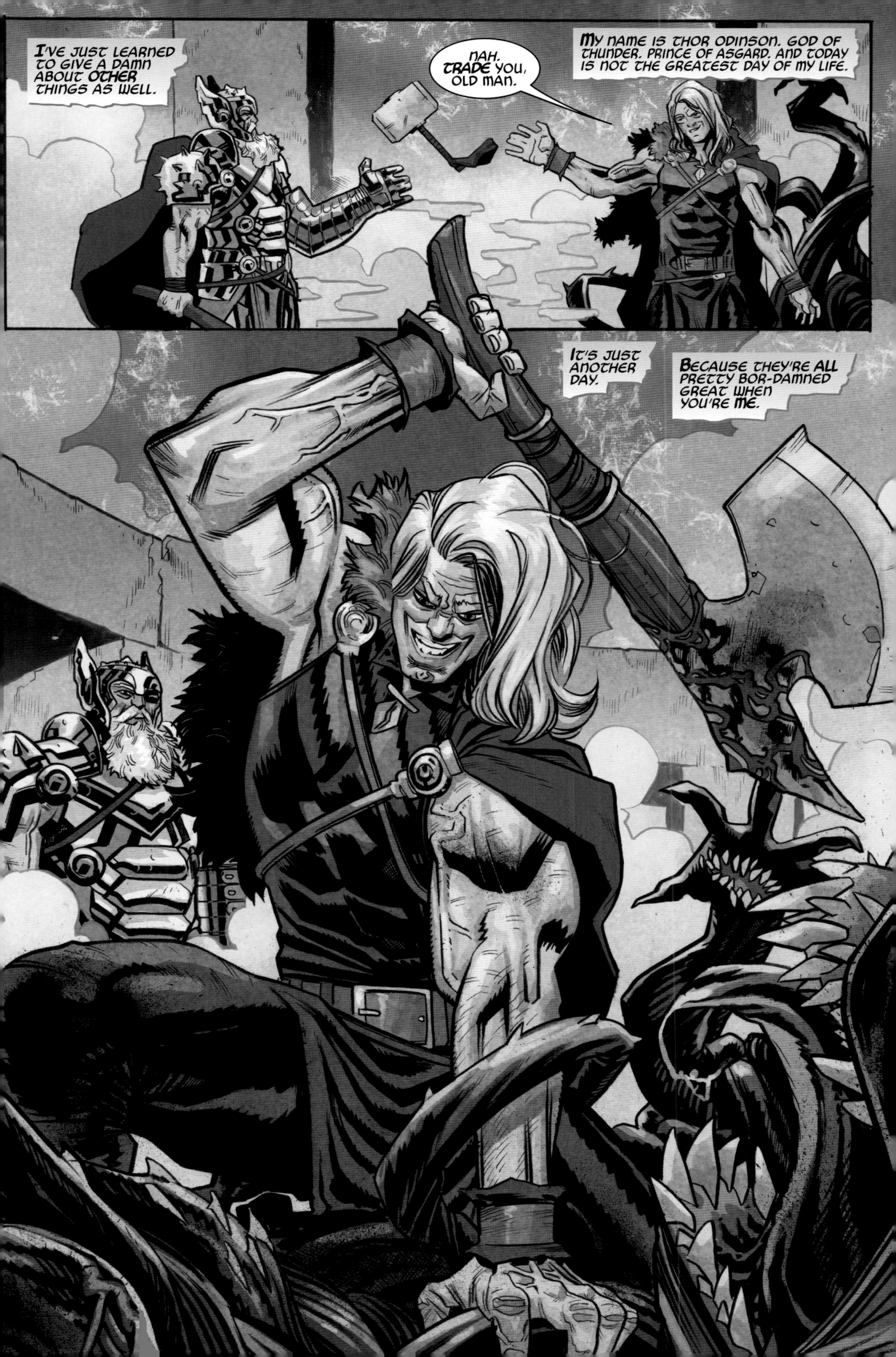

I've just learned to give a damn about OTHER things as well.
NAH. TRADE YOU, OLD MAN.
My name is Thor Odinson. God of Thunder. Prince of Asgard. And today is not the greatest day of my life.
It's just another day.
Because they're ALL pretty Bor-damned great when you're ME.

15

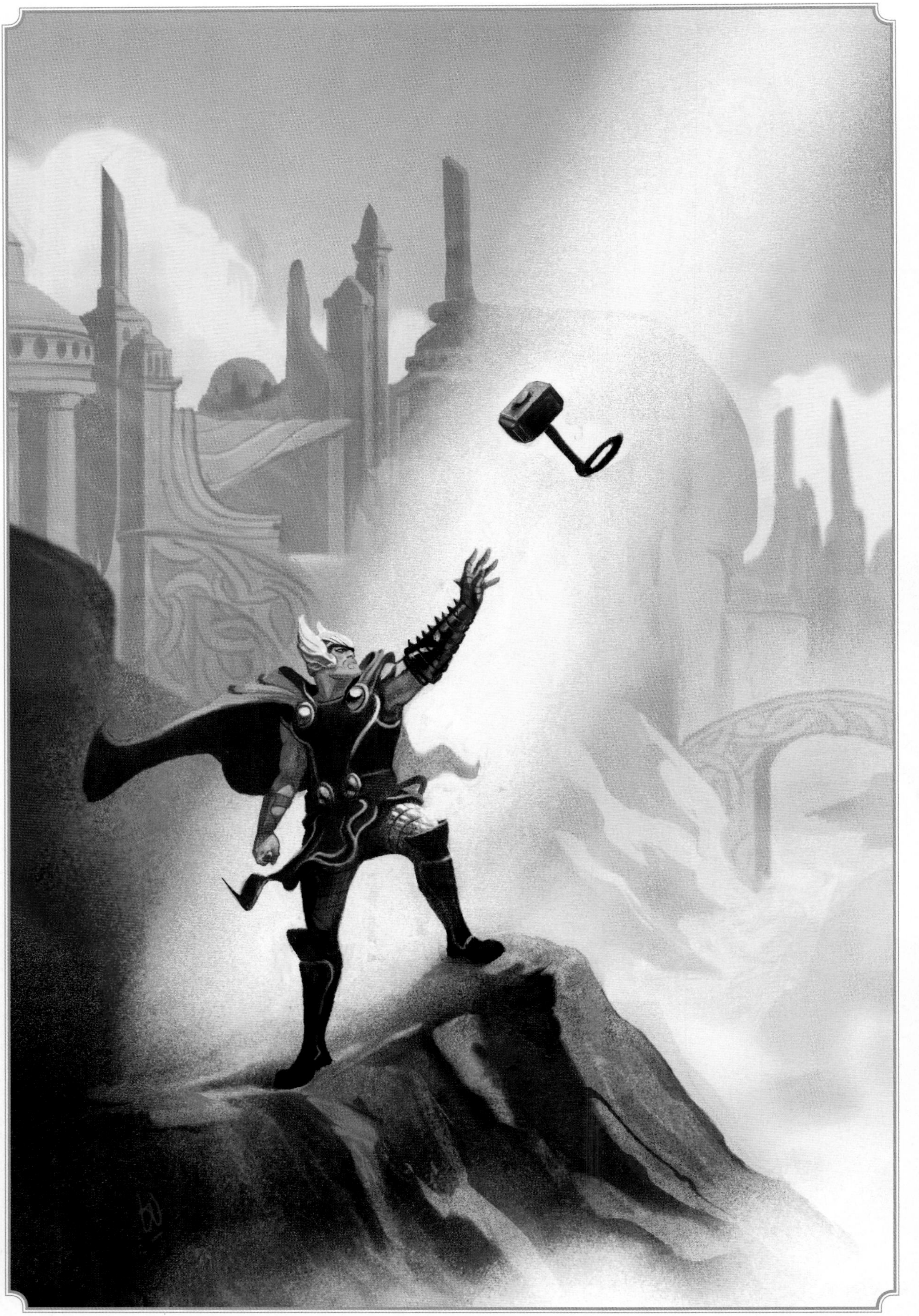

WAR'S END

THE WAR OF THE REALMS IS OVER!

WHEN THE DARK ELF KING MALEKITH GAVE THOR AN ULTIMATUM TO FACE HIM ALONE OR WITNESS THE DEATH OF HIS PARENTS, THOR SOUGHT OUT THE WORLD TREE, NOW GROWING FROM THE SUN, FOR ANSWERS.

AND HE FOUND THEM.

GATHERING THORS FROM ACROSS SPACE AND TIME—INCLUDING JANE FOSTER AS THE WAR THOR—THE GOD OF THUNDER CONFRONTED MALEKITH AND, WITH THE WISDOM OF THE WORLD TREE AND THE ENERGY OF THE MOTHER STORM, REFORGED THE LOST HAMMER MJOLNIR.

NOW MALEKITH IS DEFEATED. LOKI IS RESURRECTED AFTER BURSTING THROUGH THE STOMACH OF HIS FATHER, KING LAUFEY. JANE FOSTER IS ON THE VERGE OF A NEW TRANSFORMATION AFTER THE WAR THOR'S HAMMER BROKE APART. AND ODIN JUST DECLARED HIS SON THE NEW ALL-FATHER OF ASGARD.

THINGS ARE CHANGING IN THE TEN REALMS.

WHAT HAPPENS NEXT?

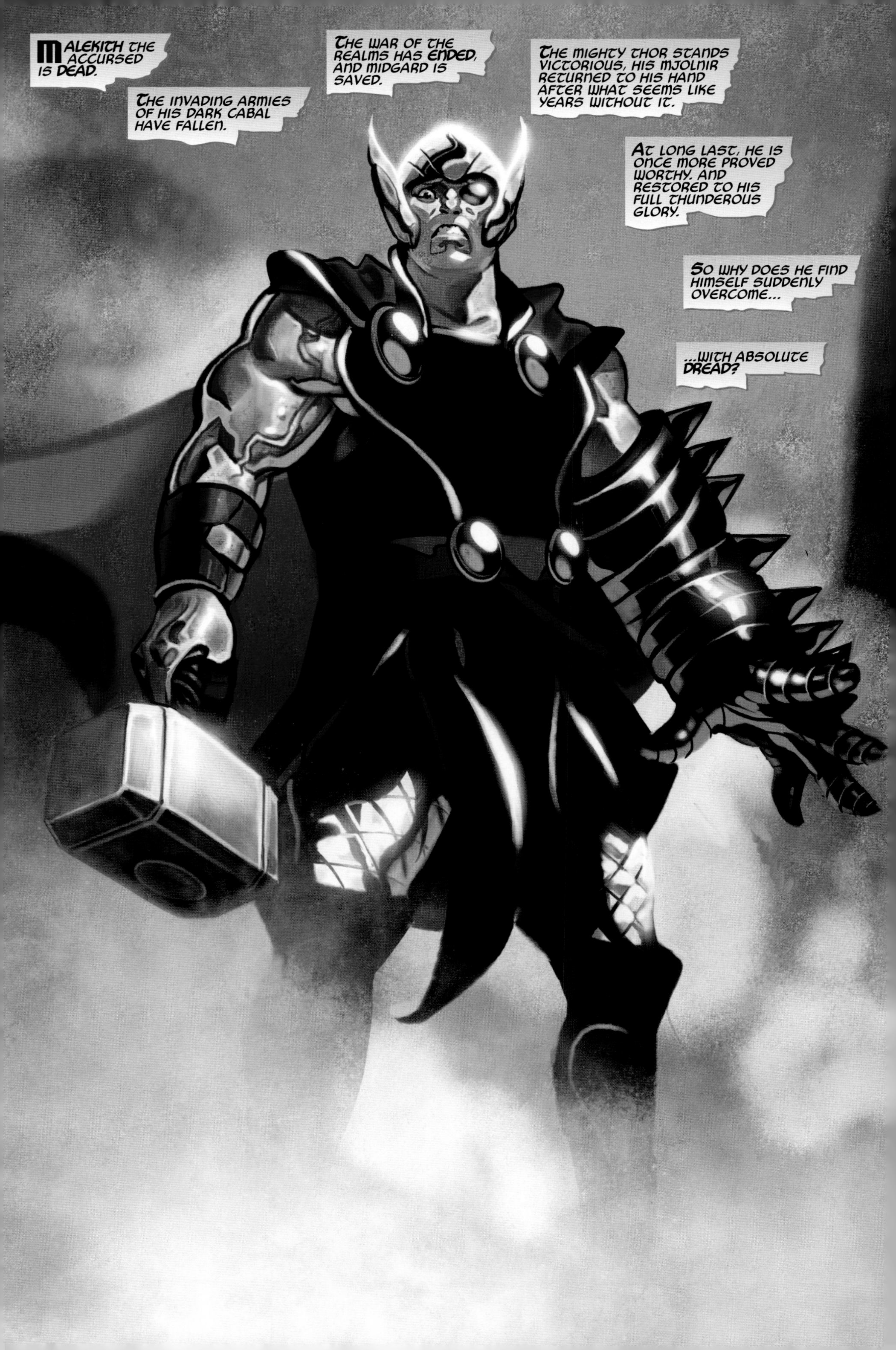
MALEKITH THE ACCURSED IS DEAD.
THE INVADING ARMIES OF HIS DARK CABAL HAVE FALLEN.
THE WAR OF THE REALMS HAS ENDED, AND MIDGARD IS SAVED.
THE MIGHTY THOR STANDS VICTORIOUS, HIS MJOLNIR RETURNED TO HIS HAND AFTER WHAT SEEMS LIKE YEARS WITHOUT IT.
AT LONG LAST, HE IS ONCE MORE PROVED WORTHY. AND RESTORED TO HIS FULL THUNDEROUS GLORY.
SO WHY DOES HE FIND HIMSELF SUDDENLY OVERCOME...
...WITH ABSOLUTE DREAD?

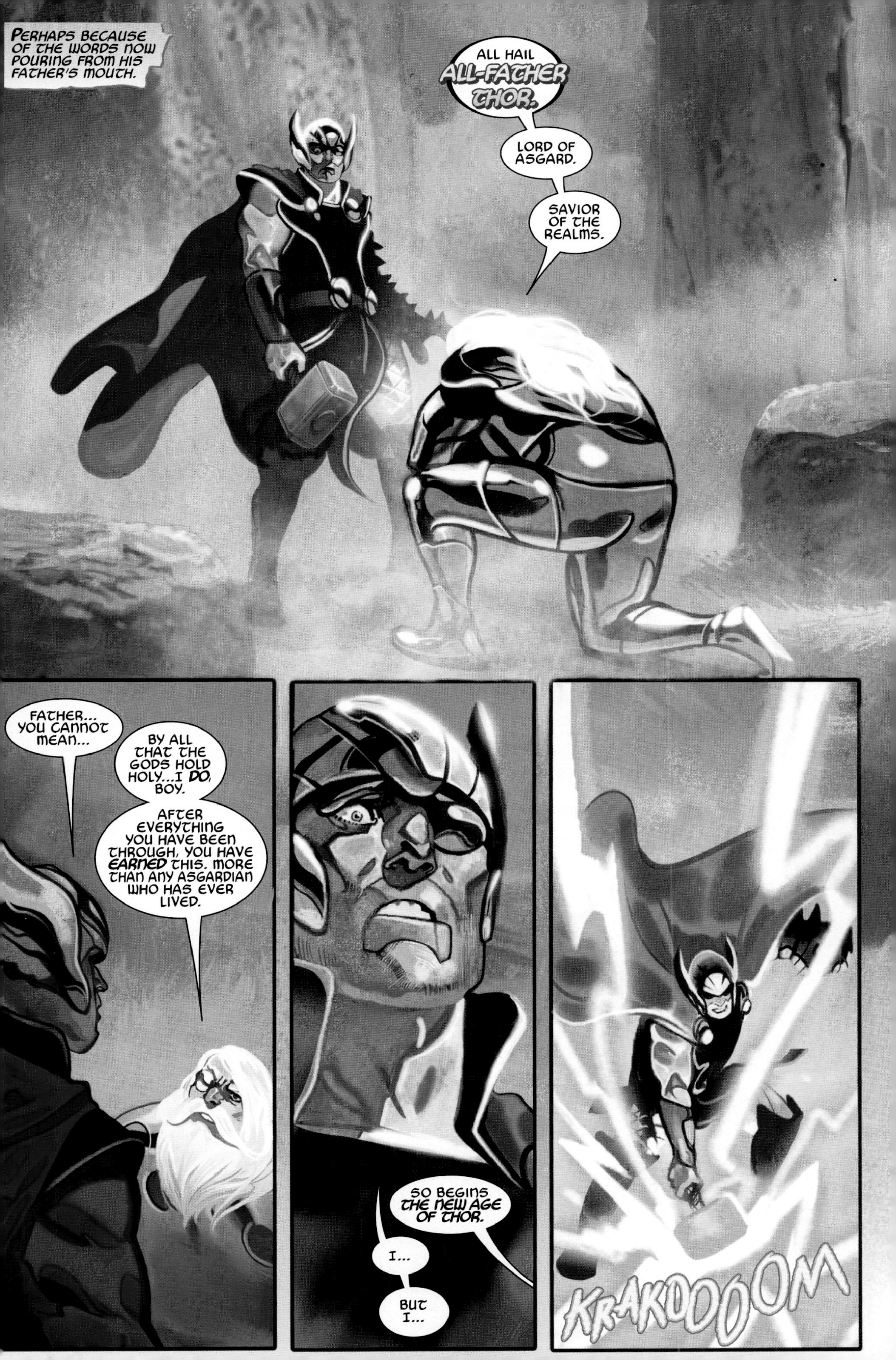
PERHAPS BECAUSE OF THE WORDS NOW POURING FROM HIS FATHER'S MOUTH.
ALL HAIL ALL-FATHER THOR.
LORD OF ASGARD.
SAVIOR OF THE REALMS.
FATHER... YOU CANNOT MEAN...
BY ALL THAT THE GODS HOLD HOLY...I DO, BOY.
AFTER EVERYTHING YOU HAVE BEEN THROUGH, YOU HAVE EARNED THIS. MORE THAN ANY ASGARDIAN WHO HAS EVER LIVED.
SO BEGINS THE NEW AGE OF THOR.
I...
BUT I...
KRAKOOOOOM

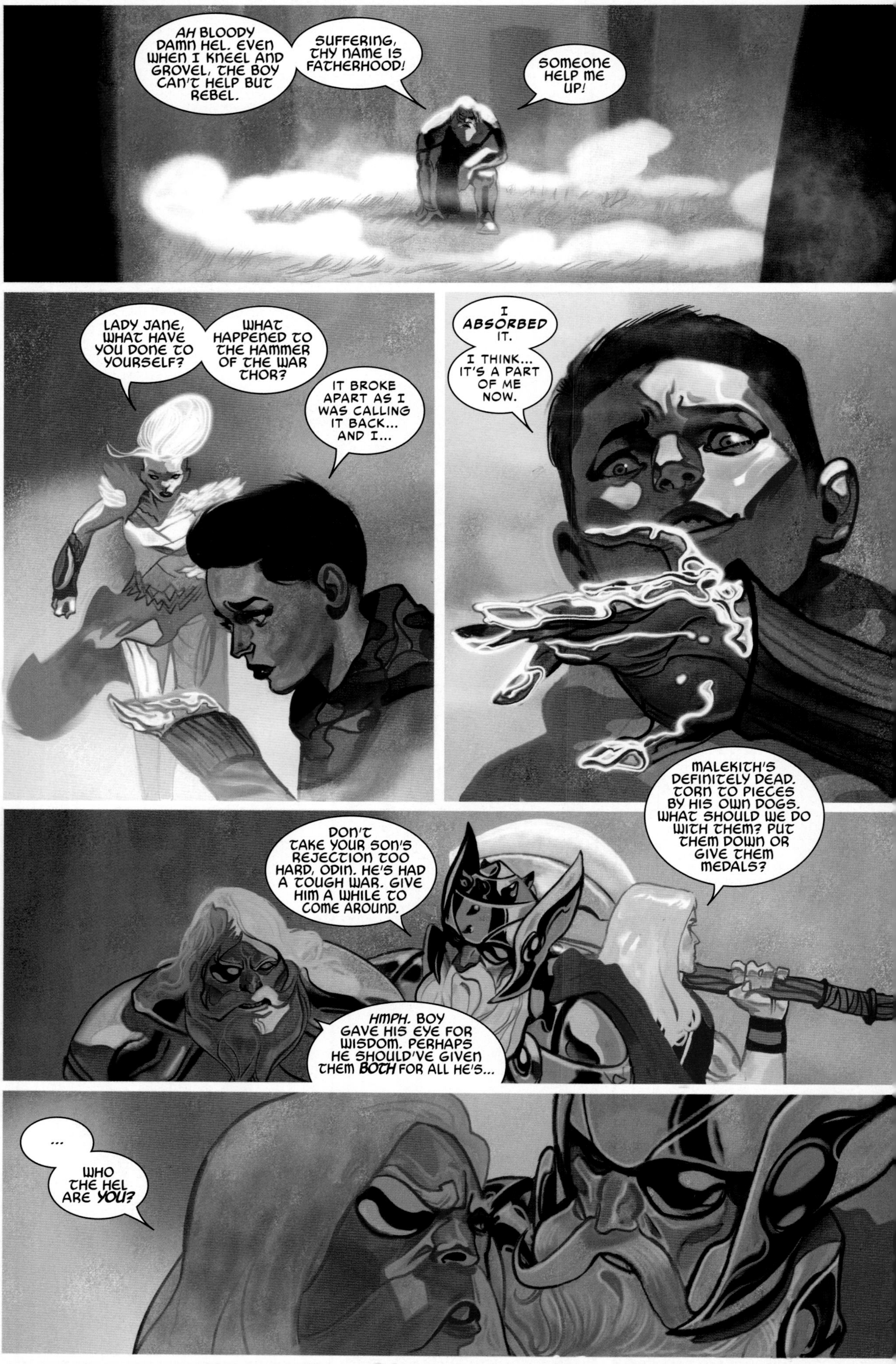
AH BLOODY DAMN HEL. EVEN WHEN I KNEEL AND GROVEL, THE BOY CAN'T HELP BUT REBEL.
SUFFERING, THY NAME IS FATHERHOOD!
SOMEONE HELP ME UP!
LADY JANE, WHAT HAVE YOU DONE TO YOURSELF?
WHAT HAPPENED TO THE HAMMER OF THE WAR THOR?
IT BROKE APART AS I WAS CALLING IT BACK... AND I...
I ABSORBED IT.
I THINK... IT'S A PART OF ME NOW.
DON'T TAKE YOUR SON'S REJECTION TOO HARD, ODIN. HE'S HAD A TOUGH WAR. GIVE HIM A WHILE TO COME AROUND.
MALEKITH'S DEFINITELY DEAD. TORN TO PIECES BY HIS OWN DOGS. WHAT SHOULD WE DO WITH THEM? PUT THEM DOWN OR GIVE THEM MEDALS?
HMPH. BOY GAVE HIS EYE FOR WISDOM. PERHAPS HE SHOULD'VE GIVEN THEM BOTH FOR ALL HE'S...
...
WHO THE HEL ARE YOU?

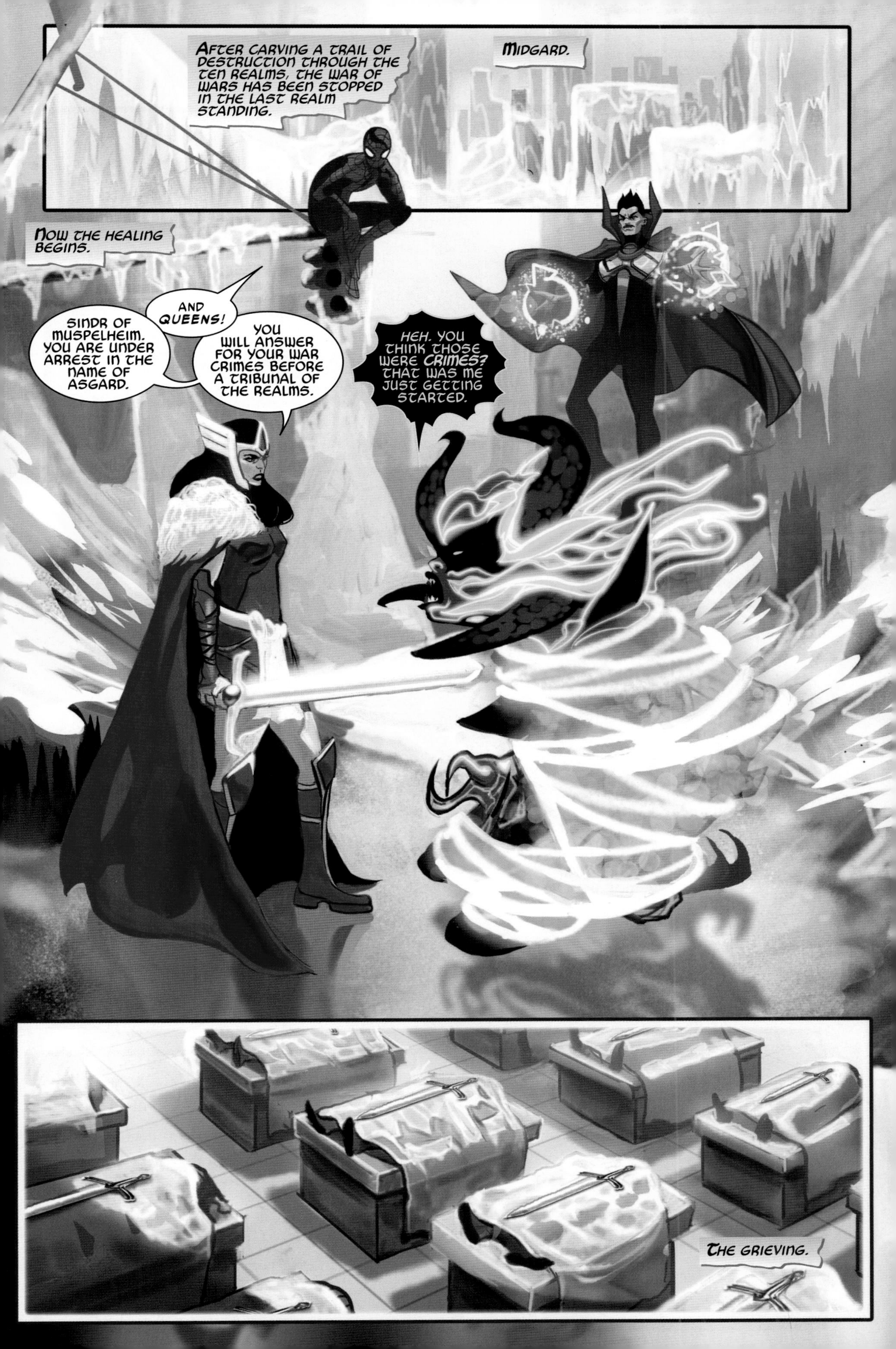
AFTER CARVING A TRAIL OF DESTRUCTION THROUGH THE TEN REALMS, THE WAR OF WARS HAS BEEN STOPPED IN THE LAST REALM STANDING.
MIDGARD.
NOW THE HEALING BEGINS.
SINDR OF MUSPELHEIM. YOU ARE UNDER ARREST IN THE NAME OF ASGARD.
AND QUEENS!
YOU WILL ANSWER FOR YOUR WAR CRIMES BEFORE A TRIBUNAL OF THE REALMS.
HEH. YOU THINK THOSE WERE CRIMES? THAT WAS ME JUST GETTING STARTED.
THE GRIEVING.

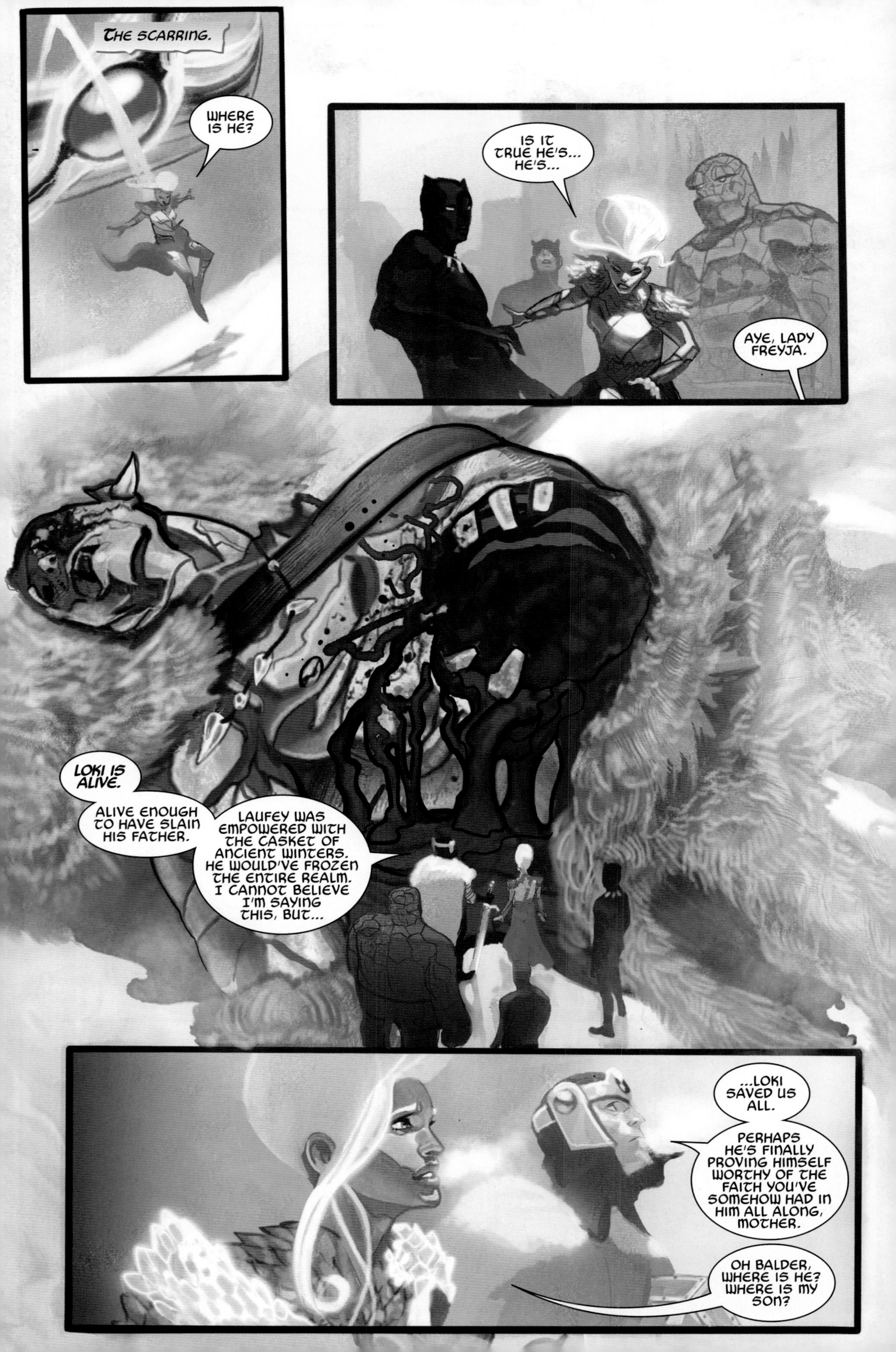
THE SCARRING.
WHERE IS HE?
IS IT TRUE HE'S... HE'S...
AYE, LADY FREYJA.
LOKI IS ALIVE.
ALIVE ENOUGH TO HAVE SLAIN HIS FATHER.
LAUFEY WAS EMPOWERED WITH THE CASKET OF ANCIENT WINTERS. HE WOULD'VE FROZEN THE ENTIRE REALM. I CANNOT BELIEVE I'M SAYING THIS, BUT...
...LOKI SAVED US ALL.
PERHAPS HE'S FINALLY PROVING HIMSELF WORTHY OF THE FAITH YOU'VE SOMEHOW HAD IN HIM ALL ALONG, MOTHER.
OH BALDER, WHERE IS HE? WHERE IS MY SON?

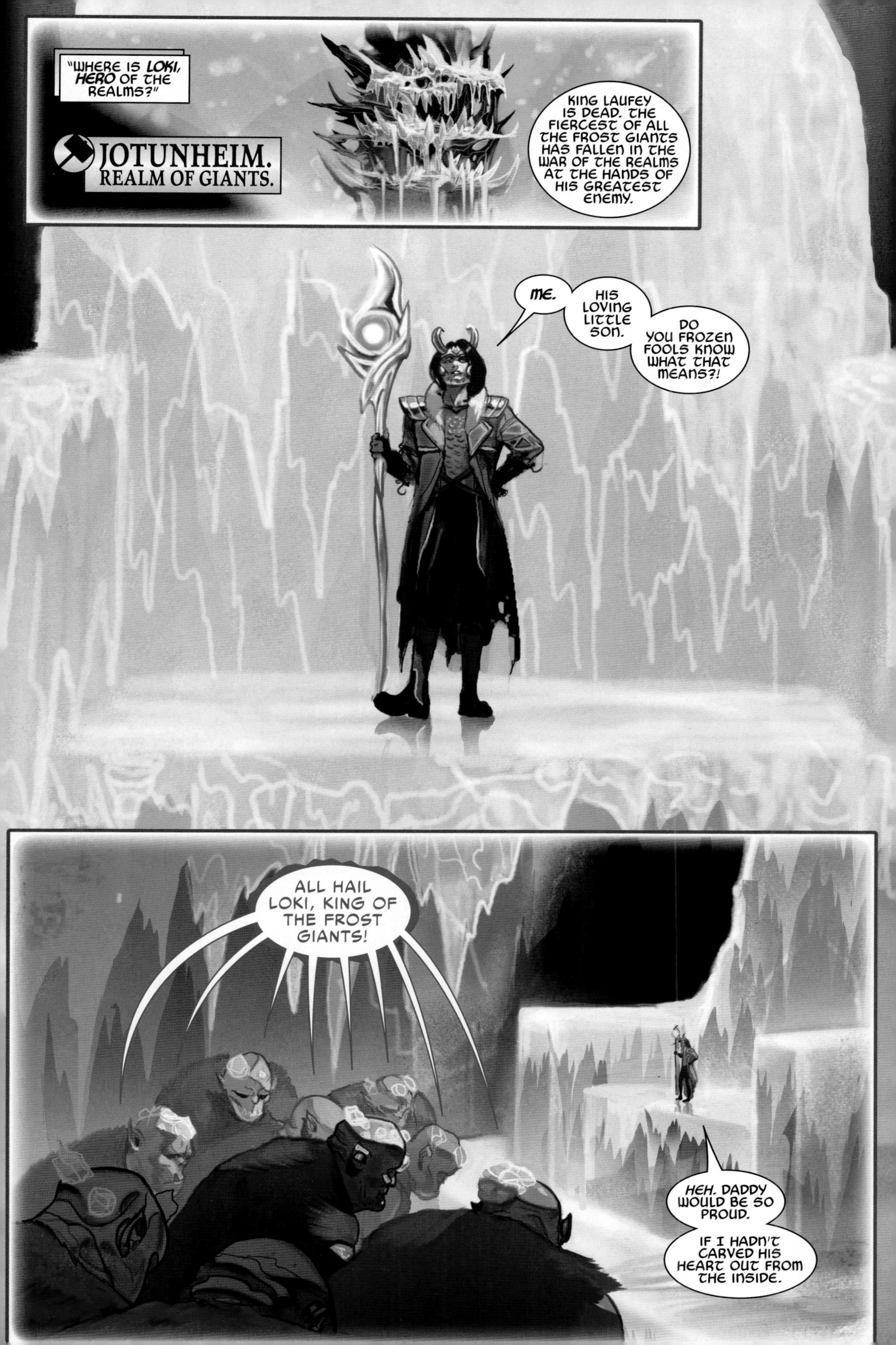
"WHERE IS LOKI, HERO OF THE REALMS?"
JOTUNHEIM. REALM OF GIANTS.
KING LAUFEY IS DEAD. THE FIERCEST OF ALL THE FROST GIANTS HAS FALLEN IN THE WAR OF THE REALMS AT THE HANDS OF HIS GREATEST ENEMY.
ME.
HIS LOVING LITTLE SON.
DO YOU FROZEN FOOLS KNOW WHAT THAT MEANS?!
ALL HAIL LOKI, KING OF THE FROST GIANTS!
HEH. DADDY WOULD BE SO PROUD.
IF I HADN'T CARVED HIS HEART OUT FROM THE INSIDE.

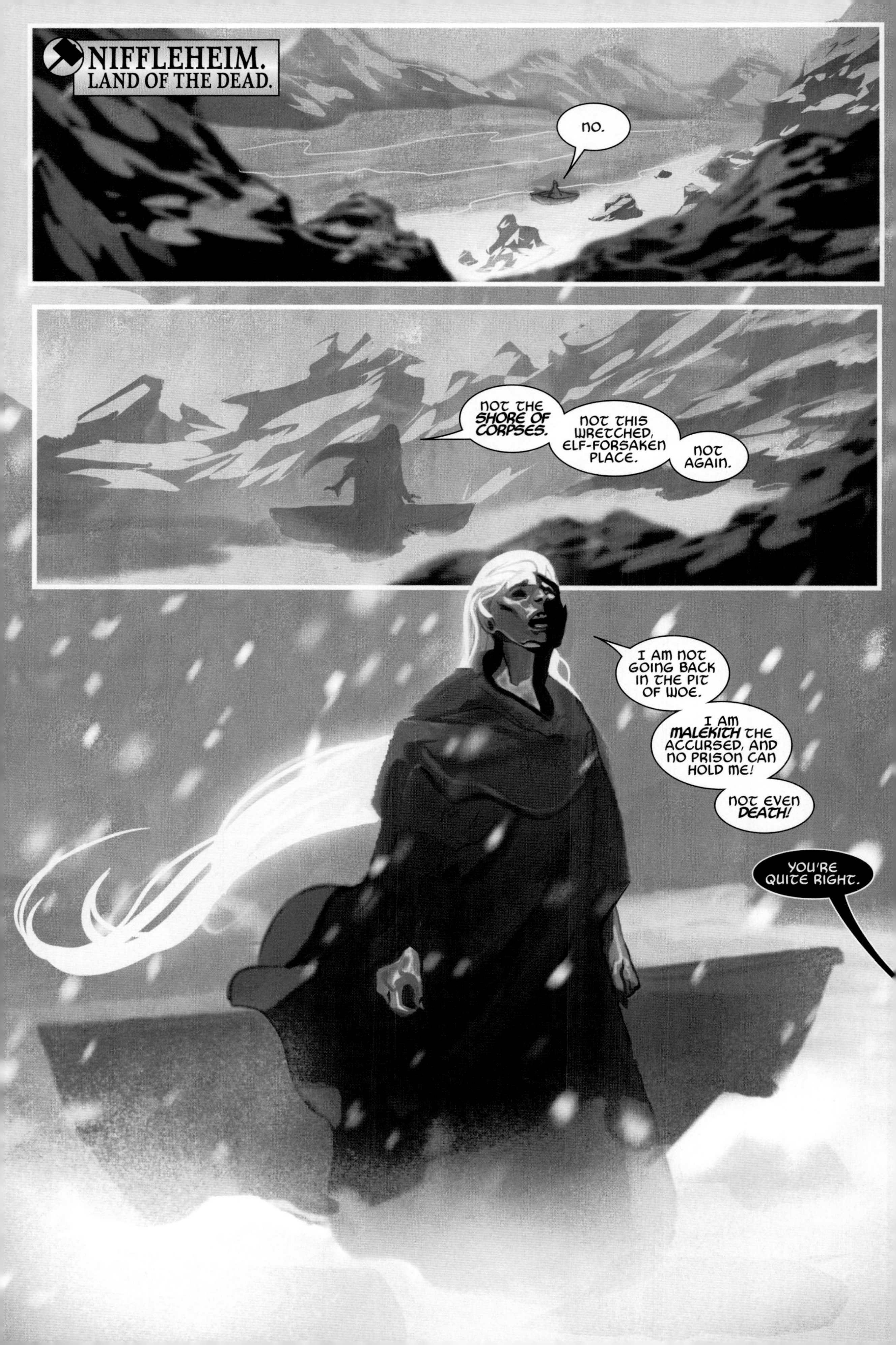
NIFFLEHEIM.
LAND OF THE DEAD.
NO.
NOT THE SHORE OF CORPSES.
NOT THIS WRETCHED, ELF-FORSAKEN PLACE.
NOT AGAIN.
I AM NOT GOING BACK IN THE PIT OF WOE.
I AM MALEKITH THE ACCURSED, AND NO PRISON CAN HOLD ME!
NOT EVEN DEATH!
YOU'RE QUITE RIGHT.

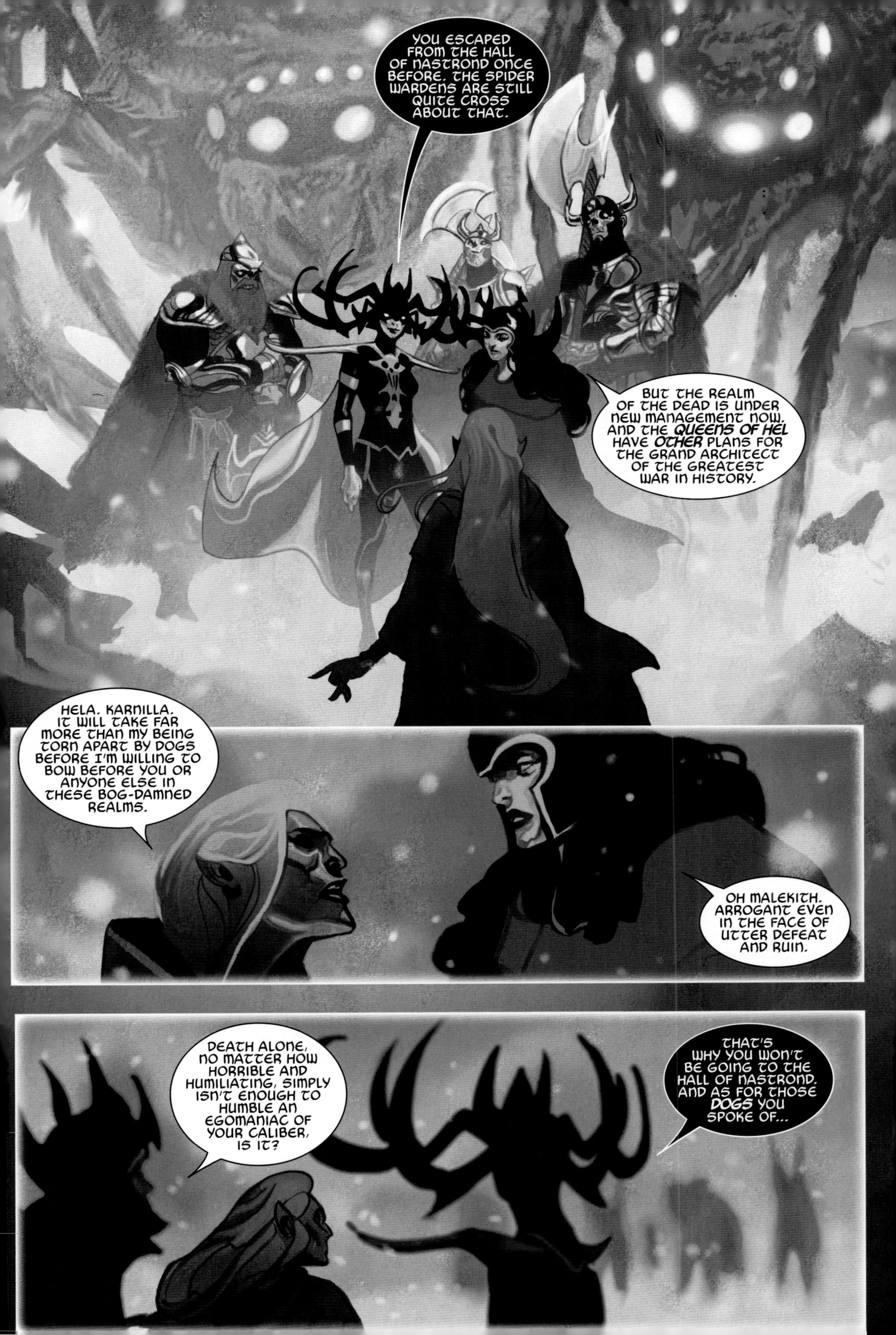
YOU ESCAPED FROM THE HALL OF NASTROND ONCE BEFORE. THE SPIDER WARDENS ARE STILL QUITE CROSS ABOUT THAT.
BUT THE REALM OF THE DEAD IS UNDER NEW MANAGEMENT NOW. AND THE QUEENS OF HEL HAVE OTHER PLANS FOR THE GRAND ARCHITECT OF THE GREATEST WAR IN HISTORY.
HELA. KARNILLA. IT WILL TAKE FAR MORE THAN MY BEING TORN APART BY DOGS BEFORE I'M WILLING TO BOW BEFORE YOU OR ANYONE ELSE IN THESE BOG-DAMNED REALMS.
OH MALEKITH. ARROGANT EVEN IN THE FACE OF UTTER DEFEAT AND RUIN.
DEATH ALONE, NO MATTER HOW HORRIBLE AND HUMILIATING, SIMPLY ISN'T ENOUGH TO HUMBLE AN EGOMANIAC OF YOUR CALIBER, IS IT?
THAT'S WHY YOU WON'T BE GOING TO THE HALL OF NASTROND. AND AS FOR THOSE DOGS YOU SPOKE OF...

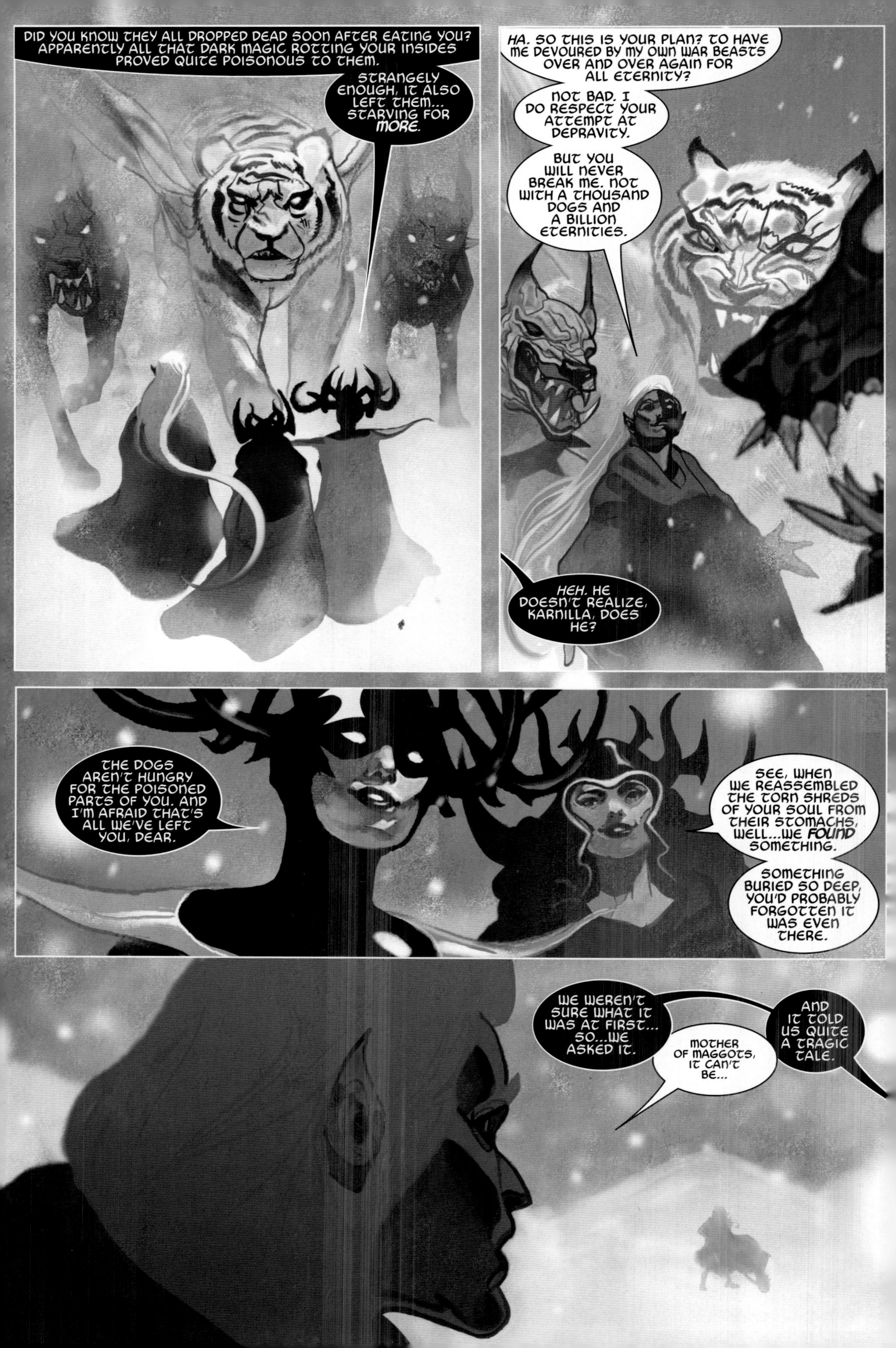
DID YOU KNOW THEY ALL DROPPED DEAD SOON AFTER EATING YOU? APPARENTLY ALL THAT DARK MAGIC ROTTING YOUR INSIDES PROVED QUITE POISONOUS TO THEM.
STRANGELY ENOUGH, IT ALSO LEFT THEM... STARVING FOR *MORE.*
HA. SO THIS IS YOUR PLAN? TO HAVE ME DEVOURED BY MY OWN WAR BEASTS OVER AND OVER AGAIN FOR ALL ETERNITY?
NOT BAD. I DO RESPECT YOUR ATTEMPT AT DEPRAVITY.
BUT YOU WILL NEVER BREAK ME. NOT WITH A THOUSAND DOGS AND A BILLION ETERNITIES.
HEH. HE DOESN'T REALIZE, KARNILLA, DOES HE?
THE DOGS AREN'T HUNGRY FOR THE POISONED PARTS OF YOU. AND I'M AFRAID THAT'S ALL WE'VE LEFT YOU, DEAR.
SEE, WHEN WE REASSEMBLED THE TORN SHREDS OF YOUR SOUL FROM THEIR STOMACHS, WELL...WE *FOUND* SOMETHING.
SOMETHING BURIED SO DEEP, YOU'D PROBABLY FORGOTTEN IT WAS EVEN THERE.
WE WEREN'T SURE WHAT IT WAS AT FIRST... SO...WE ASKED IT.
AND IT TOLD US QUITE A TRAGIC TALE.
MOTHER OF MAGGOTS, IT CAN'T BE...

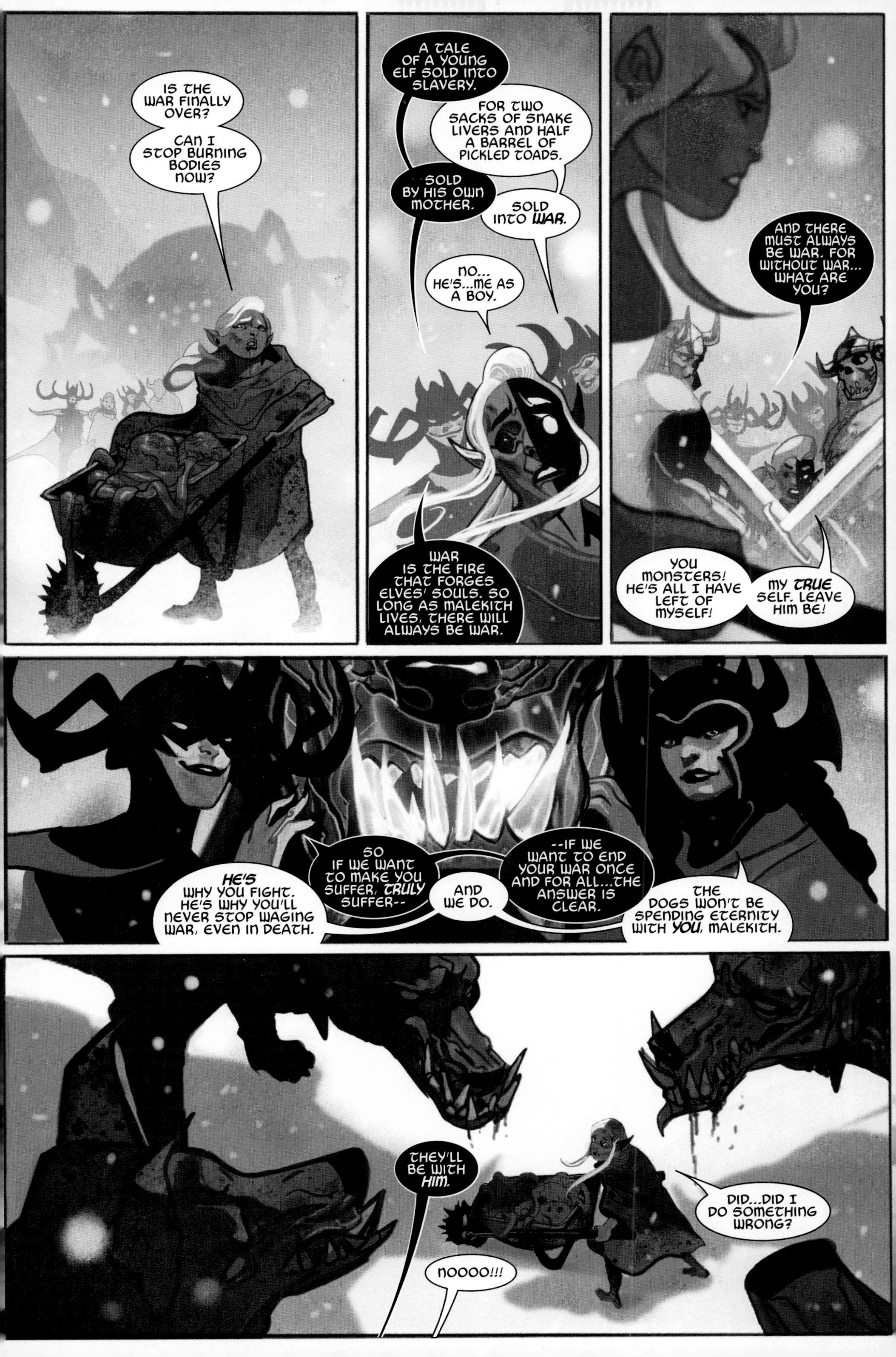
IS THE WAR FINALLY OVER?
CAN I STOP BURNING BODIES NOW?
A TALE OF A YOUNG ELF SOLD INTO SLAVERY.
FOR TWO SACKS OF SNAKE LIVERS AND HALF A BARREL OF PICKLED TOADS.
SOLD BY HIS OWN MOTHER.
SOLD INTO WAR.
NO... HE'S...ME AS A BOY.
WAR IS THE FIRE THAT FORGES ELVES' SOULS. SO LONG AS MALEKITH LIVES, THERE WILL ALWAYS BE WAR.
AND THERE MUST ALWAYS BE WAR. FOR WITHOUT WAR... WHAT ARE YOU?
YOU MONSTERS! HE'S ALL I HAVE LEFT OF MYSELF!
MY TRUE SELF. LEAVE HIM BE!
HE'S WHY YOU FIGHT. HE'S WHY YOU'LL NEVER STOP WAGING WAR, EVEN IN DEATH.
SO IF WE WANT TO MAKE YOU SUFFER, TRULY SUFFER--
AND WE DO.
--IF WE WANT TO END YOUR WAR ONCE AND FOR ALL...THE ANSWER IS CLEAR.
THE DOGS WON'T BE SPENDING ETERNITY WITH YOU, MALEKITH.
THEY'LL BE WITH HIM.
DID...DID I DO SOMETHING WRONG?
NOOOO!!!

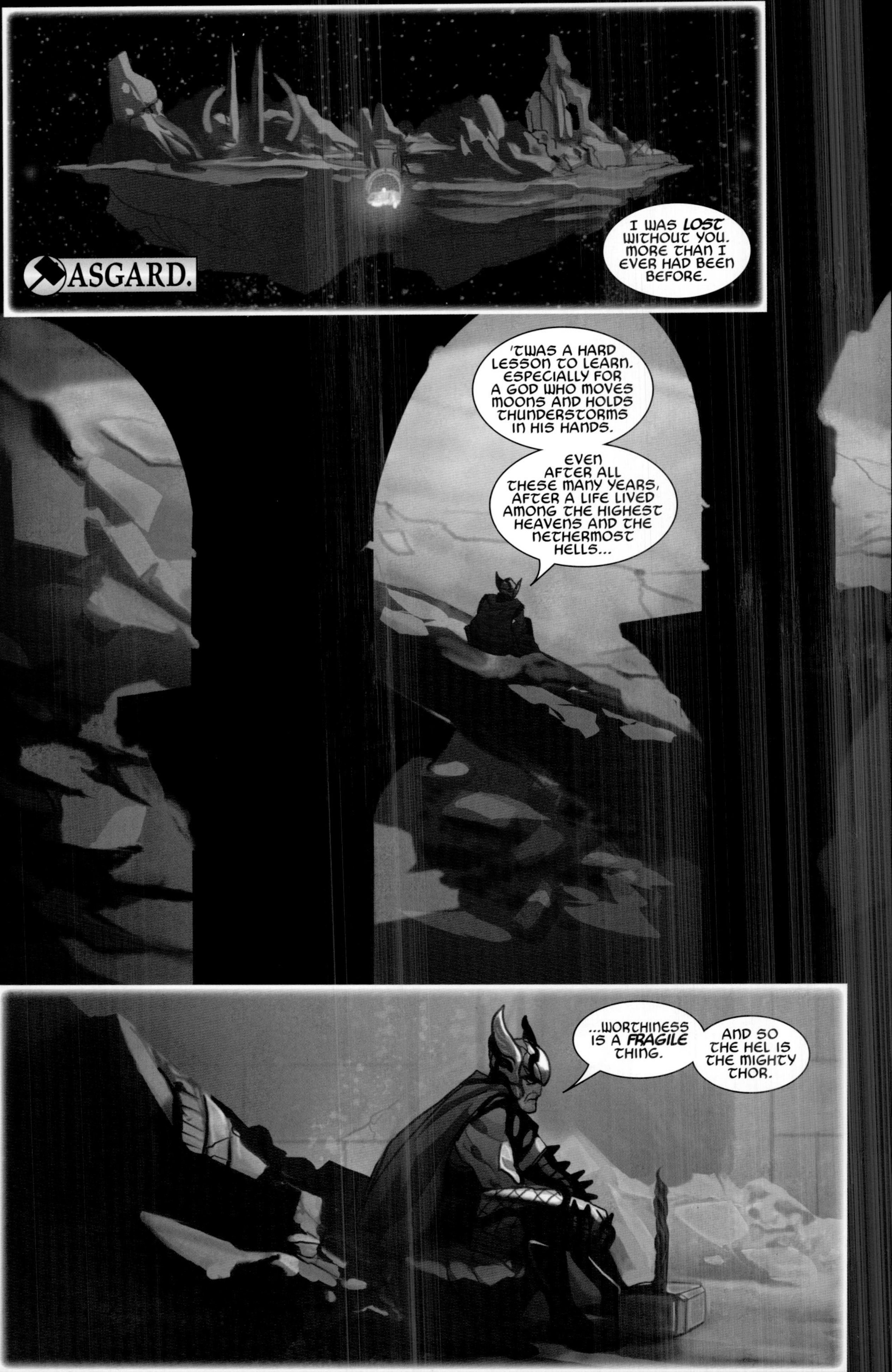
ASGARD.
I WAS LOST WITHOUT YOU. MORE THAN I EVER HAD BEEN BEFORE.
'TWAS A HARD LESSON TO LEARN. ESPECIALLY FOR A GOD WHO MOVES MOONS AND HOLDS THUNDERSTORMS IN HIS HANDS.
EVEN AFTER ALL THESE MANY YEARS, AFTER A LIFE LIVED AMONG THE HIGHEST HEAVENS AND THE NETHERMOST HELLS...
...WORTHINESS IS A FRAGILE THING.
AND SO THE HEL IS THE MIGHTY THOR.

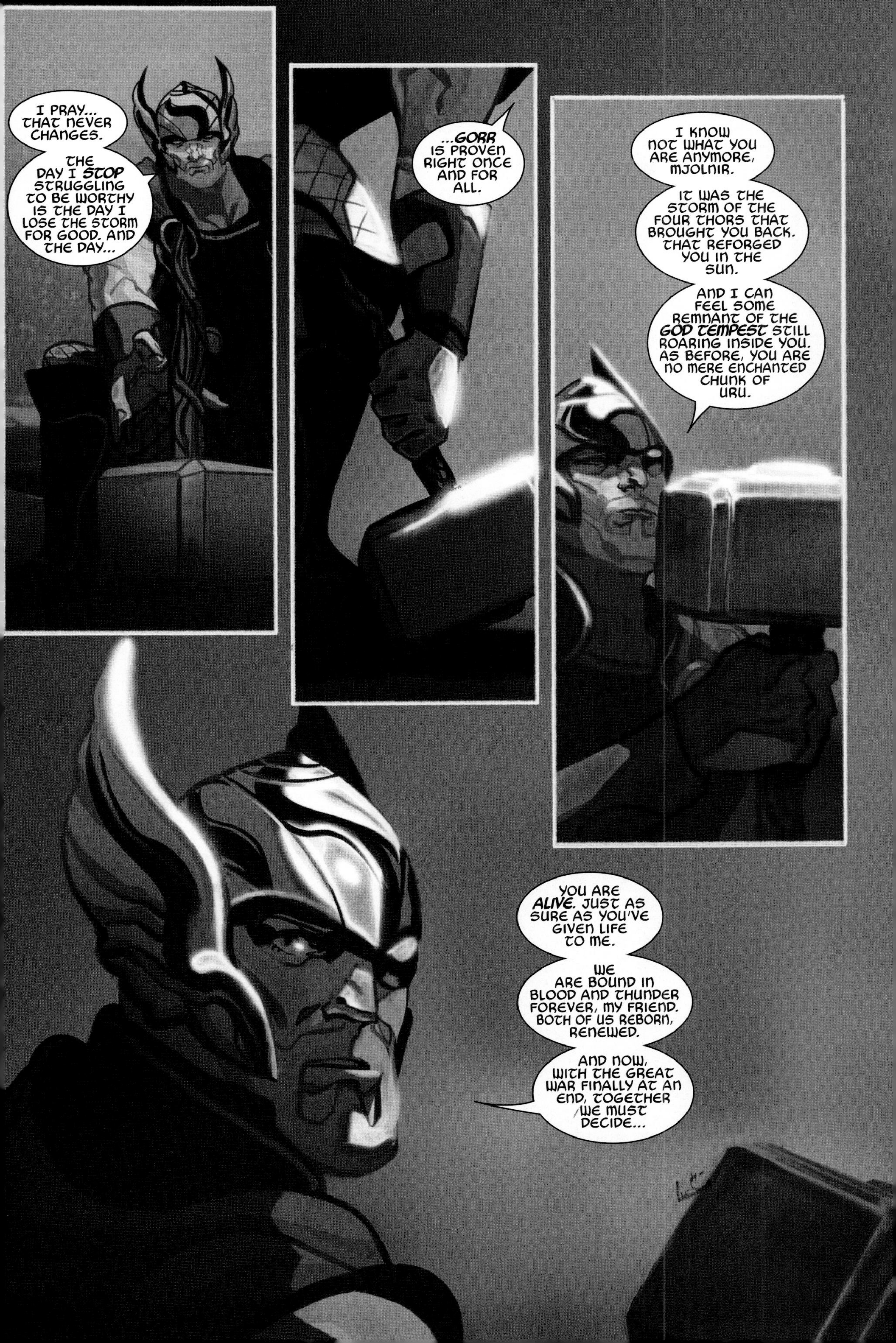
I PRAY... THAT NEVER CHANGES.
THE DAY I STOP STRUGGLING TO BE WORTHY IS THE DAY I LOSE THE STORM FOR GOOD. AND THE DAY...
...GORR IS PROVEN RIGHT ONCE AND FOR ALL.
I KNOW NOT WHAT YOU ARE ANYMORE, MJOLNIR.
IT WAS THE STORM OF THE FOUR THORS THAT BROUGHT YOU BACK. THAT REFORGED YOU IN THE SUN.
AND I CAN FEEL SOME REMNANT OF THE GOD TEMPEST STILL ROARING INSIDE YOU. AS BEFORE, YOU ARE NO MERE ENCHANTED CHUNK OF URU.
YOU ARE ALIVE. JUST AS SURE AS YOU'VE GIVEN LIFE TO ME.
WE ARE BOUND IN BLOOD AND THUNDER FOREVER, MY FRIEND. BOTH OF US REBORN, RENEWED.
AND NOW, WITH THE GREAT WAR FINALLY AT AN END, TOGETHER WE MUST DECIDE...

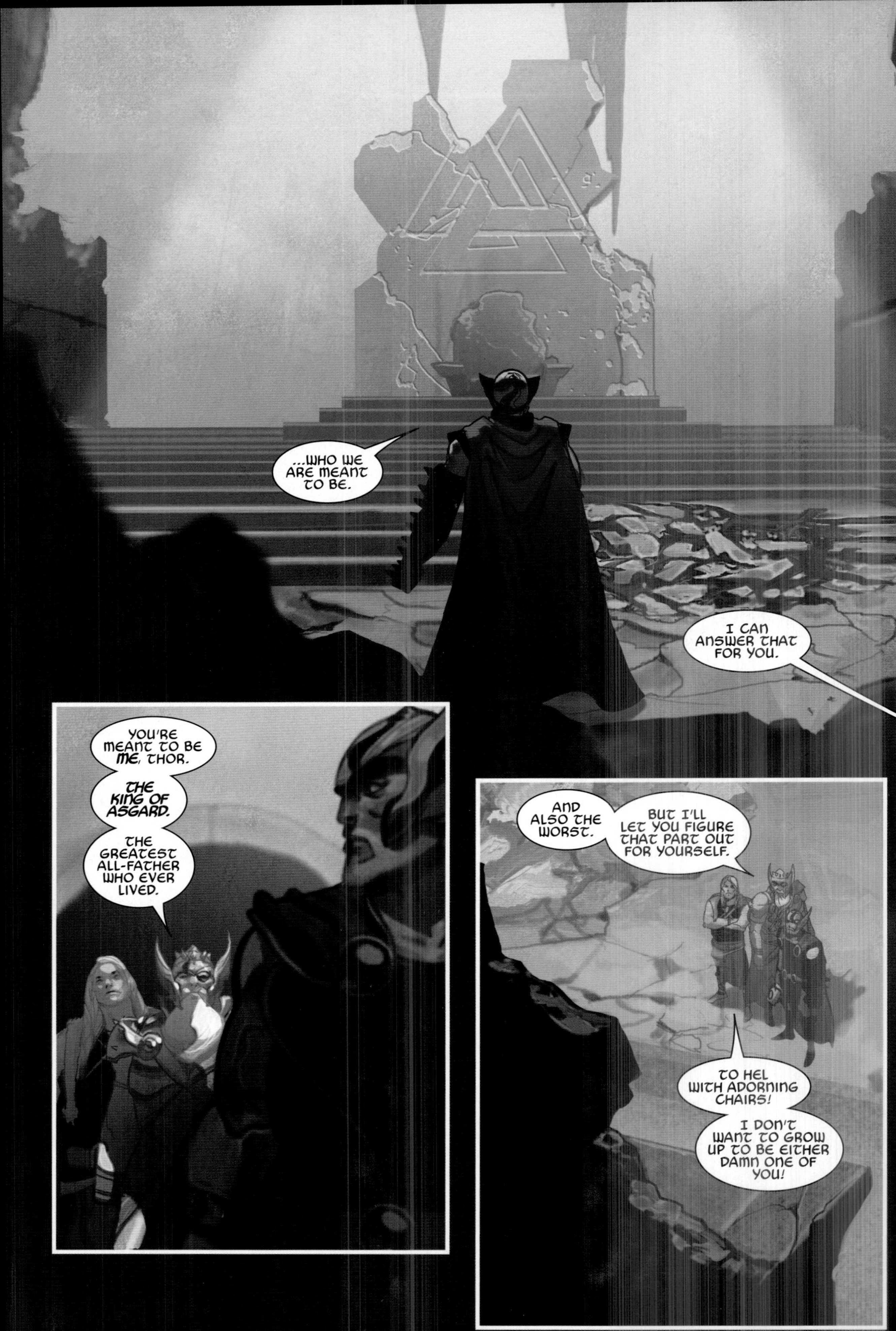
...WHO WE ARE MEANT TO BE.
I CAN ANSWER THAT FOR YOU.
YOU'RE MEANT TO BE ME, THOR.
THE KING OF ASGARD.
THE GREATEST ALL-FATHER WHO EVER LIVED.
AND ALSO THE WORST.
BUT I'LL LET YOU FIGURE THAT PART OUT FOR YOURSELF.
TO HEL WITH ADORNING CHAIRS!
I DON'T WANT TO GROW UP TO BE EITHER DAMN ONE OF YOU!

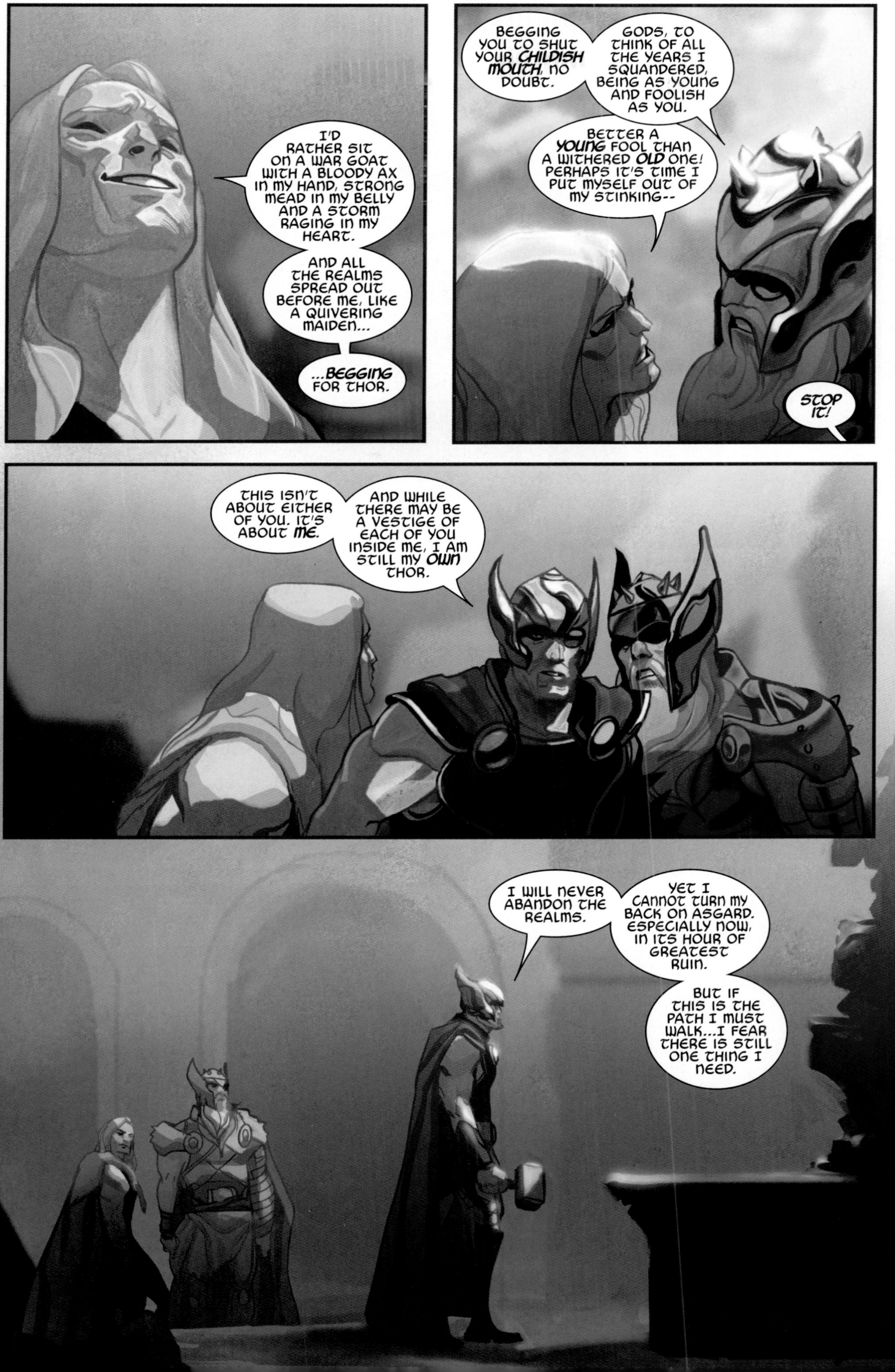
I'D RATHER SIT ON A WAR GOAT WITH A BLOODY AX IN MY HAND, STRONG MEAD IN MY BELLY AND A STORM RAGING IN MY HEART.
AND ALL THE REALMS SPREAD OUT BEFORE ME, LIKE A QUIVERING MAIDEN...
...BEGGING FOR THOR.
BEGGING YOU TO SHUT YOUR CHILDISH MOUTH, NO DOUBT.
GODS, TO THINK OF ALL THE YEARS I SQUANDERED, BEING AS YOUNG AND FOOLISH AS YOU.
BETTER A YOUNG FOOL THAN A WITHERED OLD ONE! PERHAPS IT'S TIME I PUT MYSELF OUT OF MY STINKING--
STOP IT!
THIS ISN'T ABOUT EITHER OF YOU. IT'S ABOUT ME.
AND WHILE THERE MAY BE A VESTIGE OF EACH OF YOU INSIDE ME, I AM STILL MY OWN THOR.
I WILL NEVER ABANDON THE REALMS.
YET I CANNOT TURN MY BACK ON ASGARD. ESPECIALLY NOW, IN ITS HOUR OF GREATEST RUIN.
BUT IF THIS IS THE PATH I MUST WALK...I FEAR THERE IS STILL ONE THING I NEED.

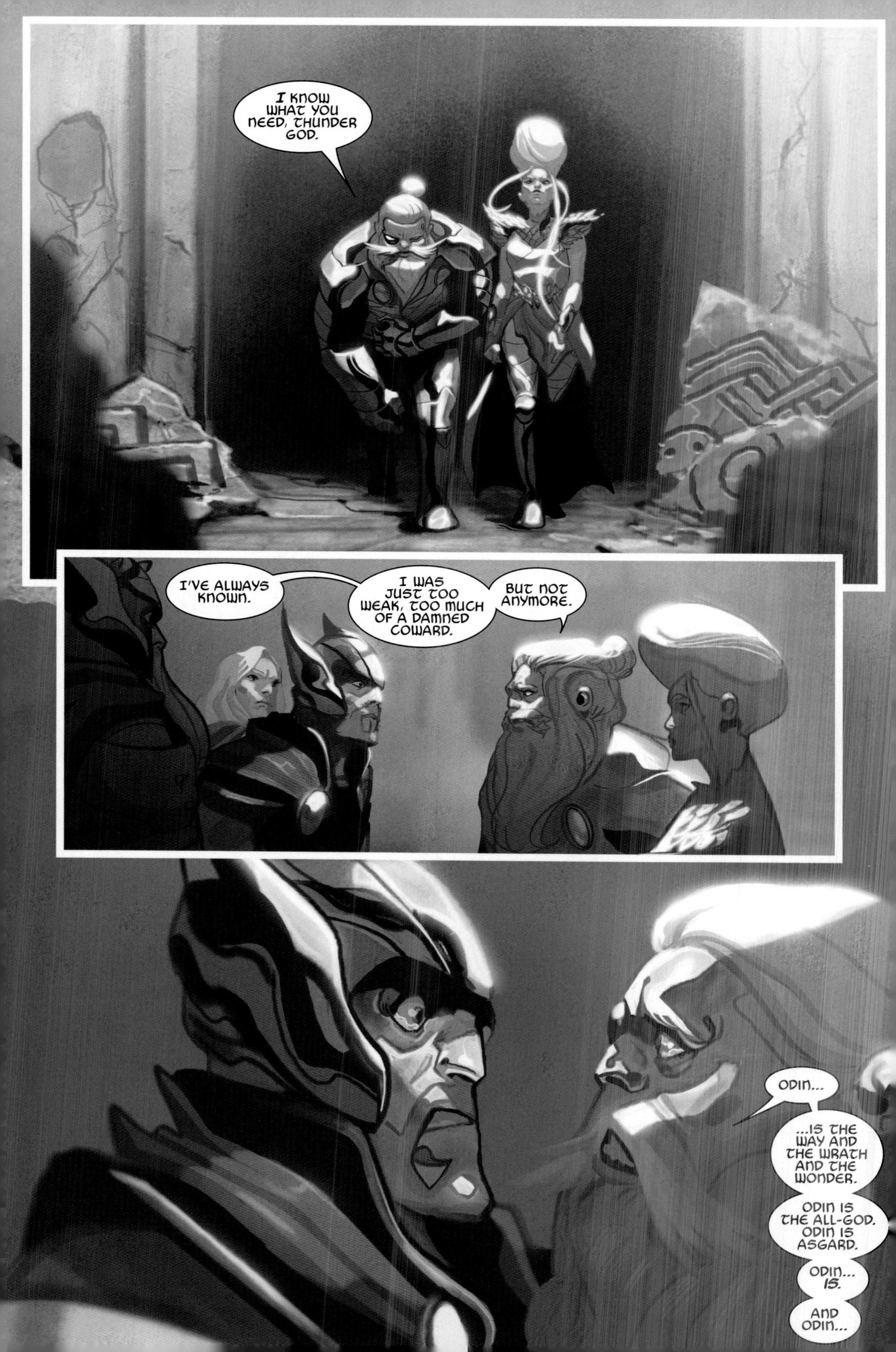
I KNOW WHAT YOU NEED, THUNDER GOD.
I'VE ALWAYS KNOWN.
I WAS JUST TOO WEAK, TOO MUCH OF A DAMNED COWARD.
BUT NOT ANYMORE.
ODIN...
...IS THE WAY AND THE WRATH AND THE WONDER.
ODIN IS THE ALL-GOD. ODIN IS ASGARD.
ODIN... IS.
AND ODIN...

ODIN IS PROUD OF YOU, THOR.
IN THE NAME OF ALL THE GODS...
...I AM PROUD OF MY SON.
THE HORRORS OF WAR SOMETIMES BRING MORE THAN RUIN.
WAR CAN GIVE BIRTH TO MIRACLES AS WELL.

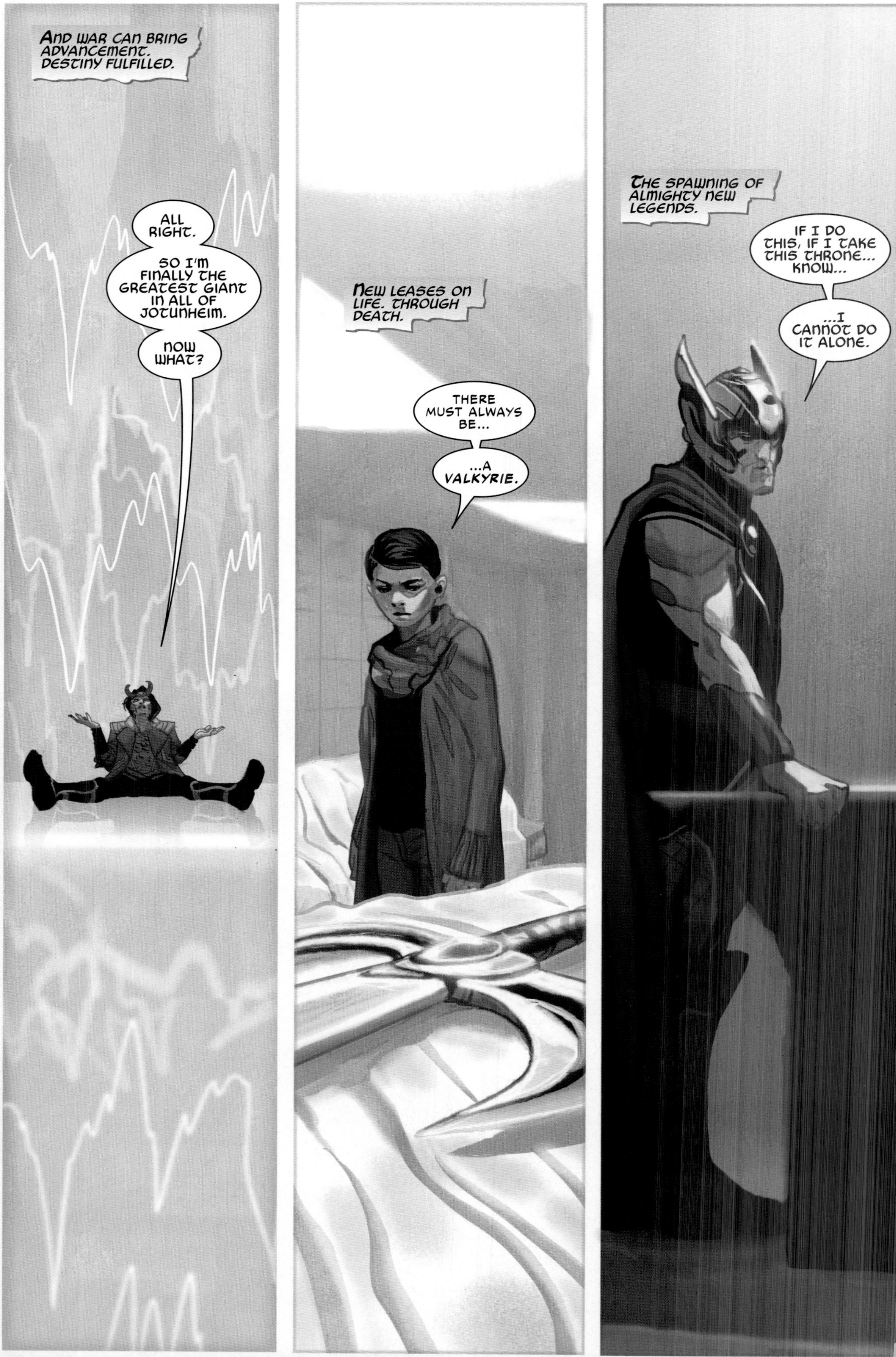
AND WAR CAN BRING ADVANCEMENT. DESTINY FULFILLED.
ALL RIGHT.
SO I'M FINALLY THE GREATEST GIANT IN ALL OF JOTUNHEIM.
NOW WHAT?
NEW LEASES ON LIFE. THROUGH DEATH.
THERE MUST ALWAYS BE...
...A VALKYRIE.
THE SPAWNING OF ALMIGHTY NEW LEGENDS.
IF I DO THIS, IF I TAKE THIS THRONE... KNOW...
...I CANNOT DO IT ALONE.

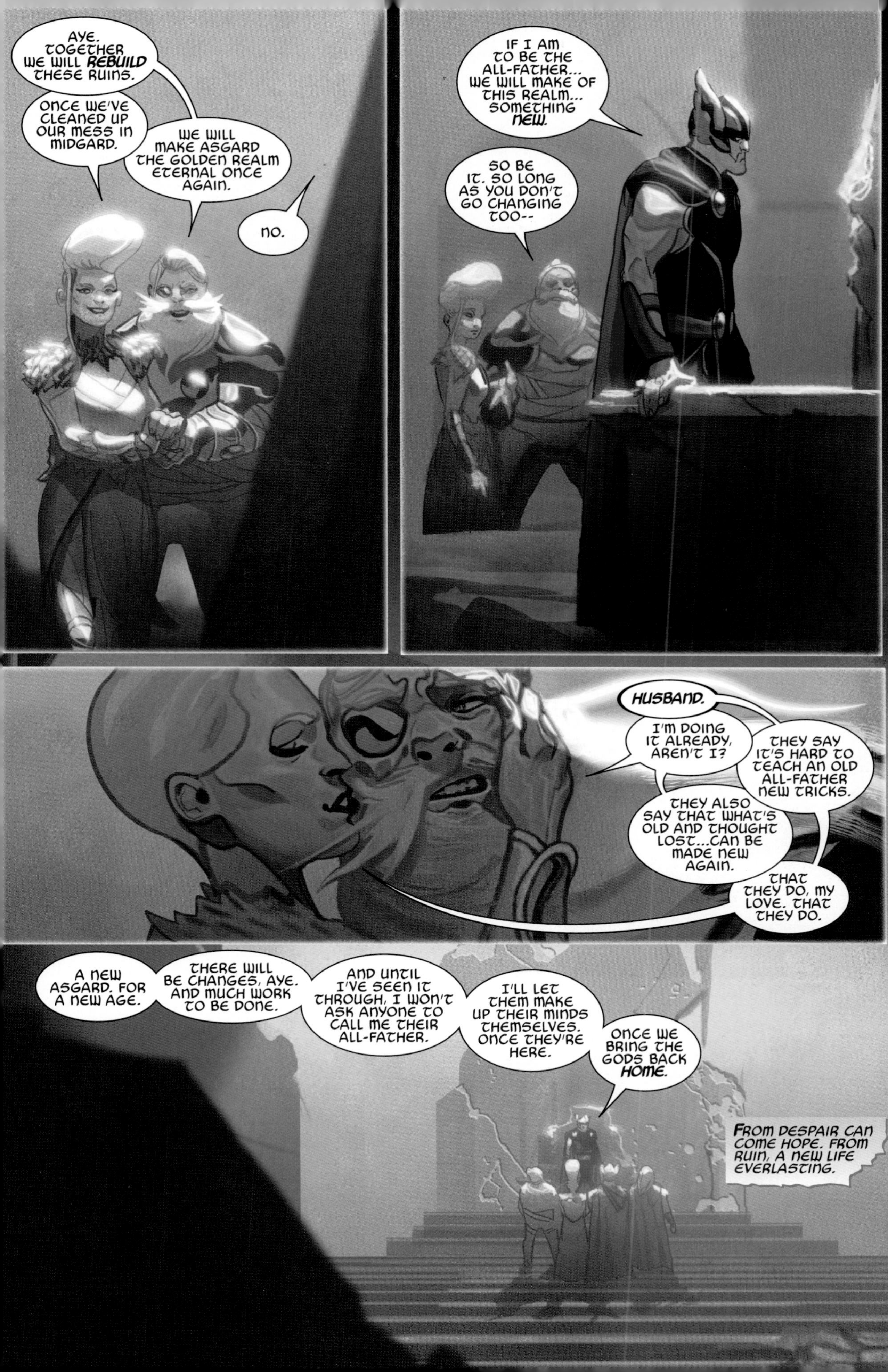
AYE. TOGETHER WE WILL REBUILD THESE RUINS.
ONCE WE'VE CLEANED UP OUR MESS IN MIDGARD.
WE WILL MAKE ASGARD THE GOLDEN REALM ETERNAL ONCE AGAIN.
NO.
IF I AM TO BE THE ALL-FATHER... WE WILL MAKE OF THIS REALM... SOMETHING NEW.
SO BE IT. SO LONG AS YOU DON'T GO CHANGING TOO--
HUSBAND.
I'M DOING IT ALREADY, AREN'T I?
THEY SAY IT'S HARD TO TEACH AN OLD ALL-FATHER NEW TRICKS.
THEY ALSO SAY THAT WHAT'S OLD AND THOUGHT LOST...CAN BE MADE NEW AGAIN.
THAT THEY DO, MY LOVE. THAT THEY DO.
A NEW ASGARD. FOR A NEW AGE.
THERE WILL BE CHANGES, AYE. AND MUCH WORK TO BE DONE.
AND UNTIL I'VE SEEN IT THROUGH, I WON'T ASK ANYONE TO CALL ME THEIR ALL-FATHER.
I'LL LET THEM MAKE UP THEIR MINDS THEMSELVES. ONCE THEY'RE HERE.
ONCE WE BRING THE GODS BACK HOME.
FROM DESPAIR CAN COME HOPE. FROM RUIN, A NEW LIFE EVERLASTING.

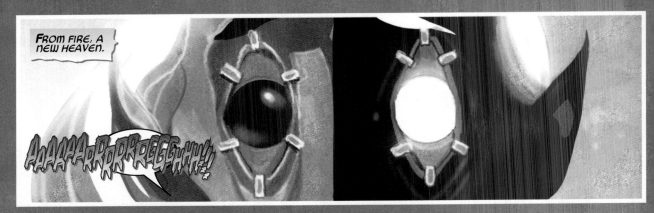

FROM FIRE, A NEW HEAVEN.

AAAARRRRRRRGGGHHH!!!

FROM HORROR, A BEAUTY TO BOGGLE THE MIND AND TAKE THE BREATH AWAY, EVEN AMONG THE BREATHLESS.

NOOOOOOO!!! MAKE IT STOP!!! PLEASE, I BEG YOU, I'LL DO ANYTHING!!!

JUST PLEASE DON'T MAKE ME WATCH!!!

FROM SUFFERING COMES JUSTICE.

HRRRAAAAGGH!!!

NICE TOUCH SEWING HIS EYES OPEN.

YES, I DO BELIEVE WE'VE FOUND THE PERFECT PUNISHMENT FOR THE ARCHITECT OF THE WAR OF THE REALMS.

FORCED TO LOOK UPON HIS GREATEST HORROR FOR ALL ETERNITY. I BELIEVE THIS CALLS FOR A TOAST.

FROM SIN, DIVINE RETRIBUTION.

HERE'S TO MALEKITH THE ACCURSED. LONG MAY HE SUFFER.

INDEED.

AND HERE'S TO MALEKITH THE ELF BOY, THE CORPSE BURNER, THE WAR SLAVE...

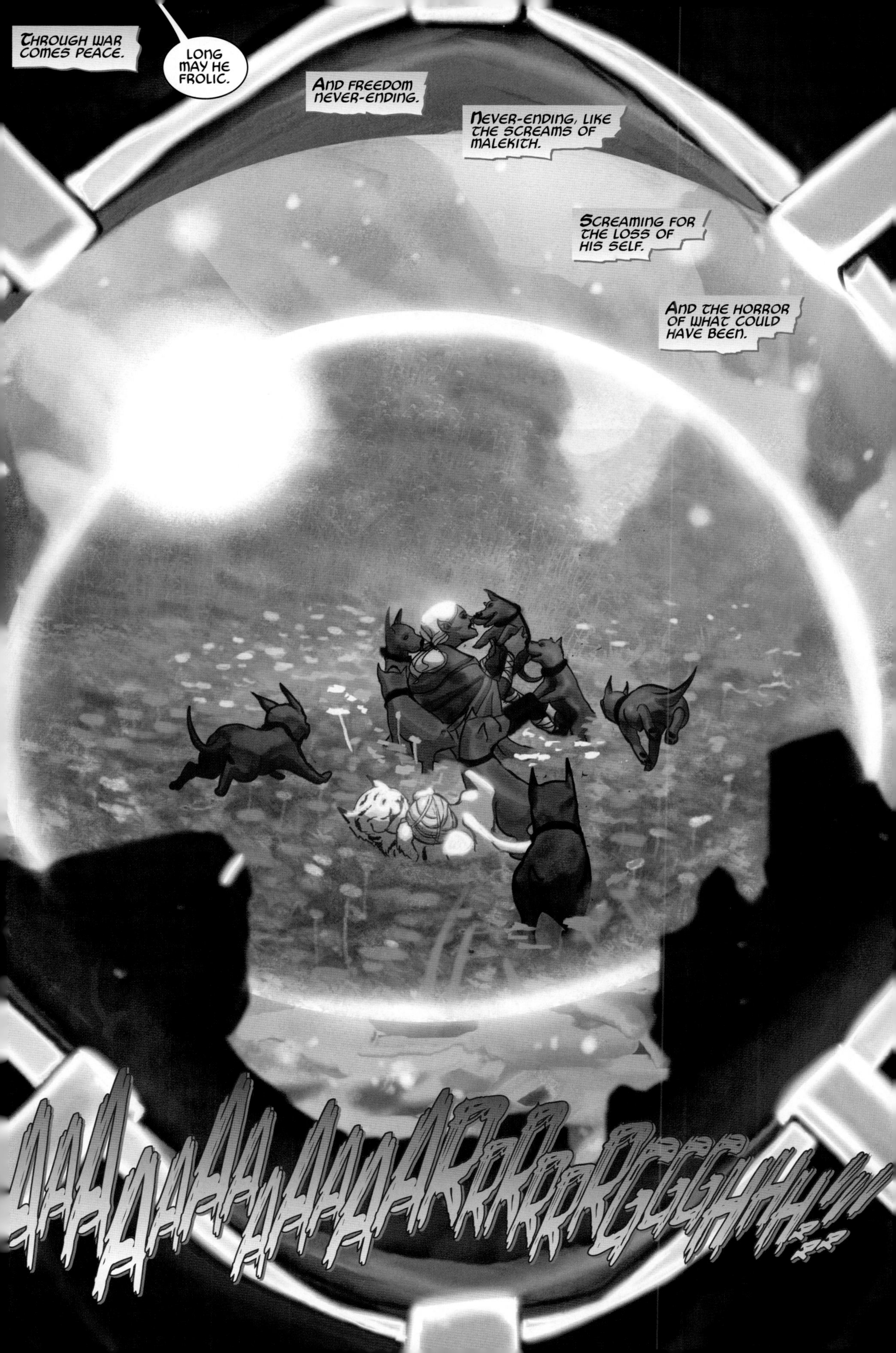
THROUGH WAR COMES PEACE.
LONG MAY HE FROLIC.
AND FREEDOM NEVER-ENDING.
NEVER-ENDING, LIKE THE SCREAMS OF MALEKITH.
SCREAMING FOR THE LOSS OF HIS SELF.
AND THE HORROR OF WHAT COULD HAVE BEEN.
AAAAAAAAAAAAARRRRRRGGGHHH!!!

16

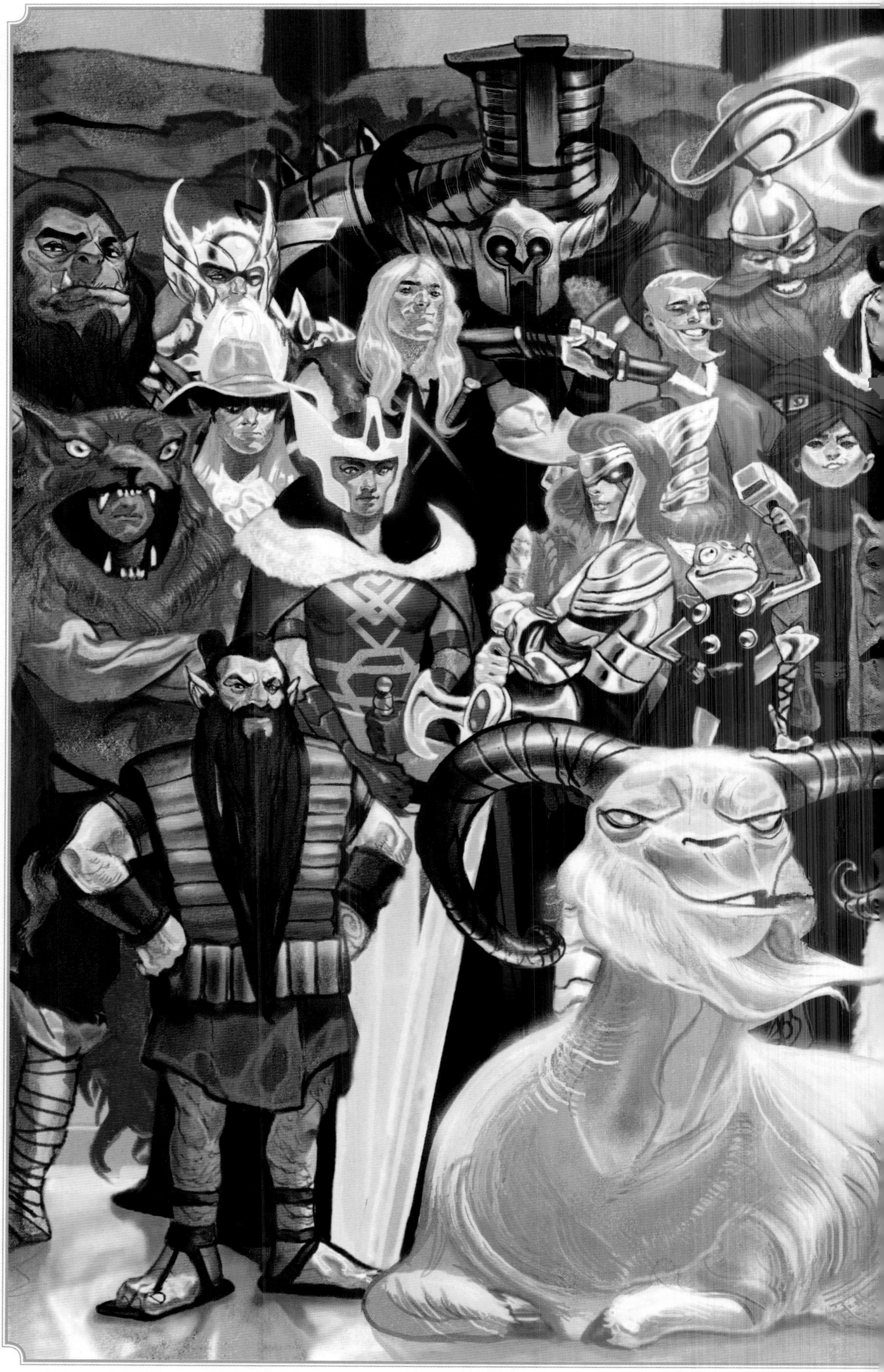

ONCE UPON A TIME IN ASGARD

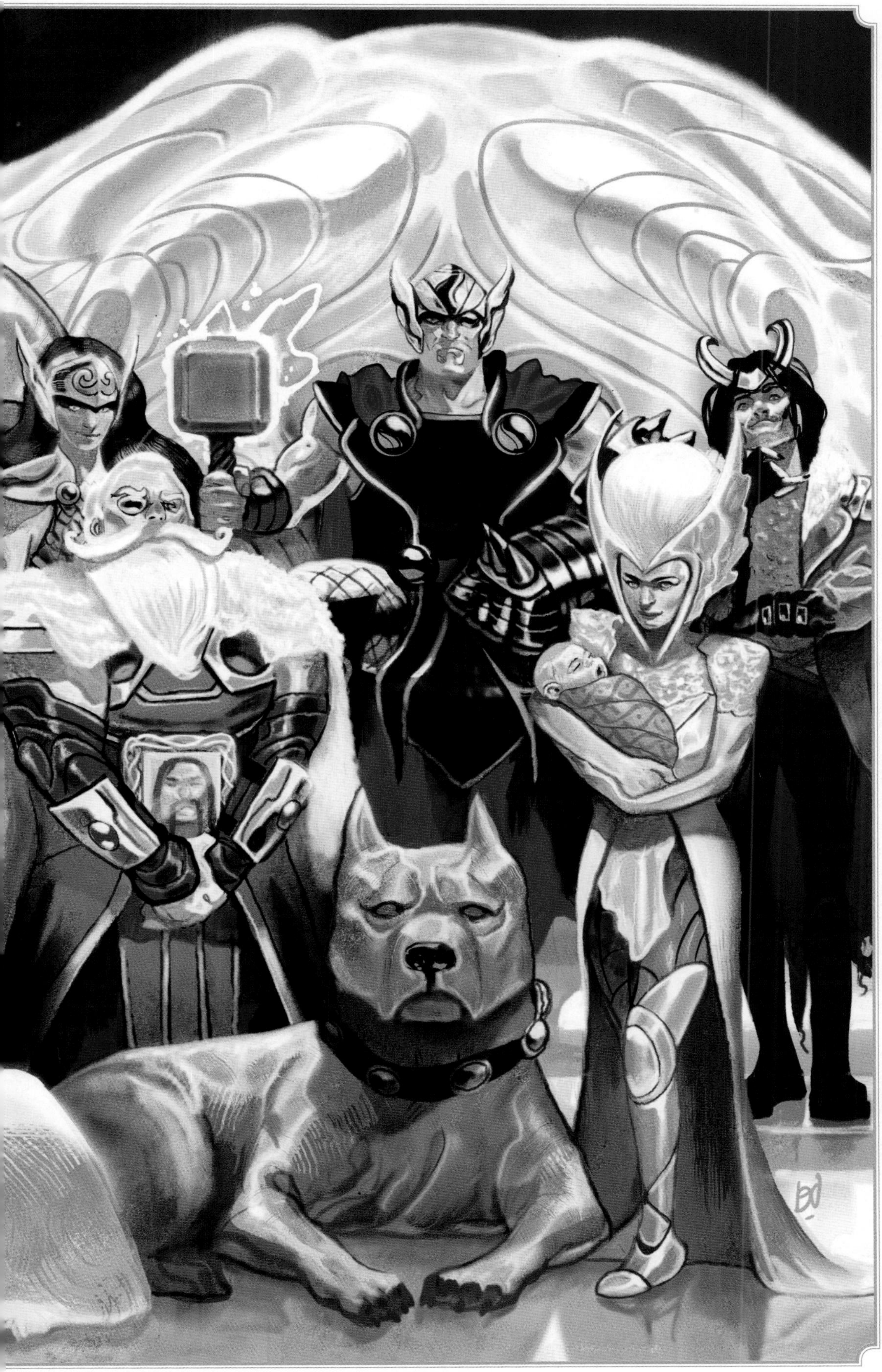

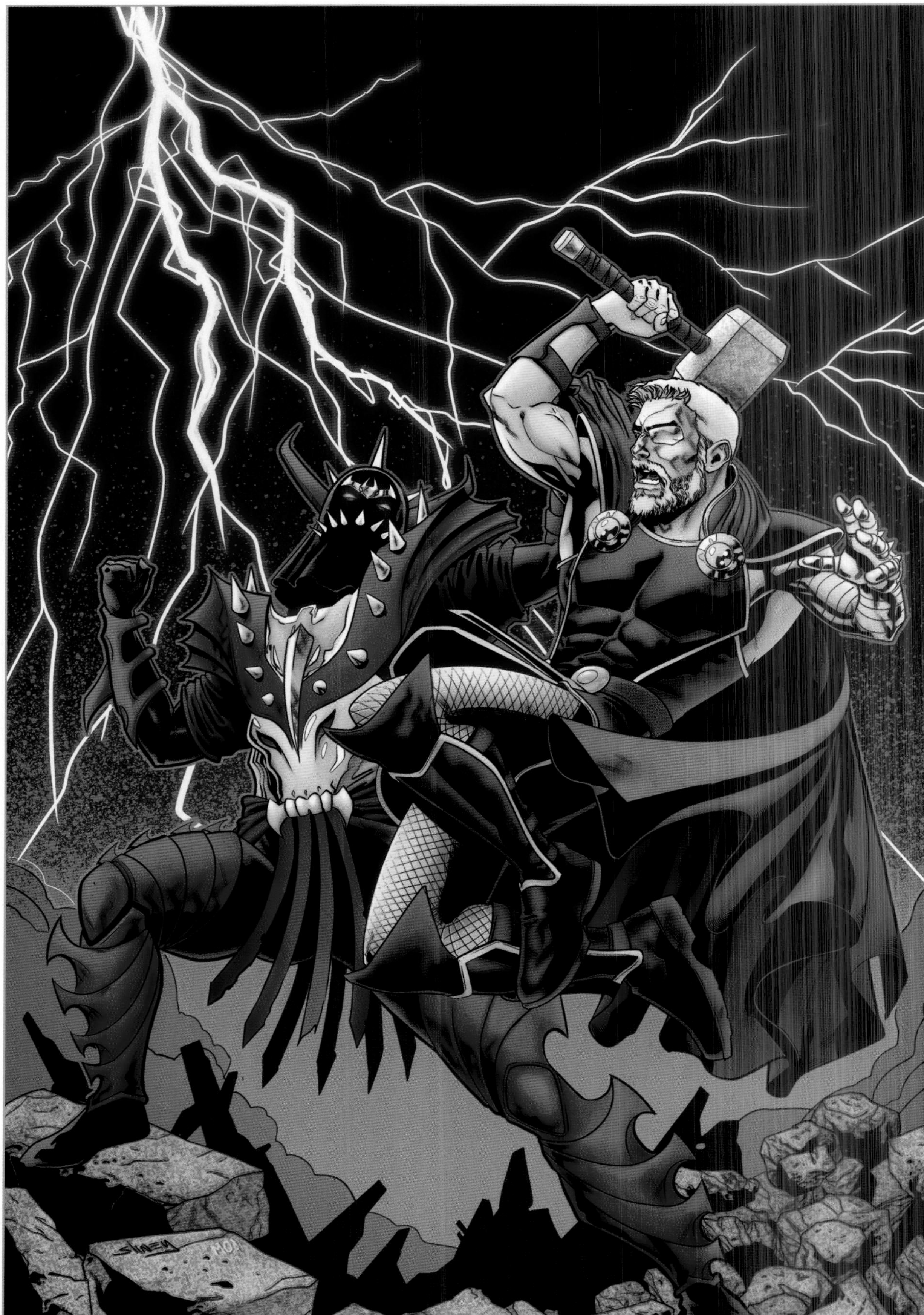

THOR #16 VARIANT
BY **WILL SLINEY** & **MORRY HOLLOWELL**

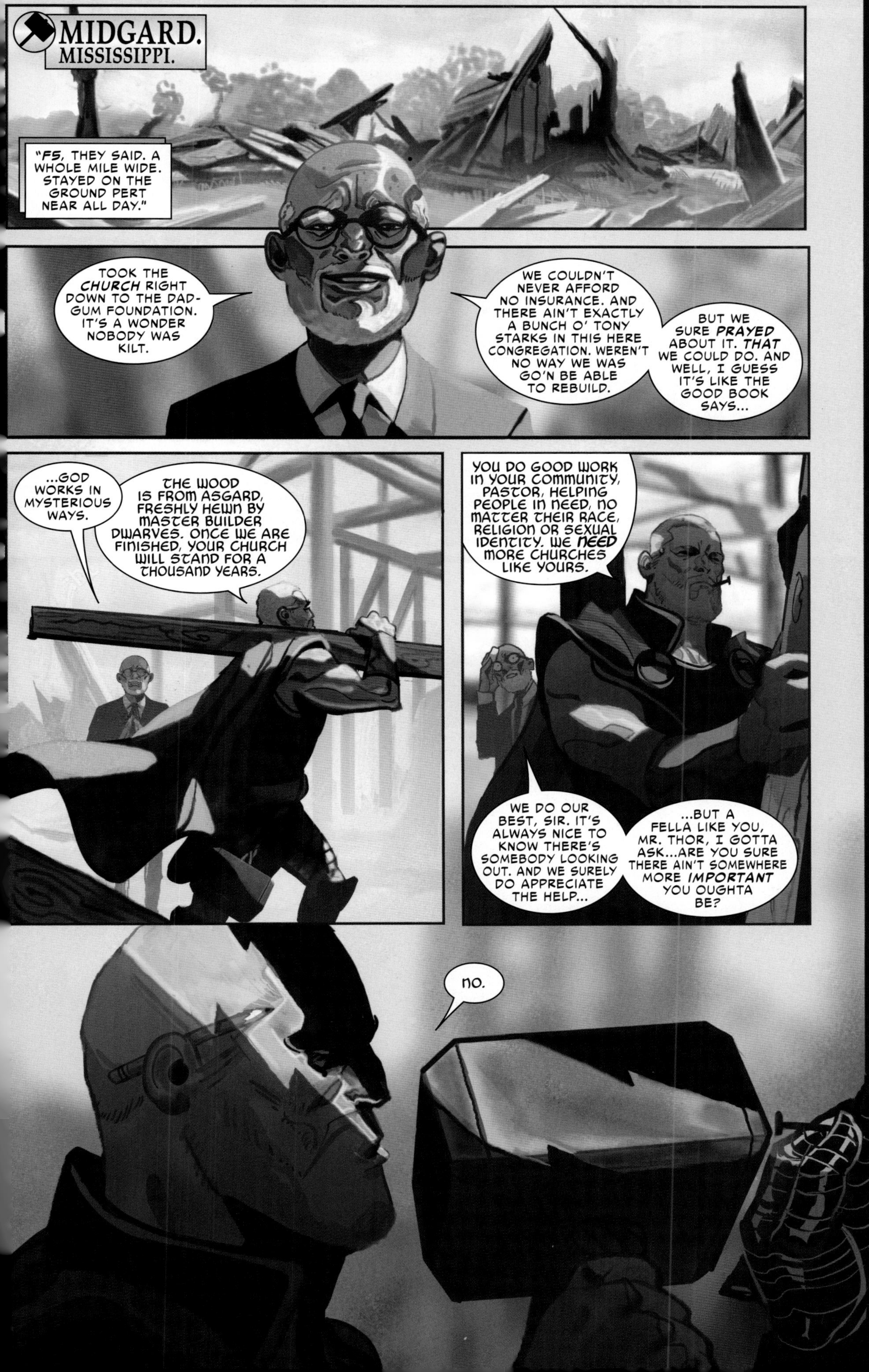

MIDGARD.
MISSISSIPPI.
"F5, THEY SAID. A WHOLE MILE WIDE. STAYED ON THE GROUND PERT NEAR ALL DAY."
TOOK THE CHURCH RIGHT DOWN TO THE DAD-GUM FOUNDATION. IT'S A WONDER NOBODY WAS KILT.
WE COULDN'T NEVER AFFORD NO INSURANCE. AND THERE AIN'T EXACTLY A BUNCH O' TONY STARKS IN THIS HERE CONGREGATION. WEREN'T NO WAY WE WAS GO'N BE ABLE TO REBUILD.
BUT WE SURE PRAYED ABOUT IT. THAT WE COULD DO. AND WELL, I GUESS IT'S LIKE THE GOOD BOOK SAYS...
...GOD WORKS IN MYSTERIOUS WAYS.
THE WOOD IS FROM ASGARD, FRESHLY HEWN BY MASTER BUILDER DWARVES. ONCE WE ARE FINISHED, YOUR CHURCH WILL STAND FOR A THOUSAND YEARS.
YOU DO GOOD WORK IN YOUR COMMUNITY, PASTOR, HELPING PEOPLE IN NEED, NO MATTER THEIR RACE, RELIGION OR SEXUAL IDENTITY. WE NEED MORE CHURCHES LIKE YOURS.
WE DO OUR BEST, SIR. IT'S ALWAYS NICE TO KNOW THERE'S SOMEBODY LOOKING OUT. AND WE SURELY DO APPRECIATE THE HELP...
...BUT A FELLA LIKE YOU, MR. THOR, I GOTTA ASK...ARE YOU SURE THERE AIN'T SOMEWHERE MORE IMPORTANT YOU OUGHTA BE?
no.

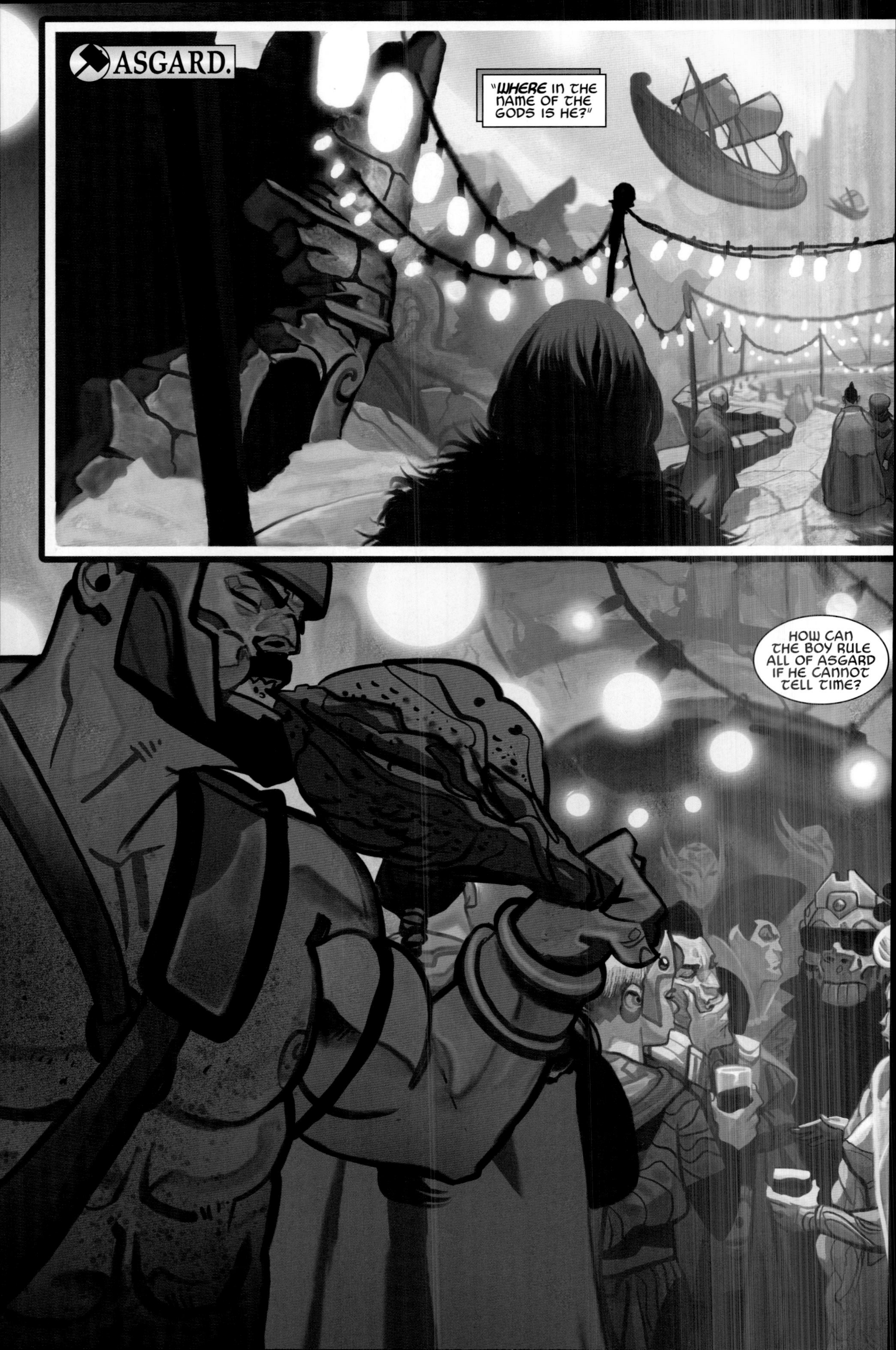
ASGARD.
"WHERE IN THE NAME OF THE GODS IS HE?"
HOW CAN THE BOY RULE ALL OF ASGARD IF HE CANNOT TELL TIME?

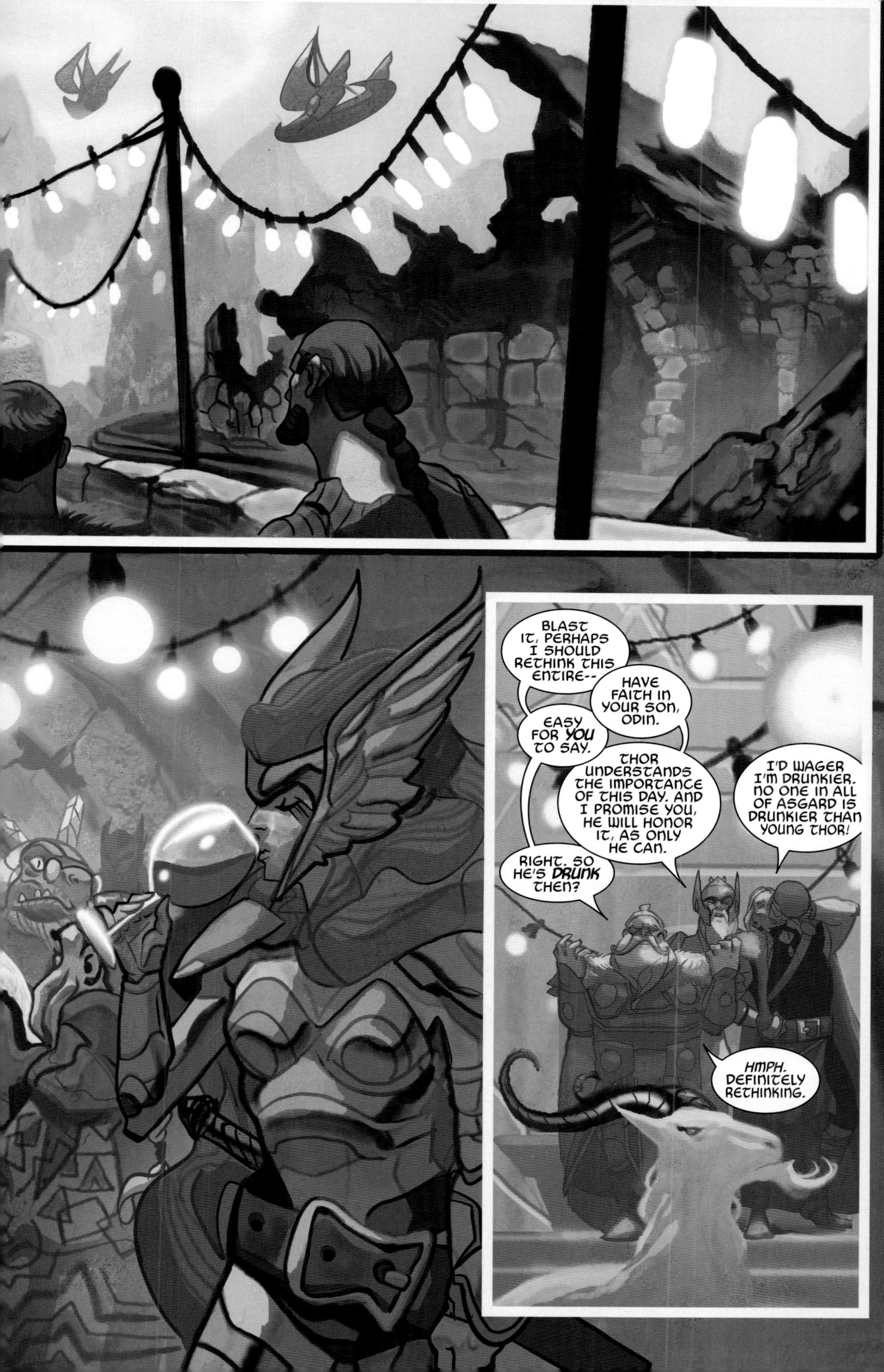
BLAST IT, PERHAPS I SHOULD RETHINK THIS ENTIRE--
HAVE FAITH IN YOUR SON, ODIN.
EASY FOR YOU TO SAY.
THOR UNDERSTANDS THE IMPORTANCE OF THIS DAY. AND I PROMISE YOU, HE WILL HONOR IT, AS ONLY HE CAN.
RIGHT. SO HE'S DRUNK THEN?
I'D WAGER I'M DRUNKIER. NO ONE IN ALL OF ASGARD IS DRUNKIER THAN YOUNG THOR!
HMPH. DEFINITELY RETHINKING.

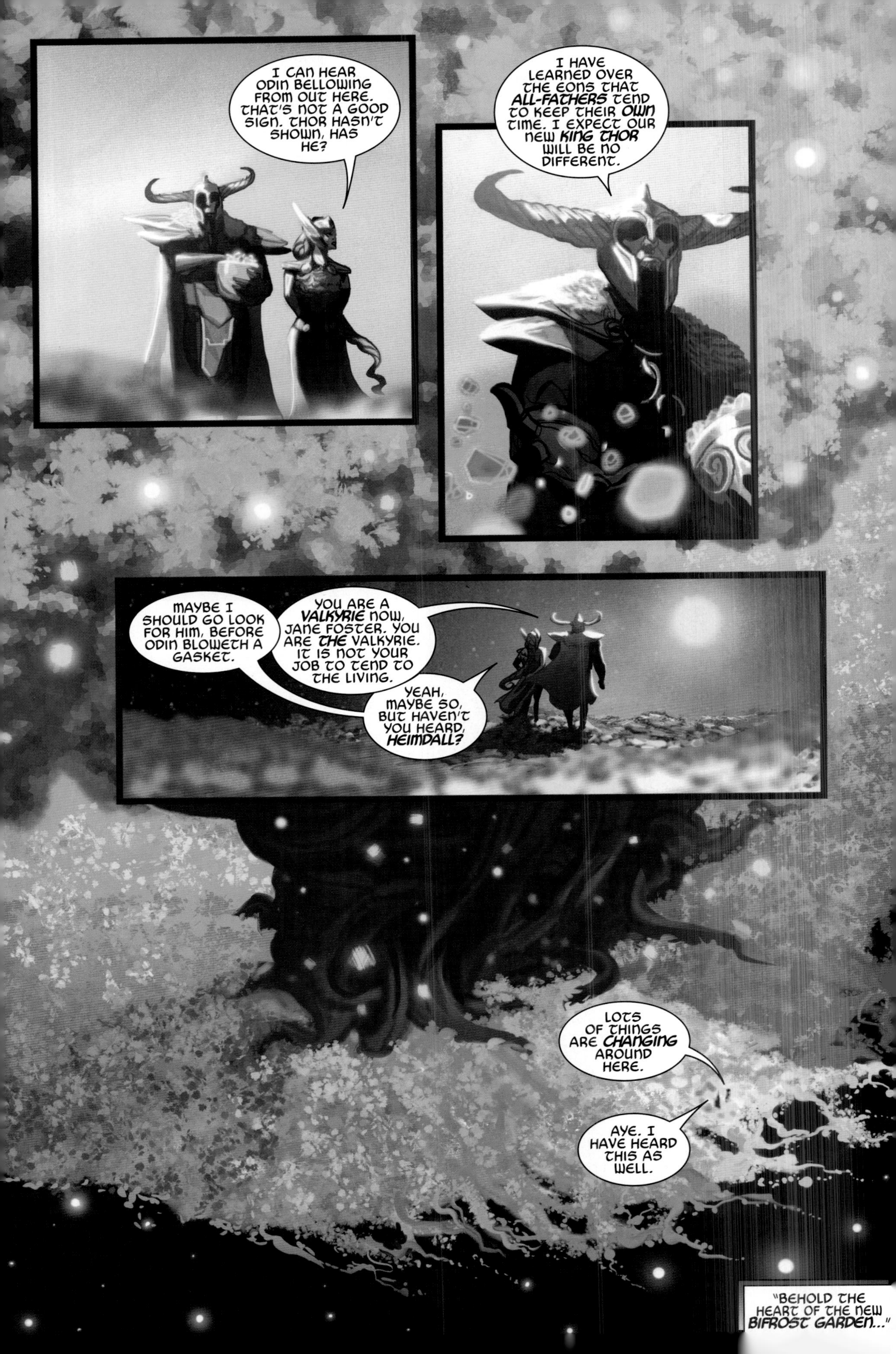
I CAN HEAR ODIN BELLOWING FROM OUT HERE. THAT'S NOT A GOOD SIGN. THOR HASN'T SHOWN, HAS HE?
I HAVE LEARNED OVER THE EONS THAT ALL-FATHERS TEND TO KEEP THEIR OWN TIME. I EXPECT OUR NEW KING THOR WILL BE NO DIFFERENT.
MAYBE I SHOULD GO LOOK FOR HIM, BEFORE ODIN BLOWETH A GASKET.
YOU ARE A VALKYRIE NOW, JANE FOSTER. YOU ARE THE VALKYRIE. IT IS NOT YOUR JOB TO TEND TO THE LIVING.
YEAH, MAYBE SO, BUT HAVEN'T YOU HEARD, HEIMDALL?
LOTS OF THINGS ARE CHANGING AROUND HERE.
AYE. I HAVE HEARD THIS AS WELL.
"BEHOLD THE HEART OF THE NEW BIFROST GARDEN..."

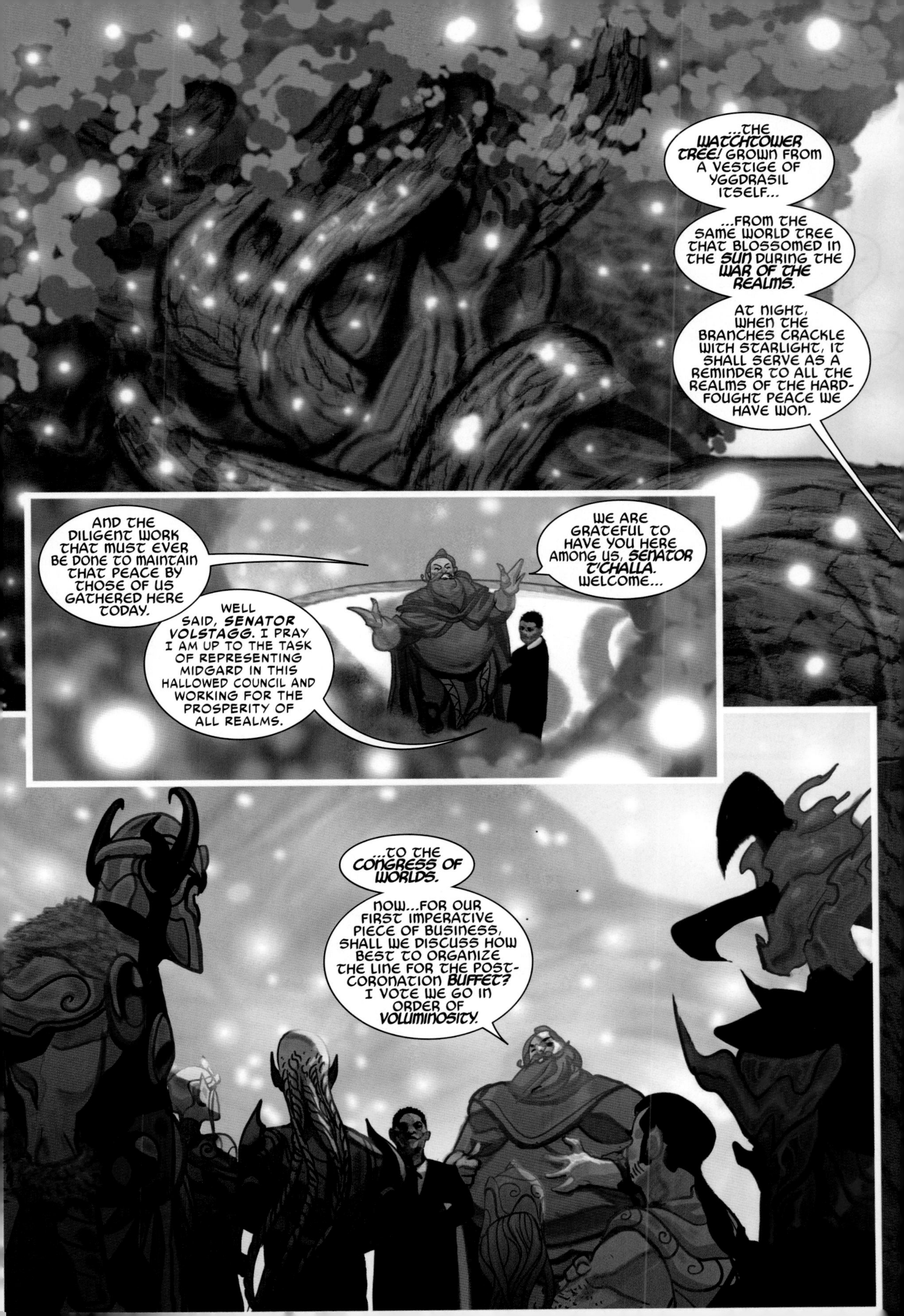
...THE WATCHTOWER TREE! GROWN FROM A VESTIGE OF YGGDRASIL ITSELF...
...FROM THE SAME WORLD TREE THAT BLOSSOMED IN THE SUN DURING THE WAR OF THE REALMS.
AT NIGHT, WHEN THE BRANCHES CRACKLE WITH STARLIGHT, IT SHALL SERVE AS A REMINDER TO ALL THE REALMS OF THE HARD-FOUGHT PEACE WE HAVE WON.
AND THE DILIGENT WORK THAT MUST EVER BE DONE TO MAINTAIN THAT PEACE BY THOSE OF US GATHERED HERE TODAY.
WELL SAID, SENATOR VOLSTAGG. I PRAY I AM UP TO THE TASK OF REPRESENTING MIDGARD IN THIS HALLOWED COUNCIL AND WORKING FOR THE PROSPERITY OF ALL REALMS.
WE ARE GRATEFUL TO HAVE YOU HERE AMONG US, SENATOR T'CHALLA. WELCOME...
...TO THE CONGRESS OF WORLDS.
NOW...FOR OUR FIRST IMPERATIVE PIECE OF BUSINESS, SHALL WE DISCUSS HOW BEST TO ORGANIZE THE LINE FOR THE POST-CORONATION BUFFET? I VOTE WE GO IN ORDER OF VOLUMINOSITY.

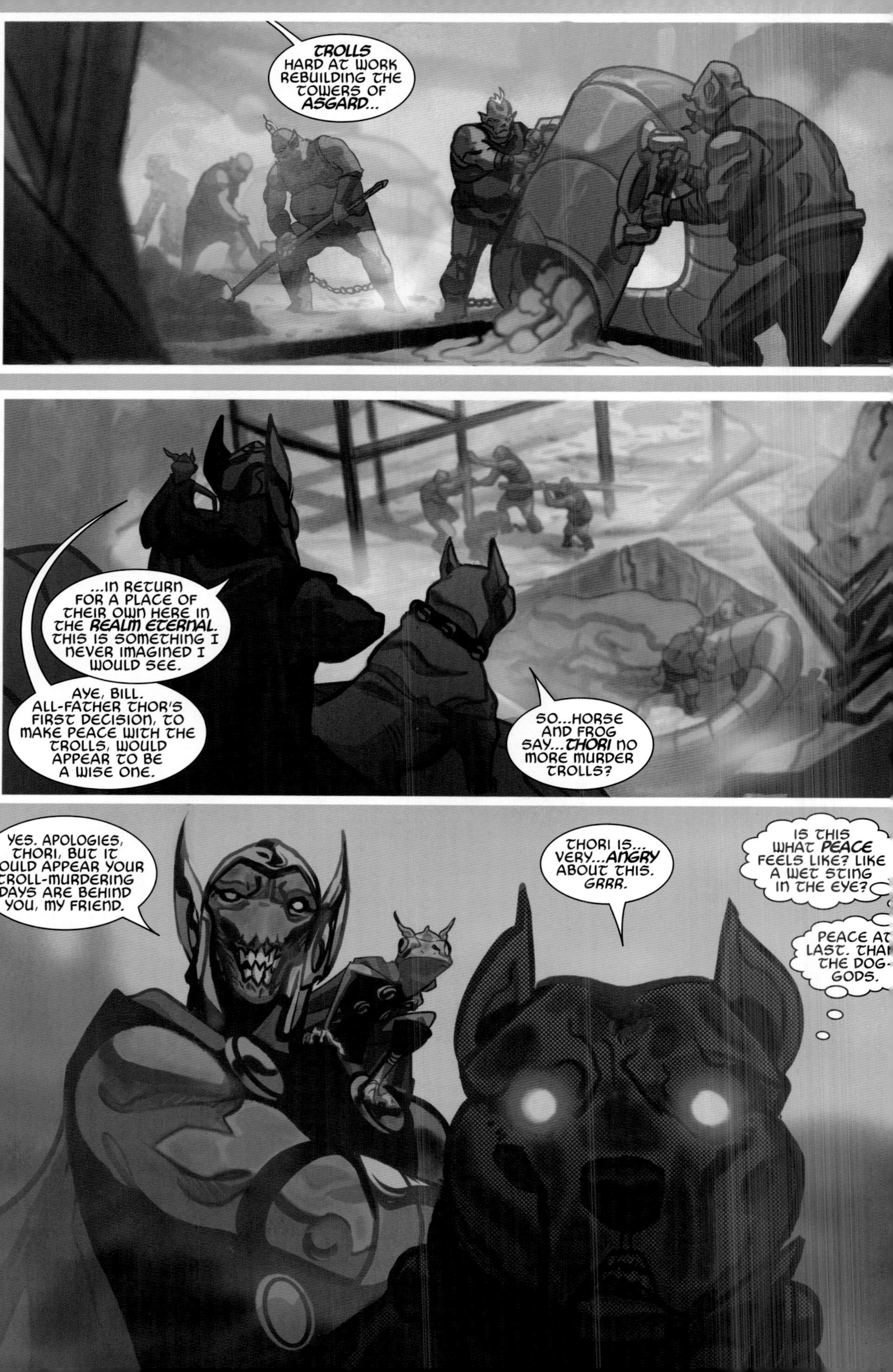
TROLLS HARD AT WORK REBUILDING THE TOWERS OF ASGARD...
...IN RETURN FOR A PLACE OF THEIR OWN HERE IN THE REALM ETERNAL. THIS IS SOMETHING I NEVER IMAGINED I WOULD SEE.
AYE, BILL. ALL-FATHER THOR'S FIRST DECISION, TO MAKE PEACE WITH THE TROLLS, WOULD APPEAR TO BE A WISE ONE.
SO...HORSE AND FROG SAY...THORI NO MORE MURDER TROLLS?
YES. APOLOGIES, THORI, BUT IT WOULD APPEAR YOUR TROLL-MURDERING DAYS ARE BEHIND YOU, MY FRIEND.
THORI IS... VERY...ANGRY ABOUT THIS. GRRR.
IS THIS WHAT PEACE FEELS LIKE? LIKE A WET STING IN THE EYE?
PEACE AT LAST. THAN THE DOG-GODS.

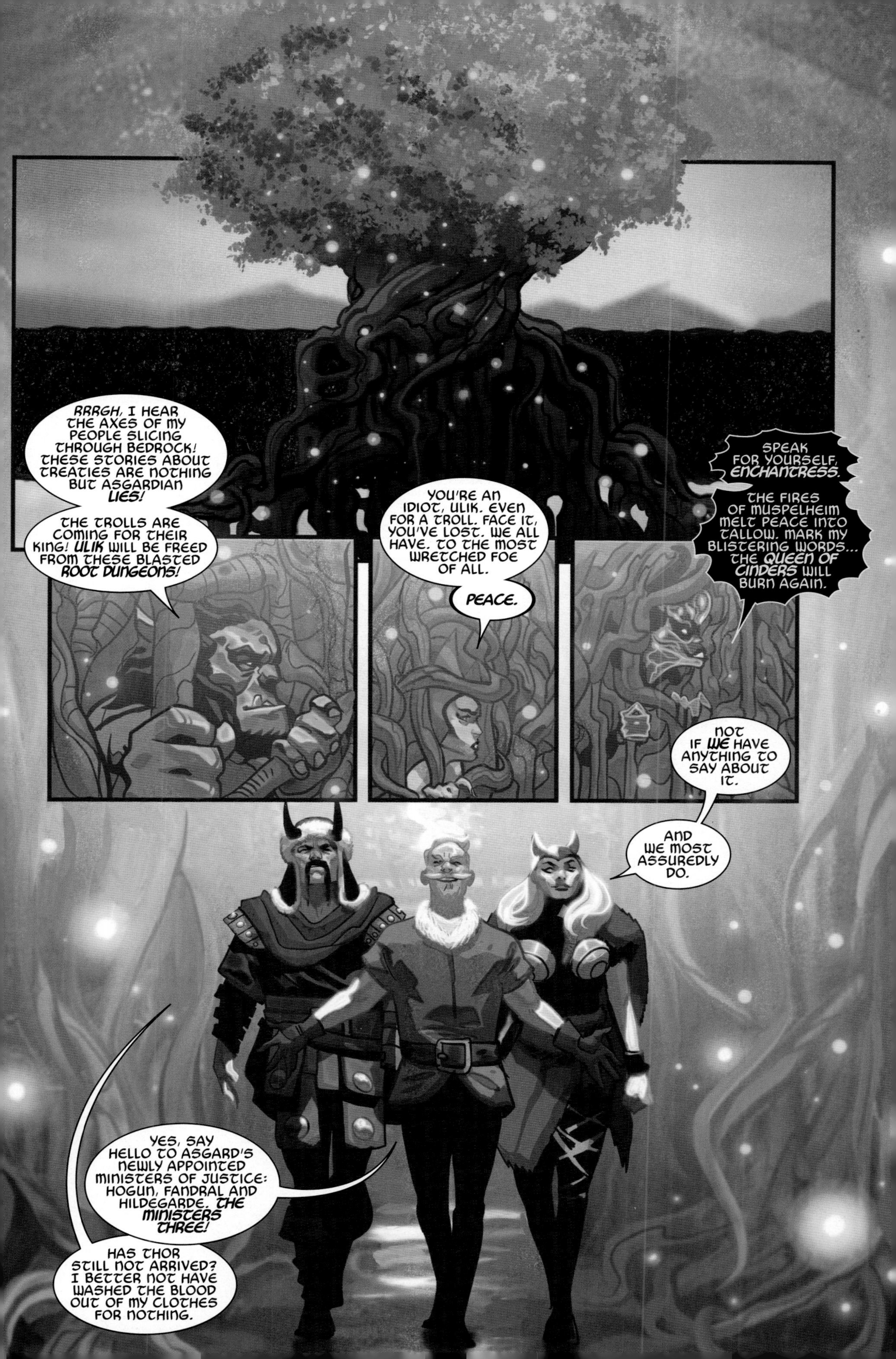
RRRGH, I HEAR THE AXES OF MY PEOPLE SLICING THROUGH BEDROCK! THESE STORIES ABOUT TREATIES ARE NOTHING BUT ASGARDIAN LIES!
THE TROLLS ARE COMING FOR THEIR KING! ULIK WILL BE FREED FROM THESE BLASTED ROOT DUNGEONS!
YOU'RE AN IDIOT, ULIK. EVEN FOR A TROLL. FACE IT, YOU'VE LOST. WE ALL HAVE. TO THE MOST WRETCHED FOE OF ALL.
PEACE.
SPEAK FOR YOURSELF, ENCHANTRESS.
THE FIRES OF MUSPELHEIM MELT PEACE INTO TALLOW. MARK MY BLISTERING WORDS... THE QUEEN OF CINDERS WILL BURN AGAIN.
NOT IF WE HAVE ANYTHING TO SAY ABOUT IT.
AND WE MOST ASSUREDLY DO.
YES, SAY HELLO TO ASGARD'S NEWLY APPOINTED MINISTERS OF JUSTICE: HOGUN, FANDRAL AND HILDEGARDE. THE MINISTERS THREE!
HAS THOR STILL NOT ARRIVED? I BETTER NOT HAVE WASHED THE BLOOD OUT OF MY CLOTHES FOR NOTHING.

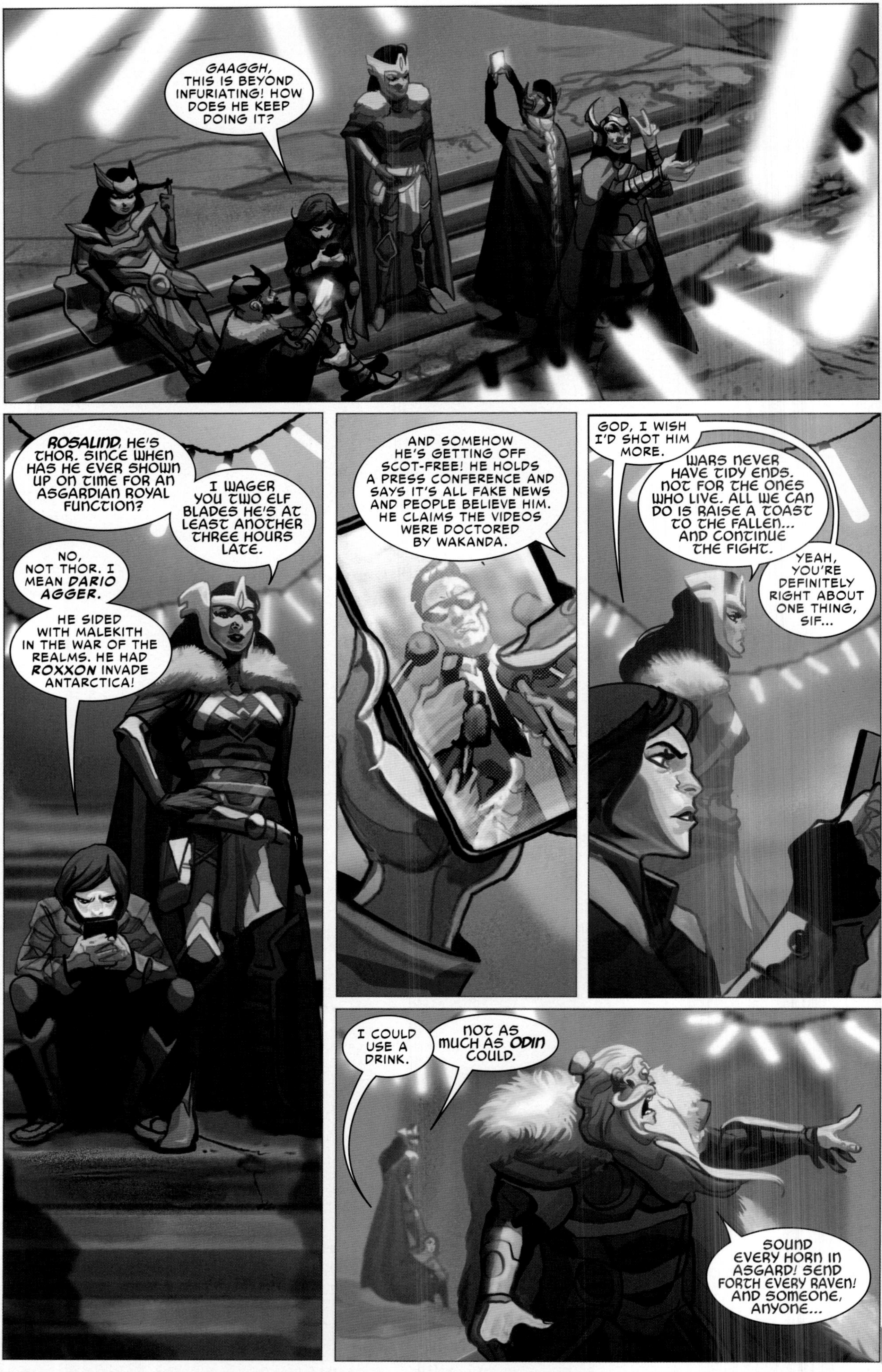
GAAGGH, THIS IS BEYOND INFURIATING! HOW DOES HE KEEP DOING IT?
ROSALIND, HE'S THOR. SINCE WHEN HAS HE EVER SHOWN UP ON TIME FOR AN ASGARDIAN ROYAL FUNCTION?
I WAGER YOU TWO ELF BLADES HE'S AT LEAST ANOTHER THREE HOURS LATE.
NO, NOT THOR. I MEAN DARIO AGGER.
HE SIDED WITH MALEKITH IN THE WAR OF THE REALMS. HE HAD ROXXON INVADE ANTARCTICA!
AND SOMEHOW HE'S GETTING OFF SCOT-FREE! HE HOLDS A PRESS CONFERENCE AND SAYS IT'S ALL FAKE NEWS AND PEOPLE BELIEVE HIM. HE CLAIMS THE VIDEOS WERE DOCTORED BY WAKANDA.
GOD, I WISH I'D SHOT HIM MORE.
WARS NEVER HAVE TIDY ENDS. NOT FOR THE ONES WHO LIVE. ALL WE CAN DO IS RAISE A TOAST TO THE FALLEN... AND CONTINUE THE FIGHT.
YEAH, YOU'RE DEFINITELY RIGHT ABOUT ONE THING, SIF...
I COULD USE A DRINK.
NOT AS MUCH AS ODIN COULD.
SOUND EVERY HORN IN ASGARD! SEND FORTH EVERY RAVEN! AND SOMEONE, ANYONE...

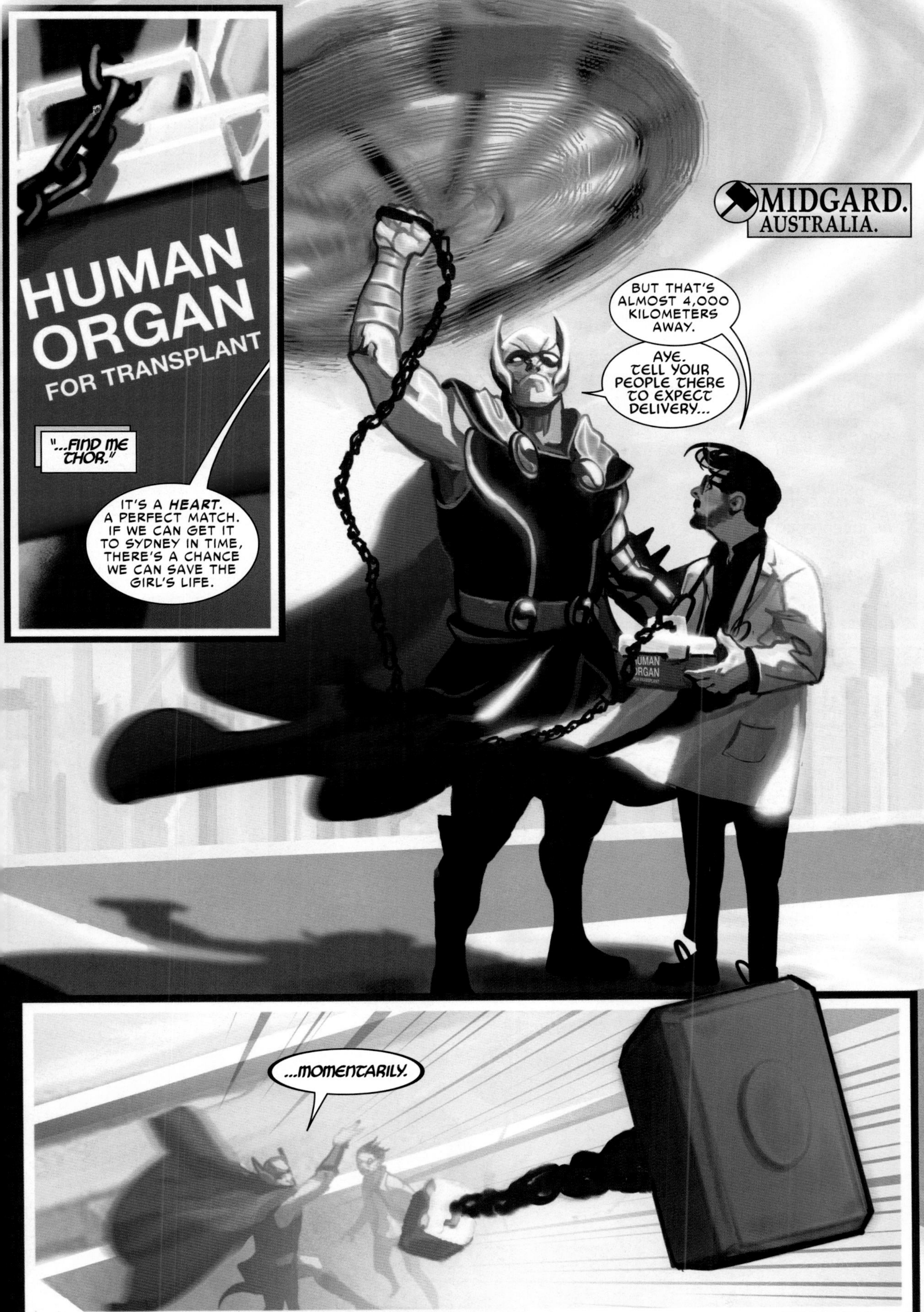
HUMAN ORGAN FOR TRANSPLANT
"...FIND ME THOR."
IT'S A HEART. A PERFECT MATCH. IF WE CAN GET IT TO SYDNEY IN TIME, THERE'S A CHANCE WE CAN SAVE THE GIRL'S LIFE.
MIDGARD. AUSTRALIA.
BUT THAT'S ALMOST 4,000 KILOMETERS AWAY.
AYE. TELL YOUR PEOPLE THERE TO EXPECT DELIVERY...
HUMAN ORGAN
...MOMENTARILY.

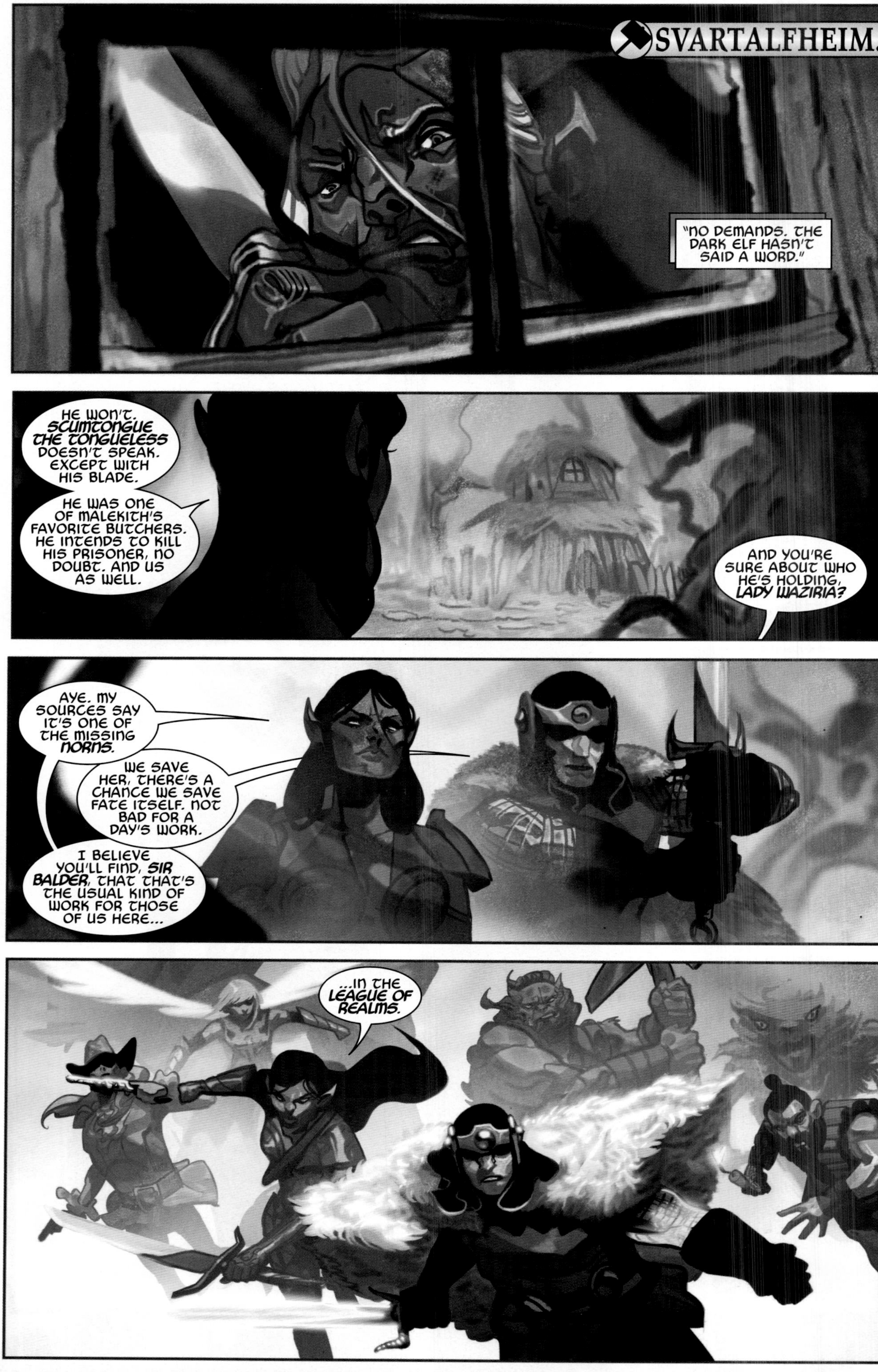
SVARTALFHEIM.
"NO DEMANDS. THE DARK ELF HASN'T SAID A WORD."
HE WON'T. SCUMTONGUE THE TONGUELESS DOESN'T SPEAK. EXCEPT WITH HIS BLADE.
HE WAS ONE OF MALEKITH'S FAVORITE BUTCHERS. HE INTENDS TO KILL HIS PRISONER, NO DOUBT. AND US AS WELL.
AND YOU'RE SURE ABOUT WHO HE'S HOLDING, LADY WAZIRIA?
AYE. MY SOURCES SAY IT'S ONE OF THE MISSING NORNS.
WE SAVE HER, THERE'S A CHANCE WE SAVE FATE ITSELF. NOT BAD FOR A DAY'S WORK.
I BELIEVE YOU'LL FIND, SIR BALDER, THAT THAT'S THE USUAL KIND OF WORK FOR THOSE OF US HERE...
...IN THE LEAGUE OF REALMS.

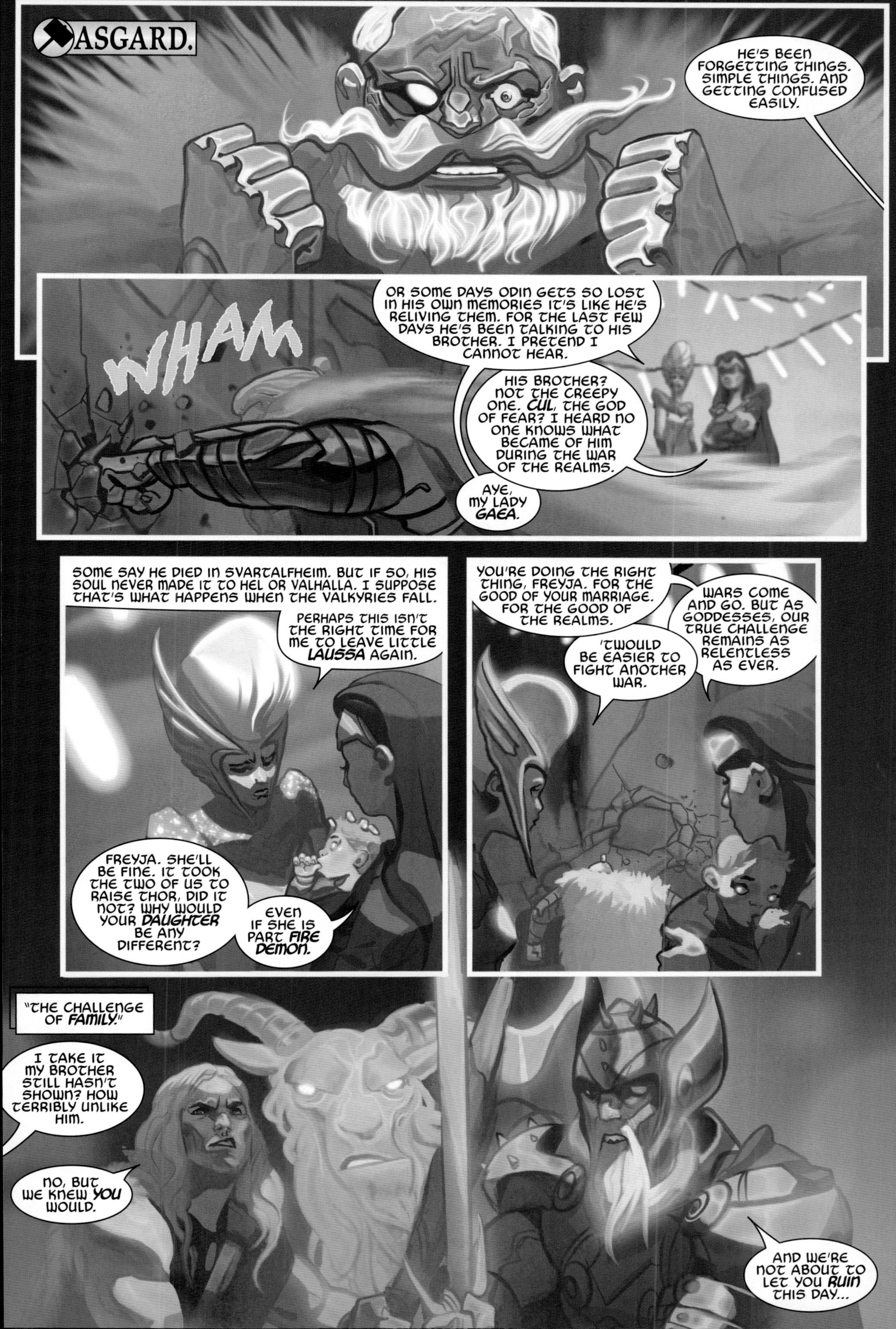
ASGARD.
HE'S BEEN FORGETTING THINGS. SIMPLE THINGS. AND GETTING CONFUSED EASILY.
WHAM
OR SOME DAYS ODIN GETS SO LOST IN HIS OWN MEMORIES IT'S LIKE HE'S RELIVING THEM. FOR THE LAST FEW DAYS HE'S BEEN TALKING TO HIS BROTHER. I PRETEND I CANNOT HEAR.
HIS BROTHER? NOT THE CREEPY ONE. CUL, THE GOD OF FEAR? I HEARD NO ONE KNOWS WHAT BECAME OF HIM DURING THE WAR OF THE REALMS.
AYE, MY LADY GAEA.
SOME SAY HE DIED IN SVARTALFHEIM. BUT IF SO, HIS SOUL NEVER MADE IT TO HEL OR VALHALLA. I SUPPOSE THAT'S WHAT HAPPENS WHEN THE VALKYRIES FALL.
PERHAPS THIS ISN'T THE RIGHT TIME FOR ME TO LEAVE LITTLE LAUSSA AGAIN.
FREYJA. SHE'LL BE FINE. IT TOOK THE TWO OF US TO RAISE THOR, DID IT NOT? WHY WOULD YOUR DAUGHTER BE ANY DIFFERENT?
EVEN IF SHE IS PART FIRE DEMON.
YOU'RE DOING THE RIGHT THING, FREYJA. FOR THE GOOD OF YOUR MARRIAGE. FOR THE GOOD OF THE REALMS.
'TWOULD BE EASIER TO FIGHT ANOTHER WAR.
WARS COME AND GO. BUT AS GODDESSES, OUR TRUE CHALLENGE REMAINS AS RELENTLESS AS EVER.
"THE CHALLENGE OF FAMILY."
I TAKE IT MY BROTHER STILL HASN'T SHOWN? HOW TERRIBLY UNLIKE HIM.
NO, BUT WE KNEW YOU WOULD.
AND WE'RE NOT ABOUT TO LET YOU RUIN THIS DAY...

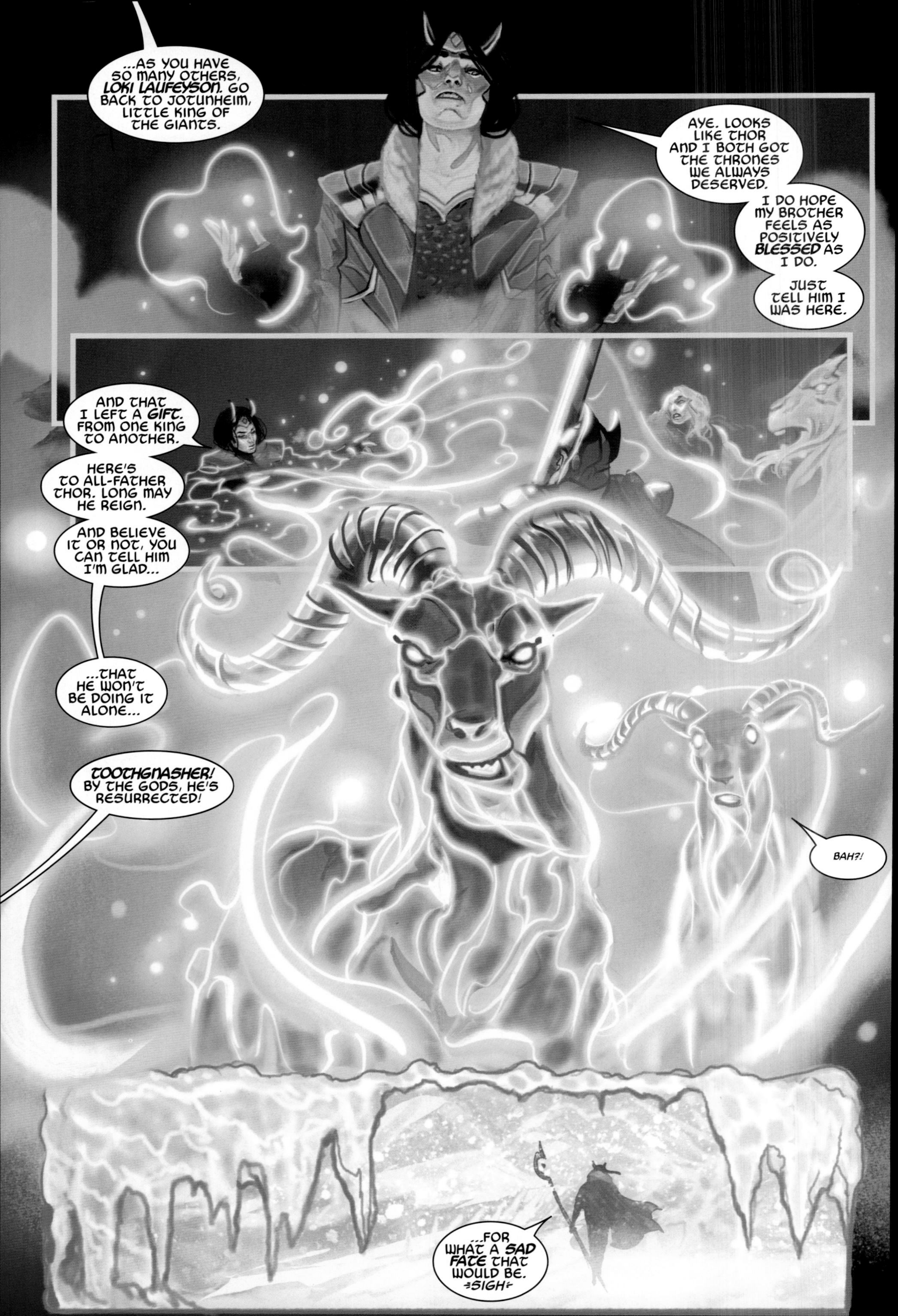

...AS YOU HAVE SO MANY OTHERS, LOKI LAUFEYSON. GO BACK TO JOTUNHEIM, LITTLE KING OF THE GIANTS.
AYE. LOOKS LIKE THOR AND I BOTH GOT THE THRONES WE ALWAYS DESERVED.
I DO HOPE MY BROTHER FEELS AS POSITIVELY BLESSED AS I DO.
JUST TELL HIM I WAS HERE.
AND THAT I LEFT A GIFT. FROM ONE KING TO ANOTHER.
HERE'S TO ALL-FATHER THOR. LONG MAY HE REIGN.
AND BELIEVE IT OR NOT, YOU CAN TELL HIM I'M GLAD...
...THAT HE WON'T BE DOING IT ALONE...
TOOTHGNASHER! BY THE GODS, HE'S RESURRECTED!
BAH?!
...FOR WHAT A SAD FATE THAT WOULD BE.
SIGH

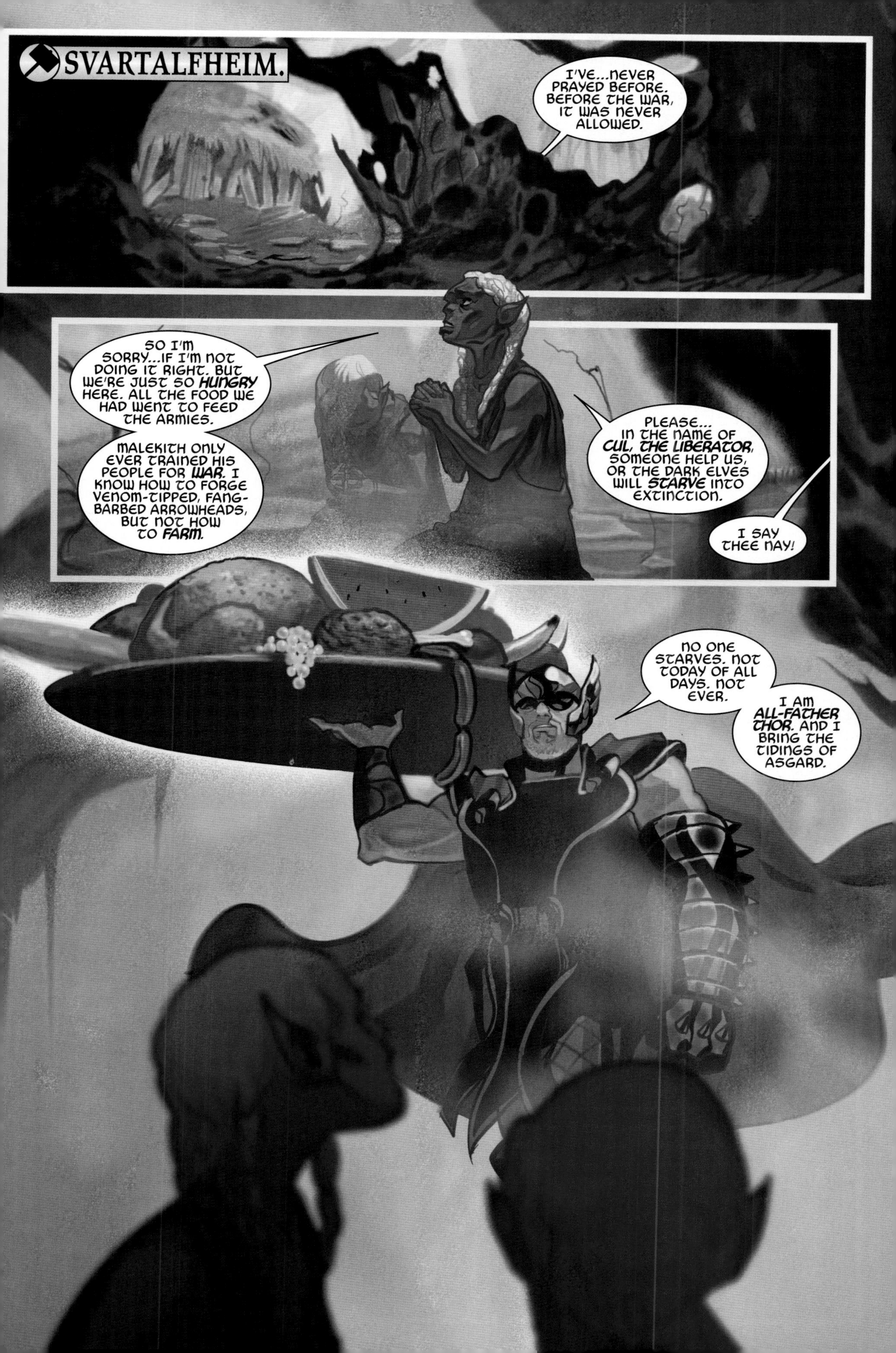
SVARTALFHEIM.
I'VE...NEVER PRAYED BEFORE. BEFORE THE WAR, IT WAS NEVER ALLOWED.
SO I'M SORRY...IF I'M NOT DOING IT RIGHT. BUT WE'RE JUST SO HUNGRY HERE. ALL THE FOOD WE HAD WENT TO FEED THE ARMIES.
MALEKITH ONLY EVER TRAINED HIS PEOPLE FOR WAR. I KNOW HOW TO FORGE VENOM-TIPPED, FANG-BARBED ARROWHEADS, BUT NOT HOW TO FARM.
PLEASE... IN THE NAME OF CUL, THE LIBERATOR, SOMEONE HELP US, OR THE DARK ELVES WILL STARVE INTO EXTINCTION.
I SAY THEE NAY!
NO ONE STARVES. NOT TODAY OF ALL DAYS. NOT EVER.
I AM ALL-FATHER THOR. AND I BRING THE TIDINGS OF ASGARD.

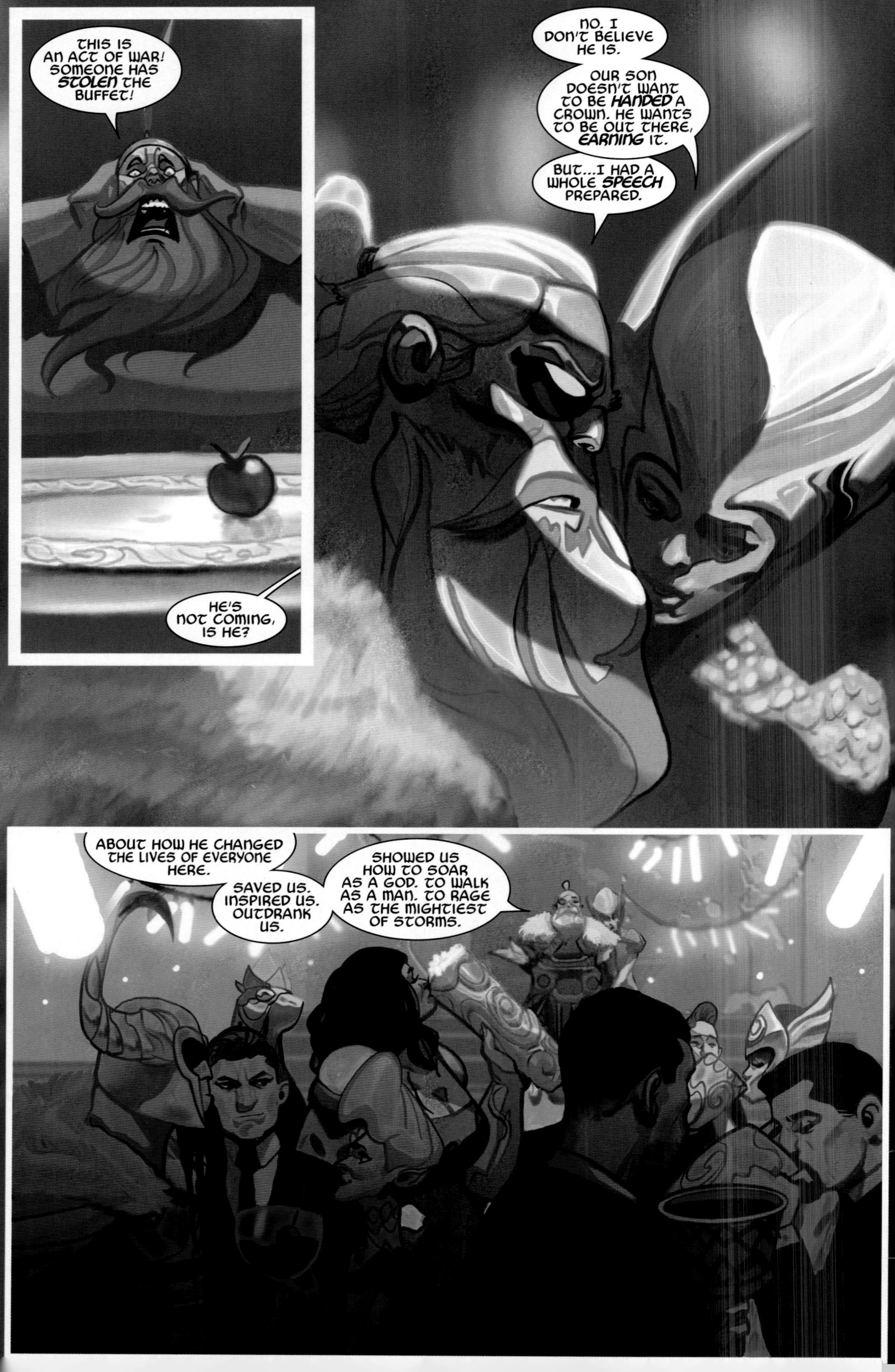
THIS IS AN ACT OF WAR! SOMEONE HAS STOLEN THE BUFFET!
HE'S NOT COMING, IS HE?
NO. I DON'T BELIEVE HE IS.
OUR SON DOESN'T WANT TO BE HANDED A CROWN. HE WANTS TO BE OUT THERE, EARNING IT.
BUT...I HAD A WHOLE SPEECH PREPARED.
ABOUT HOW HE CHANGED THE LIVES OF EVERYONE HERE.
SAVED US. INSPIRED US. OUTDRANK US.
SHOWED US HOW TO SOAR AS A GOD. TO WALK AS A MAN. TO RAGE AS THE MIGHTIEST OF STORMS.

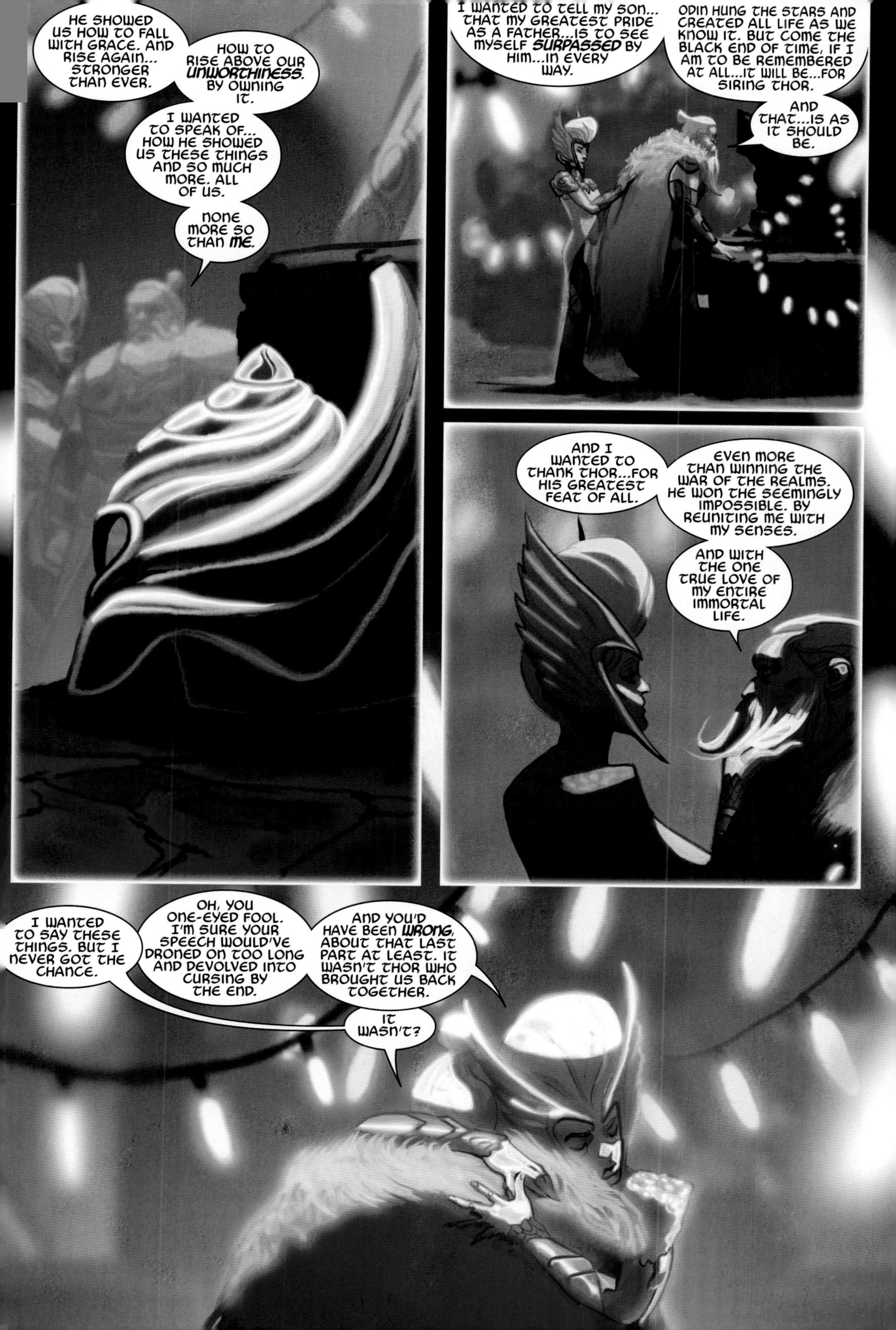
HE SHOWED US HOW TO FALL WITH GRACE. AND RISE AGAIN... STRONGER THAN EVER.
HOW TO RISE ABOVE OUR UNWORTHINESS. BY OWNING IT.
I WANTED TO SPEAK OF... HOW HE SHOWED US THESE THINGS AND SO MUCH MORE. ALL OF US.
NONE MORE SO THAN ME.
I WANTED TO TELL MY SON... THAT MY GREATEST PRIDE AS A FATHER...IS TO SEE MYSELF SURPASSED BY HIM...IN EVERY WAY.
ODIN HUNG THE STARS AND CREATED ALL LIFE AS WE KNOW IT. BUT COME THE BLACK END OF TIME, IF I AM TO BE REMEMBERED AT ALL...IT WILL BE...FOR SIRING THOR.
AND THAT...IS AS IT SHOULD BE.
AND I WANTED TO THANK THOR...FOR HIS GREATEST FEAT OF ALL.
EVEN MORE THAN WINNING THE WAR OF THE REALMS. HE WON THE SEEMINGLY IMPOSSIBLE. BY REUNITING ME WITH MY SENSES.
AND WITH THE ONE TRUE LOVE OF MY ENTIRE IMMORTAL LIFE.
I WANTED TO SAY THESE THINGS. BUT I NEVER GOT THE CHANCE.
OH, YOU ONE-EYED FOOL. I'M SURE YOUR SPEECH WOULD'VE DRONED ON TOO LONG AND DEVOLVED INTO CURSING BY THE END.
AND YOU'D HAVE BEEN WRONG, ABOUT THAT LAST PART AT LEAST. IT WASN'T THOR WHO BROUGHT US BACK TOGETHER.
IT WASN'T?

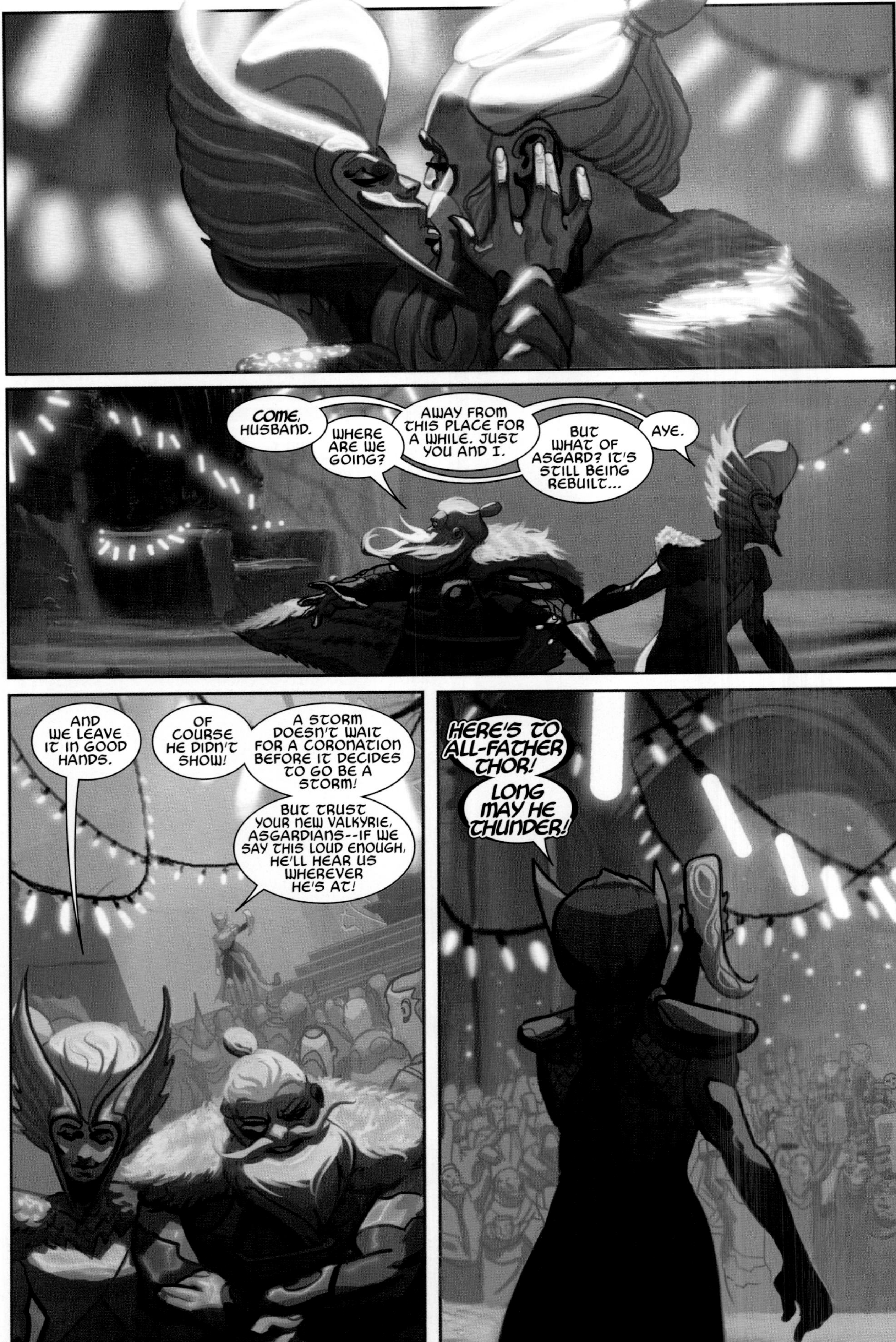

COME, HUSBAND.
WHERE ARE WE GOING?
AWAY FROM THIS PLACE FOR A WHILE. JUST YOU AND I.
BUT WHAT OF ASGARD? IT'S STILL BEING REBUILT...
AYE.
AND WE LEAVE IT IN GOOD HANDS.
OF COURSE HE DIDN'T SHOW!
A STORM DOESN'T WAIT FOR A CORONATION BEFORE IT DECIDES TO GO BE A STORM!
BUT TRUST YOUR NEW VALKYRIE, ASGARDIANS--IF WE SAY THIS LOUD ENOUGH, HE'LL HEAR US WHEREVER HE'S AT!
HERE'S TO ALL-FATHER THOR!
LONG MAY HE THUNDER!

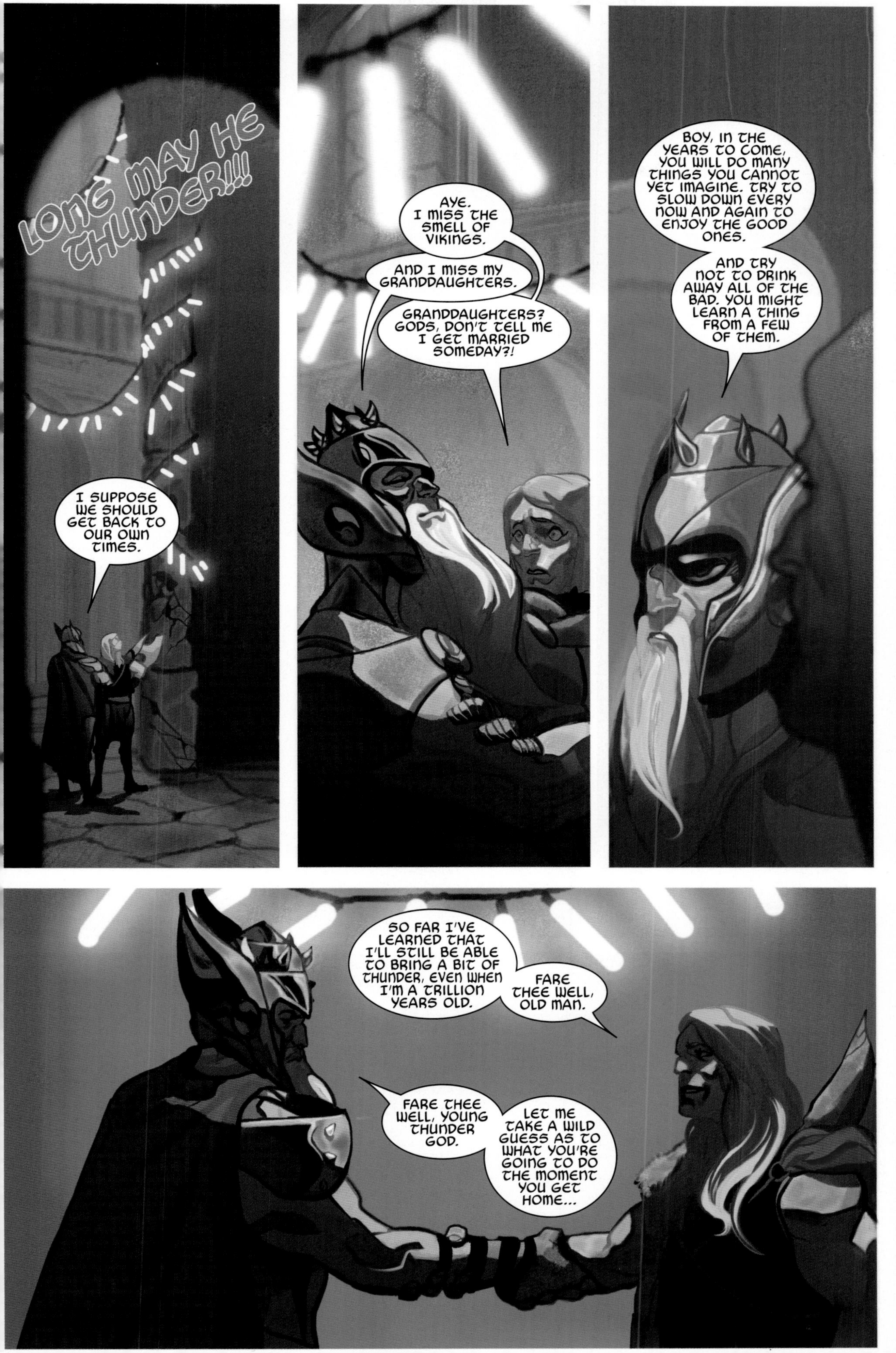
LONG MAY HE THUNDER!!!
I SUPPOSE WE SHOULD GET BACK TO OUR OWN TIMES.
AYE. I MISS THE SMELL OF VIKINGS.
AND I MISS MY GRANDDAUGHTERS.
GRANDDAUGHTERS? GODS, DON'T TELL ME I GET MARRIED SOMEDAY?!
BOY, IN THE YEARS TO COME, YOU WILL DO MANY THINGS YOU CANNOT YET IMAGINE. TRY TO SLOW DOWN EVERY NOW AND AGAIN TO ENJOY THE GOOD ONES.
AND TRY NOT TO DRINK AWAY ALL OF THE BAD. YOU MIGHT LEARN A THING FROM A FEW OF THEM.
SO FAR I'VE LEARNED THAT I'LL STILL BE ABLE TO BRING A BIT OF THUNDER, EVEN WHEN I'M A TRILLION YEARS OLD.
FARE THEE WELL, OLD MAN.
FARE THEE WELL, YOUNG THUNDER GOD.
LET ME TAKE A WILD GUESS AS TO WHAT YOU'RE GOING TO DO THE MOMENT YOU GET HOME...

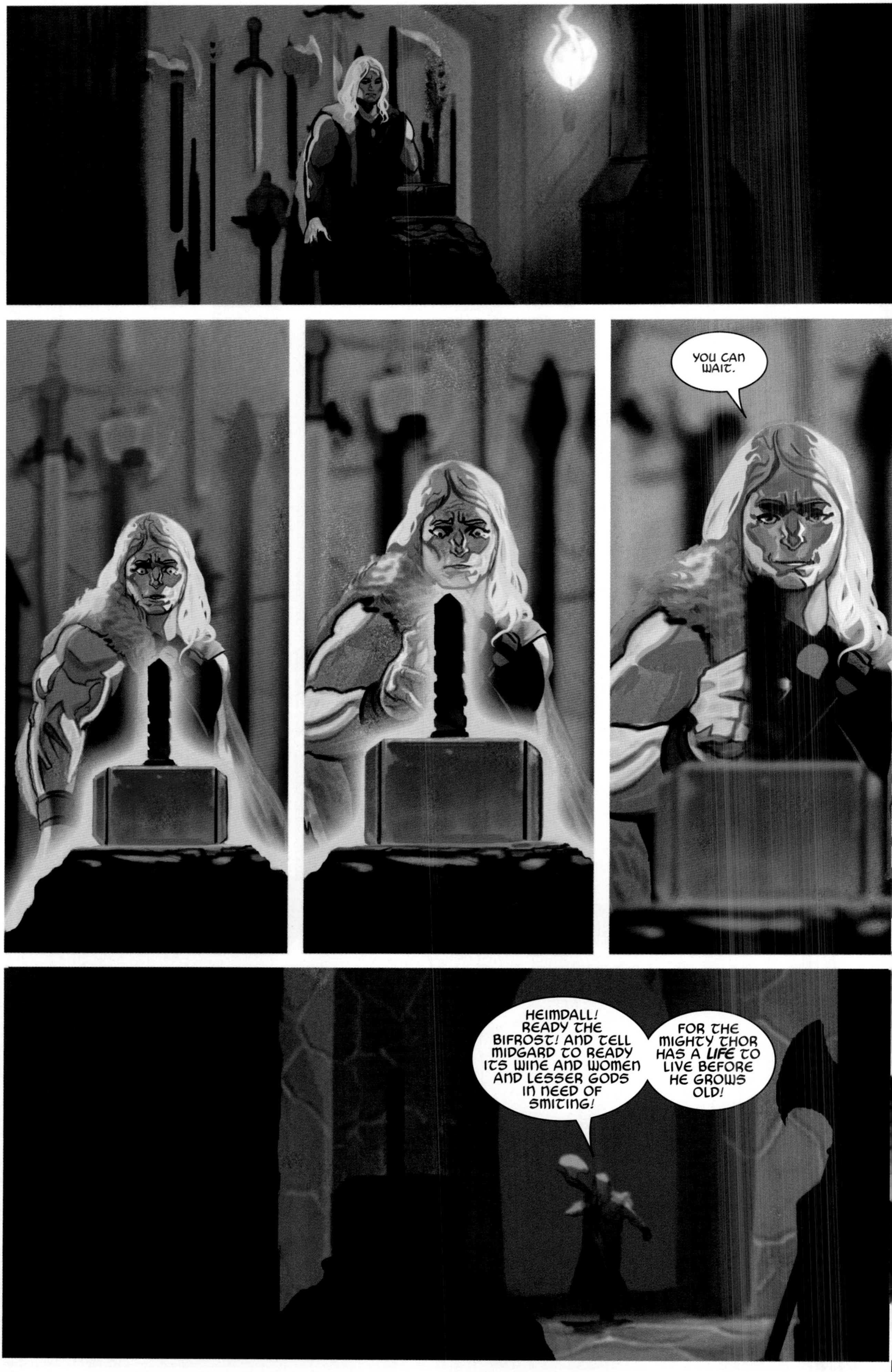

YOU CAN WAIT.
HEIMDALL! READY THE BIFROST! AND TELL MIDGARD TO READY ITS WINE AND WOMEN AND LESSER GODS IN NEED OF SMITING!
FOR THE MIGHTY THOR HAS A *LIFE* TO LIVE BEFORE HE GROWS OLD!

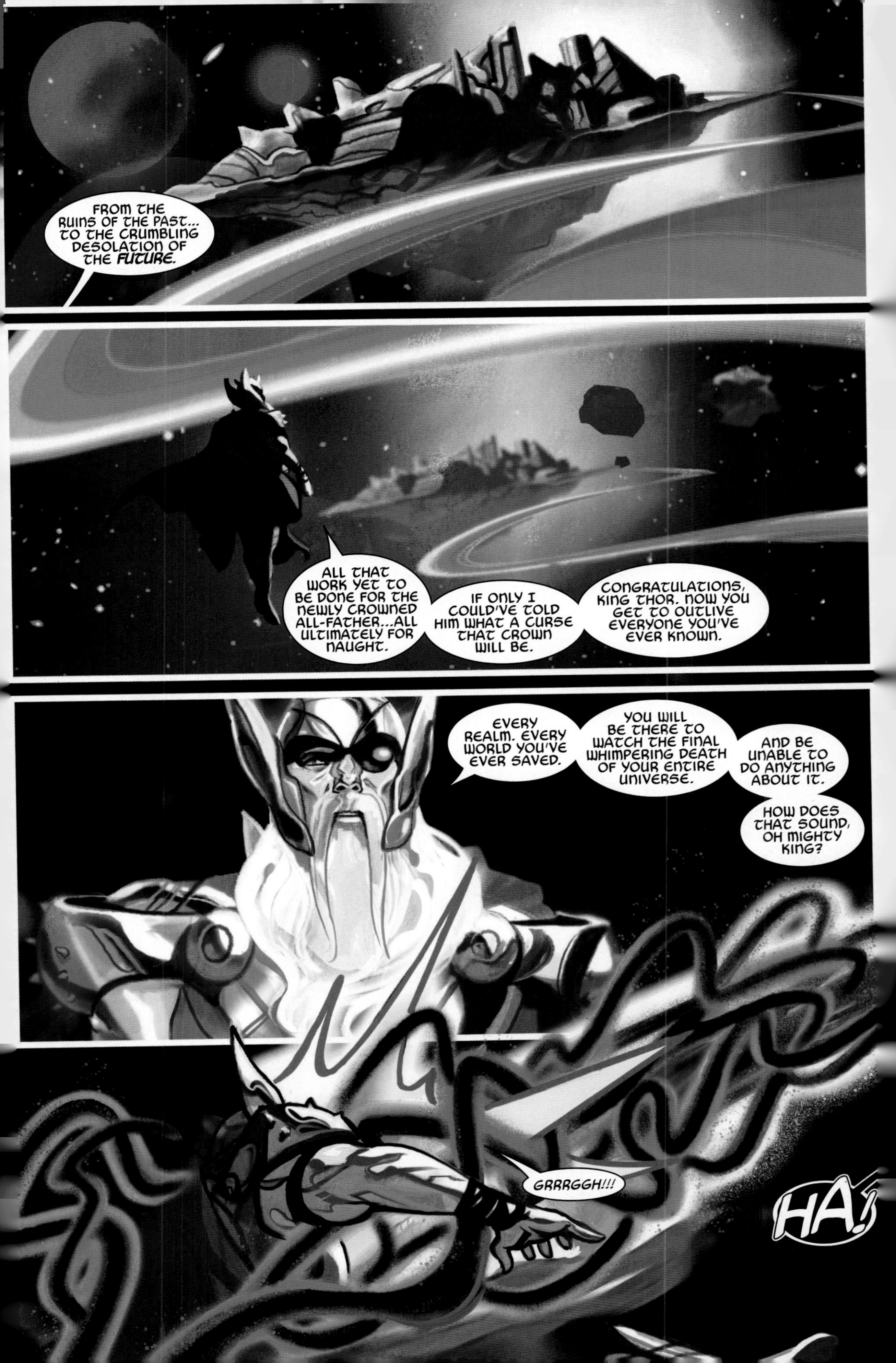
FROM THE RUINS OF THE PAST... TO THE CRUMBLING DESOLATION OF THE *FUTURE*.
ALL THAT WORK YET TO BE DONE FOR THE NEWLY CROWNED ALL-FATHER...ALL ULTIMATELY FOR NAUGHT.
IF ONLY I COULD'VE TOLD HIM WHAT A CURSE THAT CROWN WILL BE.
CONGRATULATIONS, KING THOR. NOW YOU GET TO OUTLIVE EVERYONE YOU'VE EVER KNOWN.
EVERY REALM. EVERY WORLD YOU'VE EVER SAVED.
YOU WILL BE THERE TO WATCH THE FINAL WHIMPERING DEATH OF YOUR ENTIRE UNIVERSE.
AND BE UNABLE TO DO ANYTHING ABOUT IT.
HOW DOES THAT SOUND, OH MIGHTY KING?
GRRRGGH!!!
HA!

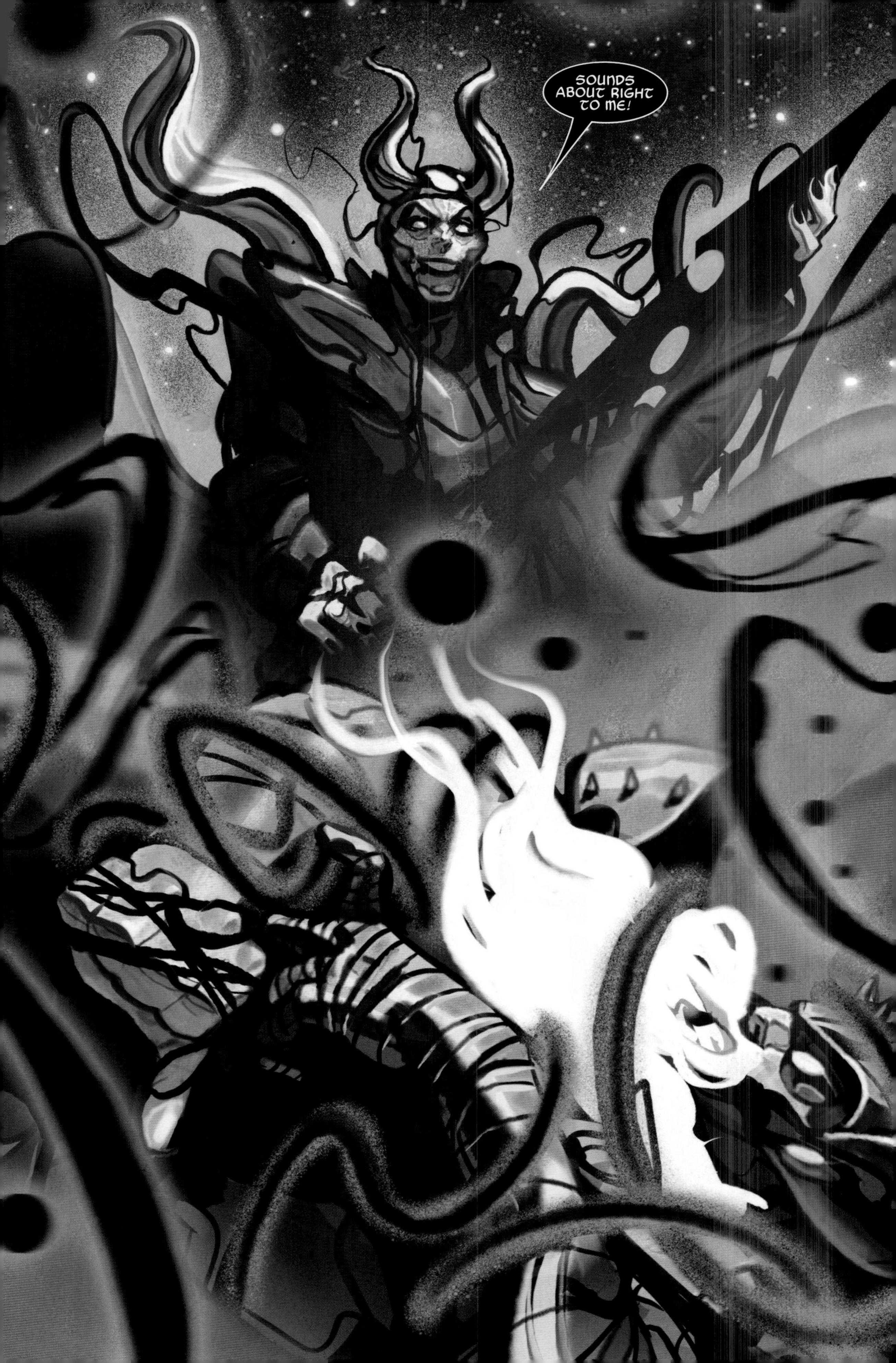
SOUNDS ABOUT RIGHT TO ME!

KING THOR 1

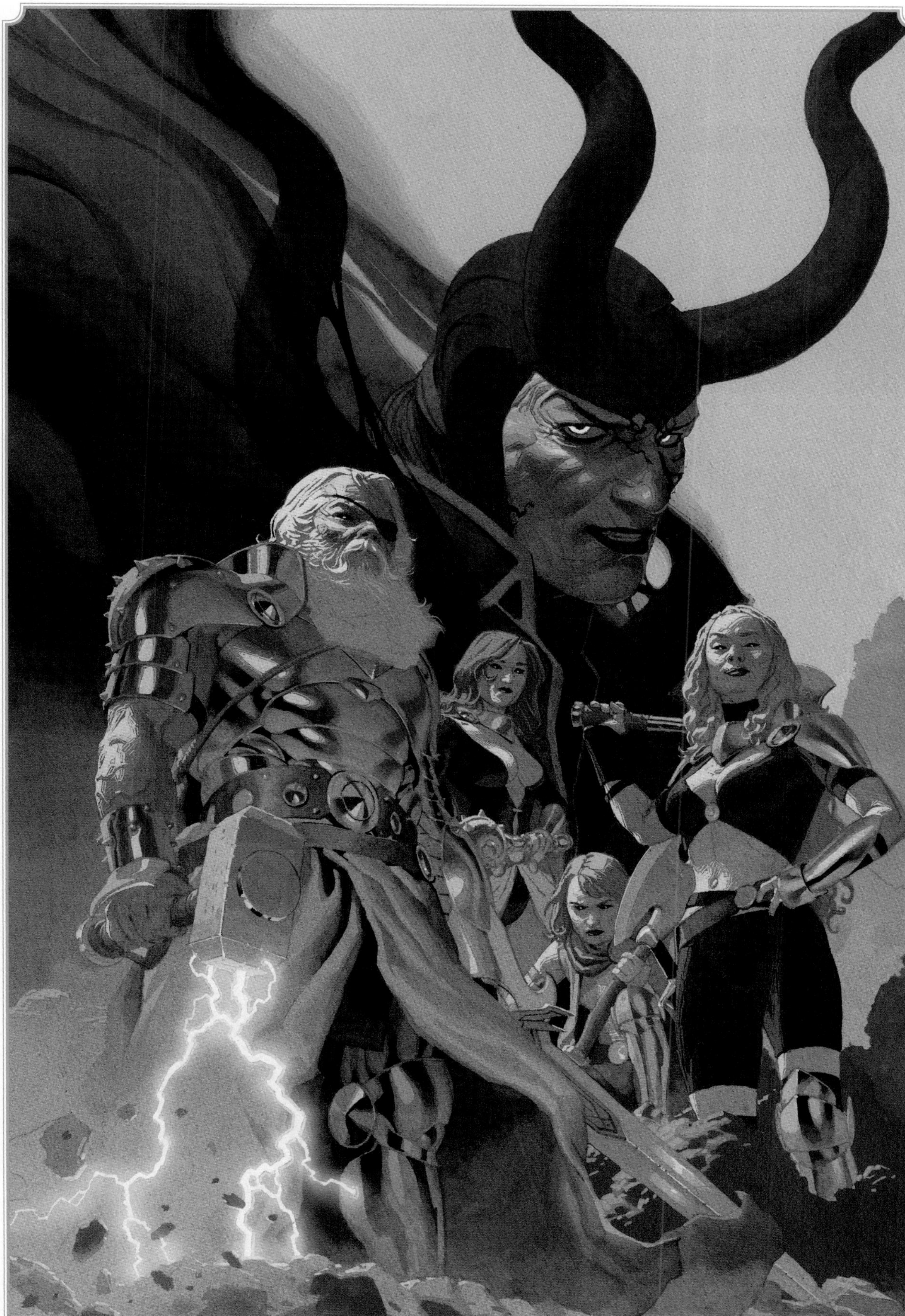

TWILIGHT OF THE THUNDER GOD

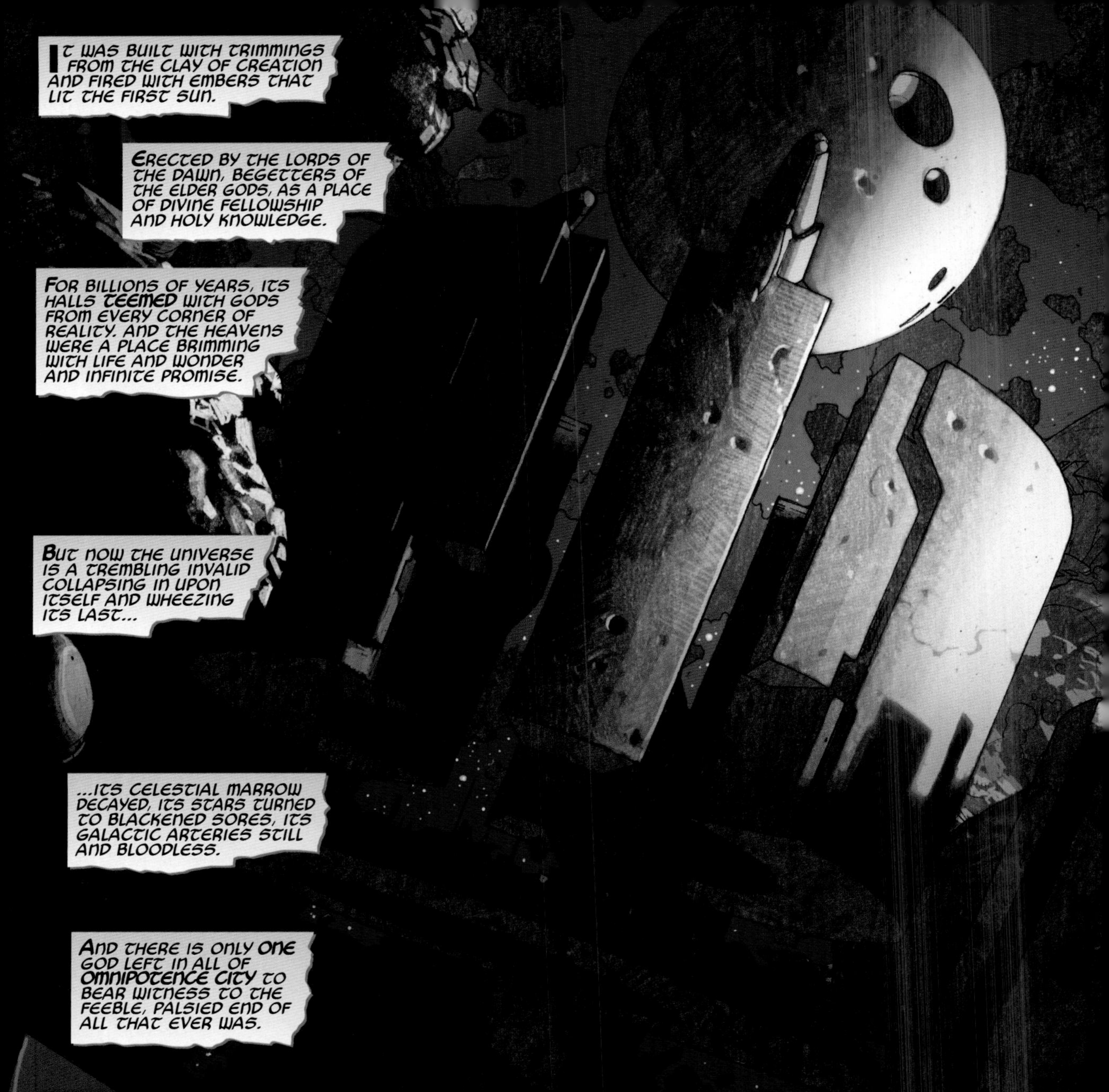
IT WAS BUILT WITH TRIMMINGS FROM THE CLAY OF CREATION AND FIRED WITH EMBERS THAT LIT THE FIRST SUN.
ERECTED BY THE LORDS OF THE DAWN, BEGETTERS OF THE ELDER GODS, AS A PLACE OF DIVINE FELLOWSHIP AND HOLY KNOWLEDGE.
FOR BILLIONS OF YEARS, ITS HALLS TEEMED WITH GODS FROM EVERY CORNER OF REALITY. AND THE HEAVENS WERE A PLACE BRIMMING WITH LIFE AND WONDER AND INFINITE PROMISE.
BUT NOW THE UNIVERSE IS A TREMBLING INVALID COLLAPSING IN UPON ITSELF AND WHEEZING ITS LAST...
...ITS CELESTIAL MARROW DECAYED, ITS STARS TURNED TO BLACKENED SORES, ITS GALACTIC ARTERIES STILL AND BLOODLESS.
AND THERE IS ONLY ONE GOD LEFT IN ALL OF OMNIPOTENCE CITY TO BEAR WITNESS TO THE FEEBLE, PALSIED END OF ALL THAT EVER WAS.
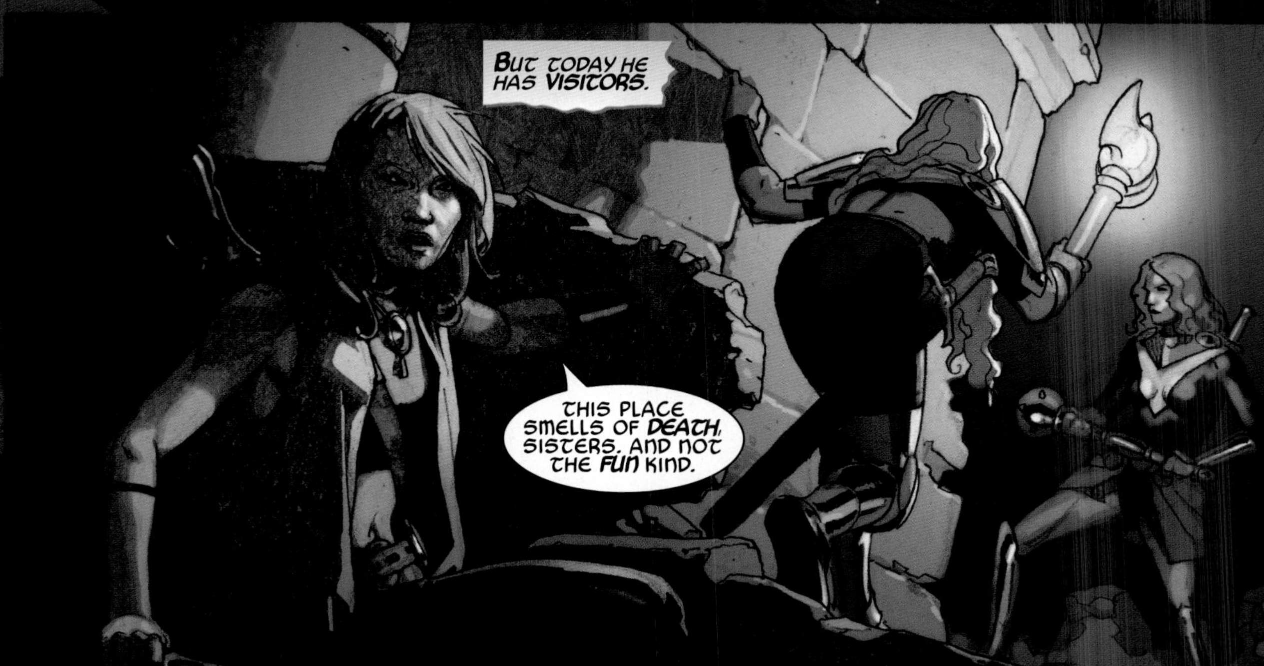
BUT TODAY HE HAS VISITORS.
THIS PLACE SMELLS OF DEATH, SISTERS. AND NOT THE FUN KIND.

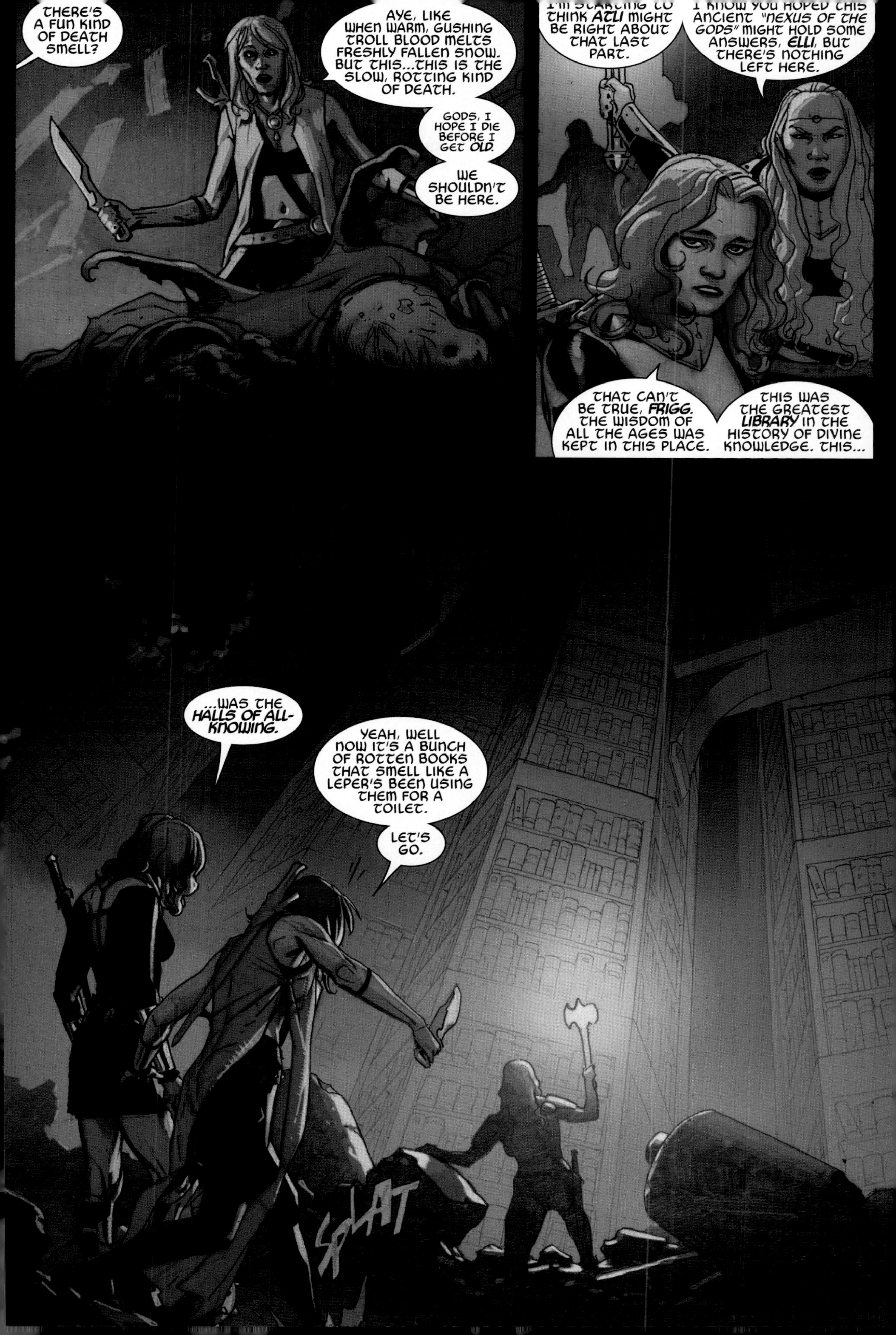
THERE'S A FUN KIND OF DEATH SMELL?
AYE, LIKE WHEN WARM, GUSHING TROLL BLOOD MELTS FRESHLY FALLEN SNOW. BUT THIS...THIS IS THE SLOW, ROTTING KIND OF DEATH.
GODS, I HOPE I DIE BEFORE I GET OLD.
WE SHOULDN'T BE HERE.
I'M STARTING TO THINK ATLI MIGHT BE RIGHT ABOUT THAT LAST PART.
I KNOW YOU HOPED THIS ANCIENT "NEXUS OF THE GODS" MIGHT HOLD SOME ANSWERS, ELLI, BUT THERE'S NOTHING LEFT HERE.
THAT CAN'T BE TRUE, FRIGG. THE WISDOM OF ALL THE AGES WAS KEPT IN THIS PLACE.
THIS WAS THE GREATEST LIBRARY IN THE HISTORY OF DIVINE KNOWLEDGE. THIS...
...WAS THE HALLS OF ALL-KNOWING.
YEAH, WELL NOW IT'S A BUNCH OF ROTTEN BOOKS THAT SMELL LIKE A LEPER'S BEEN USING THEM FOR A TOILET.
LET'S GO.
SPLAT

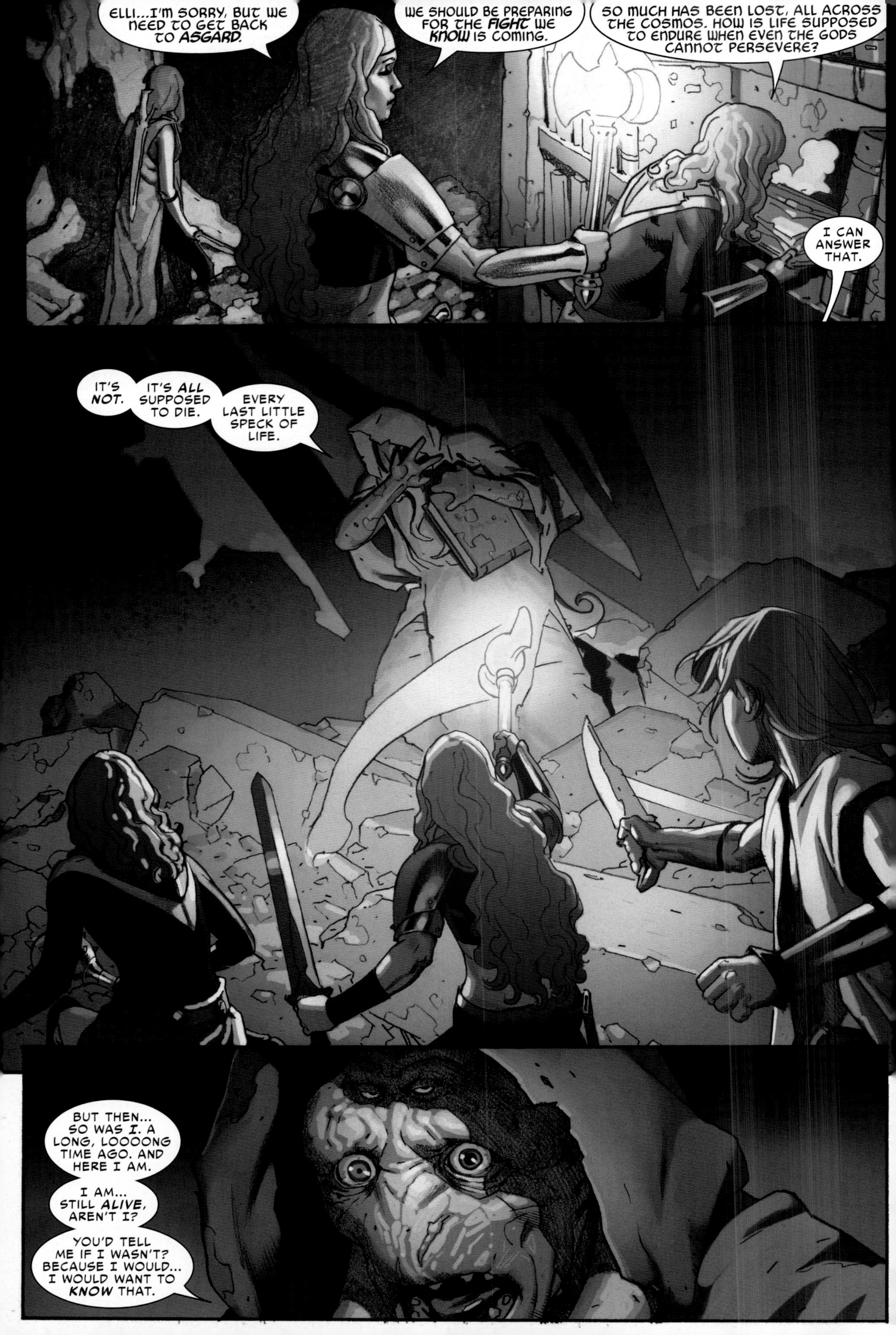
ELLI...I'M SORRY, BUT WE NEED TO GET BACK TO ASGARD.
WE SHOULD BE PREPARING FOR THE FIGHT WE KNOW IS COMING.
SO MUCH HAS BEEN LOST, ALL ACROSS THE COSMOS. HOW IS LIFE SUPPOSED TO ENDURE WHEN EVEN THE GODS CANNOT PERSEVERE?
I CAN ANSWER THAT.
IT'S NOT.
IT'S ALL SUPPOSED TO DIE.
EVERY LAST LITTLE SPECK OF LIFE.
BUT THEN... SO WAS I. A LONG, LOOOONG TIME AGO. AND HERE I AM.
I AM... STILL ALIVE, AREN'T I?
YOU'D TELL ME IF I WASN'T? BECAUSE I WOULD... I WOULD WANT TO KNOW THAT.

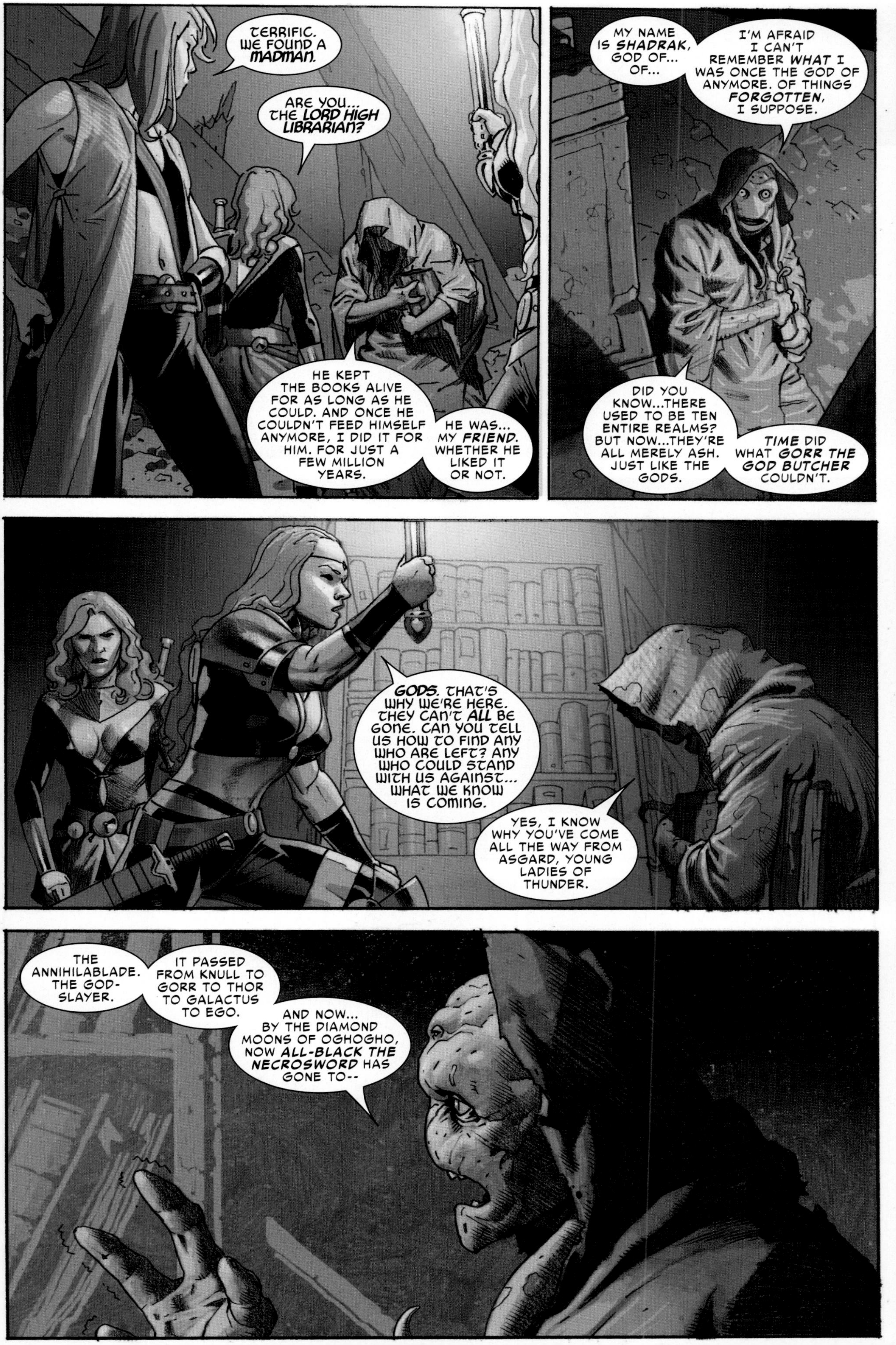
TERRIFIC. WE FOUND A MADMAN.
ARE YOU... THE LORD HIGH LIBRARIAN?
HE KEPT THE BOOKS ALIVE FOR AS LONG AS HE COULD. AND ONCE HE COULDN'T FEED HIMSELF ANYMORE, I DID IT FOR HIM. FOR JUST A FEW MILLION YEARS.
HE WAS... MY FRIEND. WHETHER HE LIKED IT OR NOT.
MY NAME IS SHADRAK, GOD OF... OF...
I'M AFRAID I CAN'T REMEMBER WHAT I WAS ONCE THE GOD OF ANYMORE. OF THINGS FORGOTTEN, I SUPPOSE.
DID YOU KNOW...THERE USED TO BE TEN ENTIRE REALMS? BUT NOW...THEY'RE ALL MERELY ASH. JUST LIKE THE GODS.
TIME DID WHAT GORR THE GOD BUTCHER COULDN'T.
GODS. THAT'S WHY WE'RE HERE. THEY CAN'T ALL BE GONE. CAN YOU TELL US HOW TO FIND ANY WHO ARE LEFT? ANY WHO COULD STAND WITH US AGAINST... WHAT WE KNOW IS COMING.
YES, I KNOW WHY YOU'VE COME ALL THE WAY FROM ASGARD, YOUNG LADIES OF THUNDER.
THE ANNIHILABLADE. THE GOD-SLAYER.
IT PASSED FROM KNULL TO GORR TO THOR TO GALACTUS TO EGO.
AND NOW... BY THE DIAMOND MOONS OF OGHOGHO, NOW ALL-BLACK THE NECROSWORD HAS GONE TO--

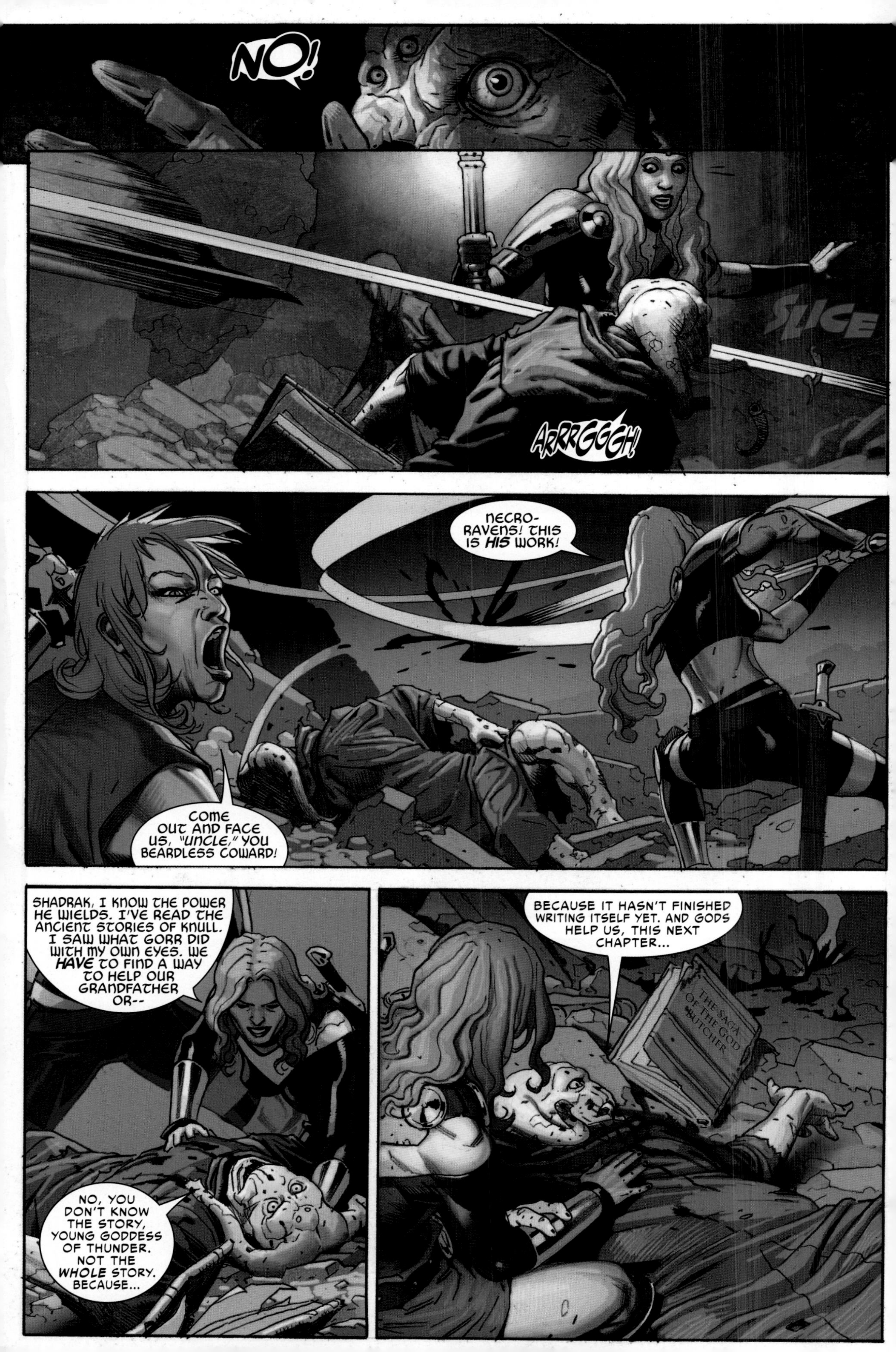
NO!
SLICE
ARRRGGGH!
NECRO-RAVENS! THIS IS HIS WORK!
COME OUT AND FACE US, "UNCLE," YOU BEARDLESS COWARD!
SHADRAK, I KNOW THE POWER HE WIELDS. I'VE READ THE ANCIENT STORIES OF KNULL. I SAW WHAT GORR DID WITH MY OWN EYES. WE HAVE TO FIND A WAY TO HELP OUR GRANDFATHER OR--
NO, YOU DON'T KNOW THE STORY, YOUNG GODDESS OF THUNDER. NOT THE WHOLE STORY. BECAUSE...
BECAUSE IT HASN'T FINISHED WRITING ITSELF YET. AND GODS HELP US, THIS NEXT CHAPTER...
THE SAGA OF THE GOD BUTCHER

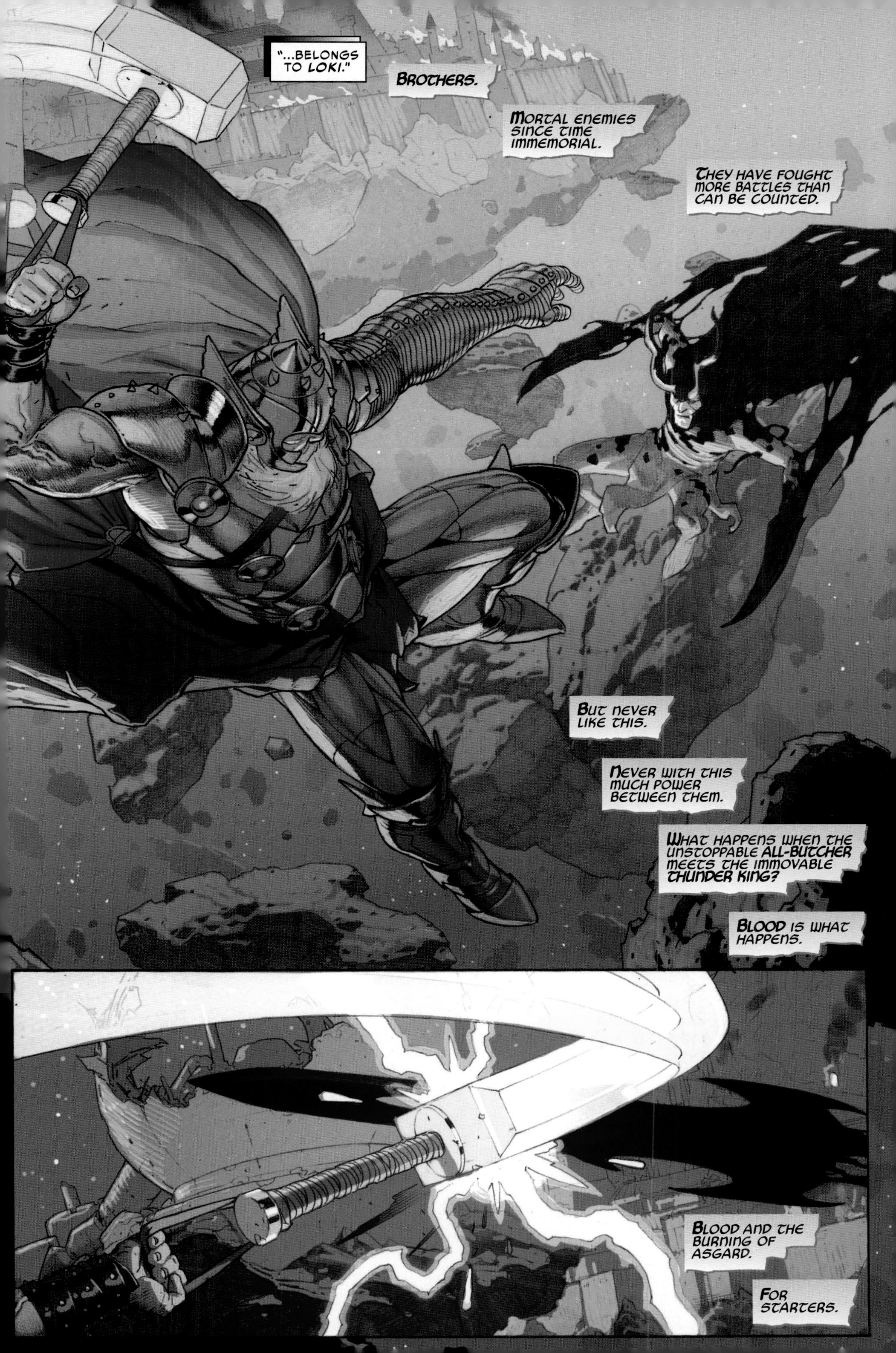
"...BELONGS TO LOKI."
BROTHERS.
MORTAL ENEMIES SINCE TIME IMMEMORIAL.
THEY HAVE FOUGHT MORE BATTLES THAN CAN BE COUNTED.
BUT NEVER LIKE THIS.
NEVER WITH THIS MUCH POWER BETWEEN THEM.
WHAT HAPPENS WHEN THE UNSTOPPABLE ALL-BUTCHER MEETS THE IMMOVABLE THUNDER KING?
BLOOD IS WHAT HAPPENS.
BLOOD AND THE BURNING OF ASGARD.
FOR STARTERS.

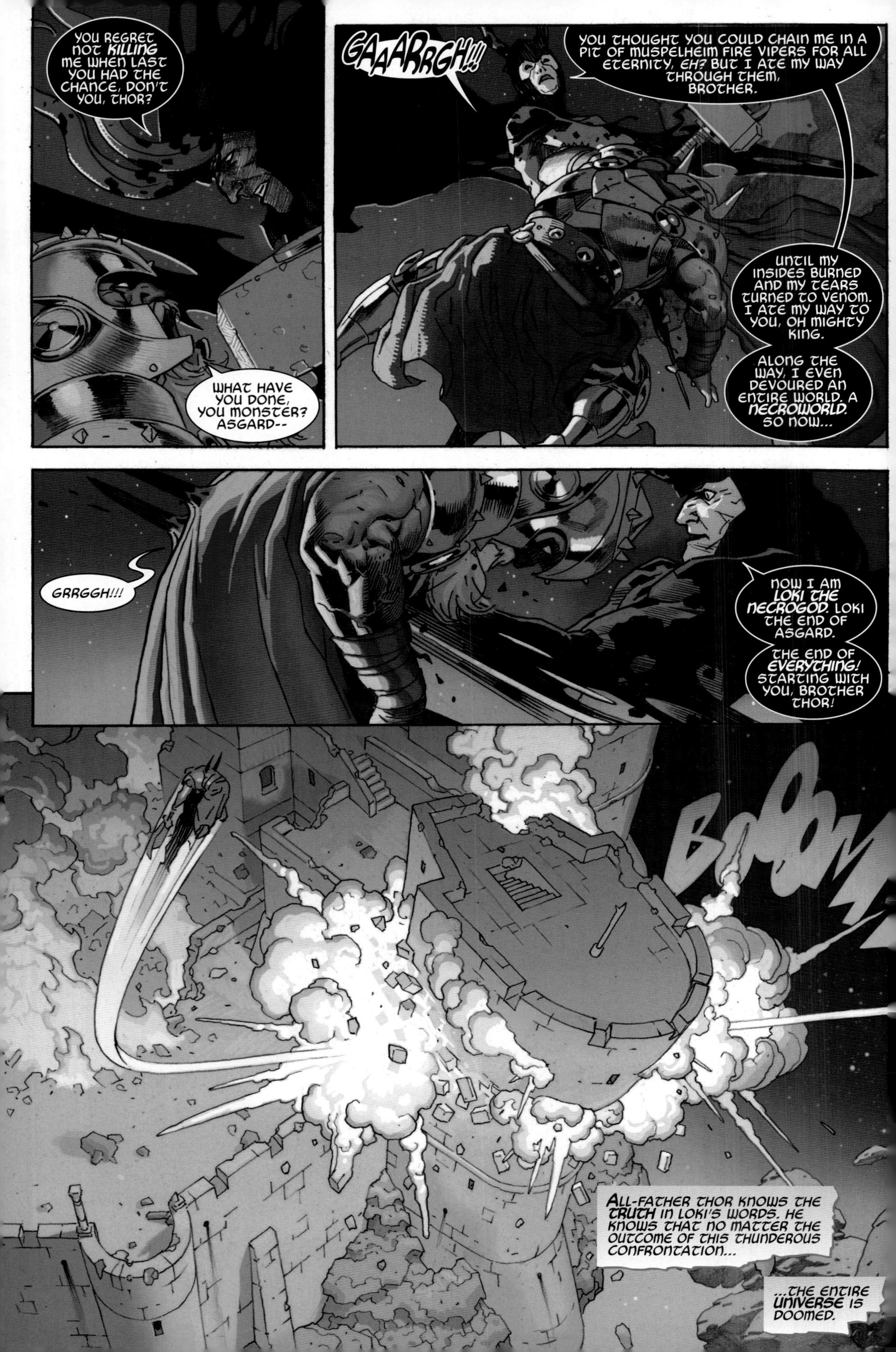
YOU REGRET NOT KILLING ME WHEN LAST YOU HAD THE CHANCE, DON'T YOU, THOR?
WHAT HAVE YOU DONE, YOU MONSTER? ASGARD--
GAAARRGH!!!
YOU THOUGHT YOU COULD CHAIN ME IN A PIT OF MUSPELHEIM FIRE VIPERS FOR ALL ETERNITY, EH? BUT I ATE MY WAY THROUGH THEM, BROTHER.
UNTIL MY INSIDES BURNED AND MY TEARS TURNED TO VENOM. I ATE MY WAY TO YOU, OH MIGHTY KING.
ALONG THE WAY, I EVEN DEVOURED AN ENTIRE WORLD. A NECROWORLD. SO NOW...
GRRGGH!!!
NOW I AM LOKI THE NECROGOD. LOKI THE END OF ASGARD.
THE END OF EVERYTHING! STARTING WITH YOU, BROTHER THOR!
ALL-FATHER THOR KNOWS THE TRUTH IN LOKI'S WORDS. HE KNOWS THAT NO MATTER THE OUTCOME OF THIS THUNDEROUS CONFRONTATION...
...THE ENTIRE UNIVERSE IS DOOMED.

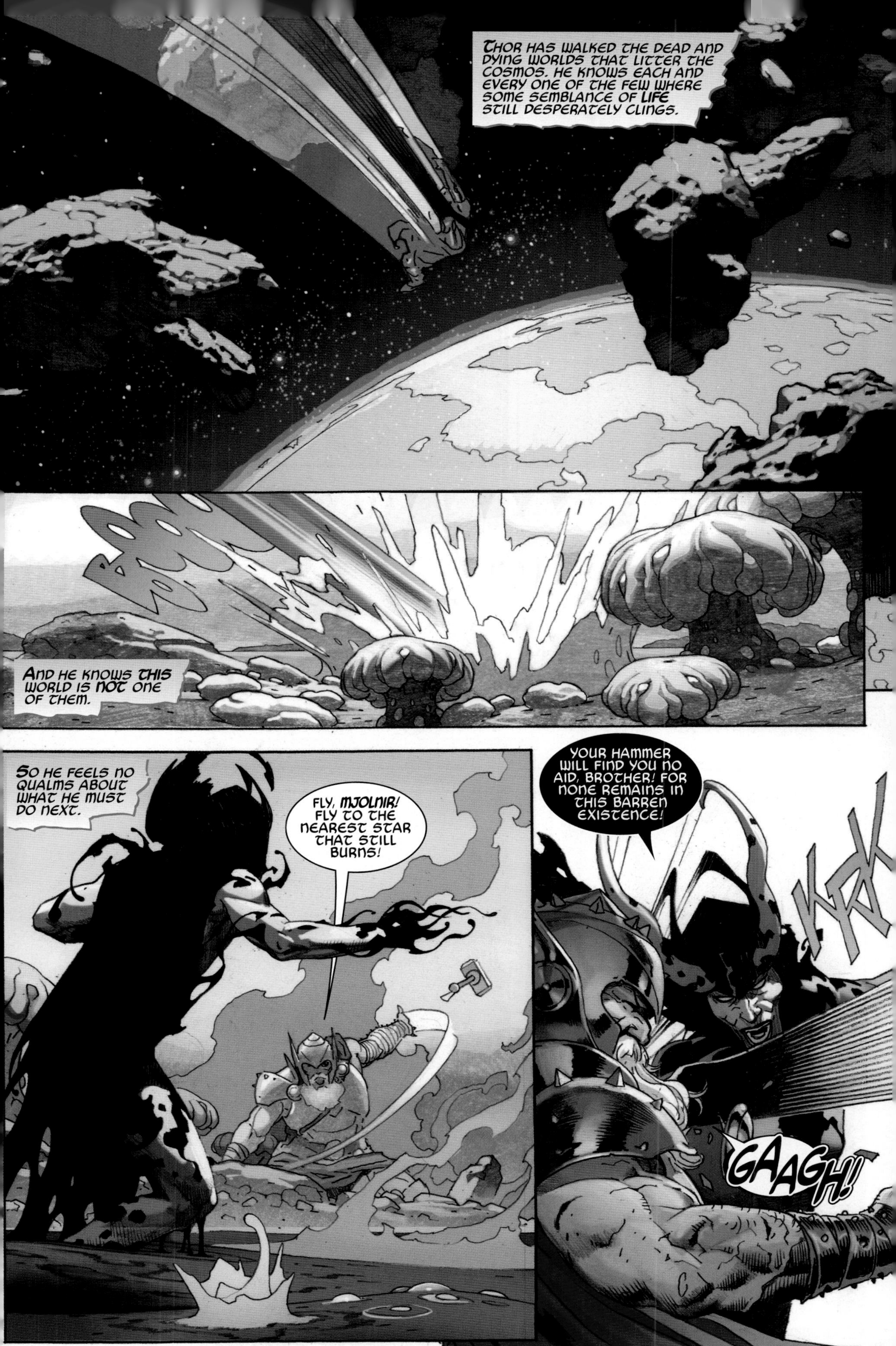
THOR HAS WALKED THE DEAD AND DYING WORLDS THAT LITTER THE COSMOS. HE KNOWS EACH AND EVERY ONE OF THE FEW WHERE SOME SEMBLANCE OF LIFE STILL DESPERATELY CLINGS.
AND HE KNOWS THIS WORLD IS NOT ONE OF THEM.
SO HE FEELS NO QUALMS ABOUT WHAT HE MUST DO NEXT.
FLY, MJOLNIR! FLY TO THE NEAREST STAR THAT STILL BURNS!
YOUR HAMMER WILL FIND YOU NO AID, BROTHER! FOR NONE REMAINS IN THIS BARREN EXISTENCE!
GAAGH!

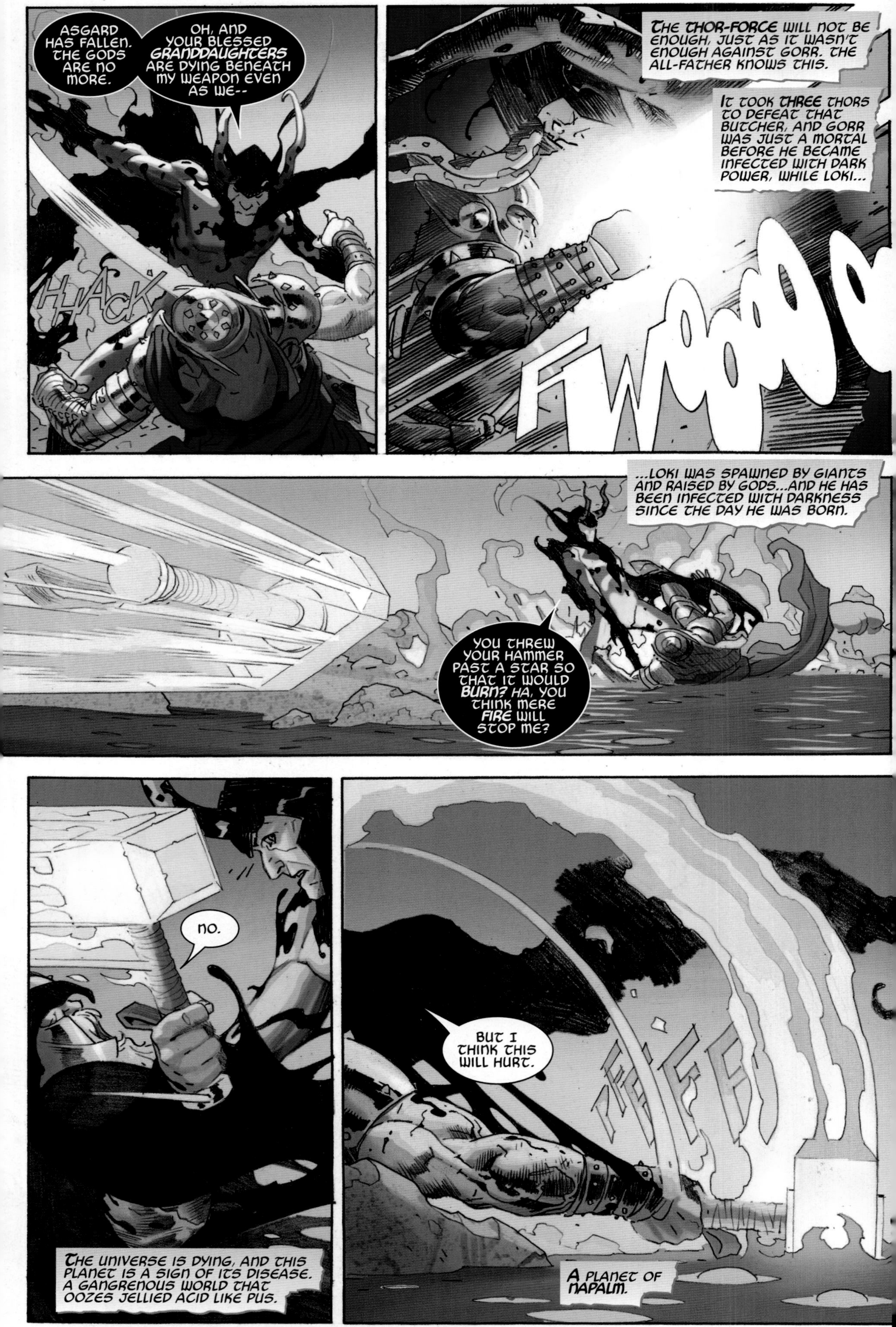

ASGARD HAS FALLEN. THE GODS ARE NO MORE.
OH, AND YOUR BLESSED GRANDDAUGHTERS ARE DYING BENEATH MY WEAPON EVEN AS WE--
THHACK
THE THOR-FORCE WILL NOT BE ENOUGH, JUST AS IT WASN'T ENOUGH AGAINST GORR. THE ALL-FATHER KNOWS THIS.
IT TOOK THREE THORS TO DEFEAT THAT BUTCHER, AND GORR WAS JUST A MORTAL BEFORE HE BECAME INFECTED WITH DARK POWER, WHILE LOKI...
FWOOOO
...LOKI WAS SPAWNED BY GIANTS AND RAISED BY GODS...AND HE HAS BEEN INFECTED WITH DARKNESS SINCE THE DAY HE WAS BORN.
YOU THREW YOUR HAMMER PAST A STAR SO THAT IT WOULD BURN? HA, YOU THINK MERE FIRE WILL STOP ME?
NO.
THE UNIVERSE IS DYING, AND THIS PLANET IS A SIGN OF ITS DISEASE. A GANGRENOUS WORLD THAT OOZES JELLIED ACID LIKE PUS.
BUT I THINK THIS WILL HURT.
A PLANET OF NAPALM.

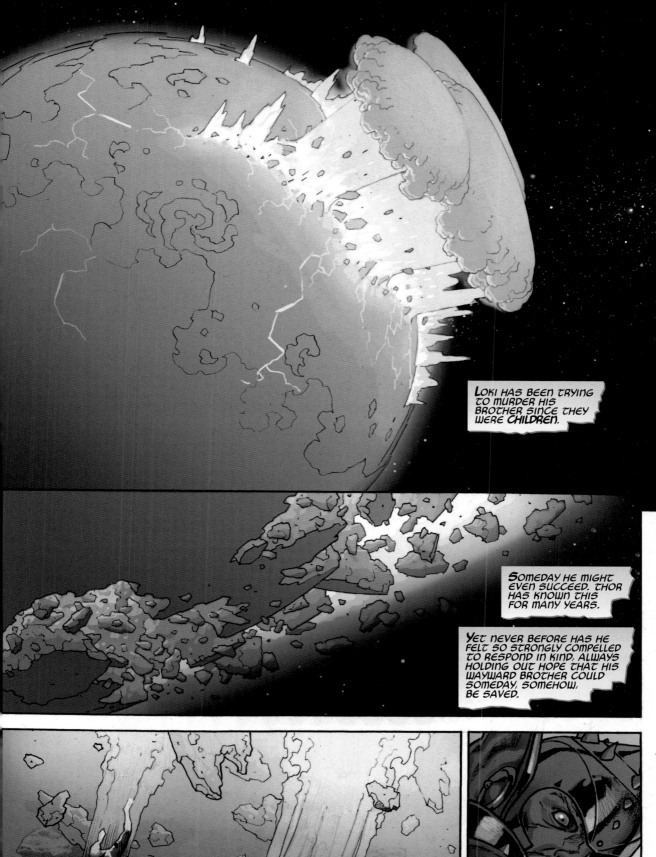

LOKI HAS BEEN TRYING TO MURDER HIS BROTHER SINCE THEY WERE CHILDREN.

SOMEDAY HE MIGHT EVEN SUCCEED. THOR HAS KNOWN THIS FOR MANY YEARS.

YET NEVER BEFORE HAS HE FELT SO STRONGLY COMPELLED TO RESPOND IN KIND, ALWAYS HOLDING OUT HOPE THAT HIS WAYWARD BROTHER COULD SOMEDAY, SOMEHOW, BE SAVED.

BUT FOR THE UNIVERSE TO SURVIVE, FOR MANKIND TO OUTLIVE ITS GODS, KING THOR NOW ACCEPTS THE DARK TRUTH...

...THAT LOKI MUST DIE.

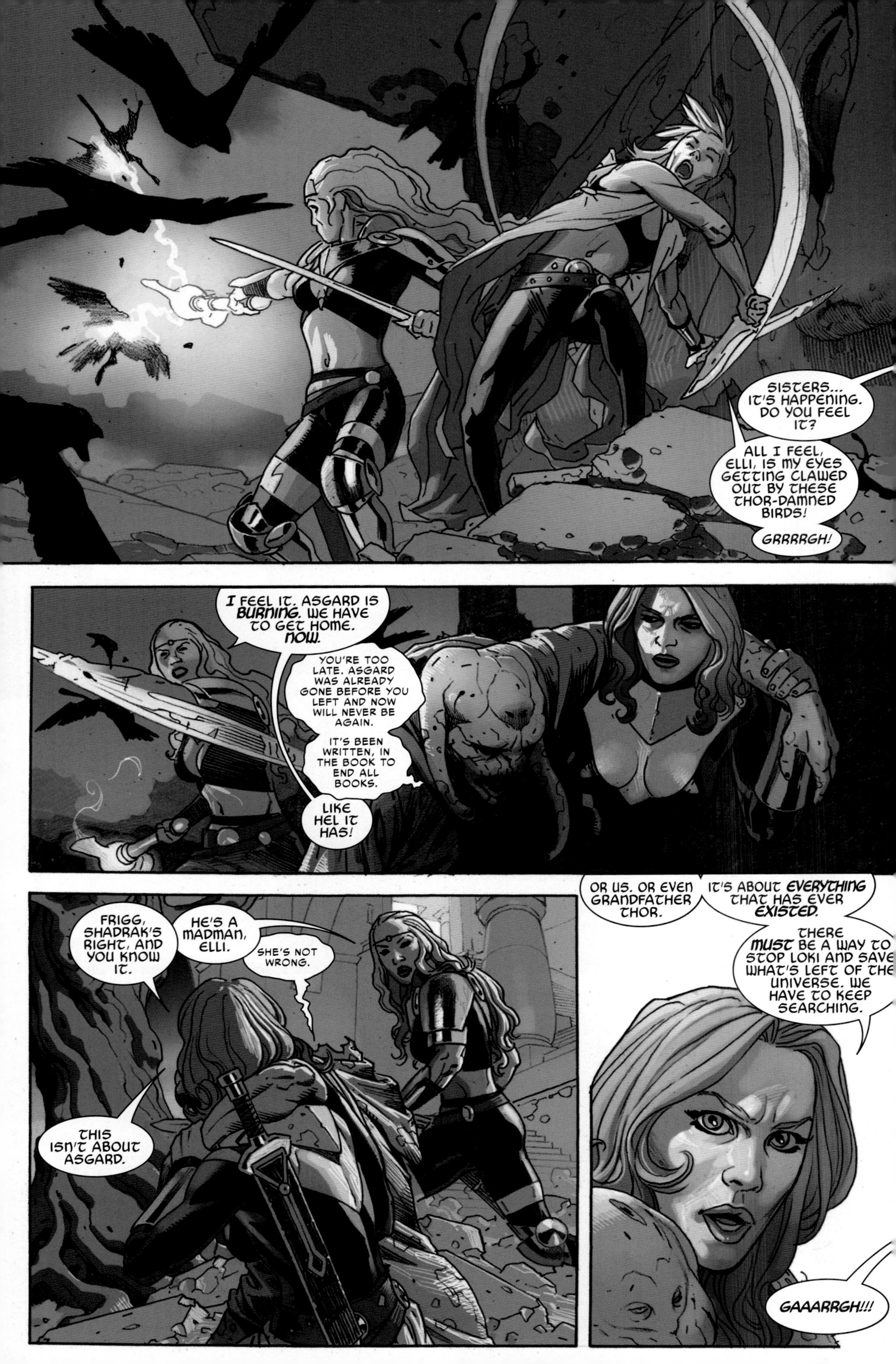
SISTERS... IT'S HAPPENING. DO YOU FEEL IT?
ALL I FEEL, ELLI, IS MY EYES GETTING CLAWED OUT BY THESE THOR-DAMNED BIRDS!
GRRRRGH!
I FEEL IT. ASGARD IS BURNING. WE HAVE TO GET HOME. NOW.
YOU'RE TOO LATE. ASGARD WAS ALREADY GONE BEFORE YOU LEFT AND NOW WILL NEVER BE AGAIN.
IT'S BEEN WRITTEN, IN THE BOOK TO END ALL BOOKS.
LIKE HEL IT HAS!
FRIGG, SHADRAK'S RIGHT, AND YOU KNOW IT.
HE'S A MADMAN, ELLI.
SHE'S NOT WRONG.
THIS ISN'T ABOUT ASGARD.
OR US. OR EVEN GRANDFATHER THOR.
IT'S ABOUT EVERYTHING THAT HAS EVER EXISTED.
THERE MUST BE A WAY TO STOP LOKI AND SAVE WHAT'S LEFT OF THE UNIVERSE. WE HAVE TO KEEP SEARCHING.
GAAARRGH!!!

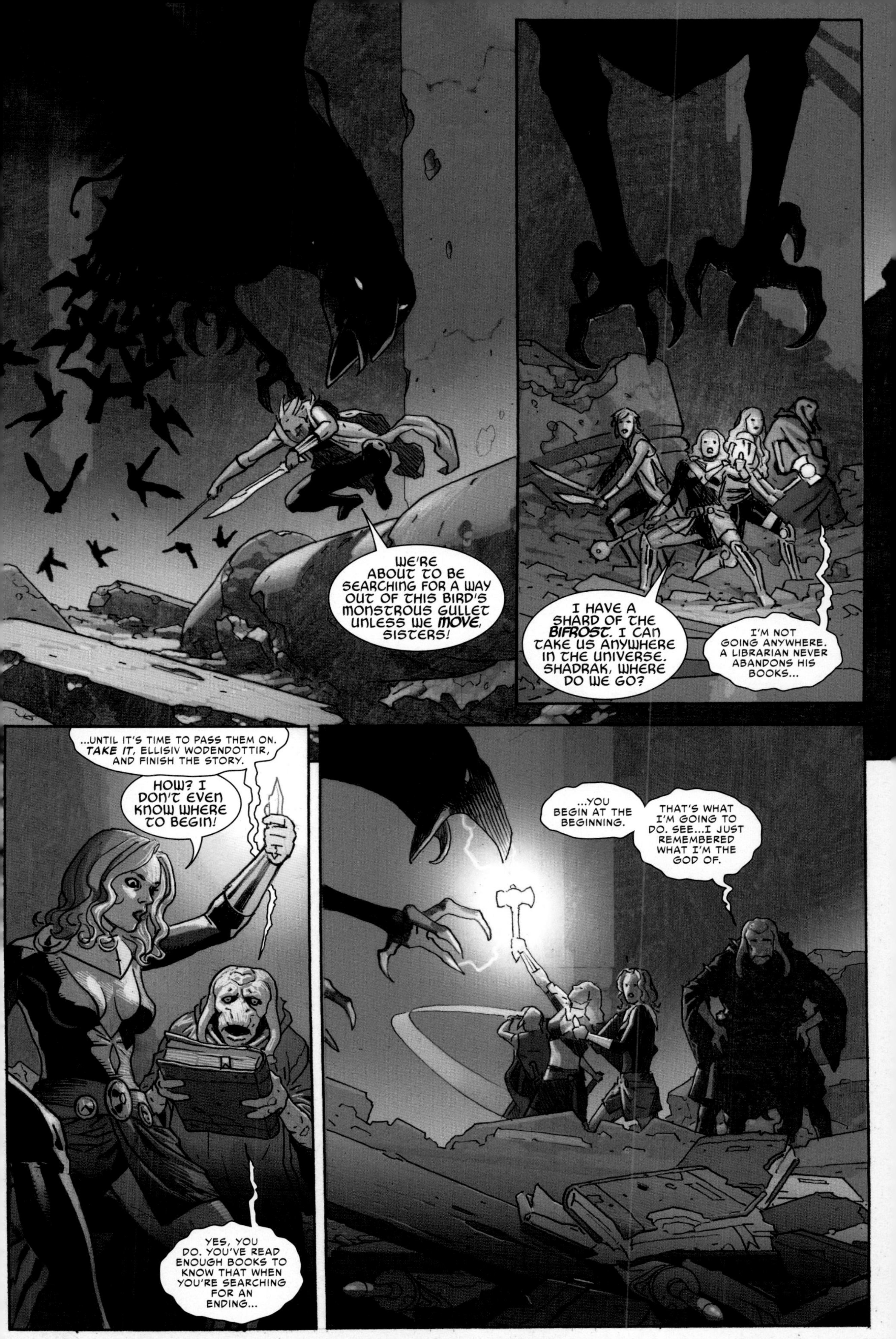
WE'RE ABOUT TO BE SEARCHING FOR A WAY OUT OF THIS BIRD'S MONSTROUS GULLET UNLESS WE *MOVE*, SISTERS!
I HAVE A SHARD OF THE *BIFROST*. I CAN TAKE US ANYWHERE IN THE UNIVERSE. SHADRAK, WHERE DO WE GO?
I'M NOT GOING ANYWHERE. A LIBRARIAN NEVER ABANDONS HIS BOOKS...
...UNTIL IT'S TIME TO PASS THEM ON. *TAKE IT*, ELLISIV WODENDOTTIR, AND FINISH THE STORY.
HOW? I DON'T EVEN KNOW WHERE TO BEGIN!
YES, YOU DO. YOU'VE READ ENOUGH BOOKS TO KNOW THAT WHEN YOU'RE SEARCHING FOR AN ENDING...
...YOU BEGIN AT THE BEGINNING.
THAT'S WHAT I'M GOING TO DO. SEE...I JUST REMEMBERED WHAT I'M THE GOD OF.

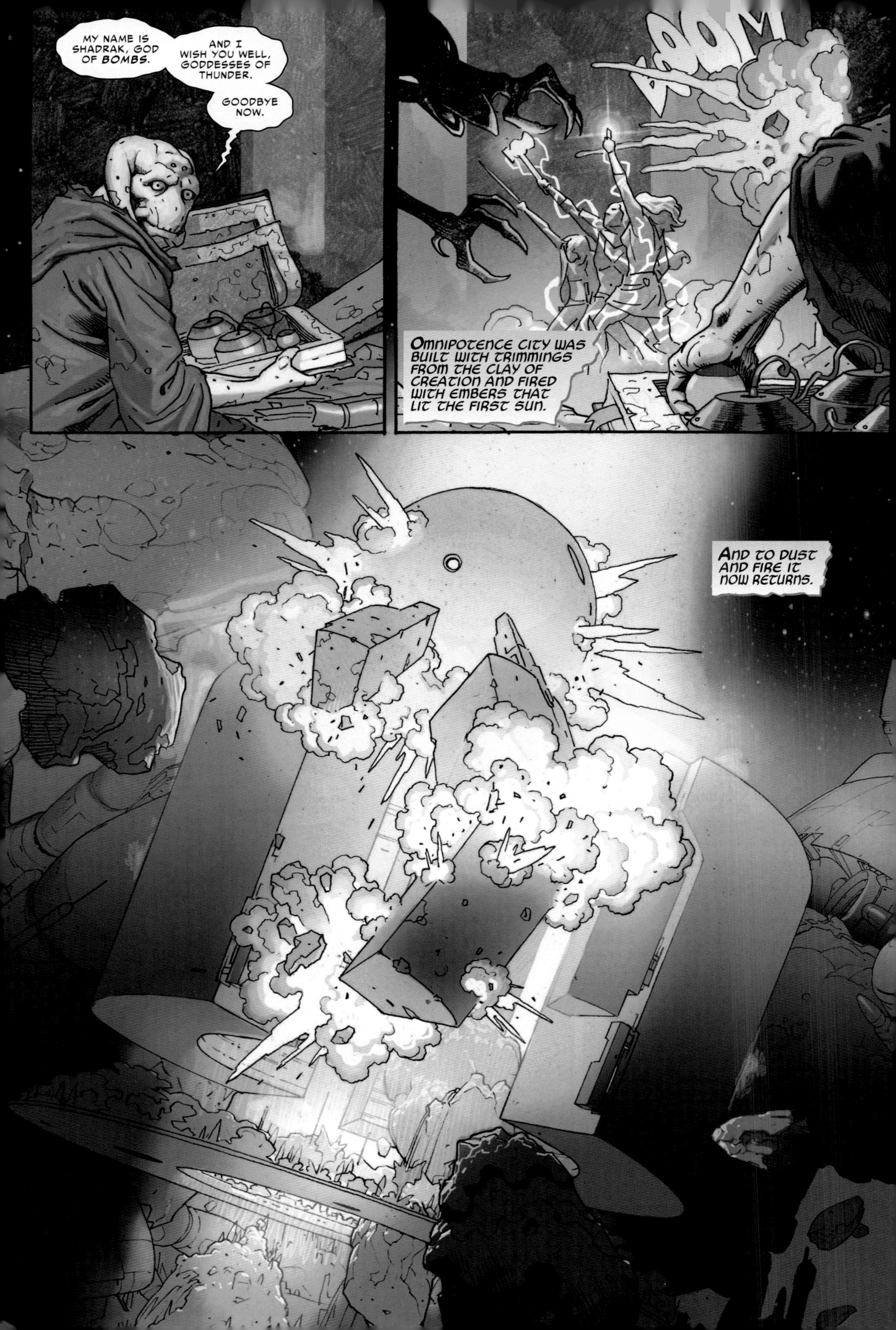
MY NAME IS SHADRAK, GOD OF BOMBS.
AND I WISH YOU WELL, GODDESSES OF THUNDER.
GOODBYE NOW.
BOOM
OMNIPOTENCE CITY WAS BUILT WITH TRIMMINGS FROM THE CLAY OF CREATION AND FIRED WITH EMBERS THAT LIT THE FIRST SUN.
AND TO DUST AND FIRE IT NOW RETURNS.

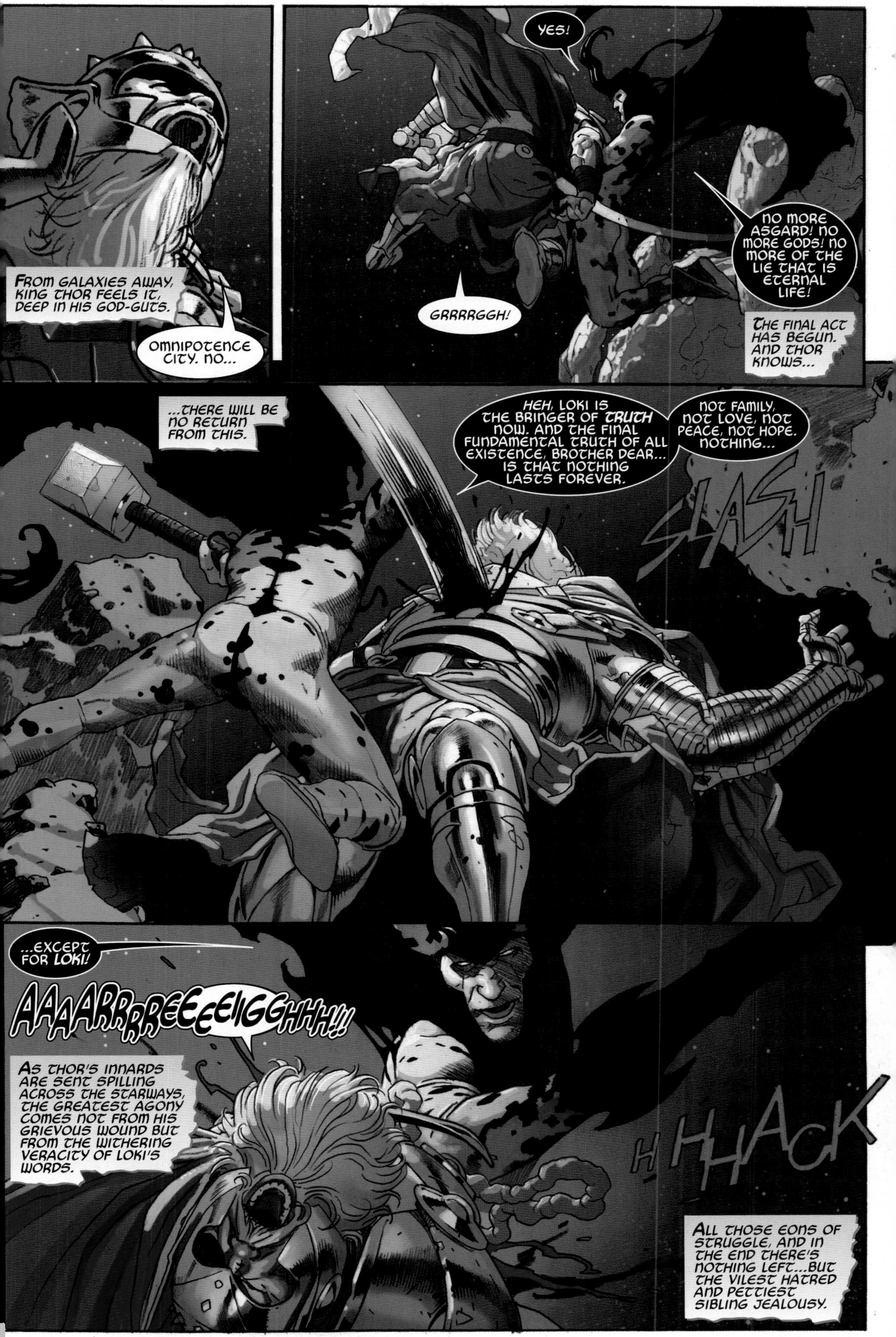
FROM GALAXIES AWAY, KING THOR FEELS IT, DEEP IN HIS GOD-GUTS.
OMNIPOTENCE CITY. NO...
YES!
GRRRRGGH!
NO MORE ASGARD! NO MORE GODS! NO MORE OF THE LIE THAT IS ETERNAL LIFE!
THE FINAL ACT HAS BEGUN. AND THOR KNOWS...
...THERE WILL BE NO RETURN FROM THIS.
HEH, LOKI IS THE BRINGER OF TRUTH NOW. AND THE FINAL FUNDAMENTAL TRUTH OF ALL EXISTENCE, BROTHER DEAR... IS THAT NOTHING LASTS FOREVER.
NOT FAMILY, NOT LOVE, NOT PEACE, NOT HOPE. NOTHING...
SLASH
...EXCEPT FOR LOKI!
AAAARRRRREEEEEIIGGHHH!!
AS THOR'S INNARDS ARE SENT SPILLING ACROSS THE STARWAYS, THE GREATEST AGONY COMES NOT FROM HIS GRIEVOUS WOUND BUT FROM THE WITHERING VERACITY OF LOKI'S WORDS.
HHHACK
ALL THOSE EONS OF STRUGGLE, AND IN THE END THERE'S NOTHING LEFT...BUT THE VILEST HATRED AND PETTIEST SIBLING JEALOUSY.

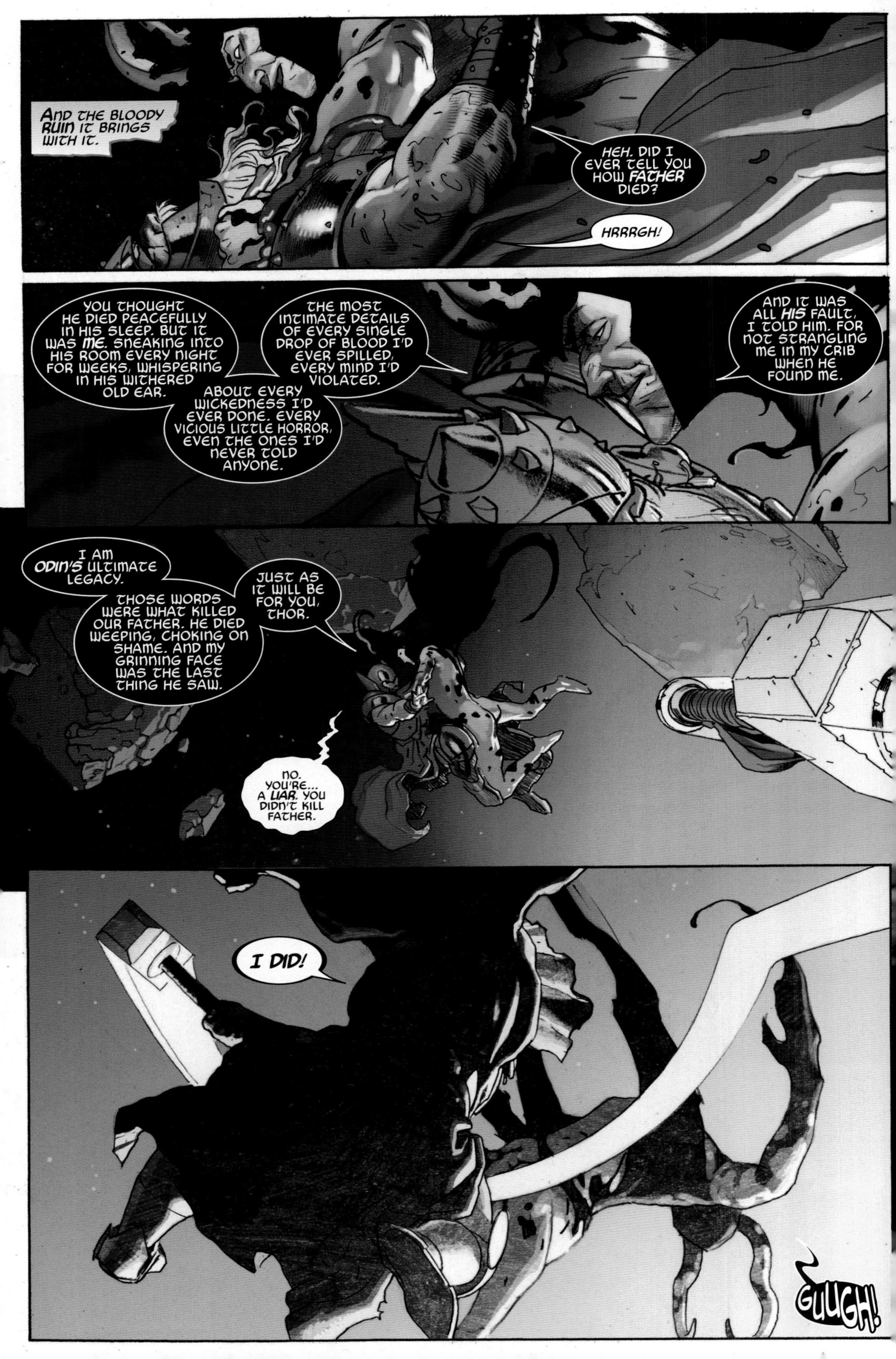
AND THE BLOODY RUIN IT BRINGS WITH IT.
HEH. DID I EVER TELL YOU HOW FATHER DIED?
HRRRGH!
YOU THOUGHT HE DIED PEACEFULLY IN HIS SLEEP. BUT IT WAS ME. SNEAKING INTO HIS ROOM EVERY NIGHT FOR WEEKS, WHISPERING IN HIS WITHERED OLD EAR.
ABOUT EVERY WICKEDNESS I'D EVER DONE. EVERY VICIOUS LITTLE HORROR, EVEN THE ONES I'D NEVER TOLD ANYONE.
THE MOST INTIMATE DETAILS OF EVERY SINGLE DROP OF BLOOD I'D EVER SPILLED, EVERY MIND I'D VIOLATED.
AND IT WAS ALL HIS FAULT, I TOLD HIM. FOR NOT STRANGLING ME IN MY CRIB WHEN HE FOUND ME.
I AM ODIN'S ULTIMATE LEGACY.
THOSE WORDS WERE WHAT KILLED OUR FATHER. HE DIED WEEPING, CHOKING ON SHAME. AND MY GRINNING FACE WAS THE LAST THING HE SAW.
JUST AS IT WILL BE FOR YOU, THOR.
NO. YOU'RE... A LIAR. YOU DIDN'T KILL FATHER.
I DID!
GUUGH!

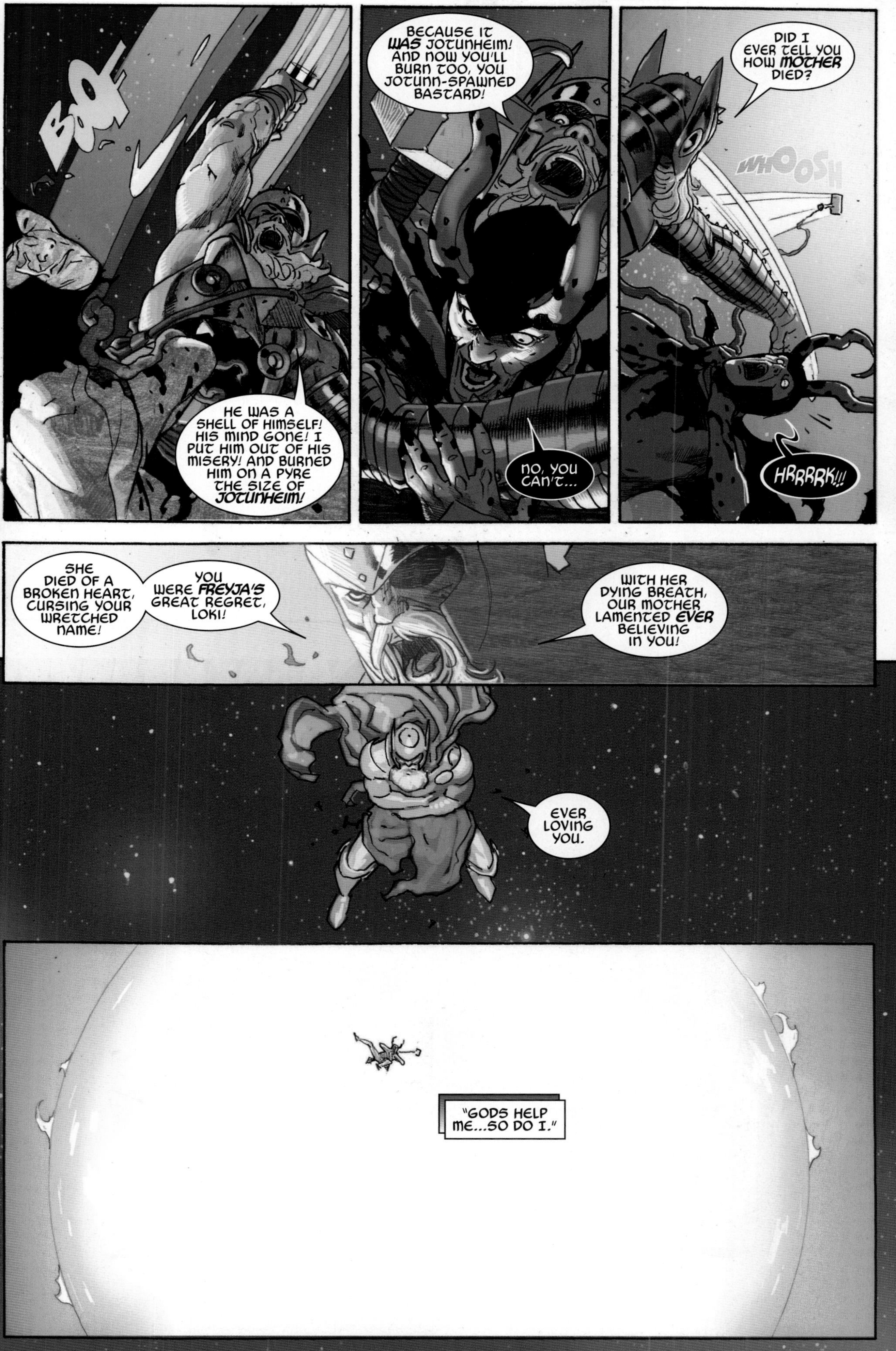
BOOM
HE WAS A SHELL OF HIMSELF! HIS MIND GONE! I PUT HIM OUT OF HIS MISERY! AND BURNED HIM ON A PYRE THE SIZE OF JOTUNHEIM!
BECAUSE IT WAS JOTUNHEIM! AND NOW YOU'LL BURN TOO, YOU JOTUNN-SPAWNED BASTARD!
NO, YOU CAN'T...
DID I EVER TELL YOU HOW MOTHER DIED?
WHOOSH
HRRRRK!!!
SHE DIED OF A BROKEN HEART, CURSING YOUR WRETCHED NAME!
YOU WERE FREYJA'S GREAT REGRET, LOKI!
WITH HER DYING BREATH, OUR MOTHER LAMENTED EVER BELIEVING IN YOU!
EVER LOVING YOU.
"GODS HELP ME...SO DO I."

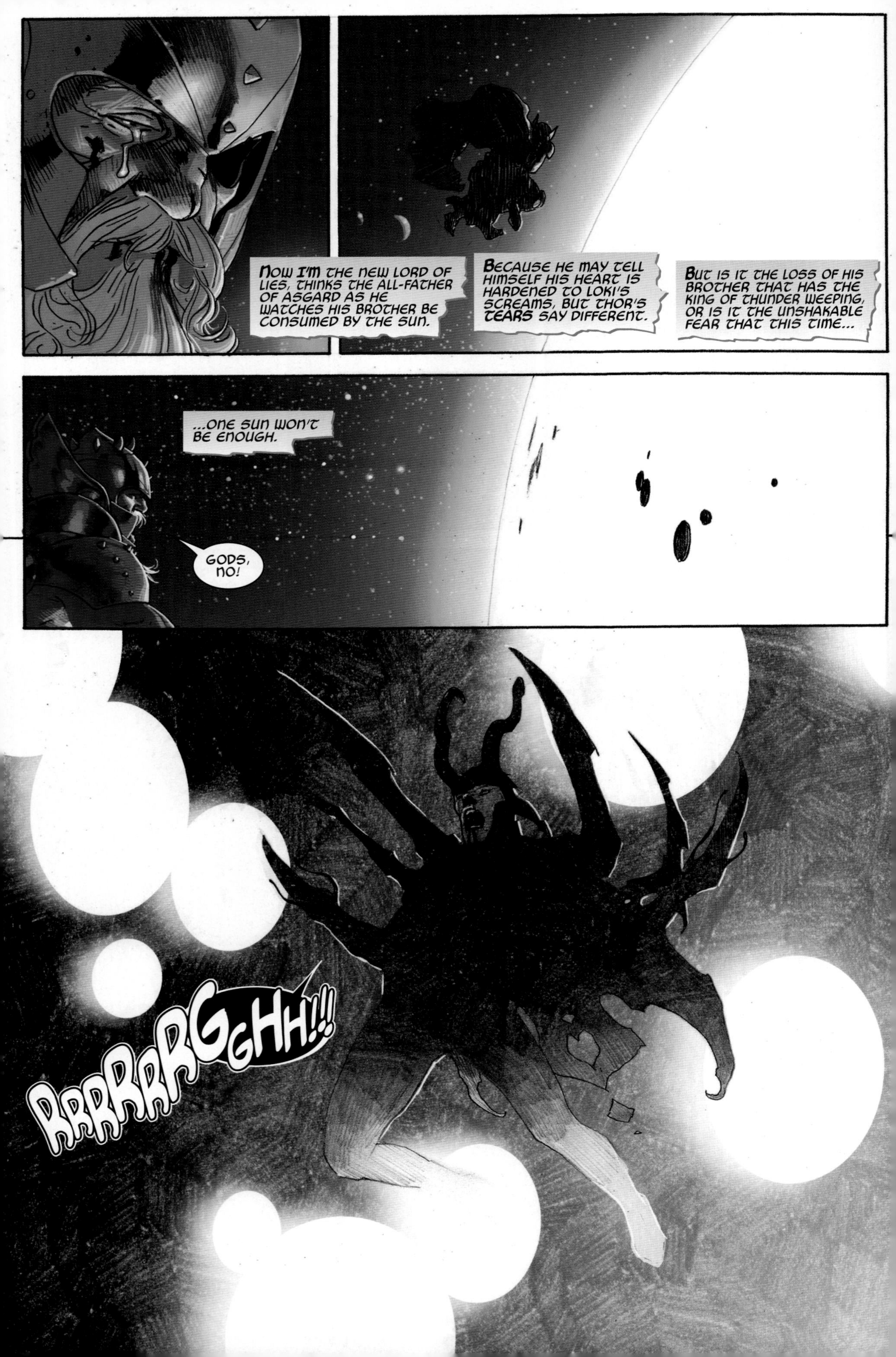
NOW I'M THE NEW LORD OF LIES, THINKS THE ALL-FATHER OF ASGARD AS HE WATCHES HIS BROTHER BE CONSUMED BY THE SUN.
BECAUSE HE MAY TELL HIMSELF HIS HEART IS HARDENED TO LOKI'S SCREAMS, BUT THOR'S TEARS SAY DIFFERENT.
BUT IS IT THE LOSS OF HIS BROTHER THAT HAS THE KING OF THUNDER WEEPING, OR IS IT THE UNSHAKABLE FEAR THAT THIS TIME...
...ONE SUN WON'T BE ENOUGH.
GODS, NO!
RRRRRRGGHH!!!

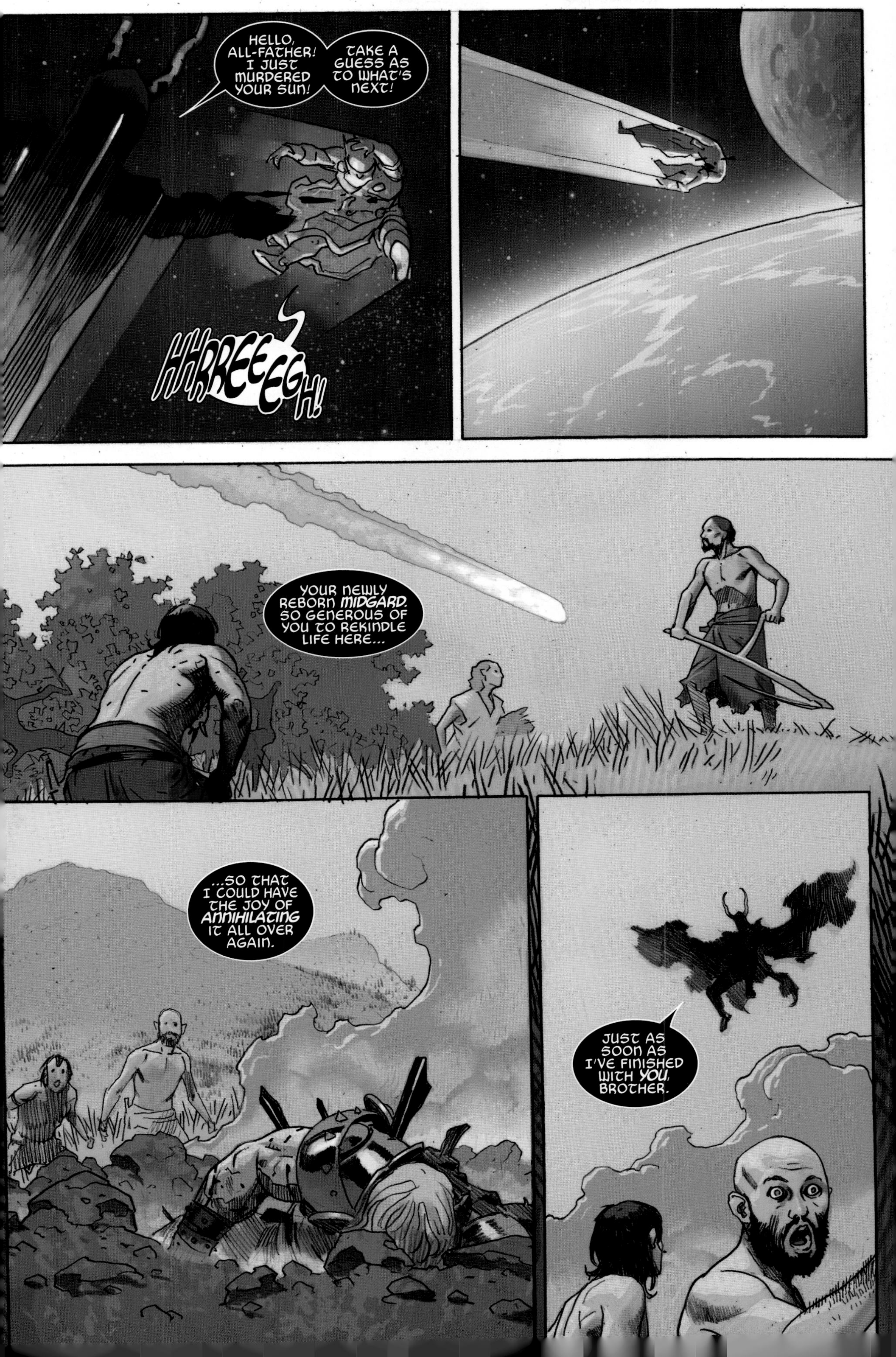
HELLO, ALL-FATHER! I JUST MURDERED YOUR SUN!
TAKE A GUESS AS TO WHAT'S NEXT!
HHRREEEGH!
YOUR NEWLY REBORN MIDGARD. SO GENEROUS OF YOU TO REKINDLE LIFE HERE...
...SO THAT I COULD HAVE THE JOY OF ANNIHILATING IT ALL OVER AGAIN.
JUST AS SOON AS I'VE FINISHED WITH YOU, BROTHER.

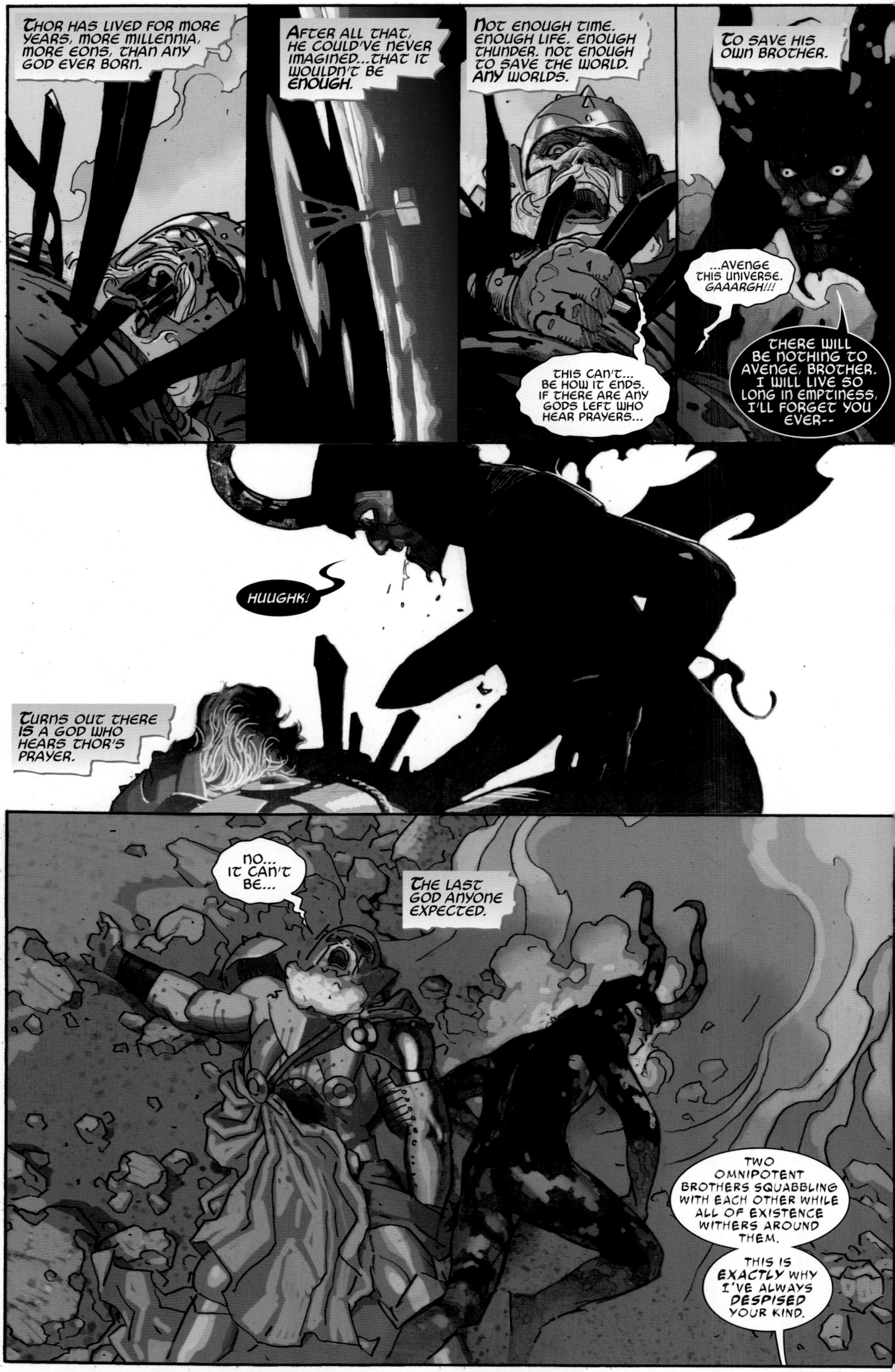

THOR HAS LIVED FOR MORE YEARS, MORE MILLENNIA, MORE EONS, THAN ANY GOD EVER BORN.
AFTER ALL THAT, HE COULD'VE NEVER IMAGINED...THAT IT WOULDN'T BE ENOUGH.
NOT ENOUGH TIME. ENOUGH LIFE. ENOUGH THUNDER. NOT ENOUGH TO SAVE THE WORLD. ANY WORLDS.
THIS CAN'T... BE HOW IT ENDS. IF THERE ARE ANY GODS LEFT WHO HEAR PRAYERS...
TO SAVE HIS OWN BROTHER.
...AVENGE THIS UNIVERSE. GAAARGH!!!
THERE WILL BE NOTHING TO AVENGE, BROTHER. I WILL LIVE SO LONG IN EMPTINESS, I'LL FORGET YOU EVER--
HUUGHK!
TURNS OUT THERE IS A GOD WHO HEARS THOR'S PRAYER.
NO... IT CAN'T BE...
THE LAST GOD ANYONE EXPECTED.
TWO OMNIPOTENT BROTHERS SQUABBLING WITH EACH OTHER WHILE ALL OF EXISTENCE WITHERS AROUND THEM.
THIS IS EXACTLY WHY I'VE ALWAYS DESPISED YOUR KIND.

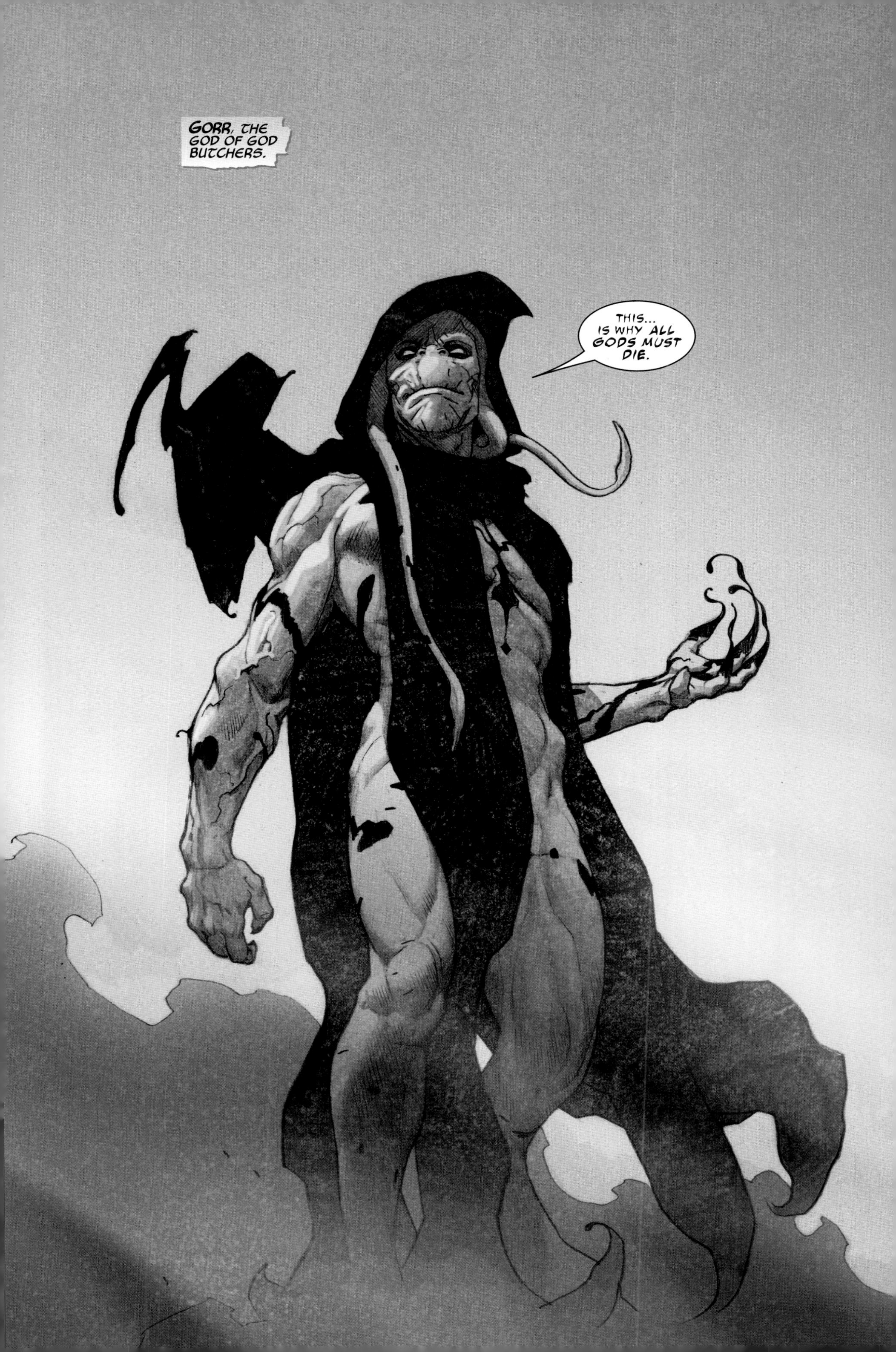
GORR, THE GOD OF GOD BUTCHERS.
THIS... IS WHY ALL GODS MUST DIE.

KING THOR 2

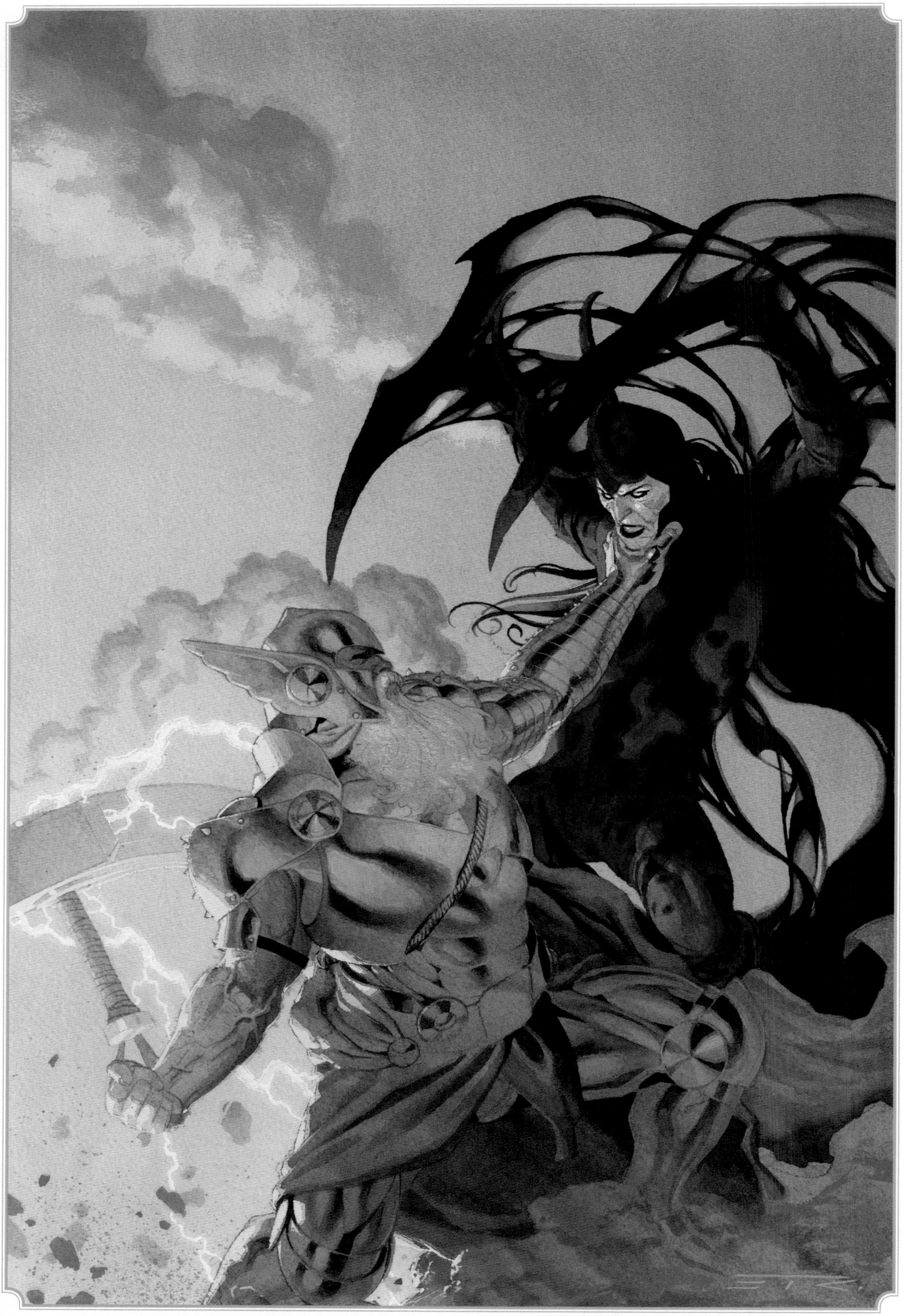

GORR AND THE LAST OF THE GODS

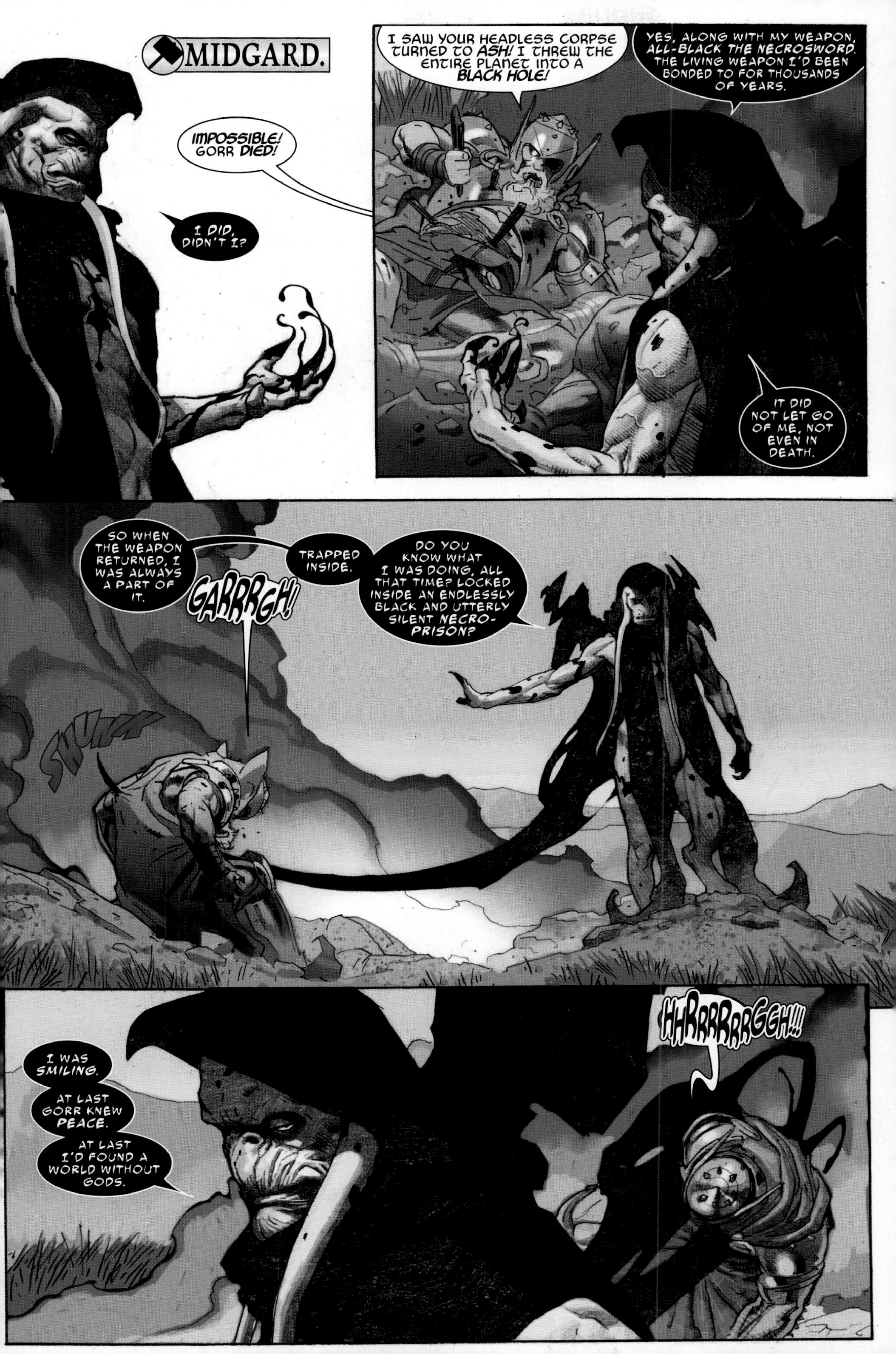
MIDGARD.
IMPOSSIBLE! GORR DIED!
I DID, DIDN'T I?
I SAW YOUR HEADLESS CORPSE TURNED TO ASH! I THREW THE ENTIRE PLANET INTO A BLACK HOLE!
YES, ALONG WITH MY WEAPON, ALL-BLACK THE NECROSWORD. THE LIVING WEAPON I'D BEEN BONDED TO FOR THOUSANDS OF YEARS.
IT DID NOT LET GO OF ME, NOT EVEN IN DEATH.
SO WHEN THE WEAPON RETURNED, I WAS ALWAYS A PART OF IT.
TRAPPED INSIDE.
DO YOU KNOW WHAT I WAS DOING, ALL THAT TIME? LOCKED INSIDE AN ENDLESSLY BLACK AND UTTERLY SILENT NECRO-PRISON?
GARRRGH!
SHUNK
I WAS SMILING.
AT LAST GORR KNEW PEACE.
AT LAST I'D FOUND A WORLD WITHOUT GODS.
HHRRRRRRRGGH!!!

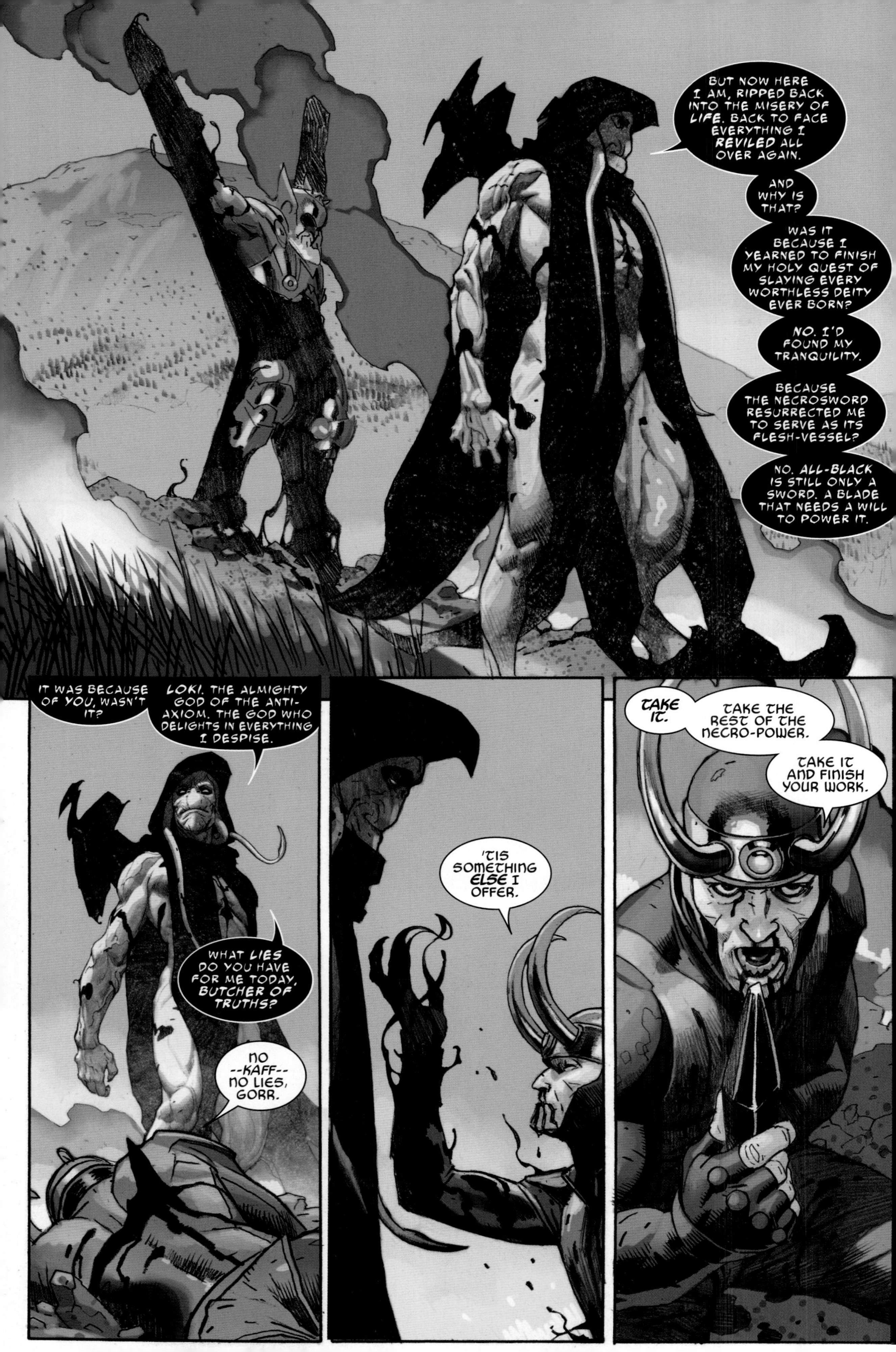

BUT NOW HERE I AM, RIPPED BACK INTO THE MISERY OF LIFE. BACK TO FACE EVERYTHING I REVILED ALL OVER AGAIN.
AND WHY IS THAT?
WAS IT BECAUSE I YEARNED TO FINISH MY HOLY QUEST OF SLAYING EVERY WORTHLESS DEITY EVER BORN?
NO. I'D FOUND MY TRANQUILITY.
BECAUSE THE NECROSWORD RESURRECTED ME TO SERVE AS ITS FLESH-VESSEL?
NO. ALL-BLACK IS STILL ONLY A SWORD. A BLADE THAT NEEDS A WILL TO POWER IT.
IT WAS BECAUSE OF YOU, WASN'T IT?
LOKI. THE ALMIGHTY GOD OF THE ANTI-AXIOM. THE GOD WHO DELIGHTS IN EVERYTHING I DESPISE.
WHAT LIES DO YOU HAVE FOR ME TODAY, BUTCHER OF TRUTHS?
NO --KAFF-- NO LIES, GORR.
'TIS SOMETHING ELSE I OFFER.
TAKE IT.
TAKE THE REST OF THE NECRO-POWER.
TAKE IT AND FINISH YOUR WORK.

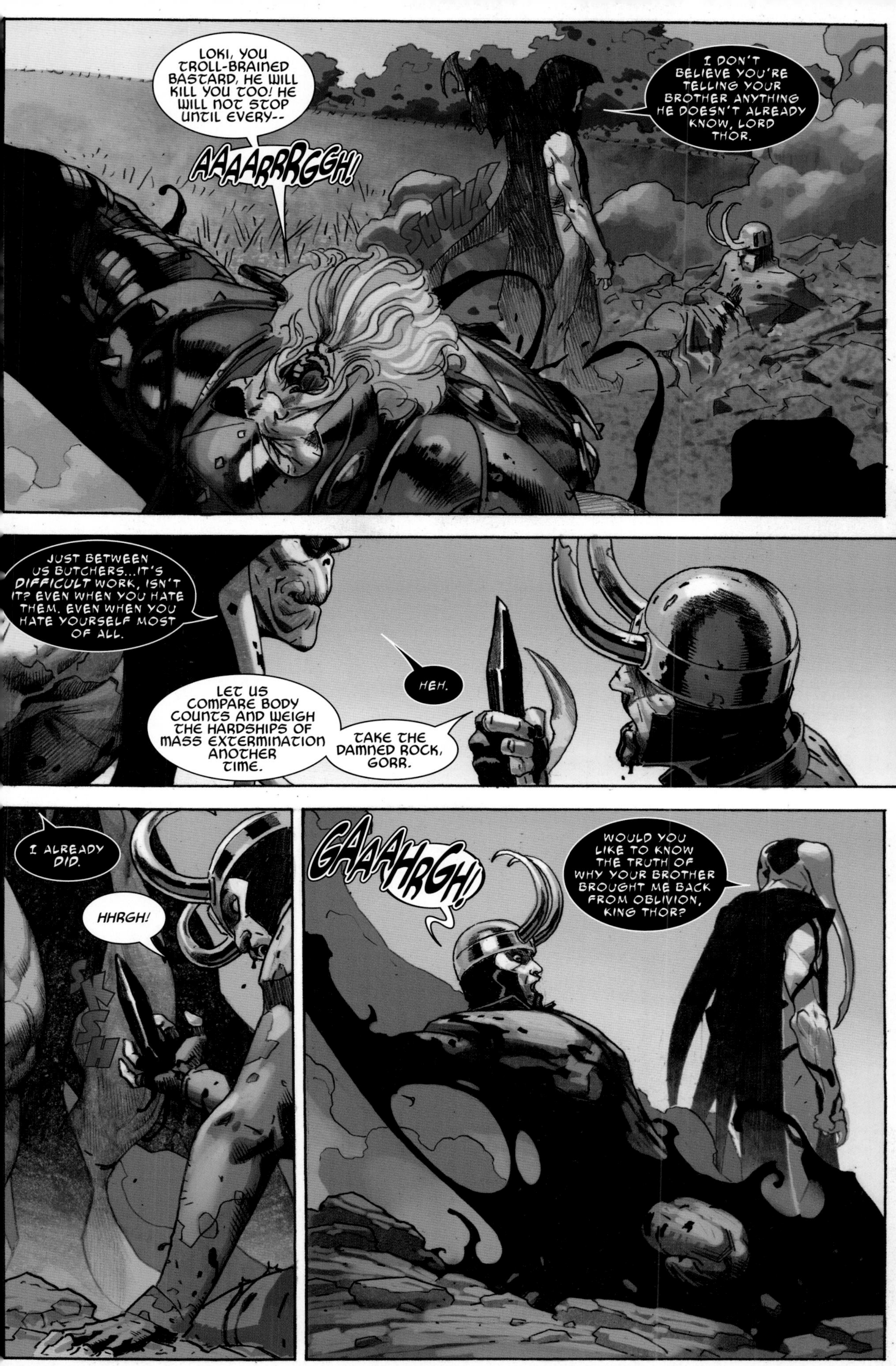
LOKI, YOU TROLL-BRAINED BASTARD, HE WILL KILL YOU TOO! HE WILL NOT STOP UNTIL EVERY--
AAAARRRGGH!
SHUNK
I DON'T BELIEVE YOU'RE TELLING YOUR BROTHER ANYTHING HE DOESN'T ALREADY KNOW, LORD THOR.
JUST BETWEEN US BUTCHERS...IT'S DIFFICULT WORK, ISN'T IT? EVEN WHEN YOU HATE THEM. EVEN WHEN YOU HATE YOURSELF MOST OF ALL.
HEH.
LET US COMPARE BODY COUNTS AND WEIGH THE HARDSHIPS OF MASS EXTERMINATION ANOTHER TIME.
TAKE THE DAMNED ROCK, GORR.
I ALREADY DID.
HHRGH!
SKSH
GAAAHRGH!
WOULD YOU LIKE TO KNOW THE TRUTH OF WHY YOUR BROTHER BROUGHT ME BACK FROM OBLIVION, KING THOR?

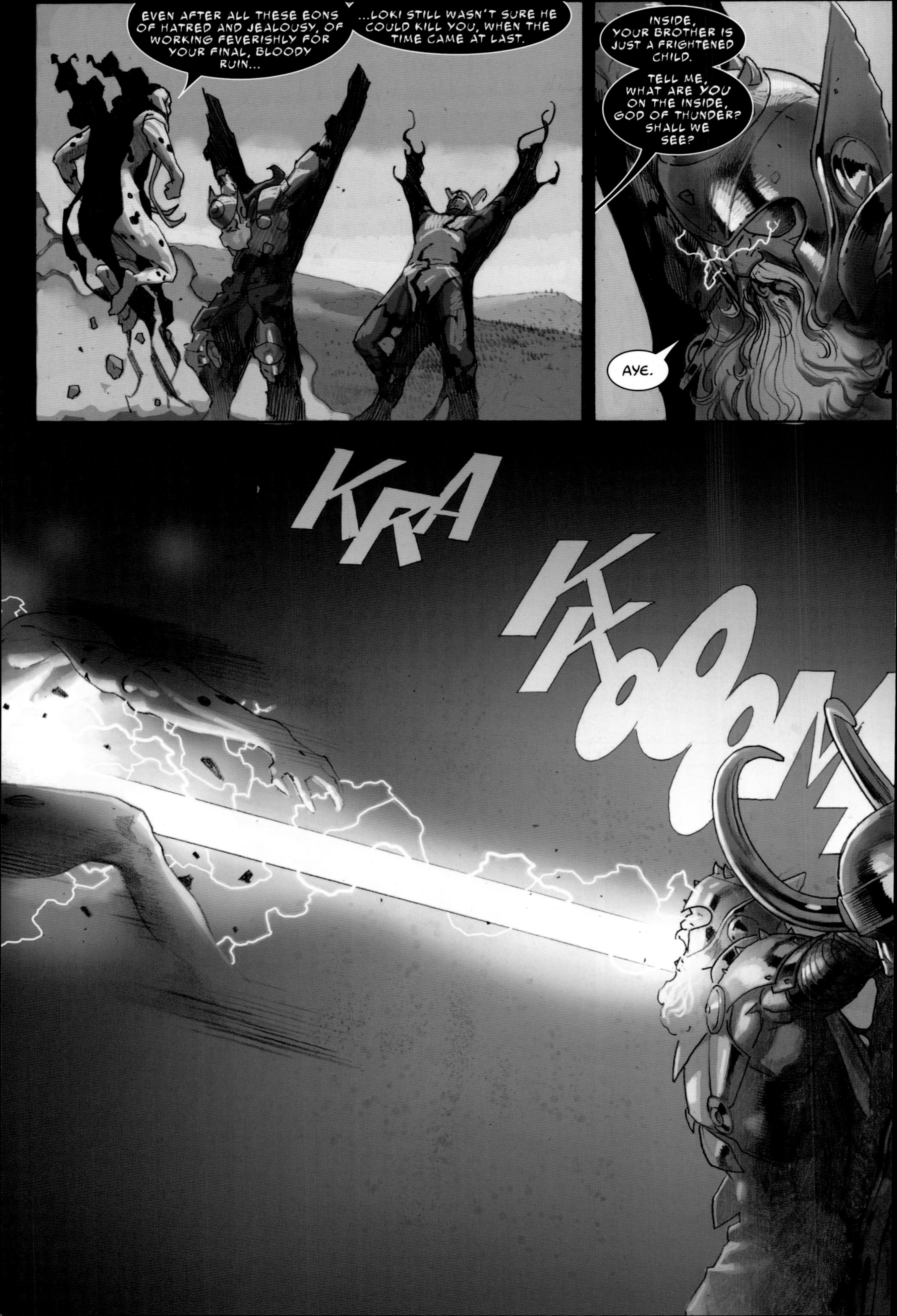
EVEN AFTER ALL THESE EONS OF HATRED AND JEALOUSY, OF WORKING FEVERISHLY FOR YOUR FINAL, BLOODY RUIN...
...LOKI STILL WASN'T SURE HE COULD KILL YOU, WHEN THE TIME CAME AT LAST.
INSIDE, YOUR BROTHER IS JUST A FRIGHTENED CHILD.
TELL ME, WHAT ARE YOU ON THE INSIDE, GOD OF THUNDER? SHALL WE SEE?
AYE.
KRA
KTHOOOM

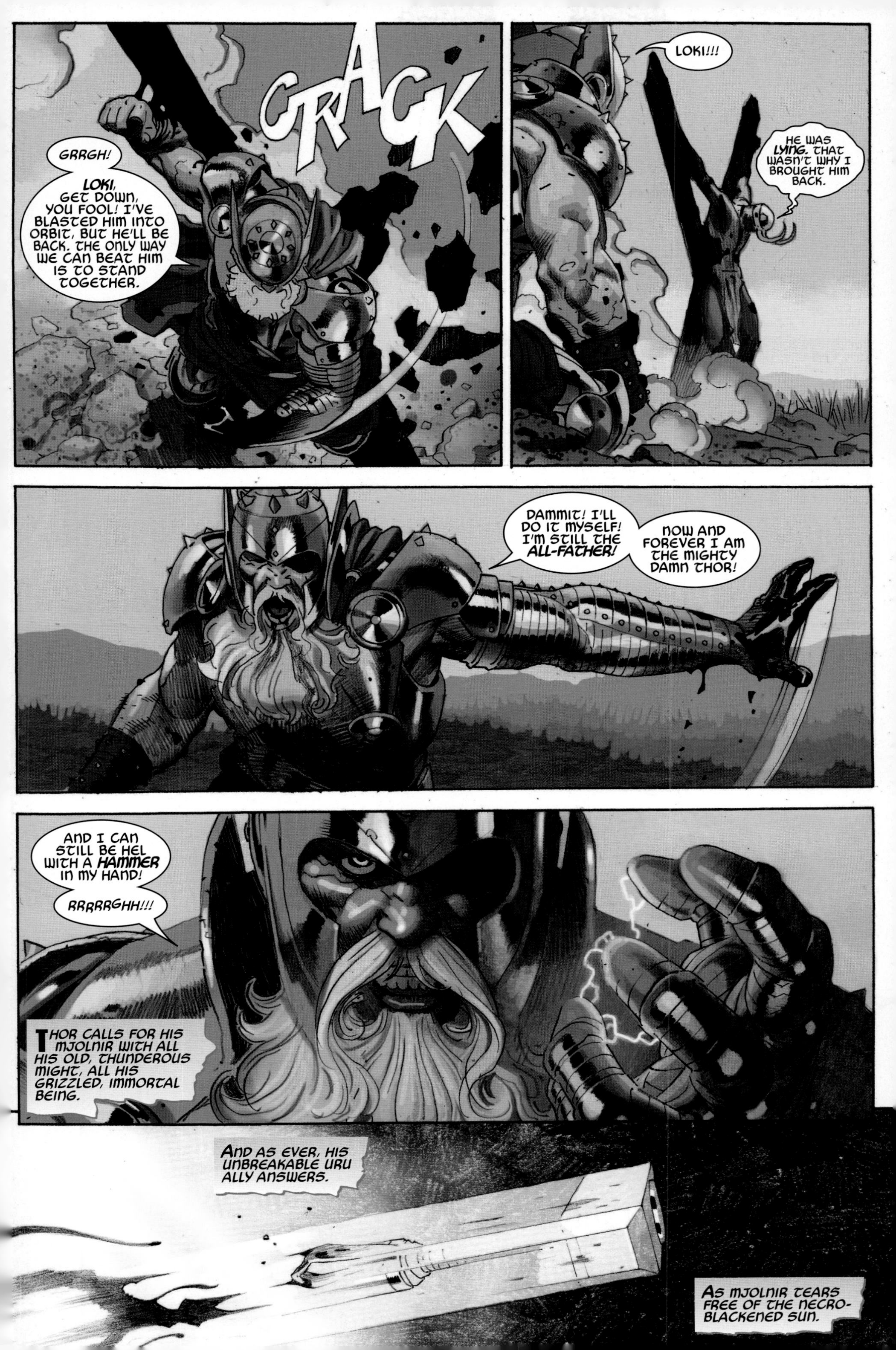
CRACK
GRRGH!
LOKI, GET DOWN, YOU FOOL! I'VE BLASTED HIM INTO ORBIT, BUT HE'LL BE BACK. THE ONLY WAY WE CAN BEAT HIM IS TO STAND TOGETHER.
LOKI!!!
HE WAS LYING. THAT WASN'T WHY I BROUGHT HIM BACK.
DAMMIT! I'LL DO IT MYSELF! I'M STILL THE ALL-FATHER!
NOW AND FOREVER I AM THE MIGHTY DAMN THOR!
AND I CAN STILL BE HEL WITH A HAMMER IN MY HAND!
RRRRRGHH!!!
THOR CALLS FOR HIS MJOLNIR WITH ALL HIS OLD, THUNDEROUS MIGHT, ALL HIS GRIZZLED, IMMORTAL BEING.
AND AS EVER, HIS UNBREAKABLE URU ALLY ANSWERS.
AS MJOLNIR TEARS FREE OF THE NECRO-BLACKENED SUN.

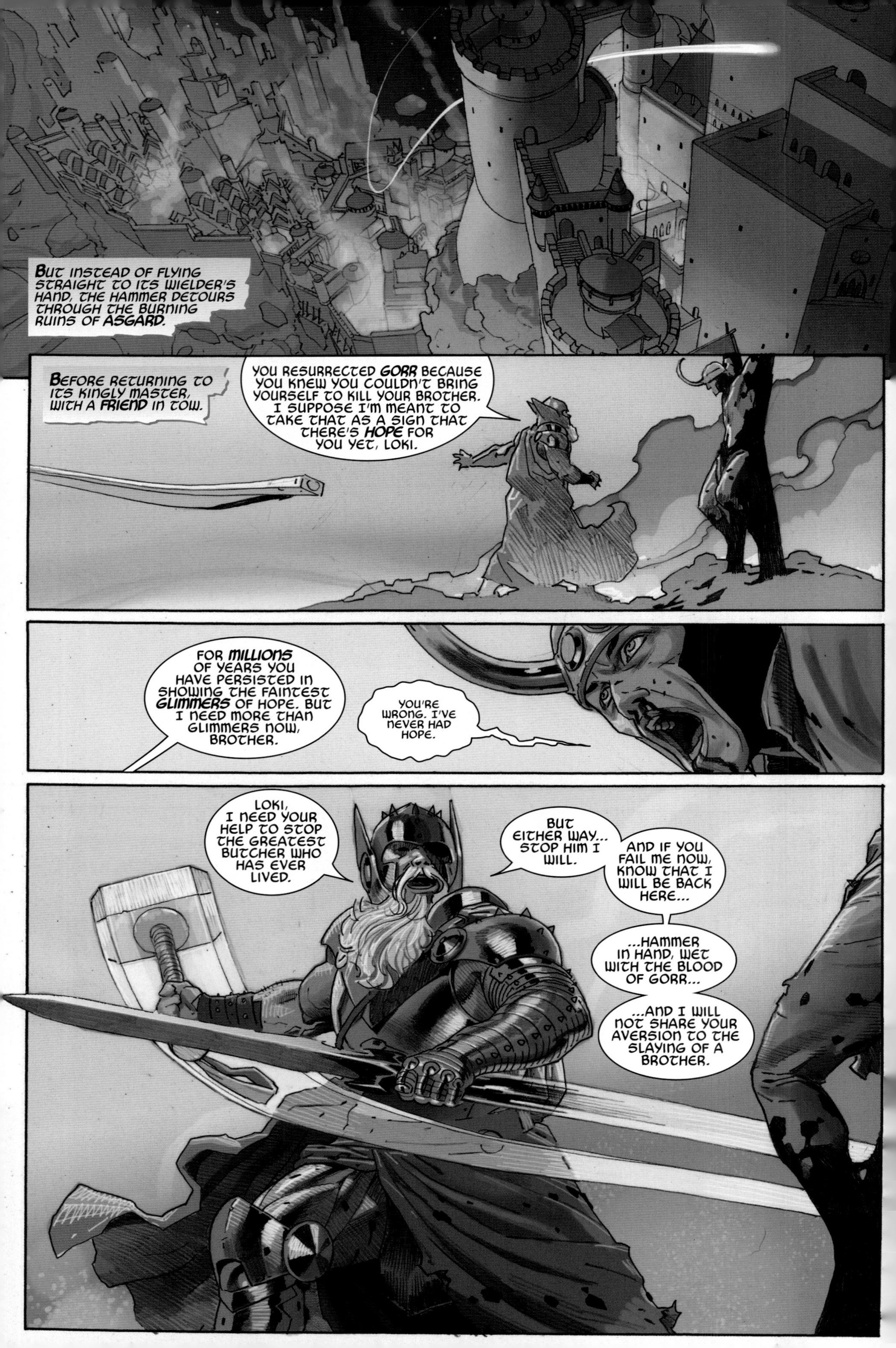

BUT INSTEAD OF FLYING STRAIGHT TO ITS WIELDER'S HAND, THE HAMMER DETOURS THROUGH THE BURNING RUINS OF ASGARD.
BEFORE RETURNING TO ITS KINGLY MASTER, WITH A FRIEND IN TOW.
YOU RESURRECTED GORR BECAUSE YOU KNEW YOU COULDN'T BRING YOURSELF TO KILL YOUR BROTHER. I SUPPOSE I'M MEANT TO TAKE THAT AS A SIGN THAT THERE'S HOPE FOR YOU YET, LOKI.
FOR MILLIONS OF YEARS YOU HAVE PERSISTED IN SHOWING THE FAINTEST GLIMMERS OF HOPE. BUT I NEED MORE THAN GLIMMERS NOW, BROTHER.
YOU'RE WRONG. I'VE NEVER HAD HOPE.
LOKI, I NEED YOUR HELP TO STOP THE GREATEST BUTCHER WHO HAS EVER LIVED.
BUT EITHER WAY... STOP HIM I WILL.
AND IF YOU FAIL ME NOW, KNOW THAT I WILL BE BACK HERE...
...HAMMER IN HAND, WET WITH THE BLOOD OF GORR...
...AND I WILL NOT SHARE YOUR AVERSION TO THE SLAYING OF A BROTHER.

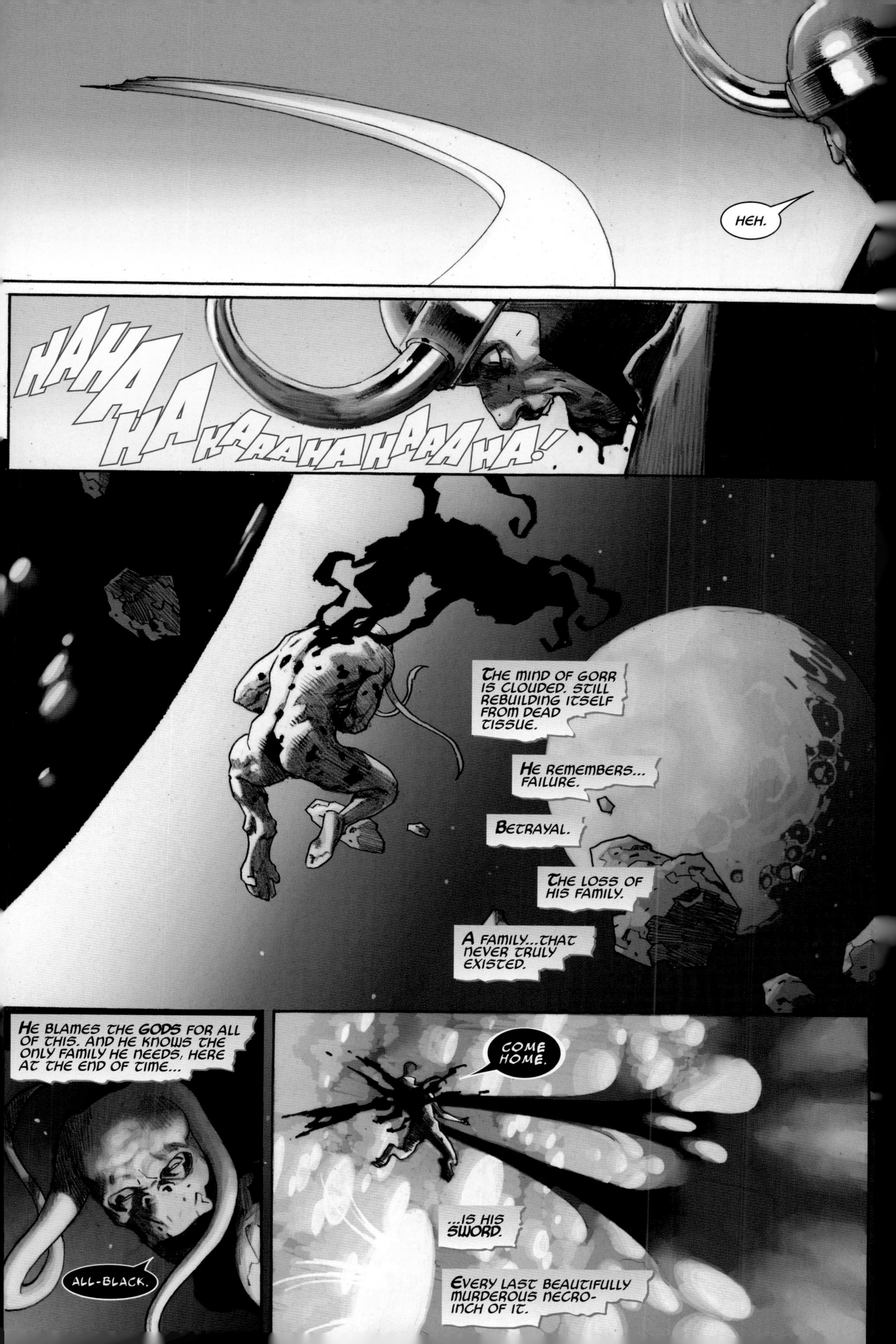
HEH.
HAHAHAHAKAAAHAHAAAAHA!
THE MIND OF GORR IS CLOUDED. STILL REBUILDING ITSELF FROM DEAD TISSUE.
HE REMEMBERS... FAILURE.
BETRAYAL.
THE LOSS OF HIS FAMILY.
A FAMILY...THAT NEVER TRULY EXISTED.
HE BLAMES THE GODS FOR ALL OF THIS. AND HE KNOWS THE ONLY FAMILY HE NEEDS, HERE AT THE END OF TIME...
ALL-BLACK.
COME HOME.
...IS HIS SWORD.
EVERY LAST BEAUTIFULLY MURDEROUS NECRO-INCH OF IT.

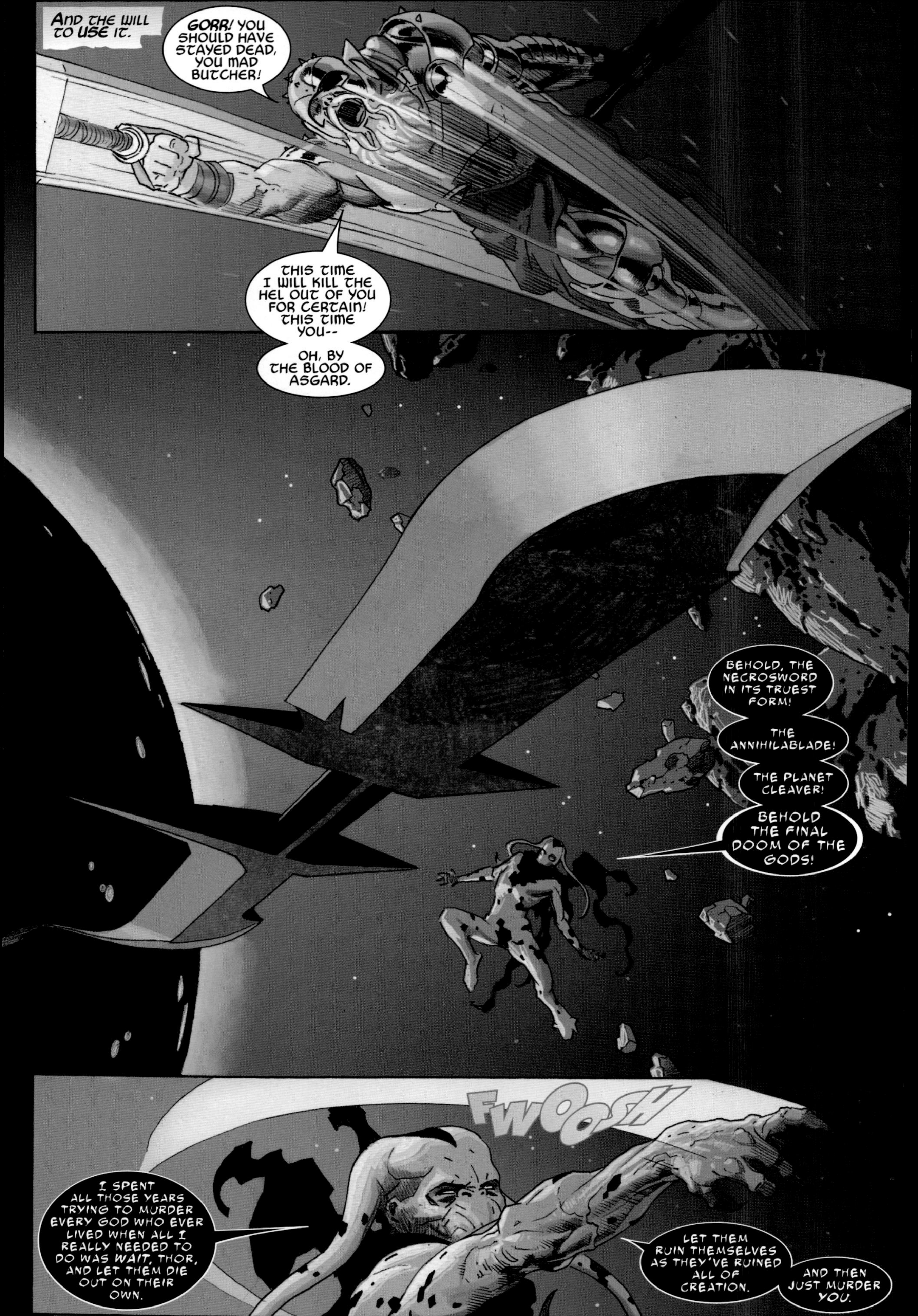

AND THE WILL TO USE IT.
GORR! YOU SHOULD HAVE STAYED DEAD, YOU MAD BUTCHER!
THIS TIME I WILL KILL THE HEL OUT OF YOU FOR CERTAIN! THIS TIME YOU--
OH, BY THE BLOOD OF ASGARD.
BEHOLD, THE NECROSWORD IN ITS TRUEST FORM!
THE ANNIHILABLADE!
THE PLANET CLEAVER!
BEHOLD THE FINAL DOOM OF THE GODS!
FWOOSH
I SPENT ALL THOSE YEARS TRYING TO MURDER EVERY GOD WHO EVER LIVED WHEN ALL I REALLY NEEDED TO DO WAS WAIT, THOR, AND LET THEM DIE OUT ON THEIR OWN.
LET THEM RUIN THEMSELVES AS THEY'VE RUINED ALL OF CREATION.
AND THEN JUST MURDER YOU.

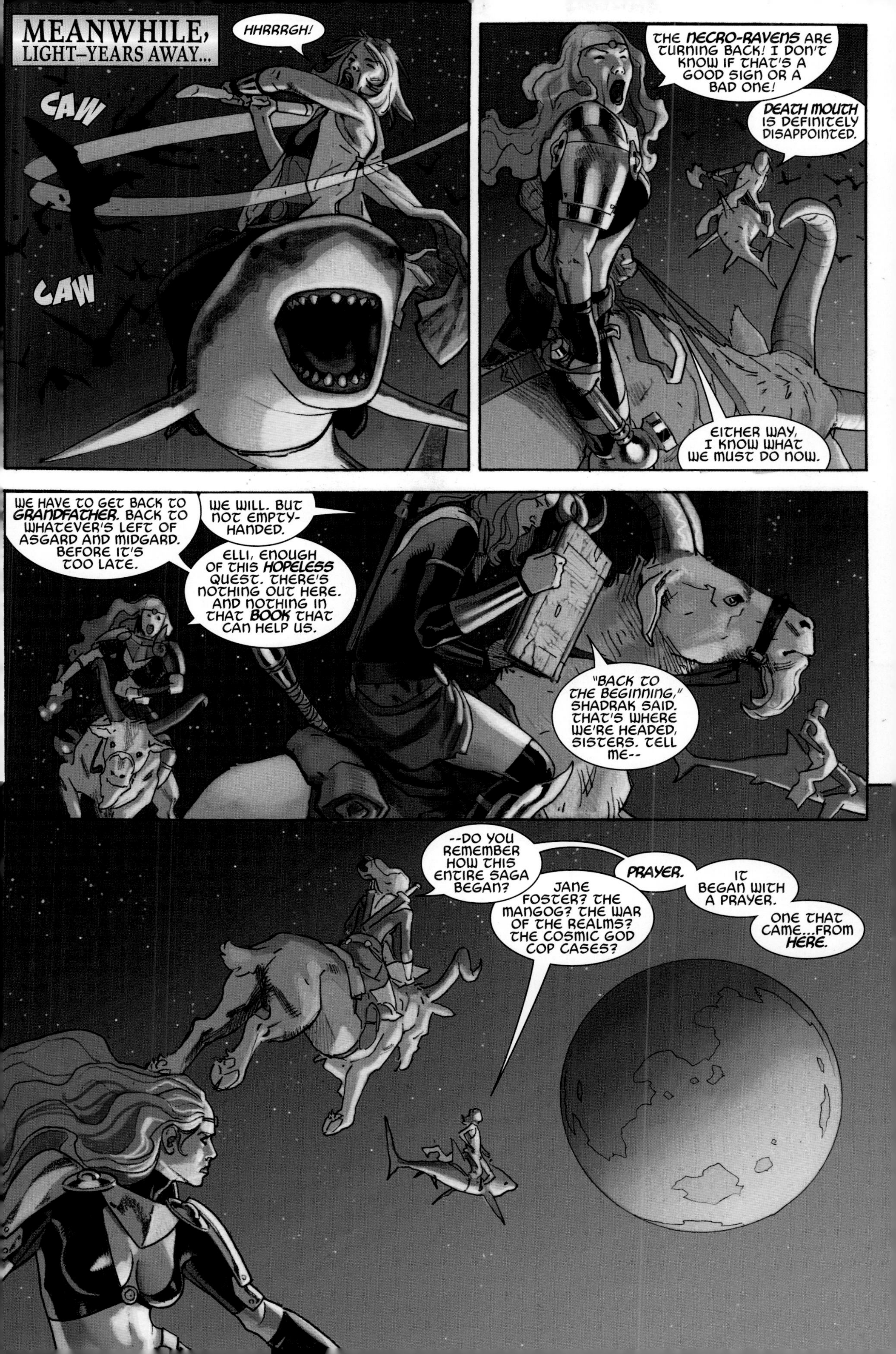

MEANWHILE, LIGHT-YEARS AWAY...
HHRRRGH!
CAW
CAW
THE NECRO-RAVENS ARE TURNING BACK! I DON'T KNOW IF THAT'S A GOOD SIGN OR A BAD ONE!
DEATH MOUTH IS DEFINITELY DISAPPOINTED.
EITHER WAY, I KNOW WHAT WE MUST DO NOW.
WE HAVE TO GET BACK TO GRANDFATHER. BACK TO WHATEVER'S LEFT OF ASGARD AND MIDGARD. BEFORE IT'S TOO LATE.
WE WILL. BUT NOT EMPTY-HANDED.
ELLI, ENOUGH OF THIS HOPELESS QUEST. THERE'S NOTHING OUT HERE. AND NOTHING IN THAT BOOK THAT CAN HELP US.
"BACK TO THE BEGINNING," SHADRAK SAID. THAT'S WHERE WE'RE HEADED, SISTERS. TELL ME--
--DO YOU REMEMBER HOW THIS ENTIRE SAGA BEGAN?
JANE FOSTER? THE MANGOG? THE WAR OF THE REALMS? THE COSMIC GOD COP CASES?
PRAYER.
IT BEGAN WITH A PRAYER.
ONE THAT CAME...FROM HERE.

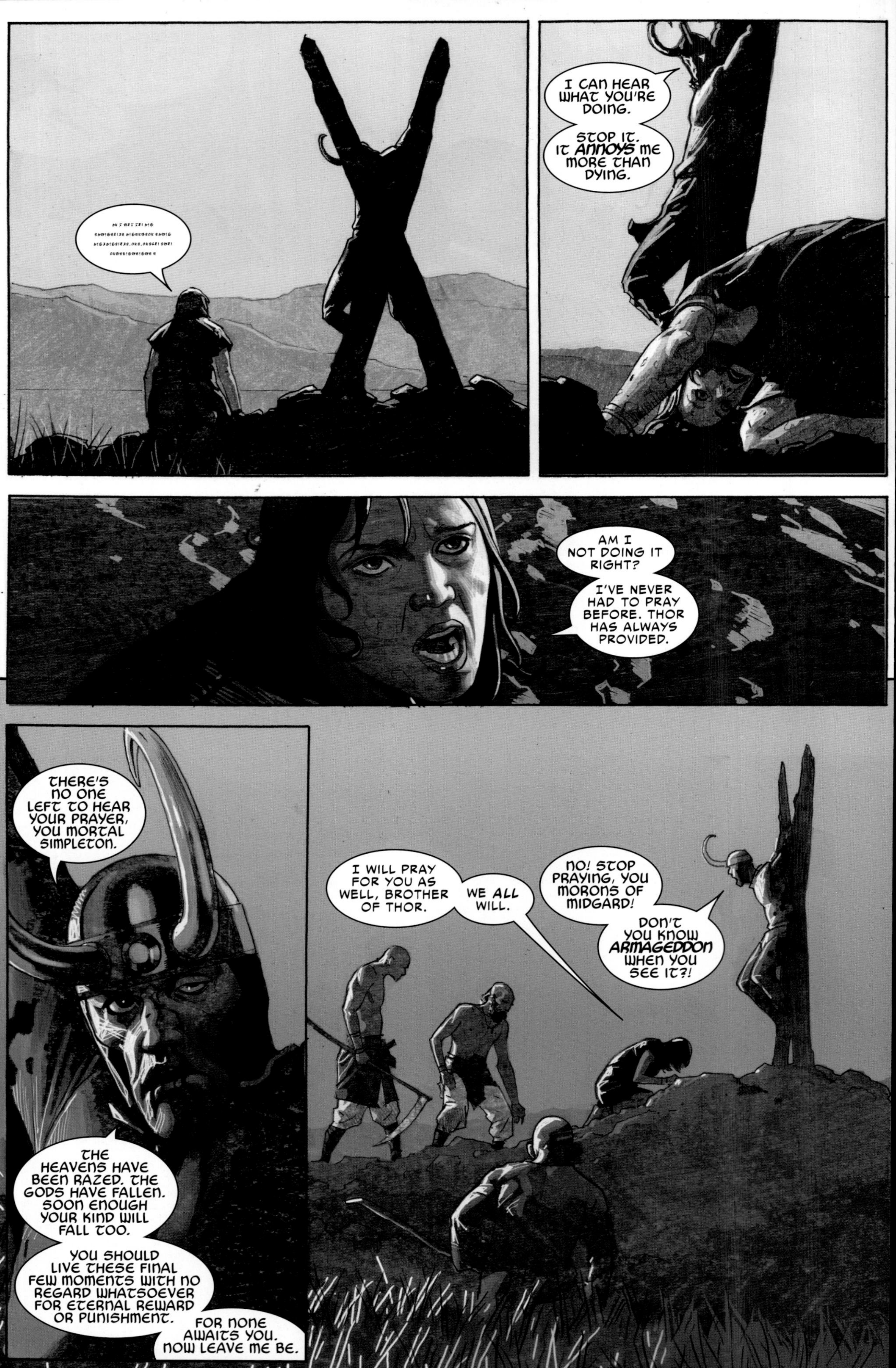
I CAN HEAR WHAT YOU'RE DOING.
STOP IT. IT ANNOYS ME MORE THAN DYING.
AM I NOT DOING IT RIGHT?
I'VE NEVER HAD TO PRAY BEFORE. THOR HAS ALWAYS PROVIDED.
THERE'S NO ONE LEFT TO HEAR YOUR PRAYER, YOU MORTAL SIMPLETON.
I WILL PRAY FOR YOU AS WELL, BROTHER OF THOR.
WE ALL WILL.
NO! STOP PRAYING, YOU MORONS OF MIDGARD!
DON'T YOU KNOW ARMAGEDDON WHEN YOU SEE IT?!
THE HEAVENS HAVE BEEN RAZED. THE GODS HAVE FALLEN. SOON ENOUGH YOUR KIND WILL FALL TOO.
YOU SHOULD LIVE THESE FINAL FEW MOMENTS WITH NO REGARD WHATSOEVER FOR ETERNAL REWARD OR PUNISHMENT.
FOR NONE AWAITS YOU. NOW LEAVE ME BE.

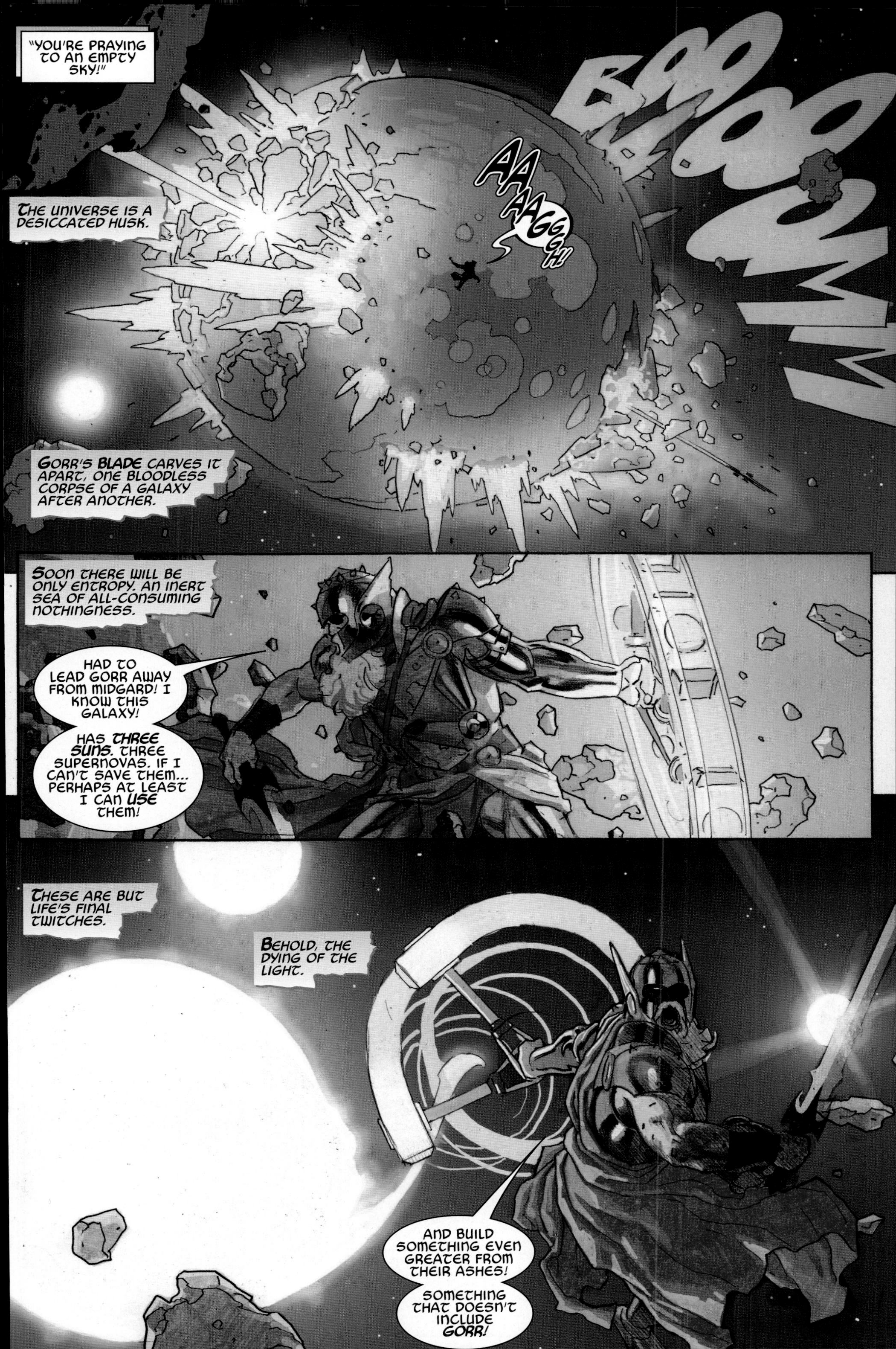
"YOU'RE PRAYING TO AN EMPTY SKY!"
BOOOOOM
AAAAGGH!
THE UNIVERSE IS A DESICCATED HUSK.
GORR'S BLADE CARVES IT APART, ONE BLOODLESS CORPSE OF A GALAXY AFTER ANOTHER.
SOON THERE WILL BE ONLY ENTROPY. AN INERT SEA OF ALL-CONSUMING NOTHINGNESS.
HAD TO LEAD GORR AWAY FROM MIDGARD! I KNOW THIS GALAXY!
HAS THREE SUNS. THREE SUPERNOVAS. IF I CAN'T SAVE THEM... PERHAPS AT LEAST I CAN USE THEM!
THESE ARE BUT LIFE'S FINAL TWITCHES.
BEHOLD, THE DYING OF THE LIGHT.
AND BUILD SOMETHING EVEN GREATER FROM THEIR ASHES!
SOMETHING THAT DOESN'T INCLUDE GORR!

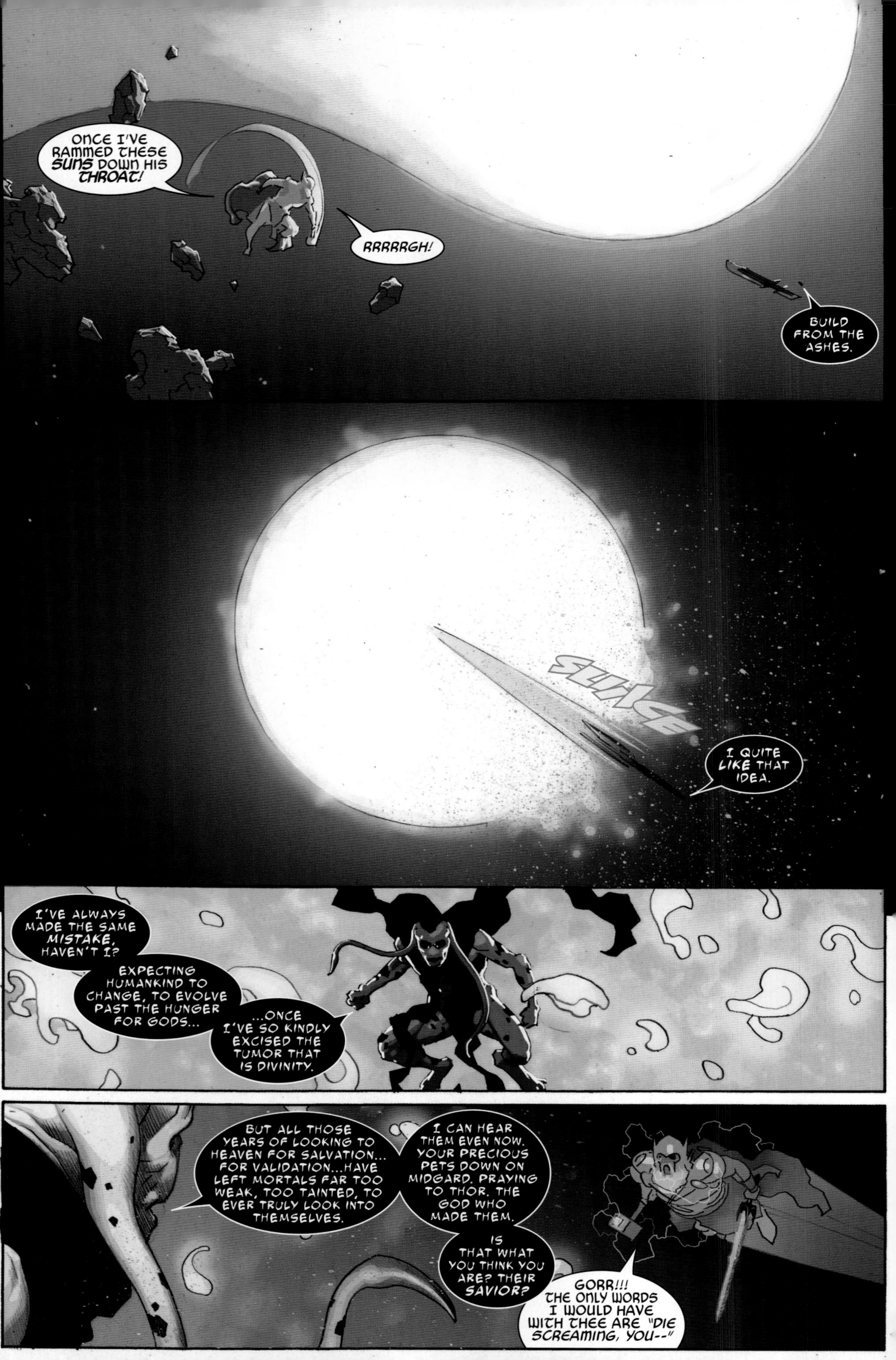
ONCE I'VE RAMMED THESE SUNS DOWN HIS THROAT!
RRRRRGH!
BUILD FROM THE ASHES.
SLIICE
I QUITE LIKE THAT IDEA.
I'VE ALWAYS MADE THE SAME MISTAKE, HAVEN'T I?
EXPECTING HUMANKIND TO CHANGE, TO EVOLVE PAST THE HUNGER FOR GODS...
...ONCE I'VE SO KINDLY EXCISED THE TUMOR THAT IS DIVINITY.
BUT ALL THOSE YEARS OF LOOKING TO HEAVEN FOR SALVATION... FOR VALIDATION...HAVE LEFT MORTALS FAR TOO WEAK, TOO TAINTED, TO EVER TRULY LOOK INTO THEMSELVES.
I CAN HEAR THEM EVEN NOW. YOUR PRECIOUS PETS DOWN ON MIDGARD. PRAYING TO THOR. THE GOD WHO MADE THEM.
IS THAT WHAT YOU THINK YOU ARE? THEIR SAVIOR?
GORR!!! THE ONLY WORDS I WOULD HAVE WITH THEE ARE "DIE SCREAMING, YOU--"

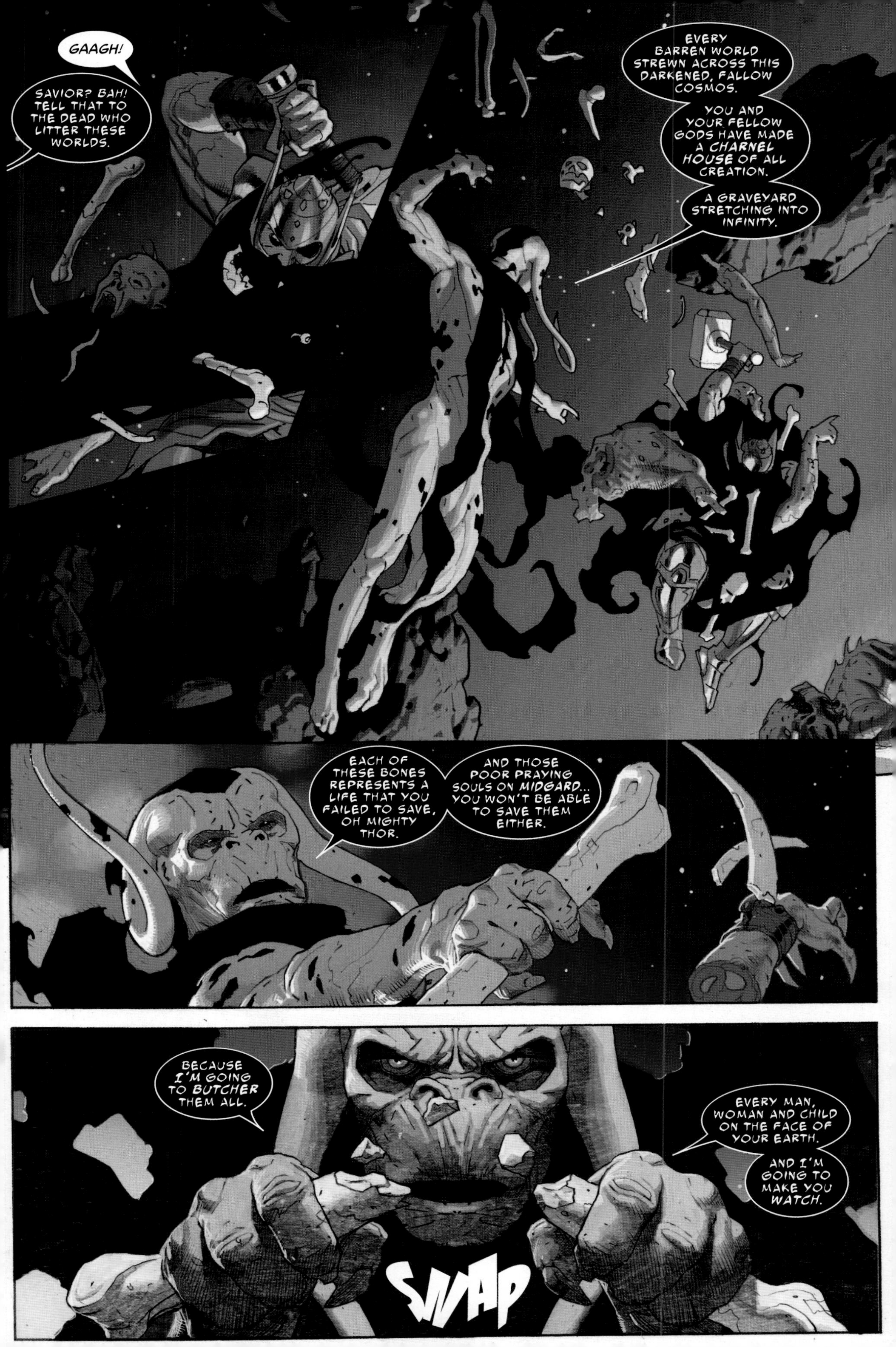
GAAGH!
SAVIOR? BAH! TELL THAT TO THE DEAD WHO LITTER THESE WORLDS.
EVERY BARREN WORLD STREWN ACROSS THIS DARKENED, FALLOW COSMOS.
YOU AND YOUR FELLOW GODS HAVE MADE A CHARNEL HOUSE OF ALL CREATION.
A GRAVEYARD STRETCHING INTO INFINITY.
EACH OF THESE BONES REPRESENTS A LIFE THAT YOU FAILED TO SAVE, OH MIGHTY THOR.
AND THOSE POOR PRAYING SOULS ON MIDGARD... YOU WON'T BE ABLE TO SAVE THEM EITHER.
BECAUSE I'M GOING TO BUTCHER THEM ALL.
EVERY MAN, WOMAN AND CHILD ON THE FACE OF YOUR EARTH.
AND I'M GOING TO MAKE YOU WATCH.
SNAP

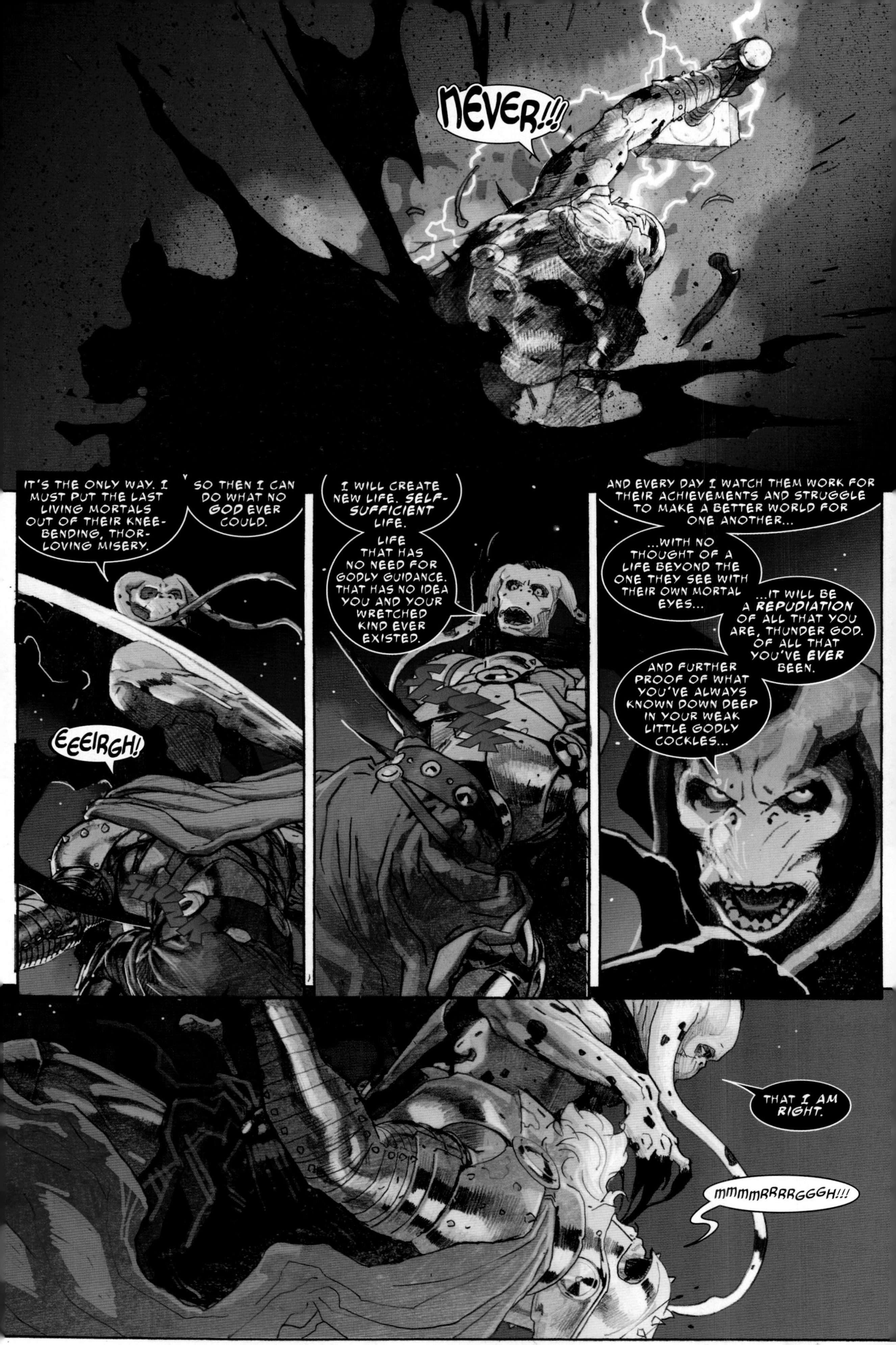
NEVER!!!
IT'S THE ONLY WAY. I MUST PUT THE LAST LIVING MORTALS OUT OF THEIR KNEE-BENDING, THOR-LOVING MISERY.
SO THEN I CAN DO WHAT NO GOD EVER COULD.
EEEIRGH!
SHUNK
I WILL CREATE NEW LIFE. SELF-SUFFICIENT LIFE.
LIFE THAT HAS NO NEED FOR GODLY GUIDANCE. THAT HAS NO IDEA YOU AND YOUR WRETCHED KIND EVER EXISTED.
SHUNK
AND EVERY DAY I WATCH THEM WORK FOR THEIR ACHIEVEMENTS AND STRUGGLE TO MAKE A BETTER WORLD FOR ONE ANOTHER...
...WITH NO THOUGHT OF A LIFE BEYOND THE ONE THEY SEE WITH THEIR OWN MORTAL EYES...
...IT WILL BE A REPUDIATION OF ALL THAT YOU ARE, THUNDER GOD. OF ALL THAT YOU'VE EVER BEEN.
AND FURTHER PROOF OF WHAT YOU'VE ALWAYS KNOWN DOWN DEEP IN YOUR WEAK LITTLE GODLY COCKLES...
THAT I AM RIGHT.
MMMMRRRRGGGH!!!

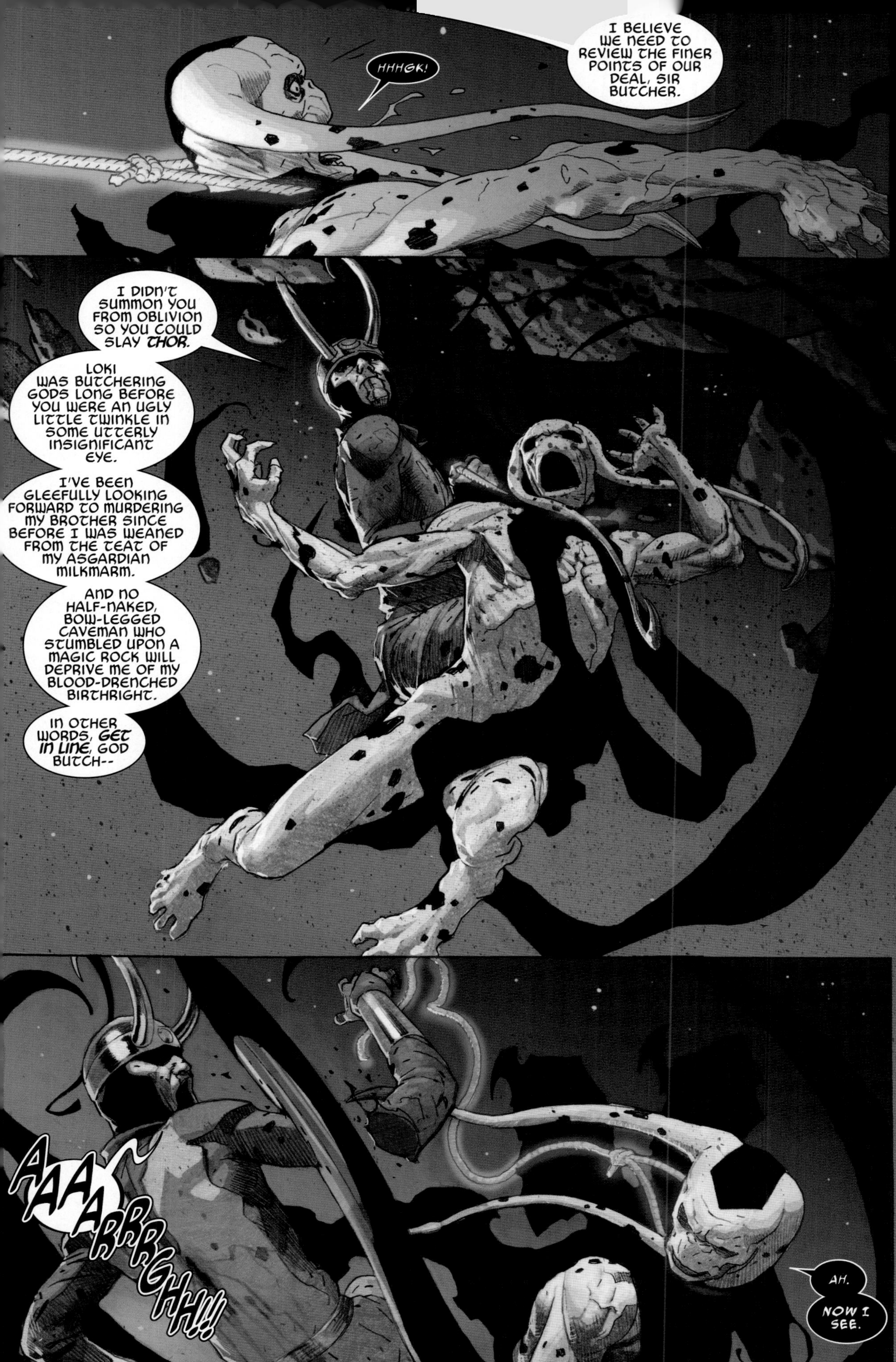

HHHGK!
I BELIEVE WE NEED TO REVIEW THE FINER POINTS OF OUR DEAL, SIR BUTCHER.
I DIDN'T SUMMON YOU FROM OBLIVION SO YOU COULD SLAY THOR.
LOKI WAS BUTCHERING GODS LONG BEFORE YOU WERE AN UGLY LITTLE TWINKLE IN SOME UTTERLY INSIGNIFICANT EYE.
I'VE BEEN GLEEFULLY LOOKING FORWARD TO MURDERING MY BROTHER SINCE BEFORE I WAS WEANED FROM THE TEAT OF MY ASGARDIAN MILKMARM.
AND NO HALF-NAKED, BOW-LEGGED CAVEMAN WHO STUMBLED UPON A MAGIC ROCK WILL DEPRIVE ME OF MY BLOOD-DRENCHED BIRTHRIGHT.
IN OTHER WORDS, GET IN LINE, GOD BUTCH--
AAAARRRGHH!!
AH.
NOW I SEE.

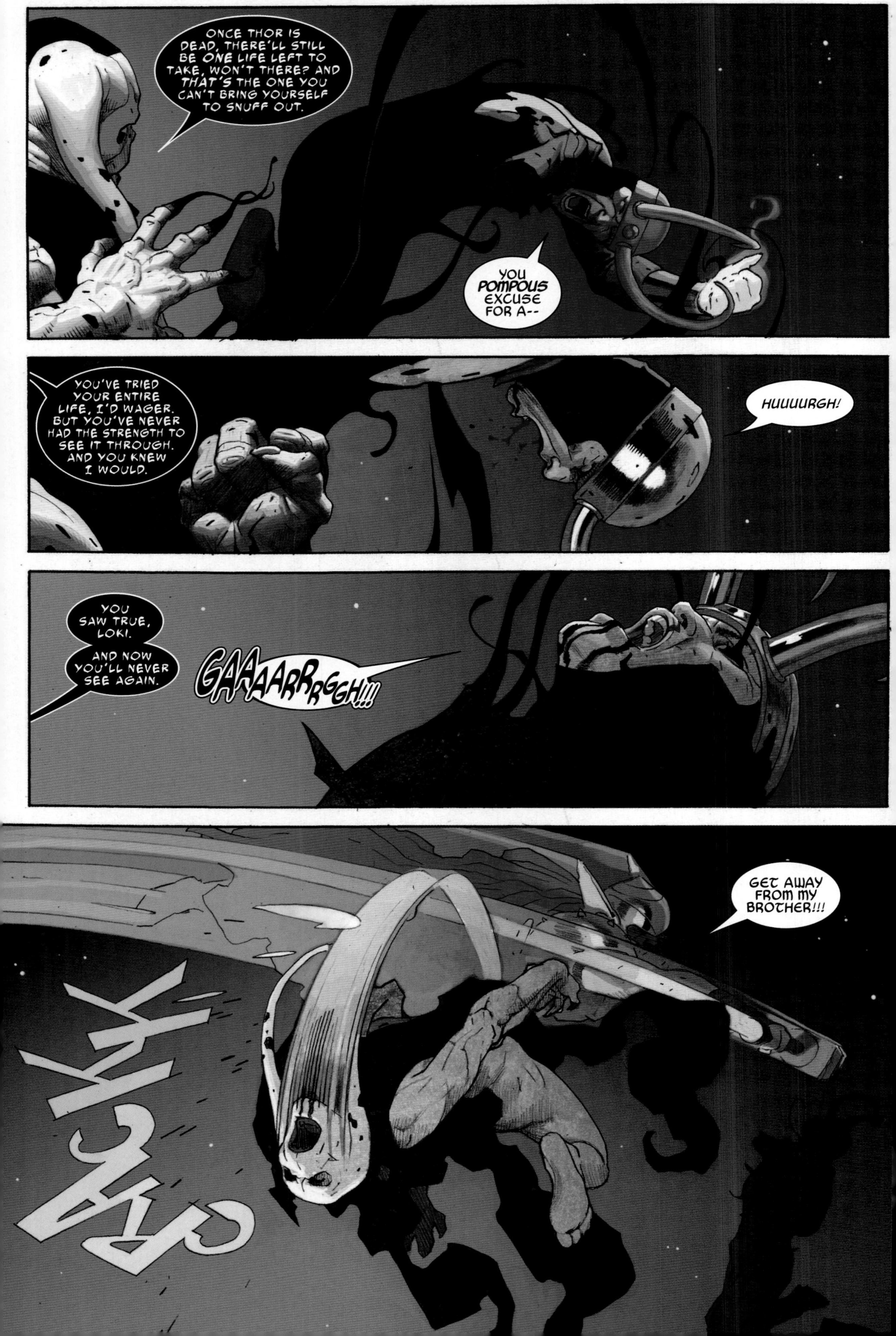

ONCE THOR IS DEAD, THERE'LL STILL BE ONE LIFE LEFT TO TAKE, WON'T THERE? AND THAT'S THE ONE YOU CAN'T BRING YOURSELF TO SNUFF OUT.
YOU POMPOUS EXCUSE FOR A--
YOU'VE TRIED YOUR ENTIRE LIFE, I'D WAGER. BUT YOU'VE NEVER HAD THE STRENGTH TO SEE IT THROUGH. AND YOU KNEW I WOULD.
HUUUURGH!
YOU SAW TRUE, LOKI.
AND NOW YOU'LL NEVER SEE AGAIN.
GAAAARRRGGH!!!
GET AWAY FROM MY BROTHER!!!
CRACK

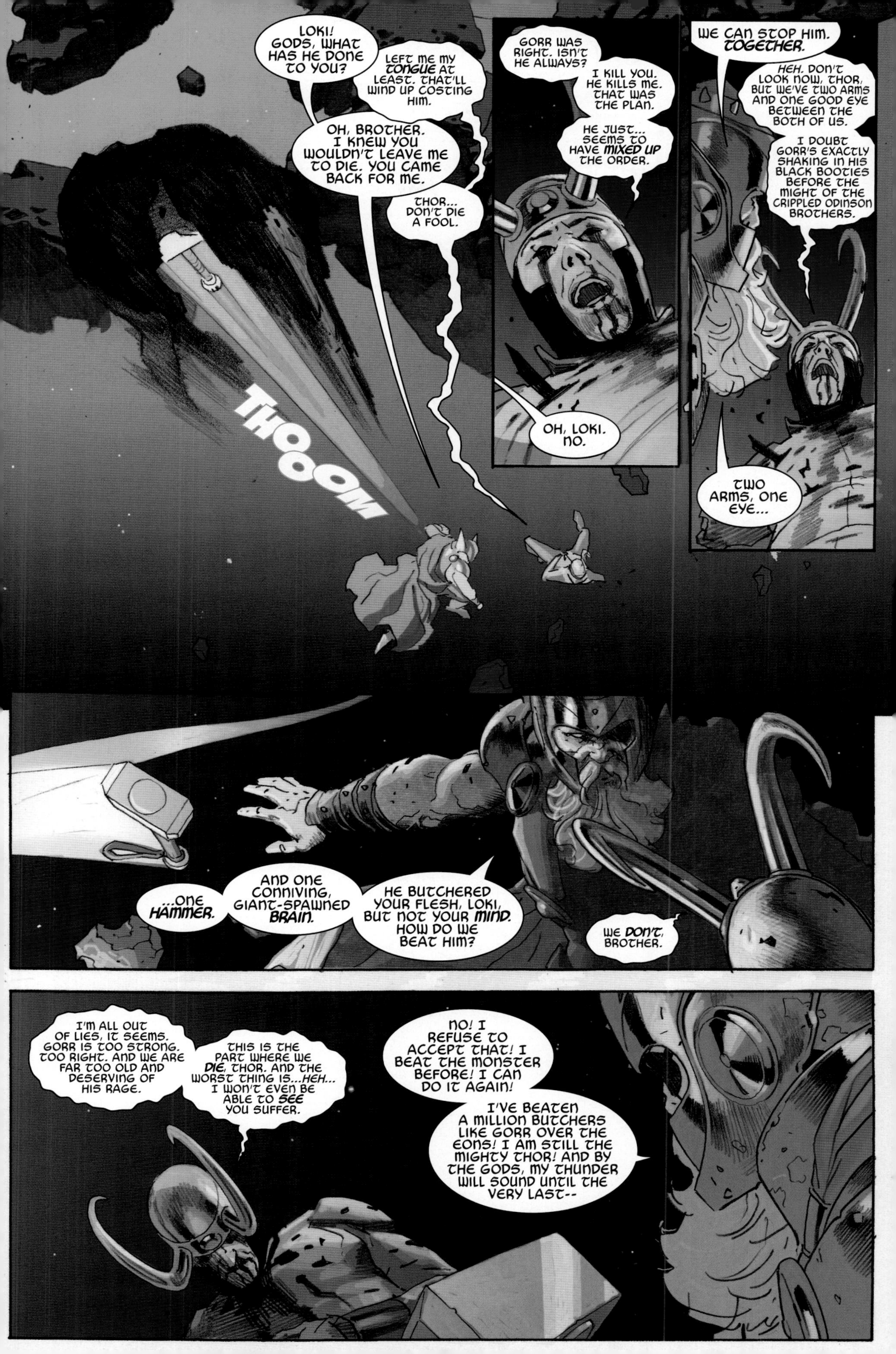
LOKI! GODS, WHAT HAS HE DONE TO YOU?
LEFT ME MY TONGUE AT LEAST. THAT'LL WIND UP COSTING HIM.
OH, BROTHER. I KNEW YOU WOULDN'T LEAVE ME TO DIE. YOU CAME BACK FOR ME.
THOR... DON'T DIE A FOOL.
THOOOM
GORR WAS RIGHT. ISN'T HE ALWAYS?
I KILL YOU. HE KILLS ME. THAT WAS THE PLAN.
HE JUST... SEEMS TO HAVE MIXED UP THE ORDER.
OH, LOKI. NO.
WE CAN STOP HIM. TOGETHER.
HEH. DON'T LOOK NOW, THOR, BUT WE'VE TWO ARMS AND ONE GOOD EYE BETWEEN THE BOTH OF US.
I DOUBT GORR'S EXACTLY SHAKING IN HIS BLACK BOOTIES BEFORE THE MIGHT OF THE CRIPPLED ODINSON BROTHERS.
TWO ARMS, ONE EYE...
...ONE HAMMER.
AND ONE CONNIVING, GIANT-SPAWNED BRAIN.
HE BUTCHERED YOUR FLESH, LOKI, BUT NOT YOUR MIND. HOW DO WE BEAT HIM?
WE DON'T, BROTHER.
I'M ALL OUT OF LIES, IT SEEMS. GORR IS TOO STRONG. TOO RIGHT. AND WE ARE FAR TOO OLD AND DESERVING OF HIS RAGE.
THIS IS THE PART WHERE WE DIE, THOR. AND THE WORST THING IS...HEH... I WON'T EVEN BE ABLE TO SEE YOU SUFFER.
NO! I REFUSE TO ACCEPT THAT! I BEAT THE MONSTER BEFORE! I CAN DO IT AGAIN!
I'VE BEATEN A MILLION BUTCHERS LIKE GORR OVER THE EONS! I AM STILL THE MIGHTY THOR! AND BY THE GODS, MY THUNDER WILL SOUND UNTIL THE VERY LAST--

GHHHRRH!
THERE ARE NO OTHER BUTCHERS LIKE ME, GOD OF THUNDER.
GORR, YOU COWARD! SHOW YOURSELF! FIGHT LIKE A--HHRH!
LIKE A MAN? I CEASED BEING ONE OF THOSE LONG AGO.
BUT I WILL NEVER BE ONE OF YOU. I AM SO MUCH MORE THAN A GOD. I AM A FORCE OF NATURE.
GODS MAY WALK ON WATER.
BUT GORR IS THE SEA.
AND THE SEA IS TIRED OF BEING TROD UPON.
YOU HAVE MY PERMISSION TO DROWN NOW, GODS OF ASGARD.

HRRRRRRGH!!!

LOKI! I CAN'T HOLD BACK THE DARKNESS!

I NEVER ASKED YOU TO! LET ME DIE, DAMMIT!

JUST AS LONG AS OUR FATHER'S BLOODLINE DIES RIGHT BY MY SIDE!

IF THIS IS IT, BROTHER...I WANT YOU TO KNOW...

I LIED.

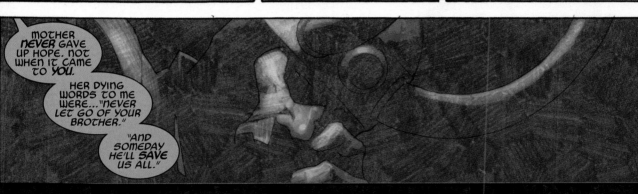

MOTHER NEVER GAVE UP HOPE. NOT WHEN IT CAME TO YOU.

HER DYING WORDS TO ME WERE..."NEVER LET GO OF YOUR BROTHER."

"AND SOMEDAY HE'LL SAVE US ALL."

I'M SORRY I FAILED YOU, MOTHER.

I'M SORRY I FAILED US BOTH, LOKI. I'M SORRY FOR--

GHUUUGH!

THE UNIVERSE IS A DESICCATED HUSK.

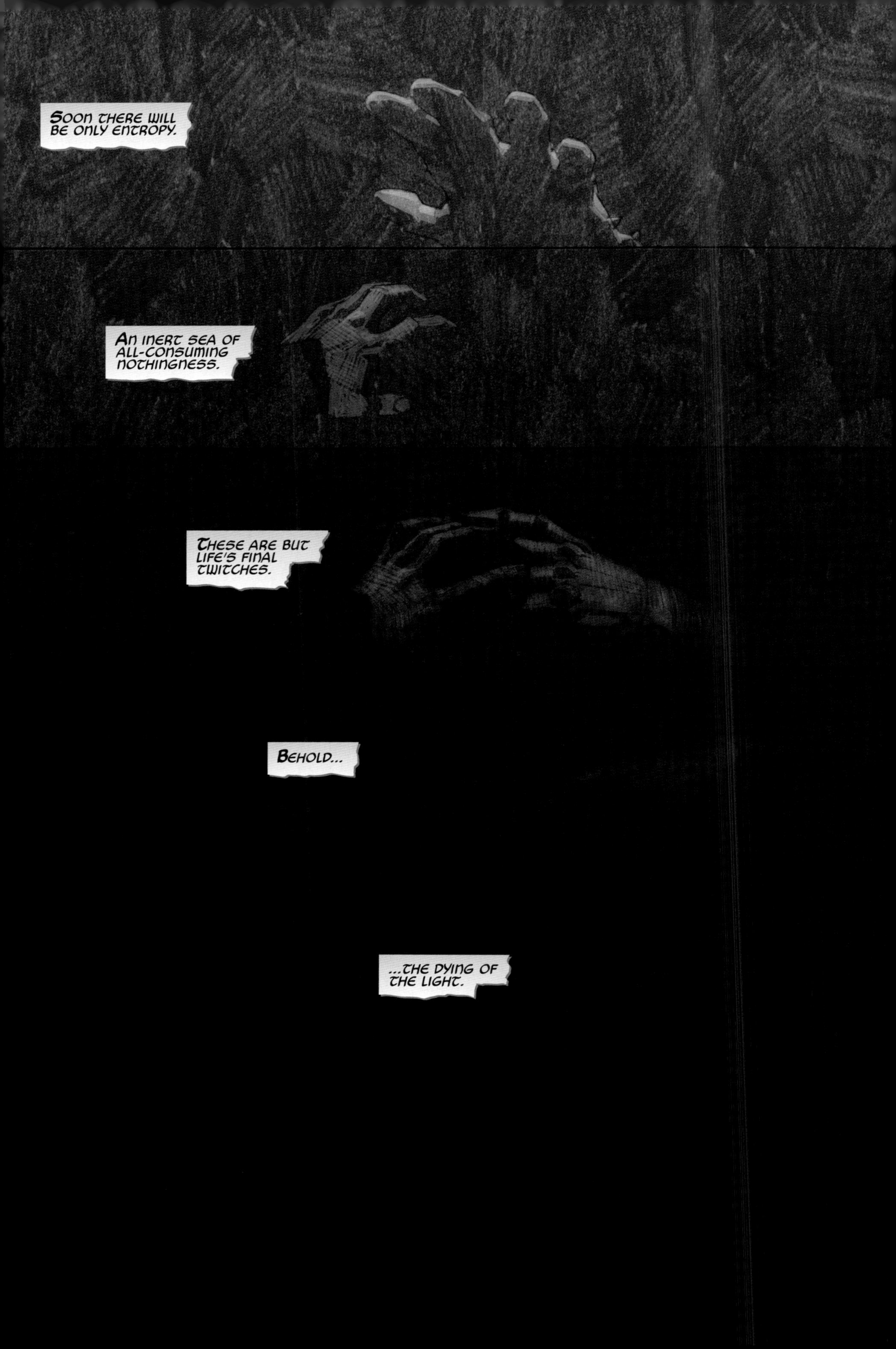
SOON THERE WILL BE ONLY ENTROPY.
AN INERT SEA OF ALL-CONSUMING NOTHINGNESS.
THESE ARE BUT LIFE'S FINAL TWITCHES.
BEHOLD...
...THE DYING OF THE LIGHT.

KING THOR 3

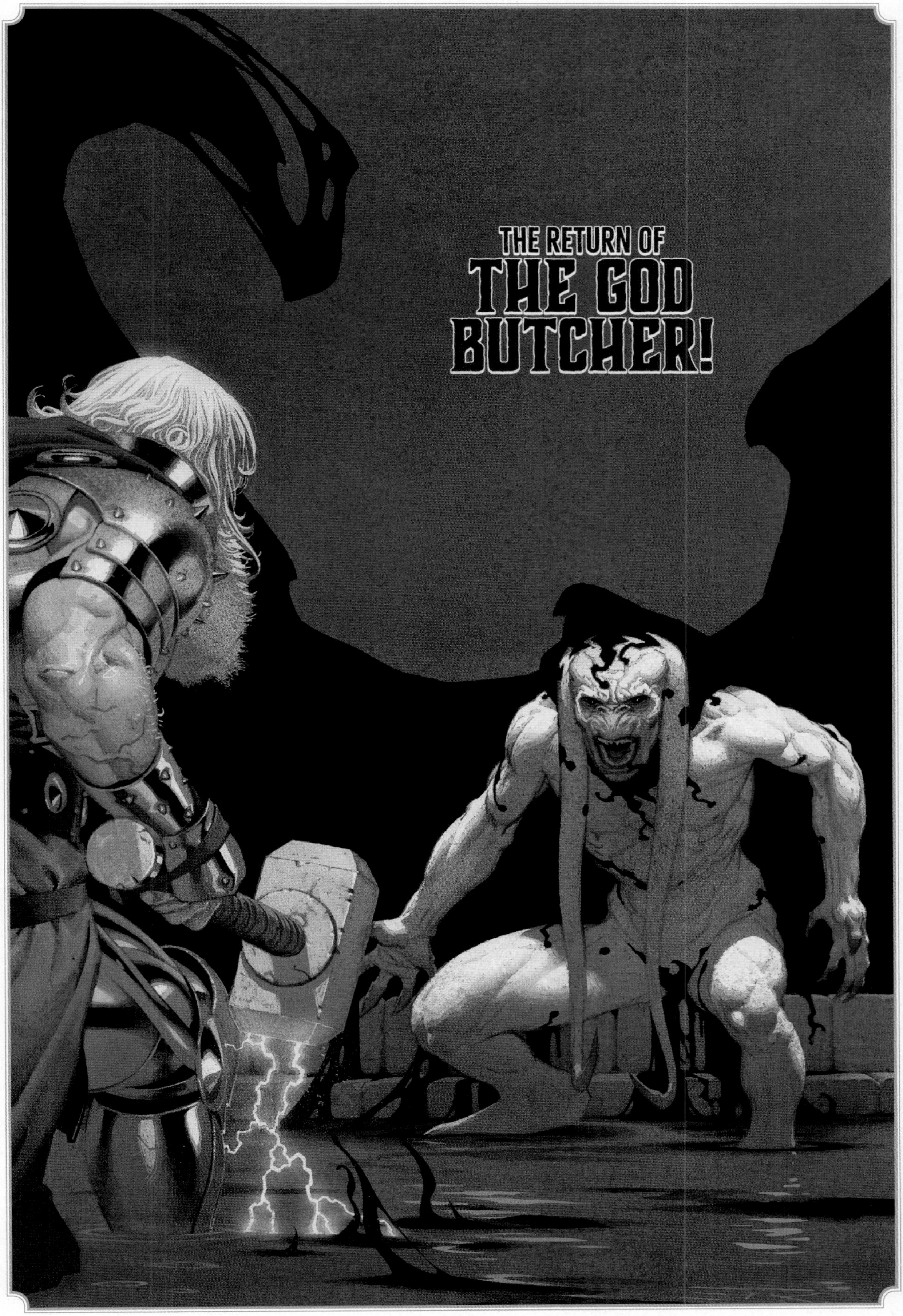
THE RETURN OF
THE GOD BUTCHER!

A STORM OF PRAYERS

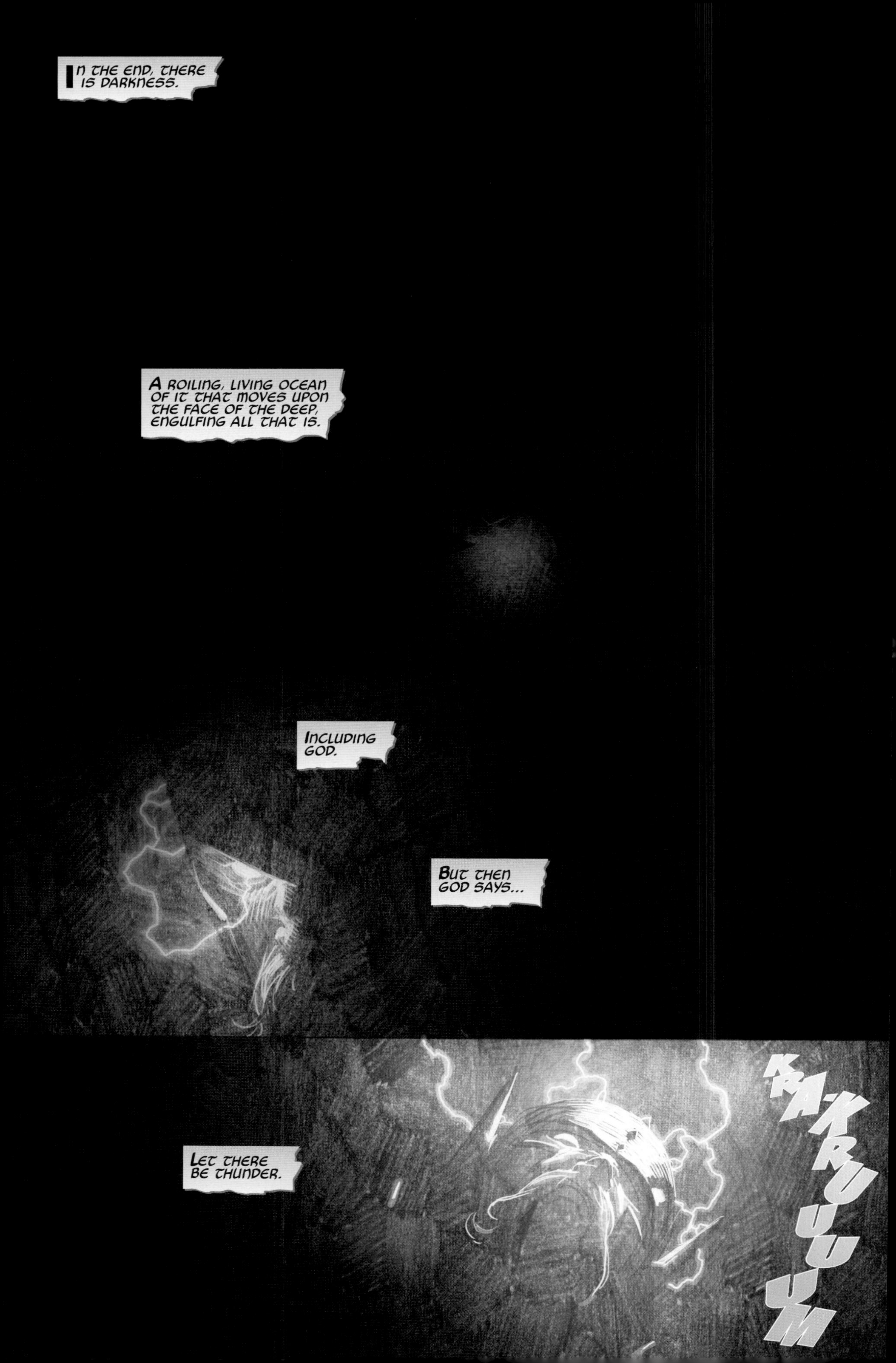
In the end, there is darkness.
A roiling, living ocean of it that moves upon the face of the deep, engulfing all that is.
Including God.
But then God says...
Let there be thunder.
KRA-KRUUUUM

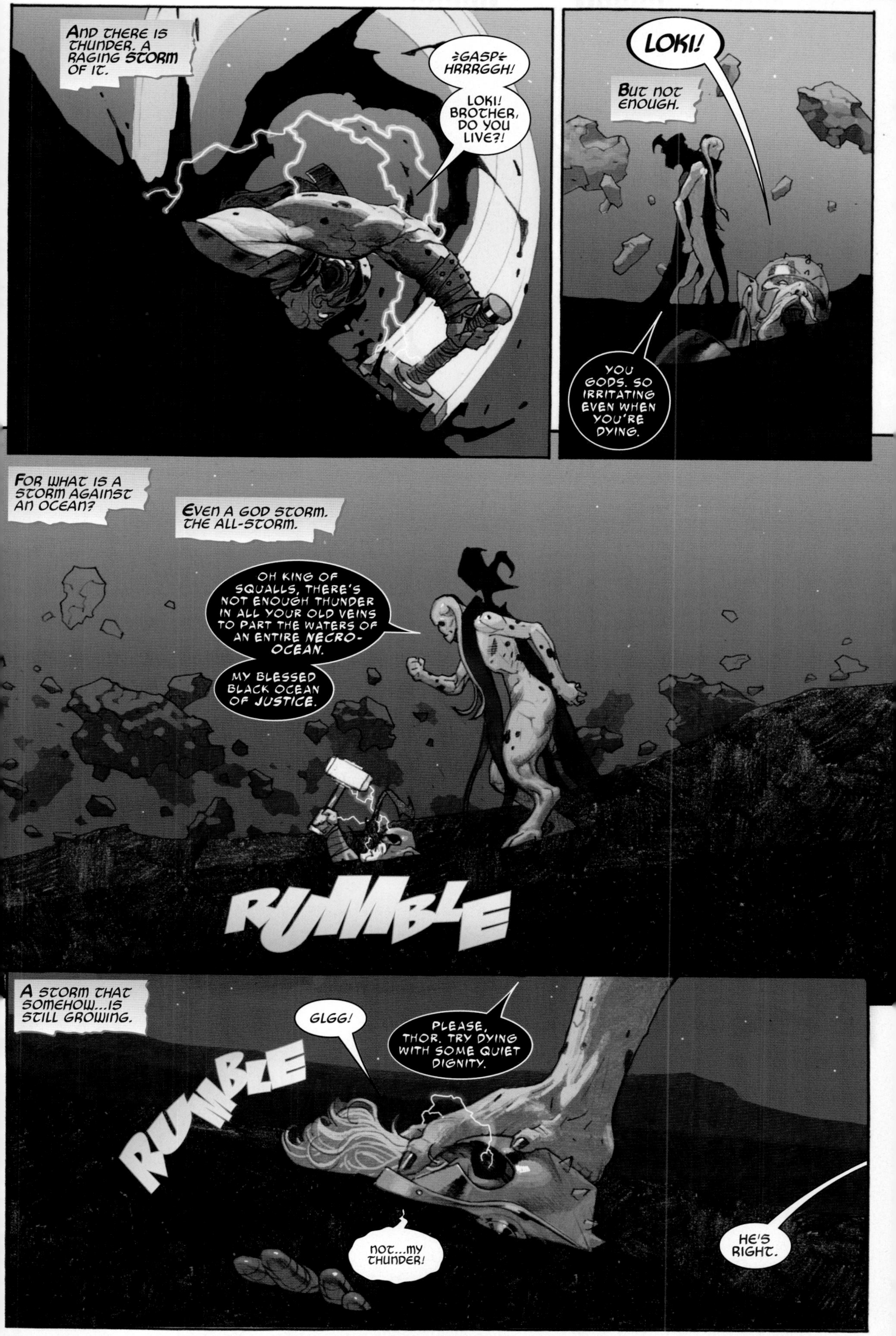

AND THERE IS THUNDER. A RAGING STORM OF IT.
≠GASP≠ HRRRGGH!
LOKI! BROTHER, DO YOU LIVE?!
LOKI!
BUT NOT ENOUGH.
YOU GODS. SO IRRITATING EVEN WHEN YOU'RE DYING.
FOR WHAT IS A STORM AGAINST AN OCEAN?
EVEN A GOD STORM. THE ALL-STORM.
OH KING OF SQUALLS, THERE'S NOT ENOUGH THUNDER IN ALL YOUR OLD VEINS TO PART THE WATERS OF AN ENTIRE NECRO-OCEAN.
MY BLESSED BLACK OCEAN OF JUSTICE.
RUMBLE
A STORM THAT SOMEHOW....IS STILL GROWING.
GLGG!
PLEASE, THOR. TRY DYING WITH SOME QUIET DIGNITY.
RUMBLE
NOT...MY THUNDER!
HE'S RIGHT.

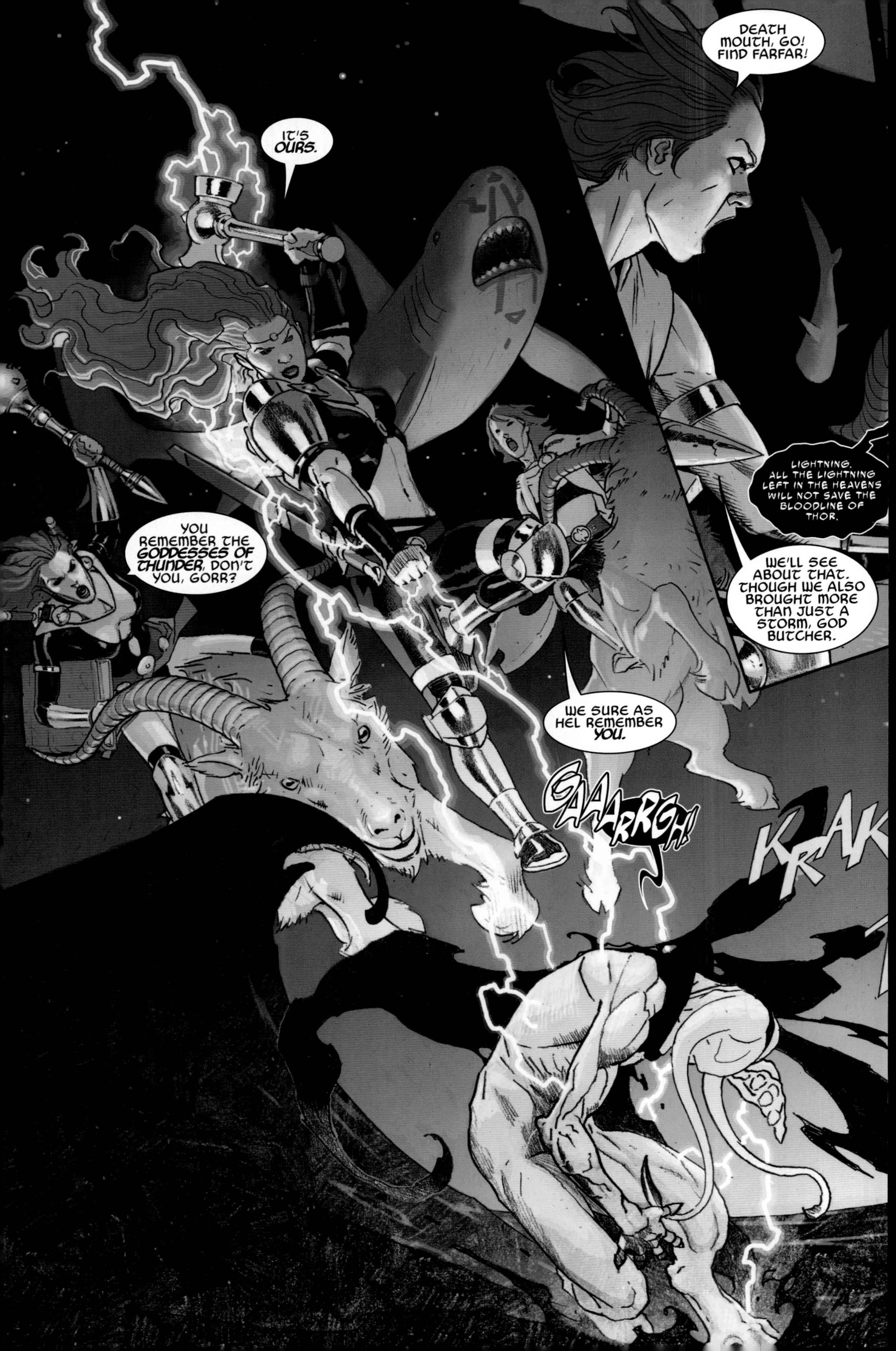
DEATH MOUTH, GO! FIND FARFAR!
IT'S OURS.
LIGHTNING. ALL THE LIGHTNING LEFT IN THE HEAVENS WILL NOT SAVE THE BLOODLINE OF THOR.
WE'LL SEE ABOUT THAT. THOUGH WE ALSO BROUGHT MORE THAN JUST A STORM, GOD BUTCHER.
YOU REMEMBER THE GODDESSES OF THUNDER, DON'T YOU, GORR?
WE SURE AS HEL REMEMBER YOU.
GAAARRGH!
KRAK

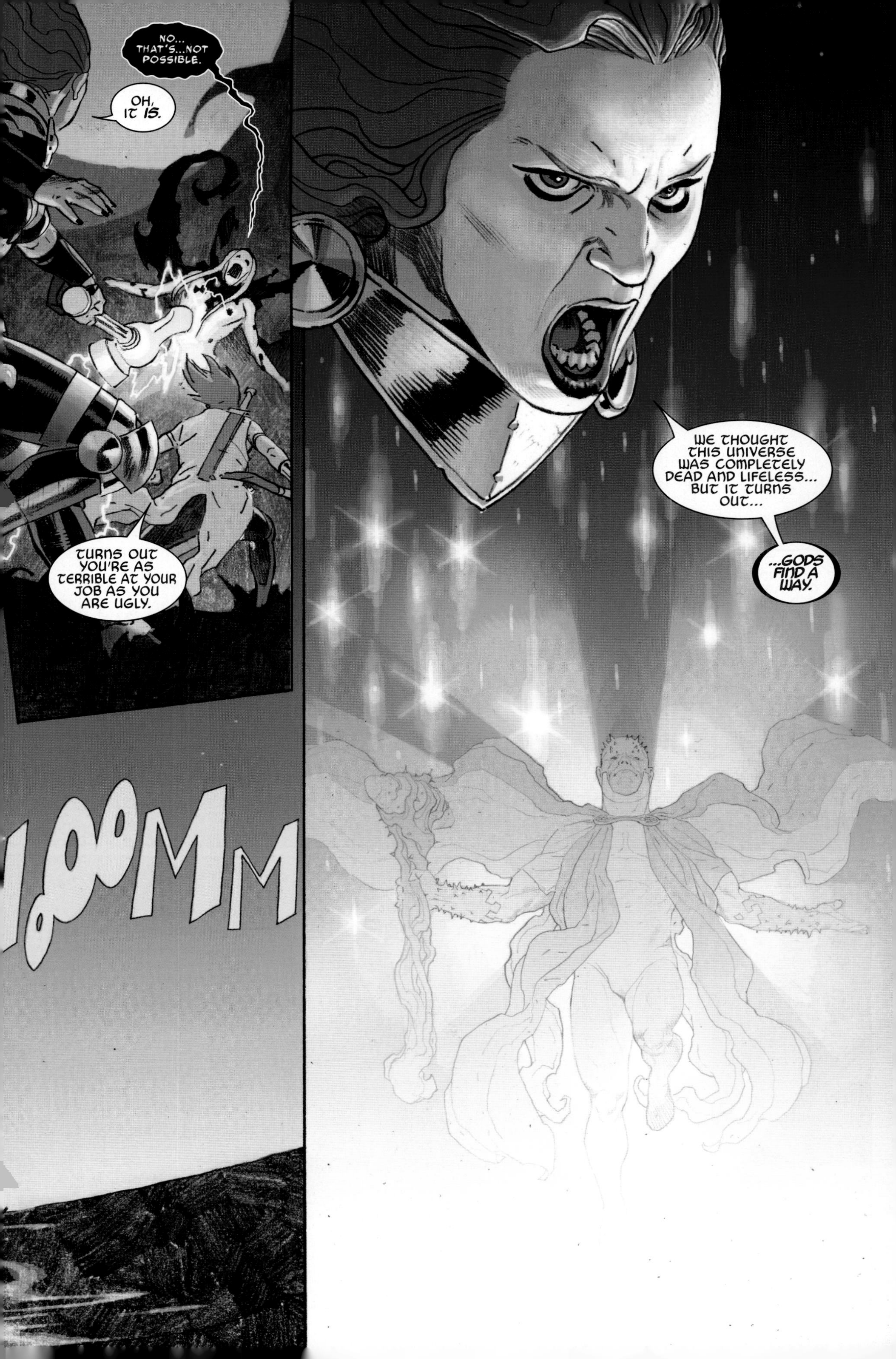
NO... THAT'S...NOT POSSIBLE.
OH, IT IS.
TURNS OUT YOU'RE AS TERRIBLE AT YOUR JOB AS YOU ARE UGLY.
WE THOUGHT THIS UNIVERSE WAS COMPLETELY DEAD AND LIFELESS... BUT IT TURNS OUT...
...GODS FIND A WAY.

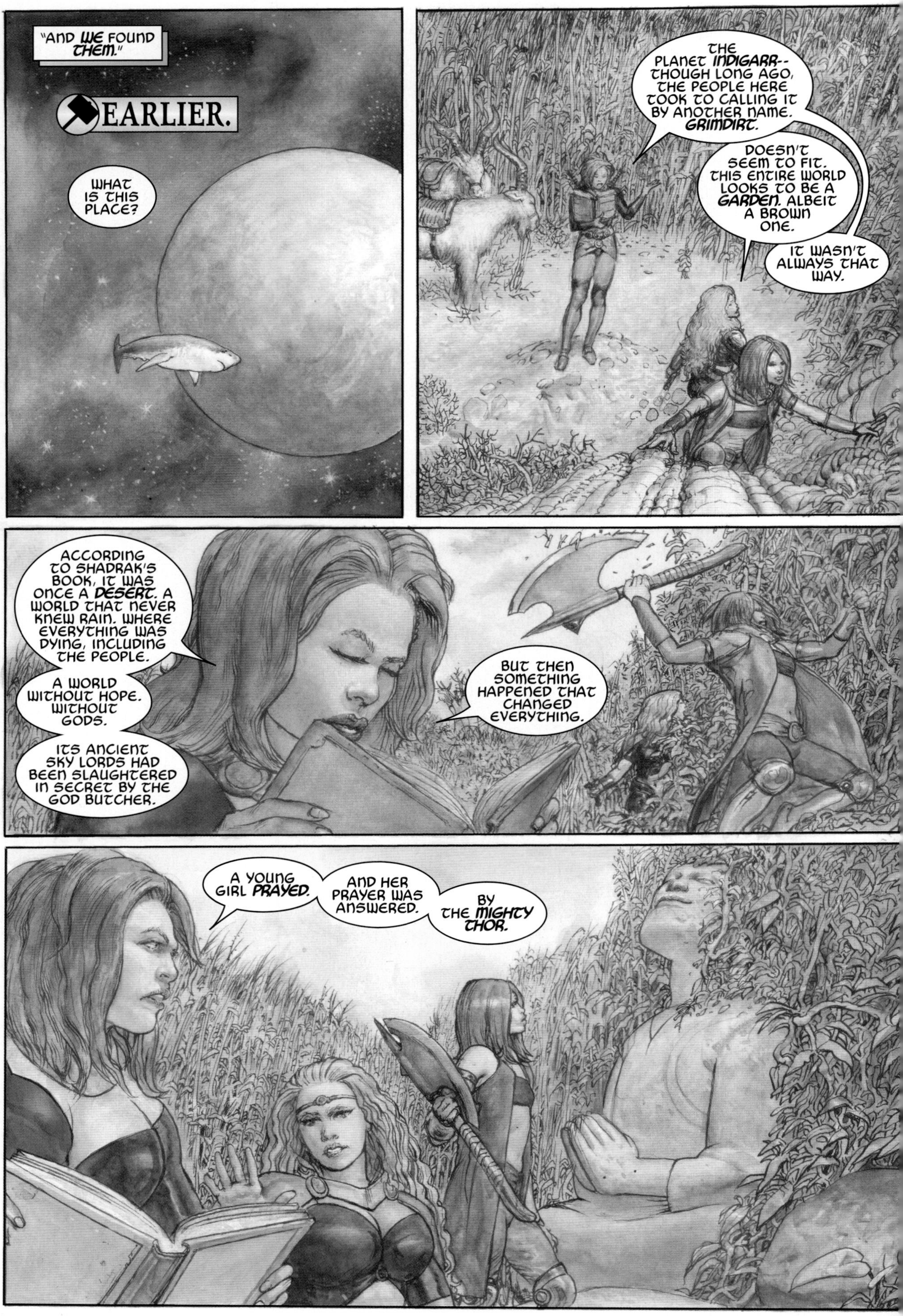
"AND WE FOUND THEM."
EARLIER.
WHAT IS THIS PLACE?
THE PLANET INDIGARR--THOUGH LONG AGO, THE PEOPLE HERE TOOK TO CALLING IT BY ANOTHER NAME. GRIMDIRT.
DOESN'T SEEM TO FIT. THIS ENTIRE WORLD LOOKS TO BE A GARDEN. ALBEIT A BROWN ONE.
IT WASN'T ALWAYS THAT WAY.
ACCORDING TO SHADRAK'S BOOK, IT WAS ONCE A DESERT. A WORLD THAT NEVER KNEW RAIN. WHERE EVERYTHING WAS DYING, INCLUDING THE PEOPLE.
A WORLD WITHOUT HOPE. WITHOUT GODS.
ITS ANCIENT SKY LORDS HAD BEEN SLAUGHTERED IN SECRET BY THE GOD BUTCHER.
BUT THEN SOMETHING HAPPENED THAT CHANGED EVERYTHING.
A YOUNG GIRL PRAYED.
AND HER PRAYER WAS ANSWERED.
BY THE MIGHTY THOR.

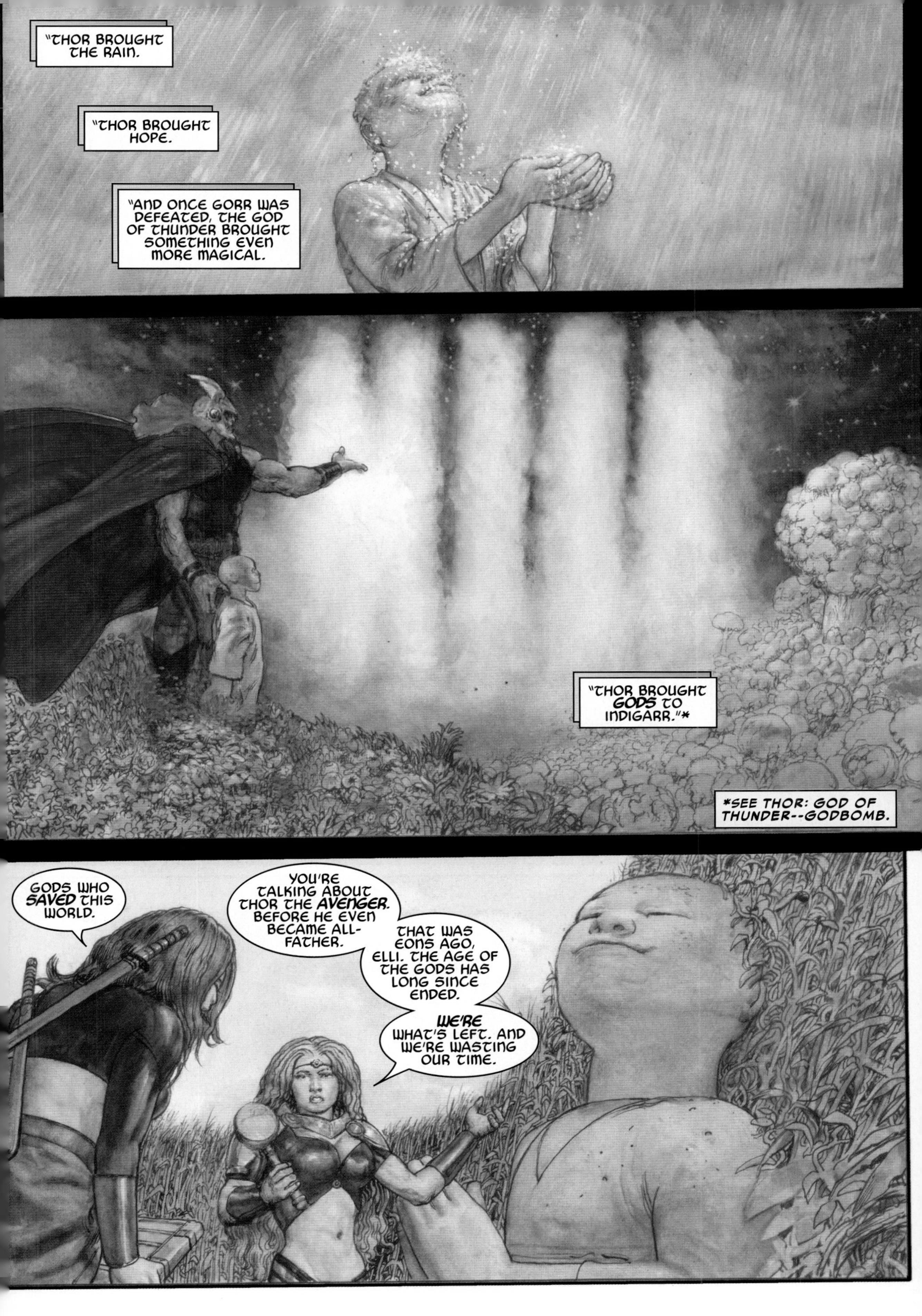
"THOR BROUGHT THE RAIN.
"THOR BROUGHT HOPE.
"AND ONCE GORR WAS DEFEATED, THE GOD OF THUNDER BROUGHT SOMETHING EVEN MORE MAGICAL.
"THOR BROUGHT **GODS** TO INDIGARR."*
*SEE THOR: GOD OF THUNDER--GODBOMB.
GODS WHO **SAVED** THIS WORLD.
YOU'RE TALKING ABOUT THOR THE **AVENGER**. BEFORE HE EVEN BECAME ALL-FATHER.
THAT WAS EONS AGO, ELLI. THE AGE OF THE GODS HAS LONG SINCE ENDED.
WE'RE WHAT'S LEFT. AND WE'RE WASTING OUR TIME.

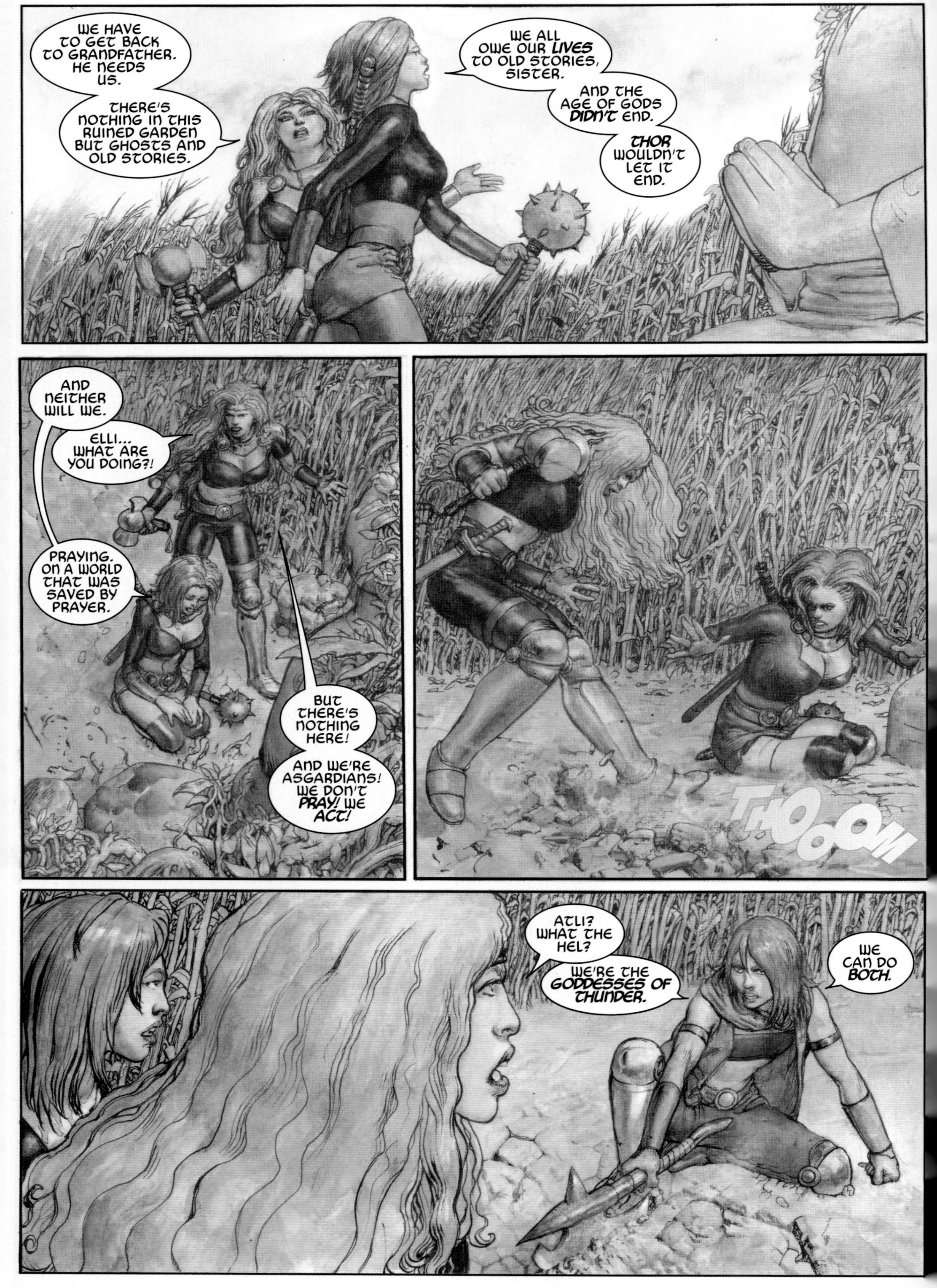
WE HAVE TO GET BACK TO GRANDFATHER. HE NEEDS US.
THERE'S NOTHING IN THIS RUINED GARDEN BUT GHOSTS AND OLD STORIES.
WE ALL OWE OUR LIVES TO OLD STORIES, SISTER.
AND THE AGE OF GODS DIDN'T END.
THOR WOULDN'T LET IT END.
AND NEITHER WILL WE.
ELLI... WHAT ARE YOU DOING?!
PRAYING. ON A WORLD THAT WAS SAVED BY PRAYER.
BUT THERE'S NOTHING HERE!
AND WE'RE ASGARDIANS! WE DON'T PRAY! WE ACT!
THOOOOM
ATLI? WHAT THE HEL?
WE'RE THE GODDESSES OF THUNDER.
WE CAN DO BOTH.

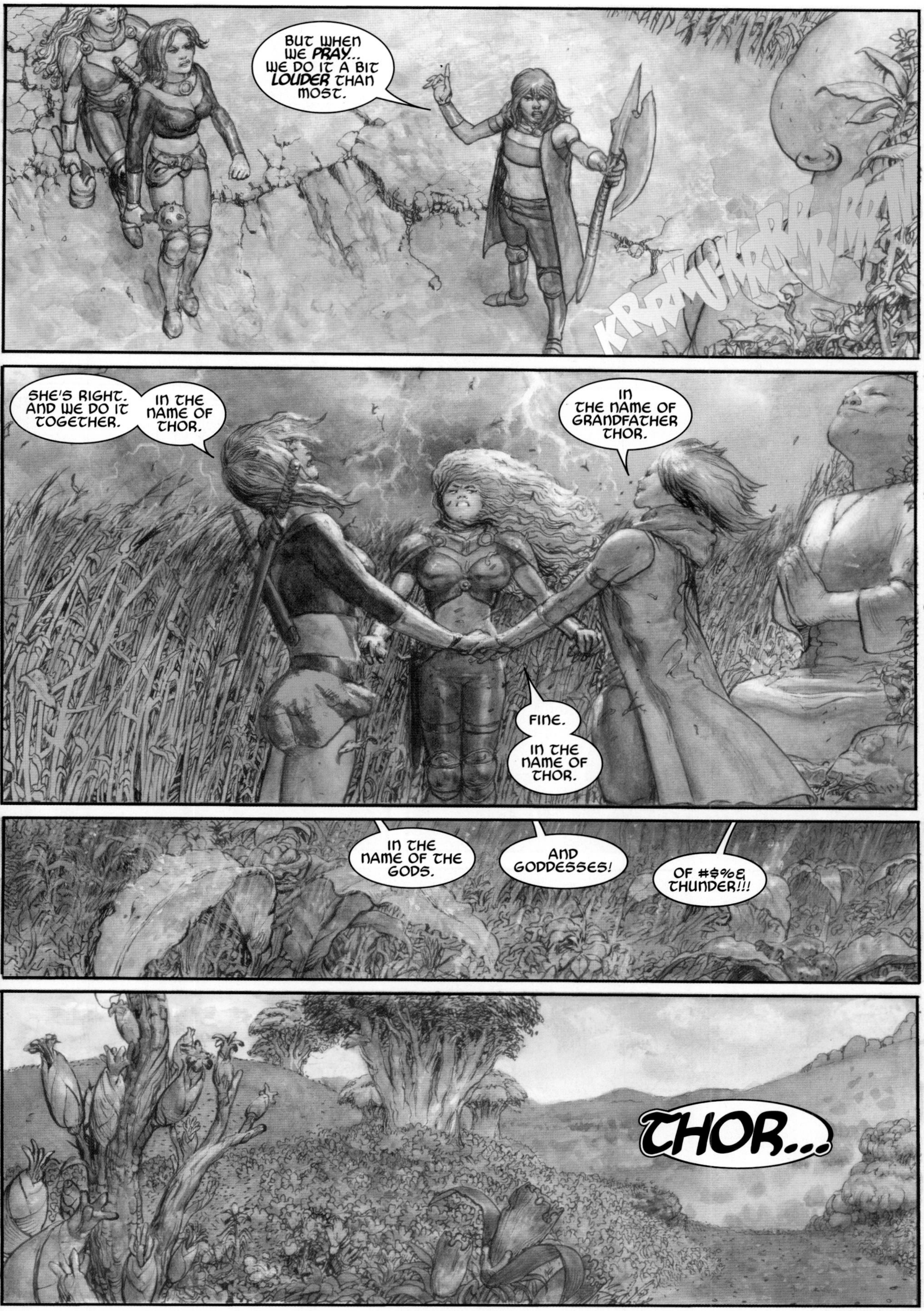
BUT WHEN WE PRAY... WE DO IT A BIT LOUDER THAN MOST.
SHE'S RIGHT. AND WE DO IT TOGETHER.
IN THE NAME OF THOR.
IN THE NAME OF GRANDFATHER THOR.
FINE. IN THE NAME OF THOR.
IN THE NAME OF THE GODS.
AND GODDESSES!
OF #$%& THUNDER!!!
THOR...

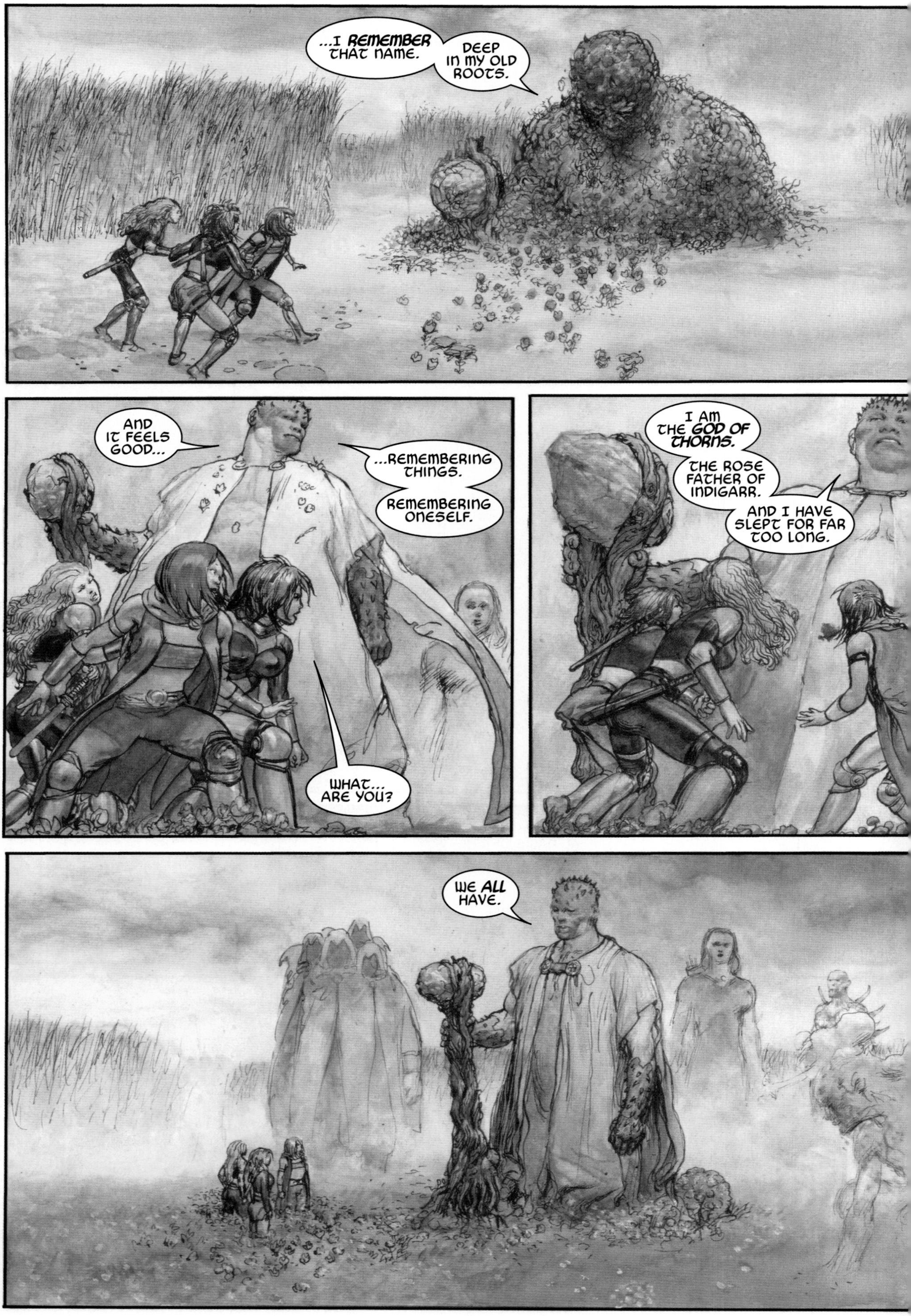
...I REMEMBER THAT NAME.
DEEP IN MY OLD ROOTS.
AND IT FEELS GOOD...
...REMEMBERING THINGS.
REMEMBERING ONESELF.
WHAT... ARE YOU?
I AM THE GOD OF THORNS.
THE ROSE FATHER OF INDIGARR.
AND I HAVE SLEPT FOR FAR TOO LONG.
WE ALL HAVE.

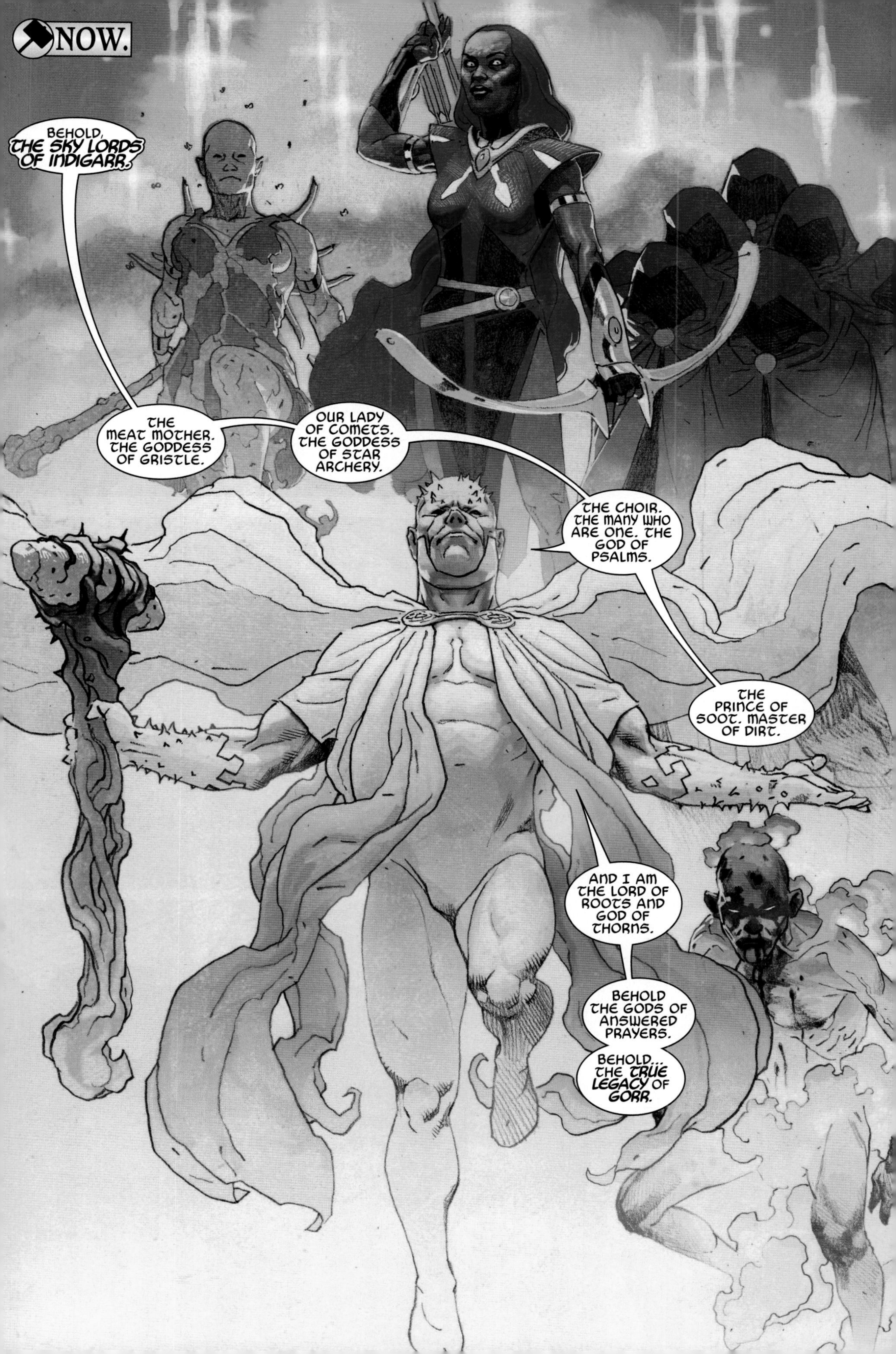
NOW.
BEHOLD, THE SKY LORDS OF INDIGARR.
THE MEAT MOTHER. THE GODDESS OF GRISTLE.
OUR LADY OF COMETS. THE GODDESS OF STAR ARCHERY.
THE CHOIR. THE MANY WHO ARE ONE. THE GOD OF PSALMS.
THE PRINCE OF SOOT. MASTER OF DIRT.
AND I AM THE LORD OF ROOTS AND GOD OF THORNS.
BEHOLD THE GODS OF ANSWERED PRAYERS.
BEHOLD... THE TRUE LEGACY OF GORR.

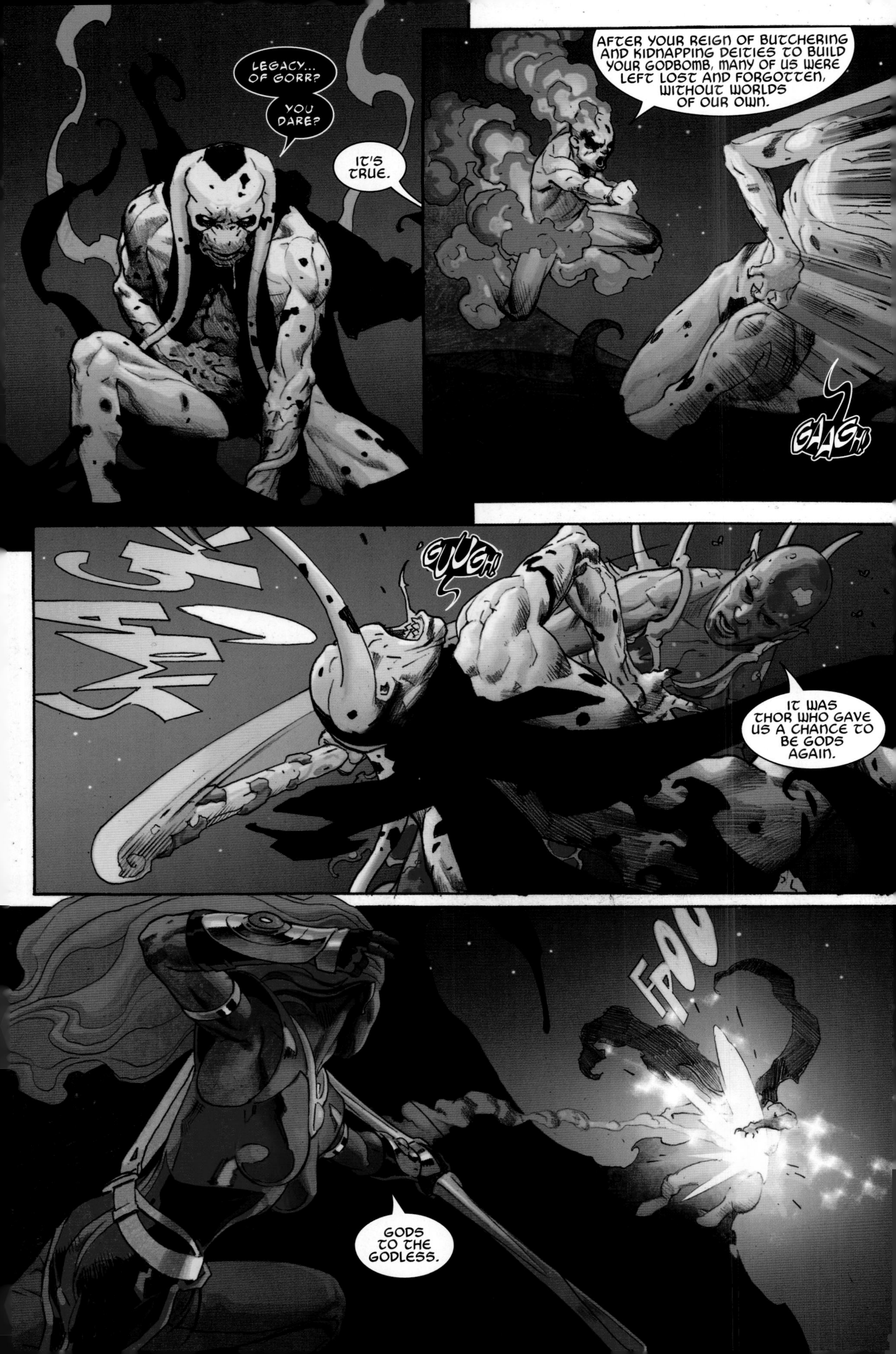
LEGACY... OF GORR?
YOU DARE?
IT'S TRUE.
AFTER YOUR REIGN OF BUTCHERING AND KIDNAPPING DEITIES TO BUILD YOUR GODBOMB, MANY OF US WERE LEFT LOST AND FORGOTTEN, WITHOUT WORLDS OF OUR OWN.
GAAGH!
GUUGH!
IT WAS THOR WHO GAVE US A CHANCE TO BE GODS AGAIN.
GODS TO THE GODLESS.

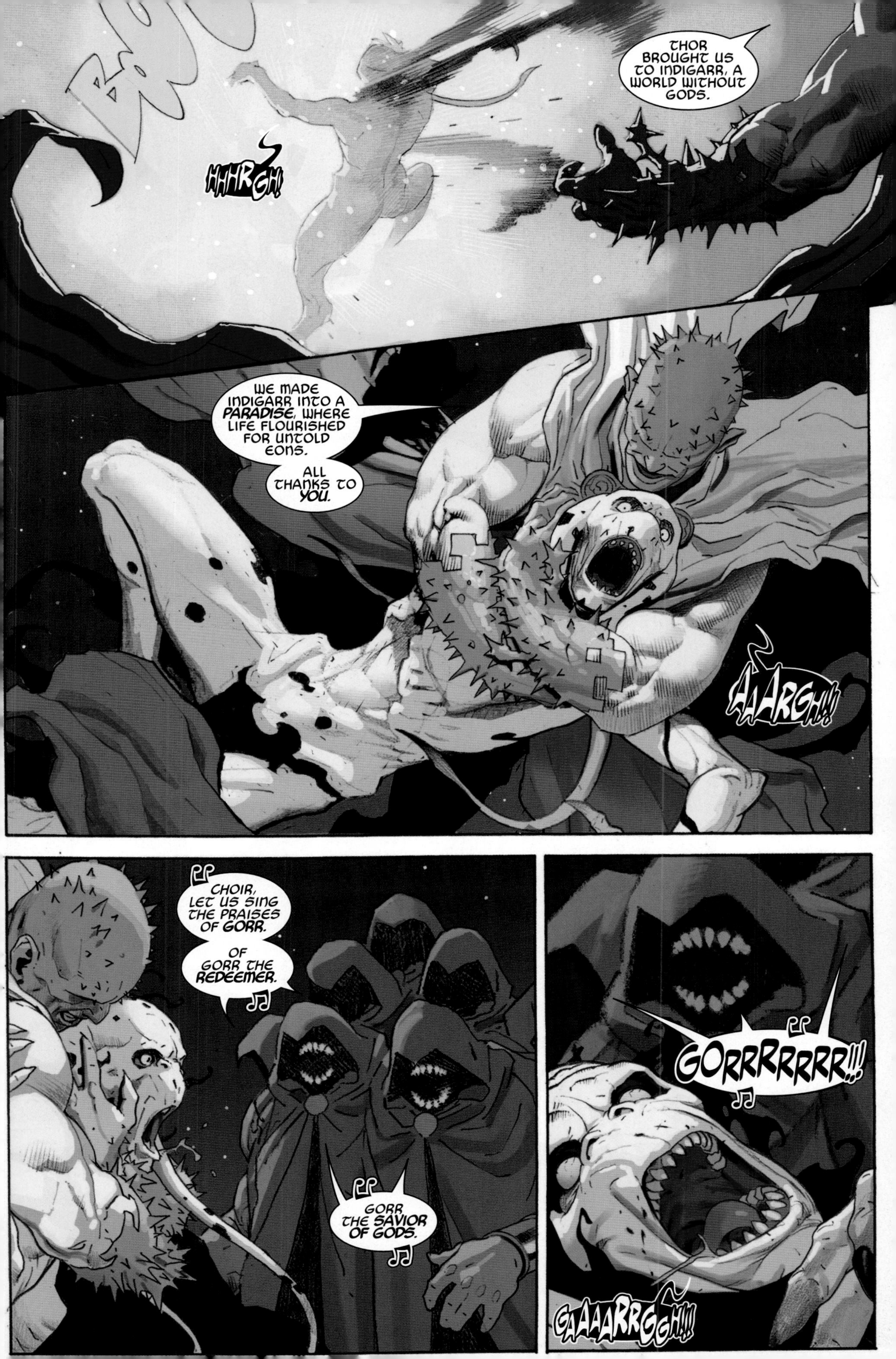
THOR BROUGHT US TO INDIGARR, A WORLD WITHOUT GODS.
HHHRGH!
WE MADE INDIGARR INTO A *PARADISE*, WHERE LIFE FLOURISHED FOR UNTOLD EONS.
ALL THANKS TO *YOU*.
AAARGH!!
♫ CHOIR, LET US SING THE PRAISES OF **GORR**.
OF GORR THE **REDEEMER**. ♫
♫ GORR THE **SAVIOR OF GODS**. ♫
♫ GORRRRRRR!! ♫
GAAAARRGGH!!!

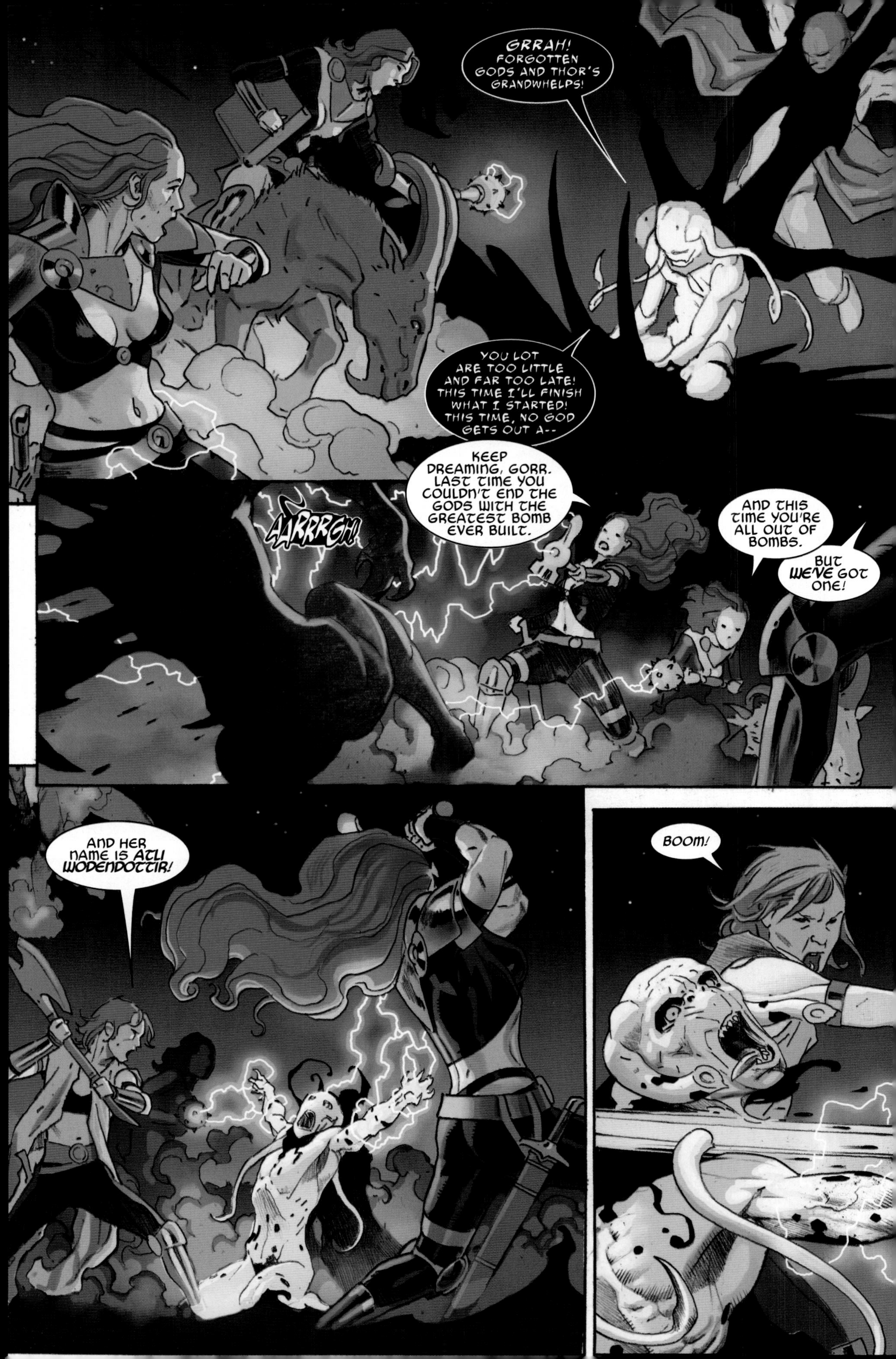
GRRAH! FORGOTTEN GODS AND THOR'S GRANDWHELPS!
YOU LOT ARE TOO LITTLE AND FAR TOO LATE! THIS TIME I'LL FINISH WHAT I STARTED! THIS TIME, NO GOD GETS OUT A--
AARRRGH!
KEEP DREAMING, GORR. LAST TIME YOU COULDN'T END THE GODS WITH THE GREATEST BOMB EVER BUILT.
AND THIS TIME YOU'RE ALL OUT OF BOMBS.
BUT WE'VE GOT ONE!
AND HER NAME IS ATLI WODENDOTTIR!
BOOM!

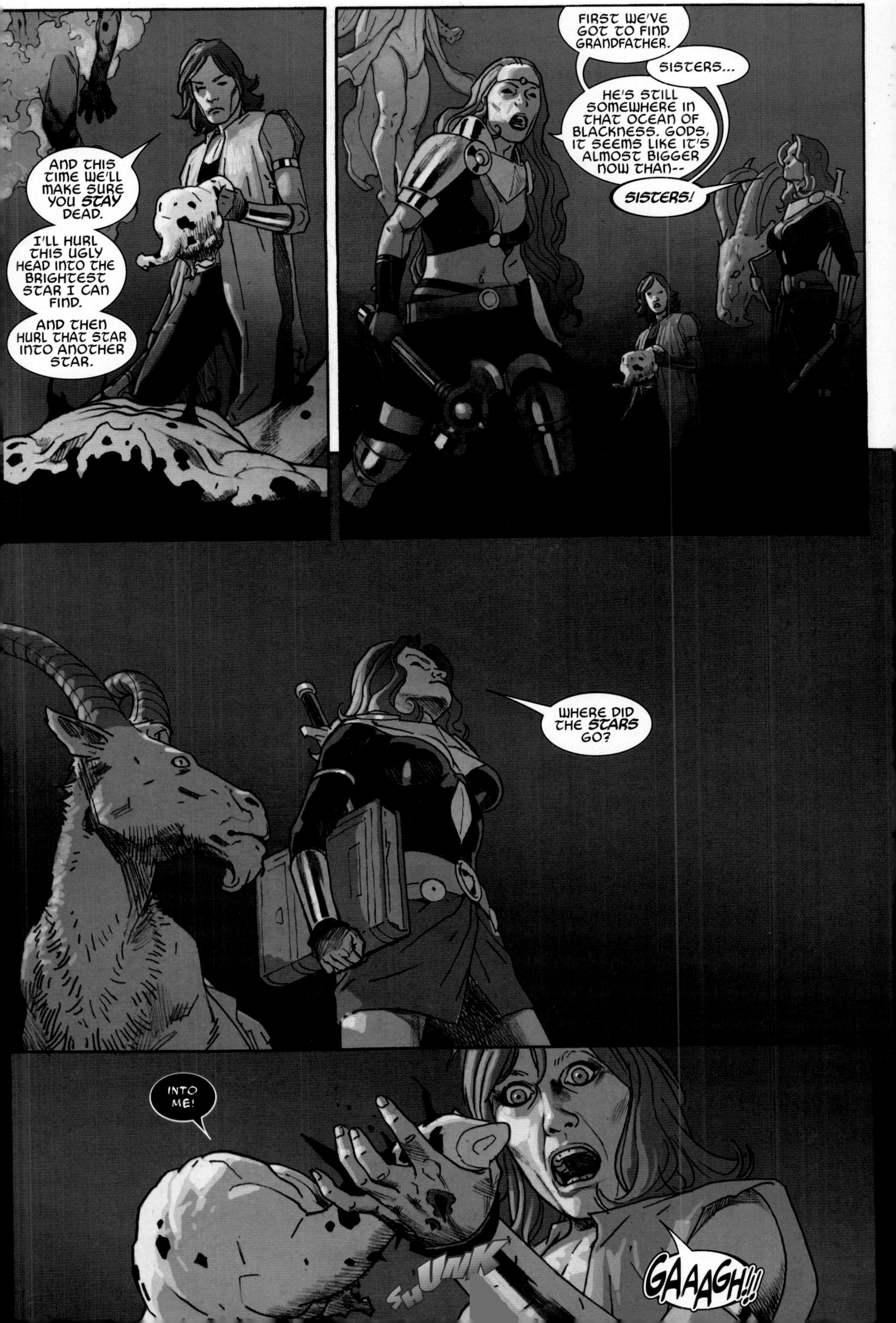
AND THIS TIME WE'LL MAKE SURE YOU STAY DEAD.
I'LL HURL THIS UGLY HEAD INTO THE BRIGHTEST STAR I CAN FIND.
AND THEN HURL THAT STAR INTO ANOTHER STAR.
FIRST WE'VE GOT TO FIND GRANDFATHER.
SISTERS...
HE'S STILL SOMEWHERE IN THAT OCEAN OF BLACKNESS. GODS, IT SEEMS LIKE IT'S ALMOST BIGGER NOW THAN--
SISTERS!
WHERE DID THE STARS GO?
INTO ME!
SHUNK
GAAAGH!!!

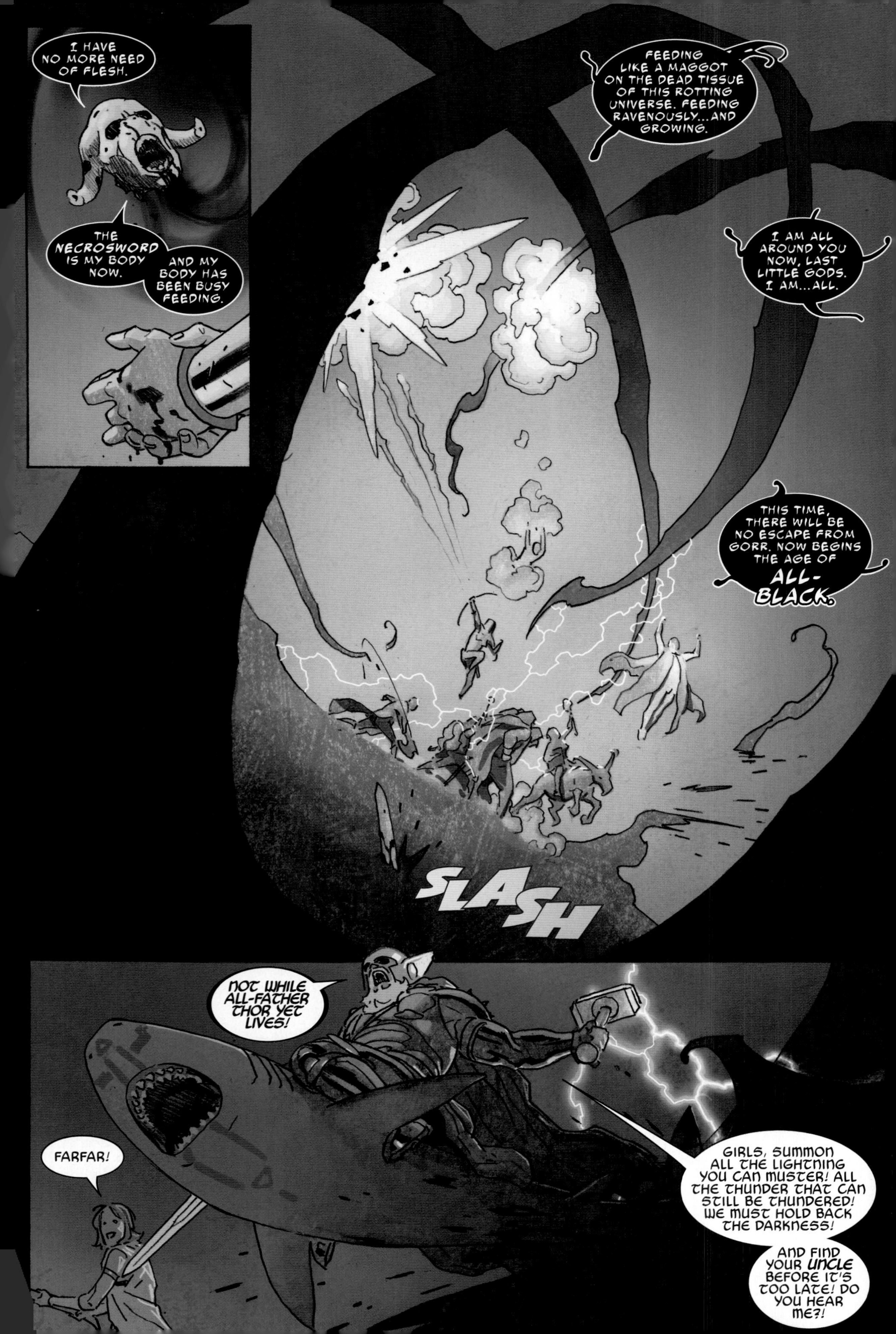

I HAVE NO MORE NEED OF FLESH.
THE NECROSWORD IS MY BODY NOW.
AND MY BODY HAS BEEN BUSY FEEDING.
FEEDING LIKE A MAGGOT ON THE DEAD TISSUE OF THIS ROTTING UNIVERSE. FEEDING RAVENOUSLY...AND GROWING.
I AM ALL AROUND YOU NOW, LAST LITTLE GODS. I AM...ALL.
THIS TIME, THERE WILL BE NO ESCAPE FROM GORR. NOW BEGINS THE AGE OF ALL-BLACK.
SLASH
NOT WHILE ALL-FATHER THOR YET LIVES!
FARFAR!
GIRLS, SUMMON ALL THE LIGHTNING YOU CAN MUSTER! ALL THE THUNDER THAT CAN STILL BE THUNDERED! WE MUST HOLD BACK THE DARKNESS!
AND FIND YOUR UNCLE BEFORE IT'S TOO LATE! DO YOU HEAR ME?!

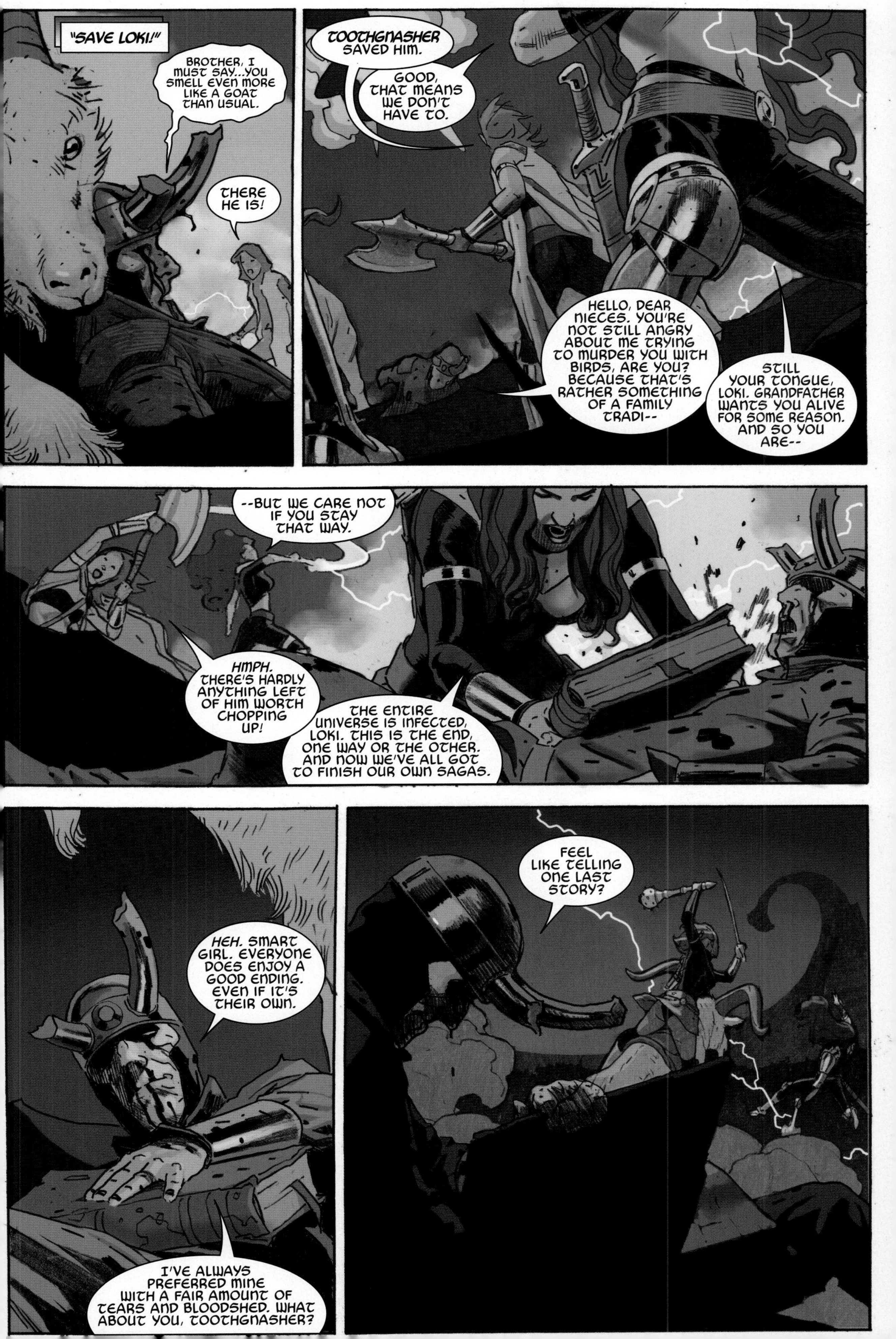
"SAVE LOKI!"
BROTHER, I MUST SAY...YOU SMELL EVEN MORE LIKE A GOAT THAN USUAL.
THERE HE IS!
TOOTHGNASHER SAVED HIM.
GOOD, THAT MEANS WE DON'T HAVE TO.
HELLO, DEAR NIECES. YOU'RE NOT STILL ANGRY ABOUT ME TRYING TO MURDER YOU WITH BIRDS, ARE YOU? BECAUSE THAT'S RATHER SOMETHING OF A FAMILY TRADI--
STILL YOUR TONGUE, LOKI. GRANDFATHER WANTS YOU ALIVE FOR SOME REASON. AND SO YOU ARE--
--BUT WE CARE NOT IF YOU STAY THAT WAY.
HMPH. THERE'S HARDLY ANYTHING LEFT OF HIM WORTH CHOPPING UP!
THE ENTIRE UNIVERSE IS INFECTED, LOKI. THIS IS THE END, ONE WAY OR THE OTHER. AND NOW WE'VE ALL GOT TO FINISH OUR OWN SAGAS.
HEH. SMART GIRL. EVERYONE DOES ENJOY A GOOD ENDING. EVEN IF IT'S THEIR OWN.
I'VE ALWAYS PREFERRED MINE WITH A FAIR AMOUNT OF TEARS AND BLOODSHED. WHAT ABOUT YOU, TOOTHGNASHER?
FEEL LIKE TELLING ONE LAST STORY?

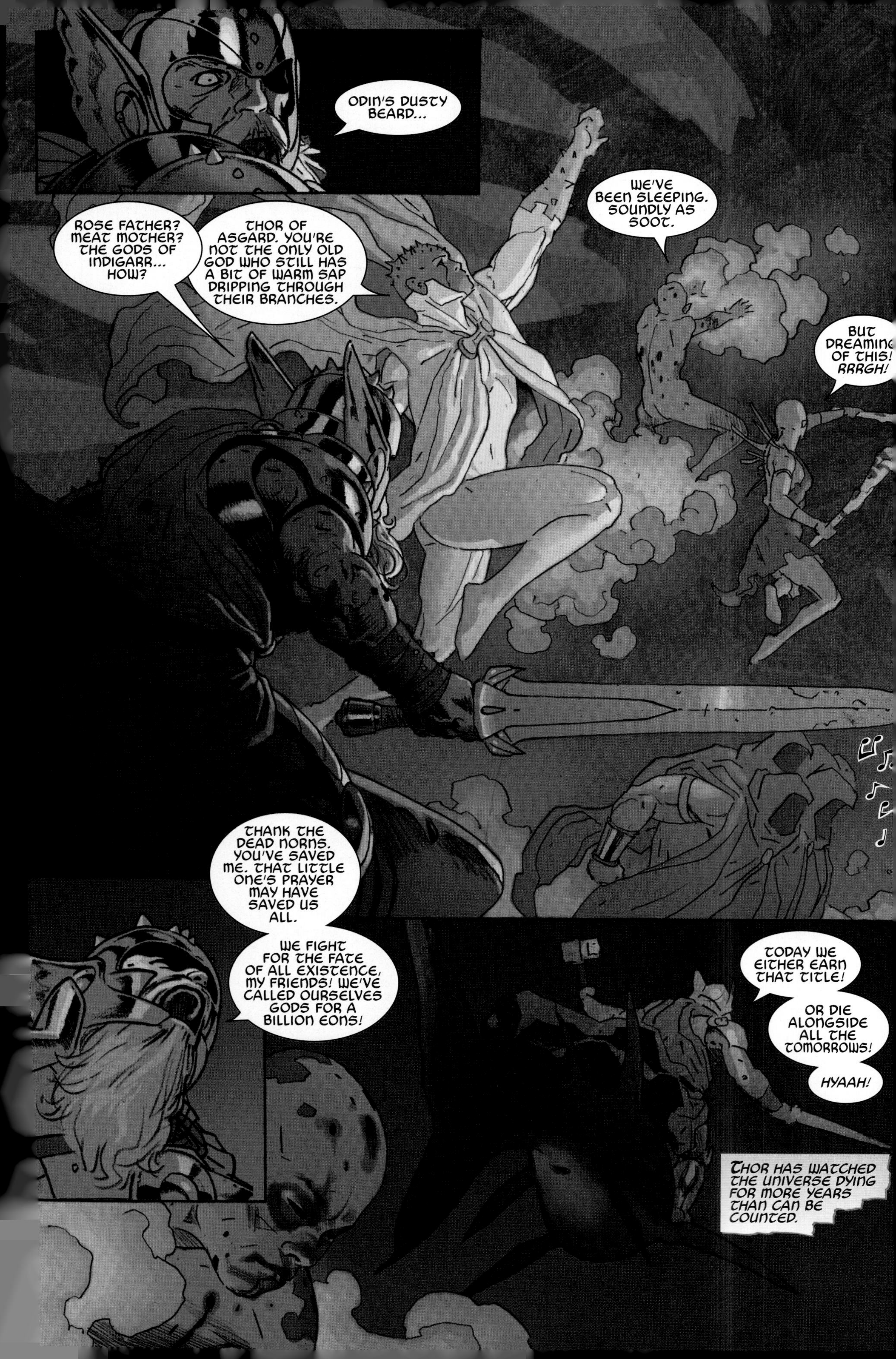
ODIN'S DUSTY BEARD...
ROSE FATHER? MEAT MOTHER? THE GODS OF INDIGARR... HOW?
THOR OF ASGARD. YOU'RE NOT THE ONLY OLD GOD WHO STILL HAS A BIT OF WARM SAP DRIPPING THROUGH THEIR BRANCHES.
WE'VE BEEN SLEEPING. SOUNDLY AS SOOT.
BUT DREAMING OF THIS! RRRGH!
THANK THE DEAD NORNS. YOU'VE SAVED ME. THAT LITTLE ONE'S PRAYER MAY HAVE SAVED US ALL.
WE FIGHT FOR THE FATE OF ALL EXISTENCE, MY FRIENDS! WE'VE CALLED OURSELVES GODS FOR A BILLION EONS!
TODAY WE EITHER EARN THAT TITLE!
OR DIE ALONGSIDE ALL THE TOMORROWS!
HYAAH!
THOR HAS WATCHED THE UNIVERSE DYING FOR MORE YEARS THAN CAN BE COUNTED.

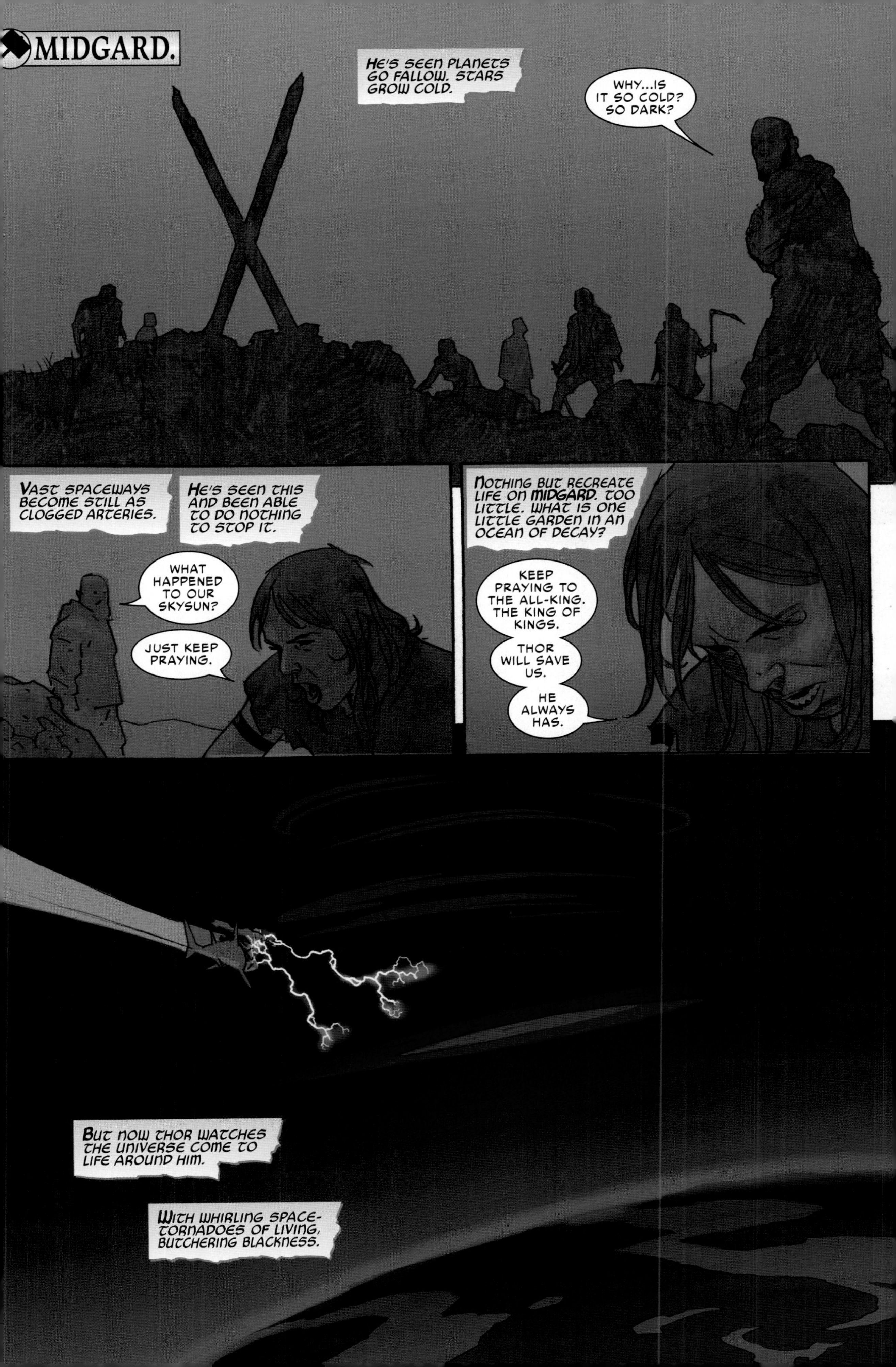
MIDGARD.
HE'S SEEN PLANETS GO FALLOW. STARS GROW COLD.
WHY...IS IT SO COLD? SO DARK?
VAST SPACEWAYS BECOME STILL AS CLOGGED ARTERIES.
HE'S SEEN THIS AND BEEN ABLE TO DO NOTHING TO STOP IT.
WHAT HAPPENED TO OUR SKYSUN?
JUST KEEP PRAYING.
NOTHING BUT RECREATE LIFE ON MIDGARD. TOO LITTLE. WHAT IS ONE LITTLE GARDEN IN AN OCEAN OF DECAY?
KEEP PRAYING TO THE ALL-KING. THE KING OF KINGS.
THOR WILL SAVE US.
HE ALWAYS HAS.
BUT NOW THOR WATCHES THE UNIVERSE COME TO LIFE AROUND HIM.
WITH WHIRLING SPACE-TORNADOES OF LIVING, BUTCHERING BLACKNESS.

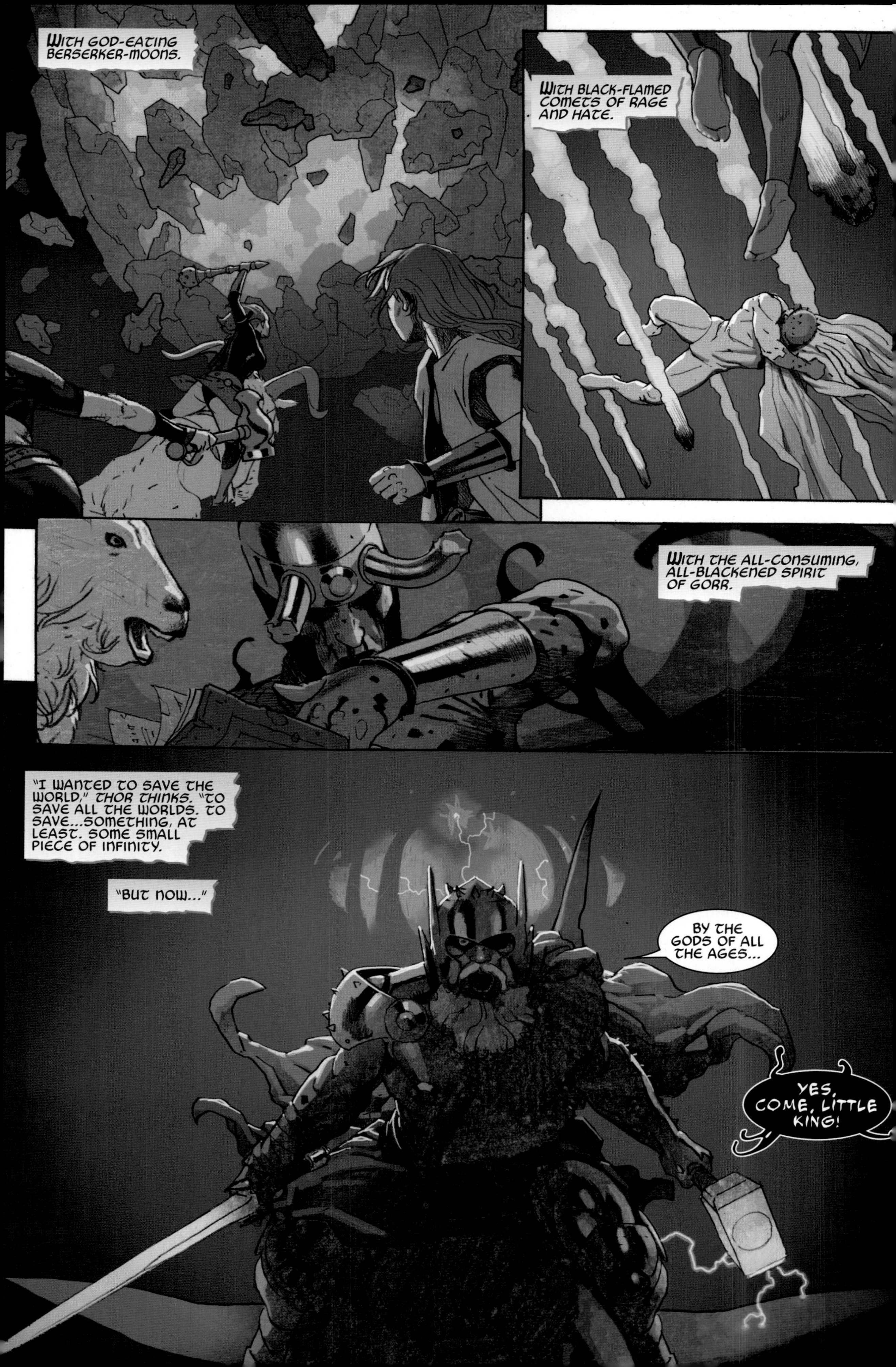
WITH GOD-EATING BERSERKER-MOONS.
WITH BLACK-FLAMED COMETS OF RAGE AND HATE.
WITH THE ALL-CONSUMING, ALL-BLACKENED SPIRIT OF GORR.
"I WANTED TO SAVE THE WORLD," THOR THINKS. "TO SAVE ALL THE WORLDS. TO SAVE...SOMETHING, AT LEAST. SOME SMALL PIECE OF INFINITY.
"BUT NOW..."
BY THE GODS OF ALL THE AGES...
YES, COME, LITTLE KING!

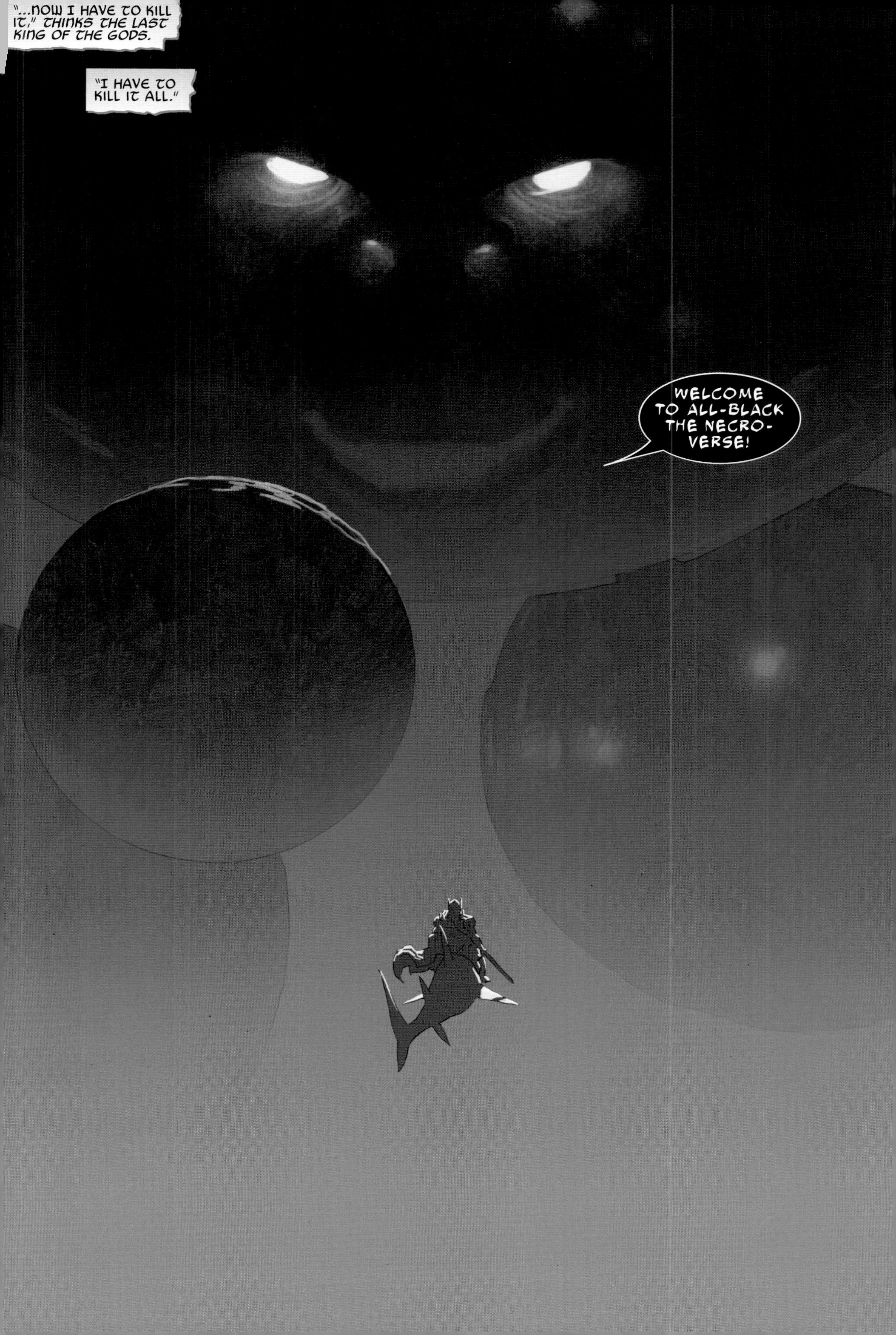
"...NOW I HAVE TO KILL IT," THINKS THE LAST KING OF THE GODS.
"I HAVE TO KILL IT ALL."
WELCOME TO ALL-BLACK THE NECRO-VERSE!

KING THOR 4

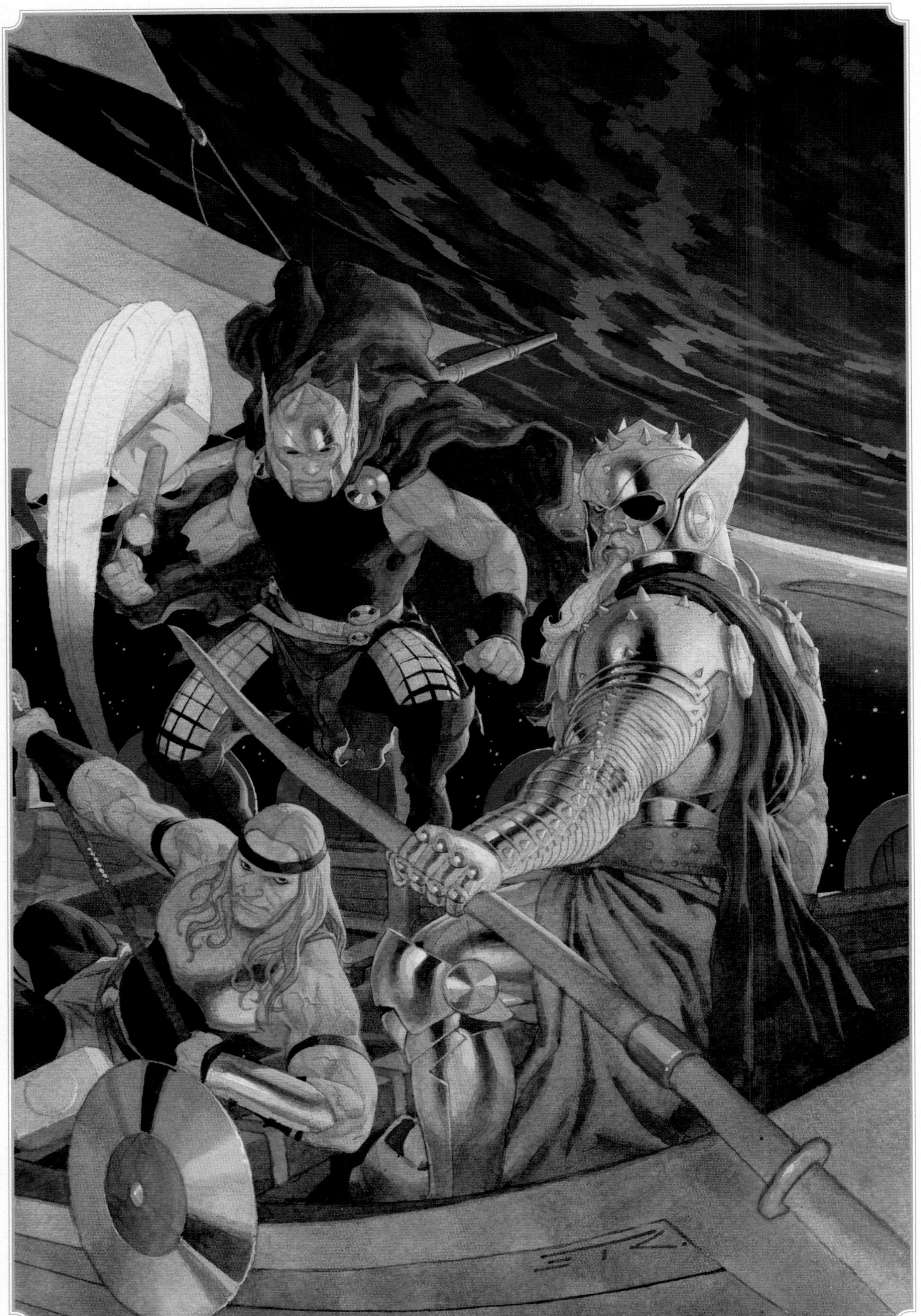

WHAT IS THE SPIRIT OF THUNDER?

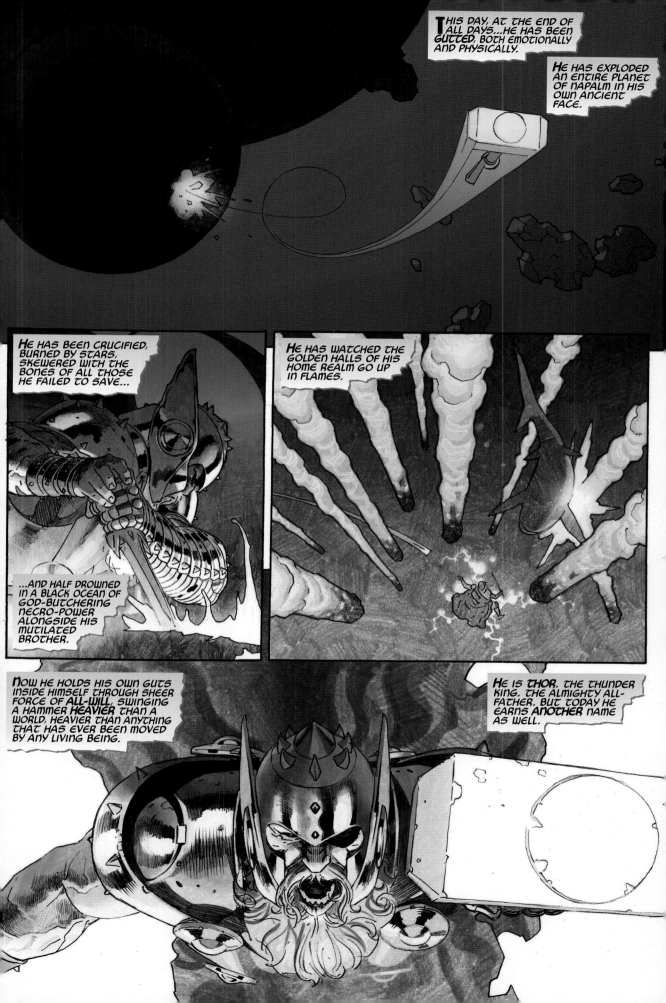

THIS DAY, AT THE END OF ALL DAYS...HE HAS BEEN GUTTED, BOTH EMOTIONALLY AND PHYSICALLY.

HE HAS EXPLODED AN ENTIRE PLANET OF NAPALM IN HIS OWN ANCIENT FACE.

HE HAS BEEN CRUCIFIED, BURNED BY STARS, SKEWERED WITH THE BONES OF ALL THOSE HE FAILED TO SAVE...

...AND HALF DROWNED IN A BLACK OCEAN OF GOD-BUTCHERING NECRO-POWER ALONGSIDE HIS MUTILATED BROTHER.

HE HAS WATCHED THE GOLDEN HALLS OF HIS HOME REALM GO UP IN FLAMES.

NOW HE HOLDS HIS OWN GUTS INSIDE HIMSELF THROUGH SHEER FORCE OF ALL-WILL, SWINGING A HAMMER HEAVIER THAN A WORLD, HEAVIER THAN ANYTHING THAT HAS EVER BEEN MOVED BY ANY LIVING BEING.

HE IS THOR. THE THUNDER KING. THE ALMIGHTY ALL-FATHER. BUT TODAY HE EARNS ANOTHER NAME AS WELL.

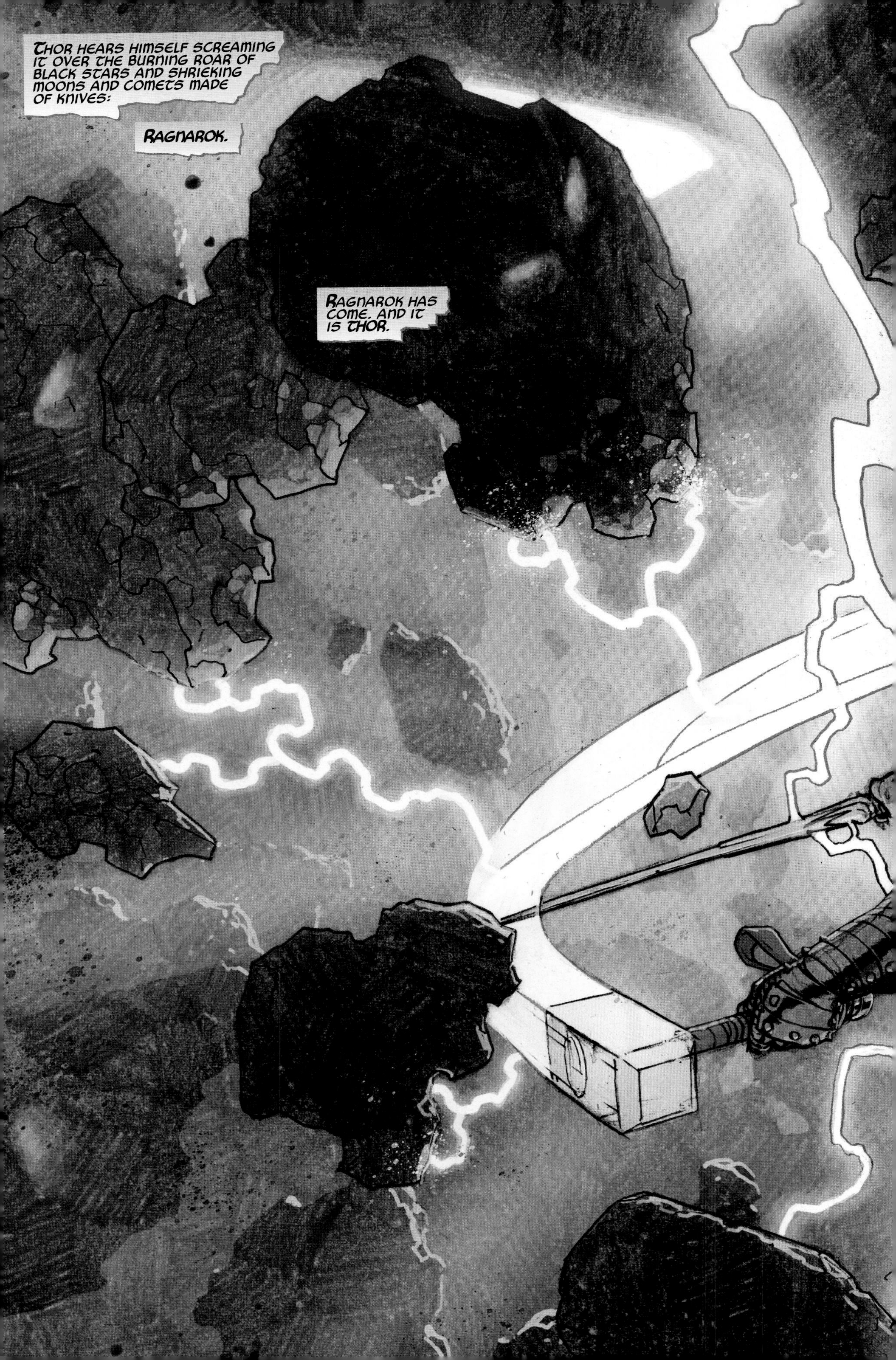

THOR HEARS HIMSELF SCREAMING IT OVER THE BURNING ROAR OF BLACK STARS AND SHRIEKING MOONS AND COMETS MADE OF KNIVES:
RAGNAROK.
RAGNAROK HAS COME. AND IT IS THOR.

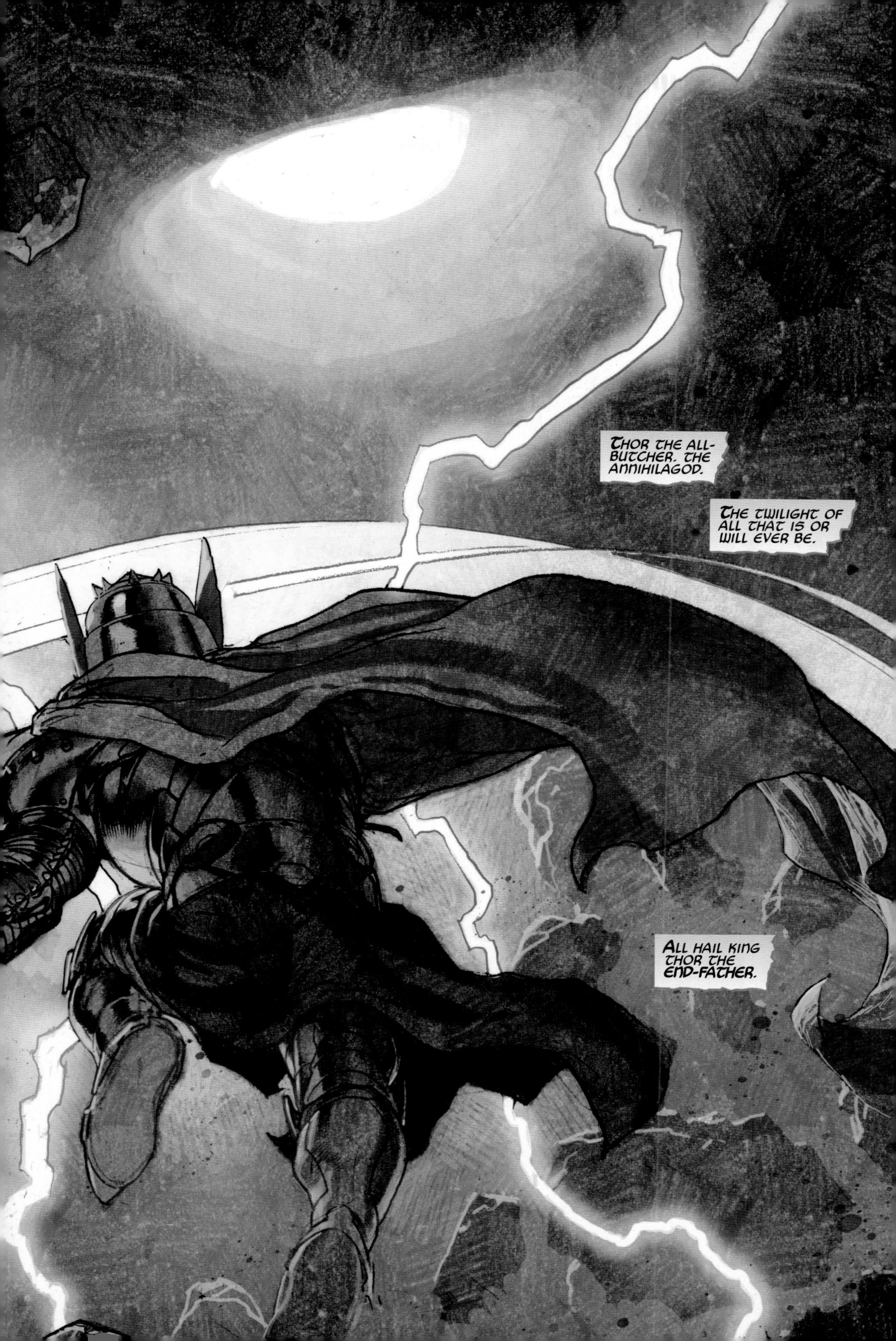
THOR THE ALL-BUTCHER. THE ANNIHILAGOD.
THE TWILIGHT OF ALL THAT IS OR WILL EVER BE.
ALL HAIL KING THOR THE END-FATHER.

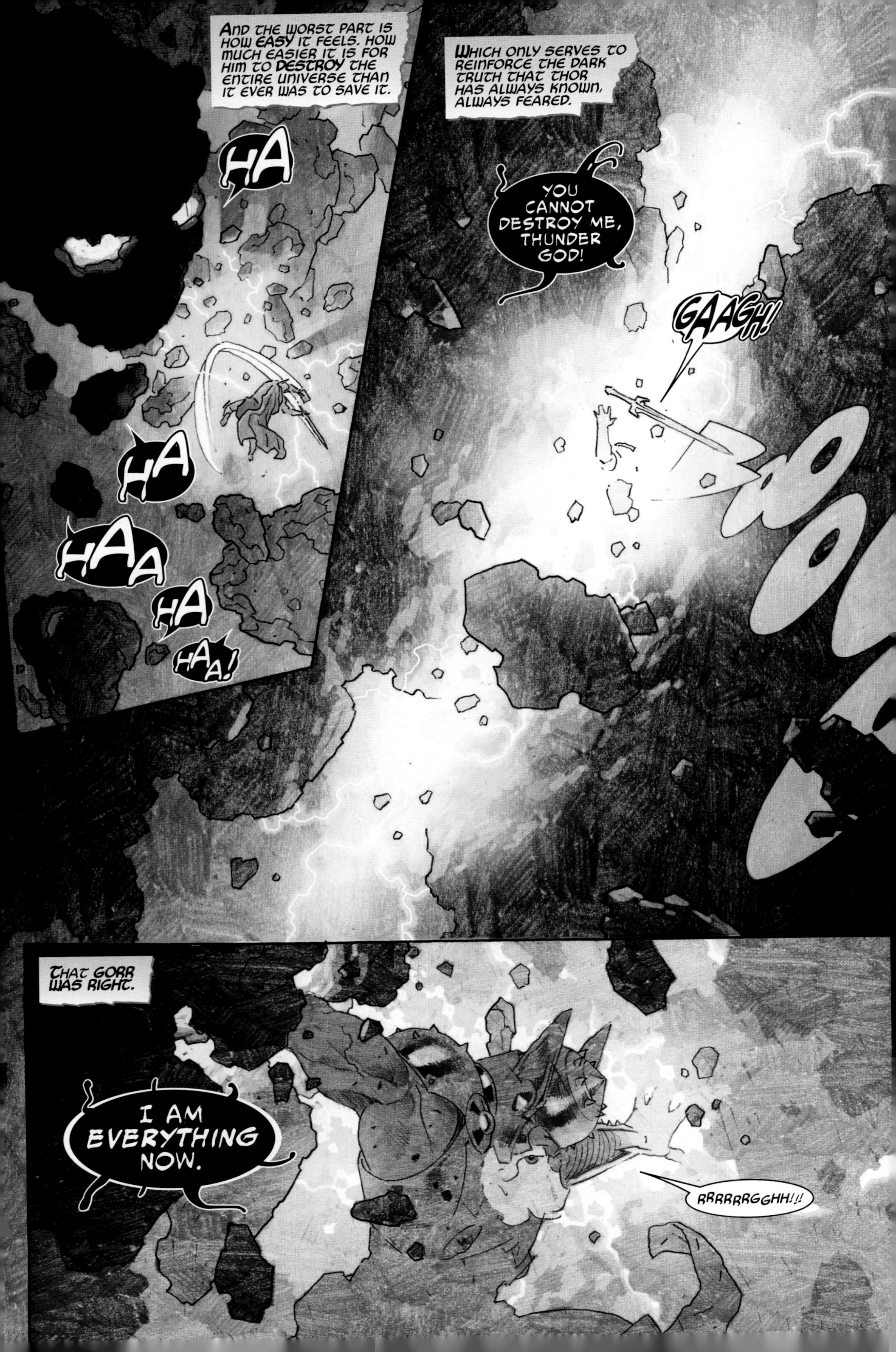
And the worst part is how EASY it feels. How much easier it is for him to DESTROY the entire universe than it ever was to save it.
HA
HA
HAA
HA
HAA!
Which only serves to reinforce the dark truth that Thor has always known, always feared.
YOU CANNOT DESTROY ME, THUNDER GOD!
GAAGH!
That Gorr was right.
I AM EVERYTHING NOW.
RRRRRRGGHH!!!

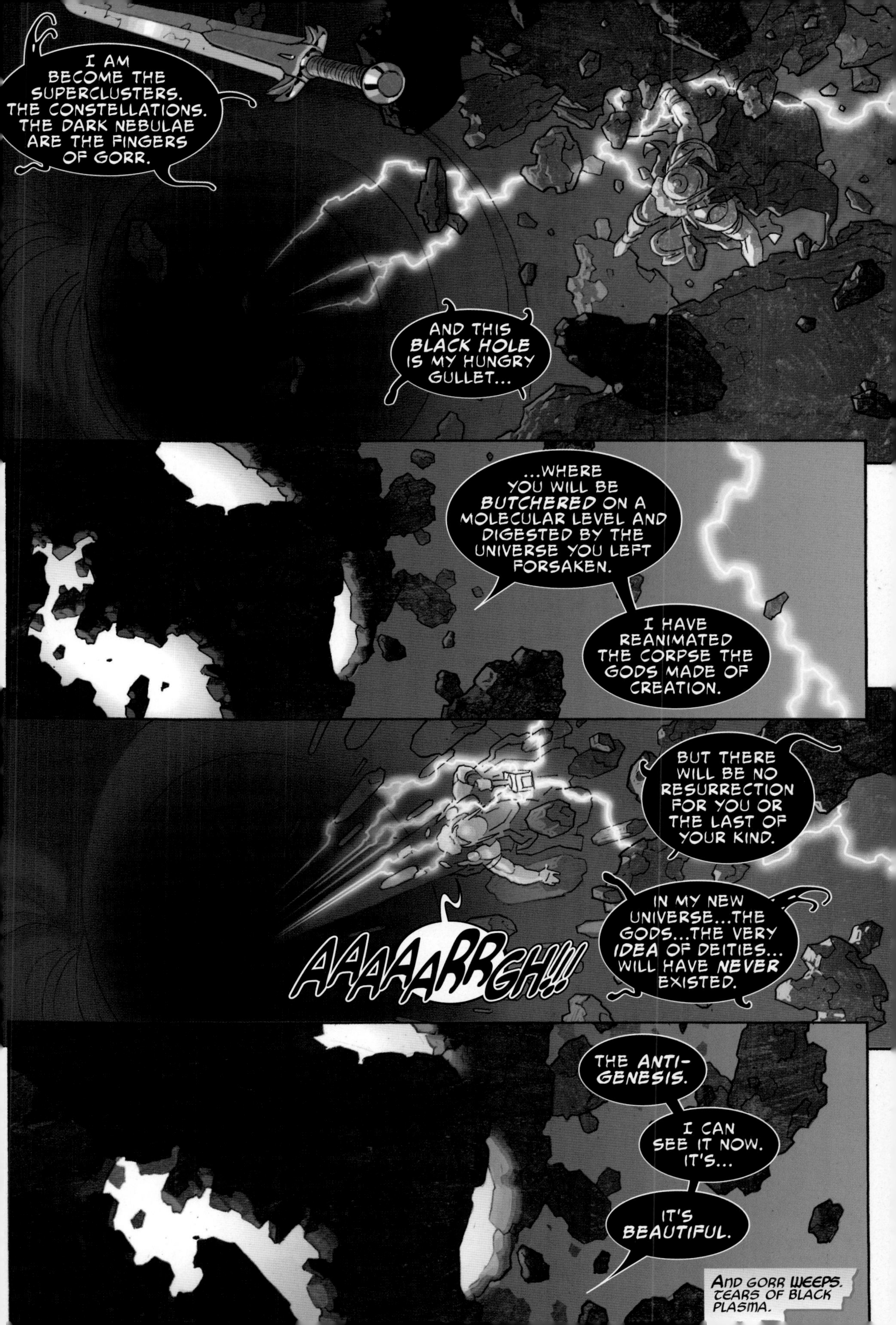
I AM BECOME THE SUPERCLUSTERS. THE CONSTELLATIONS. THE DARK NEBULAE ARE THE FINGERS OF GORR.
AND THIS BLACK HOLE IS MY HUNGRY GULLET...
...WHERE YOU WILL BE BUTCHERED ON A MOLECULAR LEVEL AND DIGESTED BY THE UNIVERSE YOU LEFT FORSAKEN.
I HAVE REANIMATED THE CORPSE THE GODS MADE OF CREATION.
BUT THERE WILL BE NO RESURRECTION FOR YOU OR THE LAST OF YOUR KIND.
AAAAARRGH!!!
IN MY NEW UNIVERSE...THE GODS...THE VERY IDEA OF DEITIES... WILL HAVE NEVER EXISTED.
THE ANTI-GENESIS.
I CAN SEE IT NOW. IT'S...
IT'S BEAUTIFUL.
AND GORR WEEPS. TEARS OF BLACK PLASMA.

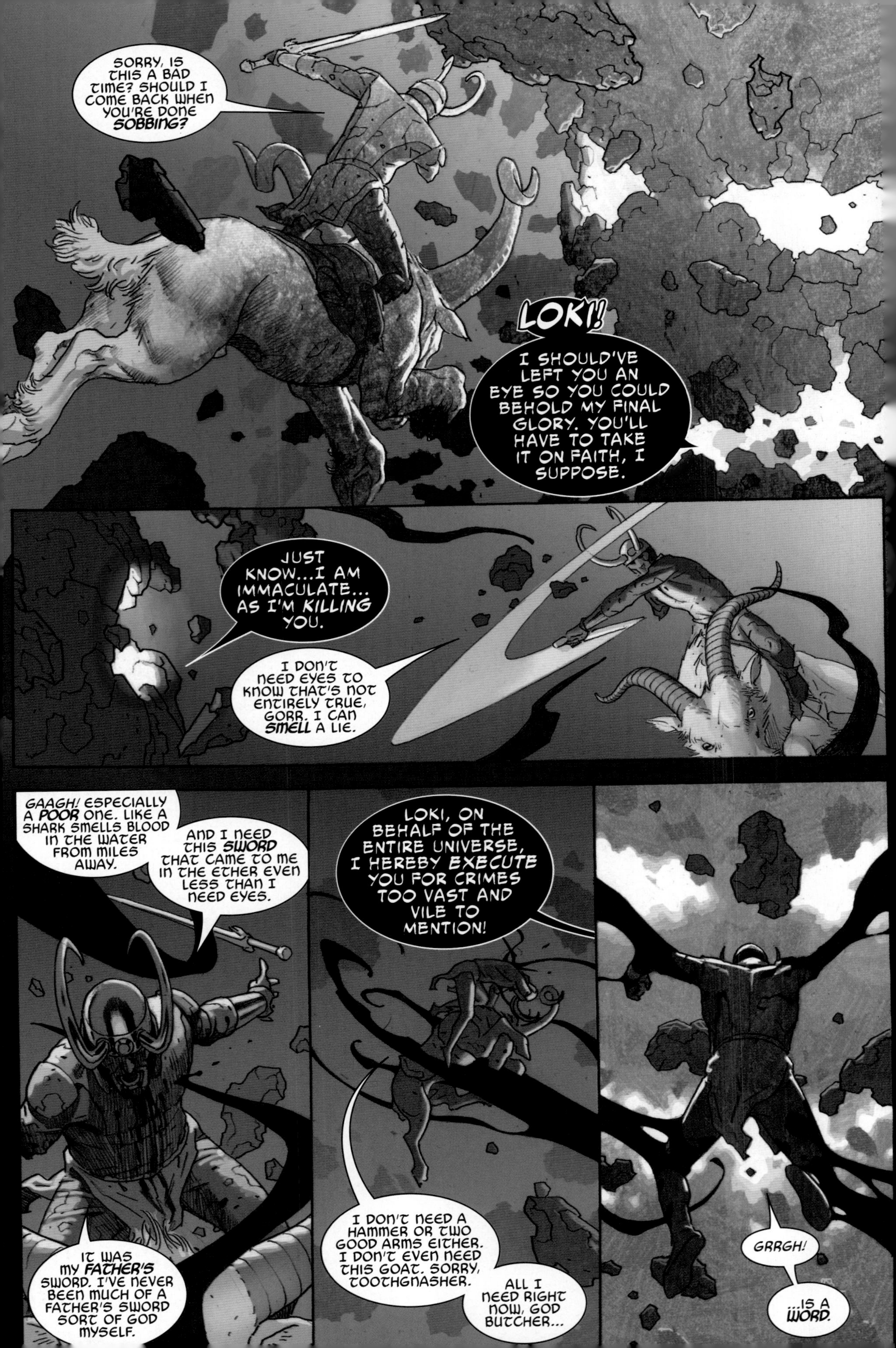
SORRY, IS THIS A BAD TIME? SHOULD I COME BACK WHEN YOU'RE DONE SOBBING?
LOKI!
I SHOULD'VE LEFT YOU AN EYE SO YOU COULD BEHOLD MY FINAL GLORY. YOU'LL HAVE TO TAKE IT ON FAITH, I SUPPOSE.
JUST KNOW...I AM IMMACULATE... AS I'M KILLING YOU.
I DON'T NEED EYES TO KNOW THAT'S NOT ENTIRELY TRUE, GORR. I CAN SMELL A LIE.
GAAGH! ESPECIALLY A POOR ONE. LIKE A SHARK SMELLS BLOOD IN THE WATER FROM MILES AWAY.
AND I NEED THIS SWORD THAT CAME TO ME IN THE ETHER EVEN LESS THAN I NEED EYES.
IT WAS MY FATHER'S SWORD. I'VE NEVER BEEN MUCH OF A FATHER'S SWORD SORT OF GOD MYSELF.
LOKI, ON BEHALF OF THE ENTIRE UNIVERSE, I HEREBY EXECUTE YOU FOR CRIMES TOO VAST AND VILE TO MENTION!
I DON'T NEED A HAMMER OR TWO GOOD ARMS EITHER. I DON'T EVEN NEED THIS GOAT. SORRY, TOOTHGNASHER.
ALL I NEED RIGHT NOW, GOD BUTCHER...
GRRGH!
...IS A WORD.

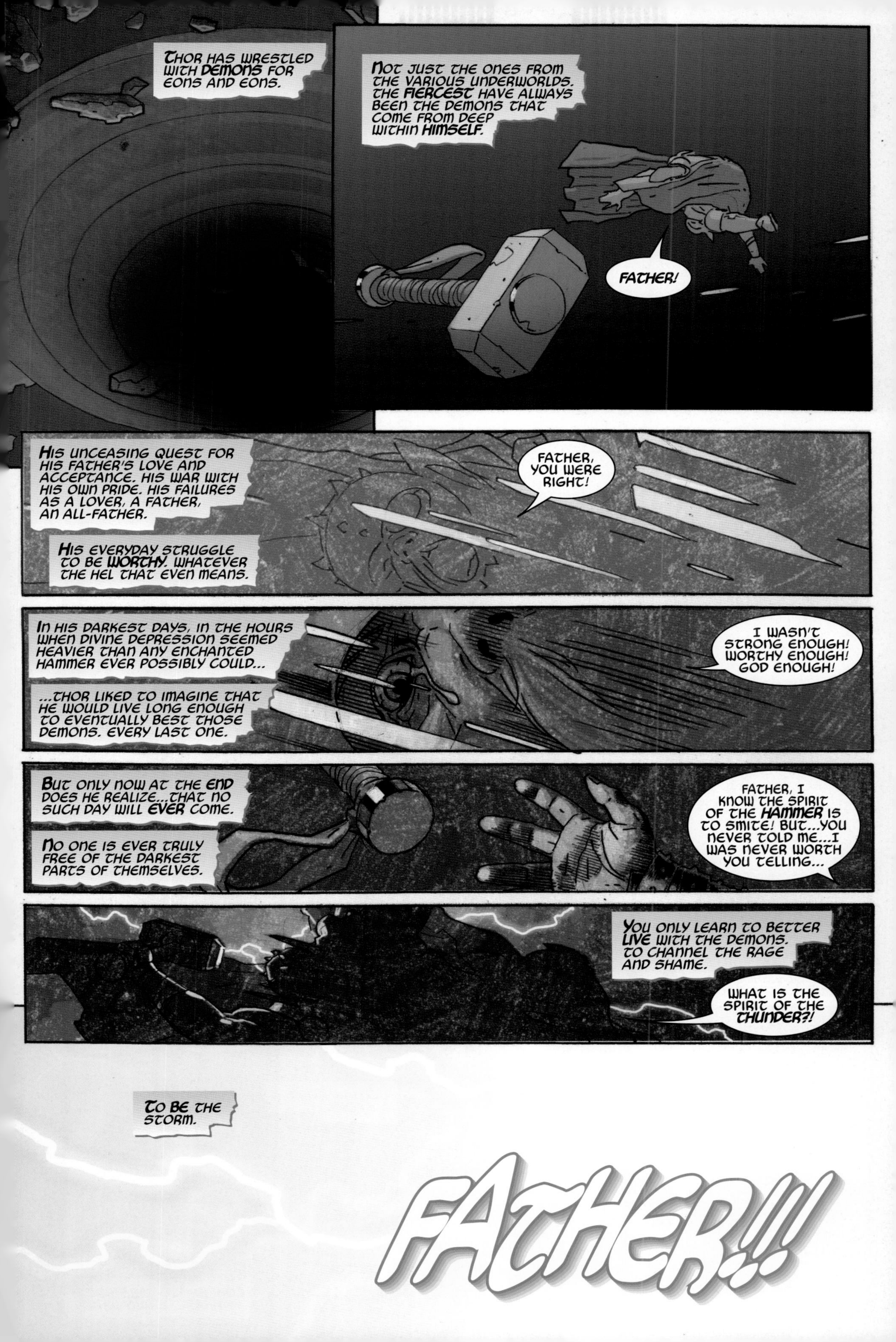
THOR HAS WRESTLED WITH DEMONS FOR EONS AND EONS.
NOT JUST THE ONES FROM THE VARIOUS UNDERWORLDS. THE FIERCEST HAVE ALWAYS BEEN THE DEMONS THAT COME FROM DEEP WITHIN HIMSELF.
FATHER!
HIS UNCEASING QUEST FOR HIS FATHER'S LOVE AND ACCEPTANCE. HIS WAR WITH HIS OWN PRIDE. HIS FAILURES AS A LOVER, A FATHER, AN ALL-FATHER.
HIS EVERYDAY STRUGGLE TO BE WORTHY. WHATEVER THE HEL THAT EVEN MEANS.
FATHER, YOU WERE RIGHT!
IN HIS DARKEST DAYS, IN THE HOURS WHEN DIVINE DEPRESSION SEEMED HEAVIER THAN ANY ENCHANTED HAMMER EVER POSSIBLY COULD...
...THOR LIKED TO IMAGINE THAT HE WOULD LIVE LONG ENOUGH TO EVENTUALLY BEST THOSE DEMONS. EVERY LAST ONE.
I WASN'T STRONG ENOUGH! WORTHY ENOUGH! GOD ENOUGH!
BUT ONLY NOW AT THE END DOES HE REALIZE...THAT NO SUCH DAY WILL EVER COME.
NO ONE IS EVER TRULY FREE OF THE DARKEST PARTS OF THEMSELVES.
FATHER, I KNOW THE SPIRIT OF THE HAMMER IS TO SMITE! BUT...YOU NEVER TOLD ME...I WAS NEVER WORTH YOU TELLING...
YOU ONLY LEARN TO BETTER LIVE WITH THE DEMONS. TO CHANNEL THE RAGE AND SHAME.
WHAT IS THE SPIRIT OF THE THUNDER?!
TO BE THE STORM.
FATHER!!

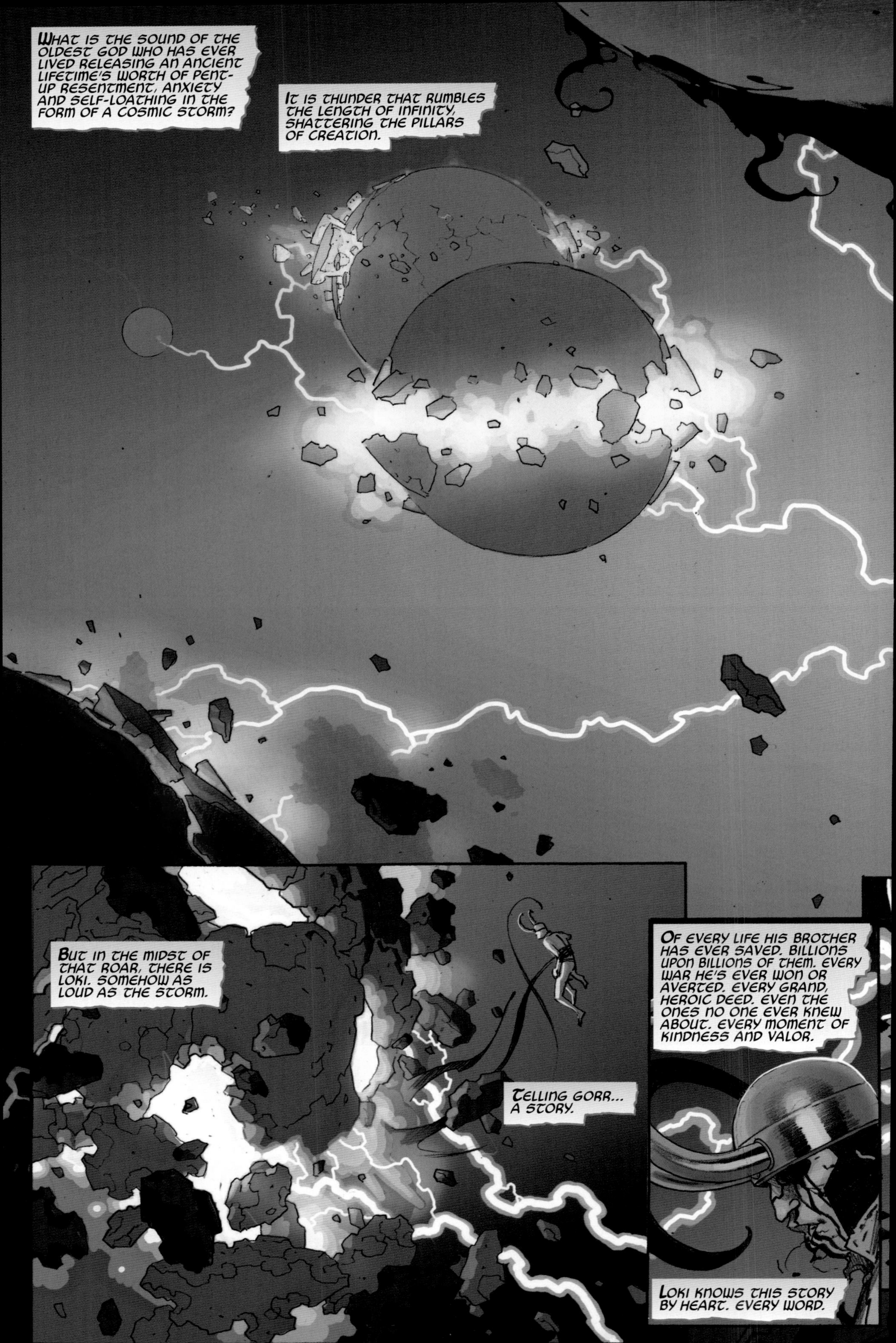
WHAT IS THE SOUND OF THE OLDEST GOD WHO HAS EVER LIVED RELEASING AN ANCIENT LIFETIME'S WORTH OF PENT-UP RESENTMENT, ANXIETY AND SELF-LOATHING IN THE FORM OF A COSMIC STORM?
IT IS THUNDER THAT RUMBLES THE LENGTH OF INFINITY, SHATTERING THE PILLARS OF CREATION.
BUT IN THE MIDST OF THAT ROAR, THERE IS LOKI. SOMEHOW AS LOUD AS THE STORM.
TELLING GORR... A STORY.
OF EVERY LIFE HIS BROTHER HAS EVER SAVED. BILLIONS UPON BILLIONS OF THEM. EVERY WAR HE'S EVER WON OR AVERTED. EVERY GRAND, HEROIC DEED. EVEN THE ONES NO ONE EVER KNEW ABOUT. EVERY MOMENT OF KINDNESS AND VALOR.
LOKI KNOWS THIS STORY BY HEART. EVERY WORD.

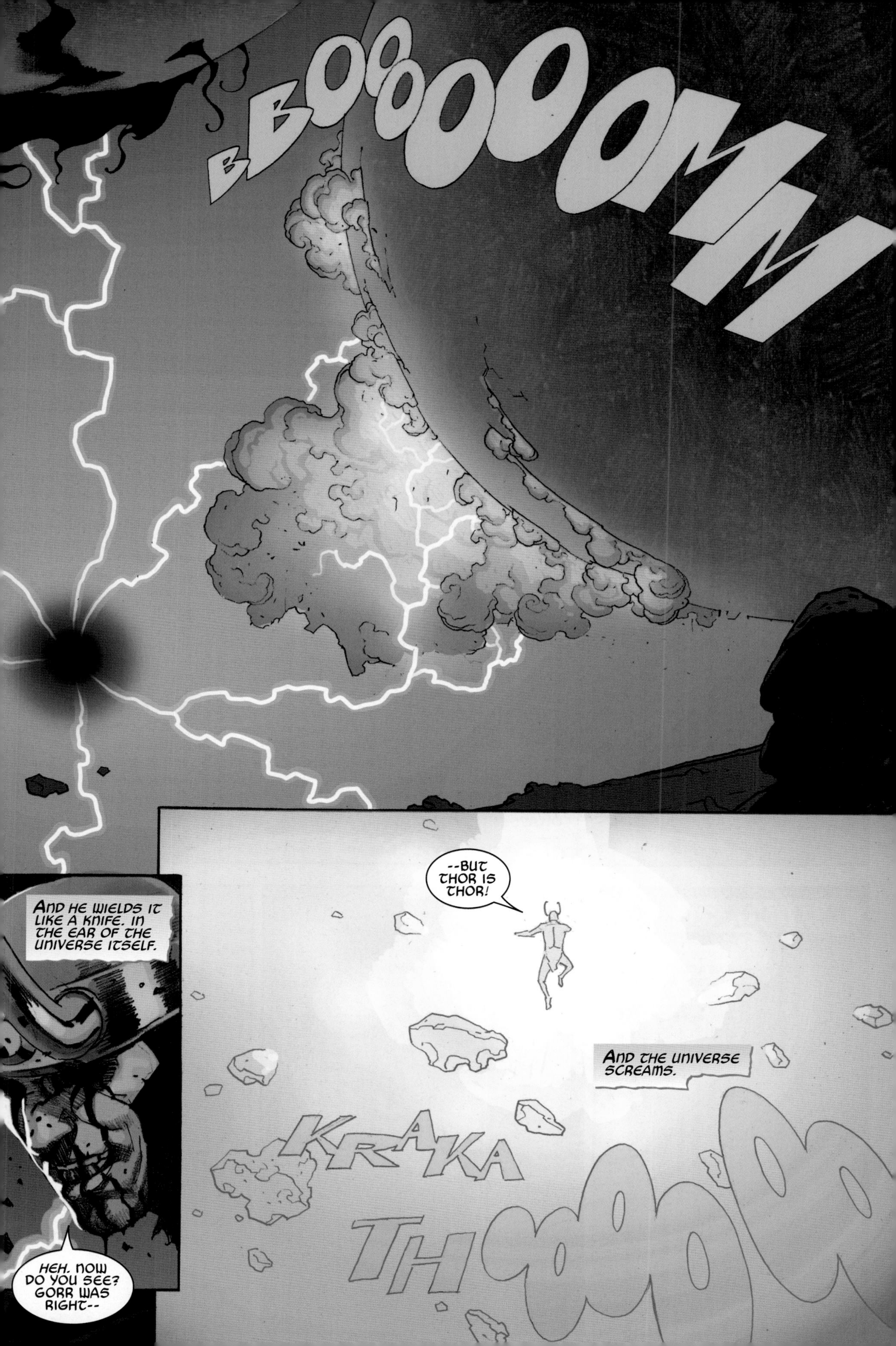
BBOOOOOOMM
AND HE WIELDS IT LIKE A KNIFE. IN THE EAR OF THE UNIVERSE ITSELF.
HEH. NOW DO YOU SEE? GORR WAS RIGHT--
--BUT THOR IS THOR!
AND THE UNIVERSE SCREAMS.
KRAKA
THOOOOOOM

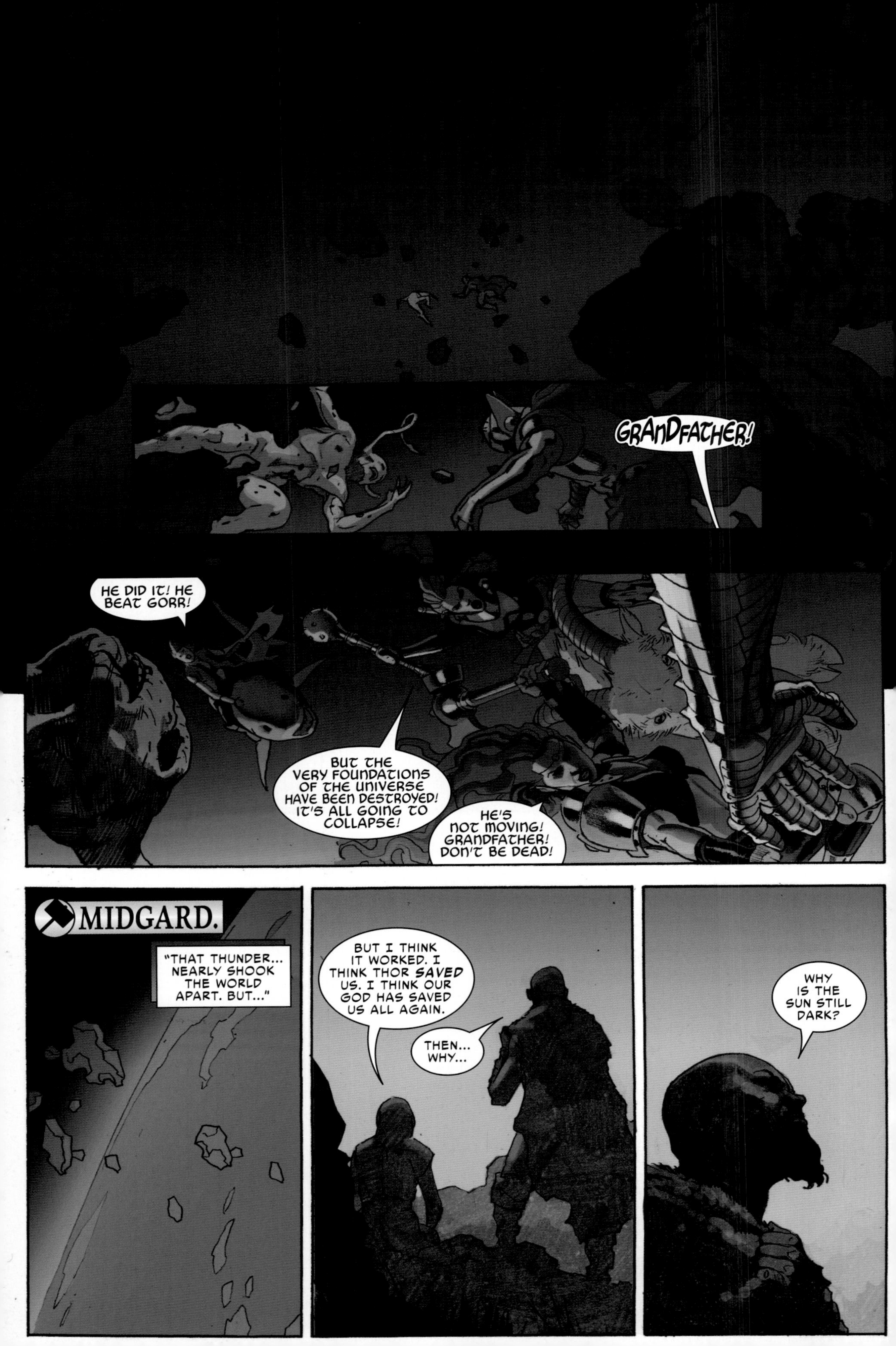

GRANDFATHER!
HE DID IT! HE BEAT GORR!
BUT THE VERY FOUNDATIONS OF THE UNIVERSE HAVE BEEN DESTROYED! IT'S ALL GOING TO COLLAPSE!
HE'S NOT MOVING! GRANDFATHER! DON'T BE DEAD!
MIDGARD.
"THAT THUNDER... NEARLY SHOOK THE WORLD APART. BUT..."
BUT I THINK IT WORKED. I THINK THOR SAVED US. I THINK OUR GOD HAS SAVED US ALL AGAIN.
THEN... WHY...
WHY IS THE SUN STILL DARK?

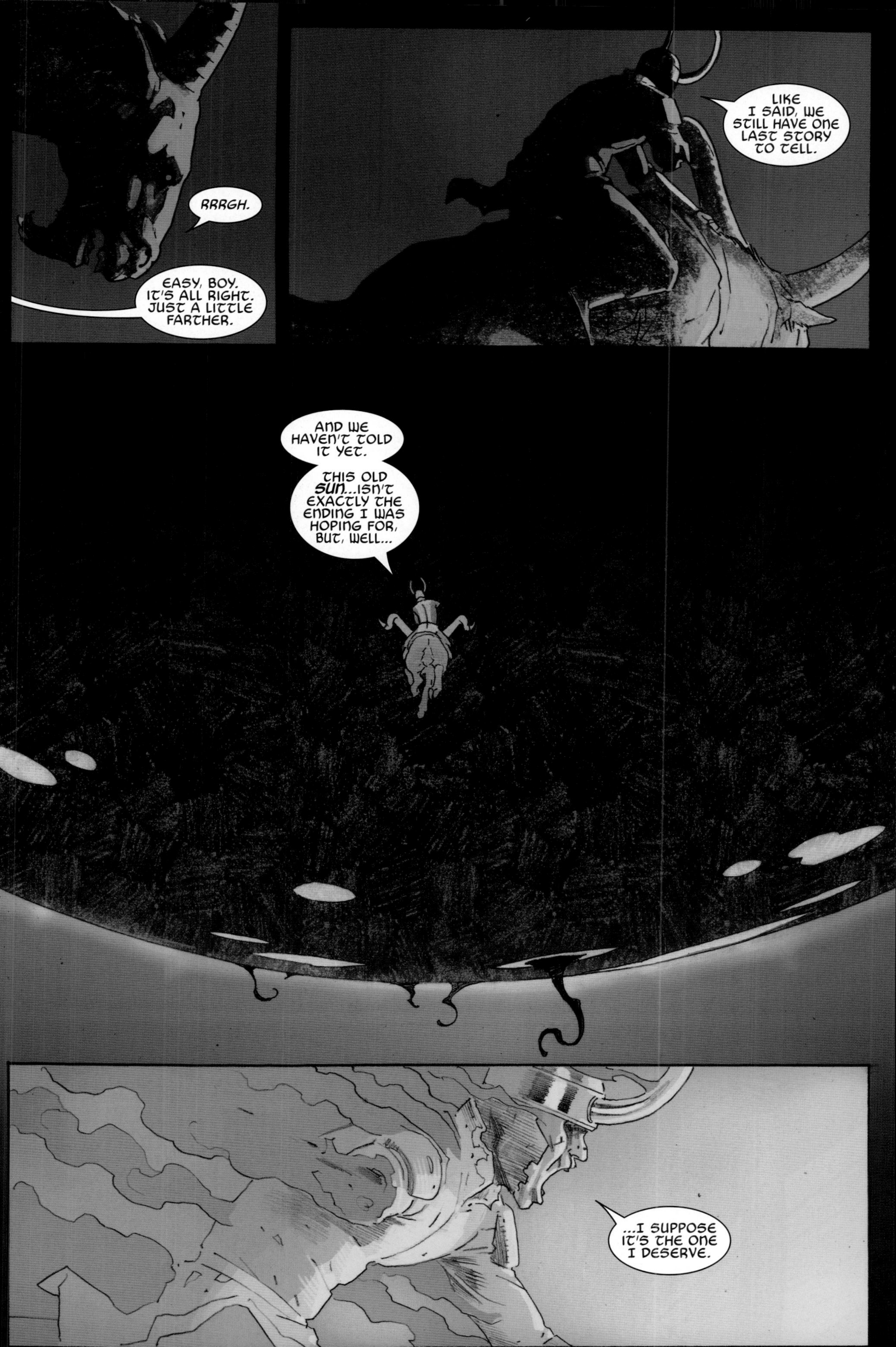
RRRGH.
EASY, BOY. IT'S ALL RIGHT. JUST A LITTLE FARTHER.
LIKE I SAID, WE STILL HAVE ONE LAST STORY TO TELL.
AND WE HAVEN'T TOLD IT YET.
THIS OLD SUN...ISN'T EXACTLY THE ENDING I WAS HOPING FOR, BUT, WELL...
...I SUPPOSE IT'S THE ONE I DESERVE.

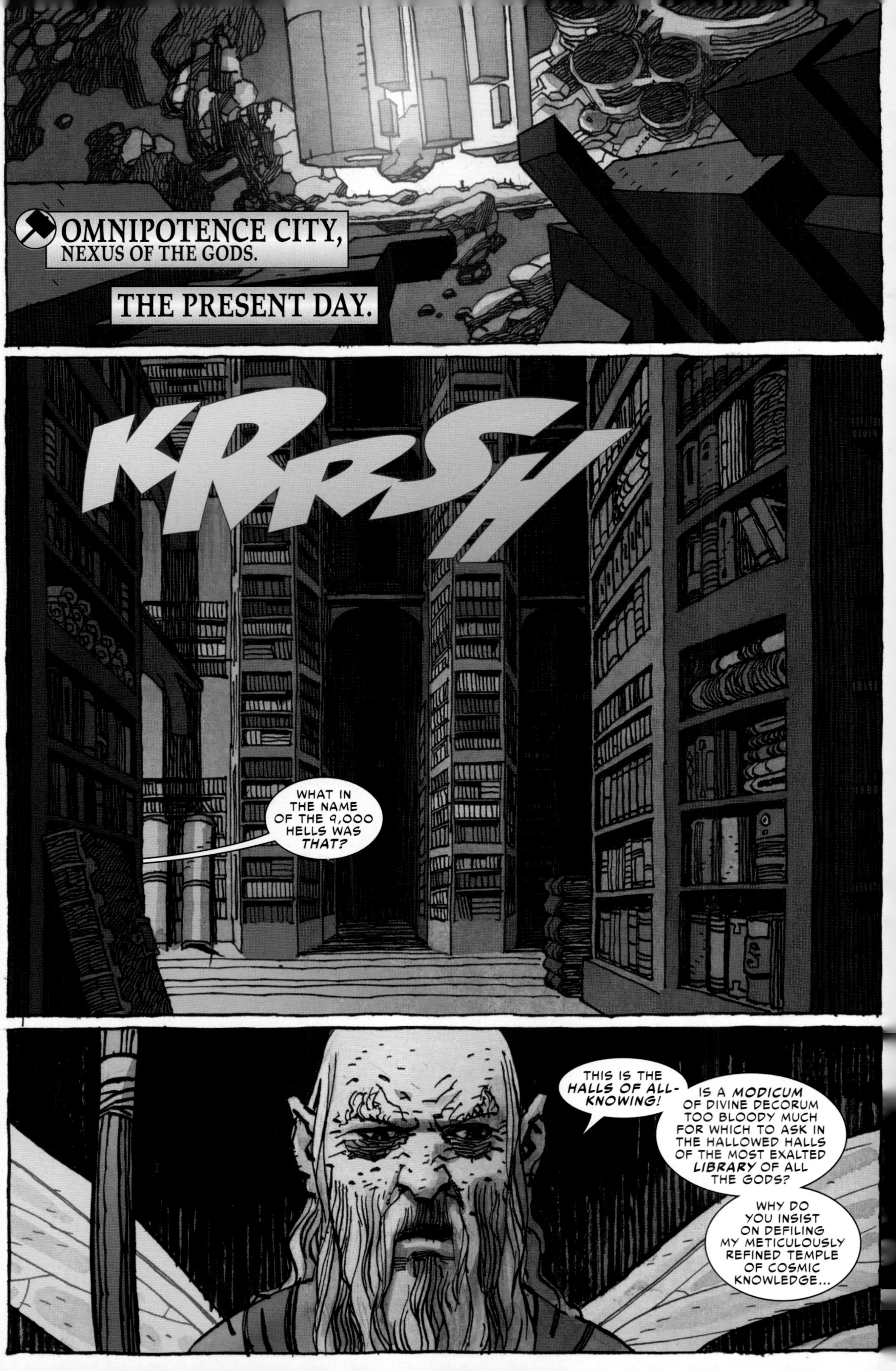
OMNIPOTENCE CITY, NEXUS OF THE GODS.
THE PRESENT DAY.
KRRSH
WHAT IN THE NAME OF THE 9,000 HELLS WAS THAT?
THIS IS THE HALLS OF ALL-KNOWING!
IS A MODICUM OF DIVINE DECORUM TOO BLOODY MUCH FOR WHICH TO ASK IN THE HALLOWED HALLS OF THE MOST EXALTED LIBRARY OF ALL THE GODS?
WHY DO YOU INSIST ON DEFILING MY METICULOUSLY REFINED TEMPLE OF COSMIC KNOWLEDGE...

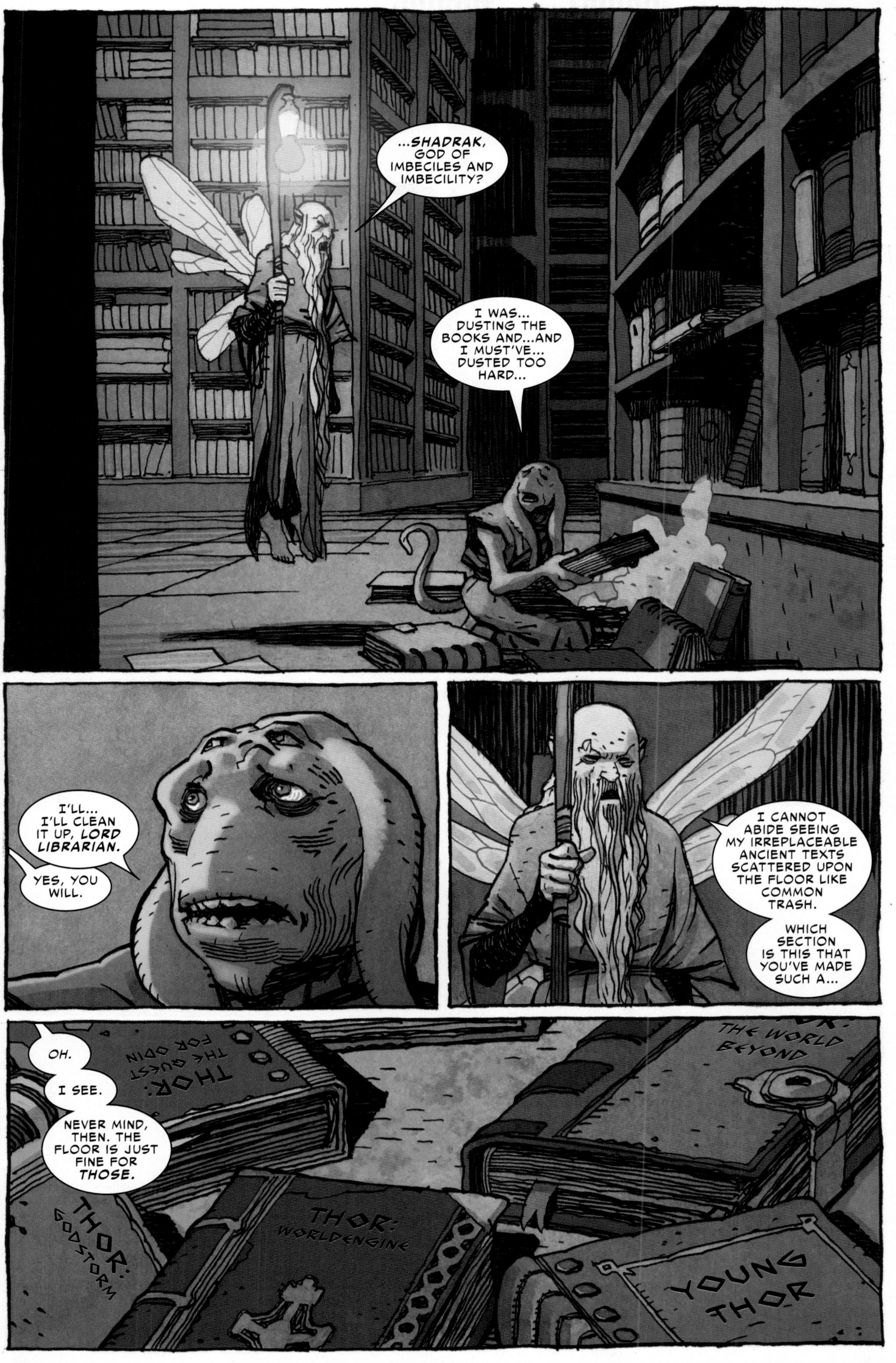
...SHADRAK, GOD OF IMBECILES AND IMBECILITY?
I WAS... DUSTING THE BOOKS AND...AND I MUST'VE... DUSTED TOO HARD...
I'LL... I'LL CLEAN IT UP, LORD LIBRARIAN.
YES, YOU WILL.
I CANNOT ABIDE SEEING MY IRREPLACEABLE ANCIENT TEXTS SCATTERED UPON THE FLOOR LIKE COMMON TRASH.
WHICH SECTION IS THIS THAT YOU'VE MADE SUCH A...
OH.
I SEE.
NEVER MIND, THEN. THE FLOOR IS JUST FINE FOR THOSE.
THOR: THE QUEST FOR ODIN
THE WORLD BEYOND
THOR: GODSTORM
THOR: WORLDENGINE
YOUNG THOR

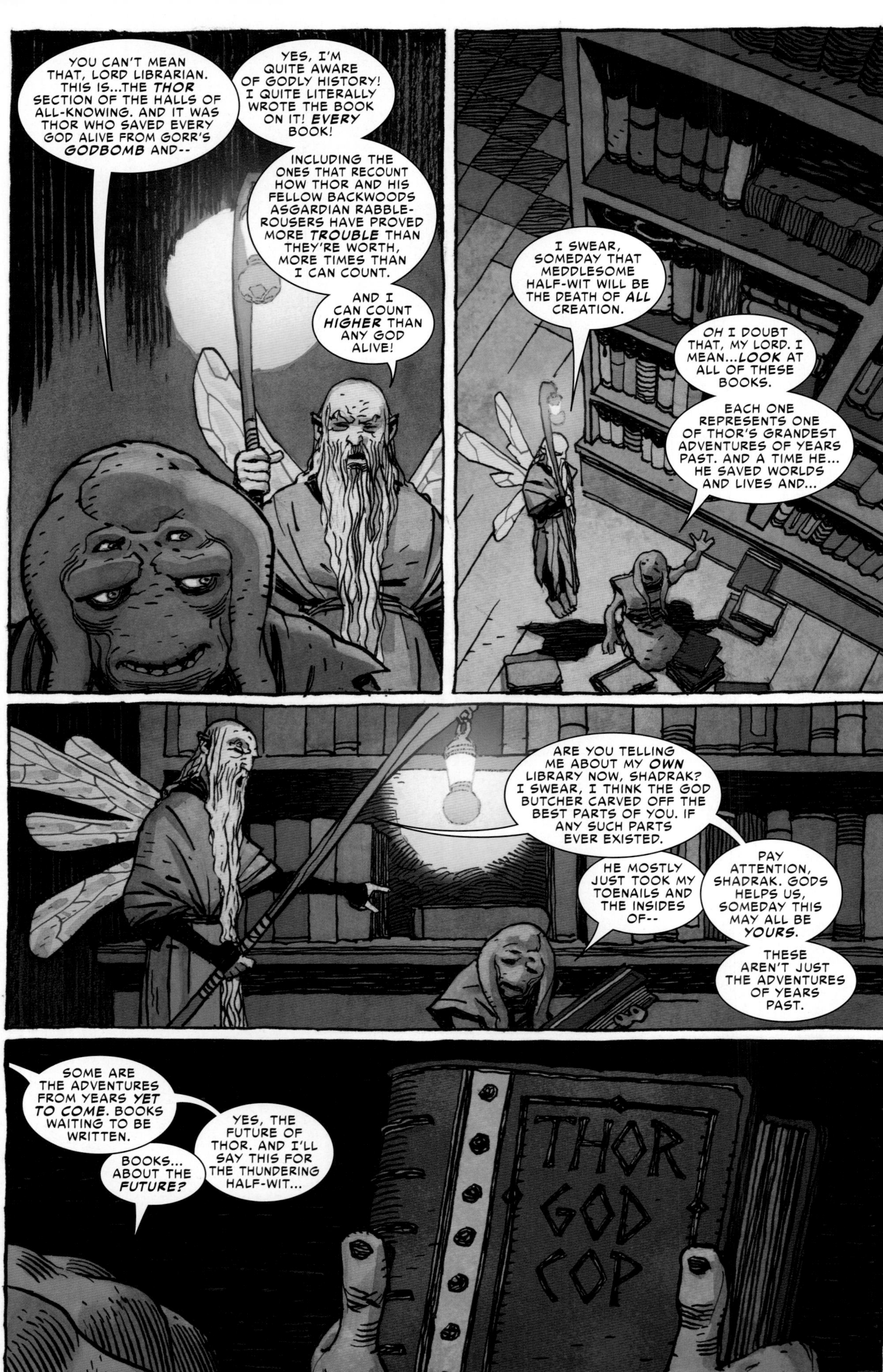
YOU CAN'T MEAN THAT, LORD LIBRARIAN. THIS IS...THE THOR SECTION OF THE HALLS OF ALL-KNOWING. AND IT WAS THOR WHO SAVED EVERY GOD ALIVE FROM GORR'S GODBOMB AND--
YES, I'M QUITE AWARE OF GODLY HISTORY! I QUITE LITERALLY WROTE THE BOOK ON IT! EVERY BOOK!
INCLUDING THE ONES THAT RECOUNT HOW THOR AND HIS FELLOW BACKWOODS ASGARDIAN RABBLE-ROUSERS HAVE PROVED MORE TROUBLE THAN THEY'RE WORTH, MORE TIMES THAN I CAN COUNT.
AND I CAN COUNT HIGHER THAN ANY GOD ALIVE!
I SWEAR, SOMEDAY THAT MEDDLESOME HALF-WIT WILL BE THE DEATH OF ALL CREATION.
OH I DOUBT THAT, MY LORD. I MEAN...LOOK AT ALL OF THESE BOOKS.
EACH ONE REPRESENTS ONE OF THOR'S GRANDEST ADVENTURES OF YEARS PAST. AND A TIME HE... HE SAVED WORLDS AND LIVES AND...
ARE YOU TELLING ME ABOUT MY OWN LIBRARY NOW, SHADRAK? I SWEAR, I THINK THE GOD BUTCHER CARVED OFF THE BEST PARTS OF YOU. IF ANY SUCH PARTS EVER EXISTED.
HE MOSTLY JUST TOOK MY TOENAILS AND THE INSIDES OF--
PAY ATTENTION, SHADRAK. GODS HELPS US, SOMEDAY THIS MAY ALL BE YOURS.
THESE AREN'T JUST THE ADVENTURES OF YEARS PAST.
SOME ARE THE ADVENTURES FROM YEARS YET TO COME. BOOKS WAITING TO BE WRITTEN.
BOOKS... ABOUT THE FUTURE?
YES, THE FUTURE OF THOR. AND I'LL SAY THIS FOR THE THUNDERING HALF-WIT...
THOR GOD COP

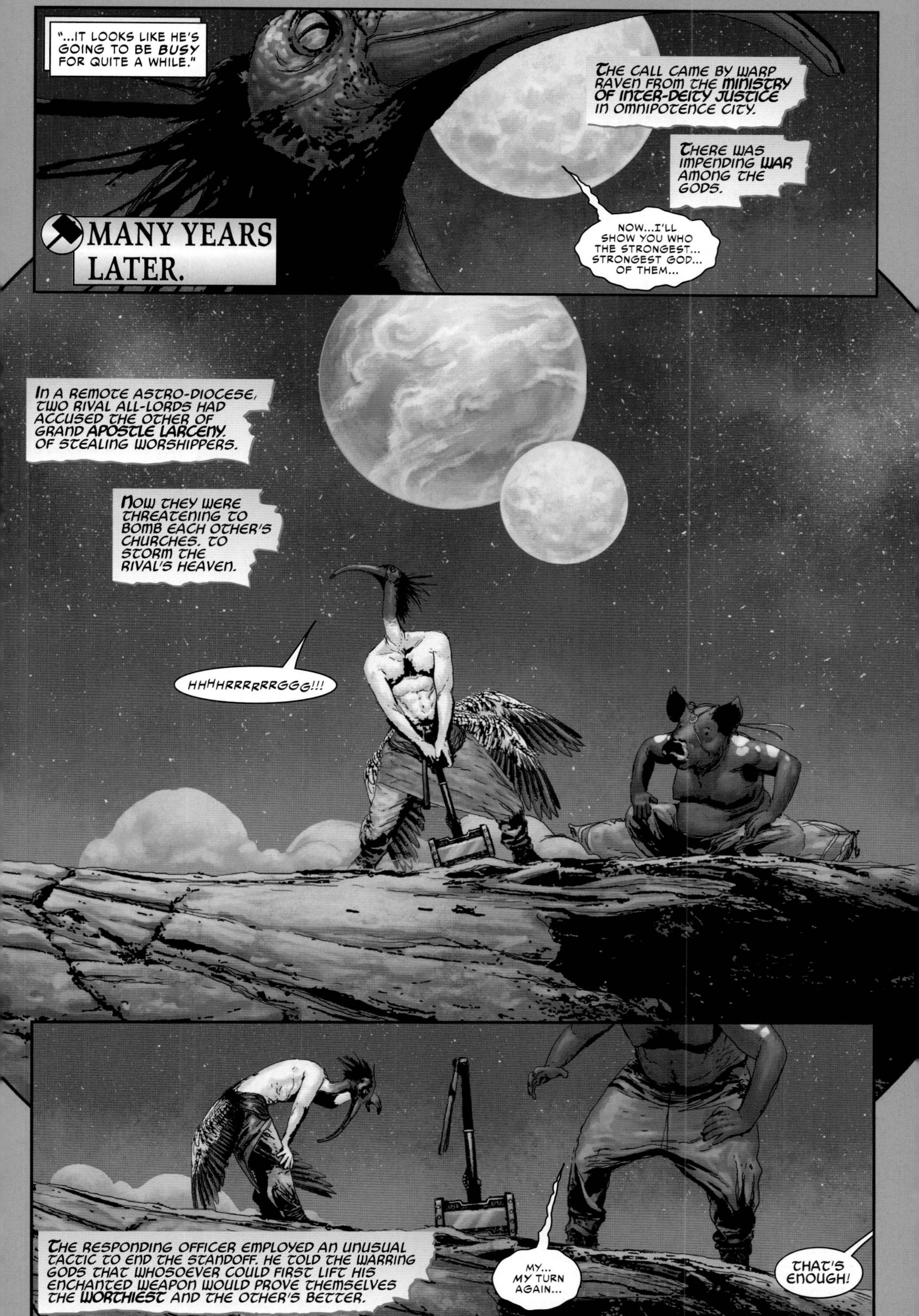
"...IT LOOKS LIKE HE'S GOING TO BE BUSY FOR QUITE A WHILE."
MANY YEARS LATER.
THE CALL CAME BY WARP RAVEN FROM THE MINISTRY OF INTER-DEITY JUSTICE IN OMNIPOTENCE CITY.
THERE WAS IMPENDING WAR AMONG THE GODS.
NOW...I'LL SHOW YOU WHO THE STRONGEST... STRONGEST GOD... OF THEM...
IN A REMOTE ASTRO-DIOCESE, TWO RIVAL ALL-LORDS HAD ACCUSED THE OTHER OF GRAND APOSTLE LARCENY. OF STEALING WORSHIPPERS.
NOW THEY WERE THREATENING TO BOMB EACH OTHER'S CHURCHES. TO STORM THE RIVAL'S HEAVEN.
HHHHRRRRRRGGG!!!
THE RESPONDING OFFICER EMPLOYED AN UNUSUAL TACTIC TO END THE STANDOFF. HE TOLD THE WARRING GODS THAT WHOSOEVER COULD FIRST LIFT HIS ENCHANTED WEAPON WOULD PROVE THEMSELVES THE WORTHIEST AND THE OTHER'S BETTER.
MY... MY TURN AGAIN...
THAT'S ENOUGH!

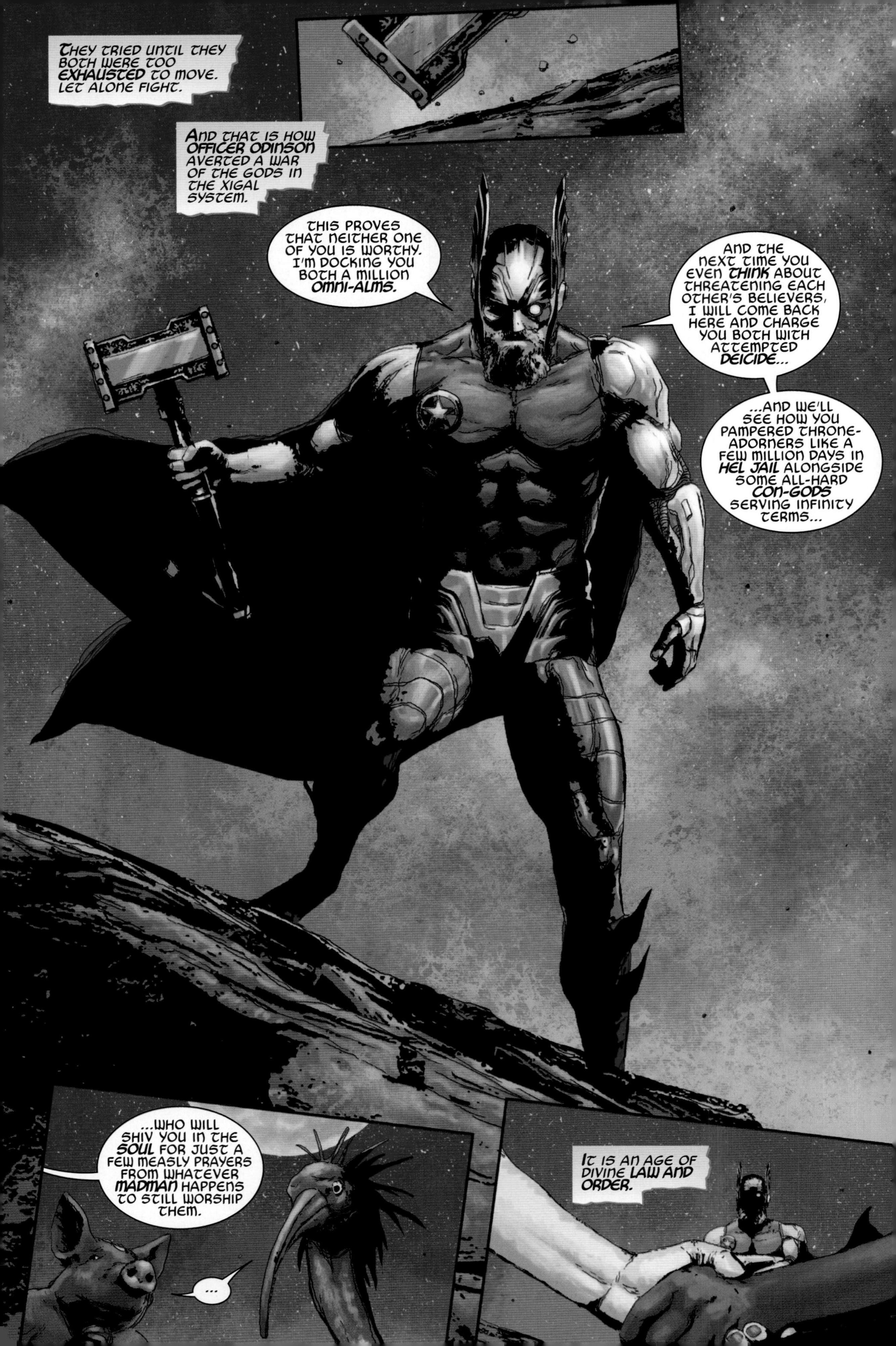
They tried until they both were too EXHAUSTED to move. Let alone fight.
And that is how OFFICER ODINSON averted a war of the gods in the Xigal system.
THIS PROVES THAT NEITHER ONE OF YOU IS WORTHY. I'M DOCKING YOU BOTH A MILLION OMNI-ALMS.
AND THE NEXT TIME YOU EVEN THINK ABOUT THREATENING EACH OTHER'S BELIEVERS, I WILL COME BACK HERE AND CHARGE YOU BOTH WITH ATTEMPTED DEICIDE...
...AND WE'LL SEE HOW YOU PAMPERED THRONE-ADORNERS LIKE A FEW MILLION DAYS IN HEL JAIL ALONGSIDE SOME ALL-HARD CON-GODS SERVING INFINITY TERMS...
...WHO WILL SHIV YOU IN THE SOUL FOR JUST A FEW MEASLY PRAYERS FROM WHATEVER MADMAN HAPPENS TO STILL WORSHIP THEM.
...
It is an age of divine LAW AND ORDER.

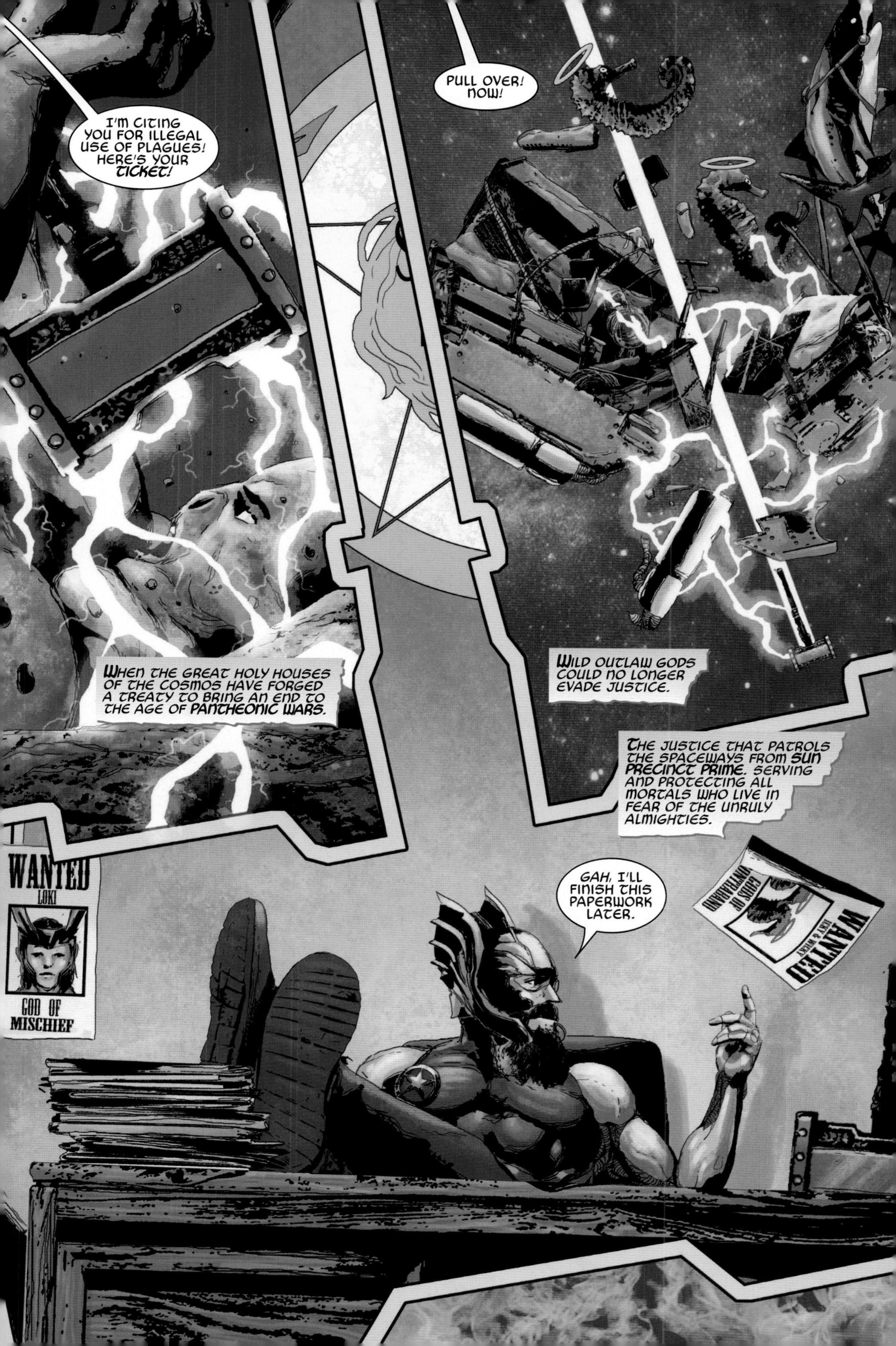

I'M CITING YOU FOR ILLEGAL USE OF PLAGUES! HERE'S YOUR TICKET!
WHEN THE GREAT HOLY HOUSES OF THE COSMOS HAVE FORGED A TREATY TO BRING AN END TO THE AGE OF PANTHEONIC WARS.
PULL OVER! NOW!
WILD OUTLAW GODS COULD NO LONGER EVADE JUSTICE.
THE JUSTICE THAT PATROLS THE SPACEWAYS FROM SUN PRECINCT PRIME. SERVING AND PROTECTING ALL MORTALS WHO LIVE IN FEAR OF THE UNRULY ALMIGHTIES.
WANTED
LOKI
GOD OF MISCHIEF
GAH, I'LL FINISH THIS PAPERWORK LATER.

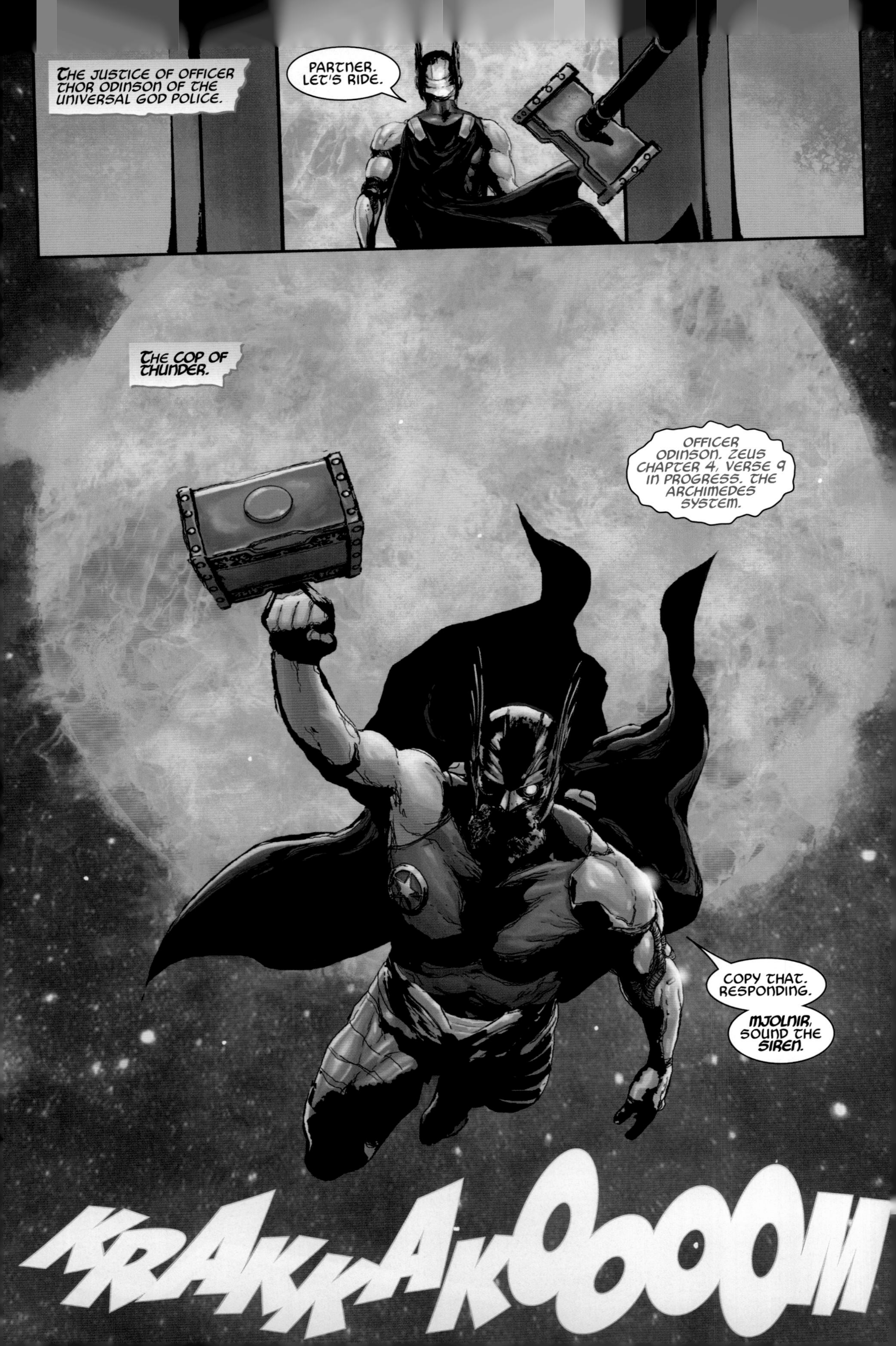
THE JUSTICE OF OFFICER THOR ODINSON OF THE UNIVERSAL GOD POLICE.
PARTNER. LET'S RIDE.
THE COP OF THUNDER.
OFFICER ODINSON. ZEUS CHAPTER 4, VERSE 9 IN PROGRESS. THE ARCHIMEDES SYSTEM.
COPY THAT. RESPONDING.
MJOLNIR, SOUND THE SIREN.
KRAKKAKOOOOM

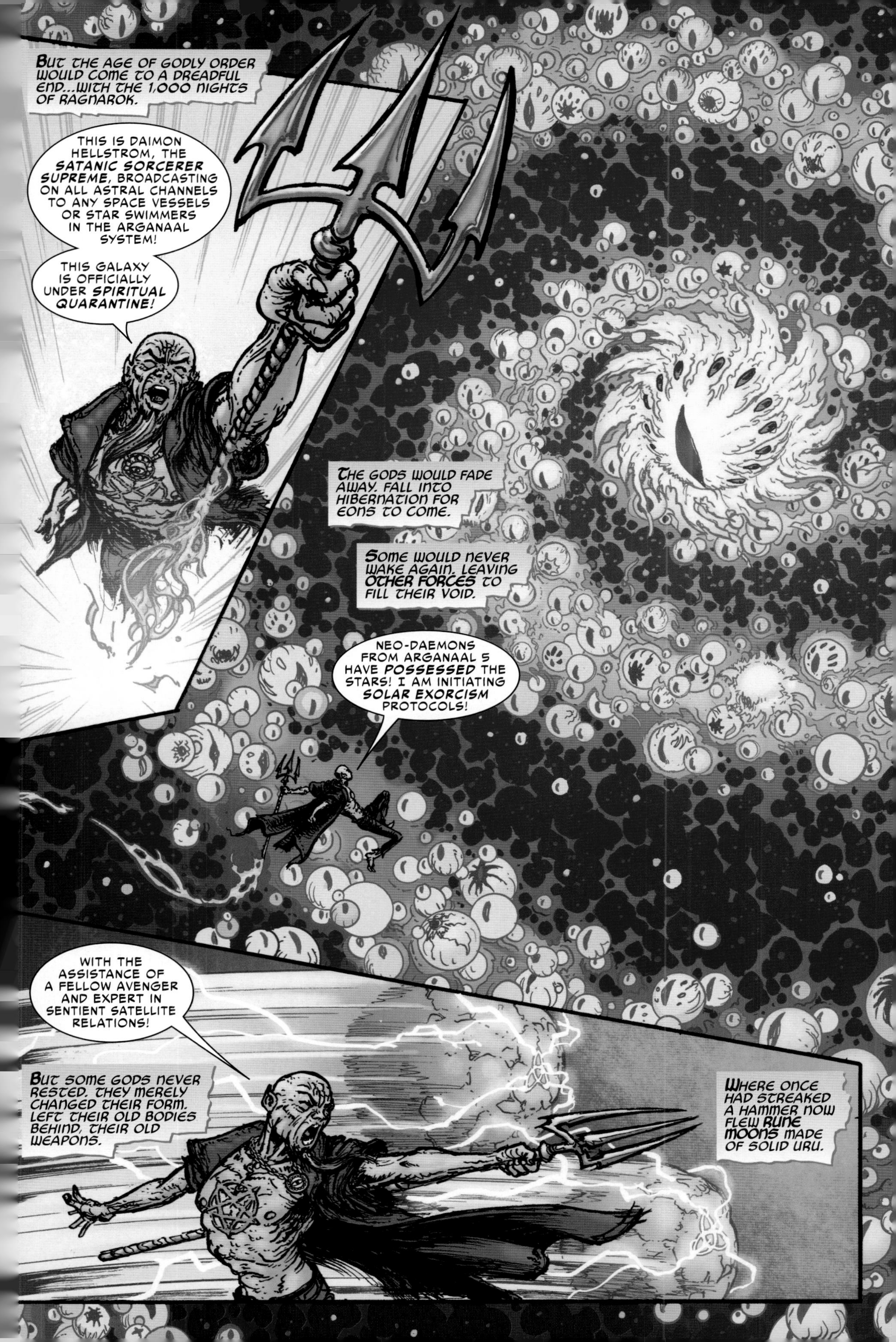
BUT THE AGE OF GODLY ORDER WOULD COME TO A DREADFUL END...WITH THE 1,000 NIGHTS OF RAGNAROK.
THIS IS DAIMON HELLSTROM, THE SATANIC SORCERER SUPREME, BROADCASTING ON ALL ASTRAL CHANNELS TO ANY SPACE VESSELS OR STAR SWIMMERS IN THE ARGANAAL SYSTEM!
THIS GALAXY IS OFFICIALLY UNDER SPIRITUAL QUARANTINE!
THE GODS WOULD FADE AWAY. FALL INTO HIBERNATION FOR EONS TO COME.
SOME WOULD NEVER WAKE AGAIN. LEAVING OTHER FORCES TO FILL THEIR VOID.
NEO-DAEMONS FROM ARGANAAL 5 HAVE POSSESSED THE STARS! I AM INITIATING SOLAR EXORCISM PROTOCOLS!
WITH THE ASSISTANCE OF A FELLOW AVENGER AND EXPERT IN SENTIENT SATELLITE RELATIONS!
BUT SOME GODS NEVER RESTED. THEY MERELY CHANGED THEIR FORM. LEFT THEIR OLD BODIES BEHIND, THEIR OLD WEAPONS.
WHERE ONCE HAD STREAKED A HAMMER NOW FLEW RUNE MOONS MADE OF SOLID URU.

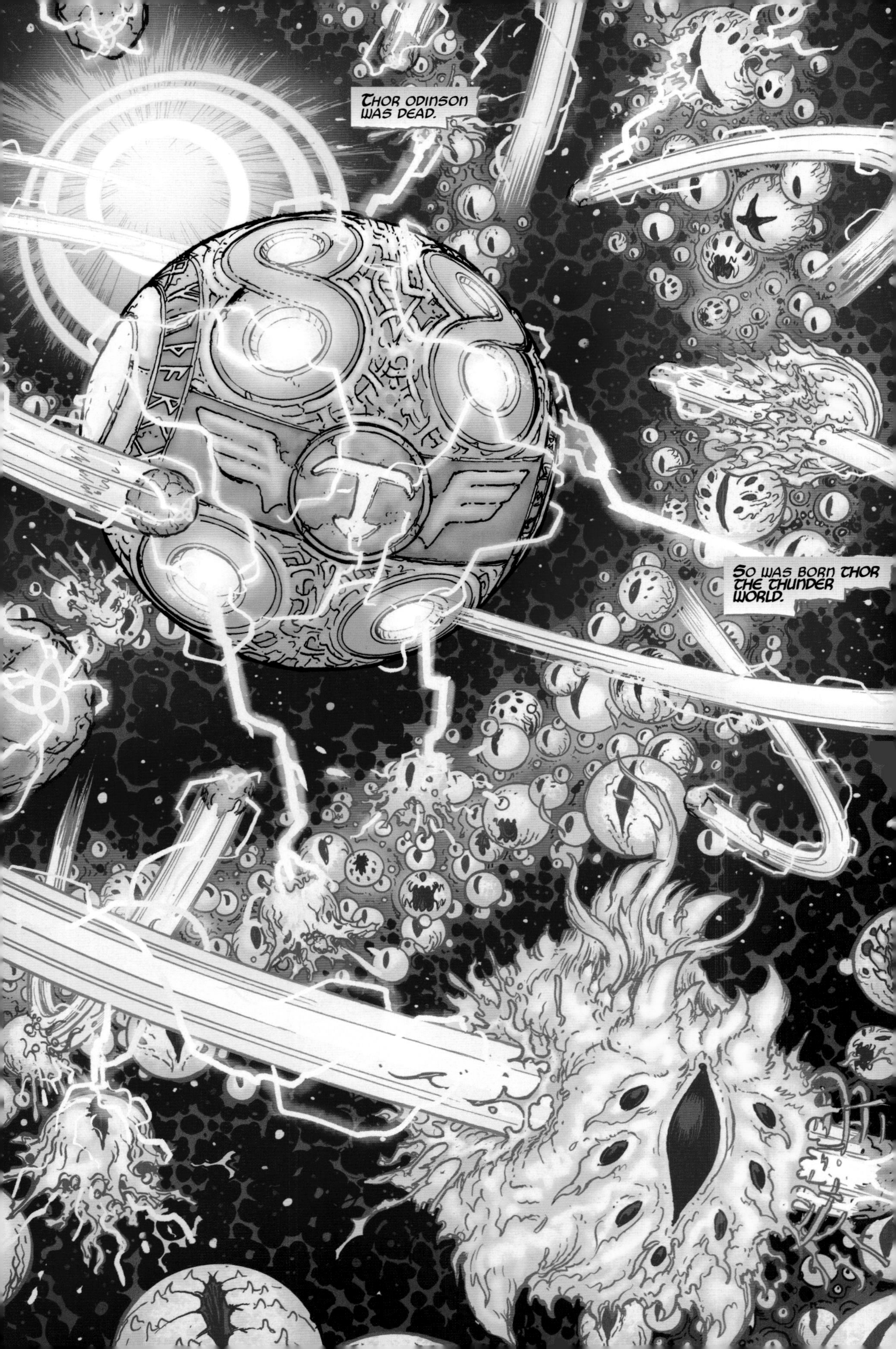
THOR ODINSON WAS DEAD.
SO WAS BORN THOR THE THUNDER WORLD.

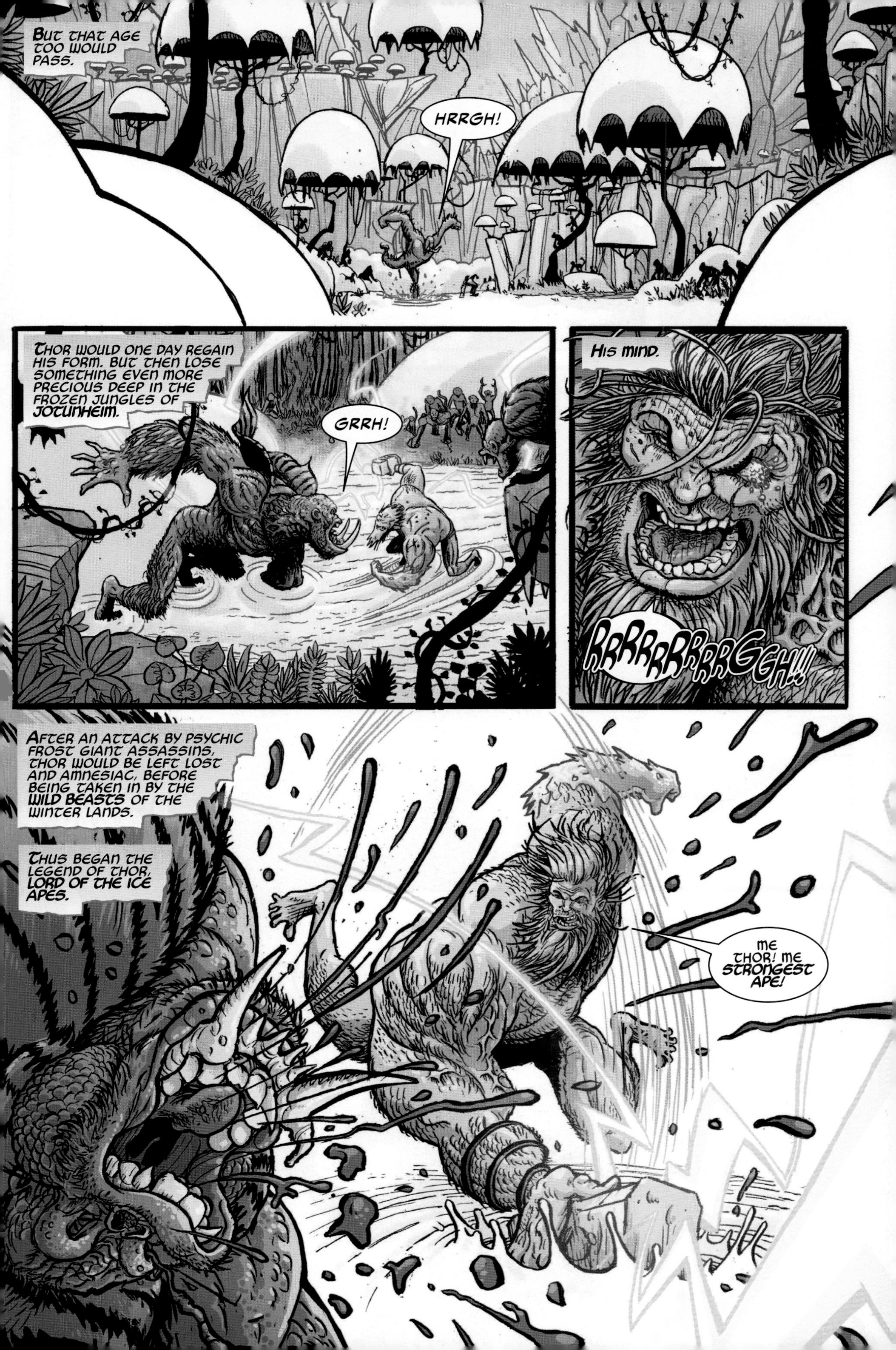

But that age too would pass.
HRRGH!
Thor would one day regain his form. But then lose something even more precious deep in the frozen jungles of **Jotunheim**.
GRRH!
His mind.
RRRRRRRRRGGH!!
After an attack by psychic frost giant assassins, Thor would be left lost and amnesiac, before being taken in by the **wild beasts** of the winter lands.
Thus began the legend of Thor, **Lord of the Ice Apes**.
Me Thor! Me **strongest** ape!

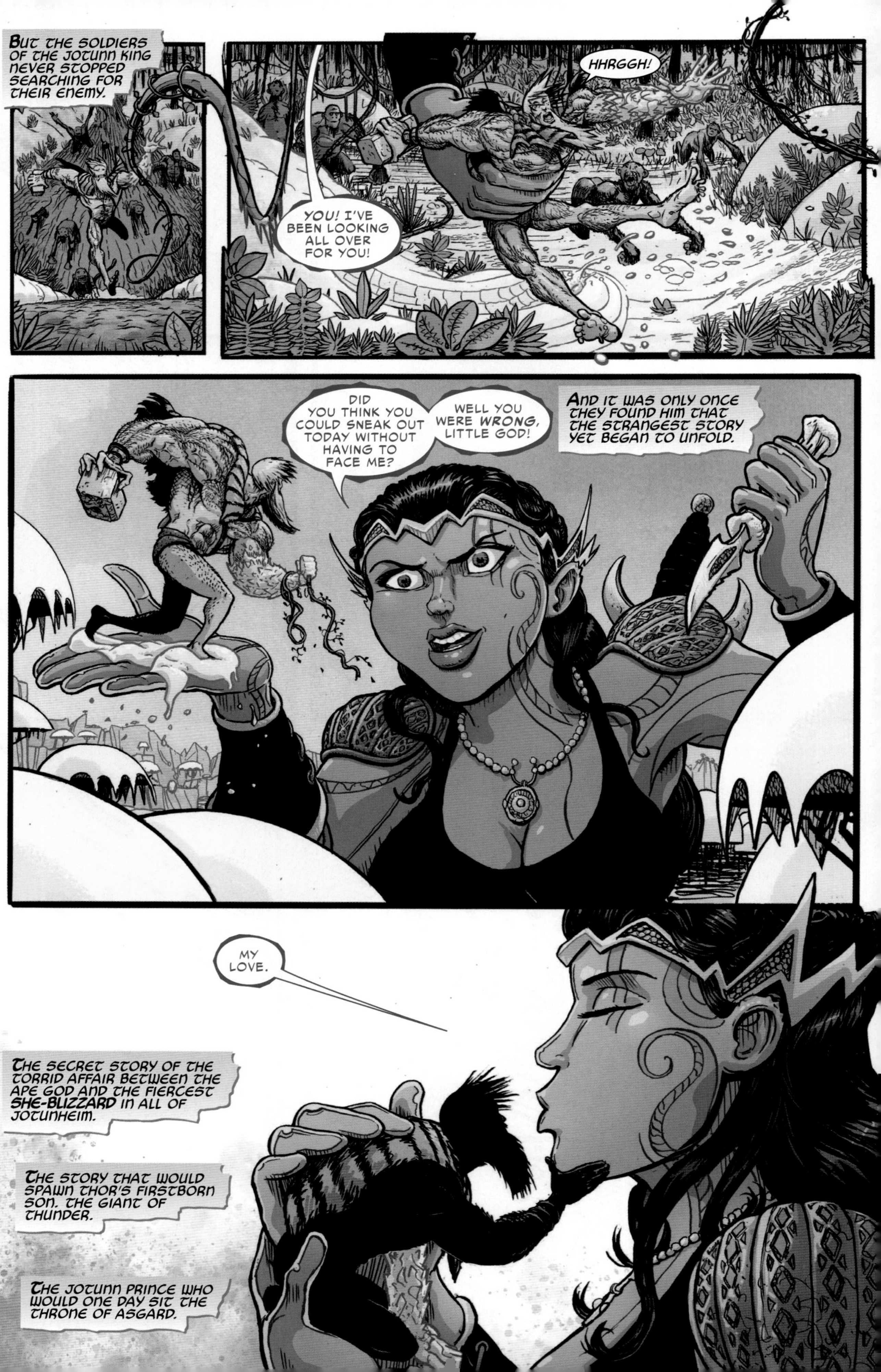

BUT THE SOLDIERS OF THE JOTUNN KING NEVER STOPPED SEARCHING FOR THEIR ENEMY.
HHRGGH!
YOU! I'VE BEEN LOOKING ALL OVER FOR YOU!
DID YOU THINK YOU COULD SNEAK OUT TODAY WITHOUT HAVING TO FACE ME?
WELL YOU WERE WRONG, LITTLE GOD!
AND IT WAS ONLY ONCE THEY FOUND HIM THAT THE STRANGEST STORY YET BEGAN TO UNFOLD.
MY LOVE.
THE SECRET STORY OF THE TORRID AFFAIR BETWEEN THE APE GOD AND THE FIERCEST SHE-BLIZZARD IN ALL OF JOTUNHEIM.
THE STORY THAT WOULD SPAWN THOR'S FIRSTBORN SON. THE GIANT OF THUNDER.
THE JOTUNN PRINCE WHO WOULD ONE DAY SIT THE THRONE OF ASGARD.

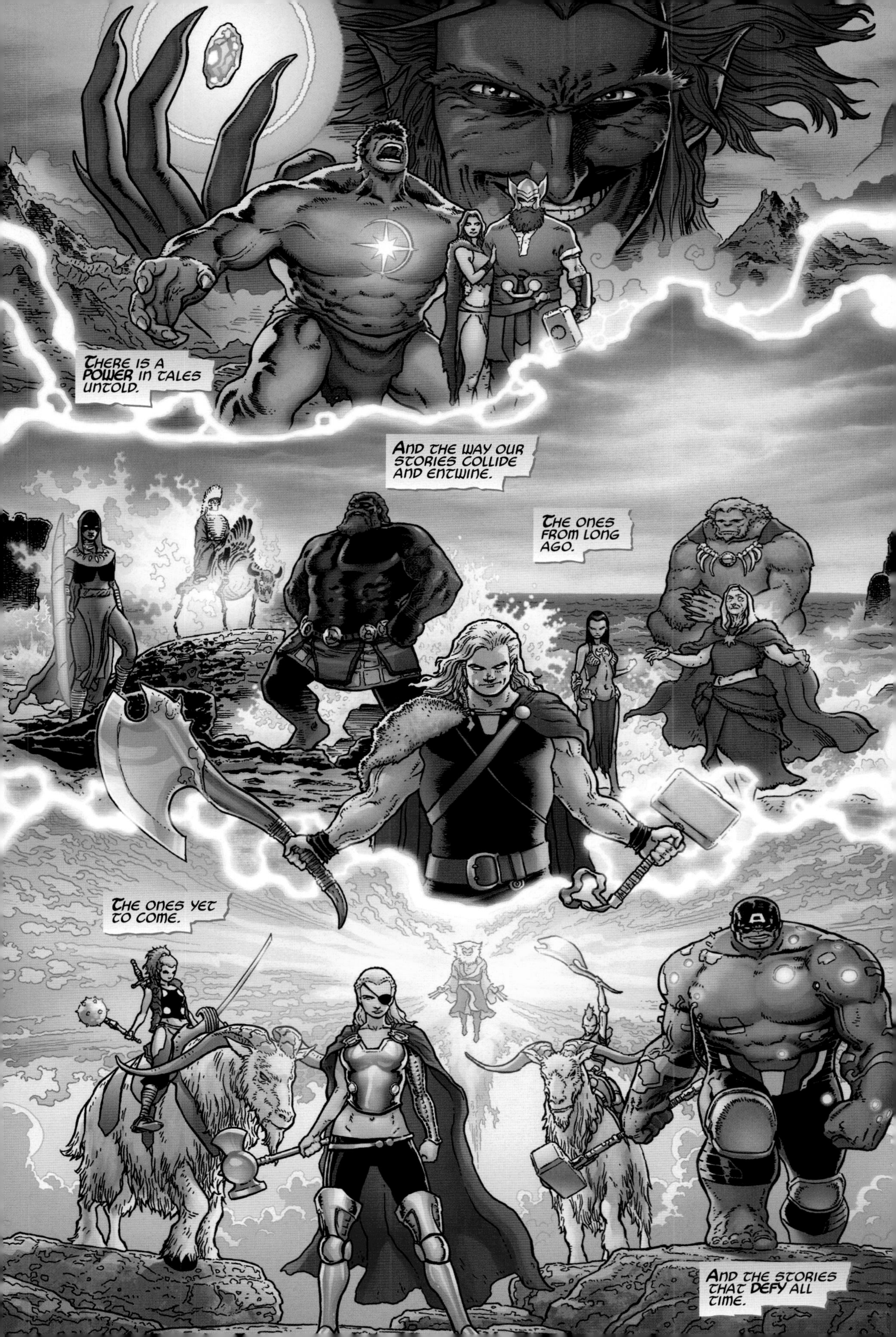
THERE IS A POWER IN TALES UNTOLD.
AND THE WAY OUR STORIES COLLIDE AND ENTWINE.
THE ONES FROM LONG AGO.
THE ONES YET TO COME.
AND THE STORIES THAT DEFY ALL TIME.

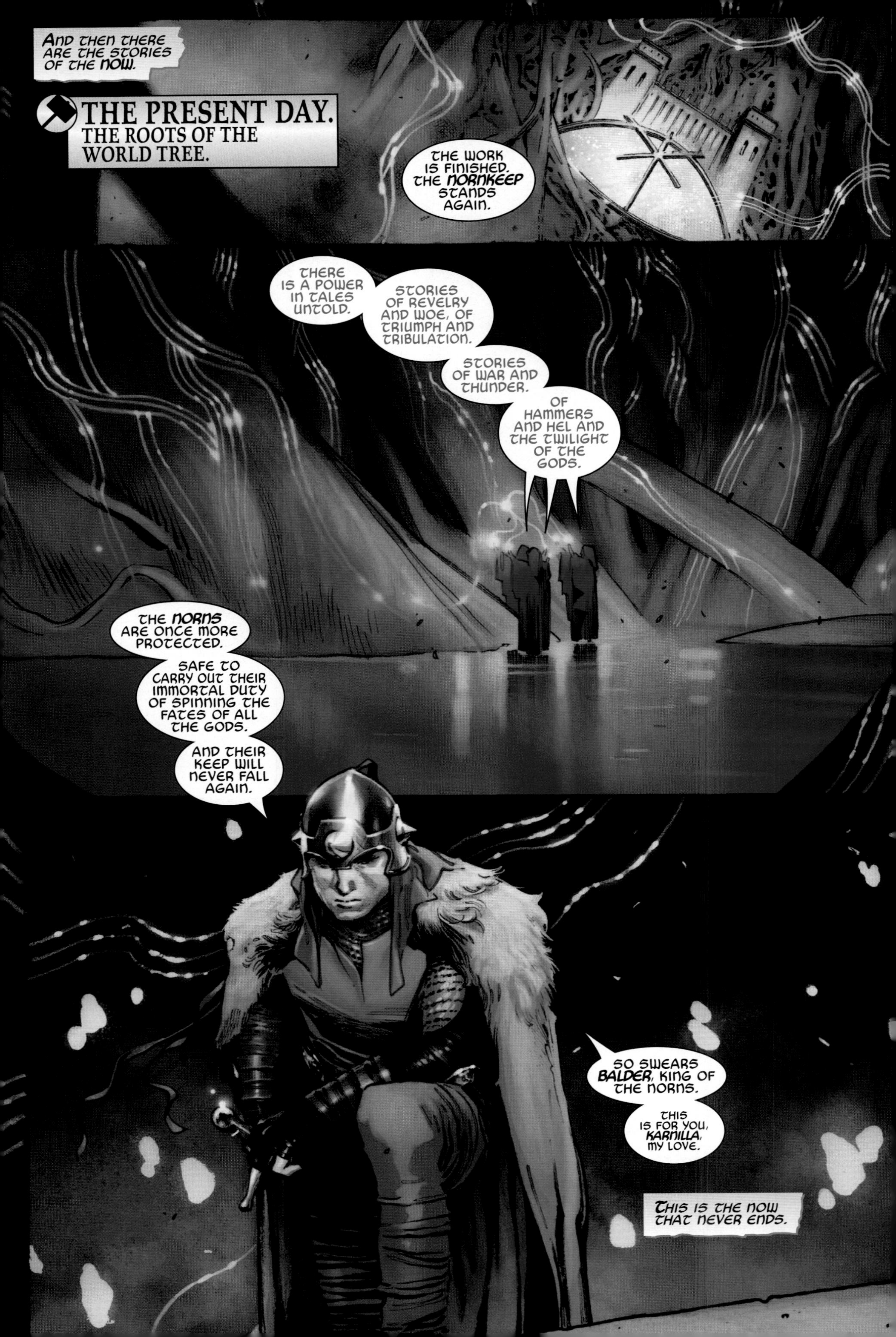
AND THEN THERE ARE THE STORIES OF THE NOW.
THE PRESENT DAY. THE ROOTS OF THE WORLD TREE.
THE WORK IS FINISHED. THE NORNKEEP STANDS AGAIN.
THERE IS A POWER IN TALES UNTOLD.
STORIES OF REVELRY AND WOE, OF TRIUMPH AND TRIBULATION.
STORIES OF WAR AND THUNDER.
OF HAMMERS AND HEL AND THE TWILIGHT OF THE GODS.
THE NORNS ARE ONCE MORE PROTECTED.
SAFE TO CARRY OUT THEIR IMMORTAL DUTY OF SPINNING THE FATES OF ALL THE GODS.
AND THEIR KEEP WILL NEVER FALL AGAIN.
SO SWEARS BALDER, KING OF THE NORNS.
THIS IS FOR YOU, KARNILLA, MY LOVE.
THIS IS THE NOW THAT NEVER ENDS.

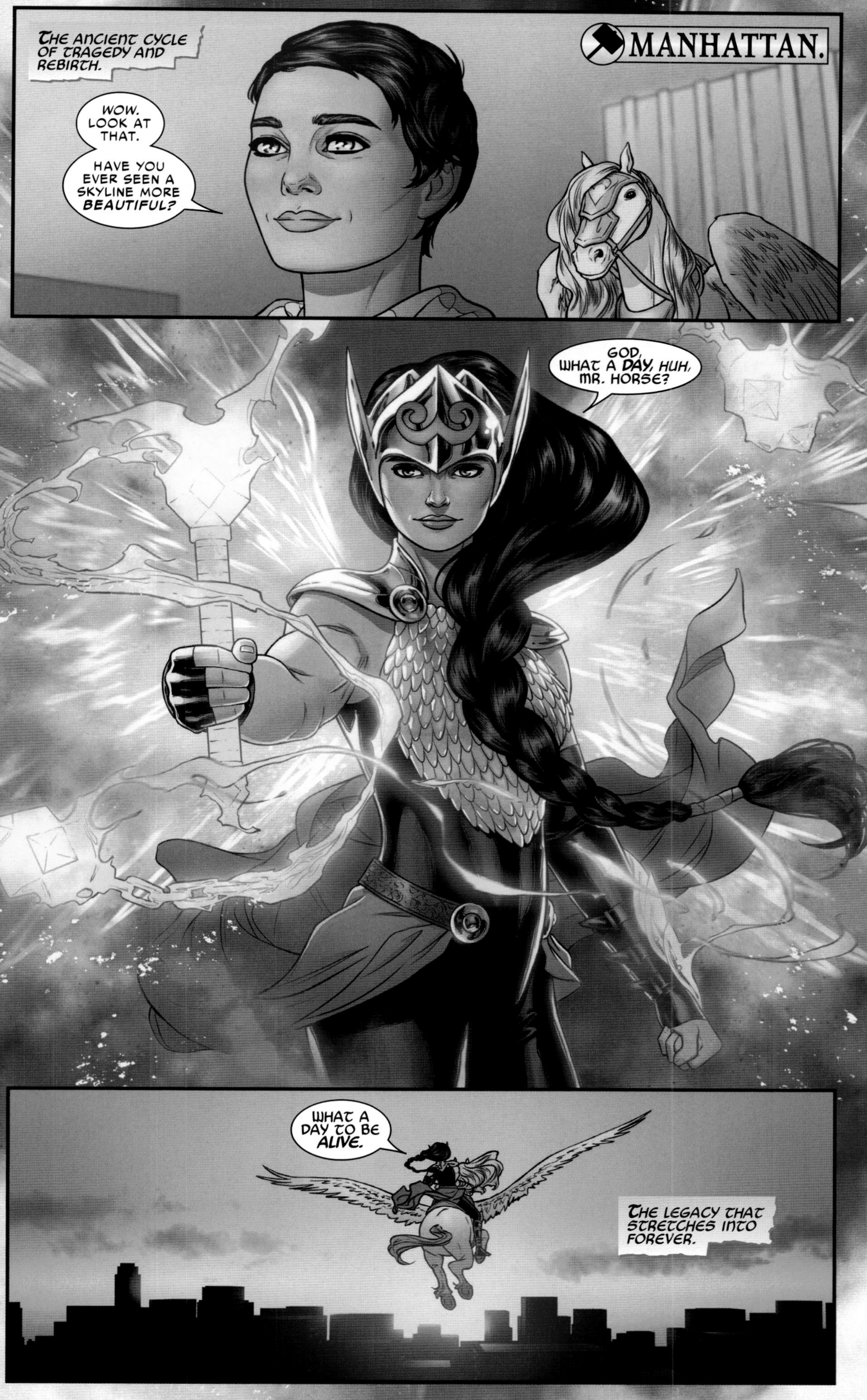
THE ANCIENT CYCLE OF TRAGEDY AND REBIRTH.
MANHATTAN.
WOW. LOOK AT THAT.
HAVE YOU EVER SEEN A SKYLINE MORE BEAUTIFUL?
GOD, WHAT A DAY, HUH, MR. HORSE?
WHAT A DAY TO BE ALIVE.
THE LEGACY THAT STRETCHES INTO FOREVER.

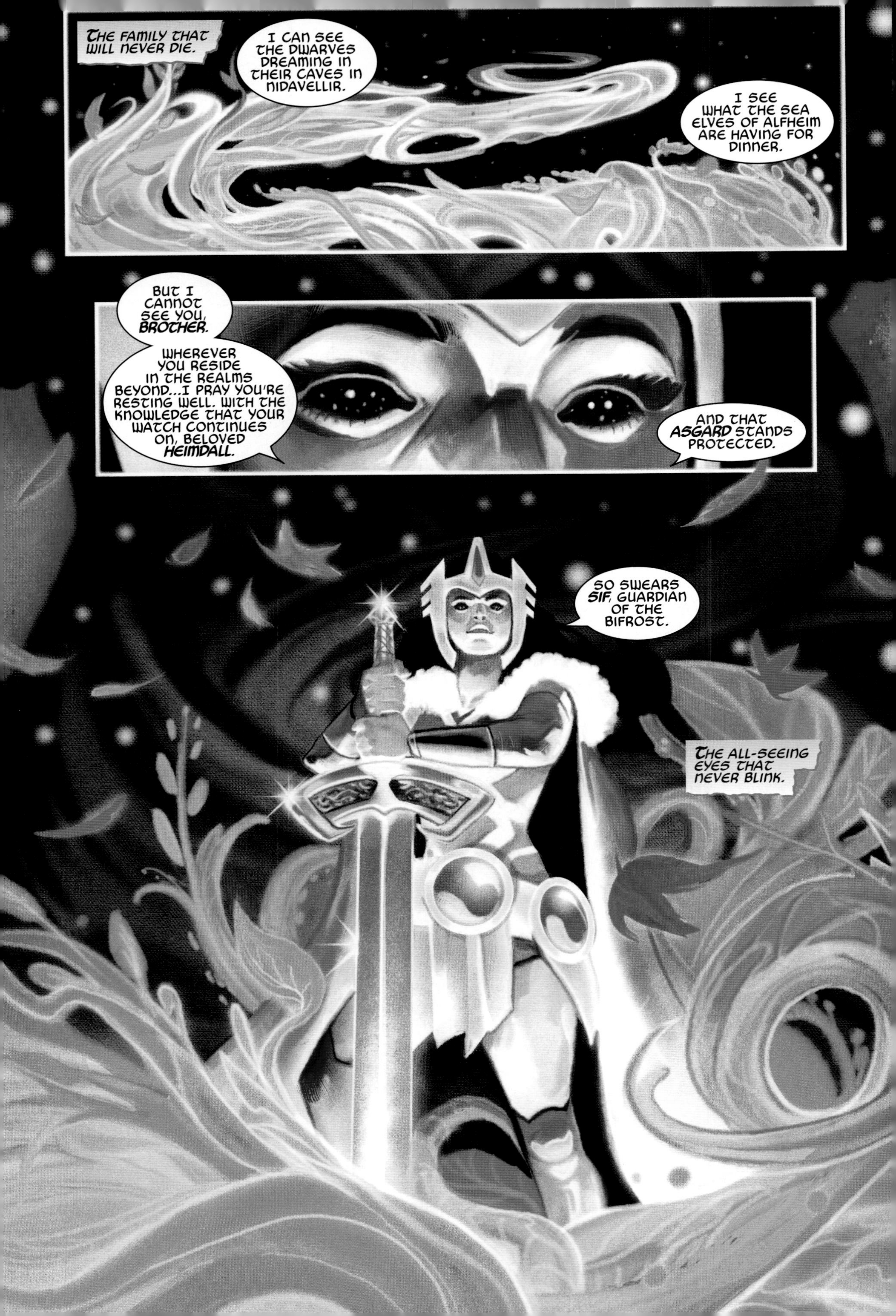

THE FAMILY THAT WILL NEVER DIE.
I CAN SEE THE DWARVES DREAMING IN THEIR CAVES IN NIDAVELLIR.
I SEE WHAT THE SEA ELVES OF ALFHEIM ARE HAVING FOR DINNER.
BUT I CANNOT SEE YOU, BROTHER.
WHEREVER YOU RESIDE IN THE REALMS BEYOND...I PRAY YOU'RE RESTING WELL. WITH THE KNOWLEDGE THAT YOUR WATCH CONTINUES ON, BELOVED HEIMDALL.
AND THAT ASGARD STANDS PROTECTED.
SO SWEARS SIF, GUARDIAN OF THE BIFROST.
THE ALL-SEEING EYES THAT NEVER BLINK.

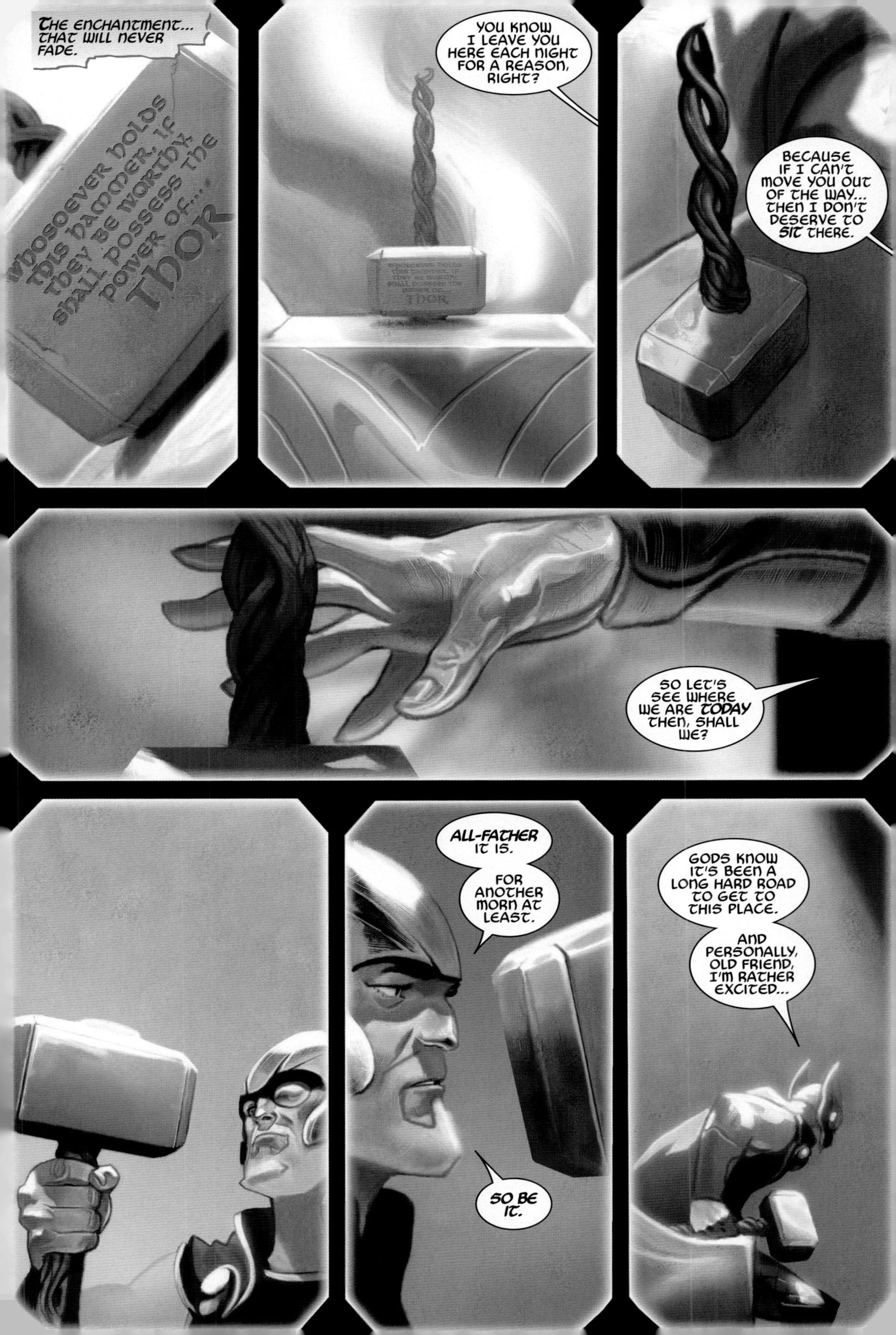
THE ENCHANTMENT... THAT WILL NEVER FADE.
WHOSOEVER HOLDS THIS HAMMER, IF THEY BE WORTHY, SHALL POSSESS THE POWER OF... THOR
YOU KNOW I LEAVE YOU HERE EACH NIGHT FOR A REASON, RIGHT?
BECAUSE IF I CAN'T MOVE YOU OUT OF THE WAY... THEN I DON'T DESERVE TO SIT THERE.
SO LET'S SEE WHERE WE ARE TODAY THEN, SHALL WE?
ALL-FATHER IT IS.
FOR ANOTHER MORN AT LEAST.
SO BE IT.
GODS KNOW IT'S BEEN A LONG HARD ROAD TO GET TO THIS PLACE.
AND PERSONALLY, OLD FRIEND, I'M RATHER EXCITED...

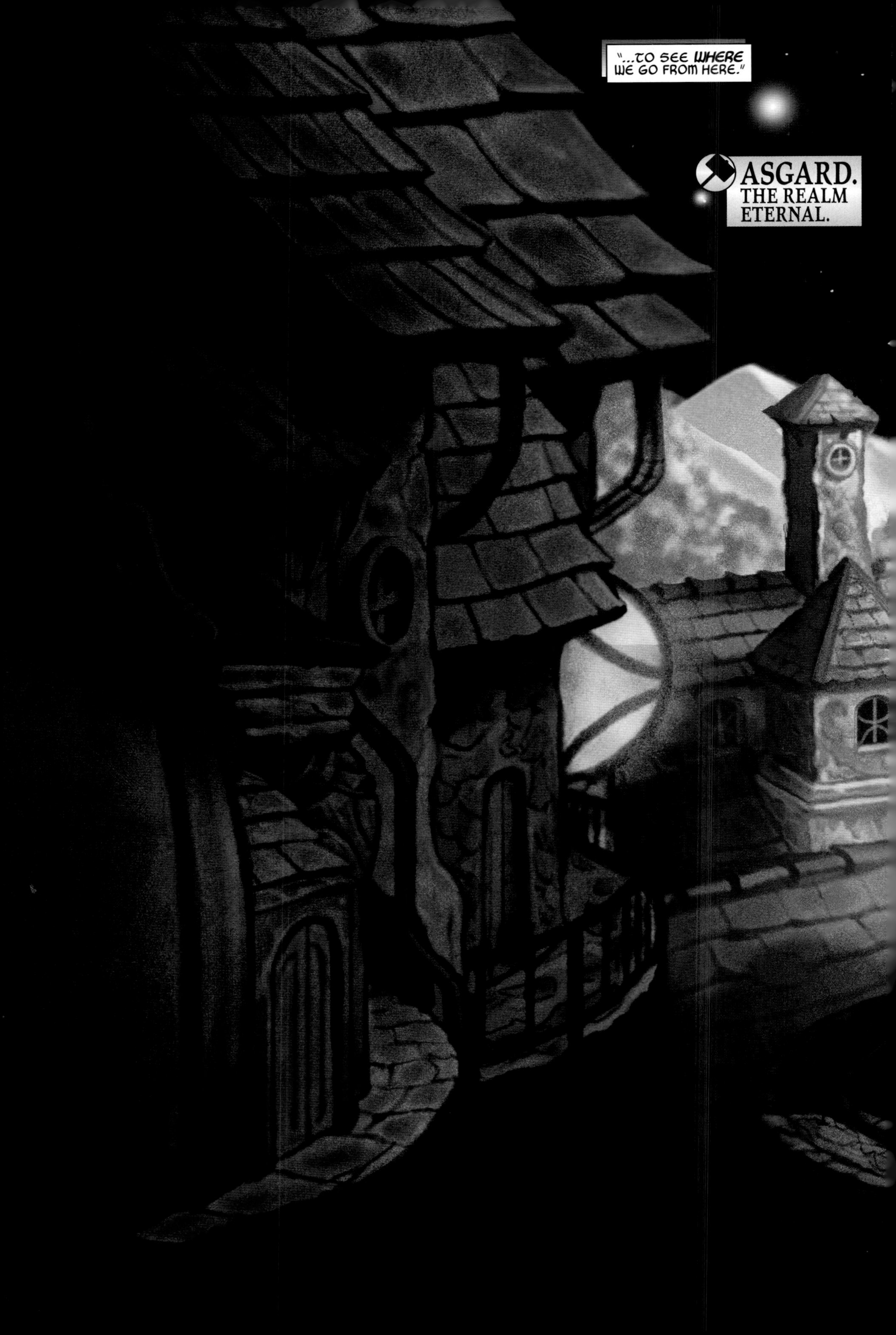
"...TO SEE WHERE WE GO FROM HERE."
ASGARD. THE REALM ETERNAL.

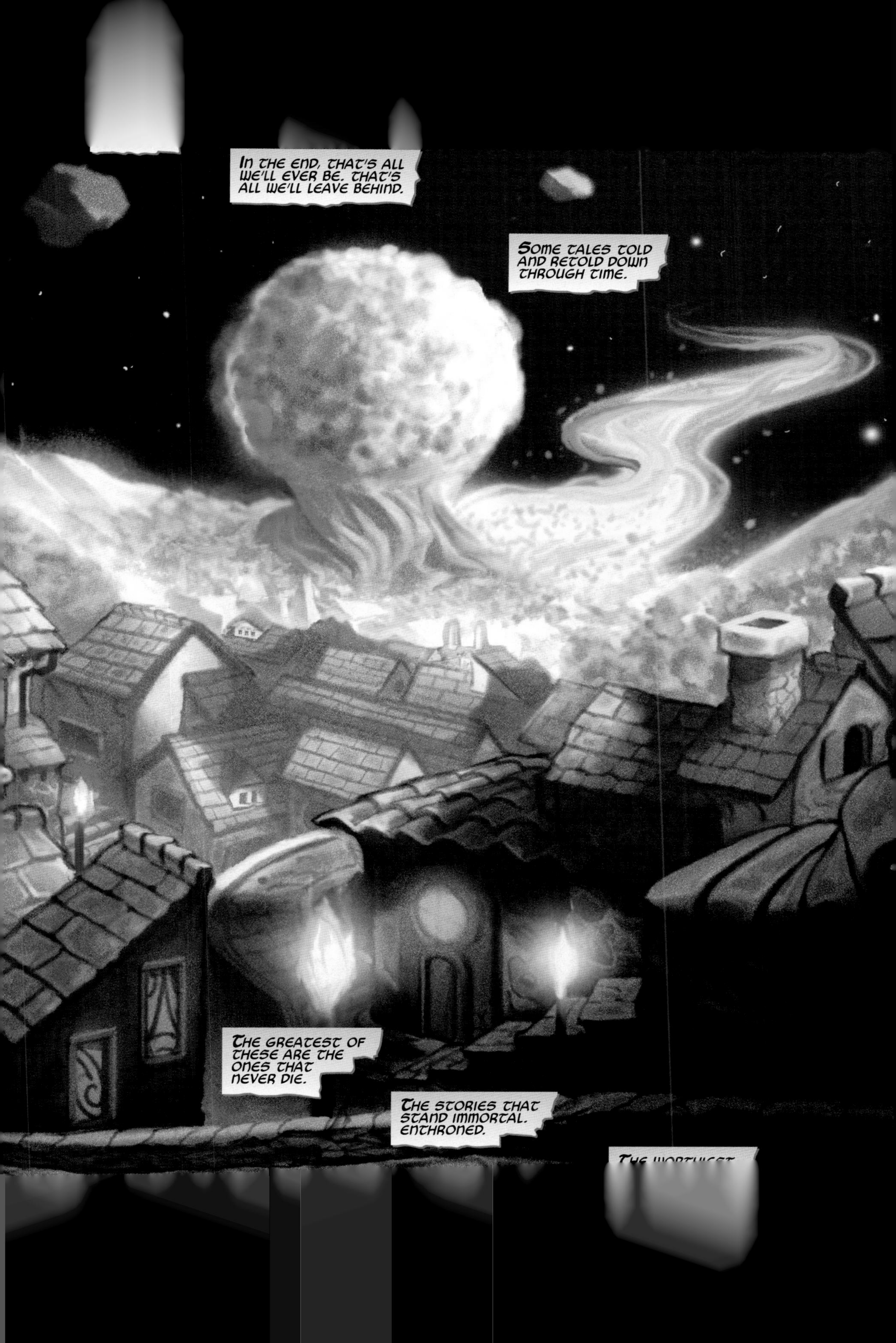
In the end, that's all we'll ever be. That's all we'll leave behind.
Some tales told and retold down through time.
The greatest of these are the ones that never die.
The stories that stand immortal. Enthroned.

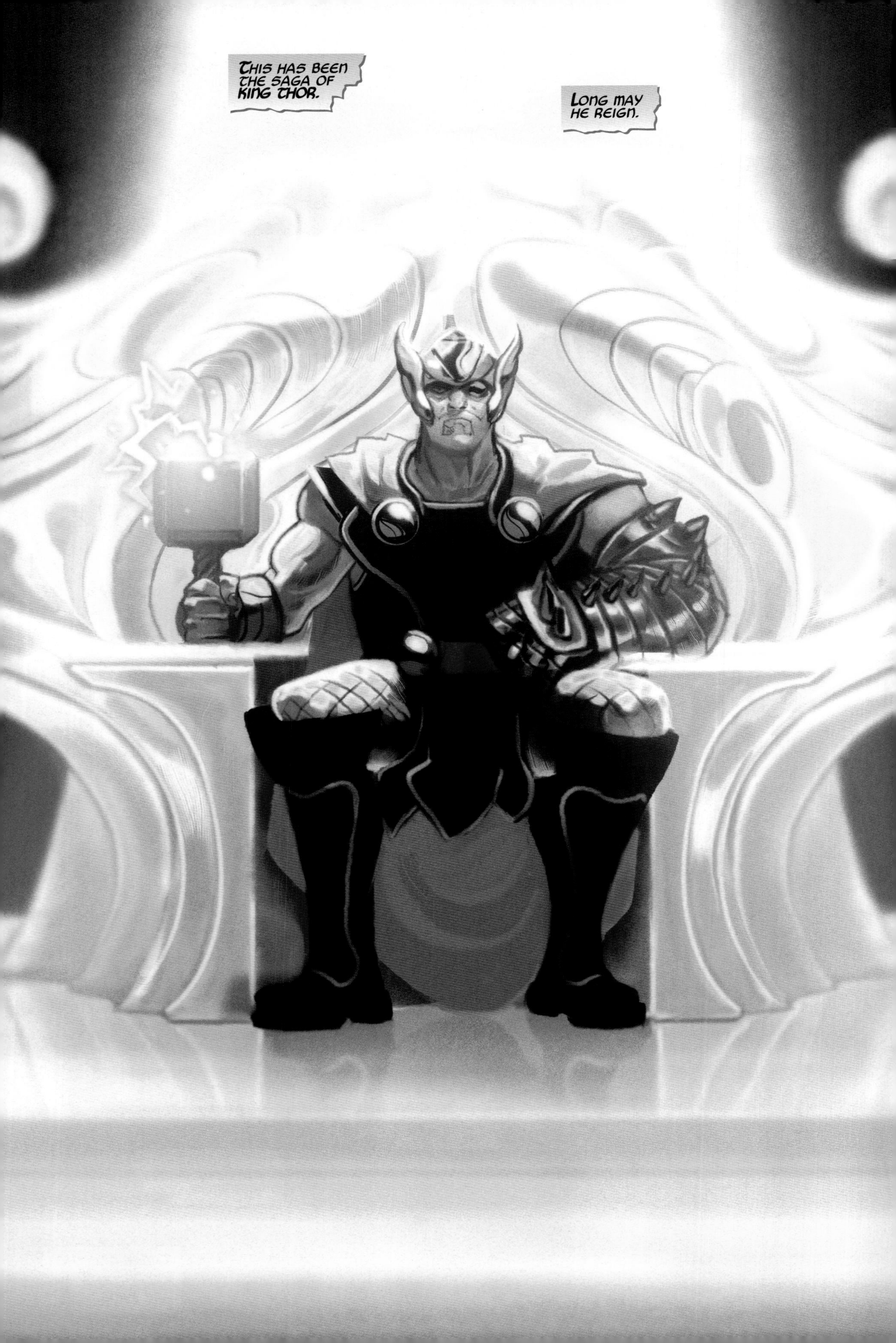
THIS HAS BEEN THE SAGA OF KING THOR.
LONG MAY HE REIGN.

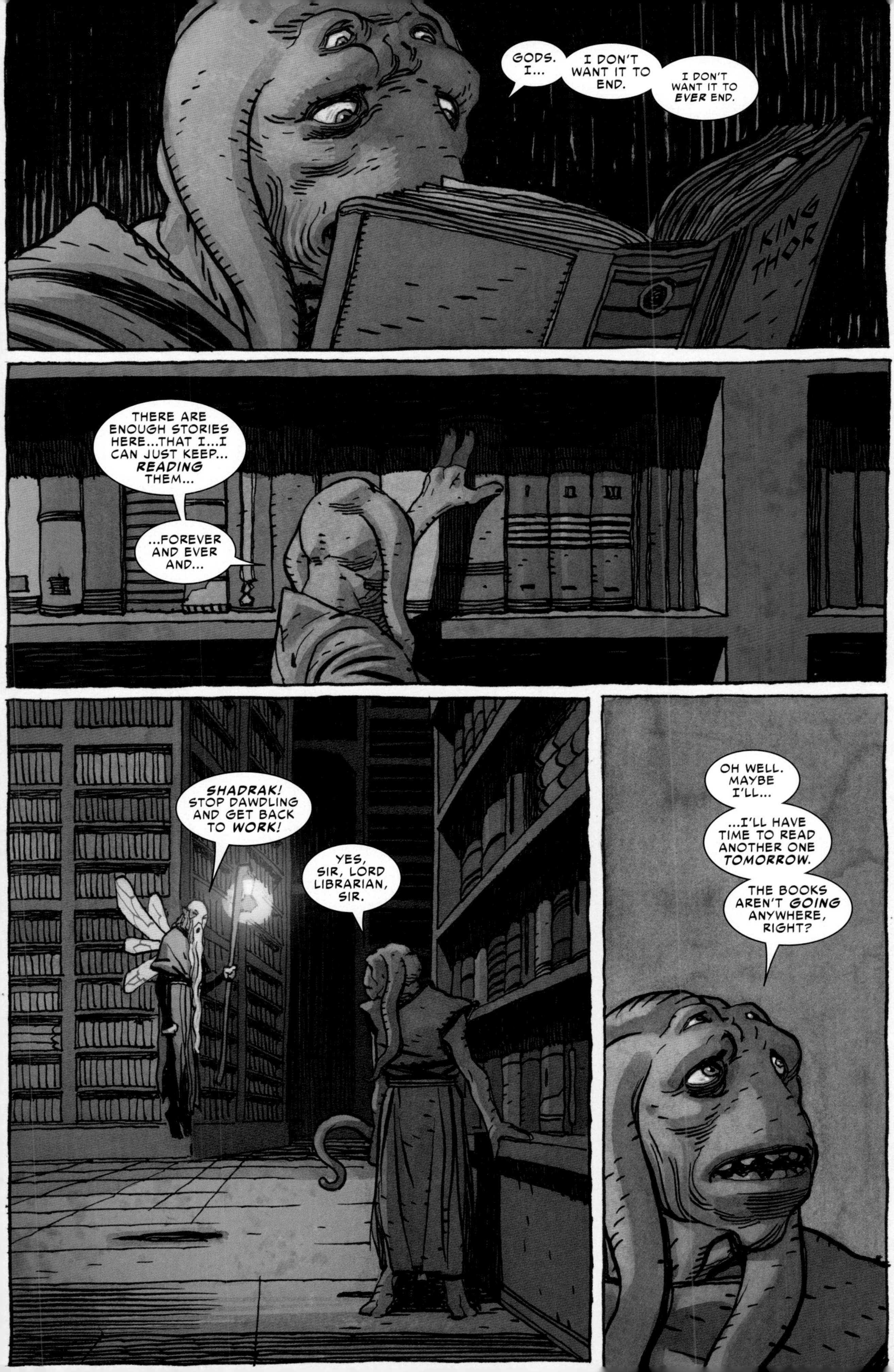
GODS. I...
I DON'T WANT IT TO END.
I DON'T WANT IT TO EVER END.
KING THOR
THERE ARE ENOUGH STORIES HERE...THAT I...I CAN JUST KEEP... READING THEM...
...FOREVER AND EVER AND...
SHADRAK! STOP DAWDLING AND GET BACK TO WORK!
YES, SIR, LORD LIBRARIAN, SIR.
OH WELL. MAYBE I'LL...
...I'LL HAVE TIME TO READ ANOTHER ONE TOMORROW.
THE BOOKS AREN'T GOING ANYWHERE, RIGHT?

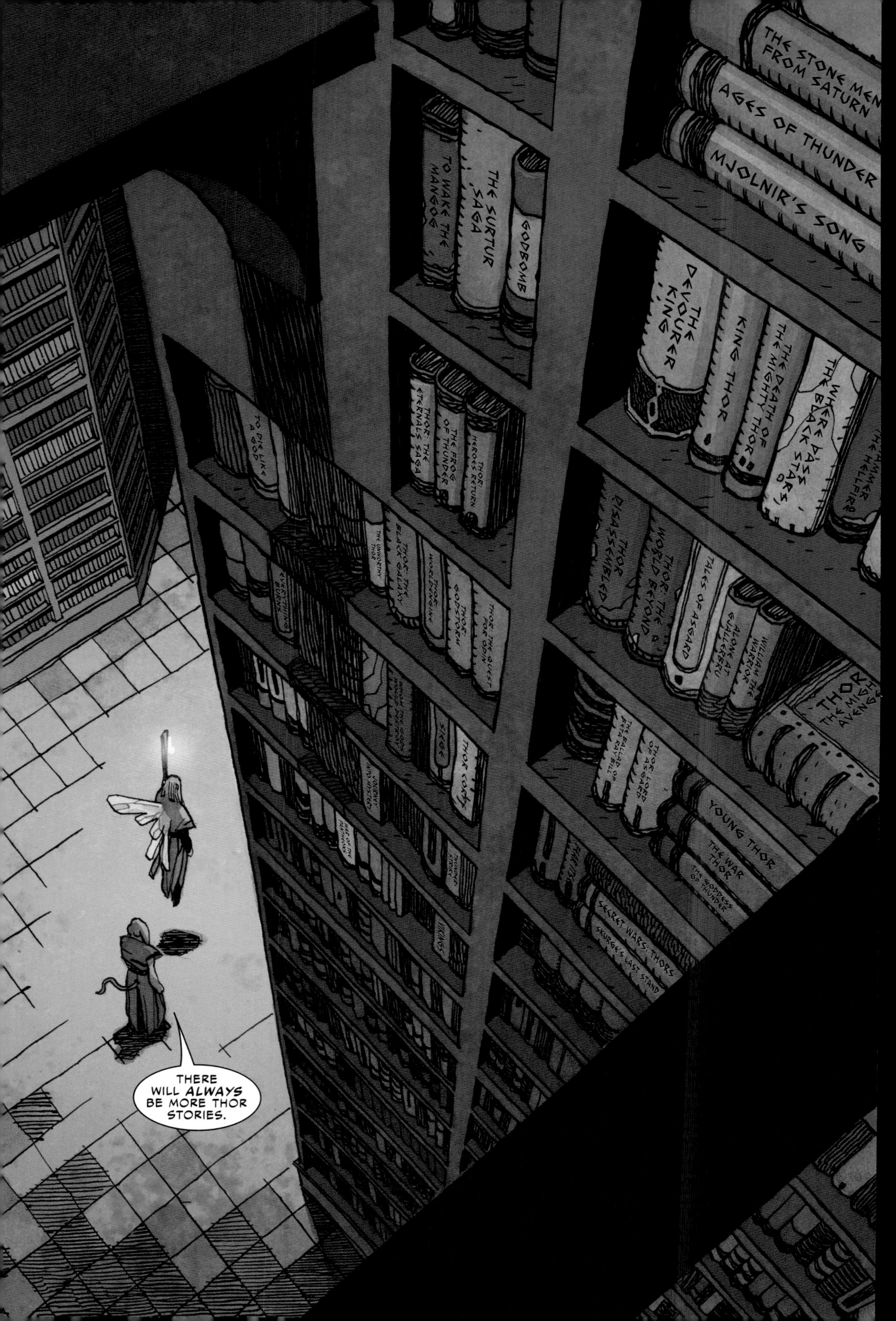
AGES OF THUNDER
MJOLNIR'S SONG
THE SURTUR SAGA
TO WAKE THE MANGOG
GODBOMB
THE DEVOURER KING
KING THOR
THE DEATH OF THE MIGHTY THOR
WHERE PASS THE BLACK STARS
TO DIE LIKE A GOD
THOR: ETERNALS SAGA
THOR: THE FROG OF THUNDER
THOR: HEROES RETURN
THE UNWORTHY THOR
THOR: THE BLACK GALAXY
THOR: GODSTORM
THOR: THE QUEST FOR ODIN
SIEGE
THOR CORPS
VIKINGS
THOR DISASSEMBLED
THOR: THE WORLD BEYOND
TALES OF ASGARD
ALONE AT GJALLERBRU
WILLIAM THE WARRIOR
THE BALLAD OF BETA RAY BILL
THOR: LORD OF ASGARD
YOUNG THOR
THE WAR THOR
THE GODDESS OF THUNDER
SECRET WARS: THORS
SKURGE'S LAST STAND
THERE WILL ALWAYS BE MORE THOR STORIES.

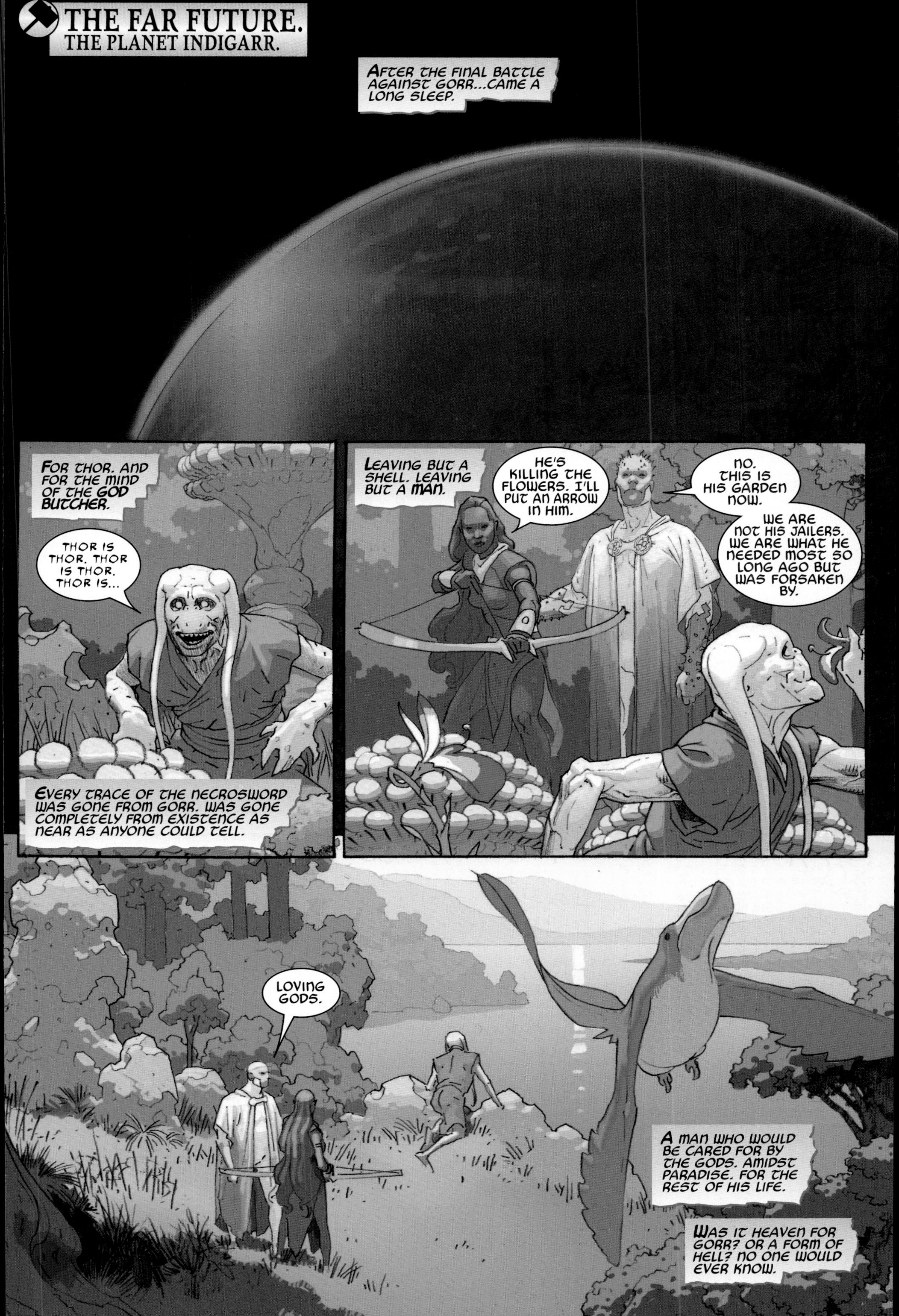
THE FAR FUTURE.
THE PLANET INDIGARR.
AFTER THE FINAL BATTLE AGAINST GORR...CAME A LONG SLEEP.
FOR THOR. AND FOR THE MIND OF THE GOD BUTCHER.
THOR IS THOR. THOR IS THOR. THOR IS...
EVERY TRACE OF THE NECROSWORD WAS GONE FROM GORR. WAS GONE COMPLETELY FROM EXISTENCE AS NEAR AS ANYONE COULD TELL.
LEAVING BUT A SHELL. LEAVING BUT A MAN.
HE'S KILLING THE FLOWERS. I'LL PUT AN ARROW IN HIM.
NO. THIS IS HIS GARDEN NOW.
WE ARE NOT HIS JAILERS. WE ARE WHAT HE NEEDED MOST SO LONG AGO BUT WAS FORSAKEN BY.
LOVING GODS.
A MAN WHO WOULD BE CARED FOR BY THE GODS. AMIDST PARADISE. FOR THE REST OF HIS LIFE.
WAS IT HEAVEN FOR GORR? OR A FORM OF HELL? NO ONE WOULD EVER KNOW.

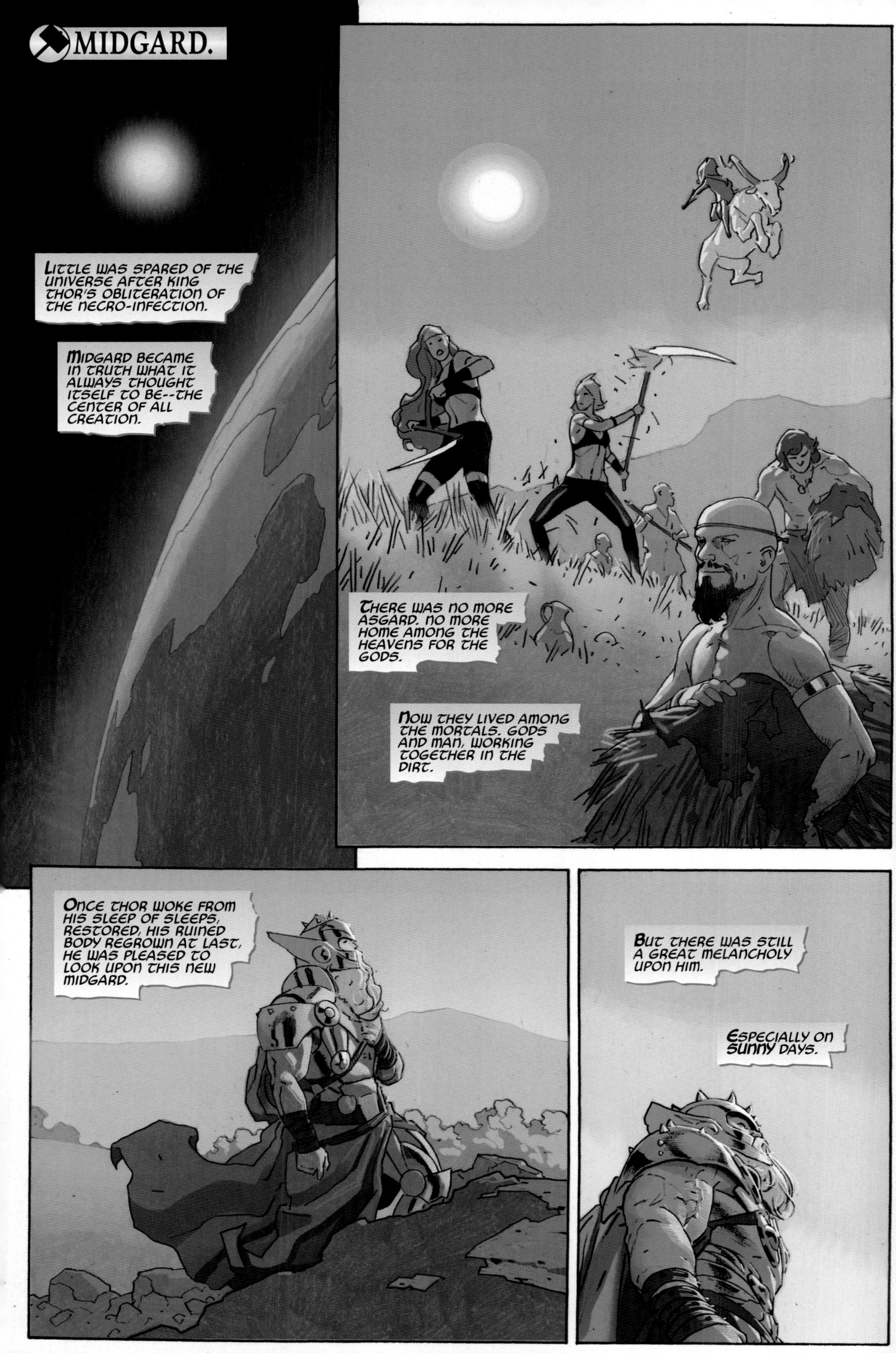

MIDGARD.
LITTLE WAS SPARED OF THE UNIVERSE AFTER KING THOR'S OBLITERATION OF THE NECRO-INFECTION.
MIDGARD BECAME IN TRUTH WHAT IT ALWAYS THOUGHT ITSELF TO BE--THE CENTER OF ALL CREATION.
THERE WAS NO MORE ASGARD. NO MORE HOME AMONG THE HEAVENS FOR THE GODS.
NOW THEY LIVED AMONG THE MORTALS. GODS AND MAN, WORKING TOGETHER IN THE DIRT.
ONCE THOR WOKE FROM HIS SLEEP OF SLEEPS, RESTORED, HIS RUINED BODY REGROWN AT LAST, HE WAS PLEASED TO LOOK UPON THIS NEW MIDGARD.
BUT THERE WAS STILL A GREAT MELANCHOLY UPON HIM.
ESPECIALLY ON SUNNY DAYS.

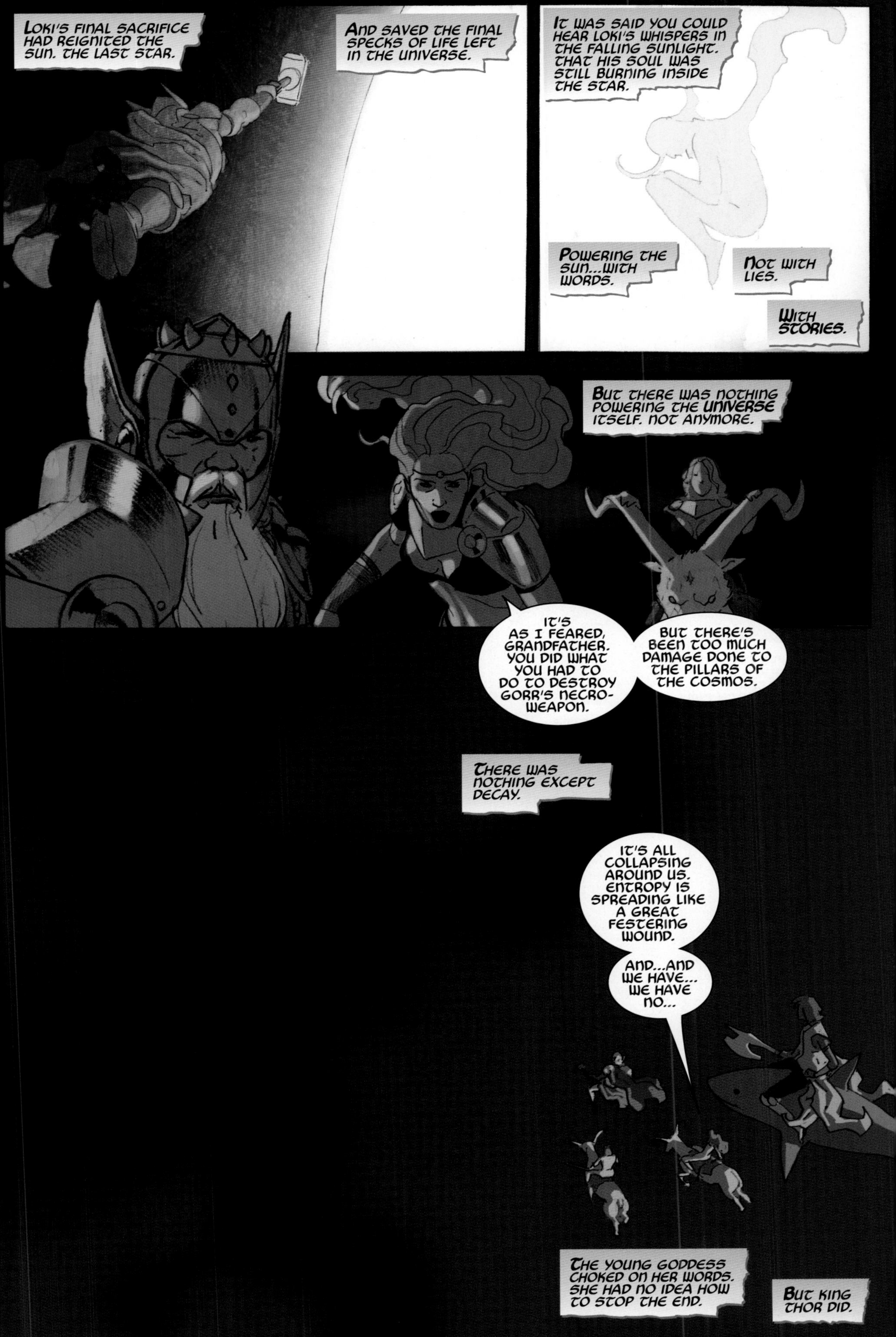

LOKI'S FINAL SACRIFICE HAD REIGNITED THE SUN. THE LAST STAR.
AND SAVED THE FINAL SPECKS OF LIFE LEFT IN THE UNIVERSE.
IT WAS SAID YOU COULD HEAR LOKI'S WHISPERS IN THE FALLING SUNLIGHT. THAT HIS SOUL WAS STILL BURNING INSIDE THE STAR.
POWERING THE SUN...WITH WORDS.
NOT WITH LIES.
WITH STORIES.
BUT THERE WAS NOTHING POWERING THE UNIVERSE ITSELF. NOT ANYMORE.
IT'S AS I FEARED, GRANDFATHER. YOU DID WHAT YOU HAD TO DO TO DESTROY GORR'S NECRO-WEAPON.
BUT THERE'S BEEN TOO MUCH DAMAGE DONE TO THE PILLARS OF THE COSMOS.
THERE WAS NOTHING EXCEPT DECAY.
IT'S ALL COLLAPSING AROUND US. ENTROPY IS SPREADING LIKE A GREAT FESTERING WOUND.
AND...AND WE HAVE... WE HAVE NO...
THE YOUNG GODDESS CHOKED ON HER WORDS. SHE HAD NO IDEA HOW TO STOP THE END.
BUT KING THOR DID.

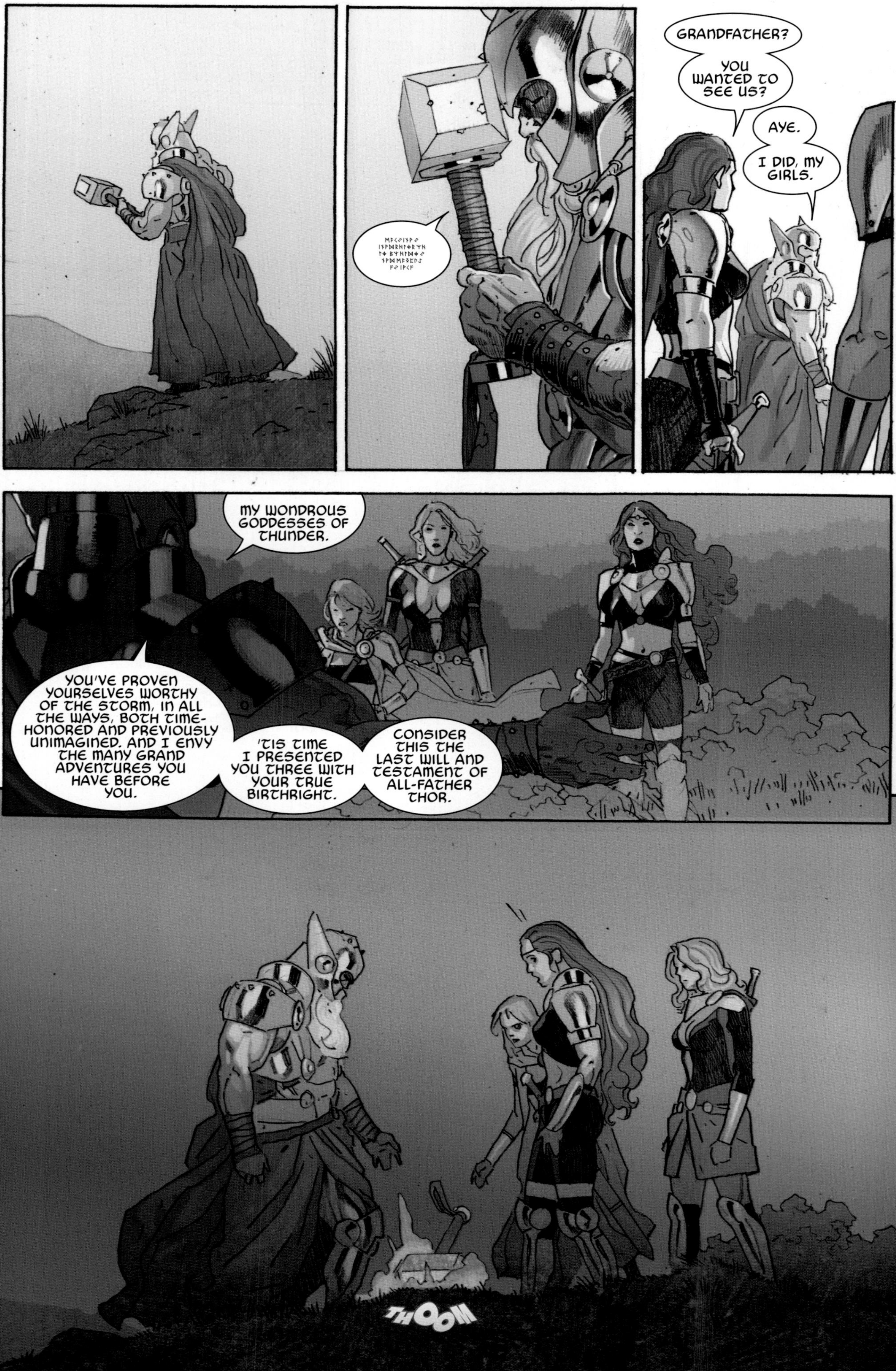
GRANDFATHER?
YOU WANTED TO SEE US?
AYE.
I DID, MY GIRLS.
MY WONDROUS GODDESSES OF THUNDER.
YOU'VE PROVEN YOURSELVES WORTHY OF THE STORM, IN ALL THE WAYS, BOTH TIME-HONORED AND PREVIOUSLY UNIMAGINED. AND I ENVY THE MANY GRAND ADVENTURES YOU HAVE BEFORE YOU.
'TIS TIME I PRESENTED YOU THREE WITH YOUR TRUE BIRTHRIGHT.
CONSIDER THIS THE LAST WILL AND TESTAMENT OF ALL-FATHER THOR.
THOOM

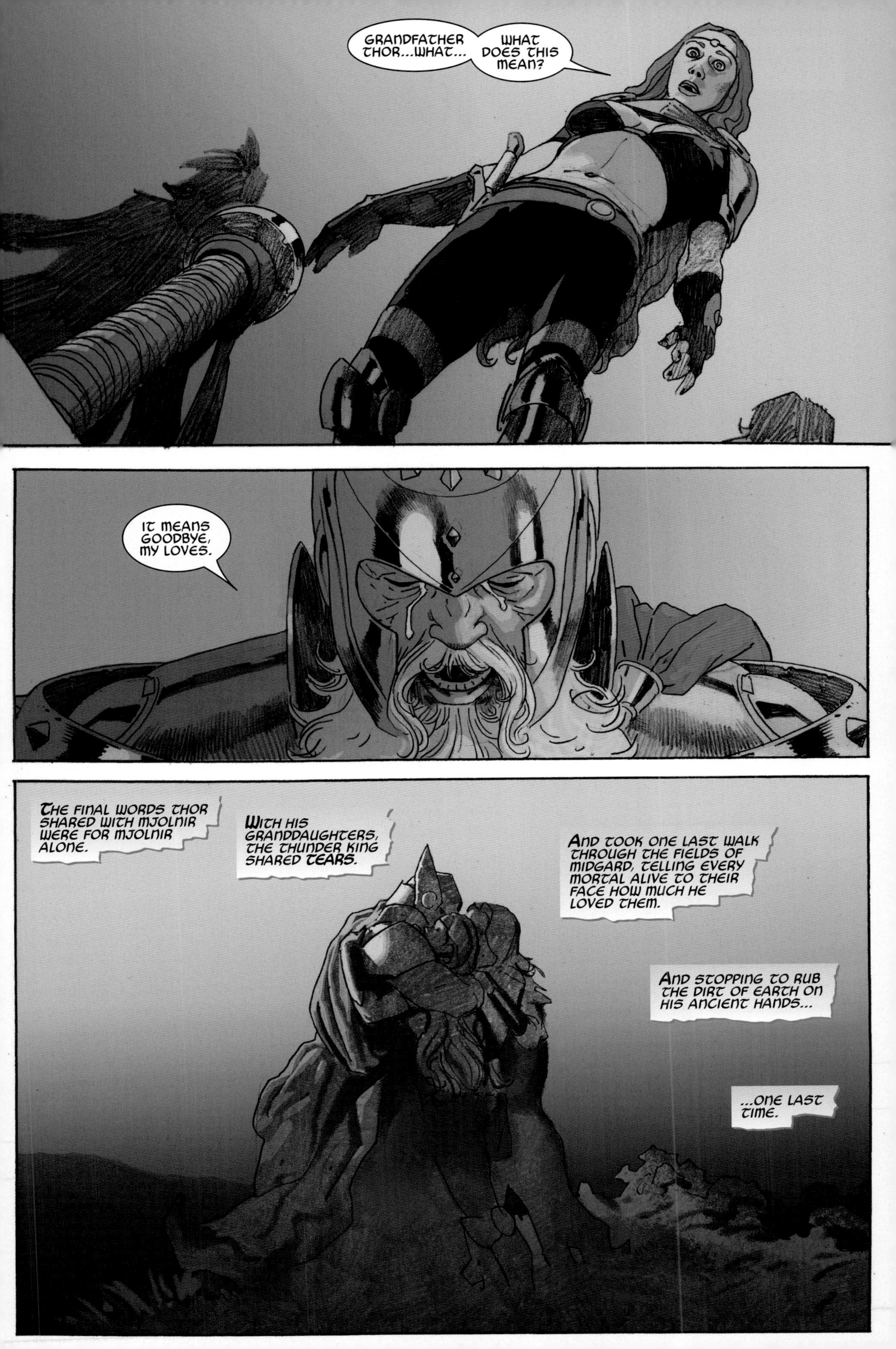
GRANDFATHER THOR...WHAT...
WHAT DOES THIS MEAN?
IT MEANS GOODBYE, MY LOVES.
THE FINAL WORDS THOR SHARED WITH MJOLNIR WERE FOR MJOLNIR ALONE.
WITH HIS GRANDDAUGHTERS, THE THUNDER KING SHARED TEARS.
AND TOOK ONE LAST WALK THROUGH THE FIELDS OF MIDGARD, TELLING EVERY MORTAL ALIVE TO THEIR FACE HOW MUCH HE LOVED THEM.
AND STOPPING TO RUB THE DIRT OF EARTH ON HIS ANCIENT HANDS...
...ONE LAST TIME.

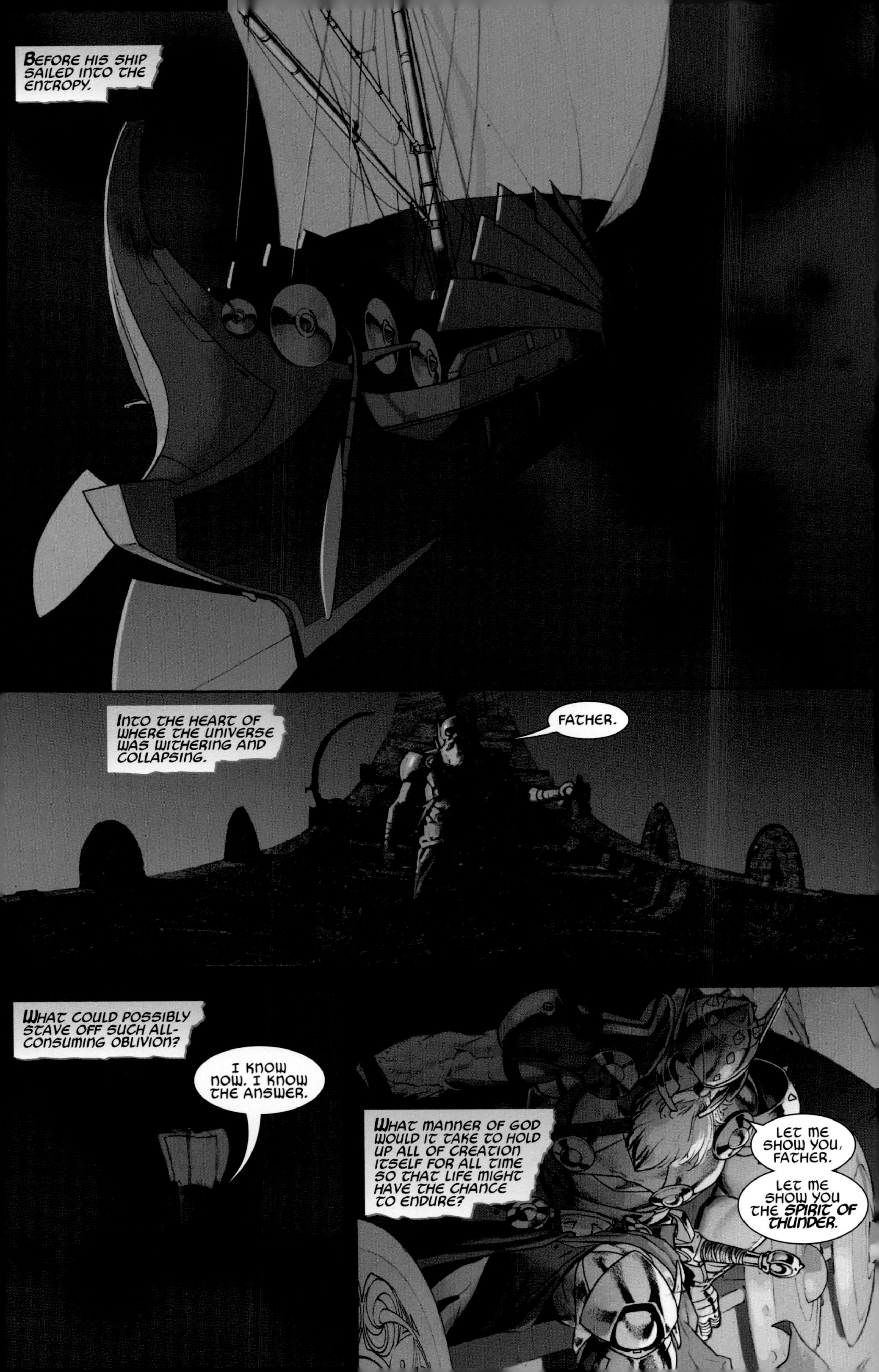
BEFORE HIS SHIP SAILED INTO THE ENTROPY.
INTO THE HEART OF WHERE THE UNIVERSE WAS WITHERING AND COLLAPSING.
FATHER.
WHAT COULD POSSIBLY STAVE OFF SUCH ALL-CONSUMING OBLIVION?
I KNOW NOW. I KNOW THE ANSWER.
WHAT MANNER OF GOD WOULD IT TAKE TO HOLD UP ALL OF CREATION ITSELF FOR ALL TIME SO THAT LIFE MIGHT HAVE THE CHANCE TO ENDURE?
LET ME SHOW YOU, FATHER.
LET ME SHOW YOU THE SPIRIT OF THUNDER.

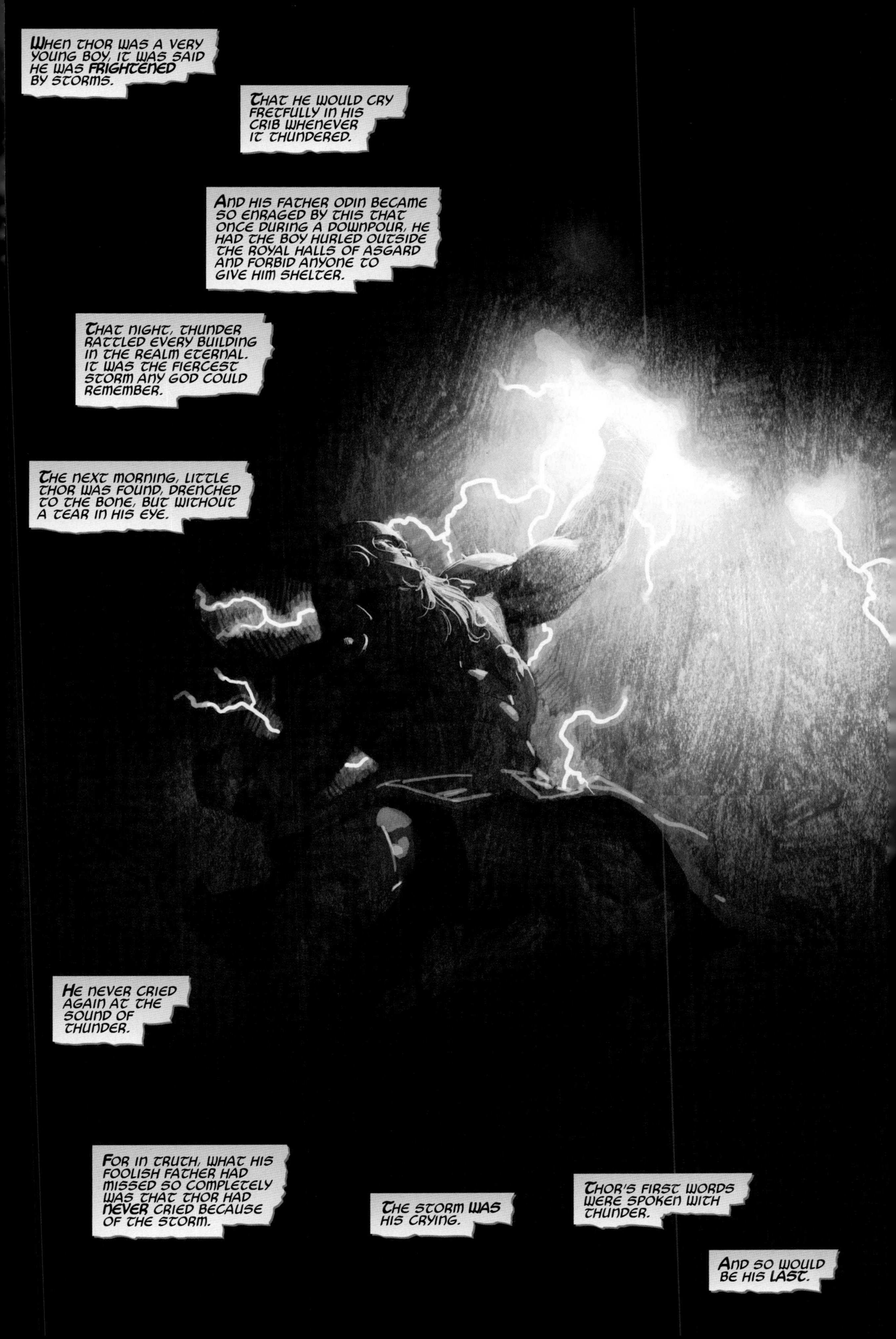
When Thor was a very young boy, it was said he was **FRIGHTENED** by storms.
That he would cry fretfully in his crib whenever it thundered.
And his father Odin became so enraged by this that once during a downpour, he had the boy hurled outside the royal halls of Asgard and forbid anyone to give him shelter.
That night, thunder rattled every building in the realm eternal. It was the fiercest storm any god could remember.
The next morning, little Thor was found, drenched to the bone, but without a tear in his eye.
He never cried again at the sound of thunder.
For in truth, what his foolish father had missed so completely was that Thor had **NEVER** cried because of the storm.
The storm **WAS** his crying.
Thor's first words were spoken with thunder.
And so would be his **LAST**.

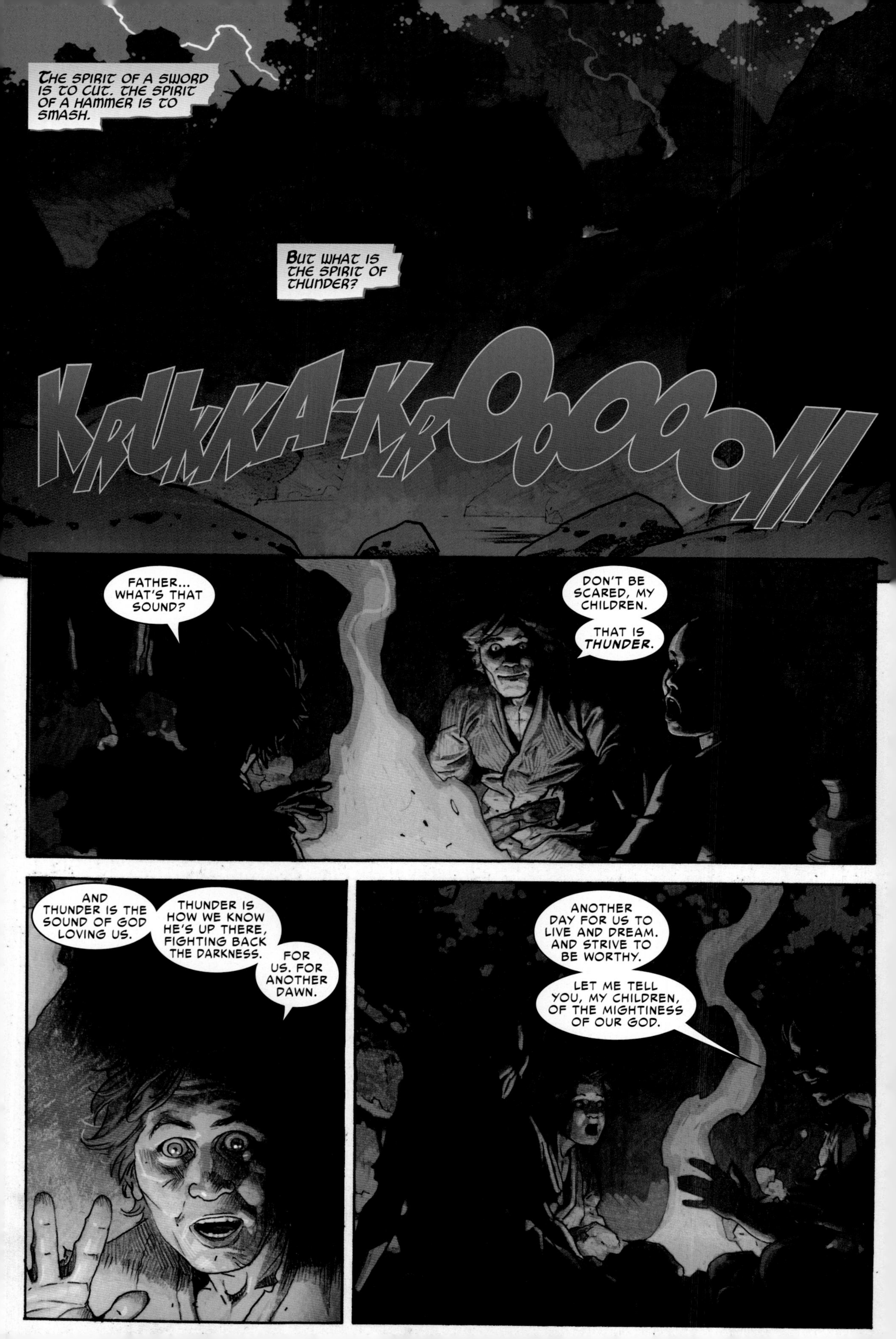
THE SPIRIT OF A SWORD IS TO CUT. THE SPIRIT OF A HAMMER IS TO SMASH.
BUT WHAT IS THE SPIRIT OF THUNDER?
KRUKKA-KROOOOOM
FATHER... WHAT'S THAT SOUND?
DON'T BE SCARED, MY CHILDREN.
THAT IS *THUNDER*.
AND THUNDER IS THE SOUND OF GOD LOVING US.
THUNDER IS HOW WE KNOW HE'S UP THERE, FIGHTING BACK THE DARKNESS.
FOR US. FOR ANOTHER DAWN.
ANOTHER DAY FOR US TO LIVE AND DREAM. AND STRIVE TO BE WORTHY.
LET ME TELL YOU, MY CHILDREN, OF THE MIGHTINESS OF OUR GOD.

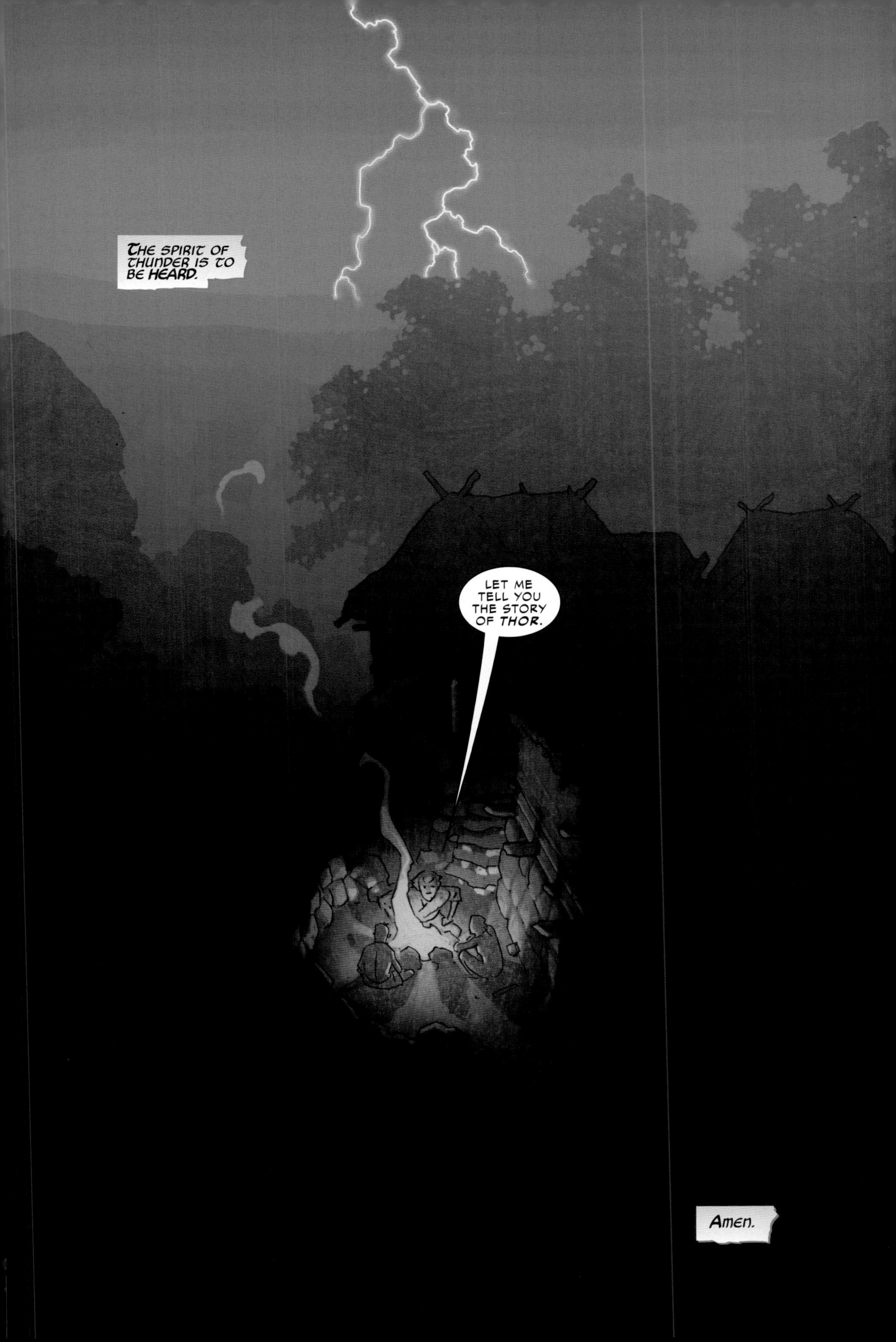
THE SPIRIT OF THUNDER IS TO BE HEARD.
LET ME TELL YOU THE STORY OF THOR.
Amen.

I'm not gonna lie.
It was hard to let go.

I don't know that I'm very good at letting go in general. But especially after seven years and 100 or so issues of being the "Thor guy" at Marvel, I found it was really hard to put this final one to bed. I held on to those last few pages for as long as I possibly could. Even though that last scene had been sitting in my head, waiting to be written, for many years.

I put a lot of myself into those 100 issues. A lot of who I was growing up, playing alone in the woods of the Deep South, breathing in stories like the purest of pine-scented oxygen, dreaming my way in the roundabout direction of the life I wanted. And a lot of who I became when I grew up, lost religion, almost lost myself, moved away, found love, found fatherhood, found the man I wanted to be, a man I'm still working to more fully realize every day.

Thor helped with that. Thor literally changed my life. And I just hope I returned the favor in some way that mattered.

Personally, I haven't believed in God, in any gods, for a long time. Faith hasn't been a part of who I am for many years. But I still have ideas and values that are precious and fundamental to me in ways that feel almost religious in nature. Even as an atheist, I still have things I worship.

And I wrote about all of them with Thor.

Thor is truly the sort of god (or gods, I guess, as I wrote a whole bunch of Thors) that I would like to believe in. The god who wakes up every single day and looks at that hammer, with its worthiness enchantment, and doesn't know if they will be able to lift it. Who lives every day questioning their own worthiness, aspiring for it, while also embracing their unworthiness, their failings. The kind of god who delights and takes unbridled joy from the wild, unimaginable beauty all around them. A god who sometimes drinks too much, sometimes loves too recklessly, who thinks both too highly and too lowly of themselves, who laughs big and weeps bigger, who thunders and broods and feels things deeply, even through near-impenetrable flesh. Who would die a thousand times to save what's most precious to them, which is us. Like the Vikings of old weaving their sagas, I was fortunate enough to be able to dream that very god into being, while standing on the shoulders of god-spawning giants with names like Lee and Kirby and Simonson. And now Thor will always be very real to me. The God of Thunder will always be a profound presence in my life.

I wasn't a huge Thor fan growing up. This *Thor* run of mine was never really the plan. Until suddenly it was. Back in 2012, there was a moment when every major title at Marvel was up for grabs all at once. I'd already been penciled in to take over a different solo Avenger series. But for some reason, it didn't feel right. And something else did. I'd really loved Matt Fraction's *Thor: Ages of Thunder* one-shots. Something about them really resonated with me at that moment in time. And so I asked if I could take over *Thor*. I didn't have a story. Didn't have a direction. Didn't know who Thor was to me. But suddenly, he was mine. And if nothing else, I hope it still shows seven years later that I have thoroughly enjoyed our time together.

So if there's a lesson in there, I guess it's to be who you are and follow what feels right in the moment.

And dream your own gods.

Speaking of gods, there's a long list of the artistic variety whom I was lucky enough to collaborate with over the course of this run. It's too large a pantheon for me to list every single deified one of them here, but I would like to acknowledge a few. Before I ever had my first Thor story idea, I knew Esad Ribić was going to draw it, and that truly helped define everything to me. The scope, the power, the feel. Everything I've done with the character goes back to Esad's initial designs and the power of his opening pencils (along with Ive Svorcina's breathtaking colors). Esad was the spark, the fiery cosmic genesis, the jaw-dropping spectacle. And he was a tough damn act to follow. But Russell Dauterman still managed to swoop in and make the character and the world so completely and utterly his own. Along with the near-omnipotently talented colorist Matthew Wilson, Russell became the heart, the soul, the beauty and Uru-strong emotion of the series. I've never cried so much looking at a comic page as I still do with Russell and Matthew's work on the Jane Foster storyline. And I expect that will always be the case. And then the amazing Mike del Mundo took the reins for the last big series and brought his own unique, staggeringly imaginative and inventive style to Thor's world. Mike managed to weave together the spectacle and the heart, the power and the passion, in a way that felt like both a progression of what had come before and something wildly new and different. I will owe these artists free drinks for the rest of my life. And I look forward to them collecting.

I also owe unending thanks to everyone at Marvel who's helped make this happen, from former EiC Axel Alonso and my original editor, Lauren Sankovitch, to the current chief, C.B. Cebulski, and my longtime editorial collaborators and infinitely patient creative partners, editors Wil Moss and Sarah Brunstad. Those artists I mentioned before are the reason this run has looked so incredible for so long. But Wil and Sarah are the power behind that. It's been their eyes and impeccable tastes guiding the look of all these gorgeous series. So we all owe them free drinks for that.

And there's one other vitally important person who's been an even bigger part of my run than anyone else.

And that's letterer Joe Sabino. Joe has brought his letters and creativity to every single issue of my time on *Thor*. And even more than that, he's been a part of Thor history for even longer, working on the character all the way back to the JMS days. And thankfully Joe will still be here after I'm gone.

Which I guess means it's time to pass the Mjolnir on to its new caretakers, Donny Cates and Nic Klein, so I can step aside and enjoy the cosmic epicness that I know for a fact they're about to bestow upon us.

And enjoy it; I will. Because I'll be right there with all of you now. The people I owe the most thanks to. The fans who read and supported this entire tale. I don't know how I could ever possibly convey to you just how deeply I've cherished and appreciated the connection we've forged from across the pages. If nothing else, I hope that connection has earned me the honor of standing alongside you. As a Thor fan. Eagerly awaiting the next issue. The next grand adventure. The next chance to spend a little more time with a dear old friend.

I love you, Thor. Most verily, I do. Thanks for the chance to share that love with the world.

I'll look for you in the storm clouds, friend.

Stay worthy.
Jason Aaron
KC, November 14, 2019

KING THOR #4 VARIANT
BY **MIKE DEL MUNDO**

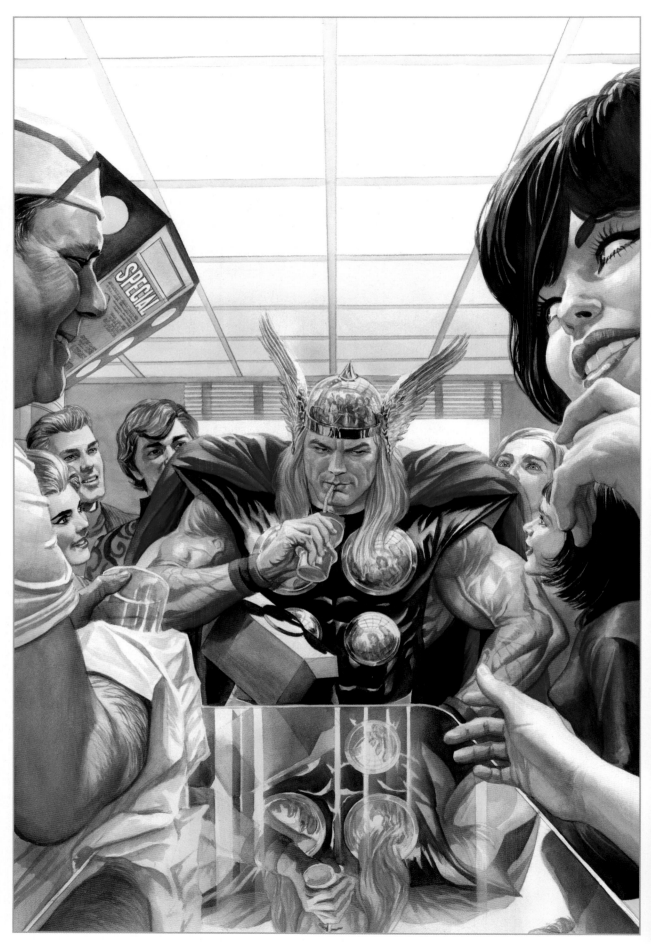

#13 MARVELS 25TH ANNIVERSARY VARIANT
BY **ALEX ROSS**

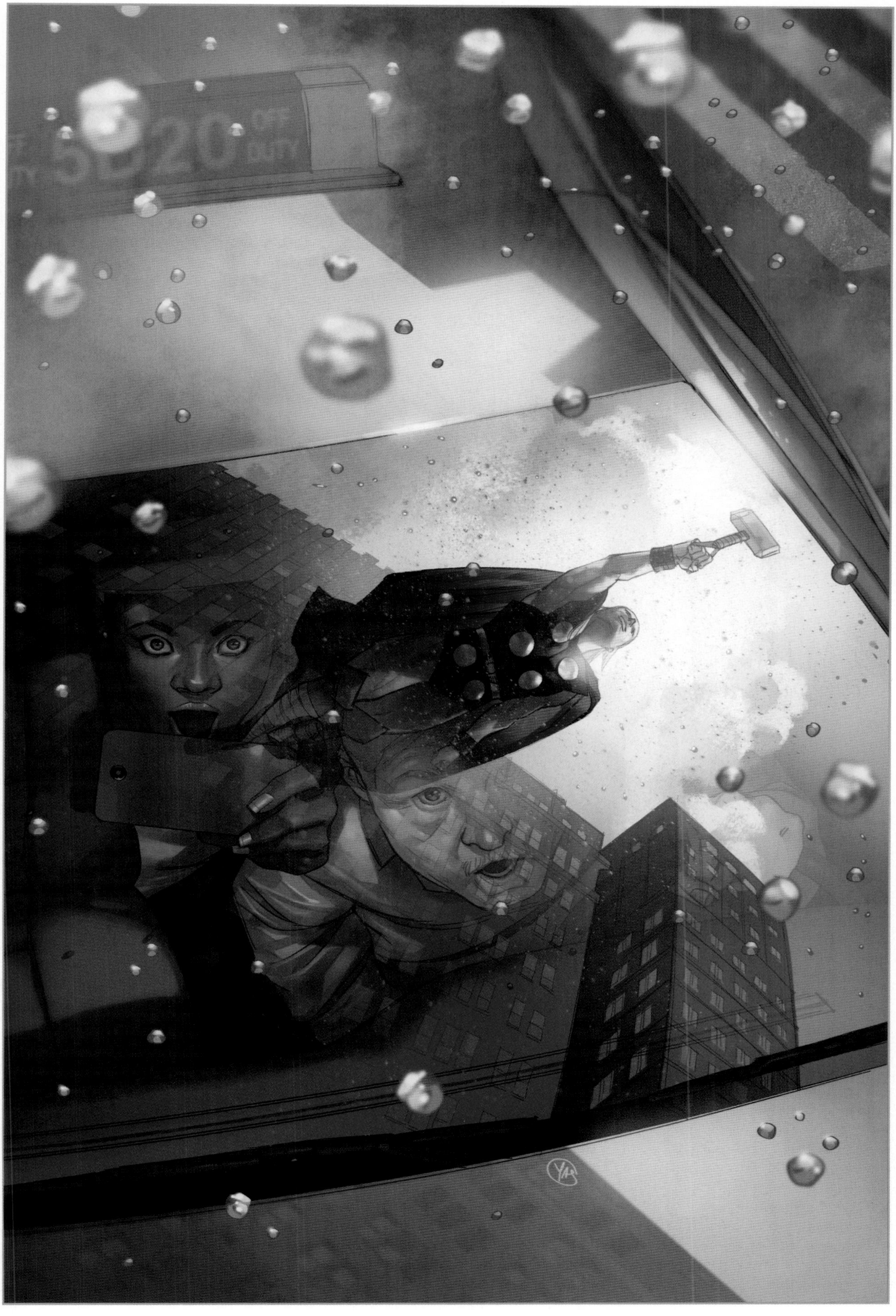
5D20
OFF DUTY

#14 MARVELS 25TH VARIANT
BY **YASMINE PUTRI**

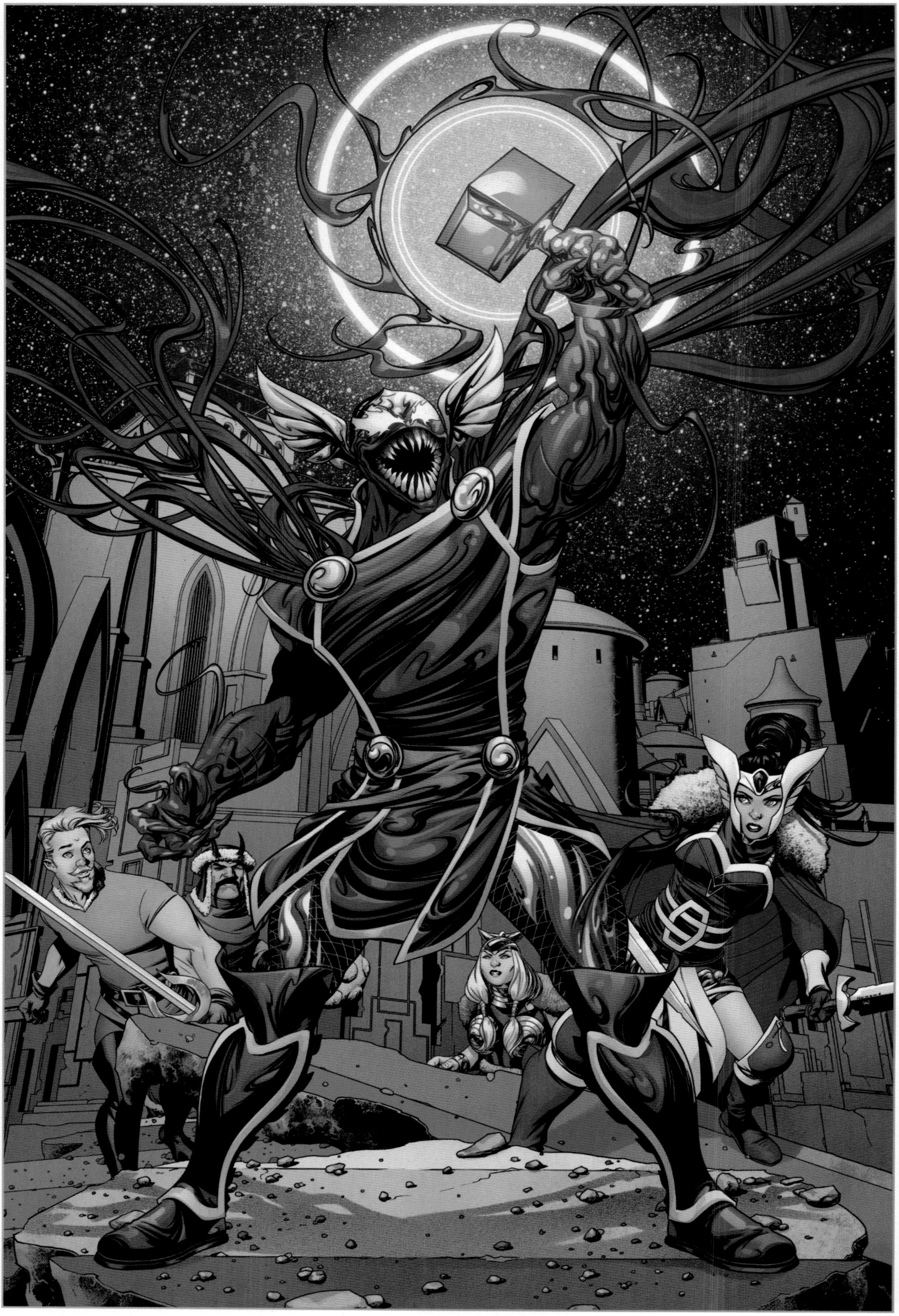

#15 CARNAGE-IZED VARIANT
BY **MIKE McKONE** & **NOLAN WOODARD**

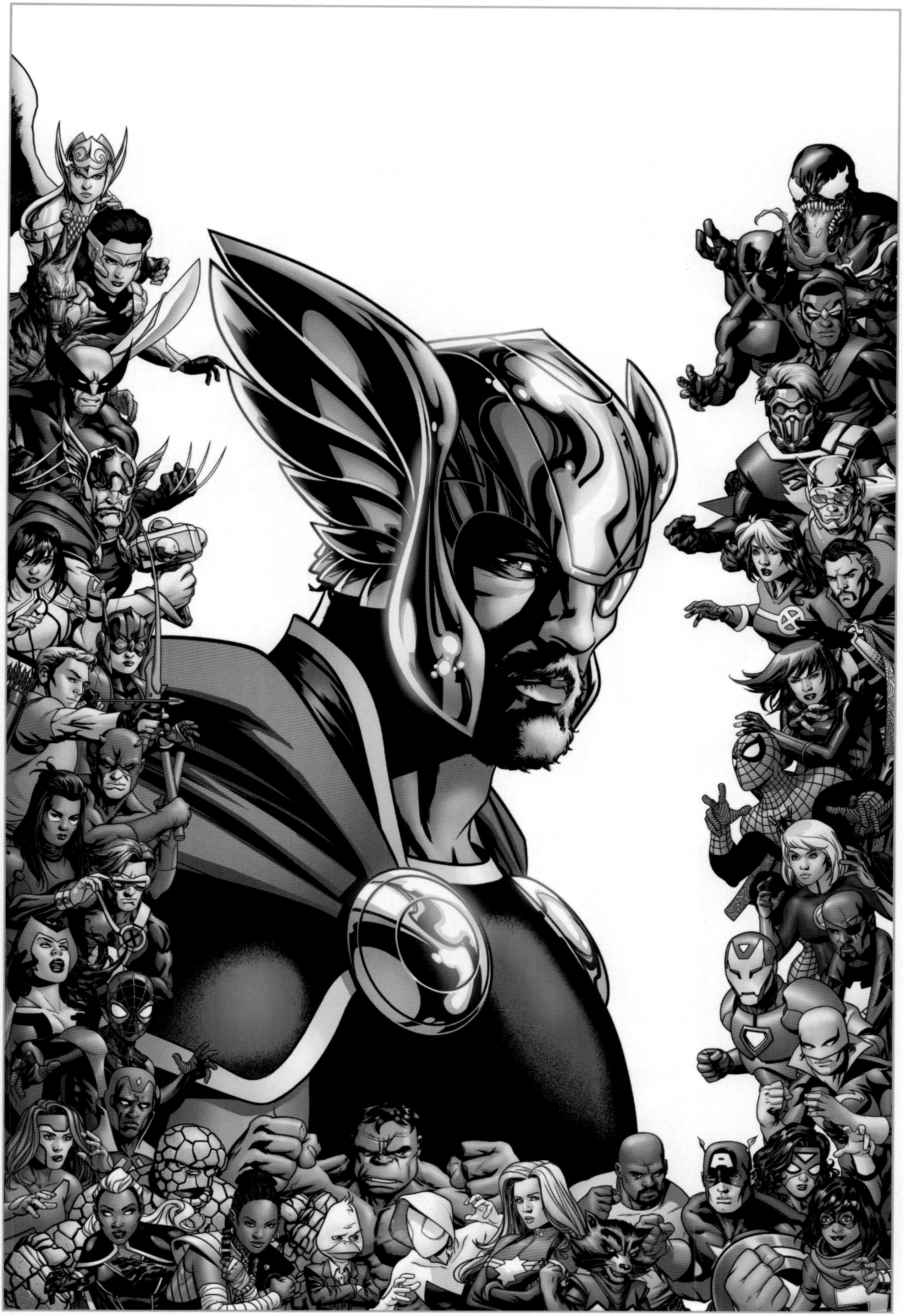

#16 80TH FRAME VARIANT
BY **MIKE McKONE** & **EDGAR DELGADO**

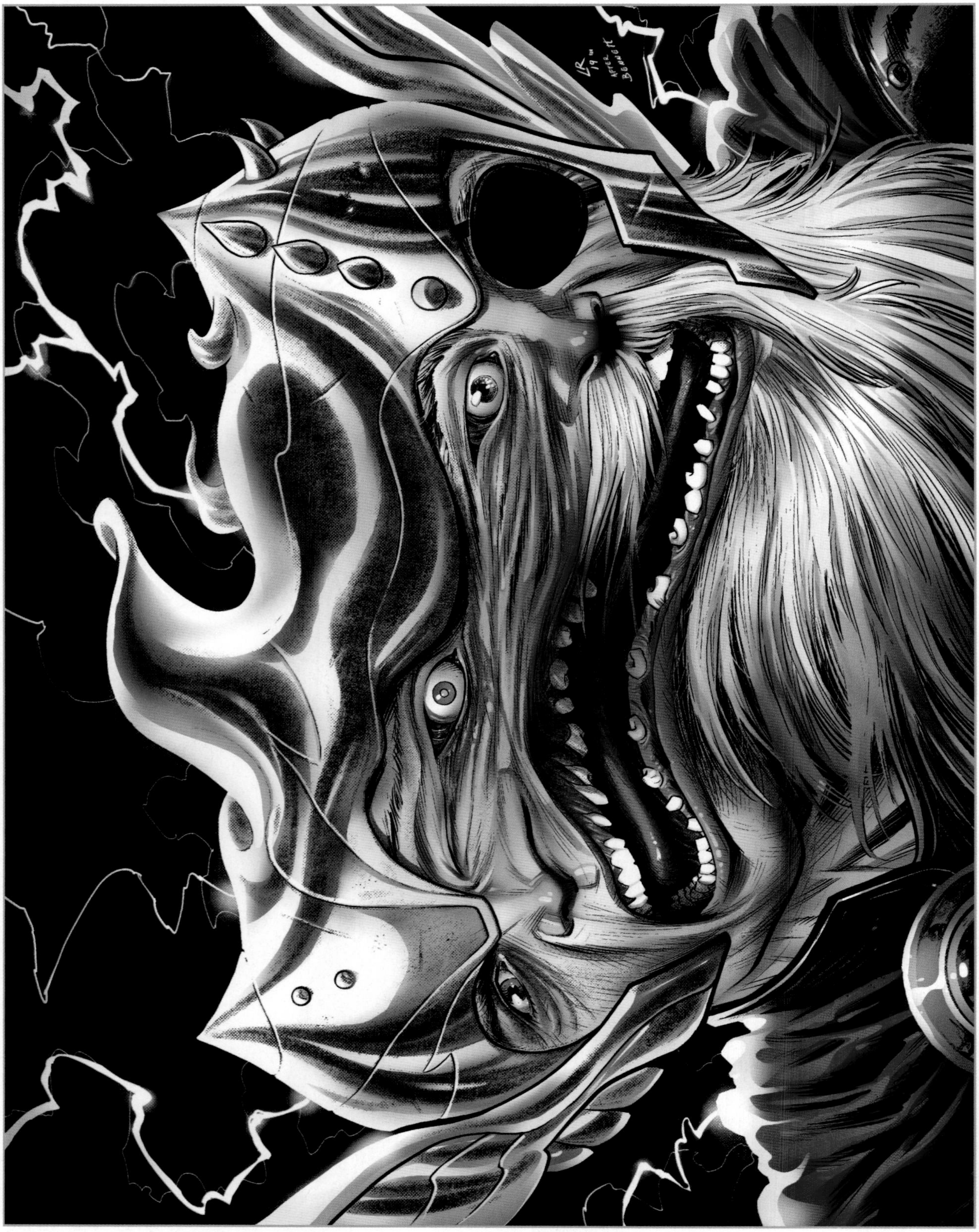

KING THOR #1 IMMORTAL VARIANT
BY **GERARDO ZAFFINO**

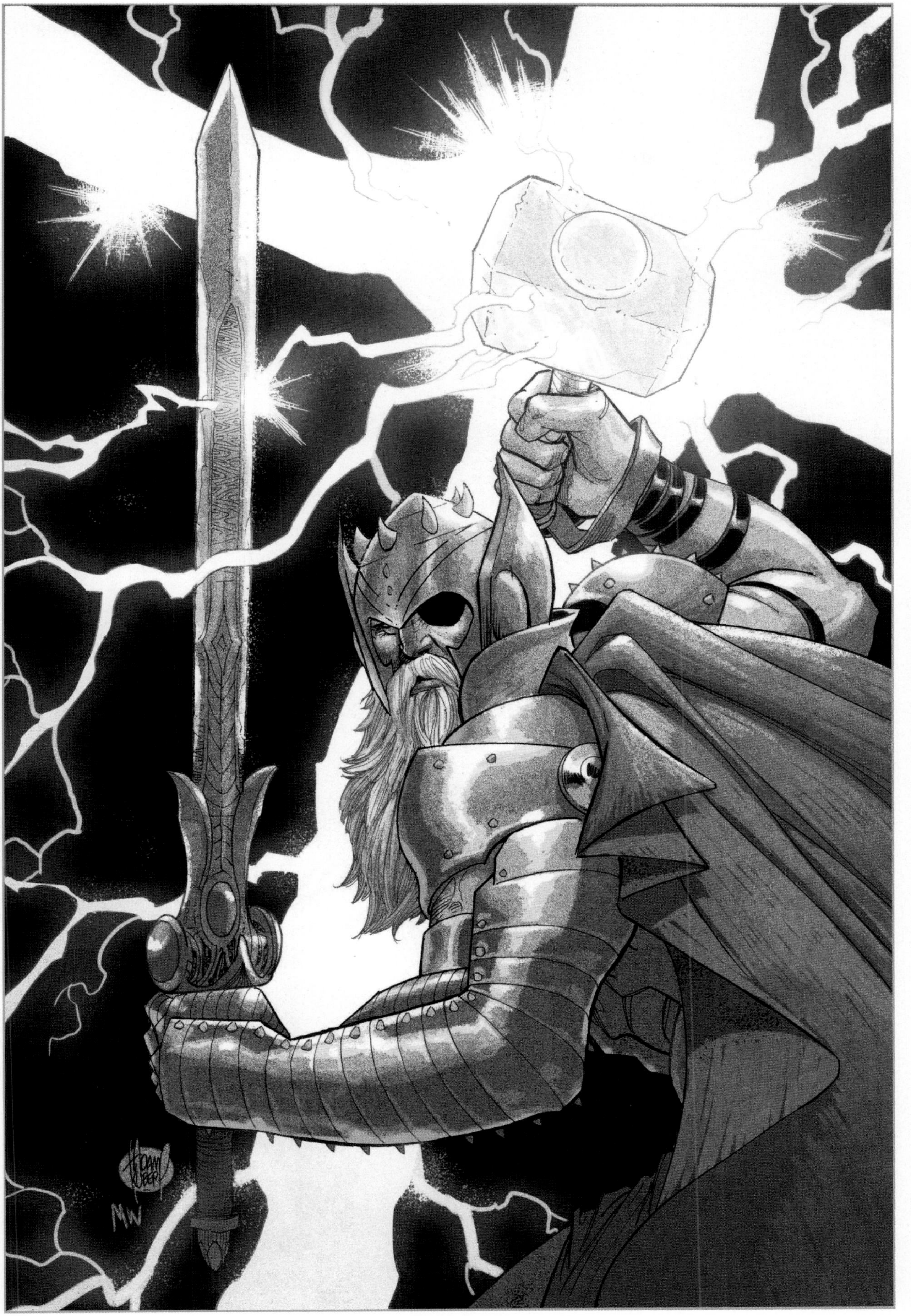

KING THOR #1 VARIANT
BY **ADAM KUBERT** & **MATTHEW WILSON**

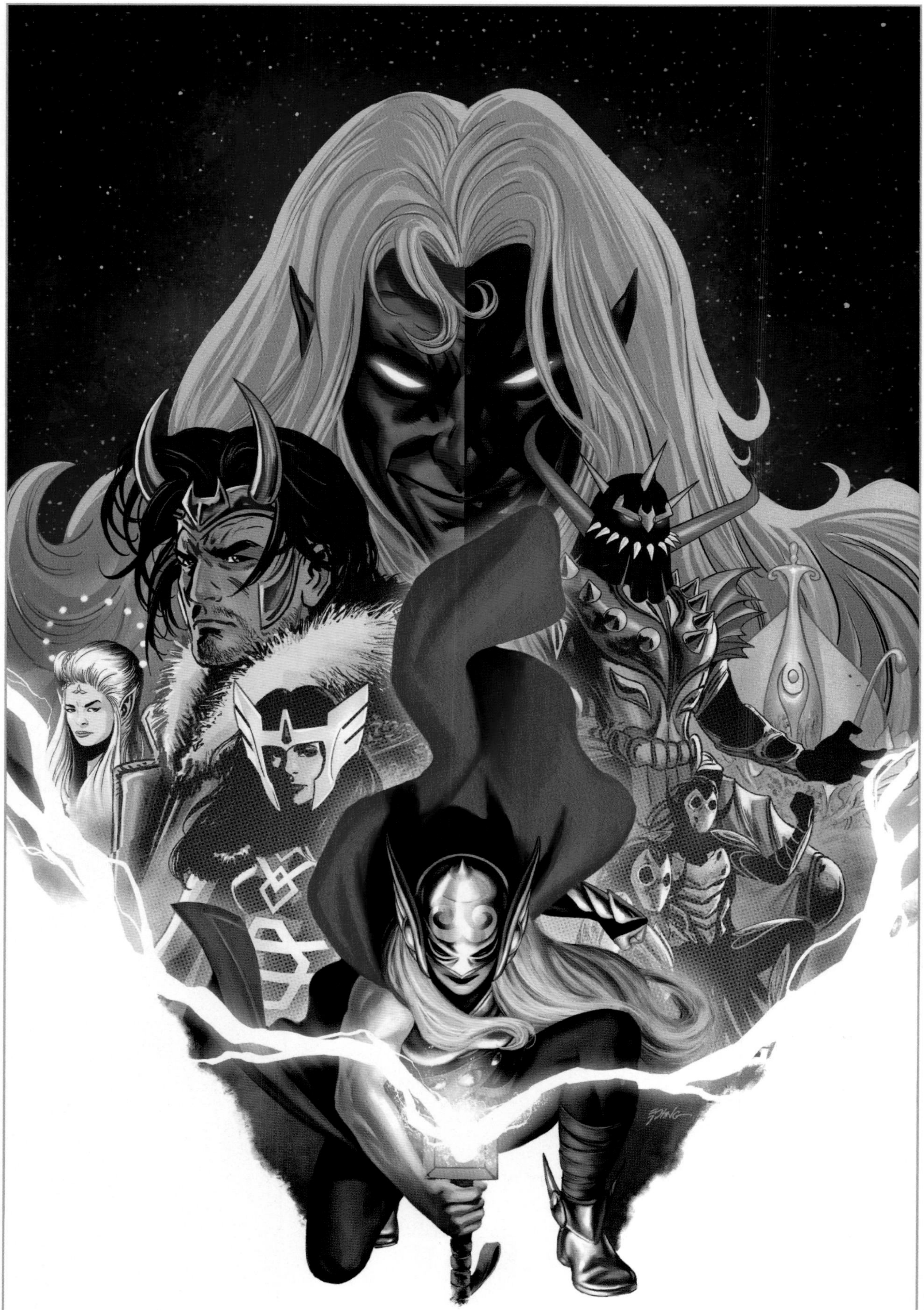

KING THOR #4 VARIANT
BY **STEVE EPTING**

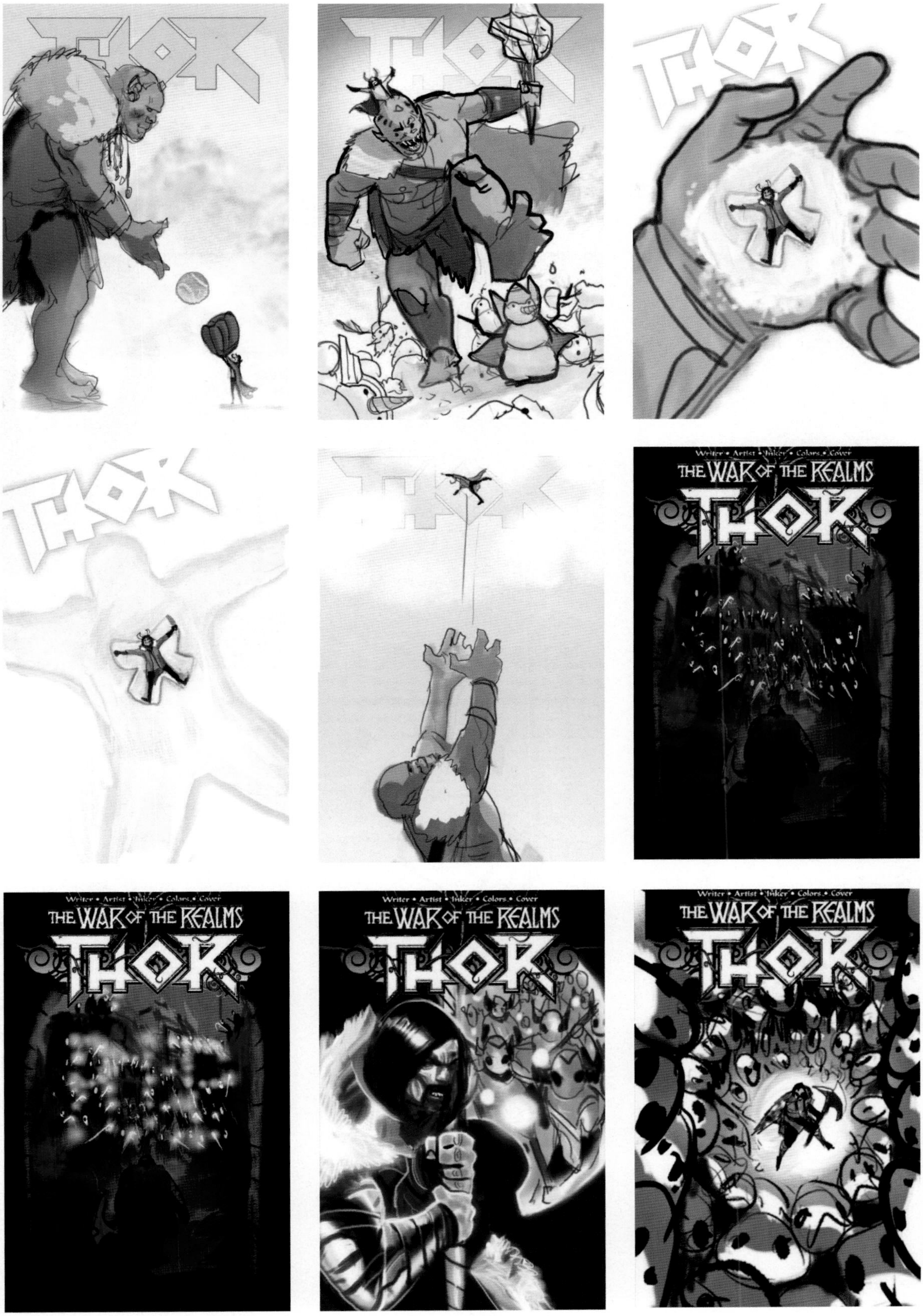
THOR
THOR
THOR
THOR
THOR
Writer • Artist • Inker • Colors • Cover
THE WAR OF THE REALMS
THOR
Writer • Artist • Inker • Colors • Cover
THE WAR OF THE REALMS
THOR
Writer • Artist • Inker • Colors • Cover
THE WAR OF THE REALMS
THOR
Writer • Artist • Inker • Colors • Cover
THE WAR OF THE REALMS
THOR

#12 & #13 COVER SKETCHES
BY **MIKE DEL MUNDO**

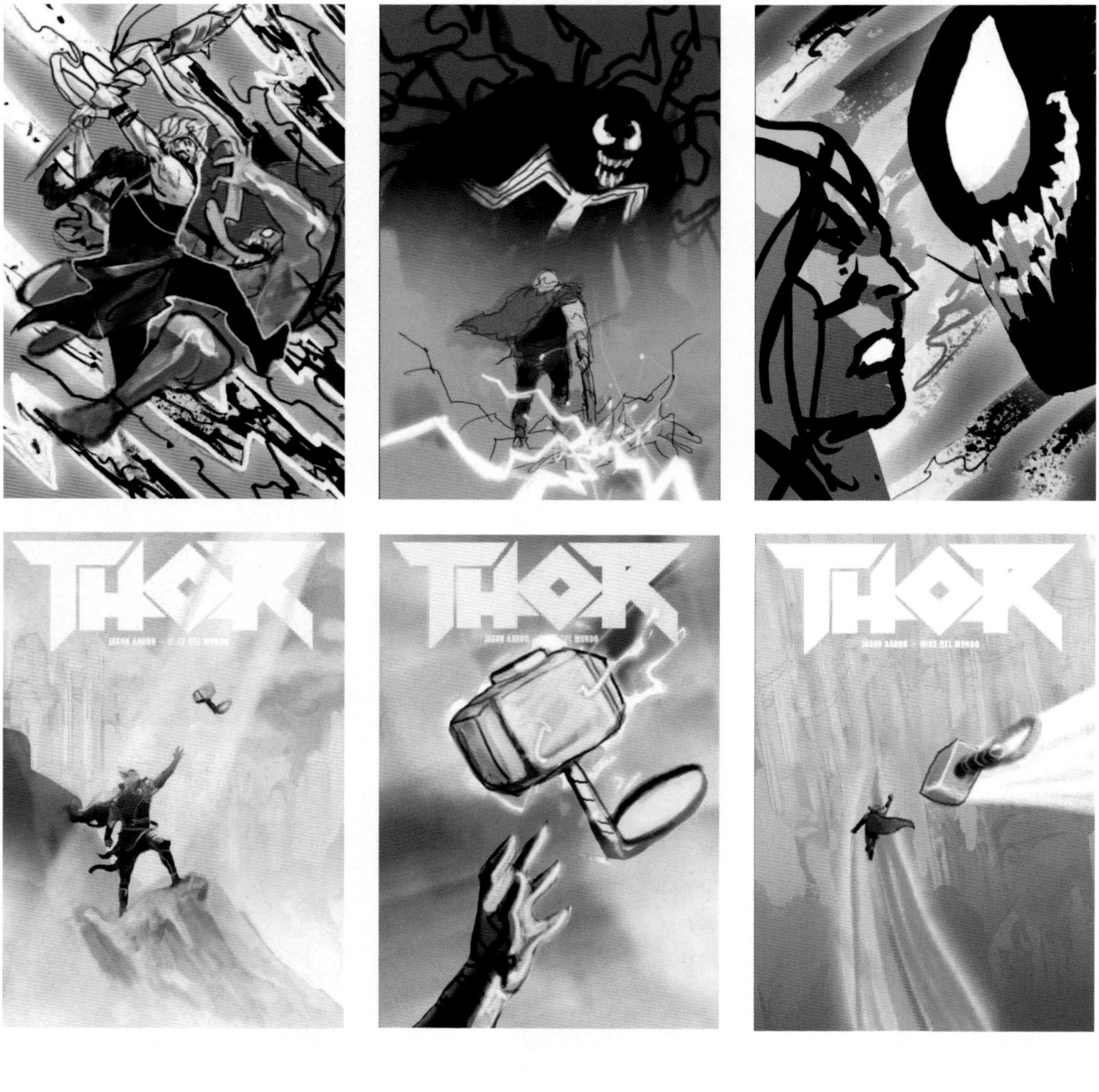
THOR
THOR
THOR

#14 & #15 COVER SKETCHES
BY **MIKE DEL MUNDO**

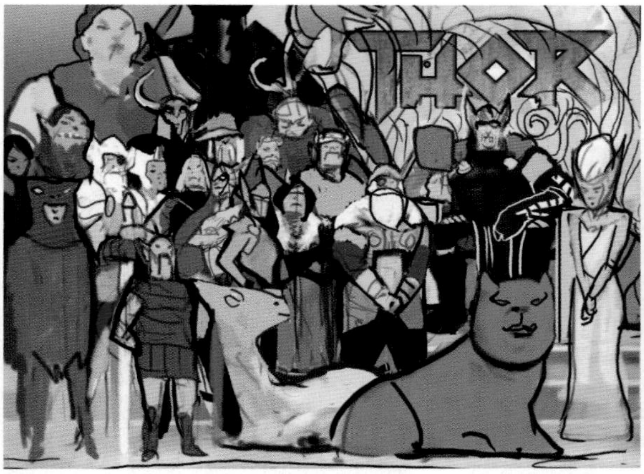
THOR
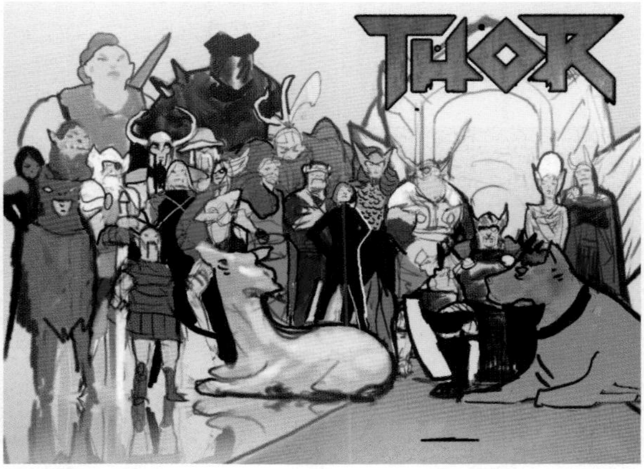
THOR
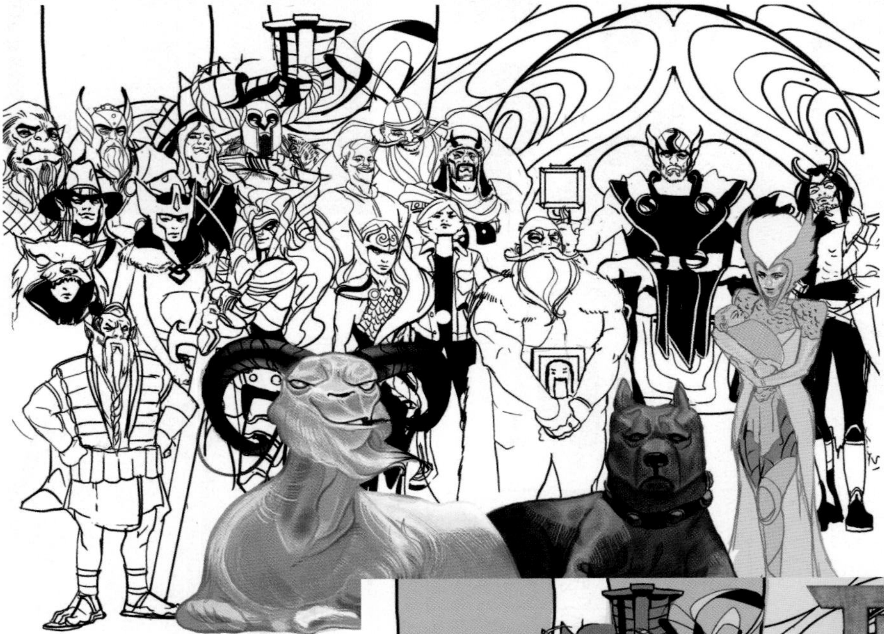
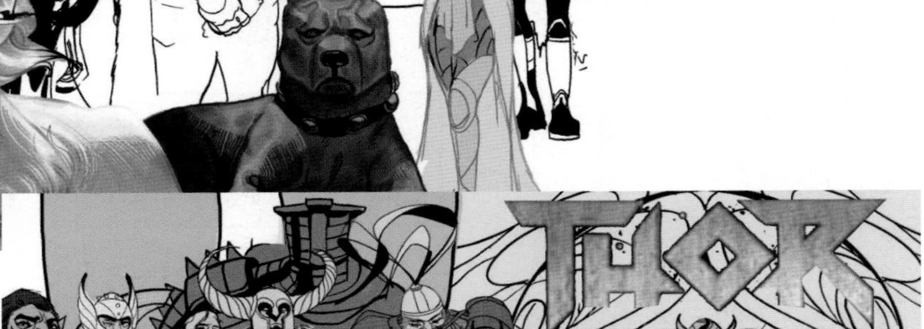
THOR
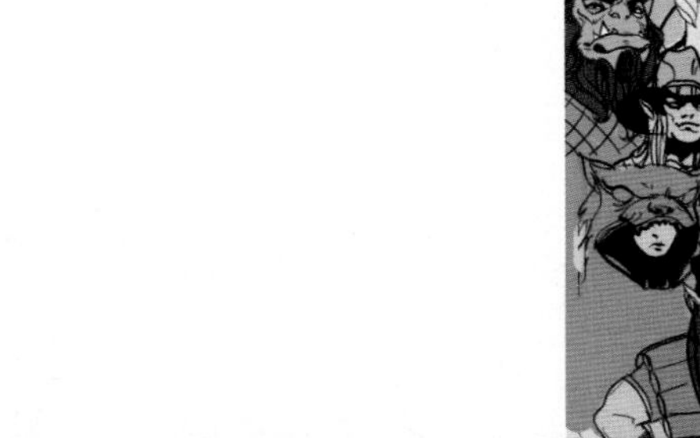

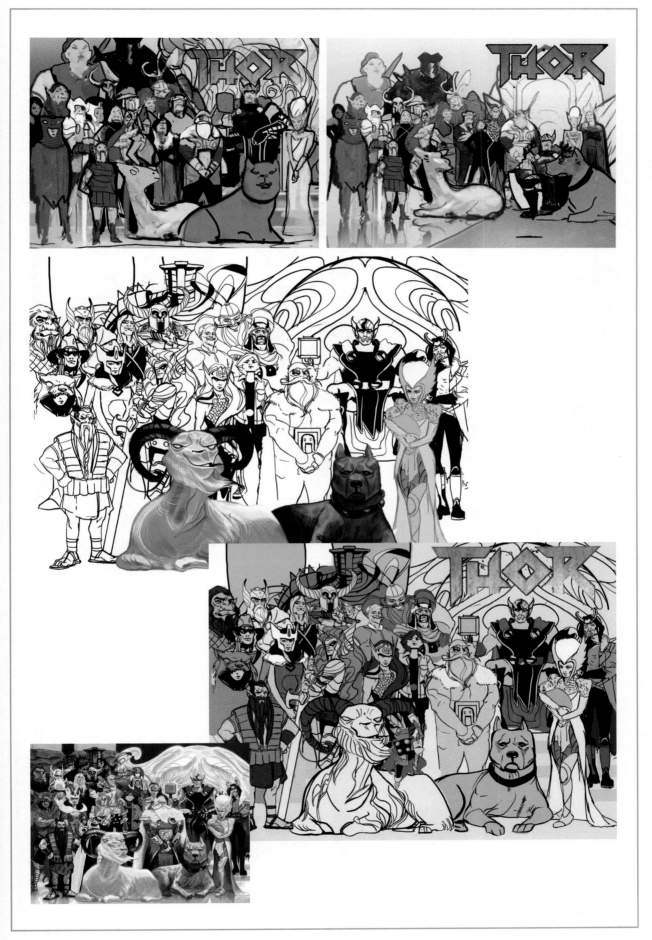

#16 COVER PROCESS
BY **MIKE DEL MUNDO**

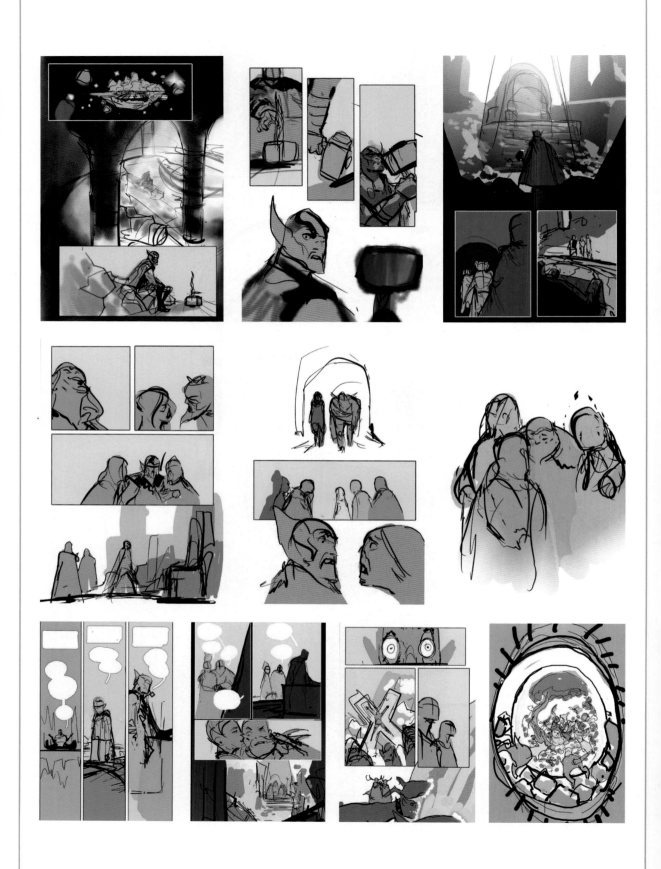

#15, PAGES 11-20 LAYOUTS BY
BY **MIKE DEL MUNDO**

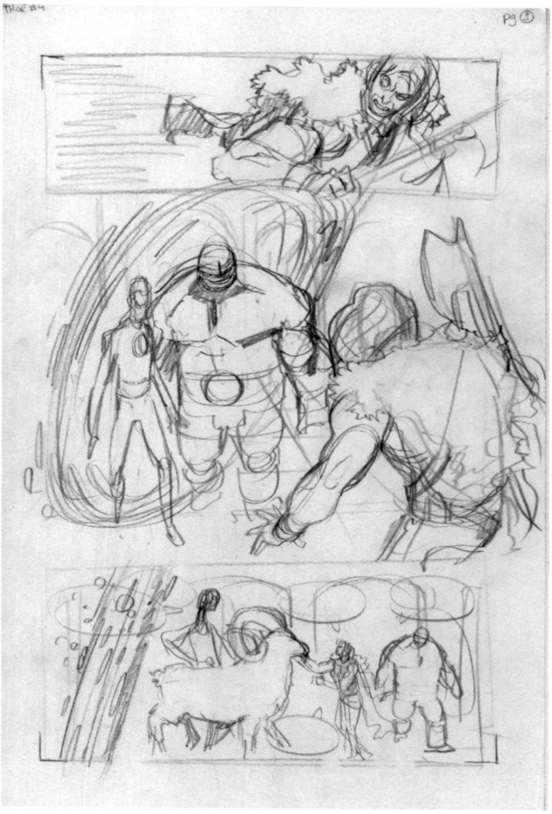
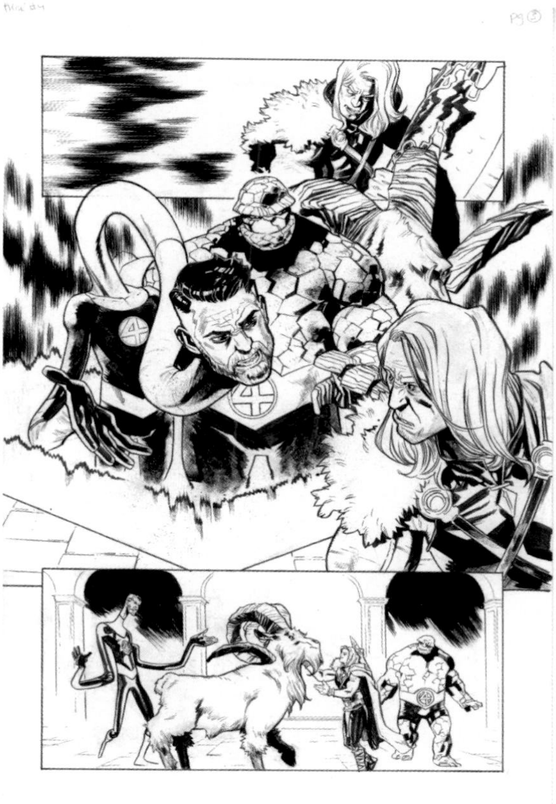
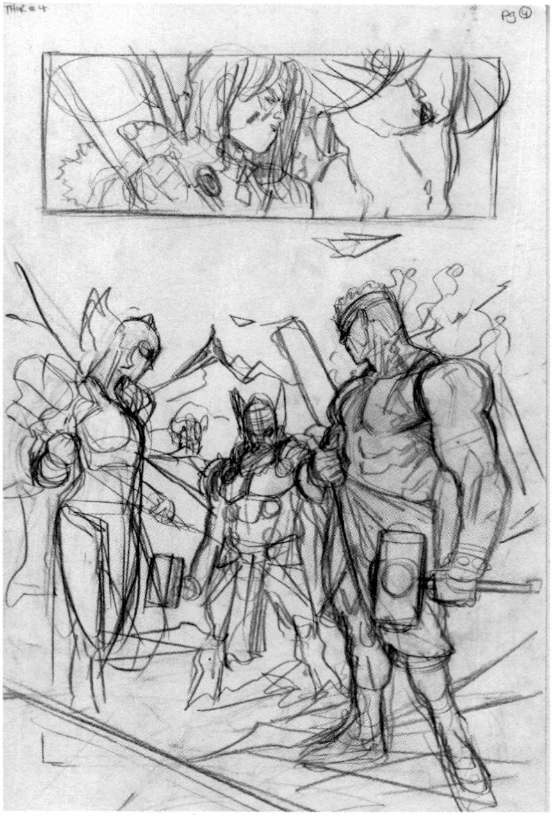
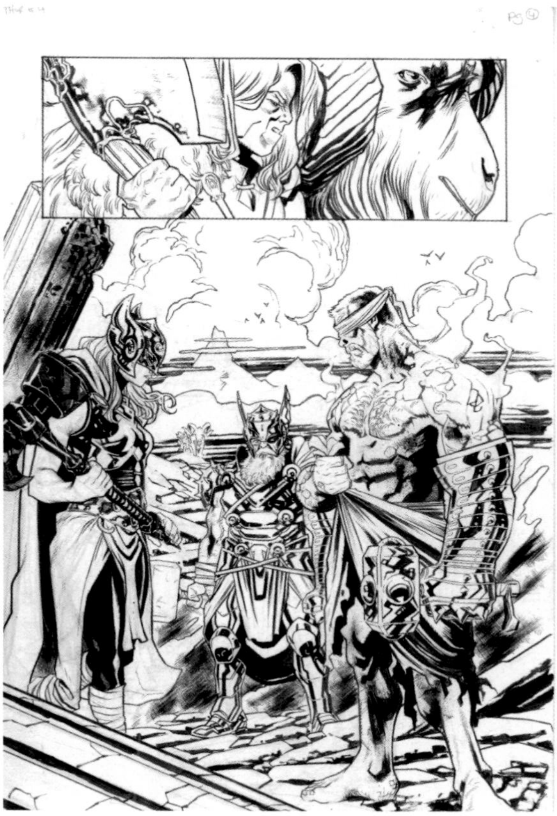

#14, PAGES 3 & 4 ART PROCESS
BY **SCOTT HEPBURN**

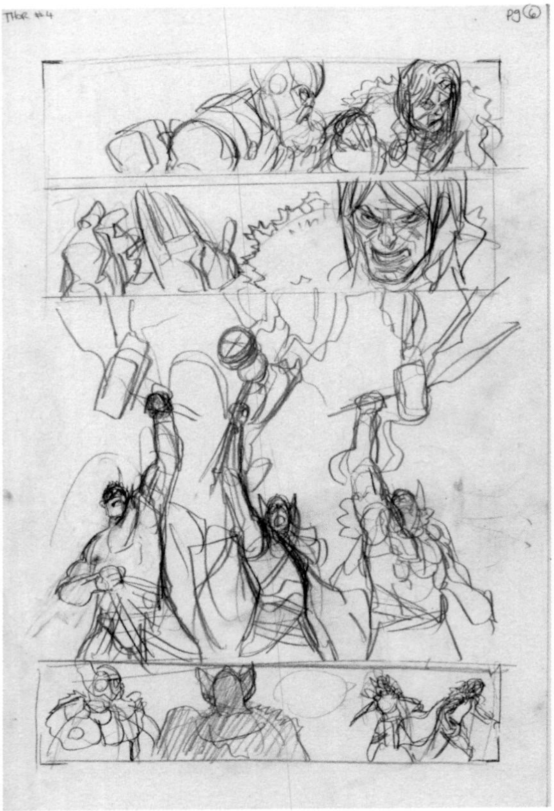

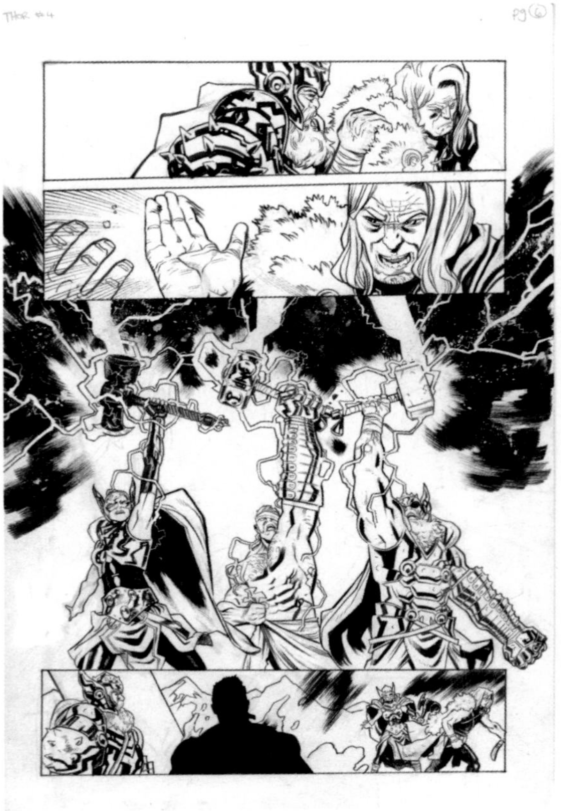

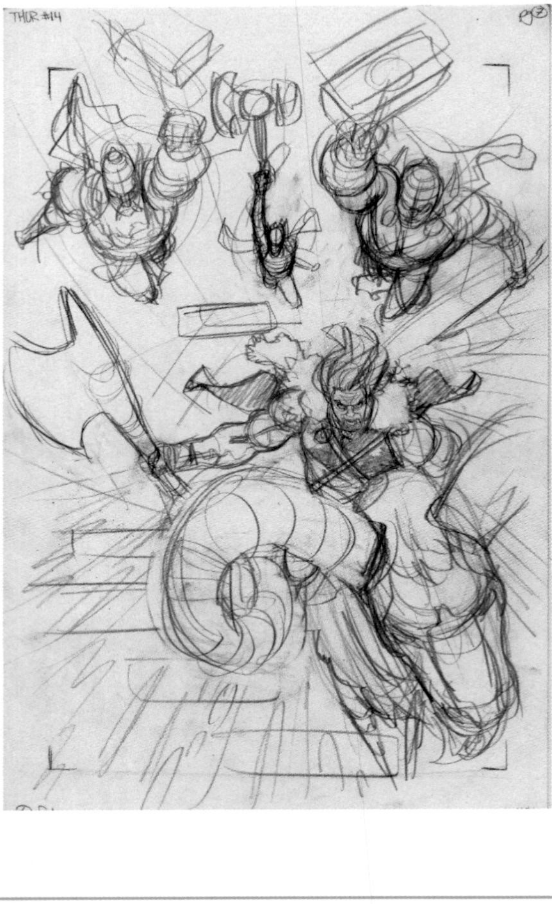

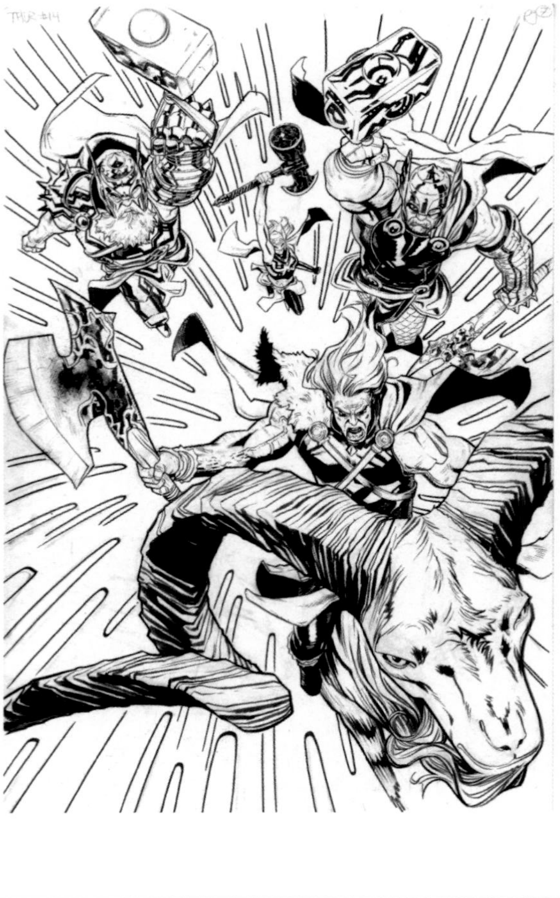

#14, PAGES 6 & 7 ART PROCESS
BY **SCOTT HEPBURN**